EMOTIONAL PROBLEMS OF LIVING

EMOTIONAL PROBLEMS OF LIVING

Avoiding the Neurotic Pattern

O. SPURGEON ENGLISH, M. D.
and
GERALD H. J. PEARSON, M. D.

THIRD EDITION

The Norton Library
W·W·NORTON & COMPANY·INC·
NEW YORK

First published in the Norton Library 1976

Library of Congress Catalog Card No. 62-12280

W. W. Norton & Company, Inc. is also the publisher of the works of Erik H. Erikson, Otto Fenichel, Karen Horney, Harry Stack Sullivan, and The Standard Edition of the Complete Psychological Works of Sigmund Freud.

ISBN 0 393 00806 1

Contents

Section B.

The Years Between—the Period of Sexual Latency

SECTION C.
The Approach to Adulthood—Adolescence

SECTION D.
Emotional Problems of Living

Preface

IN RECENT years much knowledge has been added to the study of the development of the human personality. We have long felt the need to gather some of this new material together and revise this book in order to make it a more inclusive study of the emotional problems that beset us all. We still direct this book toward the medical student, teacher, clergyman, psychologist, nurse, social worker, and others working in the field of interpersonal relations. But an attempt has been made to make the book readable for and understandable to a large number of interested lay people. We see no incongruity but rather an advantage in this, since in that field of medicine which deals with the problems of children and psychoneurosis and psycho-physiologic disease there is a great need for both the doctor and the layman to have an understanding of many of the same facts concerning the functioning of human beings. The better these groups of interested people understand the fundamentals of human personality the sooner they will understand each other as treatment is attempted. They will have a common language for expressing what they mean and thus be better able to work together to bring about a cure of the disorder.

This book is oriented to psychoanalytic thinking, since we feel that Freudian psychoanalysis is the best approach to understanding personality. Consequently we are deeply in debt to Sigmund Freud and all of his fellow workers and pupils who have made contributions to the many facets of human personality and the problems that arise in connection with it. We have made specific reference to some of these contributions. If we have also omitted some who have made contributions to the subjects under discussion in this book we hereby acknowledge that lack of space or some other reason did not make it possible to include every reference.

We have tried, however, to be more eclectic and less dogmatic in our treatment recommendations—not because we feel any less convinced about the importance of psychoanalytic concepts in the understanding of human personality but because we feel that, with the passage of time, much that was formerly regarded as Freudian, and consequently alien, has been accepted and imperceptibly interwoven into all thinking to become what is generally alluded to as "common sense."

We have discussed the development of the personality chronologically from birth to old age and in so doing we have followed the normal or average phenomena of emotional growth with a discussion of the commoner deviations from the normal occurring at each particular phase of development.

We found upon writing such a book how difficult it was to make even a discussion of the commoner emotional disturbances all-inclusive. We have, however, included new material in most chapters, particularly the chapter on mental disorders. We feel that a thoughtful population cannot ignore its outstanding medical problem—mental illness—and that perceptive adults want to know more about what it is and what can be done about it. Here and elsewhere we have drawn some material from our other books.

We are greatly indebted to Dr. Maurice E. Linden, Director, Division of Mental Health, Department of Public Health, City of Philadelphia, for his section, so graciously contributed, on the problems of later life. We are also indebted greatly to Mrs. Jeanne Jaffee for her thoughtful and painstaking work of correcting manuscript, arranging and editing material, and contributing ideas to the book as a whole to enhance its total usefulness.

For the basic work of transmitting the original ideas to paper, bearing with additions, deletions, and corrections and, seeing the book through its reformulation to a finished manuscript we are indebted to Miss Marion Mayer, Mrs. Dorothy Abel, and Mrs. Samuel E. Bucher.

O. Spurgeon English
Gerald H. J. Pearson

EMOTIONAL PROBLEMS OF LIVING

Introduction: The Meaning of a Neurosis

ONE HEARS more and more talk these days about neuroses. We hear of the neurosis of civilization and the neurosis of peoples of other countries and within our own country. We hear of a better world we must create, with security for all, greater advantages for all. We hear that a greater maturity on the part of everyone will be necessary to create that healthier, happier, more useful, effectual life.

Books are written and papers are delivered on national psychoses, on the lack of logic and reason in civilization. War has done much to convince us all that there must be some good reason for the growing murmur that we are not individually or collectively "using our heads" to the extent we should. In short, we must be either childish or a little sick that we do not manage better. Mother earth gives us abundant advantages and we either fail to use them or we misuse them. We suffer too much, we become ill too often. We have conquered the potent force of a few bacteria and have learned how to keep the body functioning with various surgical skills. But even though we apply the old drugs and many new ones, we cannot find the total secret to health, happiness, and a richer, fuller life. Too often we struggle anxiously from the cradle to the grave in order to enjoy briefly a questionable success before we begin to dread the loss of what we have acquired through illness, separation or death.

No one wants to have things work this way, but a satisfactory remedy is not easily forthcoming. The great religious leaders of all time have only helped, not saved, the situation. Philosophers and literary men have exposed human weaknesses and made suggestions for their improvement, but few people have read or listened.

Medical science reached out and took a hand in the problem in the person of Sigmund Freud nearly a half century ago. He was the first to make a scheme or chart of the fundamentals in human personality development and to make a working plan of treatment. As time went on he modified his original ideas to some degree, and his colleagues and pupils have also modified and revised them. But the bulk of his original framework remains as a guide to the study of the human mind and how to influence it. He tried to set down what he believed to be the structure of the human personality and what caused people to behave the way they do.

If we read the history of Freud's career, we can probably understand why no doctor reached out earlier to take hold of this problem. Freud got his knuckles rapped for doing what he did; a great deal of hostility arose and was directed against him and his theories about human beings. He was regarded as immoral, fantastic, and unscientific. People claimed he was being articulate about things better left unsaid. He went on many years before he achieved recognition for his work. Human beings did not and still do not want to face the truth about themselves. Human beings prefer to live in a blind, self-deluded way, ignoring their fundamental impulses. So any study of human personality proceeds very slowly.

The reader may nevertheless ask, "If a means of understanding and influencing human nature was discovered fifty years ago, why has not more been done about it?" The answer cannot be given tersely and glibly. One might say flippantly that "nobody cares about improving," and there would be a great deal of truth in that statement. Yet this does not represent the whole truth by any means, for we believe that actually people do want to behave better, more nobly, more generously, less selfishly. But to do so requires effort—an effort that cannot be put forth because the feelings and ideas that would make that effort possible are not a large enough part of the emotional and ideational nourishment of the average human being to make such effort possible in his everyday life.

For nearly two thousand years a large portion of the world has given lip service to Christian principles, yet how many professed Christians have had the inspiration to actually live from day to day according to Christ's principles? A part of the answer must lie in the fact that man is not easily inspired to such behavior as following the golden rule. Perhaps Christ seemed too far away and man needed inspiration from closer range. At any rate, the example of religion indicates that man finds it difficult to achieve his ideals. Some force holds him back, makes him indolent, selfish, cold, indifferent to a more friendly, enjoyable, co-operative existence.

FRUSTRATION AND PROGRESS

Freud observed that the force that holds the individual back from achieving the best of his potentialities is the result of the frustration of pleasure needs early in life, resulting in hostility, pain and hatred. This pain of frustration and the resulting hatred engendered gradually form a wall, a barrier within an individual so that the friendship and joy of living which he surely must encounter some day are unable to get to him and give him the happiness, peace, comfort, and desire to do for others. This same frustration and resulting hatred build up to form the *wall* of pessimism, depression of spirits, indifference and lack of generosity, and even active cruelty and oppression of others, which retard human progress and postpone the day of the better world.

While we believe a great deal of truth lies in these sentences, we realize that to many they seem like a formula or at best an explanation to be intellectually grasped but not necessarily understood in the deepest and best sense of understanding. At any rate, the authors wish in this book to take the reader chapter by chapter through certain common life experiences, so that by a process of *living with* the forces that go to make up a human personality (as well as we can make personality live in these chapters) he will emerge toward the end of the book a little closer to an understanding of human nature.

Psychiatry has taught us that the neurotic person is immature, that he is childish, that he has not grown up, that he has conflicts, all of which are true even though the facts need amplification. Growing up is a very difficult process. The human being is born into the world with certain needs which must be met by those about him. The journey through life is long and difficult, and it is the lucky person who can start under as auspicious circumstances as possible. Grownups have the responsibility for taking care of the young human being and for seeing that he is comfortable and emotionally contented in so far as possible.

If the human being from the start of life is made physically comfortable, if he is made happy, and if he has a chance to express himself without too much unnecessary frustration, he is a fortunate individual indeed, because it is the person with this kind of start who becomes the optimistic, hopeful individual, the one who can contribute something to the world at large and to those nearest to him. The human being whose needs are not met when he comes into the world, who is an unwelcome addition to the family, who is neglected and who lives in an environment that is indifferent and cold toward him, will develop hostility, resentment, hate, pessimism—all of which make it very difficult for him to function.

So when Freud as a physician directed our attention to the early life of the individual and turned our thoughts to the needs of the newborn human being, he was making an extremely important contribution to human progress. However, people did not like what he said. They did not like to be reminded of their childhood, they did not like to be reminded of their asocial impulses and they wished Freud would not say any more about it. However, psychoanalysis has continued to spread and has come to occupy a very prominent place in psychiatry, medicine, and education. More and more the theories of Freud are coming to be used in the fields of social work, psychology, sociology, and anthropology and, in short, in any field where people are attempting to understand human behavior with a keener insight and a more human approach.

Man seems to be unnecessarily thwarted in his goals of happiness and health. He does not seem to get the right start toward a free exercising of his potentialities for happiness, peace of mind, and constructive social and personal effort. He becomes fearful, doubtful, perplexed, in conflict, confused. In this state of mind he cannot act simply and constructively and his body may distress him as well as his mind. When he is in this state we say he has a neurosis.

A neurosis does not necessarily stem from one specific thing. It may stem from several things. It may stem from deprivation of love and interest as a child. It may stem from an inadequate acquaintance with the realities of the world. It may stem from an inadequate set of values for participation in the world. It may stem from an inability to love and hate effectively. It means that the individual has not matured or developed emotionally and ideationally to meet life. He may have poor control of his emotions, possibly reacting too passively or too violently. He may be either too prejudiced or have no opinions at all. He is either too sensitive to certain experiences or has too little feeling for them. He often gets distresses in his body. In short, his personality, that tool for social adjustment, is not well integrated to function smoothly, and the unnecessary emotional friction generated results in unhappiness, unpopularity, spiritual emptiness, strife with his fellow men, or illness.

In the succeeding chapters we shall endeavor to describe how these different frictions can be generated within the self or through contacts of the individual with his environment. We shall also try to give a point of view and a therapeutic approach which will reduce to a minimum these conflicts that produce the neurotic pattern.

SECTION
A

The Formative Years— from Birth to Seven

I

Development of Personality during the Oral Period

SINCE personality develops simultaneously with physical growth, the factors that enter into personality development are linked up rather closely with physiological processes. This connection makes for a physiological psychology, an approach that is best suited to medical thinking and to the solution of medical problems, and one, moreover, that is best suited to the understanding of personality whether one is a doctor or not. Most people have considerable feelings of anxiety—even shame, disgust, and prejudice against their own former helplessness and about their needs of childhood. People seem to want to forget about their bodies and their functions. Yet if they are ever going to understand themselves adequately, they must turn back and look at what they went through as children and accept it as natural and normal, and try to do away with their embarrassment and rejection of it.

The first phase of personality development is referred to as the *oral* period of development. It is not a particularly attractive or exciting name to give to this first development period, but it does convey meaning, and we hope sooner or later the reader will agree it is a good one to use, since the needs and interests of the newborn human being center around this particular part of the body, his desires being satisfied largely in the area of the mouth, esophagus, and stomach. Taking food, being fed, being made comfortable through the nursing process are to a great extent what satisfy the child and make life endurable and bearable for him—assuming, of course, that he is wanted and loved, that his skin is kept warm and comfortable. It has been clearly shown that the newborn child needs fondling and affection in much the same rhythm that he is fed. Being wanted, being loved, enjoyed, and played with, are an important part of the human psychological diet, so to speak. The intake of nourishment and the intake and acceptance of good-will should proceed simultaneously, the latter being no less important in the eventual well-being of the person than the former. Also he should not be left for long periods without the security of the presence of someone with whom he has made trustful emotional ties. A child, in addition to being fed and cuddled, needs to cling to a mother's presence and follow her about and prevent her getting too far way from him. The child also has a *need to be enjoyed* in order that he gain some sense of his importance as a human being.

CONSTITUTION AND PERSONALITY

Before going too far with the oral period, we ought to think for just a moment about the physical makeup of the individual who goes through the experiences that have so much to do with the forming of personality.

A person's makeup is referred to as his *constitution*. We say people are born with a certain constitution, which means several things. It means that people are born destined to have a certain type of stature which may be tall or short, thin or obese; it means they have light skin or dark skin; it means they have a brain with a cellular structure that is capable of absorbing and handling much factual knowledge or one that is capable of absorbing very little. In other words, they may be potentially intelligent individuals or they may be feebleminded. They may be born with a cardiovascular system that fulfills its function with a certain strength until well into old age, or they may be born with a weaker cardiovascular system that develops sclerosis (hardening of the arteries) or some other disease of the cardiovascular system early in life. In some the cardiovascular system will begin to wear out as early as thirty-five or forty and in others it will still be functioning well when the individual is ninety. The lungs may have a tendency to break down easily and become infected with an organism like the tubercle bacillus. In some families the kidney structure seems not to endure so long as in others. In other families the glandular system seems to have its own limited potentialities which are transmitted from generation to generation. This tendency to have varying strengths in the various systems of the body is transmitted through the germ plasm, and these varying physical factors in human beings we allude to as their constitutional endowment.

The more we observe human behavior in its beginnings the more we observe things which when combined with the world outside the child are important to consider in personality formation. These observations are that some children are more sensitive than others to stimuli such as light, sound, heat, cold, and being moved, while some are phlegmatic as regards these things; that some children by their very earliest life reaction have a great "will to live and get"—a great tenacity to struggle for what they want and need. Others have a weak will to live and get and enjoy (possibly related to the sensitivity alluded to above) and easily turn away from frustrating experiences into apathy, inertia, and even death. What determines this quality we do not know, but it is probably constitutional to some degree. Moreover, while we feel this quality is modifiable by environmental events after birth, it should be further studied and reckoned with in the whole problem of personality formation.

CONFLICT IN LIFE

Throughout the world a constant struggle is being waged. On the one hand there are living creatures constantly striving to remain alive and to keep their species alive, and on the other the elemental forces whose action is inimical to life. Each living creature is forced constantly to wrest its livelihood and protect its life and the life of its species from these inimical forces, and its survival depends on its ability to accomplish this struggle successfully.

Not only must the living creature wage an unceasing struggle with these hostile forces but at the same time it must contend with forces within itself whose action is to break down the complex molecule consistent with life into simpler, nonliving molecular constellations in order that the energy required for life itself may be liberated. We do not understand just what constitutes life; therefore we do not understand the nature of the forces that strive to preserve life, both personally and racially, or the nature of the forces within the organism that tend to destroy it. We can only observe the manifestations of their presence. Freud referred to these forces as instinctive and classified them into two groups: (1) the erotic or life instincts, whose presence is coexistent with life, and whose purpose is to maintain the life of the individual and to create and maintain the life of the species, and (2) the death or aggressive instincts, whose presence is also coexistent with life, and whose purpose is to reduce the complex living molecule to simpler, inorganic ones.

Thus all life is subject to two groups of conflicts, those between the living creature and the elemental forces of the physical world, and those between the opposing instinct drives within the living organism itself. In these struggles the living organism eventually succumbs and is reduced to inorganic substance. Life is maintained only by the propagation of new individuals, often differing in some degree from their parents and so gradually becoming new species.

As one ascends the biological scale from the vegetable to the animal life, a new conflict is encountered. Most animals cannot maintain their existence without assimilating molecules that are or have been alive themselves. Except for water and salt, the human being feeds exclusively on substances that are or have recently been alive. Therefore, the third conflict is the struggle for existence between the various forms of life. In this struggle the species, race, or individual that is better equipped at the time is victorious and continues to live, while the vanquished dies.

A fourth conflict is found among the higher animals, including man. These animals tend to live in a social organization, whose purpose is to protect better their existence against the inimical forces of the physical world and of other living creatures. Such a social organization can only function if each individual comprising it is willing to inhibit certain of his needs at those times when their immediate gratification would injure another member of the group or interfere too seriously with the gratification of his needs. To accomplish this inhibition, certain rules of conduct are formulated by the group, and each individual must learn to conform to them lest he lose the protection and assistance of the group organization. At the very best, these rules curtail the individual's freedom in living and maintaining the life of the species. There arises a conflict between the individual's instinctive drives and the group's rules of conduct. This conflict becomes most marked in the case of man, whose social organization has formulated a large number of rules of conduct which are handed down from generation to generation. In this conflict the basic rules of conduct that preserve the existence of the social organization must always be victorious, and the conflict results in the individual's curtailing his liberty of action at the expense of some pain and suffering to himself for which he tries to find compensations. If he will not do this, he may be excluded from the benefits of group life or be killed.

Every human being, therefore, is exposed to these four conflicts, and his happiness and success throughout his life depend on his ability to deal adequately with them all. This ability at any given point will be a complex of his biological inheritance, his physical and intellectual constitution, and the skills he has developed as a result of the conditioning experiences because of the nature of his actual contacts with the physical world, with other forms of life, and with the other people of his social organization. It is our purpose in this book to discuss this ability during the various periods of life from childhood to mature age.

EXPERIENCE AND PERSONALITY

We used to blame a great many diseases on constitution when we did not know what caused the malady. However, as we gained more knowledge about the cardiovascular diseases, the respiratory diseases, the mental diseases, we put less and less blame on the constitutional factors in disease. In other words, we hide less of our ignorance under the cloak of constitution. The constitutional factor in disease grows smaller as our knowledge grows larger, though it is unlikely that it will ever come to the point where the factor of the constitution does not exist. Therefore, we have to consider the factor of the constitution but we must not use it as a catch-all, a convenient label for things we cannot explain.

A great deal that occurs in personality formation comes by way of the human experience that is due to environmental factors and very little to the constitution. For instance, we used to say glibly that if a man were irritable, or if he were depressed, the reason was perfectly understandable because his father was that way. Today we look upon the matter differently, and doubt if he inherited anything of his depression and irritability from his father. Certainly he *did inherit* his brain from his father but we do not now say that he inherited his irritability and moody experiences. If he is like his father, it is because of his *contact with* his father. All through his childhood he observed his father hour by hour and day by day and saw that his father was big, strong, brave, capable and able to do anything he wanted—in short he was everything that the little boy admired and wanted to be. The father may not have been any of these things if judged by adult standards but to the boy he was so in comparison with the little boy himself. The son's disposition therefore is what it is because of his identification with his father and not because he inherited being a depressed individual through the germ plasm.

Let us discuss some of the early life experiences and the effects produced upon the young human being. Our first experience in extrauterine living is birth itself. Birth is an experience of short duration but it is the first and one of the most profound shocks the human being receives. In fact, there are a growing number of workers in the field of human relations who feel that they see evidences of prenatal influence on the fetus by way of chemical changes that take place in the mother, effecting anxiety and anger, and possibly depression. Such possibilities used to be regarded as "old wives' tales," but the research work of today promises to reveal how truly early the mind is influenced by forces that can make it healthy or unhealthy.

Experiments have proved that for at least two months previous to birth the fetus has been able to receive sensory impressions, to react to them, and to become sensitized to them, so that when the stimulus is reapplied, months after birth has taken place, the reaction is more vigorous than if the previous experience had not occurred. So the child at birth is capable of receiving impressions, of reacting to them, and of storing up memories of the impressions and the reactions in his nervous system. Birth is definitely a shock to the young organism and requires some quick physiological and psychological readjustments—the use of the lungs; a change in circulation of the blood; the taking of food in a new way; the adjustment to changes in the external temperature, to those in the moisture of the skin, to those brought about by relative freedom of movement, the handling and movement of the body, and the impact of sound and light. All these new factors in the environment of the newborn child bring about tension within him. We do not know how vivid or how conscious these impressions are but as experiences they are registered, along with many others that follow, to make up a person's impression of life. The young organism's reactions to these experiences become part of his habitual methods of reacting throughout the rest of his life.

The reader may think ascribing so much to birth shock is carrying things back too far, that the theory is a little fantastic. Yet the idea is no more fantastic than the stories we hear of a person who has been in an accident and has a fear of riding in an automobile afterward, the assumption being that the fear grew directly out of the accident experience. But a person who has reached the age of seventeen or twenty-seven has a great many mental qualities with which to evaluate such an experience, and he should have capacities for reasoning that might dispel the sense of dread. Yet we are ready to accept and understand his fear. If we accept that, we should also be ready to accept the fact that birth imposes lasting emotional experiences; for although the mind of the infant is undeveloped, the painful birth experiences are registered on his brain; they do not pass into thin air.

Impressions of past experience should not be regarded too lightly, whether the person was fully aware of the entire import of what was happening or not. Most of the wisest and most of the most foolish things we do in our lives we do as the result of present impressions associated in our minds with many other past experiences and our former methods of reacting to them rather than of carefully thought-out planning. Although it cannot be proven, it seems likely that the startling shock of the experiences of birth and the newborn's physiological reactions to them may lay down the pattern for the complex combination of physiological and psychological reactions that we feel in any situation that seems to us to be dangerous—the reaction patterns which we call states of fear and of anxiety. There seem reasons why this concept may have validity. Some people like the psychologist Otto Rank go further; he has put forth the theory that birth and the type of birth are the original causes of the neuroses, since all psychoneuroses start with a state of anxiety. In this theory, birth is a kind of primary experience which starts the individual off badly by giving him an early anxiety from which he never completely recovers. We cannot see that there is any basis for placing quite so much emphasis on this one experience.

EXPERIENCE OF THE NEWBORN

A few hours after birth the baby begins to feel sensations, hunger and thirst, which are new and unpleasant, and therefore must be frightening to him. To remove these sensations he must be fed. Often we do not recognize the vital importance of these first days, weeks, and months of life—the importance of the nursing experience itself and of the attitude of the one who is taking care of the child during this time of the development of the personality of the individual. It may seem we are stressing this idea overmuch, but the purpose is to stress matters that might be passed by as inconsequential, matters that our studies of personality indicate are of great consequence. We must take our minds back to childhood and keep them on that age period in order to get used to thinking of the events of this age and of their importance. If we do not think back upon this time, we will have great difficulty in understanding the often erratic behavior of our patients, if we are doctors, and the sensitive emotions in all people we deal with. Moreover, something must be done about this erratic behavior and sensitiveness in people we meet if we are going to be successful doctors in the larger sense. We have not only the responsibility to cure aches and pains but also to be leaders in imparting some information that will help to cure a sick, unhappy, contentious society.

We cannot do all this if we are going to limit our knowledge to anatomy, physiology, and pathology and trust to the effects of the pharmacopoeia and surgical techniques—no matter how important they may be. All sick people are sensitive and they retrogress to the feelings of childhood. Whether the patient's sickness be of an organic nature or of psychological origin, doctors need to be in tune with the feeling and needs of childhood, since they express themselves at every age period in the life span of an individual.

The satisfaction of the demands of the newborn child through nursing is extremely important to the child, because this act is practically his only source of satisfaction. We should realize that the child's world is small, and that he has no sense of time. He has only rhythms set up by his physiological apparatus. He enjoys the flow of milk into the mouth, down the esophagus, and into the stomach. He enjoys the act of sucking, which incidentally helps the rhythms of breathing and digestion. He enjoys the nearness to the mother and the feel of the nipple in his mouth. We can say he also has a "hunger" for contact with the mother's body—for the security of touch with her or some other human being—and enjoys the rhythm of being rocked and handled. Babies left too much to themselves do not thrive, as has been noted by many pediatricians long since. As the child grows older other senses come into play and he can do many things to gain satisfaction: he can go out of doors, play games, go to the movies, and thus gain a variety of pleasant sensations in a very short time—sensations that are satisfying and make the person feel that life is worth living. The infant has largely one satisfaction: being fed and, supplemental to it, being in contact with his mother and having her affection. During this stage of life the mother—or in special situations the nurse—is the major part of the environment and is the main object for the child. It is only later that the father becomes an important object. There is a tendency at present to consider the mother and her attitudes more important for the child's development than the father. They are so only in the first twelve months.

Children need to be fed regularly, and they need to be fed in accordance with their own natural rhythm rather than by schedule. If a child is on a two-hour schedule, or a three-hour schedule, and if, before the time of his next feeding, he gets into a state of discomfort, the proper thing is to feed him and not attempt any discipline at that time. When the child cries and manifests hunger some mothers say to themselves, "Oh, no! I mustn't give in to him. The doctor said he was to eat only every three hours, and I must stick to his schedule." When a doctor, mother, or nurse makes too much ritual of the child's schedule and ignores his own rhythm, the child becomes anxious and greatly concerned about whether his fundamental needs are going to be met. Infants allowed to remain too often in such a state of uncertainty tend to develop into the kind of person who later in life is always uncertain about whether specific persons or fate will be kind. They are prone to assume they must be disappointed in plans or aspirations. They doubt their ability to influence the environment by any means whatever because their earliest human environment did not adjust itself to their basic needs. Let us allude again to these basic needs of the human organism.

HUNGER-AFFECTION TENSIONS

It is part of the nature of living human protoplasm to build up tensions as a result of the physiochemical processes of metabolism. These tensions as they increase make themselves felt as a discomfort (pain) and they demand release through some process. Food hunger is an example—the hunger is felt as pain and the taking of food gives the gratification or release of tension. The energy continuously exerted to keep body tensions relieved is termed libidinal energy or *libido*. It is energy manifested in the activities of the erotic group of instincts. *Instincts* in turn are psychic representations of somatic processes. Instinct is a term applied to a sensation lying somewhere between cellular metabolism and psychological feeling. For instance, if a person is hungry, exactly where is his hunger? Is the person uncomfortable in his stomach or is he uncomfortable in his mind? The answer is that he is uncomfortable in both places. But if a person were challenged to say exactly where his discomfort lay when he is hungry, he would not find the sensation entirely easy to locate.

Actually, stomach and cellular activities do produce local sensations which are promptly carried to the mind, and the feeling of hunger goes with these sensations. The hungry person is indeed hungry all over. Therefore, hunger is one of the tensions demanding satisfaction. This tension builds up in the newborn infant every few hours and food satisfies it. If the tension mounts too high, the infant cries, wiggles, and makes known to the persons around that he is hungry. Ordinarily he gets relief. The *pleasure principle* is the name given to the tendency in the human being to regulate these tensions so that unpleasant accumulations of energy are discharged at intervals and a state of comfort maintained.

The newborn being who has these tensions soon comes to realize that it is the people around him who can satisfy his needs or reduce his tension and they do so with varying attitudes. Here we begin to speak about the importance of the attitudes of those who take care of children, our next generation. A child comes to associate the feeding process (nursing) with the attitude the mother takes as she feeds him and we assume, often without justification, that the attitude of the mother toward her child is a loving one. Whatever attitude is shown by the mother in the feeding process (environment) is the attitude the child is likely to associate with food, feeding, and the nursing process. Moreover, the child not only associates this environmental attitude with food and the taking of food but psychologically he also gathers much about life in general and makes it important in his mind in connection with food. The newborn child is a newcomer into the world and whatever attitude he meets in his environment he is likely to adopt and to carry throughout his life to a large degree.

The combination of the mental attitude and the feeding process or the psychological process of eating contains many implications. In the first place, when a person is depressed in spirits he cares little about eating. During mourning, after the loss of some loved one or relative, or when a person is under an emotional distress and suffering, his appetite may be very poor. Under better conditions he may eat heartily. Certain restaurants endeavor to intrigue the fancy of the public by advertising the warmth of the atmosphere and the geniality of the personnel, both of which are supposed to put the customer in a special frame of mind so he can enjoy his food the more. In certain homes—the custom differing from place to place—it is unheard-of to visit for a few moments and not be served something to eat or at least a glass of something to drink. A person would be considered very impolite to refuse. Anyone desiring to insult another need only walk away from his host's table and refuse to eat with him. Friendship, goodwill, affection, and the eating process are connected in many ways.

FEEDING AND SECURITY

The behavior and the attitude of those taking care of the child can produce important long-run trends. Some of these trends can be illustrated by the following examples. A person can have been fed in such a way or with such an attitude that later he will feel very insecure about his livelihood or his place in the esteem of those around him. He may feel insecure about whether he will have enough to eat, or whether he will be able to survive by holding his job. If in business, he will constantly fear business failure.

Anxiety concerning food has been shown recently in some sections of the country by the way people became anxious because of a dread that there would not be enough to eat; they bought huge stocks and filled their cellars. What is the difference between those who went along and took chances about food and those who felt special anxiety about food? The difference is related to early experiences, going back to the first few days, weeks, and months of life. If a baby has had to go hungry because of feeding difficulties, or because his needs for food have not been taken care of, perhaps because of a feeling that he may be spoiled, then in later childhood or in adult life he may have undue anxiety about food, or undue anxiety about attention to himself. He may react by eating too much daily or by having a pressing, clinging attitude to those around him, demanding attention and reassurance all the time. He is afraid he will not have enough food or enough recognition and love. He will be very jealous of the recognition and love shown other people, and even may go so far as never to be satisfied with what he has and never to want anyone else to have anything even if he does not want it himself.

Another attitude can be produced by a still different cause. Some mothers put too much emphasis on food. They make the child feel that eating is the most important thing in life, perhaps by feeding him every time he cries regardless of the real cause of his agony or by breastfeeding him for an excessively long time; food then may become all-important to him, and other things of too little importance. Not only does good food become too important, but the child may also be given the feeling that he need never worry, that he will always be taken care of. Those who do take care of him go out of their way to assure him that the good things of life will always come his way without effort. Such an attitude is not made complete in the early years but it is started there. Much, of course, depends upon what responsibilities are given in the child's third and fourth years, upon what he is taught in school, upon how he is encouraged to get a job in adolescence. Nevertheless, the attitude of taking a dependent position toward society is laid down in the oral period. Such a person may say, "I am going to get a job. I am going to do well." However, he always puts it off because he has the feeling he will be taken care of, which is just the opposite from the feeling of the person who fears he will not be taken care of. The person who has had too great assurance that he will never need to take care of himself may be a baffling social problem during adulthood as a result.

A special disorder which has always been fairly common is alcoholism. Excessive, uncontrollable drinking has more than one cause. One of the reasons people drink to excess is to gratify an oral need. The psychoanalysis of alcoholics regularly shows that the patient did not care about the taste of liquor, and he could, with little hardship to himself, be put on Coca-Cola or coffee or tea and be just about as content as when drinking alcohol. A second reason for drinking is to dull a sense of loneliness, which is a feeling tone in the alcoholic that is very difficult to affect favorably. This sense of loneliness may go back to the sense of loneliness in the early weeks and months of life. Drinking dulls the pain of loneliness and puts the alcoholic in a state where he is able to fantasy that he can love and be loved. This urge to keep up to the early pattern of the first years continues to play a role in people's attitudes for a long time. It persists particularly in respect to the addictions, which moreover become complicated by the fact that the particular drug used by an addict may —by chemical means—produce wished-for changes in the balance of instinctual conflicts, diminish inhibitions, heighten self-esteem, and ward off anxiety to a certain degree and for a short time.

INFANTILE TENSIONS IN ADULTS

Unless there are young children in the home under our very eyes, people pay little attention to them and their behavior, which is perfectly natural because people's interests have been turned in other directions and they have not bothered to look at young children or be interested in them. We hope the reader will be able to project himself backward into that early period of childhood and appreciate the situations in it which are being alluded to. For instance, in addition to his regular food a child will frequently put his thumb in his mouth, or his whole fist, or a piece of bread, possibly a dirty stick from the floor, or anything within reach. Each thing goes to his mouth as if his mouth were the testing apparatus of everything in his environment—clean or dirty. Part of the reason is that he can use his hands to convey things to the mouth and part that there is a satisfaction in sucking on these things. This satisfaction in sucking has two sources. It gratifies special instinctual needs found not only in the human being but also in animals, and it relieves tension.

The urge to seek gratification by oral means and to allay tension thereby is seen in later life in alcoholism, in the enjoyment of food, in drinking, in smoking, or in chewing gum. In adults the important reason for these habits is that they are tension reducers. A person who feels a little uneasy or a little depressed may go out and buy a good meal or go to a soda fountain for a double-decker. Afterward he feels better. This better feeling is not all due to the sugar he has eaten; it is due to the pleasure he has had in the oral activity. In subtler ways people often show this early infantile trend for oral gratification. Such a person seems to be of a clinging, beseeching, dependent disposition who frequently makes requests of those he is associated with, or just hangs around and talks as if he needed to be near another person and live a part of his life. His own life is too empty to sustain him so he leans on other people. His attitude is one of seeming to try to eat up the other person. It might appear that he is trying to establish a psychological umbilical cord with words, to attach himself thereby to someone else, and to maintain that attachment through speech. The presence of such a person, although felt, may not be bothersome for a while; but after it goes on for a time his group or his individual associate wishes this person would be more self-sustaining.

Often our first impression of certain people is that they are attractive, that they make a pleasing impression, that they are interesting talkers and that they have many winning personality traits, but later their friends say that they do not wear well. There may be many reasons; a common one is that the person whose conversations were brilliant and interesting in the beginning never stops, never lets go. He attaches himself too completely to people and the result is that his newly made friends grow "fed up" or tired of him. In many instances the attitude that causes such estrangement is very difficult to isolate and describe. However, it often is due to the dependency which may arise out of an oral phase of development in which the essential needs of the infant child have not been sufficiently gratified; thus, instead of having an attitude of basic confidence and trust in himself in relation to his environment, he basically is distrustful of himself and his environment. In order to overcome this feeling of mistrust he tries too pressingly to draw from others in adulthood the attention he has lacked in infancy. While it may be hard on those around him, to such a person this behavior is a lifesaving mechanism.

These people who attach themselves to others have considerable advantage over the ones who are too anxious and too mistrustful even to try to make contact with others or to try to use them for emotional sustenance. The lives of the latter resemble the life of an individual who lacks the outer horny protective layers of the skin. The former get along in society fairly well by frequent changes in friendships unless they estrange too many people.

ANXIETY AND ITS CONSEQUENCES

We have used the word anxiety so far without attempting to define clearly what we mean by it. *Anxiety* is an affect. By *affect* we mean an emotion or feeling tone. Some of the affects are happiness and sadness, elation and depression, and euphoria. Anxiety is a special affective state which grows out of the conflict between instinctual needs and a society that is unwilling or unable to gratify the needs. Instincts are energy that is released as a result of the physiochemical processes of the body, the life processes themselves, which produce tension for which relief is required right from the onset of the first breath. Because of his helplessness the young child can only partially relieve himself of these tensions and gratify his instincts and so is under the necessity of being at the mercy of other humans in accomplishing this end. He has a fairly well-developed sensory nervous system that makes the pain of his instinctual tensions felt, but a relatively undeveloped motor nervous system with which to effect a relief of tension by himself. Hence, these instincts require an *object,* something animate or inanimate in the environment which will gratify the child's instinctual needs. When the instinctual tension manifests itself in the child and when the environment, in the form of the mother or nurse, meets the demand with indifference, with refusal, with annoyance, with threats, or with punishment, that painful state has to find some release other than the object. The child has to find some more direct method of expression or he has to endure the tension. In other words, the child just may have to suffer hunger, loneliness, or the discomfort of lying too long in one place. The necessity of enduring this tension too long by himself creates affects which, multiplied with the passing of time, result eventually in an apathy or emotional coldness.

The parental attitude of letting children "cry it out" too often and too long is bad; it requires the child to deal with too much pain and loneliness by himself and he fails to develop that most necessary psychic function of being able to relate to and use the warmth and friendliness of others. These attitudes on the part of the upbringers tend to give children the impression that they are alone in the world, that they are likely to be neglected, that their needs will probably not be met anyway. The baffling lack of emotional response in depression and in schizophrenic reactions is undoubtedly due to this cause. As a result, society has many uninspired persons who do not wish to try to be successful or to make any imprint on the world around them. Lack of attention in the early weeks of life is probably one of the greatest stultifiers of ambition.

As the child continues to live, instincts continue to seek gratification. Some of them are gratified, and those that are not gratified act as a signal to the child that he has impulses within himself that he would like to gratify but must not because of loss of love or punishment. To keep love and avoid punishment the human being erects in his mind *defenses* against this unpleasant affect of anxiety—worry, fretfulness, apprehension, uneasiness, overconcern about small matters—or certain other defenses. One of these common defenses against anxiety is a *phobia*. For example, a child may become afraid of an animal or afraid to go on the street alone; perhaps he cannot be in a closed room, or cannot go to sleep without a light. This anxiety is a derivative of instinctual tension or the result of an instinctual tension within a human being which has not been mastered in an appropriate way at the appropriate time.

Another big area in which anxiety may find release—rather than in a direct expression of the instinctual impulses—is in symptom formation. This area should be of serious concern to medical students and doctors. The anxiety that has accumulated within a human being brings into action many symptom pictures with a great amount of psychopathology underlying them. For this reason it is important that we focus our attention upon the very early activities of the human being so we can know just as much as possible about the recognition of anxiety and its many manifestations.

For the purposes of discussion and understanding we can relate anxiety to fear, but the two are different in certain ways. We speak of fear in connection with something of which the person is definitely and consciously aware. If a man starts to cross a street and does not see a car that whizzes by and from whose path he must jump out of the way, he probably gets a fright as a result that will make his heart beat faster, bring out perspiration and leave him with a feeling of weakness. In that case he is afraid of something definite and that object has caused specific temporary changes in the body physiology. The effect from anxiety may be the same as that resulting from fear. Both fear and anxiety have similar functions. Both are signals to the person that he is in some serious danger. The difference between fear and anxiety is that the actual cause of neurotic anxiety is not conscious and we usually do not know why we feel the discomfort from it. In every neurosis and in every mental disease anxiety is present. Those who have suffered from mental conditions, such as depression of spirits, or from an obsessive compulsive reaction, say that mental suffering is most intense and that no physical suffering can compare with it. Anxiety is a very distressing state and the suffering from it can be far worse than the suffering from a physical disease because it can last so long and because relief can be so difficult to obtain.

Anxiety is not confined to the mind. Anxiety is an all-over sensation and is felt in the body as well as in the mind. We shall discuss the various distresses of mind and body resulting from anxiety as we proceed. Having introduced the subject of anxiety, however, and having indicated its importance and some of the ill effects when it is excessive, we would like to stress that to keep it at a minimum in each individual the infant should have love, affection, interest, attention, and fondling by a close contact with devoted parents, should not be allowed to be hungry too long, and should be allowed the satisfaction of sucking. If these needs are frustrated excessively, the child's development may be arrested or he may retain more characteristics of a particular stage of development than is normal and so be less capable of undergoing the next step in his growth. A fixation on that phase of his development has occurred. In general we should not fear that the baby will be spoiled by too much love and as a result later not accept socialization values. The result of experiencing excessive satisfactions at a given level of development, that is, of over-indulgence or spoiling, is not dangerous if the parents know how to ask for the child's co-operation in the requirements appropriate to his age. Moreover, the question of spoiling is not as important during this first period of development as it may be during later stages. On the contrary, the more the child experiences affection and understanding of his early instinctual needs the easier will be his later responses to family demands and the progress of his socialization.

Reading the papers these days, it would seem that our future depends upon well-planned, well-constructed and well-launched rockets. Does it not depend more upon well-constructed and well-launched personalities? And cannot the young profitably study personality as well as mathematics? The oral stage of personality development, we see, contains many variables. Father is important to the child in the first year of life. But, he is important in two different applications of himself. First, what he does directly for the child by feeding, taking care and playing with him, and, second, how he makes mother happy, contented and aware of the importance of the job she is doing in her role of mother. A husband and father must certainly apply himself in one of these ways and if he is to be the most help, he will apply himself in both. "Personal-making" is not a job that can be satisfactorily done by mother alone. What is more, she should not bear all the blame if she is forced to do it all alone and the results turn out unfavorably.

SUMMARY

We have discussed only the first year of life and have tried to show that the "baby" is a very sensitive and knowing human being. He is going through various experiences that are laying down some of the basic, automatic emotional patterns of the personality. He is learning that other human beings can or cannot be trusted. He is learning that they can be kind, reasonable, gentle, dependable, and consistent, or that they can be evasive, cruel, loud, capricious, and unreasonable. And we know from thousands of observations that what he learns in the first year is not easy to unlearn.

We have seen how the infant grows during the first year, if conditions are favorable, to have a healthy sense of his own importance. He learns of security from the hands of other people and how to win their co-operation in meeting his needs. He can learn many patterns of mutual satisfaction (giving-taking) that are almost entirely nonverbal. Or, on the other hand, he may have received so little nourishment of his emotional needs, not to mention his physical needs, that his emotional emptiness and hunger leaves him empty, isolated, lonely and estranged from his fellow man all his life.

Finally, we see that not only do important learnings occur in this first year having to do with social adaptation, but that there should be also healthy, secure emotional forces of *mutual concern between mother and child* that serve to keep the body physiology in a state of healthy equilibrium. The well-related child, i.e., the one who feels himself an important, appreciated part of a well-functioning family, is not so likely to have the sensitive skin, the queasy stomach, the irritable colon, or frequent headaches later, because his body is regarded is the vehicle which carries his personality around and not the sounding board for all the personality's aches, pains, irritations, and strains. One might say that if the baby's body is a joy and a delight in the mother's arms, that same body will become a joy and a delight to its owner later on. There are, of course, some exceptions to this rule, but it is still a rule worth bearing in mind for those who are rearing young people. The groundwork laid down the first year of life has more possibilities for good or bad results than most people have an awareness of.

BIBLIOGRAPHY FOR CHAPTER I

Abraham, Karl, *Selected Papers on Psychoanalysis,* Hogarth, 1927.
Bernfeld, Siegfried, *The Psychology of the Infant,* Kegan Paul, 1929.
Freud, Sigmund, *The Problem of Anxiety,* Norton, 1936.
Gesell, Arnold, *The First Five Years of Life,* Harper, 1940.
Ribble, Margaret A., *The Rights of Infants,* Columbia, 1943.

II

Emotional Disturbances that Occur during the Oral Period

W E ALL have in our minds a picture of the behavior of an ideal human being. This picture is different for the behavior of an infant, a child, an adolescent, an adult, or an old person. No two persons present exactly the same picture, but in a particular culture these differences are not very great, although they may be so between different cultures. If we observe some person acting too differently from our ideal pattern we feel that he is maladjusted, and according to the view that we may hold as to the reason for this maladjustment we label him as sick, unhappy, or perverse. If we have the task of trying to help him to a better adjustment we do so by dealing with the situation according to our idea of its cause; that is, we look for the cause of his sickness or unhappiness, or we scold or punish him for his perversity.

There are few people today who believe that the maladjusted person is innately bad and perverse, but there are many who feel baffled because they cannot easily determine the cause of the maladjustment. The reason is that they forget that the individual has basic instinctual and emotional needs; if he cannot satisfy them adequately—because of some physical or intellectual defect either acquired or inherited, because of some difficulties in his present environment, or because of the development of reaction patterns as a result of his infantile and childhood experiences, which prevent him satisfying his needs or force him to demand only the type of satisfaction that was reasonable in early childhood but now is unreasonable—he has to suffer pain and discomfort and must try to do something to relieve himself of these unpleasant feelings. In fact, we can say that if the behavior of a child deviates too much from the normal pattern, then we must investigate his physical and intellectual status and what, outside or inside himself, is frustrating the satisfaction of one or more of his basic instinctual and emotional needs.

As this book deals mainly with psychological processes relating to personality, it is necessary to discuss what we mean by *frustration*. All of us experience frustrations. As we mentioned earlier, some may be due to external causes—either from situations or from other people in our environment. We may have to frustrate our desires and wishes because our judgment tells us this is the wisest course. A man may be completely aware that he is angry at his boss but his judgment tells him that he would be foolish to try to do anything about expressing it. Some needs, wishes, and desires may be frustrated because the form of their expression would be regarded as wrong or improper or childish by our conscience—perhaps even before we are aware we have them. Such frustrated needs, wishes, and desires often are expressed and gratified in a distorted fashion in our dreams the night after the frustration has occurred. Some people who suffer from neuroses, from neurotic characters, or from psychoses have developed reaction patterns and unreasonable concepts of what is right and wrong and what is dangerous or not dangerous because of their childhood experiences. As they grow up these concepts have become unconscious but still govern their behavior and force them to forgo perfectly proper and reasonable methods of gratification for their instinctual needs and desires and so frustrate themselves.

During each period of development, the child may experience two types of frustration—those that are inevitable and those that are unnecessary. Every child experiences many inevitable frustrations because he lives largely by the pleasure principle and desires what he wants when he wants it. He may desire to continue being suckled rather than learn to eat in other ways. He may want to be carried by his parents rather than learn to walk by himself. He may be hungry at a time when it is impossible to feed him, but he has to endure the pain of hunger because he cannot be fed immediately. He feels disappointed and hurt if these wants are not satisfied. Gradually he learns that he can overcome his feelings of pain and discomfort by adopting new methods of behavior. He can learn to eat a greater variety of food and to use other methods of eating than sucking. He can learn to walk instead of being carried. Also, he will have to learn that he may have to postpone his desire for immediate gratification—even if this causes him to suffer some pain—and to wait until he has an opportunity to gratify his wishes and his needs. In his way he learns gradually to adapt his desire for immediate pleasure—the pleasure principle—to the demands of reality—the reality principle. Each new method of behavior is a step forward in his development; these forward steps eventually bring him more pleasure and enable him to have less pain and discomfort than if he had been able to continue with his old patterns.

Each step in the individual's development is inaugurated by a frustration, partly as a result of his progression in biological maturation and partly as a result of his necessary training. These frustrations give him a feeling of discomfort, and this feeling causes him to develop new skills in his ability to live. This is the process we anticipate will happen to every child, but it can occur only if the child first has an optimum period of the method of getting satisfaction for his inner needs, then becomes deprived of this method gradually so that although he experiences discomfort the suffering is mild and causes him to stir himself into activity instead of overwhelming him. The child should experience the necessary and inevitable frustrations in life in small doses and gradually, and should not be exposed to the necessary frustrations in sudden large doses or to unnecessary and unusual ones.

We said earlier that a frustration produces a feeling of pain and discomfort. The child is disturbed by this feeling and expresses his displeasure with whatever methods he has at his disposal. If he is a young infant who cannot talk, walk, or stand up, then he lies in his crib and cries, beats with his clenched fists, and kicks. He must express his reaction to his feeling of displeasure with the skill he has at his disposal at the time and with the methods his training has taught him are proper. If his training has been such that the child really cannot react to his discomfort, he will perceive the discomfort as what we called a feeling of anxiety—a signal that some need or desire is being frustrated and that he is in danger. He will react either to his feelings of discomfort or to his feelings of anxiety.

Basically, all his reactions will be one of, or a combination of, four types: he will fight the cause of the discomfort; he will run away from it in some way; he may become so overwhelmed by the frustration that he will remain immobile; or he may give up the skills and abilities adequate to his age and try to go back to the pleasures or behavior of an earlier period of development. (Freud has called this attempt to go back to an earlier stage of development in the face of present difficulties *regression,* believing that it stems partly from the innate desire to seek pleasure, and partly from the *repetition compulsion,* an innate tendency to repeat previous experiences, even though they may have been unpleasant.) These reactions to a feeling of discomfort produce behavior we regard as different from the normal and call *problem behavior.*

UNNECESSARY FRUSTRATIONS DURING THE ORAL STAGE

In the first chapter we described the behavior that we expect to find during the oral period of the average child's life. We stated also that he has certain emotional needs that he himself cannot satisfy because of his helplessness, and that therefore he has to depend on someone else for his satisfaction. If the infant has had parents on whom he can depend, he has experienced the inevitable frustrations in gradual small doses. He develops a feeling of social trust which he demonstrates by the ease of his feeding, the depth of his sleep, the relaxation of his bowels, and by his being interested and appearing happy and comfortable during the greater part of his waking hours. His first social achievement is his willingness to let his mother out of his sight without undue anxiety or rage. He will not really achieve this until he has progressed to the next stage of development.

What happens if these needs are frustrated severely or unnecessarily? The child suffers pain and discomfort and may react in the present against the process that produces the pain and suffering, against the person whom he holds responsible for the discomfort, or against both. This may result in the child's being unable to progress adequately to the next stage of development. It is as if, under the influence of the repetition compulsion, instead of progressing he is forced to remain to a greater or lesser extent at the oral stage of development in his unconscious need to find adequate pleasure there. He becomes fixated at the oral stage, and under the influence of his biologically determined course of development, he progresses only weakly to the next stage. This happens at any stage of development in childhood if the needs of that stage are frustrated unnecessarily. It also happens if he finds too much and too constant pleasure in one stage. It is not the constant great pleasure he feels that causes the fixation but the fact that he is too suddenly deprived of that pleasure by the force of circumstances.

A marked fixation at any stage of development means that the child does not grow up satisfactorily. He is not as well able to meet the difficulties he must find in his life and either in later childhood or adult life when faced with a usual difficulty of adjustment may tend to regress to the stage where the fixation occurred—in this case the oral stage. In the oral stage the child may suffer frustrations in the actual process of feeding, in his needs for being touched, moved, carried, spoken and sung to, and in his needs to be mothered.

FRUSTRATION ASSOCIATED WITH FEEDING

If the supply of breast milk is inadequate, if its chemical composition makes for difficulties in assimilation, if the nipples are inverted or are so constituted that sufficient milk is not obtained until the child becomes very fatigued, he experiences a frustration and feels dissatisfied and uncomfortable. Sometimes he reacts by vigorous protest. He cries and squirms. He regurgitates what he has in his stomach as if to say, "If I can't have what I want I don't want anything." He is more liable to do this if the ingested food produces cramps or colic. Sometimes he reacts by turning away and refusing to take the food offered him. Sometimes he reacts by ceasing to suck, and although the process of sucking is a reflex one he seems able to inhibit it so that it requires very strong stimulation to his lips in order to make him suck a few times more. Sometimes he reacts by rather quickly losing all feelings of hunger. When he should be hungry he tends to fall asleep as if he said, "Because my hunger has brought me only pain it is better that I do not feel this painful desire again."

As we mentioned earlier if the child is born with what is probably a constitutional activity type, he will tend to react to these discomforts with his activity type. The vigorously active child will protest vigorously while the inactive type will tend to fall asleep. It is important to note that the inactive types often are regarded as good babies. They seldom cry or complain and as a result sometimes they are really neglected by a busy but good and loving mother. Such babies need more stimulation than the active type. In fact, the very active type are helped more by being held firmly than by being stimulated.

Similar discomforts and the reactions to them occur if breast-feeding is complemented by new articles of food presented in an improper manner. If the complementary foods are served too hot, if their consistency makes digestion difficult, if, as the child gets his teeth, the food given him requires too much chewing so that he becomes fatigued, any of the reactions discussed above can occur, as if the child were saying through these reactions, "I don't want to eat if eating produces discomfort and pain." If the baby is very young he will retain the disorganized, irregular type of breathing, which is normal in the newborn, for a very long time. (This reaction will occur in all very young babies not only in respect to eating difficulties but also as a reaction to the other frustrating experiences mentioned in this section.)

These reactions directly affect the process of eating. If, because of the discomfort engendered by this eating situation, the child blames the mother for his trouble he will begin to turn away from her when she approaches, refuse her breast when it is offered to him, cry in her presence, and, as he gets a little older, refuse to do anything she suggests, often doing the opposite instead. This behavior resembles that of an older girl who said that because she became angry with her mother she resolved to go as far away from her as possible and to do everything her mother said was wrong.

As the reader can well understand, the mother can prevent some of these unnecessary discomforts. Others such as inverted nipples or breast milk inadequate in amount or composition she cannot. Whether the baby is breast-fed or bottle-fed, he should be held against the mother's body—perhaps preferably against her naked body—while he is being fed. When unpreventable but unusual discomforts occur during the feeding process the baby needs to be held more to make up to him for the uncomfortable feelings he had in satisfying his need to eat.

The child's desire to suck may also be frustrated. If the mother's breast produces an oversupply of milk the child does not have to suck much on the nipple because the slightest pressure of the lips causes the milk to flow freely down his throat. The same frustration may occur also if the child is bottle-fed from a nipple whose aperture is very large. In these instances the child does not get enough satisfaction for his need to suck and will have to suck nonnutritive objects—his fingers, his bedclothes, toys, and the like, for a much longer period than the two hours daily that he should devote to nonnutritive sucking. His finger sucking also will tend to continue for several months or years past the time when it is usually relinquished (between the second and third year). If he is allowed these extra periods of sucking he does not show any reactions of displeasure. However, if the parents disapprove and try to stop the finger sucking either because it disgusts them or because they have the superstition that it will deform the child's mouth, the child will suffer considerable discomfort and will react with a feeling of displeasure. He may begin to reject the ingestion of food in ways similar to those discussed above. He may act antagonistically to his mother. He may conform to the parent's wishes after a more or less prolonged struggle, and from that point on try to make a virtue of the fact that he does not suck. This means that he makes a virtue out of his ability to suffer the pain of the frustration of an inner desire or need and thus becomes able to extract pleasure out of his suffering. If such a mechanism becomes very well developed the child as he grows older may actually seek situations that will cause him pain in order to obtain the pleasure he finds in suffering, as he had learned to do when he found that if he rubbed his painful gums while his teeth were erupting there was an increase of pain followed by a greater feeling of comfort.

FRUSTRATIONS IN SENSORY STIMULATION
AND IN MOTHERING

We already have mentioned a number of times the baby's need to be touched, to be held, to be moved, to have objects to look at and touch, to be sung to, and read to. He needs these from the time he is born. In the first three or four months these teach him to feel and be aware of his feelings. Later, they teach him to know that he can obtain pleasure from his own actions and also pleasure from his mother. The newborn baby cannot distinguish very well between his own self and his surroundings, but as his sensory organs become better developed he begins to make a distinction between himself and his mother—who to him is the source of all pleasure and comfort—and he yearns for her attentions and presence. In her daily routine care of him during washing and dressing she touches the sensitive parts of his body—his arms, hands, face, the skin around his anus, his genitals, his feet and legs, and his trunk. All of these touches are pleasurable and he learns this and begins to remember the pleasure and to yearn for more of it. Similarly, he finds pleasure in being moved and carried. If he got none of this stimulation, his intellectual and physical development would only proceed slowly if at all.

It has long been known that the death rate among babies in orphanages and foundling homes even though they are well fed and well cared for physically is much higher than among children in their own homes. Those children who live develop personalities in which the use of their intellectual abilities and initiative are limited. They seem to lack basic identifications and so either cling to authoritarian rules during their lives or have periods when their impulses break through in an uncontrolled fashion as delinquent episodes. Pediatricians also have known for a long time that babies who have to be hospitalized for a long period of time do not develop as well as those that remain in their homes and with their mothers. Both groups suffer from the lack of needful stimulation. For adequate development the baby needs an optimal amount of sensory stimulation. We say an *optimal* amount because too much stimulation causes him to cry and suffer discomfort. This readily can be observed when the parent rushes at the baby in the crib, hauls him out, and swings him around or tosses him in the air and catches him. At first the baby may coo and smile but if this is repeated too often and done too strenuously, he will start to cry and later will begin to cry when he sees the parent come toward him. Everybody knows that the arrival of grandparents or other well-known relatives who wish to talk to and hold the baby may cause him to be uncomfortable and to cry, particularly if he is somewhat fatigued. We think that too much or too strenuous throwing up in the air and catching the baby or small child is much too stimulating for him and may have adverse effects on his development.

When the mother really loves her baby he senses this in her and he responds to her and tries to please her even if this means occasionally that he has to undergo the discomfort of some frustration—which will be gentle, slow, and careful because the loving mother intuitively understands how the child feels. Of course every mother who loves her baby has her own individual pattern of mothering and her own psychological reasons for this pattern, as Sylvia Brody has described very well; if the reader is interested, he will find her book of value.

Due to certain profound though temporary psychological changes in every mother which accompany the processes of pregnancy, childbirth, and the early post partum period, many mothers begin to feel slightly depressed when the baby is about two to four months of age. This usually ceases when her baby shows response to her care, but if he does not or she thinks he does not, her depression may deepen and her interest in mothering him diminish. We will discuss some of the reasons for the mother's dislike of her baby in Chapter Six. The baby senses this lack of love through her handling of him and feels very frustrated and upset.

Disturbances in her patterns of mothering may develop if the mother loves the baby but if the circumstances of her life have upset her emotionally so that she becomes too worried by her own problems to be able to respond fully to her love for the child. A little girl about seven months of age was referred for study of her compulsive masturbation which was performed by pressing her thighs together tightly in a rhythmical manner and which occupied most of her waking time. This started shortly after a period of severe feeding difficulty accompanied by colic and vomiting had subsided. The feeding difficulty, which started when the baby was about four months old and lasted until the baby was a little over six months old, began rather suddenly following a serious quarrel between the mother and her brother-in-law, which severely disturbed the mother emotionally. The child became so ill that she had to be weaned, and only when a formula that agreed with her was found did the gastrointestinal disturbance cease, to be replaced immediately by the compulsive masturbation. It seemed that this child reacted first to the frustration occasioned by the change in the mother's attitude by developing a feeding difficulty and when this was corrected continued to react by endeavoring to be an older child and to be sufficient unto herself. It was as if she said, "I can get all the gratification I need from my own body. I do not need my mother because at her hands all I experience is pain and suffering." She reacted to her feelings of pain and suffering by attempting to grow up too quickly and to obtain satisfaction for herself through methods which she was not ready either physiologically or psychologically to find really satisfying. This meant that her development during the oral stage became confused intraphysically with a phase of development which should appear during a later stage of her life.

Of course, the mother who is an ambulant schizophrenic, who suffers from a psychotic depression during the first year of a child's life or who has a severe psychoneurosis finds it difficult to care for her baby adequately. She is too concerned with herself and has little or no real love to give to him. Physical illnesses of the mother which require hospitalization or confine her to bed, even although she is at home, for several weeks or months mean that she cannot take care of her baby. No matter how mature and loving a mother is, fate may step in and she may die. Also, although the mother may love the child and although she may not be upset emotionally she may go off for a vacation or on business and leave the child to the care of someone else. The absence may be a brief one, of only a week or two, but the child regards the separation as a sign that the mother does not love him. Even though well cared for, he may feel neglected and lonely, with very much the same feeling that the adult has when someone he loves dearly goes away.

Except for the perhaps rather sudden weaning from breast-feeding, separation from the mother does not matter so much to the baby during the first three or four months. Studies on animal behavior show that newborn birds follow the first moving object they see, whether it is the mother or not, and will remain close to that object rather than the real mother throughout the rest of their baby life, and the newborn human baby in its first weeks or months has the same undiscerning attitude. However, after the fourth month, when the baby begins to recognize the mother, and particularly at eight months, when the signs of separation anxiety are at their peak, the child reacts greatly to such a separation. When older children or adults feel homesick, they are experiencing only a pale replica of the separation anxiety that the baby feels.

Painful or very frightening experiences, such as operations or very painful long-continued illnesses, particularly if they occur in the second six months of life, sometimes cause serious disturbances in the development of the child's confidence in himself. Instead of developing a knowledge of himself as a pleasurable going concern who occasionally suffers certain unpleasurable feelings, such a child suddenly is forced to use a great deal of energy to avoid the memory of the painful shock that he has suffered, and he has to keep himself constantly wary of any unfamiliar or only partly familiar environmental situation which might presage a recurrence of the terrifying experience. Both of these attitudes expend a great deal of his energy, so that the amount of energy at his disposal for his development will be severely curtailed. He will be constantly apprehensive, and so his capacity to explore and learn of new situations and abilities and to relate them to previous remembered pleasurable experiences will be greatly hindered. Instead of being confident and trustful he will be untrustful and unconfident.

In some cases of childhood psychoses, which we will describe more fully later, the cause of the illness seemed to have been an operation that took place in the latter half of the first year.

THE BABY'S REACTIONS TO AN UNLOVING MOTHER AND OTHER ADVERSE TYPES OF MOTHERING

When the mother's attitude to the baby is based on lack of love for him—whether this lack of love is real, as when the mother actually dislikes the child, suffers from a schizophrenic psychosis or a depression, or when she seems so involved with her own emotional problem that she is indifferent to him—when her patterns of mothering are very inadequate, when she is separated from her baby whatever the cause, when he suffers serious disturbances in his feeding or has been unfortunate enough to have had a very painful or frightening illness or operation, the baby soon senses that he is being exposed to a climate that seems filled with discomfort and pain.

Of course the degree of his reactions to this displeasurable situation will depend on the degree of deprivation and discomfort that he actually receives. However, in general, the child's symptoms as a result of these adverse environmental climates fall into several groups. He may react with anxiety symptoms, such as frequent crying, restlessness, insomnia, vomiting, and diarrhea. The chronic restlessness frequently causes the child to rock himself in the knee-chest position or to bang his head. It might be noted that when a baby persistently rocks, and particularly if he does it in the position we have just described, or when he bangs his head constantly, the parents should consult a child psychiatrist to ascertain the cause of the behavior. When the reaction is quite severe, a real depression occurs, with weeping, unappeasable screaming at the approach of strangers, refusal to show any interest or any need for food, etc., or interest or need for any person—with resulting developmental arrest. Such a reaction is designated as an *anaclitic depression*.

In a third type of reaction, the baby becomes negativistic and antagonistic to the parents, and all his reactions are disturbed to the point of what looks like paranoid suspiciousness. He rejects all toys except his own feces, which he often eats (*coprophagia*).

In all cases, he may express his displeasure by developing reactions against the taking of food—the main activity in which he knows his mother is interested—or by direct antagonistic reactions to her (instead of trying to please her he does nothing or does the opposite), or by falling into a condition of semistupor where he pays no attention either to food or to her. These feeding disorders range all the way from simple refusal of food to prolonged vomiting and may reach the degree of marasmus, which produces an arrest of psychic development that may result in mental impairment or death.

Refusal to eat or vomiting after eating may occur also if the environment in the home is one in which there is too much strife, if there is quarreling between husband and wife or between mother and grandmother, if there is tension between the mother and her mother-in-law, if there is too much noise and interference from other children—all of which wreak a constant bombardment upon the psyche of the newborn child.

We have said before that incorporation is the psychological process of taking into the body, through the mouth, the objects, human and otherwise, in the environment. Naturally we do not take in everything by way of the mouth; we take in ideas and principles through the eyes and ears, for example, but certainly a great deal of what we take in goes in with the taking of food. The taking of communion in a Christian church is an example from everyday life of the value and importance of incorporation. We are told that in communion we partake of the body of Christ. This is a symbolism which means taking Christ's ideas as well as his Body within us, and we are supposed to make new commitments to the religious principles connected with the Church. In other words, we have here the process of taking in a person, and the principles and cause that He stood for. In the symbolism of communion the Church must long ago have recognized that ideas are taken in along with food by way of the mouth.

At the time when the child has his attention centered on the oral part of the body, people are inextricably bound up with his oral activity. He incorporates both the pleasant and the unpleasant features of the environment; this produces within the child what are known as good and bad *objects*. The incorporation of the pleasant features in his environment—of the good object—makes him feel that he is a good and lovable person, and gives him self-confidence. When the people in the environment are unpleasant, irritating, or obnoxious, when they are not kind to the infant, he may eat his meals but he feels he has something inside him that is unpleasant. This unpleasantness is not undigested milk or an unsuitable formula but is the unpleasantness in his environment—the bad object—which he has incorporated along with his meals. We have the expression in our language, "I am sick of this job." The expression grows from experience; people have had to become ill and vomit when in a difficult situation in an attempt to rid themselves of obnoxious people or circumstances.

This incorporation of an unpleasant part of the environment produces a bad object in the child which makes him feel that he is bad, that he is the cause of his sufferings. This makes him lose confidence in himself. He realizes to some extent that his suffering comes upon him from without and that he really had nothing to do with its cause; it is as if an adverse fate had fallen upon him. In his apprehension lest he re-experience the discomfort, he dreads lest fate again be unkind to him. This apprehension gives him a sense of impending disaster and as he grows up and as an adult, he tends to view the future as if a malignant fate were waiting to pounce on him. He becomes a true pessimist. He begins to behave in ways that will avoid the disaster he anticipates. Since he has reacted to a frustrating experience in a specific way—by desiring to eat constantly or by clinging to his mother, etc.—that specific way of reacting is more something belonging to him than other methods might be. Hence he tends thereafter to react to frustrations in the same general pattern perhaps by clinging to some one or two persons, perhaps by overeating, perhaps by the abuse of alcohol, and perhaps by an addiction to drugs.

SUICIDAL DEFENSES

Under these circumstances as a little baby, he may not wish to go on with the life process. We say "wish," as if the child had the decision, which he does not have as we think of decision, according to our standards. But this small piece of protoplasm, from all we can observe, can seem actually to decide that living under too much frustration and pain is not worth the effort. It has been known that babies who have been very distressed and who have not had life made pleasant for them in the beginning have seemed to turn away from life, from sucking, from eating, from the taking of food. The baby does not turn away wilfully; he does so because he has suffered too much pain. Some adults who have gone through a great number of painful vicissitudes may come to the conclusion that they cannot stand any more, and they jump off a bridge or out of the window of a high building. The rational mind does not have much to do with the reasoning of people in this state. They feel that they have got to get out of a world that has been too painful up to now, and they cannot see any hope that it is going to be less so. Even though an adult person's work and other activities may have brought him to the point of considerable success in spite of obstacles, something else may go wrong. He loses his money, or a member of his family, and he feels he must turn away from the disappointment of life. If an adult with all the memories of his past pleasures and his knowledge of the possibility of present pleasures and advantages can do this it should not be difficult to understand why a child who has had a very little pleasure, who has had to live in a cold, frustrating environment, should have sufficient pain of anxiety from what he has suffered to make him stop functioning. The same mechanism is at work in the child who does not want to eat that is at work in the person who commits suicide. In the case of the suicidal adult, however, besides wanting to get away from his sufferings he also is killing some person whom he has deeply loved and bitterly hated and who now has disappointed him in some way. As the result of his disappointment he has incorporated the other person in himself and so when he kills himself, he also, in his mind, kills the other person.

THE EXPERIENCE OF WEANING

No matter how carefully the child is cared for he has to experience one major frustration in his early life—he has to be weaned from the breast and later from the bottle. If the weaning is done suddenly the child shows all the reactions already discussed, in a rather severe form. It is important, therefore, that weaning be a gradual process. This can be done if the child receives complementary feedings of semisolids very early in his life. It is desirable that he be breast-fed, even if breast-feeding has to be complemented, for as many months as possible, and that complete weaning not take place until after the ninth or tenth month.

Another character type resulting from fixation at the oral stage is the person who acts as if he believed he didn't have to do anything himself in order to be successful in his life, as if the world owed him a living and all he had to do was to sit and it would be brought to him. His attitude is one of unrealistic optimism in the constant beneficence of "fate" but is not one of real self-confidence. This type of character is the result of breast-feeding and babying prolonged much beyond the end of the first year. The fixation, however, occurs because of the necessary sudden termination which brings it to an end. Such situations may also result in a symbiotic psychosis in later childhood or in those children who later show serious separation anxiety.

We have observed very cruel and unnecessary types of weaning which have had disastrous effects on the child's later development. One mother decided she would not spoil her child, so at the age of two months weaned him suddenly from the breast and went on a vacation of several weeks, leaving him to the care of a total stranger. Thus, the child was frustrated not only in the feeding process but also in his relation to his mother. Another mother weaned her son by putting him to the breast and then pinching him painfully. Of course, as the boy grew up he consciously did not remember this occurrence. However, he knew the story from his mother, who told it to him on several occasions. During his treatment when an adult, it was noticeable that he regularly fell in love with women whom he knew would treat him cruelly. If he made a mistake and fell in love with a kind woman, he would act toward her in such a manner that eventually she would become cruel to him. In another case the mother became concerned because the child was so anxious and fearful; she had weaned him suddenly at the age of two months. At the age of six months she broke his habit of finger sucking by a painful punishment—the application of mittens that tied his hands to his sides. In the face of these frustrations it was no wonder that the child became anxious and fearful.

PSYCHOTHERAPY FOR ILLNESS
DURING THE ORAL PERIOD

The physician who is consulted about problem behavior in a child in the first year of life should remember that prevention is much better than cure, and that at this time the climate in which the child usually lives will be the cause of the pathology. The child himself will contribute little. In later periods of development, the pathology may be within the child himself and may not be due to the environment. This is not so during the first year. The physician should understand that the problem behavior arises from one of four sources or a combination of them: (1) the child has undergone a series of painful experiences, most commonly during his feeding; (2) his need to suck for pleasure and not for nutrition has been frustrated; (3) his certainty that he can depend on his mother for the satisfaction of his needs has been destroyed because of her attitude toward him, her behavior with him, or the circumstances of her life; (4) his emotional comfort has been destroyed by wrangling in his environment. The first and third show the most violent and immediate effects because they are in reality a threat to his life. We do not mean that he can formulate in his mind the clear idea that if his mother leaves him or if he can't eat without hurting himself he will die; we mean rather that he shows a reaction which, if it could be translated into a concept, would have that content. He is able to suppress the desire for nonnutritive sucking more easily because it does not put him in danger of immediate death. His reaction seems less important because it comes more slowly, but it may continue over a long period of time.

How is the doctor to proceed in the treatment of these conditions? When the illness—that is, the reaction of the child to the frustrating situation—has started, the procedure of approach is first to ascertain the cause (namely, the frustrating situation) and the need that is being frustrated. The physician who is called to treat a child with a gastrointestinal disturbance should inquire as fully into the emotional experience of the child as he does into the chemical composition of the food the baby has been receiving.

When the frustrating experience has been ascertained it is important that the mother and physician start handling the child as if he were a little younger than he was when he experienced the pain.

If the difficulty was started because a supplemental food was given when it was too hot, it is desirable to take him off all supplemental feedings, and then after a period of time to introduce the supplemental feedings gradually without forcing them on him. It has been demonstrated experimentally that if a baby is forced to put something in his mouth before he is ready to, he reacts by signs of discomfort and by developing colic. If the illness has been caused by the mother's preventing the baby from doing nonnutritive sucking it will be necessary for her not only to allow the sucking to begin again, but also to try to encourage him to start sucking nonnutritive objects. If the frustration has occurred because of the mother's attitude or behavior toward the child this will have to be changed, and the mother for a time will have to go further in the opposite direction than she would usually.

Feeding difficulties in a baby, either vomiting or refusal to eat, may cause serious emergencies in which there is danger of the child's dying. The child will not eat because he feels hostility around him or because his needs have not been properly met. In order to get the baby to return to his proper eating habits he needs a warmer environment or a friendlier person to take care of him. As his life may be in danger, it may take too long for safety to change the mother's attitude or the behavior of the adults in the environment. Such a situation requires a change in environment. This may be provided by leaving him in his own home but placing him in the complete charge of a more understanding, more loving, and more serene person than his mother; or the child must be taken out of his home and put in a warmer, more loving, and more affectionate environment than his own home has furnished. During the period of separation, treatment for the home situation should be continued so that the baby will return to a more loving and peaceful environment and be able to remain well.

As always, the best treatment would be to prevent the occurrence of the illness. The physician should weigh carefully the actual need to use any painful and uncomfortable medical procedure or operation, particularly in the second half of the first year. Unless it is absolutely necessary for the child's life or well-being that it be done at this time, it should be avoided. The mature, loving mother can depend on her own intuitive reactions to prevent the baby's undergoing the unnecessary frustrations we have discussed.

Many mothers really love their children but are either not aware of the importance of their intuitive reactions to the child or are afraid to depend on them. Such conflict is very evident along two lines, breast-feeding and separation. Many mothers actually long to nurse their babies but fear they are doing the wrong thing in insisting upon it, if either the doctor or the nurse tends to disagree, or that their friends or relatives will laugh at them for being too old-fashioned. Other mothers are not so aware of their own longing to suckle the infant or feel there is something too animal about such a desire, and so are very easily persuaded to wean the child. Similarly, although the mother may love the child and be quite heartsick at the thought of leaving her baby when she goes on vacation, she may try to disregard her own feelings because her husband might not have as good a time if the baby were taken along, or because her friends might think her foolish and antiquated to be such a doting mother. She goes on vacation, stifling her own feelings by being sure that the child will get good physical care and by the pleasant feelings engendered by the new surroundings and experiences. In both instances the mother interferes with her own intuitively correct feelings because she dreads some external condemnation and the child suffers as a result.

These types of mothers could be helped greatly to be less sensitive to external disapproval by the support of their doctor or by intellectual knowledge. For such, a course during the period of pregnancy in the essentials of child care and the fundamental emotional needs of the child would be very helpful. This could be given directly by the obstetrician to groups of pregnant women as part of prenatal care, or in clinics as part of the prenatal preparation. We are not of the opinion that intellectual knowledge in itself is a cure-all for these problems. We believe, however, that many women at present show an increasing dread of believing in their own feelings lest they appear foolish in the eyes of friends or lest the expression of their feelings in some way injure the child. Such women may be more certain of the adequacy of their feelings as guides if they feel the support of outside authority.

Of course we are aware that this fact (that a woman may stifle her own feelings because she dreads outside criticisms) does not account for the majority of mothers who refuse to nurse their children or who go off and leave their young babies in the care of other people. All too often the behavior is the result of a conflict between the feelings of love toward the baby and the selfish desire to do things that give the mother more pleasure, and in the conflict the latter impulse wins, often to the point that the mother is aware only of her desire for pleasure for herself and unaware of her feeling of love for the child. Such women cannot be good mothers regardless of the amount of intellectual education they receive.

There is no question that in the first year of life severe organic feeding disturbances, severe and painful illnesses, and marked disturbances in mothering—due to the death, serious organic illness, or severe depression in the mother (none of which are preventable)—may produce serious and perhaps irreversible disturbances in the child which may affect adversely the remainder of his life. However, it should be remembered one swallow does not make a summer nor do what seem serious situations in any one period of development necessarily become irreversible. We have known people who as babies had very severe organic gastrointestinal disturbances, who during their later childhood and adult life have been quite happy and successful people. The early disturbance has been corrected by adequate handling and sufficient mothering during this and throughout the later stages of development.

Anna Freud and Sophie Dann have reported a group of children who spent their first four or five years in a Nazi extermination camp. Some of their parents were exterminated when the children were only a few months old. These children were ill fed and there was a succession of women who mothered them, each for a short period prior to her own extermination, each knowing before she died that she had only a few days left to live. These children did not die. They seemed to develop their personalities through reliance on the group of children with whom they lived. When they were released, they showed fairly adequate personality development and were getting along pretty well. Miss Freud and Mrs. Dann have had these children studied—and many of them by psychoanalysts—since they became older. They have not published the results of their studies, but it would seem that most of them are adjusting moderately well. So, although as much care and prevention of trauma during the oral period as is possible should be desired, parents, physicians, and social workers should not be too pessimistic as to the future of a baby who has lived through unpreventable adverse experiences.

SUMMARY

The problems which arise during the oral period are essentially difficulties in feeding, in mothering, in too much or too little stimulation, painful illnesses and operations, and separation of the child from his mother, particularly after five months of age. Whether these needs of the child are frustrated by unpreventable situations (acts of fate) or by the mother's conscious or unconscious attitudes, including her own disturbance by unsolved intrapsychic conflicts or her environment, the child feels pain and discomfort and reacts to it by a greater or lesser refusal to eat and by turning away from the human beings in his environment.

In the most severe cases, the refusal to eat food may result in death. (It should be mentioned here that feeding difficulties in young children *only* cause death during the first year of life.) Also, in severe cases the turning away from persons in the environment may result in permanent intellectual impairment, in either retarded or too rapid emotional development, or later, in an autistic psychosis, or in prolonged autoerotic pleasures (head banging, rocking, and coprophagia).

Each period of psychosexual development should last an optimal period and come to a close gradually. If there is less than the optimal oral period or if the oral gratifications are insufficient, the child may attempt to cling to the psychological methods of obtaining satisfaction during that period (a fixation at the oral level may occur) and later will show oral personality traits—demandingness, extreme jealousies, a chronic pessimistic attitude and a deepseated feeling that he cannot trust finding necessary satisfactions from the environment and a lack of confidence in his ability to obtain needed satisfactions —a basic attitude of mistrust, or if experiences later in his life prove frustrating, he will turn backwards (regress) to oral methods of getting gratification. In some cases the regression may be severe, as in the depressive psychoses. In other cases with an oral fixation, the person eats or drinks whenever the least frustration occurs in his life or when he becomes anxious.

A fixation on the psychological reactions to methods normal for the oral stage may occur if the period is brought to a close too suddenly by abrupt weaning.

As the child's basic instinctual orientation during the oral period is passive-receptive and as he is not able to act on his environment very much and thus is forced to submit to the emotional climate during this period because he can do little to change it, therapeutic measures will be directed toward modifying the behavior and attitudes of the persons who are looking after him (usually the mother), toward changing the emotional climate. It may be possible to help the mother through counseling or psychotherapy. Or it may be necessary to introduce a new and better mother substitute. It has been found that in some cases the traumatic effects of the emotional climate are so severe that they become irreversible and the child remains emotionally crippled throughout his life—so crippled that even prolonged psychotherapy later cannot help him. These cases actually are few. In other instances, the effects of the adverse emotional climate can be removed to a greater or less extent later by psychotherapy. In cases in which there has been an unpreventable trauma about one of the child's needs—for example, an organically caused feeding problem—adequate mothering during the oral stage and optimal emotional climates during the later periods of psychosexual development will undo the effects of the feeding problem.

BIBLIOGRAPHY FOR CHAPTER II

Benedek, Therese, "Adaptation to Reality in Early Infancy," *Psychoanalytic Quarterly,* 7, 1938, 200.

Brody, Sylvia, *Patterns of Mothering,* International Universities Press, 1956.
(This book has a complete bibliography on the relationship of the infant and the mother.)

Davis, C. M., "Self Selection of Diet by Newly Weaned Infants," *American Journal of Diseases of Children,* 36, 1928, 651.

Erikson, Erik H., *Childhood and Society,* Norton, 1950.

Freud, Anna, "Psychoanalytic Study of Feeding Disturbances," *Psychoanalytic Study of the Child,* 2, International Universities Press, 1942.

Freud, Anna, and D. Burlingham, *Infants without Families,* International Universities Press, 1944.

Freud, Anna, and Sophie Dann, "An Experiment in Group Upbringing," *Psychoanalytic Study of the Child,* 6, 127, International Universities Press, 1951.

Greenacre, Phyllis, *Affective Disorders, Psychoanalytic Contribution to Their Study,* International Universities Press, 1953.

Levy, David M., and A. Hess, "Problems in Determining Maternal Attitudes Toward Newborn Infants," *Psychiatry,* 15, 1952, 273.

Pearson, Gerald H. J., *Emotional Disorders of Children,* Norton, 1949.

────── *Psychoanalysis and the Education of the Child,* Norton, 1954.

Spitz, Rene A., "Hospitalism: An Inquiry into the Genesis of Psychiatric Conditions in Early Childhood," *Psychoanalytic Study of the Child,* I, International Universities Press, 1945.

────── "Psychiatric Therapy in Infancy," *American Journal of Orthopsychiatry,* 20, 1950, 623.

────── "The Psychogenic Diseases in Infancy," *Psychoanalytic Study of the Child,* 6, International Universities Press, 1951.

Winnicott, D. W., "The Observation of Infants in a Set Situation," *International Journal of Psychoanalysis,* 22, 1941, 229.

III

Development of Personality during the Anal Period

THE ORAL period comes to an end about the end of the first year. This does not mean that the activities of the oral period cease at the end of the first year; in fact, the activities and the needs of the oral period continue as long as life lasts. As the child nears the end of the first year he has gained a great deal of muscular ability that he did not have at birth. The average child is creeping and actively pulling himself up by holding onto furniture, some children are standing alone, and some are beginning to take steps. At this time most children understand what is said to them and some are beginning to respond by talking. The child's interest in the world around him is expanding, and the world around him is likewise beginning to make demands upon him for conformity to certain social requirements. A biologically predetermined change in the importance of the erogenous zones also has come about. During the first year the greatest amount of pleasure was obtained through the use of the mouth, but by the end of the first year considerable pleasure begins to be obtained from the use of the anus and rectum. For this reason the second period of psychosexual development has been designated the anal stage. This stage lasts from about the end of the first year to the end of the third year and is therefore longer than the oral phase (according to paper reckoning only, of course).

We want to make clear to the reader certain points about these stages of psychosexual development. The seven stages of psychosexuality—oral, anal, genital, latency, adolescence, adulthood, and senescence—are predetermined biologically; as far as we know they are universal in all human beings and in all cultures. During each stage of psychosexual development the child has to learn how to solve certain specific problems, although all of the problems remain throughout the whole of his life. For example, as we have pointed out, during the oral stage the main problems are those of: (1) feeling important as a human being, (2) feeling secure in the matrix of human beings and, (3) building trust in human beings. During the anal stage the main achievements are those of: (1) discovering that one can accomplish something that will please others, (2) discovering that one can produce beauty in form and color, (3) discovering that one can produce power—trading power—by virtue of the concentration of his own emotional and physical forces and, (4) discovering that his mind and body can contribute to the general state of social (family) well-being. The achievement of these various capacities results in the additional development of the ego, that is, in personality development. The growth occurs in consequence of the interaction, during each period, between the child and his upbringers. The child manifests his instinctual needs and desires. The upbringers—parents and other members of the social organization—deal with the manifestations of the various stages in ways which will insure maturity of the personality. Mature personalities inevitably bring about cultural growth.

TOILET TRAINING

The most significant manner in which the child has to conform during the anal period is to go through bowel and bladder training. This activity is highly important because it is a most personal phase of his training and because it pertains to the individual's body and its feelings. Learning to dress himself or put away his toys does not "touch" the child nearly so closely in the sense of physiological tension. We must realize that our society has a great many attitudes concerning cleanliness, neatness, and the control of eliminations that are in conflict with the child's own instinctual tendencies. As far as the child's personal comfort goes, he would continue to empty his bowels and bladder as tension appeared in these organs; in short, as he became uncomfortable. The world around him does not permit this, however. Therefore, the child must begin to accept regulations; he must gain a certain control of himself with the help of others, and he must begin to take certain responsibilities.

A child who is brought up in a family where extreme value is placed on cleanliness will be in the midst of keener conflict than the one in a home where the people are more relaxed about things of that kind. In many homes cleanliness has a moral aspect; a dirty child is considered a wicked and bad child, so a feeling of guilt can develop in such surroundings. In all homes there is the practical matter of the mother or the nurse having to wash a great many clothes for the child. For these various reasons a great deal of pressure may be put upon the child to control his excretions as early as possible for the convenience, comfort, and esthetic gratification of those around him. This pressure puts a strain upon his psychological apparatus. At best, learning to meet the environment's expectations and demands of cleanliness is actually one of the big problems of human development. Under the most favorable conditions it is not an easy process; under unfavorable conditions it can lead to a great deal of anxiety, hostility, and other attitudes that we will take up as we go along.

Let us consider the child who has been the recipient of all bounties of the home for, roughly, a year, and who now confronts a considerable change in his environment. Now, instead of being the receiver, he is asked to begin to be the giver. Now, instead of being contributed to, he is asked to make a contribution. Now, instead of being in the position of irresponsibility, he is asked to assume a responsibility in relation to himself. He has to learn to hold in and to let go.

The bowel and bladder training is not the only thing of psychological importance that happens in the years between one and three. There are others: getting the idea of keeping the body clean through bathing and hand washing and tooth brushing; being neat about clothes; avoiding too much contamination with foreign matter in play; keeping the playroom clean and in some order; and, perhaps, learning to share toys with other children and to pay some polite attention to friends of the family who come into the home. Parents may begin to teach a great many of the social amenities at this time. The child is asked to do what the grownups want—to be a little lady or a little gentleman. However, none of these matters come quite so close to his instinctual needs and none are so personal as bowel and bladder control.

Whenever instinctual tension exists in the body there is a tendency to seek relief from that tension without regard to environmental standards. The attitude follows the pleasure principle. From the standpoint of the pleasure principle children do not want to bother with toilet training at all. It is foreign to their wishes, foreign to their comfort; but they have to accept it all the same. In certain homes the child's natural abilities are kept in mind and toilet training is not begun until the end of the first year. At least, it *should* not be begun very much before the end of the year because it has been shown by careful neuropathological study that the tracts of the spinal cord are not completely myelinated until the end of the first year. Therefore, it is rather futile—at least it is demanding a great deal—to ask the child to exercise control over his organs for which he does not have the neurological pathways completely laid down.

Nevertheless, toilet training often *is* begun somewhat earlier. Most pediatric authorities agree that toilet training should not be begun before the eighth month, better not until the tenth month or the end of a year. It should be begun by observing when the child usually has bowel movements, then placing him on a comfortable toilet seat around that time and indicating by gestures and tone of voice that he is expected to pass his eliminations in this particular place and at this particular time. This is a difficult matter to grasp because the child's mind is still incompletely formed to comprehend any ideas such as these. He achieves it as a result of repeated attempts, a great deal of patience, and a great deal of understanding on the part of those who are doing the training.

Achievement in bowel control in average, healthy, intelligent children will not have taken place until the end of the eighteenth month and possibly not until the end of the second year. Therefore, in the best cases—begun at a year with the expectation of some result at eighteen months—mothers should realize that they have quite a number of days in which to work out the problem with the child. A child that is both clean and dry at the end of the third year is a satisfactorily performing human being and, as a rough yardstick of behavior at this age, should reassure many perfectionistic mothers and permit them to soften their insistent drive toward a good machine physiologically speaking but a nervous wreck in addition.

PERSONALITY CONSEQUENCES OF TOILET TRAINING: THE CHILD'S REACTION

There are many attitudes toward excretions in various parts of the world, which show in the personality patterns of the adults. In Western civilization and particularly in England and in the United

States people tend to have a considerable feeling of shame and disgust concerning these functions. There is, of course, no need of this. Indeed, such feelings *should not* exist; yet they do exist. We trust the reader will see that the feeling of shame and disgust that surrounds toilet training is one of those unfortunate social attitudes that in later life causes people to be very ashamed of their bodies and to be ashamed of sexual functioning especially. In other words, some of the emotion that is engendered at this period over bowel and bladder functioning spreads out and encompasses sexuality, since the organs of sexual functioning and excretion are associated.

In the course of their work, doctors encounter difficulty with certain patients in the wards, in their homes, and in their offices, because these patients are reluctant to undress, reluctant to expose themselves, reluctant to be sensibly examined. They react in a way that is overmodest and inappropriate, and it is often time-consuming to get the co-operation needed for giving the best advice. This over-modesty is due largely to the way these people have been educated as children, particularly in their toilet habits. Many people, we are sure, feel that everyone ought to be ashamed and disgusted about elimination and that if people do not have shame and disgust, and a great deal of it, they are not nice persons. Some go so far as to feel that people are immoral if they are not ashamed of themselves in relation to the body and its functioning.

We hope the reader realizes that having such a feeling and having it in such intensity is not necessary at all. In the first place, children *do* wish to conform to what is expected of them and will do so in time if they are treated with consideration. *That can be relied upon.* That fact is a very important one for doctors to remember to pass on to their patients, to mothers of children, to nurses, to grandmothers, and to anyone who has charge of a child. Very often these people make the serious error of having no confidence whatever in the child's innate intelligence, in his wish to conform, in his desire to do what is asked of him if he is only allowed a reasonable time for learning. Instead, some believe he will not learn unless treated strictly, harshly, even cruelly. In other words, they ignore that which is posi-tive in the child—his ability and willingness to conform. If they allow time, if they give the child love and affection, if they give him confidence and approval when he meets their expectations, and if they refrain from scolding and browbeating when he does not, the child will eventually master the training in a satisfactory manner.

In the matter of toilet training and, incidentally, in all other little things that the child has to begin to learn in this period, his co-operation is likely to be good somewhat in proportion to the way he was treated during the oral period. In other words, the mother who has been generous, affectionate, interested in her child when he was helpless and at her mercy in the first year of life will be repaid with a much better conformity when the problem of toilet training arises than she whose child has been treated inconsiderately and already has acquired a grudge against those around him. If a child is happy and well adjusted at the end of the first year and the mother indicates what is expected of him in the matter of toilet training—does not hurry him too much, does not become too irritated, does not become unkind on too many days—she will get the desired result.

Children just will not go on soiling themselves or wetting themselves indefinitely if patience and tolerance are used. Probably very few mothers can believe this, hence a mother will become rather anxious on certain days and feel that her child is destined to be a nonconformist and that she must put on the pressure or she will have a child who seems to be feeble-minded, or at least behaves in a way that will bring criticism to her as a parent. Too often, instead of realizing some of the facts we have mentioned, the mother has not related herself to the child and his needs but has fixed her attention on some neighbor down the street who is boasting that her child is clean or dry; then the mother feels she has to become very hard on her own child in order to make him appear as clever, intelligent, and capable as the neighbor's child.

Children have their own rhythm about these things just as about eating and sleeping. In the long run what difference will it make whether a child achieves cleanliness at sixteen months or at eighteen months? Actually, none at all! But in some homes the perspective is rather short and before sixty days have elapsed the mother is sure she has the most undesirable child that ever existed because he has not become clean or dry.

Dryness is not achieved as early as bowel control and should not be expected so soon. While the average child is very likely to be clean at the end of the second year he may not become dry at night until the end of the third year and may wet the bed at night even beyond that age. The psychological mechanism by which the bowel and bladder are controlled is partly under voluntary and partly under involuntary control. It is an example of an automatic function that is achieved through the emotional contact of someone in the environment of the child, usually the mother, sometimes a nurse, but it is the *person* of the mother or the nurse that makes the child feel that he can make his body conform to what is expected.

In the course of time the impatient and distrustful mother will make the child impatient and distrustful of himself. The child needs a great deal of attention and confidence from others in order to master bladder function just as he needs patience and confidence to master the many functions that are concerned with growing up. For example, co-operation is required about going to school. The reader can probably remember something in his own life or in the lives of the children he knows that will make him realize that a child may not want to begin going to school or, if he begins, he may go a few days and because of some incident—known or unknown—wish to remain at home. Then the mother or the father or someone in whom the child has trust must come forward and reiterate the advantages of school. This person must point out that it is the upbringers' desire that the child go to school and ask him if he will do it to please them. That argument is usually won. However, an adult may have to go with him for a day or two in order to lend the strength of grownup presence to his weak ability to do the expected thing.

We are speaking now of the average child who has no anxiety problem and who has only a normal amount of reluctance to do the difficult thing. In these cases the parent has to come forward and say, "We want you to do it. It will please us if you do." So the child takes the idea within himself and being aware, consciously or unconsciously, of many nice things his parents have done for him, he goes back to school. The same thing is equally important in bowel training even though the child's vocabulary is limited. Incidentally it is to be noted that the child becomes clean at the end of the second year when he is beginning to get a fair vocabulary and a fair understanding of words.

We have described roughly how the training should take place in the average case. There are a great many cases that are not average and in which the mother has little feeling and little understanding of how to train a child so that the training will be accomplished with a minimum of trauma to him. It is to be remembered that in the matter of bowel training the child is making a sort of present or gift to those who are training him. To him the matter is just a great effort and he does not sense its social implications; he only senses that the parents are asking something of him which is difficult to achieve. Consequently, he feels that the least they could do is to be kind and appreciative of whatever efforts he makes.

There is a delicate balance in this emotional relationship. If the parents are too busy, or personally do not give the child what he feels to be a proper response in gratitude and acceptance of his efforts, he can become rebellious and stubborn, he can become indifferent, and he will not try. Then you have the efforts at training going on for many days and weeks and very little being accomplished because underneath the child is just not trying. This particular response may easily be misinterpreted, and so more pressure is put upon him to conform, and the situation which was already a little pathological becomes more so. A battle begins. The child refuses to attempt to be clean. If put on the toilet he does not move his bowels, but always moves them in some other circumstance that annoys his mother. She scolds him, reproaches him, whips him, or deprives him in some way, hoping that she will bring home to him the fact that he is displeasing her and that he must mend his ways.

In a great many instances this method does not work. The more the mother complains, scolds, and punishes, the more resistance the child has. There is a clash of wills and very often the child comes out the winner. Then the doctor comes on the scene and the mother asks what to do with a child who is not behaving himself properly. The trouble is usually not that the food is disagreeing with the child, or that he is feeble-minded, or that he is particularly bad, or a pathological child. The pathological person is the one who is handling him, who has not started the process off properly, and she is the one who needs to mend her ways.

When doctors step in and attempt to tell the mother she is not handling her child well, they should use great tact, of course. The most tactful and easy way is not to tell the mother how wrong she has been but just to give her the explanations of what has been presented so far: the limitations of the child's neurophysiological apparatus, how impressions of what is expected are conveyed to the child's mind; how these two forces work together; how the time element and the value of hope and expectation affect the child's physiological makeup. Thereby the doctor tries to get the mother to see the importance of discarding her hostile and reproachful attitude. By her hostile attitude she has already engendered some of the most unfortunate emotions human beings can develop—hostility, stubbornness and lack of co-operation.

During the course of development in the oral period, the first year of life, many events are encountered that can stir up hostility and start the child feeling unhappy, resentful, and rebellious; but generally they are less important when compared to the events that occur in this anal phase of development. The anal phase is the time in which co-operation, goodwill, and conformity are elicited from the child. This co-operation, goodwill, and conformity are brought about on the first responsibilities, which are in turn connected with the function of the lower part of the gastrointestinal tract. The basic conflicts can lead in the end to hostile or benign attitudes. "Holding on" can become a pattern of careful holding and helping or it can become a destructive and cruel retaining and restraining. "Letting go" can become a relaxing to let pass or let be or it can become an inimical letting loose of destructive forces. If in teaching control of the bowel and bladder the mother goes about it with too much harshness, or with too many reproaches, she can get a child who will give vent to his hostility not only in nonconformity in bowel and bladder function but also in other spheres of activity such as temper tantrums, disobedience, cruelty to other children and to animals, destructiveness of toys or property. In connection with bowel and bladder training a mother can build up in the child a great deal of hostility which finds its way into many diverse channels. Or if we encounter aggression or hostility, we find that it is built up during the anal period through the frustration of instincts. If the child were to do what is instinctual and most comfortable for him, he would not bother with bowel and bladder control at all; but he is able to manage the necessary compromise if he is treated considerately. When he is not treated considerately, and when he has too much frustration of instinctual needs, then aggression and hostility are built up. Culturally speaking, attitudes of goodwill and conformity or of aggression and hostility are neither good nor bad. Their importance depends on whether their hostile implications are turned against an enemy, a fellow man, or the self.

What does the child get in compensation for accepting bowel and bladder control, for doing away with the comfort of voiding or soiling at will? The answer is not difficult. He gets approval, he gets the love, or he *should* get the love, of those who are training him. If things go well, we call this process of acceptance of training "adaptation to the reality principle" as opposed to "adherence to the pleasure principle." The reality principle refers to the ability of a human being to postpone an immediate pleasure for pleasure at some distant period, or to achieve some more distant goal. In other words, the child gives up his desire to relieve the tension of his bowels and bladder at the slightest stimulus and manages the way the adults want him to in return for their immediate approval, or their approval two hours later, or two weeks later, or maybe two months later. He senses that such would be the most sensible practice and lead to the best gratification for him in the long run. However, to make it possible for him to grasp such an impression satisfactorily, it is necessary for him to have the love and goodwill and affection of his parents practically *ever present*.

This ability to postpone immediate pleasure for some future gratification is, of course, one of the necessary abilities of adults as opposed to those of the child. In the first place, the child wants an immediate gratification of his needs. His body and mind cannot stand much tension and in the beginning he does not have any realization of why he *should* stand it. He gets a feeling of the importance of this concept, gradually during growth, from those around him who make it easy for him to endure more tension as he goes along and make him see good reasons why he should.

Later in our study we will encounter many people whom we will call neurotics, psychotics, and persons with personality disorders. One of the chief difficulties of such a person is that he can never seem to postpone gratification. He leaves school because it is monotonous and because he feels he must go out and earn money to buy a new suit or to go dancing more often. Perhaps he has a fine job with a good promise of security but in a short time leaves it because he can get a few cents or a few dollars more at some job that has no promise or is only temporary. In later life people get into many varieties of trouble because they have not become masters of their instinctual tensions, because they have not been able to conform to the reality principle, because they must still act in conformity to the pleasure principle.

As the reader can see, very little is asked from the child in the first year, but a great deal that has to do with human personality development and with the development of the mind and with later conformity adjustment takes place during this so-called anal period.

Whenever material of this kind is being presented the question usually arises as to whether children cannot be spoiled by a training procedure that sounds as lenient in all aspects as this one that has just been discussed. Right away we would like to make the point that there is no such thing as *spoiling* a child *if* the child is expected to do the things required by the average environment and at the appropriate time. What he must receive is careful training by parents who have some understanding of the child's neurophysiological apparatus—who have, that is, an understanding of the child's inherent helplessness and limitations and are easy on him in the beginning, then, as time goes on, make social requirements at the appropriate point. With such a procedure there can be no process of spoiling. Spoiling cannot occur, because the balance of what is given the child and what he gives back to the parent is nicely adjusted. If the parent has been wise enough to regulate his interest *in* the child in generous proportion to what the parent is asking *of* the child, then the latter will not be rebellious, heedless, inconsiderate, or un-co-operative.

It is quite true that children are spoiled, but not because of the love and consideration that they have been given. The reason is that, even if the right kind of love and consideration has been given, the parent has never quite had the heart to make the necessary demands upon the child; has not been willing to demand that the child accept responsibilities as they arose. Thus responsibilities are postponed. Parents rationalize their attitude by saying the child is too young. Too often the attitude never changes and when the child is twenty-one he is still considered too young to be considerate of other people and to fulfill any degree of responsibility to his parents and to society. If this balance of giving and demanding were better understood, fewer parents would wonder whether they are giving their child too much attention and spoiling him and react by depriving him of necessary love and pleasure.

In fact, what you give the child in the way of understanding and affection contributes toward making him a more capable, more responsible, more competent and more able individual, provided the proper and usual responsibilities are put upon him. Children who have not been loved, who have not had friendly parents, who have not had a well-rounded education as to how to live life, will be inadequate people because they will be fearful, anxious, hateful, or un-co-operative as a result of the emptiness within them. The child who has been treated generously will respect his parents and society as a whole. The parent will get back what he has given if he knows how to ask for it at the right time and in the spirit of fair play and co-operation. Children are fair and co-operative citizens when asked to be so in the right manner. Someone has said that if a parent wants to have a well-behaved, socially well-adapted child, then the parent should figure out what kind of person that objective implies and be such a person himself; if he does, the chances are pretty good that through association with the parent the child will become much the same kind of person when he is twenty-one or thereabouts.

CONFLICT IN THE CHILD AND PARENT:
HOSTILITIES AND FRIENDLINESS

This balance between the love and generosity that are given to the young human being and that which he gives in return is bound to bring up certain attitudes in the child because a basic problem of all human beings is ambivalence. *Ambivalence* is an emotional state of feeling both love and hate toward a person at the same time. The love or hate, or even both, may be unconscious. All attitudes have some degree of ambivalence in them because we rarely completely hate or love a person for long. Yet the concept is a useful one because our reactions may become very confused if we do not understand how we feel toward each other.

Children are often ambivalent in feeling toward their parents, who in turn often are equally ambivalent toward their children. It is not a self-evident fact that children love their parents any more than it is a self-evident fact that parents love their children. Each is necessary to the other. So, if we were honest, we would probably say that in cultivating positive feelings between each other, parents and children are making a virtue of a necessity.

In thinking this matter over, we should realize that a great many adults have children just because it is being done, or because they are ignorant about contraceptives, or because they want to gain some degree of immortality through their children. We should not delude ourselves into thinking that the majority of parents have children because they love them, or that their main goal in life as parents is to help the oncoming generation to adapt to and enrich society generally. We are aiming for this goal, but we are farther from it than we realize.

Children impose a great many responsibilities upon parents. They take a great deal of their parents' time, interest, energies, and money. Thus the parents' basic ambivalence is increased by the circumstances of being a parent. These feelings in the parents are bound to be sensed by the child and the child develops and reflects a corresponding feeling during the time when he changes from his tendency to operate by the pleasure principle and begins adapting to the reality principle of postponing his gratifications to some future time. During his toilet-training period the child does not find it easy to make this change, and he does not accept the training without some degree of resentment against the person who imposes the restrictions. That attitude of resentment can always be minimized if the person in authority can talk in a way that makes people accept restrictions very readily. But some persons in authority make those subject to them want to fight. Thus some parents have the ability to bring children through the vicissitudes of childhood and get them to accept toilet training and other matters easily. They manage it in an easy good-natured way and keep the hostility, which is always there, at a minimum—and the result is that the child's feeling of friendliness and goodwill toward the parents always dominates.

An important goal in social relations is to try to increase the amount of positive feeling between people. We once heard a woman make a statement of that kind in relation to her child; she said, "When I take a gay and interested attitude toward my child's behavior, rather than a perplexed and critical one, he is much more relaxed and co-operates much better." This remark was in relation to an emotional problem of eating in her six-year-old child. Often during treatment for neurosis a parent's *real attitude* toward his children is revealed. We are prone to assume too readily that life goes on smoothly in the home, that the mother and children are living "happily" together. Actually tensions between mother and children can become very high. The mother feels greatly perplexed at times as to how to manage her children, hostilities between them spring up, unfortunate attitudes of thwarting one another go on a long time, and hatred develops which will handicap the children for years to come in ways that we will discuss as we proceed.

The drive toward as complete an instinctual gratification as possible leads the child to try to dominate those in the environment and to do as much as he can to gain his ends—even to the point of inflicting pain upon them in the process. This desire to inflict pain in order to dominate combines with an instinctual process—the desire to obtain pleasure by inflicting pain—which is called *sadism*. We see it exhibited socially in some types of "kidding," in biting sarcasm, in temper tantrums in which those who are loved are nevertheless subjected to these sadistic experiences. The remorse felt after each tirade bears witness to the fact that a large pleasurable element energizes the cruel behavior.

Just as there are those who take pleasure in inflicting pain, so there are those who like to endure pain. They, in contradistinction to the sadists, like to experience pain. It may be harder for the reader to understand why one should wish to endure pain rather than inflict pain, yet who does not know of some person who seems to like to "take a beating" or "get kicked around." The reaction of cheerfully enduring endless privation or repeated misfortune, even of taking pleasure in being beaten, pinched, or bitten very painfully in the act of lovemaking, is called *masochism*.

One of the problems in the inevitable give and take of training children during the anal period is to keep hostility at a minimum. It can be solved by exhibiting some real understanding consideration for the child, his ego limitations, and the number of responsibilities (relatively) that are being thrust upon him. Since he must control so much of himself at such an early age he feels the least he should get in return is his mother's heartfelt appreciation. Yet some mothers seem to be constantly scheming as to how they can devise some trickery that will get the child to learn what they want him to learn. Such a mother seems to lack any idea of living happily together with the child or doing things together with him—a procedure that should be important to both. Instead, she seems to take the attitude that what the child accomplishes is no concern of hers, provided he makes her as little trouble as possible.

If the mother has been generous in her attitude toward the child during the oral period, and if she is tolerant and understanding with the big problem of toilet training itself, then she will get a child who will always undertake his responsibilities, whatever they may be, with a correspondingly generous spirit. So far as the child's mind is concerned, excretions are gifts which he makes to those around him and which he makes generously if he is asked in the proper way. The whole later-life attitude of generosity gets its start here. Many people have had such a difficult time in the first two or three years of life that they always have difficulty in bringing out their generous impulses. They always have an anxiety about being imposed upon, always fear repetition of the exploitations that occurred in their childhood.

EXCRETA SUBSTITUTIONS AND SELF-EXPRESSION

The child's personal interest in the values of feces and urine in the nursery becomes *displaced* onto money and other things which have a pleasure value if possessed for their own sake or if traded for something else desired. In fact, it must be stressed against the opposition of our sense of esthetic value that the child is naturally quite intrigued by and quite enamored of his own excretions. He finds their proximity to his body when warm quite satisfying. He finds them in no way filthy, disgusting, or unpleasant to sight and touch as do adults. He would like to touch and play with them in a quite uninhibited manner, and often does so in spite of the careful vigilance of those who supervise him. Many a mother has been surprised and disconcerted to find her child occupying himself with smearing his feces over himself, the bed, and the walls of the room.

Any child is prone to do this, and no mother who experiences it should be frightened about her child's nature or worry that he has more primitive or animal heredity in him than the next child. He is merely being an average child and following the dictates of the pleasure principle. He need only be washed and told he can be given something more acceptable to play with instead of the contents of his own body. This promise should be kept by providing plasticine, molding clay, sand and water, or finger paint as substitutes for excreta in order to gratify the instinctive tendency to play with material of such consistency. This displacement of interest to something more socially acceptable forms the beginning of *sublimation,* which is defined as the process of helping the instinctual expressions inherent in childhood to find expression on a more socially valuable and accepted level.

All work has to be more or less directly a sublimation, that is, a refinement of the interests which the child of necessity finds in relation to his own body and its functions. Adults who would reject these humble beginnings of interest in social activity should do a little honest reflecting upon the interests in the human body that persist into adulthood: masturbation, overconcern with aches and pains, fussiness about what they eat and where they sleep, excessive concern with bowel movements (their regularity and consistency), overconcern with the color and amount of the urine passed, and the like. This neurotic preoccupation with the body may greatly curtail the efficacy of an individual and make him poor company to those around him. Hence, if the child of two or three is interested in playing with water and dirt even to the extent of an excessive attraction for the toilet bowl, it is but good sense to have a little patience and understanding in helping him to get interested in more socially accepted activities which do not force him to give up satisfaction to which he will only have to return later on under the guise of illness.

A clear picture of the gradual substitutions and new interests which the child adopts in his efforts to sublimate his original interest in feces has been well shown by Ferenczi when he points out that feces are brown, moist, soft, have a bad odor, and are worthless. The child turns to mud pies which have all the characteristics of feces minus the odor. He then turns to sand and relinquishes the characteristic of moisture. From there his interest turns to bright stones and trinkets, and he relinquishes softness. Next he adopts stamps, coins, and money, gaining more color than the original brown, and at the same time gaining something of social value. The adults in the environment should provide opportunities for these substitutions to take place.

Some people come out of the anal period with a feeling for orderliness, neatness, having things just so, being strictly punctual in every way as their outstanding personality traits. The mother of such a person has made him adopt these ways so strictly and thoroughly at this time that he is never able to break away from them. He feels always that he must follow this type of behavior, otherwise people will be displeased with him. He cannot believe, for instance, that he will be forgiven if he is a few minutes late, that people will accept him even if things are a little out of order. Everything has to be just so at all times. These personality traits have value, but they can be excessive. This type of person can become the kind of individual who is so intent on order that he becomes emotionally lost in being orderly, punctual, and neat. He is so much so that he ceases to be a human, warm, friendly person. He lives by the letter of the law and will not tolerate any trace of carelessness in himself or even in others.

A certain amount of this precision makes a careful worker and may make a good person to be in authority provided it is tempered with a little kindness and understanding. However, at a certain point, which is always difficult to define, it can come to be a burden to those associated with the person who evinces it. If he is a parent, he is too strict, and too little fun is allowed in family life. If he is an official or an employer, he is so strict that he makes work disagreeable for everyone. He feels that he has been severely dealt with but that severity has given him a sterling "character" and that others would profit by the same kind of treatment.

IDENTIFICATION AND PERSONALITY

A word about the personality as it is formed. We started with the instinctual needs of the human being that demand gratification regardless of the environmental forces. For purposes of written and verbal condensation, we call these instinctual forces the *id*. In the beginning, as a matter of fact, the child reacts as if he feels that he is part and parcel of the mother and her body. When he is hungry he cries and she comes to feed him, yet at the same time he seems to conclude the mother is a part of himself. Not until some time after birth—we do not know exactly when—does the child gradually gain the sense that he is a separate entity and that, if he is going to thrive and have his needs gratified, he must begin to conform to those in the environment and their expectations.

As this perception takes place we have the beginning of the ego formation, the formation of the "I" part of the personality. As time goes on, the child comes to think of himself as a separate individual and during toilet training and during the training in the other habits which must be learned during this period his realization of self is enhanced. When he becomes able to control some of his behavior in conformity with social demands, he begins to have vestiges, at least, of conscience. The conscience is still a part of the ego but a special part of it. This development of conscience takes place as a result of the child's taking over into himself the wishes and demands of grown-up people and the process is called *identification* or *introjection*. First, the child learns to do what is expected of him by reason of his proximity to the parent and being told what is expected of him. He takes in these wishes and ideas, makes them a part of his own mind, and begins to be a better and better trained individual. It is this process that is called identification. The child identifies with the mother and what she wants.

We can also use the word introjection, which to some would mean a more thoroughgoing "taking in" or incorporation of the loved object than identification, and which eventually leads to independent thinking and independent functioning. This is a long, tedious, difficult process for both the parent and the child. Parents are always giving advice and admonitions while in their homes and double or treble them if the child goes to visit friends or relatives, or is to stop at a neighbor's, or even later when he goes away from home to school or to work. The parent says, "Don't forget this," or "Don't forget that." This means that the parent fears the child will not remember what the parents have taught him—and not to remember means that the child does not take away within himself enough of the parent's thinking, feeling, or point of view. The parent feels that the child has not incorporated within him enough of these good ideas, and so keeps reiterating them.

The phenomenon can degenerate to nagging. The child does his best to swallow the ideas, to digest them, and to metabolize and deposit them in his own mind for reference. Sometimes, however, he has to regurgitate these ideas. Sometimes they give him indigestion and may be reflected in the statement, "Pop gives me a pain," or "Mom makes me sick." Sometimes he has to ignore them completely. At any rate, this taking over of social values as correct thinking and behavior for functioning in contemporary society forms a theoretical third part of the personality called the *superego,* to which we shall refer more fully in the next chapter.

Incorporation is a process that is going on continually, and we trust the reader already sees from the foregoing discussion how important a process it is. We want to make clear that before the age of three is reached much has been going on by way of personality development, and that the essential personality traits have been in the process of formation in the nursery. Parents are prone to criticize the school system for not making a better child of their offspring. Actually a great many problems in the child which parents blame on the school system are problems that should have been solved before the child was out of the nursery.

All these interactions between mother and child mean that a mother should have a good awareness of the needs of a young human being at this early age. Not only should an ability to meet these needs be part of the mentality of any female undertaking motherhood but she can exercise herself and her knowledge better if her husband also knows this much about human needs. He can help to amplify his wife's understanding and implementation of her role in meeting the child's needs as well as offer much of the same to the child himself.

SUMMARY

We have dealt with the psychological interactions between child and mother during the period when toilet training occupies an important place in the events which structure personality. In this anal phase of development, the lovely dependency of being fed, cared for and admired as a baby gives way to responsibility—the responsibility of assuming bowel and bladder control on one's own. With this go other requests for neatness and order, but bowel and bladder control is the most intimate, the most personal and interpersonal of all demands. It is a demand that involves the co-operation of will from the neurophysiological system and both its autonomic and voluntary mechanisms. The use of rewards given and withheld for good performance enter the picture with new situations which can be anxiety-producing. We have seen how positive values such as self-esteem, self-confidence and competence to achieve are started, as well as how potentially harmful values such as guilt, shame, dirtiness, badness, unworthiness, stubbornness, and aggression are born. Much can occur in this period which will condition a person either to consider himself attractive, potent, and good or to regard himself as dirty, incompetent, and destructive. These fates are not completely decided in this period, but toilet training is a phenomenon which serves to act as a vehicle for these personality traits and values. In short, we see how conscience values are forming rapidly in this age period.

BIBLIOGRAPHY FOR CHAPTER III

Abraham, Karl, *Selected Papers on Psychoanalysis,* Hogarth, 1927, pp. 370–392.

Erikson, Erik H., *Childhood and Society,* Norton, 1950.

Ferenczi, Sandor, *Contributions to Psychoanalysis,* Bedger, 1916.

Freud, Sigmund, *Three Contributions to the Theory of Sex,* Nervous and Mental Disease Publishing Co., 1930.

IV

Emotional Disturbances That Occur during the Anal Period

THERE is a distinct difference between the reactions of the casual adult observer to the baby of six months and to the child of eighteen months. The former is called "the baby" or "it." The latter is too evidently a person to be regarded so casually. The child during the anal period is a living human being. He is a person in his own right, who can walk, talk, and perform definitely purposeful actions, and who has thoughts, ideas, and fantasies which he can describe to others. In psychological terms, we recognize that he has an ego and we perceive that his ego is devoted to a difficult task—that of trying to gratify (1) his instinctual desires and needs for pleasure and, at the same time, (2) the demands of his environment and of the real world. Every minute of the day struggles are going on in the child's mind: "Will I do what I want?" "Will I be satisfied with what I can do or will I continue to attempt the impossible?" "Will I give up what I want to do in order to please someone else?" Many phases of these struggles are easily observed. Others are not so evident, particularly the deepest struggle, "How can I equally love and hate the same person at the same time?" These are the struggles that are present constantly throughout human life, but in this period the child is first really aware of them.

In the preceding chapter we have explained that because the whole question of excretion is of paramount importance to the child, at this time much of this struggle takes place around toilet training. We have shown how the methods by which these struggles are resolved lay down patterns which often remain the accustomed techniques of dealing with the problems of autonomy versus feelings of shame and doubt. If a child, toward the end of his toilet training or shortly after it is completed, suffers from some unusual situation such as a severe organic gastrointestinal illness with diarrhea which he cannot control, he will develop into an adult who is somewhat irritable, anxious, and eccentric. It is evident that if the parents use unnecessary or unusual methods of management for the child during his toilet training, their effect will be apparent not only during this period but also many years later. (We say "will" rather than "may" because psychoanalytic research has shown that one important root of a person's accustomed method of reacting—his so-called character traits—can be traced back to the struggles of the individual to adjust himself during this period.)

During this period there are two predominant psychic conflicts. One conflict in the child is between two opposing tendencies—to let go and to hold on—and the child has to decide frequently to which side he will direct his energy at a particular time. He learns to solve this conflict by trial-and-error methods and in these trials and errors he can receive little or no help from his parents. The child's other conflict is between his wish either to let go or to hold on at a particular time or place and his fear of the consequences of doing what he wants. These conflicts produce feelings of anxiety, whose ideational content during this period will be his fear that if he does what he wants his parents, particularly his mother, will not love him. As his toilet training progresses toward completion, his fear of losing his mother's love becomes internalized as an early part of his superego. At this point his fear becomes a fear that if he does what the precursors of his superego do not approve of he will lose the love of this part of his superego. The internalized image of his mother will point the finger of shame at him and he will feel humiliated. A great deal of the fretfulness, easily hurt feelings, sleeplessness, and other symptoms shown by children of this age is due to these conflicts and the fears they engender; and these, of course, will be increased to the point of pathological reactions either immediately or after an interval if the child is forced to resolve these conflicts too early or too quickly, either through circumstances or through his toilet training.

ANXIETY REACTIONS

An acute or chronic anxiety state is the sign that the child has a conflict which so far he has not been able to solve. A careful analysis of an acute anxiety situation in a two-year-old child has been reported by Bornstein. This small child developed panic when she was put to bed. She refused to lie down and when she fell asleep it was in a sitting posture. During the analysis it was learned that her acute panic was the result of her fear lest she soil herself when asleep and as a result her mother would not love her and would go away and leave her. Her toilet training had been very early and strict, and she had reasons to make her believe that she could not be certain of her mother's love. Her behavior was like that of a phobia. She tried to avoid the situation where her conflict was greatest.

The anxiety does not necessarily appear in acute attacks or as phobic avoidances of specific situations in the manner of the case we just cited, but the child may be mildly apprehensive most of the time. He may be jittery during the day and sleep restlessly at night as we have already mentioned. Parents need to be aware, however, that all children have sleep disturbances at about the age of eighteen months. For a period of several weeks at least the child will dislike going to bed, will refuse to go to sleep, or will be awake at intervals throughout the night. These disturbances of sleep are so usual as to be considered "normal." The child at this age is learning to use many new skills by which he increases his pleasures and is able to control his desires so that they do not overwhelm him and cause him to feel anxious. These skills are only partly learned. From time to time the child's new abilities fail him or he fails to accomplish what he wants to do by the use of them. As he falls asleep he feels he is losing these powers and he tries to stay awake so he may be sure to retain his controls and not suffer fears and anxieties. As he grows a little older he feels more confident in his capacities and so does not need any longer to prevent himself from sleeping.

DIRECT DISTURBANCES OF EXCRETORY FUNCTIONS

Instead of showing signs of anxiety, the child after his toilet training may show disturbances of bowel and bladder functioning. If one watches a child during the process of toilet training one can be sure that there are times when the child tries very hard to retain his excretions until he is in the proper place to void them because he wants so much to please his mother and have her love him. At other times he seems either not to care to retain them or seems to get a savage delight in not retaining them. At these times he is angry and displeased with his mother and does not love her because he feels she does not love him. One mother reported that her son of less than two years had been free from the habit of smearing his feces for several weeks. One day she had to leave him alone in the house while she went to bring the maid for the day's work. She put the child in his pen. When she returned, everything in the pen was smeared. She was intuitive enough to understand the child felt that she did not love him because she had left him alone, and in revenge he did the thing he knew would upset her. This was the use of the mechanism to expel and destroy as an expression of hate which we described in the previous chapter as one of the predominating mechanisms of the first part of the anal period. Conversely, if a child is angry at his mother he may withhold his movements even for several days, especially if she is anxious to have him produce a good movement. This is the use of the mechanism to retain and hold in, which we described as characteristic of the latter part of the anal period. In these instances it also expresses hatred. So to expel—that is to have a bowel movement—or to retain or hold in a bowel movement at a particular time or place may express either of two opposite feelings. The child can expel the movement in the toilet as a sign that he loves his mother or he can expel it in other places as a sign that he hates her. He can retain or hold in his bowel movements except on the toilet as a sign that he loves her or he can retain or hold in his bowel movement while he is on the toilet as a sign that he hates her. In certain bowel disturbances such as diarrhea or constipation for which no physical basis can be found, the bowel difficulties often are an expression of certain unconscious feelings of love or hate toward other people. Wetting in the daytime is also an expression of antagonism toward the parents. In our opinion a high percentage of day wetting is based on a conscious or nearly conscious desire to annoy, irritate, and defy the parents.

If the child has been too severely toilet trained, or toilet trained too early, he may become afraid of moving his bowels even in the toilet, and so become constipated. The young child's powers of discrimination are not very great and he may confuse his mother's demands that he move his bowels no other place than in the toilet with the idea that she does not want him to move his bowels at all. In trying to conform to this confused demand he may become constipated. If a great deal of attention has been paid to his bowels, through the use of suppositories or enemas, he may be loath to relinquish both the sexual and emotional pleasure he receives from this treatment and hold back his own movements to coax his mother to use a suppository or an enema. Constipation in young children is either the result of fear of the mother's displeasure, a desire to take revenge on her, or of a greediness to continue to get sensual pleasure at her hands. Withholding of urine is not as common in children as is withholding of feces. The probable reasons are that an overfull bladder, causing more pain than an overfull bowel, cannot be tolerated so long and that the reverse peristalsis of the large bowel allows the contents to move away from the lower part so that overdistention does not take place, while the bladder has no such capacity to escape overdistention.

DISTURBANCES OF OTHER FUNCTIONS

Human beings have a tendency to continue an experience with which they are familiar. The experience itself does not necessarily have to be a pleasurable one; it has only to be well known. If a new experience is uncomfortable and we find ourselves unable to derive from it the pleasure we desire, we tend to give it up and hark back to a previous experience with which we are familiar and from which we know by familiarity how to derive pleasure. When a child is too severely, too quickly, or too early subjected to toilet training he will find himself quite uncomfortable because of feelings of anxiety and may try to return to the pleasures he experienced during the oral stage. He cannot do so completely, since his desire for oral pleasure at this stage cannot be satisfied as a purely pleasurable experience.

Sterba has reported a series of cases in which the child's feeding problem came on shortly after his toilet training began. From certain reactions in the feeding situation Sterba deduced that the feeding problem bore a relation to the toilet training and when the latter was stopped temporarily the feeding difficulty disappeared. In this case is seemed evident that the child, bitterly resentful at being required by the mother to suppress his desires for anal pleasure, protested by refusing to eat because he knew that such behavior would disturb her, make her uncomfortable and worried about his welfare. It had the added motive that the child, feeling under the force of necessity to relinquish his anal pleasure, went back to attempting to obtain his satisfactions in an oral way. This attempt would be only partially successful because he knew that big children must not obtain their entire gratification through the activity of the mouth.

The lower end of the gastrointestinal tract can be used to make noises and smells through the passage of flatus, which may be disgusting to the adult but are enjoyable to the child. If, at his mother's stern insistence, he relinquishes this pleasure before he is ready to do so, the enjoyment he experienced at the lower end of the intestinal tract may now be transferred to enjoyment from the productions of the upper end, for example through the use of obscene and scatological speech. This is not common among children in the anal period, partly because they have not acquired the vocabulary but also because they are too proud of their newly won ego ability to control themselves and do not wish to relinquish this control for even a short time. However, this phenomenon is very common among nursery-school children, who from time to time experience epidemics of obscenity in which they delight in shocking the adults through the dirtiness of their language. This process is not regressive but is really progressive, because it is much more acceptable culturally to use obscenity in speech than to express the same feelings by the public passage of flatus.

The obscenity may be obscenity in the adult sense through the use of vulgarisms that the child has overheard from some adult, or may be obscenity in the childish sense through the use of words he knows are forbidden or not usual in his home. Thus if urination is the family word for the passage of urine he will use the word pee; if the word pee is the family word for this activity he will use the word urination as an obscene term, or he may use the simple name of an object, like dish or plate, as an obscene epithet. He may also become apprehensive lest he shout out in some place such as a church where he should be quiet. We know one child who suffered agonies of apprehension lest he yell or scream during the church service. This apprehension was not really lest he shout out but rather lest he pass flatus and so be embarrassed. His embarrassment arose from the fact that he had been severely reprimanded many times. We might mention here that parents seldom learn from the child that he is undergoing such agonizing apprehensions. Instead the child appears to be self-willed and unreasonable. He stubbornly refuses to go to church or to other public places. Like the little girl described by Bornstein, he avoids the situation in which he would have anxiety. The desire to pass flatus not only gratifies the anal needs but after toilet training takes place it serves the function of expressing contempt, anger and hatred—just as profanity and obscenity do in later life.

There are some parents who encourage the child to pass flatus in public either by acting as if it were cute or by passing flatus in public themselves. A child who is raised in such a situation will have had no help in controlling the act and when he grows old enough to mix with other children and to go to school will have to impose his controls on this too suddenly in order to avoid the ridicule of his friends and classmates.

If the child relinquishes his anal pleasures because he is too much afraid of offending his mother he may regress to the infantile method of breathing. In this the respirations are not rhythmic but are very irregular, and catching of the breath is common. When this type of respiration is re-established it produces extreme difficulty in the clear pronunciation of words. Because of the breathing difficulty the enunciation becomes irregular and arrhythmical, and stuttering often results. This stuttering portrays a conflict between the desire to express hostility and defiance toward the parents by the passage of gas from the body, and the desire to please them by not performing an improper action. The conflict has been displaced from the lower end of the gastrointestinal tract, where the child has acceded to the parent's prohibitions, to its upper end. At this part of the body the internal gases are used in the function of speech and when the conflict is displaced to it the speech function is involved. Stuttering at this age period usually is started by a sudden shock or fright. This produces a strong startle reflex, which is a marked part of the reactions of early infancy. The startle reflex is accompanied by a catching of the breath, that is, a sudden resumption of the infantile breathing arrhythmia. If the child is already in conflict between his defiance of the parent and his desire to please the parent, this startle reflex paves the way for the displacement of the conflict onto the speech function. This mechanism is not the only one at work in the stuttering of older children but is of great importance when the stuttering begins at the anal period of development. Kolansky [1] has published a detailed account of the treatment of stuttering in a three-year-old girl which illustrates very well the sources of the type of conflict we have been discussing and which the reader will find very interest-

[1] Harold Kolansky, "Treatment of a Three Year Old Girl's Severe Infantile Neurosis: Stammering and Insect Phobia," *Psychoanalytic Study of the Child,* 15, p. 261, International Universities Press, 1960.

ing and informative.

If the child suddenly gives in to the parent's toilet training he may react to her admonitions to be a good boy and grow up quickly and be clean by striving desperately to follow them out. One little boy of nearly three years of age had to have a cup or a glass taken from the cupboard and rewashed until he was sure it was clean before the liquid he wished to drink was poured into it. To him the cleanliness of the cup or glass was more important than his desire to drink. Along with this excessive need to be clean the child suddenly may become independent, refuse to have anything done for him and demand to be allowed to do everything for himself, even if the activity is manifestly beyond his physical powers. Instead of being interested any longer in his excretory functions he suddenly becomes interested only in masturbation. This masturbation is accompanied by conscious fantasies which are different from the fantasies that appear naturally at the next stage of development. Their content deals entirely with expressions of defiance and hostility toward other people or of other persons toward the child himself. As the child masturbates he is wishing that he were hurting, injuring, or defying the parent or that the parent were hurting, injuring, or defying him. Consciously the child is disgusted with the idea that he would really like to be dirty and do dirty things of which the parent would disapprove. He has repressed such desires completely. The full effect of the toilet training has fallen on the anal pleasures but the sadism and masochism of this stage have been unaffected. As the child strives to be more grown up he carries this sadism and masochism along and they remain as active as if he were still the cruel little savage that he was during the anal stage. We know one boy whose mother made strict demands for cleanliness and who at the same time encouraged him to be destructive and cruel. She would break up his toys and encourage him to do the same, shouting gleefully when he followed her directions. He responded to her by being overclean and by being destructive and cruel. We might note here that we consider too great independence in a two-year-old—an independence that rejects any attempt to help him—as pathological as too great dependence.

We have mentioned before that not only is the mucus membrane of the anus and the skin surfaces immediately surrounding it the chief pleasure zone during the anal period but the skin of the buttocks also has the same characteristics. The child obtains a great deal of pleasure from the touching, patting, and even slapping of his buttocks if the slapping is not too severe. If the child is spanked too often on his behind, he may be able to change the pain of the spanking into a masochistic pleasure. When this happens the child becomes constantly naughty, defiant, and disobedient. This is not due to negativism but to the desire to be spanked. The parent does so but it results in no diminution of his naughtiness. Instead the child behaves worse, for the spanking becomes a favor, like a piece of candy that the child craves. As such a child grows older, his masochistic desires become more firmly entrenched and he seeks constantly to be hurt and punished. Occasional spankings may be necessary during the anal period, but they should not be administered too often.

PHOBIAS AND COMPULSIONS

The child is unable to differentiate between situations that resemble each other too closely. In this respect he behaves like the sheep that has been subjected to certain conditioning experiments. The sheep through repetition is conditioned to anticipate being fed when he sees a circle. After this conditioned reflex has been well established the animal is conditioned to expect a painful electric shock when it is shown an ellipse. After this conditioned reflex is well established the circle which is shown the animal at feeding time is gradually flattened. A point is reached where the sheep is unable to distinguish between a circle and an ellipse and at this point the animal loses both of his conditioned reflexes and shows a complete change in his daily behavior.

Parents often forget that the child stands midway between the animal and the adult in his powers of discrimination between situations that resemble each other but are not exactly the same. If the child becomes frightened about soiling himself with excreta he may be unable to distinguish between soiling himself with excreta and soiling himself in other socially acceptable ways. A girl of eight was referred by her mother because she seemed to be intellectually retarded although her I.Q. was 108. When her school work was closely examined it was found that her difficulty lay in the fact that she never completed any assignment. She was unable to do so because she spent too much time making each word she wrote on the paper exactly perfect. Her bedroom was always arranged in perfect order. She had a specific location for every object and would become angry if the object was not just where it ought to be. She would become upset if there was one small spot on her dress and would immediately have to change it. She never played with other children because she could not stand getting her hands dirty, and had to run in the house about every ten or fifteen minutes to wash them. She had one game with which she occupied herself endlessly, spending entire Saturdays and Sundays with it. She tore a newspaper into small pieces, placed them in a heap on the floor under a chair, took them out and put them back again. She had little appetite. It can be seen readily from her behavior that she spent her entire time preventing herself from being anything but clean and meticulous. This was more important than having a good time or being successful with her work. Her play was an open representation of moving her bowels in the toilet—"on the chair."

These reactions by this child had started rather suddenly when she was about four years old. Up to that time she had behaved in a fairly normal manner except that she was difficult to toilet train. The reason for her slow response to toilet training was not evident. One may suspect a constitutional predisposition to desire more pleasure from excretory activities than is usual.[2] Her mother had tried all forms of training. They were not successful. At last in exasperation she had seized the child's soiled panties and rubbed them on the child's face.

The child never soiled herself again, but within a short time her activities and behavior changed to the way she was when we first saw her. Because she was unable to distinguish clearly between soiling with feces and soiling with other materials, the humiliation

[2] There seems little question that there are constitutional predispositions that cause a child to need more of one of the infantile pleasure activities than other children do. In certain families the children tend to suck their fingers longer than usual. In other families all of the children wet the bed for much longer than the customary period. We commonly say that such things run in families, by which we mean there is a constitutional predisposition to need more than the ordinary amount of the infantile pleasure. We know very little about the physiological basis of a constitutional predisposition. A small boy has many of his father's traits and mannerisms. Uusually analysis will show that these are not inherited but are the result of constant conscious and unconscious identifications with the father. One can say definitely only that body habitus, and some types of handedness, are constitutional. For most other forms of behavior the probability is that they are the result of the individual's life and are not inherited.

of the severe punishment forced her to regard as prohibited not only soiling with feces but also all other types of being soiled. In order to avoid a repetition of the humiliating punishment she avoided indulging in any type of soiling. In short, as a result of her inability to differentiate between soiling with excreta and soiling with other types of dirt the punishment compelled her not only to cease the former but also to stop the latter sublimatory activities.

During toilet training the child experiments frequently with his ability to hold on and to let go. These are not only muscular actions but also are important types of psychological social reactions. Basic conflicts about them can lead to either hostile or benign expectations and attitudes: "to hold on" can be either "to value and possess" or "to cruelly restrain and retain"; to let go can be either to let be or to let pass or it can be a hate charge, a letting-loose of destructive forces. The cultural value of these attitudes differs according to whether their hostile implications are directed in an adequate and appropriate manner toward an object in the external world or against oneself. This little girl turned against herself all her urges to discriminate and to manipulate. Instead of taking possession of things in order to test them by purposeful repetition she became obsessed by her own repetitiveness. She ruled herself by the letter rather than by the spirit. In short, she had developed a precocious conscience which caused her to be too ashamed of herself and her productions and too filled with doubt as to her abilities and her social acceptance. Doubting her capacity to avoid making an error interfered with her ability to learn from trial and error. Thus she was rapidly developing personality traits whose sole purpose was to prevent her experiencing further shame and humiliation and were not to help her utilize her physical and psychological abilities in a more and more cultured manner. This girl suffered from an obsessional neurosis, as is indicated by her compulsive behavior.

We have already cited Mrs. Bornstein's intensively studied case of a phobic reaction due to the child's fear of soiling herself when she fell asleep. Phobic reactions appear during this period but as they are more common during the next period of development we will leave further discussion of them until later.

Older children, long after their toilet training has been completed, seem to fall into two groups in their reactions to urination. Some children, after a period following toilet training during which they were somewhat apprehensive lest they wet themselves during the day and more so lest they wet themselves during the night, seem to become certain of the surety of their unconscious urinary control system and of the efficacy of their sphincters. After this, they no longer seem to worry, fall asleep readily, and sleep throughout the night without going to the toilet. In the daytime, they usually are quite certain how long they can go without having to urinate and seem not to fear accidents. Other children and even some adults have to get up and go to the toilet two or three times before they can fall asleep. They sleep lightly—at least their sleep is disturbed by the fact that they wake one or more times to go to the toilet. Frequently, they seem slightly reluctant to go to bed. In the daytime, they are very careful to go to the toilet before they go anywhere, often have to urinate somewhat more frequently than seems necessary and always have to be sure that a toilet is within reach.

We are under the impression that the children in the first group have been toilet trained by the incorporation of the parental desires into their mind so that they and their bladder control operate as smoothly interfunctioning part of one whole. They have been sure of their mother's love and so are confident of the efficient working of their control systems. On the contrary, we are under the impression that the children and adults in the second group seem to live constantly under an unconscious fear that their urinary control will lapse, as if the incorporated parental desires were still partly a foreign body which had not been assimilated. They act as if they had not toilet trained themselves in order *to get more of their mother's love* but as if they had toilet trained themselves *through fear that they would lose their mother's love*. This fear constantly hangs over their heads, and so they feel unconfident. We have some evidence that this uncertainty over bladder control is one of the reasons that certain adults have a very pronounced and very painful type of introspection in which they are constantly thinking about everything they have said and done and worrying about its effect on the feelings of other people toward them. Such persons wake frequently during the night to worry in this way and usually urinate before they fall asleep again. Even as adults they occasionally wet themselves. Their histories show that they had a great deal of difficulty in establishing bladder control.

In our gadget-filled mechanized culture it is during the anal period that both parents and the child come face to face with the serious problem of dangers to the child's body and to his life. There are electrical outlets, gas stoves, boiling water, electric refrigerators, plastic bags, cars, etc., etc., all of which can injure the child seriously or kill him. The child, through his ignorance of the real world, does not realize that such dangers exist and he has to be trained to recognize them. The fewer gadgets there are within his reach the better, so that there are fewer occasions for the parents to curtail his activities. The child has to be trained about those that cannot be placed out of his reach but in this training the parents should remember the case of the sheep we quoted earlier. The child of this age cannot use his discrimination and judgment about the differences between things which appear too similar but are not. Too frequent admonitions and punishments may make him lose what little judgment he has, may make him overfrightened of too many harmless things or make him curtail his curiosity too much.

One of the important developmental aspects of the anal period is in the use of the voluntary muscles. The child should have sufficient opportunity and space to use them and parents have to allow him this opportunity even if his activities take him into slightly dangerous situations. Many authorities believe that the ordinary sized playpen actually is too small an area for the child during the latter part of the oral period. It really is too small for the child during the anal period. If the parent, particularly the mother, is too frightened lest the child injure himself in his exuberant activity and so restricts him too much, it may have a deleterious affect on his ability to use his muscles and to develop coordination.

THE ANAL PERSONALITY

In the course of daily life—more often in the practice of medicine, particularly of psychiatry and psychoanalysis—from time to time we meet people who have certain outstanding personality traits. Their emphasis on cleanliness, orderliness, and meticulousness sometimes borders on the point of absurdity. A very pretty girl of twenty-four had to bathe at least four times a day and after bathing always perfumed the seat of her skirt. She refused even to contemplate traveling because the places she might stay would not be clean. She could not contemplate marriage because she knew she could not get into bed with a man unless he bathed as often or more often than she did. Another woman cleaned her house from top to bottom every day of the week. One time her husband was ill and had to stay home from work, so secretly she gave him a sleeping pill so she could go on with her cleaning without being disturbed by his complaints. Often these people are very critical of others who are not as orderly and conscientious as they are and sometimes make quite a nuisance of themselves. When we get to know them better we find that they also are parsimonious. This ranges in degree from great care in keeping money and not spending any more than is absolutely necessary to real hoarding and miserliness. At the same time they are very obstinate and stubborn. If they have a point of view or a way of doing something they absolutely refuse to change their ways even if the facts have proven them wrong. When we come to know such people, we usually find them quite difficult and often unpleasant to deal with, and in general we often prefer to have our social, recreational, and work life separate from them.

When a person who shows the triad of marked personality traits of orderliness, parsimony, and obstinacy is psychoanalyzed, it has been found that these traits are the evidence of a marked struggle over toilet training—whatever the cause of the struggle may have been. Bringing the sources of these traits into consciousness often helps the patient to have a less rigid personality.

TREATMENT OF EMOTIONAL DISTURBANCES
OF THE ANAL PERIOD

Teachers are well aware how often a child on first entering school is unable to use finger paints or other forms of artistic action because he refuses to get his hands dirty. Such children have undergone severe toilet training and have displaced the fear of soiling with excreta onto all types of soiling. It is also remarkable how often after a psychoanalysis an adult begins to be interested in art and how really beautiful his productions are. We believe that there is in general too much emphasis on toilet training in the education of American children and that this overemphasis often interferes sadly with the later capacity of the adult for self-expression. It is interesting that this overemphasis usually produces overconformity. The child is little and helpless; because of his helplessness he has so much need for his parents' assistance and love that he perforce must give in to them in order to get this needed assistance and love.

As is usual in the practice of medicine, attempts to prevent the development of pathological reactions if possible are as important and perhaps more important than treatment. At the anal stage of development, as in the oral stage, the emotional climate in which the child lives is very important. Parents must realize the child needs time to toilet train himself and that efforts in this direction must not be begun too early. Conversely, they must not be started too late. From the age of two on the child needs to be encouraged to try to manage his excretory activities as his parents do, particularly as the parent of the same sex does. To this encouragement should be added an occasional mild insistence. There are some mothers who consciously but more often unconsciously desire that no toilet training take place. Fairly often we meet mothers whose children of nine, ten, or eleven are still wetting the bed at night and who say they haven't bothered making any demands on the child to stop his bed wetting because they themselves wet the bed until they were fourteen or fifteen years old. Such mothers unconsciously are tacitly encouraging the child to continue wetting the bed.

As the process of toilet training goes on, little emphasis needs to be placed on cleanliness in other directions. In fact, the child should have opportunities to play with dirt and water and to be "dirty" in this way. Also, he needs opportunities for the free use of his muscles and opportunities to be destructive. Free use of his muscles should be encouraged by his parents. Destructiveness should be neither encouraged nor discouraged, for it is a truism that in the development of the child, destructive actions will be followed by constructive ones. He should be permitted to express verbally his feelings of anger and hate which he will feel toward his parents from time to time. Again, such expressions should neither be encouraged nor discouraged.

Treatment for those children who show the effects of having over-conformed in their toilet training must lie in a retraining of the child, for the condition has become an intrapsychic one—one in which the child himself consciously or unconsciously feels over-afraid or overashamed of wanting to do or doing anything dirty regardless of what other people say or do. Changes in the emotional climate in which the child lives will not cure him completely. The child's oversevere conscience will have to be changed.

Take the case of the little girl cited above. The child has two emotional problems: (1) she feared any type of soiling so much that she had to live her life in a way that excluded soiling, and (2) she gave in to her mother, not because she desired to maintain a friendly relationship with her, but because she was humiliated and feared the loss of her mother's assistance and kindness. She had felt antagonistic to her mother for asking her to give up a pleasurable activity, but when she relinquished it through fear she was forced to suppress her feelings of antagonism from her conscious mind. Thereafter these feelings appeared only in her behavior which, by the time she came for treatment, was not of a kind to make her mother proud of her. The repression of the two impulses—the desire to soil and the hostility to the mother—caused them to become combined in the child's mind, and they were kept combined through the fear of a repetition of the humiliating experience. The same fear kept them separated from the child's conscious thinking and feeling.

The aim of treatment will be to remove the fear from the child's mind and to replace it by a desire to be cultured. Such a desire will be sufficient to enable the child to use her desires to soil and her feelings of hostility to her mother in a culturally acceptable manner for her own benefit and the benefit of the society in which she lives. How can this be accomplished? The first step will be the diagnosis, the ascertainment of the nature of the conflict that has produced the symptoms. This task is not easy and may require a considerable period of time. A careful reading of Bornstein's and of Kolansky's cases will indicate the difficulties involved. Usually the parents know only the child's symptoms that they can observe and have little or no idea as to their cause. We believe diagnosis can be made only by a psychiatrist, although a psychoanalytically well-trained physician, psychologist, social worker, or teacher also may be skilled enough to diagnose. After the diagnosis has been made, treatment, in some cases, can be carried out through several steps. The first step is that the child develop a love relationship with an adult. If the mother can be used in treatment this step is not necessary, for the love relationship already exists. If the mother cannot be used, then the love relationship must be developed with another adult—a teacher, a physician, or a psychiatrist.

As soon as the love relationship is established the adult will begin gradually to encourage the child to take part in activities which the child regards as dirty. Playing with mud and water, sand and water, plasticine, or finger paints, ordinary painting, drawing with chalk, and gardening are all such activities. No comment is made about the child's desire or attempts to be clean and neat, but the adult will praise all successful attempts at being dirty. Even if fecal soiling recurs, the child should be commended for it. This prescription seems simple as it is written, but the application of it with the child will demand much painstaking and careful labor before she will be able to do with any degree of success or pleasure the things the adult does. If the mother can be persuaded to work in this way with the child the success might be quicker and easier.

During this process the child will begin to express hostility and antagonism to the therapist and also (at home) to her mother. Again the adult attitude should be to accept without praise or comment all the child's attempts to please or ingratiate herself and to praise the successful expression of hostility. As the child becomes easier with her hostile feelings she will begin to attempt to paint or model, and any real success along this line should be encouraged. Through such methods the child gives up her idea that the only way to get on with the adult is to be clean and conforming and replaces it with the more healthy attitude that not only are her productions and opinions worthwhile and bring her pleasure but also that she can produce them and retain her friendly relationship with the adult at the same time. The therapist's approach might begin along a different line. Using dolls, the child would be encouraged to dramatize the feelings a little girl has toward her mother. Again, no comment should be made about tendencies to conformity, but the child should be encouraged to express hostile feelings and their successful expression should be praised. During this process the child will become interested in playing with materials which she has formerly regarded as dirty, and this interest should be praised.

Both methods are combined in the ordinary psychiatric treatment of children, but the therapist does not assume as much direction as has been described here, because there are often other problems which are involved in the main one but are known only to the child. These must be worked out also. As they are solved, the child comes to the solution of the main problem more easily. If they are not worked out they often interfere tremendously with the effect of the management we have described. In the case of this particular girl the treatment would have to be conducted throughout by a trained child psychiatrist.

As a successful result of such treatment we would expect the child's school work to improve tremendously, for she would be more interested in accomplishing her task instead of putting all her efforts in seeing it was done neatly; we would expect her play activities to become as varied as those of other children of her age, for she would have no further interest in the futile paper game and be able to join with other children in their play without regard to whether it got her dirty or not; we would expect the state of her room and her clothes more nearly to approximate that of a child of her own age, for she could then wear soiled clothes if desirable and would be able to move her possessions from one position to another; and we would expect that her feeding problem would vanish.

It will have been noticed that this child did not react exactly like the sheep—that is, she did not lose her conditioning; rather it became more pronounced and spread into other areas. Usually, besides losing its conditioned reflexes, the sheep becomes seclusive, stands by itself in the corner of the field, shakes, trembles, and shows tic-like movements, eats and sleeps poorly, and although it may have had a very mild disposition before the conditioning experiments, now it will attack any person or animal that approaches it. A similar reaction occurs following another type of conditioning experiment on dogs. A dog is conditioned to anticipate being fed as soon as it hears a bell. When this conditioned reflex is established, the time interval between the ringing of the bell and the feeding of the dog is lengthened. When the interval reaches the space of two minutes the dog behaves as the sheep did in the former experiment. The dog cannot stand having to postpone the gratification of a desire (to be fed) too long, so it develops a pathological reaction. Similarly, the young child cannot tolerate having to postpone too long the gratification of a desire.

If a young child is toilet trained too vigorously or too early (that is, before he is ready for it), he may become very antagonistic, negativistic, and stubborn, be a prey to fears, and develop a great restlessness. In brief, from being a moderately well-behaved child he becomes badly behaved. This reaction usually annoys his parents, who express their annoyance by punishing him for his behavior. The punishment makes him more antagonistic and negativistic; they punish more, he behaves worse, until a vicious circle is rapidly produced. This vicious circle may result in a recurrence of the original soiling. It is as if the child said, "What's the use? I try hard to please my parents but they don't seem to understand that I try. I don't seem to understand them either, because they say one thing at one time and another at another. I might as well give up and return to pleasures I know are certain."

Treatment for this condition will follow the lines laid down for the case already mentioned. It will be more difficult to establish an affectionate relationship with such a child because he has become angry and filled with hate for the adults who trained him. He anticipates that any new relationship with an adult will result in further curtailment of his gratifications and so views the therapist with suspicion and immediate hostility, being ready constantly to defend himself against any demands. He is ready at the least opportunity to take revenge on any adult for the deprivation he has suffered at his parents' hands. In addition to all these, the conformity of cleanliness has enhanced the sadomasochistic attitude which forms a great deal of the interpersonal relationship of all children of this age. This means that the main ties he has to other people lie in the pleasure he receives from hurting and being hurt. Therefore treatment will consist definitely of two steps. The first is the overcoming of the suspiciousness, defiance, and hostility through which the child operates in his relationship to adults. The adult has to refuse to react to this by hostility, for reaction would only increase the child's antagonism, gratify him masochistically, and give him a reason to be sadistic. The second step is for the therapist to make every effort to have the child like him. This can be done by being kind and considerate, by doing small favors for him, by helping him in difficulties, and by understanding his point of view. From this point on the treatment, the second step, is the same as that described above.

Even with the problems shown by these very young children—such as in the cases described by Mrs. Bornstein and Kolansky, treatment is not a simple matter that can be done by anybody. This is much more true in the case of the eight-year-old girl we described. Our description of a treatment makes it seem a very easy procedure because we have oversimplified it. These cases require treatment by a well-trained and skilled child psychiatrist—preferably a child psychoanalyst.

SUMMARY

The process of toilet training imposes severe emotional strains on the child because almost for the first time he has to force himself to postpone his desire to obtain immediate and constant pleasure in the hope of obtaining greater pleasure at a later time—he has to force himself to try to live by the reality principle instead of by the pleasure principle. Under the best circumstances he finds this difficult, and the struggle always leaves definite monuments to it in his personality, his habitual reactions, and his abilities for adjustment. When the circumstances of his life during his toilet training have not been optimal either because of organic gastrointestinal illnesses or because of parents who demand that he toilet train himself too early or who are too severe to him about his efforts, the effects may be observed at once or in his personality traits later in life.

He suddenly may develop an acute or a more or less chronic anxiety state. In order to assuage the painful feeling of anxiety he may start to avoid certain situations in which he thinks he will feel more anxious. The situations he avoids do not indicate usually what he feels anxious about—only that in that situation he tends to become anxious. This was illustrated very well by the child described by Mrs. Bornstein who avoided both going to bed and falling asleep—the real cause of the anxiety being her fear that she soil herself while she slept.

Instead of an anxiety state the child may learn to express his feelings of hatred to his mother either by continuing to soil himself, to wet himself while he is awake or by being constipated. If many suppositories or enemas have been used, he may not wish to give up the added pleasure he finds in the insertion of the suppository or the enema nozzle and his mother's ministration to him during this procedure. He may become constipated in order to force his mother to continue the use of the suppositories and the enemas.

Partly as an attempt to spite his mother and partly as an attempt to return to the pleasures of the oral stage because he is being deprived of his anal pleasures he may develop a feeding problem.

When his pleasure in the uncontrolled passage of flatus is curtailed too suddenly or too severely, he may conform to the demand not to pass the gaseous contents of his body from his anus but instead to use the gaseous contents that pass out of the upper end of his gastro-intestinal tract—his speech—to get the same type of pleasure through the use of obscenities.

Too sudden or too early toilet training may cause him to regress to the type of breathing found in young infants. When this is combined with the need to express his feelings of hatred by obscenities and by other words, and when he fears to express these feelings, he may begin to stutter.

He may show none of these reactions in a form marked enough for his parents to observe them. Instead, after his toilet training is completed, he may become unreasonably clean and meticulous and develop a compulsive personality which interferes in many ways with his happiness and success. He will grow up with this type of personality. This personality can become marked, as the anal personality described by Freud in which the quartet of meticulousness, cleanliness, parsimony, and obstinacy cause difficulties in adjustment for the individual himself and often make him unpopular and disliked by other people. Being toilet trained too early or too severely may cause the child to enter the genital period before he is psychologically and physiologically ready. He uses progression in development as a defense against anxiety about gratifying his anal needs. He gratifies himself through a great deal of masturbation, but his thoughts and fantasies during this masturbation are not those of the oedipal period but are sadomasochistic in nature. His oedipal conflicts become confused with his conflicts over sadism and masochism to the disturbance of his later sexual life.

We also have discussed how too frequent spankings on the buttocks may increase the child's desire for masochistic pleasure and which may continue as his main pleasure throughout his life.

During the process of toilet training the emotional climate is important for the child's optimal development, and preventive measures in regard to this often are of great importance. Once the toilet training is completed, whatever problems the child shows as a result become his own intrapsychic problems. As such they really are not very amenable to changes in the environment. This is true especially if the problems of toilet training are solved by the development of marked personality traits. A child with these marked and hampering personality traits needs treatment by an experienced child psychiatrist or psychoanalyst, preferably the latter.

BIBLIOGRAPHY FOR CHAPTER IV

Bornstein, Berta, "A Phobia in a Two-and-a-half-year-old Child," *Psychoanalytic Quarterly*, 4, 1935, 93.

Freud, Sigmund, *Character and Anal Erotism*, Vol. 9, The Standard Edition of the *Complete Psychological Works of Sigmund Freud*, Hogarth, 1959.

Sterba, Editha, "An Important Factor in the Eating Disturbances of Childhood," *Psychoanalytic Quarterly*, 10, 1941, 365.

V

Development of Personality during the Genital Period

WITH the genital phase of psychosexual development we enter the third phase in personality development. This phase covers roughly the time between the ages of three and six. In every child's life each successive phase has to be lived through, with incidents occurring in each which contribute to the child's attitudes and feelings toward the world around him. As the child enters the third year of life the gratifications in the oral zone have lost their predominance. Oral pleasures no longer have all the important values they had to the nursing infant. The average child is usually through the period of toilet training, the struggles to master and achieve it, and some sublimations of interest in excretions have already begun. Also the child is more aware than previously of both himself and the outside world, and his interests go beyond the gastrointestinal tract and its functions to the phenomena of the world around him and to the hows and whys of living. He is more aware of his own body and is becoming aware of the pleasurable sensations in his genitals and of the changes that occur there under certain conditions.

INFANTILE SEXUALITY

The term *psychosexual development* seems an applicable one to use for describing the interactions of body, physiology, social attitudes, and psyche. For some it is more difficult to see that the sensual pleasures in the oral period (nursing and sucking) and the pleasure of the child in the bowel and bladder function have a sexual or sensual component. This difficulty comes, no doubt, from having been accustomed to confining the thinking about sexual expression too narrowly to genital functioning.

It is generally accepted by doctors, social workers, students of social relations, and counselors in marital relationships that sexuality has two components: one of procreation and one of pleasure. Moreover, it is accepted that enjoyment should be derived from the sexual act as a means of enhancing the value of marriage and of life in general, and more and more attention is being paid to this fact. Within the last decade various cities have set up marriage agencies, an important part of whose activities is to help young people, through group or individual discussion, to obtain a more satisfactory knowledge of sexual adjustment in marriage and thus enhance the social value of the sexual act and not confine its values completely to procreation.

It is generally accepted that there are other zones of the body that are areas of sexual excitation: witness, for instance, the prejudice some parents have against the kissing, fondling, and petting in which adolescents participate. Thinking honestly through that situation, we realize that the adult fears the adolescent will be so stimulated by kissing, hugging, and close body contact that he will be led into an actual genital relationship. We can say, then, that besides the genitals there are areas of the body that are capable of erotic excitation. They are called the *erogenous zones* and when stimulated are capable of being pleasurably exciting. They are notably the mouth, the anus, the skin, and the breasts of the woman. These areas give pleasure when stimulated by touch because of their anatomical structure. They are a constant source of pleasure throughout life and are not magically innervated because a marriage is entered into, nor do they cease to be sources of pleasure when a marriage ends. Their demand for pleasurable gratification has to be reckoned with at all ages. If this process is "sexual" in the grade- or high-school student, it must be so in the infant child as well. In other words, in order to understand psychosexual development we need only to be logical in our thinking and correlate the growth phenomena of the adult and the child. There is no sudden metamorphosis from the innocence of the child to the sophistication of the adult. It is a gradual steady growth from birth onward.

THE OEDIPUS COMPLEX

It has been observed at this age period between three and six that children tend to be drawn emotionally toward the parent of the opposite sex and in a way that is erotically tinged. This phenomenon is called the *oedipus complex*—that much discussed concept of

Freudian psychology. A *complex* is an emotionally toned group of ideas. As a result of careful studies over a long period of time ample proof has been assembled that about the time the child is leaving the home and entering school he goes through the struggle of a minor love affair—with the mother if the child is a boy and with the father if the child is a girl. Some suggest that this is due to a sexual glandular activity in children. Others tend to discount this possibility and say that sexual glandular activity does not start until puberty. However, something is present within each sex which we have to call, for the time being, biological, and which draws the sexes toward each other. It has esthetic and social elements also.

Manifestations of this phenomenon can and do take place as early as the genital period which we are discussing. The boy talks about being in love with his mother, about wanting to marry his mother and, because of this feeling for her, wanting her attention to the exclusion of other members of the family. He is acting like an adult lover and has a corresponding ambivalence toward his father, partly because of this interest and feeling for his mother, and partly because his father is standing in his way and being, at the same time, a disciplinarian. In the same way the girl is drawn toward her father, courts his interest, and seems to seek to be his favorite. Also, in a corresponding way, she resents her mother and feels a hostility toward her for being in the way of her complete possession of the father.

When the reader accepts such a situation, he can see that it needs to be understood and handled wisely by the parents, since there is a tendency for some persons to remain in love with their parents indefinitely, and thus never quite be able to free themselves, or to become interested in a person of the opposite sex, or to get any idea of marriage and home formation of their own. Almost everyone knows of a woman who lives at home with her father—either with the mother on the scene or not—who keeps house for him and has never taken any interest in another man and continues to be emotionally incapable of marriage because her emotional ties to her father are so strong; she may quite consciously say that she never found anyone else good enough. In such a case, incidentally, the father may have helped her in this belief. He may have been intrigued by the interest and affection of his daughter and sought to keep his hold on her. He may have found it convenient to have her devotion and attention and may never have tried to direct her desires toward a home of her own; he may have occasionally unconsciously encouraged this emotional relationship which we call the oedipus complex.

We all know men, too, who are caught in the same dilemma, who have emotional ties to their mothers which they cannot break or relinquish. They do not marry, or if they do, they have an unsatisfactory marriage because they are trying to be a lover of two women —the wife and the mother. The result usually is that such a man satisfies neither woman and is himself in great conflict over his feelings for each.

This emotional bond between the parent of the opposite sex and the child has its first manifestation around this genital period. It has a sexual erotic basis and many ramifications, which we will see as we go along and which make it a most important phase of human development, warranting our close study and thought. It derives its name from a Greek myth concerning Oedipus, the son of Laius, king of Thebes. It was prophesied that the boy would grow up to kill his father, whereupon, to avert the tragedy, he was given by his father to a shepherd with instructions that he was to leave the boy on the mountain to die. The shepherd, instead, gave the child to the king of another realm where he grew to manhood; eventually he met his real father and, being unaware of his identity, slew him in a battle. Oedipus eventually returned to the land of his birth and, in return for solving a riddle, was given the queen, his mother, to wife. Still unaware of the identity of his real parents, he lived with his mother for a time as man and wife. When he finally learned the truth, in his guilt he put out his eyes and his mother hanged herself. He later was destroyed by the avenging deities. The theme of guilt and tragedy associated with incest has carried the name of Oedipus and is applied to the ubiquitous presence of the emotions surrounding the family emotional interactions.

In his family emotional interaction the boy with his instinctual drive and his conformity with the social pattern talks and thinks in terms of marrying his mother and of excluding his father. In the same way, the girl talks and thinks in terms of marrying her father, or being his wife and having a baby by him. Are there many readers who have never heard small children make statements such as this? If they have not, the facts can easily be verified by listening a little more closely to the conversation of small children for a while. A boy of five recently came downstairs in the morning after his father had been away on a two-day trip. He was hurt and annoyed to find the father there and he started to cry, saying, "You aren't supposed to be eating with my mummy. She is just for me. You go away again." It took considerable reassurance on the part of the mother to quiet him and to get him to accept the fact that she could love them both enough for his happiness.

Another child we know, four and a half years old, insisted one night that he sleep in his father's bed in the same room with the mother while the father slept elsewhere in the house. Some fathers find it difficult to acquiesce to such a high-handed attack upon their importance and authority; but on the occasional times that the boy or girl does show intense feeling of this kind over the family emotional interaction, it is well for them to forget their dignity and concentrate on the fact that the child is going through a critical and emotional conflict that needs help. To discipline or reprove the child at the time he is suffering jealousy can bring about an obedience only at the price of sullenness and resentment. The parent who realizes that these ideas and thoughts are going on in the child's mind is in a better position to help the child to a solution of the problems they create than if he were not aware of them. The solution of these ideas has to be reached in one of two ways, either by repression or by redirection.

Repression is the ejection from consciousness (into a hypothetical area or realm of the mind) of those ideas and feelings that are not acceptable to the conscious ego. The most frequent way in which a great number of the problems of childhood are settled is by repression, by this forcible ejection into the unconscious.

Another and better way, of course, is for the child to rearrange and reassemble his ideas and emotions so that they become acceptable to the ego or become redirected away from the parent to other persons and other activities in the environment. In this solution the child needs help.

We want the reader to understand as clearly as possible the difficult problem that both the boy and girl encounter in the oedipus complex and its eventual solution. To a varying degree the boy naturally fears his father's disapproval, anger, and possibly punishment because of his ideas and feelings toward his mother.

In the average family setting the mother is usually generous and giving, while the father is more the disciplinarian. This love relation between the boy and his mother gradually comes to be broken up by the presence of the father and by the fear of his disapproval, anger, or punishment. Among the punishments that are feared by the child for manifesting the ideas inherent in the oedipus complex is the threat of harm to the genitals specifically. Thus the boy finally renounces his mother as a love object; he gives up the idea of supplanting his father in her affections and redirects his energy toward those persons in the environment who are available. The child is usually in school at this age period. There he enters into play with his chums and at home with his brothers and sisters, if he has any, and contents himself with their companionship, giving up the hope of being the mother's lover.

At this point, the boy's feelings toward his father are mixed. He is, of course, ambivalent toward him. He does not want to give up the feeling he has for his mother but if the father is a reasonably kind man and a reasonably desirable character, the boy decides, in the solution of the oedipus complex, that since he cannot depose his father, he will imitate him, he will be like him, with the hope, thereby, that some day he, like his father, will be able to marry and enjoy the many privileges his father enjoys. The kinder the parents are, and the more aware they are of this family emotional struggle, the easier it is for children to resolve the oedipus conflict without too many difficulties.

MASTURBATION AND PSYCHOSEXUAL DEVELOPMENT

Masturbation is another phenomenon that occurs during the genital period. Masturbation is simply the act of manipulating the genital organs in order to produce pleasure. *It is a universal and normal phenomenon of human growth and development.* We want to stress the universal and normal aspect of this phenomenon because a great many people feel there must be some harm in any kind or degree of masturbation at any age. The very word masturbation frightens, disgusts or disturbs many people. Yet psychiatrists, psychologists, teachers, and educators who have made a serious study of personality development agree that masturbation is merely a normal and universal phenomenon of human development; in fact, they agree further that it is a phenomenon necessary to a satisfactory psychosexual development. Before the end of the first year, children discover that the genital area is sensitive to touch and capable of pleasurable responses. For this reason the child will play with himself in that zone at various times.

Masturbation tends to increase in intensity during two periods of the child's life: the first is during the genital period and the second is at puberty when the sexual glands become active and endocrine secretion of the sexual glands gives an added impetus to the sexual part of the personality. A mother may say that her child never masturbated. This statement cannot be true. It appears authentic to this mother because she was so disturbed and frightened and unhappy over the idea of masturbation that when her child was very young and attempted manipulation of his genitals for the first few times, she may have frightened him so severely as to have killed any further attempt at masturbation, or at least prevented his masturbating again in her presence. Therefore, she can honestly say from what she has seen of her child's behavior that he has never played with himself. However, when we question mothers who are able to answer honestly because they are not afraid to face the fact of masturbation, we find that it is a universal practice for children of both sexes to play with themselves genitally and that they will do so more or less and from time to time. In various degrees masturbation is a normal phenomenon from the first year of life up to the time a marital relation is established.

Let us speak a little about the meaning of masturbation and what our attitude can be toward it. What should be done to control it, or direct it, or have it fit in with the personality in order that it does not become either a personal or a social problem? The problem of masturbation can be compared to the problem of drinking. For some people drinking is never a problem. They drink with dignity and restraint. In the same way, for a great many people masturbation is not a problem. They indulge in it occasionally, but they never worry about it; they have no excessive mental conflict about it; it does them no physical harm, and as a piece of behavior it fits satisfactorily into their whole personality structure. However, masturbation can become excessive and can become a pathological manifestation of an underlying personality difficulty.

We feel that the attitude toward masturbation should be one of considering that the child is a pleasure-seeking animal who seeks pleasure from various sources and who, finding it in masturbation, may pursue it to too great a degree if he is not receiving sufficient affection from the people in the environment and if his energies are not being directed into other channels. If those in the environment make the child feel happy and contented, if they see that he has companions and toys to play with, he will not gravitate toward any excessive degree of masturbation. He will curtail his indulgence for much the same reason that he learns to control his bowels and bladder, for the same reason that he eventually learns to eat three meals a day instead of demanding to eat at any time or at all times.

The child will masturbate enough to further his psychosexual development. During the genital period the child's romantic interest in the parent of the opposite sex acts as an extra stimulus to excite him, or her, sexually. For this reason masturbation is more frequent at this time. Usually the child masturbates when by himself. Even if he tends to handle his genitals in the presence of others, if the relationship between the parents and child has been good up to this time, and if the parents realize that this is just a phase he is going through, then the child will come through the genital period without becoming a frequent or "chronic" masturbator. When the psychic energy remains attached to a phenomenon of psychosexual development instead of passing on to a more mature and socially accepted expression, we term such a condition a *fixation*. Individuals may remain fixated at the autoerotic stage of psychosexual development and remain self-centered, seeking pleasure in their own activity or in fantasy rather than in a warm emotional relationship with others. Persistent and excessive masturbation can be a phenomenon of this process if parents foster such fixation by condemning the habit of masturbation rather than by lovingly helping the child to go through the difficult period of socialization. Parents who are very much distressed about masturbation may tell the child that he is wicked, that he is doing something dirty and shameful, that he will ruin his health, that he will make himself feeble-minded, that the practice will harm his heart, that it will give him tuberculosis. They may threaten to mutilate the child's organ, a threat more frequently made against the boy than the girl. Such parents often say and do a great deal to scare the child out of what they consider a nasty habit and do not recognize as a normal phenomenon of development, no more and no less abnormal than trying to relieve the boredom of home life by chronic TV viewing.

We must remind the reader again that the world of the child is still very small at this age and that what the father and mother say is law. When the mother, father, and other grownup persons in the household tell a child over and over that the thing he is doing is wicked, shameful, dirty, or will harm his health indefinitely, they put an idea into his mind that may be a most painful burden for him to carry all his life. The mentally sick people in the hospitals of the United States always outnumber the patients having any other disease. When we talk with mentally sick people whose minds have grown troubled, we find frequently that one of their most common, torturing beliefs is that they have committed unpardonable sins or that they have injured their health irreparably through self-abuse.

We need not consult such troubled people but can merely question a cross section of the student body of any college to learn that fears of the harm of masturbation linger all too long. Often unconsciously and in an honest and well-meaning attempt to curb or cure what they felt to be an innate weakness and "dirtiness" in the child, parents have put lifelong ideas of inferiority and unworthiness into the minds of people when they were children going through the genital period. That kind of education is wrong during this age period; it is almost always harmful and should not be carried out.

Masturbation does not produce nervous trouble, does not weaken the mind, does not weaken the body organs. In fact, we know of no harmful effects of masturbation other than the mental conflict engendered. In an average home where the parents and the child have a good understanding, the need for masturbation can be accepted along with accepting the child's need to nurse, to suck, to evacuate, to eat, to ask questions. Masturbation, far from being any special problem, is one that responds as well as the others to the intelligent combination of gratification and direction. The adult who indulges in excessive masturbation has a neurotic problem and is sick emotionally, but he is not harming himself by the act itself. The problem that should concern the doctor in any case of excessive masturbation is why the patient needs to carry on this compulsive drive for pleasure in and on himself; for along with the compulsive masturbation the patient has many other symptoms, such as a social adjustment which is very unsatisfactory, very ungratifying, and very uninteresting.

Masturbation has at least two important aspects. In order to function sexually men and women need to have some feeling developed in the genital area. Masturbation is an aid in bring feeling to that area and centering it in the sexual organs. Children who have been made to feel ashamed of the sexual desire that leads to masturbation and who have been made afraid of sexual feeling by having been threatened about injury will as a result repress this feeling and dam it back upon themselves. By punishment and threat of injury for the practice of masturbation, the parent sets up the danger that the child grown to womanhood will be frigid and the child grown to manhood impotent. The anxiety engendered in these frightened people becomes a barrier to the process of psychosexual development and hinders the process of the libido's becoming genitalized.

Furthermore, impotent men are a threat to the whole race, for if enough men became impotent, the race could not be carried on. Frigid women can, of course, have sexual relations and become pregnant, yet it is important for the race that they not be frigid. When women become frigid and do not allow themselves to have sexual feeling, there is a danger that they will be unhappy in marriage, or fail to have warm feelings toward their children, or both. They are also more prone to develop neurosis and psychosis; they have less to contribute emotionally to the marriage and their whole joy in living is reduced.

So, if the sexual feeling that is struggling to express itself through the child's masturbation is dammed back and the development inhibited, that child will grow into a person with little interest in marriage, or, marrying reluctantly, will have a rather lukewarm interest in marriage and get an early divorce, or drift on through an unhappy married life, or suffer, after marriage, from frigidity or impotence. Thus serious problems arise from a too thorough and unrestrained condemnation of sexual feeling in the child. It is important that this restraining process not be started in childhood and that children not be frightened into a state of stagnation in their sexual development. Such treatment will inhibit not only their ability to procreate children but also, to a varying degree, their buoyancy and enthusiasm for life in every sphere; it will suppress that part of their personality which would lead to a happy home and family.

Many people by the time they reach thirty or thirty-five become discouraged with living; they wonder what they are living for and find little joy in any activity. They are not working for any person of the opposite sex, and their interest in life and persons generally is greatly diminished through having been inhibited so thoroughly in their sexual development. This can come about, *partly,* at least, by the wrong treatment of early sexual interest either before the genital period or during it. No modern psychiatrist would say that masturbation causes frigidity in women or impotence in men. The difficulty has arisen over too much attention having been directed toward the supposed evils of masturbation and at the same time disregarding the evils of the social maladjustment which was setting in when the excessive masturbation arose. Excessive masturbation in a child or an adult always arises in a somewhat pathological setting. What we want the reader to see in these cases is the nature of the pathological setting and not exclusively, in a too shortsighted way, a pathology in masturbation itself.

ANXIETIES ASSOCIATED WITH MASTURBATION

Threats that are given to children concerning masturbation may give rise to an emotional attitude described as the *castration complex.* A complex, as has been mentioned, is an emotionally toned group of ideas. The castration complex merely means that there has been implanted in the child a fear that something may happen to his genital organ, a fear that has important results for both sexes. The female has a castration complex, though its forms for her are somewhat different. One of these is the female's distress over the fact that since she has no penis she has already been castrated. She may feel that her mother cheated her out of the penis at birth or that she once possessed it and lost it through some act of "naughtiness." Later she may acquire the idea that sexual intercourse will in some way injure the vagina and that childbirth will do the same thing even more extremely.

It should be easy to see why a male child, who is threatened horribly about injury to his genitals, should have a castration complex. Anyone who gives much thought to the worries of the small child can imagine the pain of the female child, struggling alone with the fact of what she takes to be an anatomical defect. Physicians need not be in medical practice long to encounter men who can remember that their parents threatened to cut off the penis or to do it some harm, or women who feel bitterly that "men have all the advantages." The idea that the penis might be lost through some measure taken by the outside world is reinforced in the male child when he sees the female child and realizes that she does not have his organ. Then he may think the same thing may happen to him.

We have to ask for the reader's open-mindedness in discussing these concepts and putting forth these ideas. We realize that many people are skeptical about such ideas entering in, or remaining in, a child's mind. Children are naively regarded as being always gay, happy, innocent little persons concerned mainly with play. They are not often regarded as being concerned with the problems of sex, or worrying about their anatomical differences, or being envious of each other. Yet these concerns are ubiquitous. Children do a great deal of talking about these matters and actually get little help from grownups, and the sexual concerns of the child are very important to him.

It is an interesting fact that while the tolerant and enlightened mothers sees outward manifestations of the sexual ideas that are going on in the child's mind, the intolerant and unenlightened mother does not notice them. The frightened mother senses something of her child's questioning attitude, but she tries hard to silence him in an effort to discourage the ideas and get them out of his mind. She believes she can make a better person of him if he is prevented from putting the inquiries into words. Such a mother thinks she has settled the matter by ignoring it. Instead, she has merely left the child to ruminate by himself, to obtain the answers by himself or with the aid of the limited or incorrect information from other children. Some mothers refuse to see and help their children with these problems; others accept the problems and hear them but do not know how to help; others, a still smaller group, do see and do try to help the children.

SEX PROBLEMS OF GIRLS

Many a female tends to be quite concerned about the fact that she does not have a genital organ like the male, her feeling about it arousing a state of mind called *penis envy*. On seeing boys, little girls feel jealous of the fact that the boys have this "extra" tissue in the form of the phallus. More than that, the girls are jealous of the extra prerogatives which being male gives to the boys. We do not know many women who do not resent this fact in one way or another at times, for which they can hardly be blamed.

For the girl who feels that the boy has more privileges than she, the obvious procedure is to state the truth. She should be told that she has sexual organs as good as those of the male, only of a different structure; she should be told that she can have as much pleasure out of life as the boy, despite external differences; that she can grow up and become a mother, that she can produce a child, which he cannot, and that the production of children and preparing them for life is one of society's greatest achievements.

Up to the present time female children have had far too little help with their emotional problems, especially those beginning at this age. With the boy it might be enough to refrain from frightening him, because he is usually mildly confident of himself and getting some sense of worth. However, in order to make the female healthily satisfied with herself, some explanation and reassurance about the reasons for anatomical differences in the sexes should be made, and as early as she shows concern about them. This concern is likely to be manifested during the genital or phallic phase of development, if not before, to the mother who intelligently observes her children.

SEX INFORMATION FOR CHILDREN

During all the genital period, both the child's curiosity and his own feelings are expanding as he grows older and asks more and more questions about life. In asking about life he must inevitably touch upon the question of sexuality and reproduction.

When the child becomes interested in the problems pertaining to sex and birth, his questions should be answered frankly, truthfully, and without embarrassment as they arise. To answer without embarrassment is not so difficult a job as one might think. Children need and want very little information at any one time. If children ask where they come from and are told that babies grow within the mother's body, that answer will satisfy most children for that particular day and perhaps for several weeks or months to come. They just do not get around to asking any more until something in connection with their play with other children, or some event in their home life comes up which prompts a question for additional information. Very often parents make a problem for themselves by the feeling that when the child asks the first question about sex, they are obligated to tell him everything that has been written in a comprehensive treatise on sexuality. Obviously this is neither necessary nor advisable. Any parent who will put himself at ease on the subject of sex, not try to show how much he knows or be afraid of how little he knows, not be flustered with embarrassment but just answer what the child asks, will manage sex education in a very satisfactory manner.

A practical question may arise here in the minds of some readers. What will the child do with the information? Will he take it to the neighbor's children, shock them (or more precisely their parents), and get himself in disrepute? Practically, this possibility rarely causes a problem. When the parents have told a child in a frank, calm, natural way, we have not known of any case where that child has gone out to try to impress the other children with his knowledge and thereby create an emotional disturbance in the neighborhood. The implication here is clear. When a child is answered simply and without embarrassment before his curiosity has grown out of bounds, he will take it for granted that he has just learned one more fact and he does not feel any need to go out and display his knowledge. He does not mention it, because it is of no more importance than any other question he has asked that day and he has no special desire to impart this particular piece of information.

The child may handle the matter in another way. Children have a way of disregarding what they do not want to believe and letting it go at that. Sometimes parents are startled when they have told their children the truth about sexuality to find that the children tell them later that they do not believe that babies grow inside the mother but that the stork brings them. They do not choose to believe what they have heard from their parents and may not do so for some time. However, it is a wise idea for parents to have told the truth (when asked), because then the facts are there for the child to use when he is ready. The parent can combine his or her ideas about love and the sexual expression of love in any manner and at whatever times he deems fitting.

If the child is the kind who is not yet ready to face the truth of sex at three or four years, then that child is not going to be a persistent questioner. Hence, parents need not fear being troubled by the child's insatiable curiosity—that it is going to test their knowledge or ability to impart it within a short space of time. Actually parents who fail to accept their responsibility for imparting information to their children about sex and rationalize their neglect by saying the child is too young or merely being childish themselves and obeying the old dictum of their parents which was, "You must not tell those things," or "You must not talk about that nasty subject." If the child is not anxious and the parent's relationship to him is good, and if he continues as he grows older to ask about the problems of sexuality and where he comes from, then again we really mean that parents can tell the whole truth, calling the body organs by their names and telling the child what their functions are. Following the answer that he has grown inside the mother's body, the child may ask how he got there. Then the mother—for usually the mother and not the father has to answer these questions—may say, "Well, the seed was put there by daddy."

This answer may suffice for some time and, if so, no more need be said. However, if the child should press for more information and ask, "How did daddy put it there?"—it is up to the mother to explain the procedure of sexual intercourse, to say that the man's penis is put into the woman's vagina and that, in the course of that relationship, the sperm, or egg of the man is deposited into the womb and there it is united with the egg of the woman to grow into a new life. Such a statement is not shocking to the child. Only certain adults have come to feel it is a shocking phenomenon to discuss because they were told and made to feel so. The child is prepared, or is eager and willing, to accept information without anxiety, without shame, without embarrassment, and he will do so if the parents do not convey these unfortunate attitudes along with their discussion of the matter. In other words, if a child of four or five questions the way a baby does grow in the woman's body and how the seed of the male is put in the woman's body, and if the mother tells him, she does not have to respond by thinking later, "Gracious! What have I said?" She has merely told a truth which will *not* shatter her child's mind. He will simply store up the knowledge as he does other facts, and they will be in his mind for his use always. He is left free to go about his play or work without all the ruminations and preoccupations about sex which the children who do not get the facts from their parents have to struggle with. Often these children never have their curiosity satisfied no matter how much they read or how much experience they have. They are always seeking the truth about sex which they feel was withheld by the parents and spend a great deal of time in fantasies, and a great deal of emotion and energy in thought, trying to find the answer.

SOURCES OF SEX INFORMATION

Children find it difficult to believe the stories they hear from other children. The stories differ in many aspects, and even if children hear the actual facts from other children they would prefer to have them confirmed by the parents. All too often they have already been treated by the parents in such a manner that they dare not ask the questions that are going around in their minds. They feel the questions are bad, and that even if they are not reproached openly, they will have burdened the parent with an unwelcome subject. Consequently, they continue to struggle with piecing together what information they can from extraparental channels, and they may never feel at ease with the truth about sexuality, even when they become adults. A great many of the problems that beset adolescents arise because they are using up too much energy, too much thought, too many fantasies in preoccupations with the question of sexuality which has never been properly handled at the right period; namely, the period we are discussing right now—the genital period.

It seems clear from numerous case studies that many of the sex problems in adolescence are not due to the desire for sexual intercourse, nor to a great sexual hunger, but to a great unsatisfied sexual curiosity which could have been alleviated if the subject had been treated frankly and straightforwardly in childhood.

In some families the mother and father deal poorly with the child's curiosity—every phase of curiosity. Other families are willing to answer questions on every subject but specifically forbid those having to do with sexuality. For the sake of a more adequate personality and a better social adjustment and as a help in the prevention of neurosis, psychosis, and psychopathic personalities, the subject of sex should be dealt with frankly by the parent.

Obviously, from what has been said, the idea of leaving a child ignorant of the subject until puberty and then taking him to the doctor to have a "good talk" is bad practice, is evading the issue, and is practically valueless, because when a child is forbidden to deal with the sex question up to twelve years and is then brought to the office of a relative stranger he is not likely to talk about what he knows or what he wants to know or to ask or answer questions very intelligently. If the doctor rushes in and tries to "tell him all," the boy is not likely to be comfortable enough to take in and organize much of what is said. The whole setting is unnatural. The way for sexual information to be given is through as sincere and frank treatment of the subject *by the parents* as is given to any other matter that arouses his curiosity during his growth and development. Moreover, when the sex question is dealt with in this way by the parents, it denotes to the child an acceptance of himself, an acceptance of his body and of the impulses of his body.

This attitude is in line with what we said in the previous chapter concerning talking to the child about toilet training. We cannot in good sense and fairness disapprove of the child because he must excrete; we merely disapprove if he does not learn properly to control his excretions. So in the matter of sex we do not disapprove of the child because he has sex impulses; we merely ask him to accept a code of reasonable control of his impulses. Such a frank treatment of the subject tends to reduce the anxiety that people acquire about their body functions, particularly about sex and even about other body functions that have their sexual component.

Case histories indicate that information that is given to children about sexual matters and that is given early will not cause them to misuse the information or become sexually delinquent during grade-school years or during adolescence. Children do not misbehave by utilizing what they know nearly so often as they misbehave because of what they do not know. It is the unsatisfied curiosity to which we referred that causes so much of the sexual experimentations that go on during adolescence or that exerts its pull upon adolescents and makes parents suspicious that they are too interested in the subject.

Children are much calmer and more willing and able to accept a fair code of sexual behavior when they know the facts and when they get them from their parents at an early age. Out of gratitude for the information and out of the close relationship with the parents which is bound to occur when the young person is dealt with thus frankly, he as an adolescent is more likely to accept the values in behavior that the parent would like him to accept. It is not sexual information that leads to promiscuity or to the danger of illegitimate pregnancy or venereal disease. What does often lead to these results is rather the lack of proper information or of an altruistic code of behavior taught by friendly parents.

SUMMARY

As toilet training is achieved, the child becomes aware of other bodily phenomena and wonders about anatomical differences in the sexes. Opportunities for this concern are more available to all children than many parents like to think. Masturbation is common. We have seen how an erotically toned emotional relationship to the parent of the opposite sex comes about. How all this is met and evaluated and worked into the fabric of family life and personality development is crucial for the child's later concepts about the importance of the opposite sex. Whether they can be used for one's welfare and development, or whether they are to be feared and avoided, depends, it seems, on what is learned at this period.

The castration complex and oedipus complex are described and discussed in this chapter as well as the role of identification as an important means of solution, healthy or unhealthy, to the many psychosexual growth problems confronting the human being.

As in the anal period, conscience formation continues to go on during the genital period but any complete system of sexual morality is, of course, impossible. Yet, we have seen how some parents act as if they would like to induce enough anxiety, guilt, and fear during this genital period to suppress sexual interest and feeling for all time. Such haste and severity is not conducive to mental health.

BIBLIOGRAPHY FOR CHAPTER V

Freud, Sigmund, *Three Contributions to the Theory of Sex,* Nervous and Mental Disease Publishing Co., 1930.
English, O. Spurgeon, and Constance J. Foster, *Fathers Are Parents Too,* Putnam, 1951.

VI

Emotional Disturbances that Occur during the Genital Period

THE PSYCHOLOGICAL illnesses of childhood fall into two groups—fancied (by the parent, not by the child) and real. This classification applies to all age levels, but particularly to the genital period. As has been mentioned in the last chapter, a child's behavior during the genital period, and particularly during the struggle with his feelings toward his parents, is not very conforming, and is often very annoying to them. He is frequently negativistic, obstinate, stubborn, disobedient, and antagonistic. He has temper tantrums and nightmares. The adult who has lived with a child through this period will remember that neither his life nor the life of the child was entirely happy.

Some parents, particularly those who want a good, conforming child who will be a credit to them, regard these manifestations of the child's normal development as abnormal and consult the physician or psychiatrist about them. The only therapy desirable is to review the whole family constellation, including the child's behavior, and if everything seems to be normal to inform the parents of this and to instruct them in the kind of behavior which they may anticipate during these years.

In order to understand the real emotional illnesses of the genital period and of the period of latency it is necessary to discuss what causes psychological illness in children. The child has certain needs, which may be summarized as follows:

1. He needs the security and backing of both living parents.

2. He needs their love and understanding.

3. He needs an optimum period of gratification for his infantile sensual desires. We say *optimum;* it should not be too curtailed nor should it be allowed to continue too long. If it is too brief he suffers too much painful anxiety when it comes to an end. If it is too pro-

longed he does not learn how to tolerate anxiety, and when the gratification necessarily has to end, the amount of anxiety experienced
is too great. A child has to learn how to tolerate anxiety but he has
to learn this through minute doses.

4. He needs to have opportunities to express his hostilities, antagonisms, and aggressiveness in order that he may learn what these
feelings are like and how to deal with them efficiently. All children
during the period of infancy develop three fears—fear of being deserted, fear of not being loved, and fear of being punished by horrible
mutilations. If the reader doubts the presence of these fears as part
of childhood he should try to explain why most little children cry
when their parents go out for the evening, why a child has a panic
when he is lost, and why he has a panic when he is about to be punished by whipping. In regard to the fear of whipping, the reader
must realize that the average child is not really very cowardly, that
he has been spanked before, and that in the majority of instances
the previous spanking did not really hurt and that therefore he
knows it will not be worse this time.

Anything that occurs that prevents the effective satisfaction of
needs or that increases the fears mentioned above will have a deleterious effect on the development of the child's personality and is
likely to produce an illness. Such occurrences are known technically
as *traumatic events,* that is, events that are injurious. They can be
grouped into three classes: (1) acts of fate, (2) adverse parental attitudes, and (3) exposure to premature and excessive sexual stimulation.

ACTS OF FATE

We have discussed in the previous chapter why the child needs the
security and backing of the visible presence of two parents—a father
and a mother—in order to solve the problem of his conflicting feelings toward them. What happens to the child if one parent is absent
because of death, marital separation, or separation through the necessity of patriotism or business? Since there are two parents and since
their sex and the sex of the child all affect the result it seems desirable
to consider five forms of the problem:

1. The effect on the boy of the absence of the father.
2. The effect on the boy of the absence of the mother.
3. The effect on the girl of the absence of the mother.

4. The effect on the girl of the absence of the father.

5. The effect on either boy or girl of separation from both parents.

THE EFFECT ON THE BOY OF THE ABSENCE
OF THE FATHER

The small boy needs the visible presence of his father for two reasons: he needs a male person to imitate and he needs a masculine foil with whom he can learn how to temper and exercise his feelings of aggression and love, for the adult male's main difficulties of adjustment lie in his relationships with other persons of the same sex. The presence of a visible father is most necessary during the period from birth to the age of six or seven, is less necessary but still very important during the latent period, and is much less important though still desirable during adolescence. In adult life the man derives pleasure from the fact that he has a father, though there is no imperative need for his existence.

If a boy is brought up in a fatherless home he suffers from the fact that he has no father to imitate. The word *imitation* is used here loosely to express a phenomenon more properly designated as *identification*. The small boy loves his father and because of this love he desires to be exactly like him, that is, to do, think, and feel exactly as the father does. In his daily life he automatically observes his father very closely. He is not really aware that this observation is going on, but he soon finds himself behaving or attempting to behave exactly like the father. This reaction is so automatic that the child is unaware that it takes place and when confronted with the fact will often be quite surprised. The automaticity of the process is one of the reasons for the prevalent belief that the child behaves like the father because he has inherited his traits. If there is no father present with whom the boy can identify, this process does not take place; the boy is deprived of the advantage of having at his disposal the useful reaction patterns which the father has developed from his life experiences for solving his conflicts and which have contributed to his success.

This is a complicated way of stating a simple and well-known fact: that the boy who is brought up in a fatherless home is deprived of the benefit of his father's knowledge of the world and of life. He can identify with his mother but this identification is not very helpful to the *boy*. His mother has learned about life and the world only from the point of view of a female and because of her feminine needs and desires. Such a viewpoint is of little benefit to the male person, for masculine ways of thinking and feeling are different from feminine ones and vice versa. Therefore the boy who has been deprived of the visible presence of his father has to meet life with little real knowledge of how other men think and feel and so is at a constant disadvantage. Though he has not been deprived of the greater part of his ability to think and feel in a masculine fashion, since this ability rests on an instinctual basis, he is deprived of the cultural accentuation that produces its precision and definiteness.

The lack of a father with whom to identify works a deeper psychological harm on the boy than the difficulty in thinking and feeling in a definitely masculine way. The boy identifies with the father because he loves him. He would like to be his father. In order to be his father he will have to get rid of the father. But his love protests against this solution and impels him to a better one. He must not *be* his father and have and do *exactly* as his father does but he can become *like* his father and have to do things the way his father does, but in other situations and with other persons. By the identification with his father he learns to renounce through love for another person the uncultured methods of gratification for his needs and desires, realizing that such renunciation still permits him their gratification and does not expose him to the anxiety that would be his lot if they could not be gratified. This learning is important because the whole structure of civilized society is built on this renunciation, because of love for other persons, of a *method* of obtaining gratification, not of the gratification itself.

When a boy is brought up in a fatherless home there is no possibility that this renunciation through identification will occur, nor is there any need for it, because there is no father to love. The boy feels he possesses his mother. He feels that she will gratify him completely and therefore feels no need to look for his gratification elsewhere. Even if she will not gratify him completely now, he believes that if he waits long enough she will. Gratification, therefore, is his by right and he does not need to procure it through his own efforts. There is no day-by-day struggle between his jealousy, love, and fear of his father through which he learns gradually and somewhat painfully how to compete successfully. When he reaches the age when the social situation and reality demand that he compete, if he wishes to continue to live successfully, he is baffled and helpless because he has never learned how to do so. There is no possibility of real gratification for him and so he is overwhelmed with anxiety. If he attempts to abolish the anxiety he acts in a fumbling, ineffectual, unsocial manner which gets him into trouble, and now this further pain is added to his suffering of anxiety.

Often the mother contributes to the boy's difficulty. She is deprived of a husband and she may try to make up to herself for her own deprivation by trying to obtain her gratification from her son. The reader will be able to supply from his observations many examples of such doting mothers and spoiled sons.

A result as serious, if not more so, follows when the father dies during the height of the boy's oedipus conflict. The boy is jealous of his loved father, hates and fears him and wishes he would die. He believes that his wishes are magical and will avail where his actions would fail. If his wishes were effective, he thinks then life would be paradise. His father dies at the height of these feelings. He finds that the result is the opposite of what he expected. During the period of the funeral the dead father is more the center of attention than he was before. No one pays much attention to the little boy. The mother is consumed with her own grief and has little real time for the child. If he has a wish or discomfort that he feels needs attention she will attend to it but perfunctorily.

After the funeral the mother is still unhappy and concerned with her loss and does not give him all the happiness he anticipated. He often finds that he does not have as many material benefits as before because there has been a change in the financial situation. Formerly when the mother was busy or withdrawn for any reason, he could turn to his father for pleasurable activities. Now there is no father to play with, to tell him stories, or to bring him gifts. He comes quickly to realize that this event has brought him pain rather than pleasure. He remembers that he wished it to take place and that at the time he was irritated that his wishes did not act magically quickly enough. These aggressive wishes were the cause of his father's death and instead of bringing him pleasure and gratification they brought exactly the opposite. Therefore aggressive wishes are very powerful and result in suffering. Henceforth he must never permit aggressive wishes of any sort. Every time he has an aggressive impulse, which would appear in his consciousness as an aggressive wish, he must put it out of his mind. In fact it would be better if it never appeared there at all.

How can he keep such wishes away? If his father had punished him for the wish as soon as it appeared, the magical wish would not have caused the catastrophe, his father would still be alive, and he would be happier. Perhaps he can learn to punish himself for such wishes, or better still, perhaps he can learn to experience a small amount of suffering to warn him that an aggressive wish is about to appear, and thus be able to kill it in the bud. He develops an immediate feeling of guilt about any aggressive feeling or impulse; and because success in life, whether in the realm of sexuality or ambition, depends on the proper and adequate exercise of aggression, he later on finds himself failing constantly.

These disturbances of development follow the death of the father. As death to the young child is only a prolonged separation, the disturbances also follow the permanent absence of the father due to marital separation. Even when the separation is not permanent but long-continued (as when the father is away from home for long periods due to business, or during time of war due to patriotism), the effect on the boy is the same, although perhaps not so marked. It is less marked, although still present, when the father is often away from home for periods of several days at a time.

It can be seen that separation from the father constitutes a definitely injurious situation in the boy's development. We wish to point out that these reactions of the child may continue into adult life if nothing is done about the situation. If, however, other events occur in his life which make up for his deprivation, or if circumstances provide a substitute father the effect of the trauma is not so long lived.

THE EFFECT ON THE BOY OF THE ABSENCE OF THE MOTHER

From a practical point of view the absence of the mother is not so serious an injury to the small boy as the absence of the father. We have never seen a boy who was brought up in a completely motherless home, although we have seen many cases where the home had no father. Some mother substitute—a housekeeper, an aunt, or an older sister—is always present, so the boy is exposed to intimate personal relationships with some woman. Arguing from what happens when a girl is brought up in a completely fatherless home, we suppose that if the boy were raised completely isolated from women there is a probability that he would develop into an adult homosexual. Any long-continued separation from the mother has a definite effect on the small boy. Since his relationship with the mother is different from that with the father, the effect is bound to be different. The mother is the main love object of the small boy and so separation from her will affect his erotic relationships more than his aggressive, ambitional ones.

This will show itself in two directions. The very small child, whether girl or boy, slowly gives up his (or her) infantile methods of obtaining gratification and proceeds forward in his development because he feels certain of his mother's love. When realization of the mother's absence strikes home his development immediately ceases. Instead of being willing to do for others he begins to demand that everything be done for him. Instead of being as free from fears as it is possible for a small child to be, he becomes increasingly fearful. Instead of wanting to dress, feed, and bathe himself he acts as if he were unable to perform these routines and must have them done for him. He seems unable to walk as well as he used to, and makes demands to be carried. His speech becomes more babyish. If he had ceased to suck his fingers, the habit starts again. If he had been toilet trained he may begin to wet or soil himself either during the day or at night. He has temper tantrums more frequently. He develops a feeding difficulty. He whines and cries a great deal, seems unhappy, and constantly demands the attention of adults. In all of this behavior he is using every possible action to express a very simple feeling. He says in effect, "Dear mother, see, I am only a very little baby. Please love me and stay with me."

This regressive demand for the mother's love is often seen in children. It is noticed in the older child when a new child is born in the family. It occurs when the mother dies, when she leaves the family because of marital disagreements, when she goes on a long trip, when she goes to work, or when the child is placed in a nursery school or in a camp. It lasts until the child makes a love relationship with another woman, that is, until he finds a satisfactory mother substitute. When this occurs, his development starts again.

Although from this point on, the development may seem to proceed satisfactorily and even the memory of the separation from the mother seems to be forgotten, the memory of the pain of the interlude has only been repressed and, being repressed from consciousness, tends to become a governing factor in the child's future life. As he grows up he may tend to avoid having any close relationship with a woman. He has been hurt by his mother, the prototype of all women, therefore all women have a tendency to hurt men. Why should he put himself in a position where a woman can hurt him? (Witness the well-known reaction of the burnt child who dreads the fire. Technically the psychological mechanism underlying the behavior is known as *inhibition*.)

Such an inhibited grownup may fall in love with a woman and as soon as he is sure she loves him desert her or act in such a way as to break her heart. Since he had been hurt by a woman he will now take revenge on this one. Sometimes, after marrying a woman and treating her badly and then leaving her, he marries again quite satisfactorily. It is as if, having taken revenge on one woman, he now can have a decent relationship with the sex. There are two psychological mechanisms underlying this behavior. The first is known technically as *displacement:* the individual having certain emotional reactions expresses them toward a person other than the real object. The second is known as *changing an instinctual drive into its opposite.* In the instance cited above, the child had to be passive in a very painful situation. He could overcome this pain by becoming active and inflicting the pain on another person; that is, he could change passivity (one instinctual drive) into activity (its opposite). This mechanism forms one of the important reasons for children's play: A small child is taken to the dentist. He is frightened and perhaps hurt. He is compelled to sit quietly in the dentist's chair and has to force himself not to express any of his fear, resentment, or anger. When he comes home he will take his younger brother, sit him in a chair, and play that he is a dentist and the younger child the patient. In his activity he acts away, "gets out of his system," the emotional reactions engendered in the passive situation.

Alternatively, the inhibited grownup we are discussing may fall in love *only* with a woman who he is certain will desert him, who in the pursuance of her interests will be away from him a great deal, who is an invalid, or who has a serious physical condition from which he knows she will die shortly. It is as if he said, "In my first relationship with a woman I suffered much at her hands. Because I was little I was unable to react emotionally to the situation in a complete way. If I can reconstruct a similar painful situation I will be able to react more fully and so feel less tense inside." This is the psychological mechanism of the *repetition compulsion,* which we see around us all the time disguised under the concept of fate. As one watches human beings one observes certain of them acting as if they were pursued by a malignant fate. Often the individual himself feels that fate is against him. This fate arises from an unconscious need to repeat an earlier painful situation in order to react fully to it. Its manifestations can be studied most clearly in the nightmares of a patient suffering from a traumatic neurosis.

THE EFFECT ON THE GIRL OF THE ABSENCE OF THE MOTHER

Just as the boy's relationship with the father is the most important factor in his development during the oedipus period, so is the girl's relationship with the mother her greatest problem. She will react to the mother's absence in somewhat the same way the boy does to the father's. Also because, as is the case with the boy, up to the beginning of the oedipus situation the mother is the important parent, so will her reactions to the loss of the mother be to some extent similar to those of the boy when he loses the mother.

THE EFFECT ON THE GIRL OF THE ABSENCE OF THE FATHER

When the small girl loses her father she may show the same type of reactions that were described for the boy who has lost his mother. She may tend to become too strongly attached emotionally to her mother because of the strength of the very early emotional relationship. This attachment helps her to have few emotional reactions at the time of her separation from the father, and therefore regressive behavior is not so common as when the boy is separated from his mother. The effect of the separation is more likely to show itself later in life. She may become homosexual, as we stated might happen to the boy if he lost his mother and was brought up in a completely male environment.

THE EFFECT ON EITHER BOY OR GIRL OF SEPARATION FROM BOTH PARENTS

This will be a combination of all the reactions discussed above. War has brought forcibly to our attention that separation from parents is an exceedingly traumatic experience for any child. It was learned in England that the child suffered more from being separated from his parents through the evacuation scheme than he did when he remained with them and underwent the experiences of the blitz. It seems that separation from the mother is more traumatic for small children than separation from the father. This finding, however, we believe to be only an immediate one. The small child reacts immediately to separation from the mother. His reactions to separation from the father tend to go on under the surface and not to become evident for several years. We foresaw in the early 1940's (and correctly) that we would be observing as many adverse reactions as a result of separation from the father (due to his military service) as we then observed as a result of separation from the mother. We must reiterate the fact that the child is not consciously aware of all his feeling in these situations nor of the relation between his feelings and his behavior. Neither does the adult in the reactions described above say consciously to himself, "My mother deserted me, therefore I will take revenge by deserting another woman." The connections and motivations are unconscious and the individual is genuinely surprised when he finds out what is occurring beneath the surface of his conscious mind.

Since these effects are so deleterious on the child's psychological development, can anything be done to ameliorate them? We cannot prevent these situations from occurring because we never can hope to abolish death or marital disagreements. In fact, it seems to us to be the best of two bad choices, from the standpoint of the child, for the marital partners in an unhappy marriage to separate rather than to remain together for his sake. If they do the latter they are almost certain to come to regard the child as responsible for their unhappiness in the marriage and to take revenge upon him for it. The effect on the child will be better understood after we have discussed the effect on the child's development of adverse parental attitudes. We feel that when a child has been separated from one or both parents there will always remain a psychic scar which will affect his relationships, happiness, and success to a greater or less extent. However, the injuriousness of the effect can be ameliorated.

When the child is separated from a parent he passes through a period of mourning. We are not going to discuss the mechanisms and purposes of mourning here, but will do so later, in connection with adult mourning. The child's mourning has the same mechanisms and purposes as that of the adult but is often expressed differently. Children are less verbal and tend to use their vegetative and sensorimotor nervous systems rather than their psychological systems to express their emotions. A small child, if frightened, will soil himself, while the adult tends to feel frightened and to talk about his fear. Children often react to a mourning situation by regressive behavior, by disturbances of the gastrointestinal tract—vomiting, diarrhea, constipation, and the like—or by naughty behavior. These reactions may continue for several months or for the duration of the period of mourning. (In the adult it usually lasts about a year.)

The adult should abstain from scolding, punishing, or criticizing the child for these reactions. They are to be expected and should be accepted with kindness. Every attempt should be made to encourage the child to talk about the absent person, express all his feelings verbally, whether these feelings be love, resentment, or hatred. We know that hearing these expressions may put a great strain on the adult. The mother whose beloved husband has died may not like to hear her son express resentment of his father. The wife whose husband has deserted her may not like to hear her daughter eulogize her father. From the point of view of the development of the child, however, all possible verbal expression of the relationship with the absent parent will be helpful.

A parent substitute should be provided as soon as possible. Such a parent substitute is imperative. The parent substitute must realize that it may take the child some time really to accept him and he must make every effort to win the child's love and confidence. It is not as difficult to provide a father substitute if the father has died or deserted as it is when he is absent on a prolonged business trip or in the military service. The remaining parent must try not to make the child a substitute wife or husband.

These measures and the passage of time will be helpful for the child, but just as an exposure to tubercular infection renders a child potentially suspect for tuberculosis for some time, so does such a traumatic experience render the child potentially suspect for a neurosis. He should remain under skilled observation for many years. Careful observations should be recorded by his teachers, particularly as to his reactions during the change from grammar school to junior high school and from junior to senior high school. If at any time he shows any evidence of neurotic symptoms, either overt or in his personality reactions, he should be studied by a child psychiatrist, and, if deemed advisable for him, placed under treatment.

THE EFFECT ON THE CHILD OF PROLONGED, PAINFUL, OR CRIPPLING ILLNESS

Another act of fate that may seriously interfere with the child's development is the occurrence of frequent, prolonged, painful, or crippling illnesses. In an unpublished study of restlessness in children, one of us found that in a great percentage of cases the beginning of neurosis in a child follows immediately after a prolonged illness or a succession of illnesses within a short period of time. When a child is stricken with a serious illness the parents become much disturbed by the fear that he will die or become permanently disabled. This fear results in an oversolicitous attitude. They come to the child if he makes the slightest complaint and tend to do for him anything he wants. As the child becomes convalescent he begins to recognize this solicitude and to exploit it. When he wants something he wants it right away and if his parents do not provide it for him he will complain of feeling ill. His illness has given him the right to make demands and have them satisfied even when they are unreasonable. He resents any attempt to bring this situation of constant gratification to an end and feels that he is not loved if it does not continue. Eventually he may accept the reality of the situation and continue with his development, but a certain reaction pattern has been laid down.

Similarly, the parents have developed a new reaction pattern. Their solicitude tends to continue even after the child is well and they become alarmed when he shows any slight symptom of illness. This apprehensiveness may remain a long time if at the time of the child's illness the parents had a conflict in their own minds about their feelings to the child. A girl of about five years was injured severely by a truck. She had a paralysis of the right hip, was completely comatose for several weeks, and it was almost a month later before she recognized any person. During this time they had been informed that the prognosis was poor and that if she lived she might be feeble-minded or be paralyzed permanently. At this time both parents dreamed that their daughter had died and woke in horror from the dream. In fact, for many years they both recoiled in horror from any memory of the dream. They regarded the dream as an indication of a death wish against their child. Troubled by such an idea they became overapprehensive that in some way and at some other time they would be punished for this death wish by the death of the child. There is no question that the dream expressed such a death wish but the parents' difficulty arose because they were unable to see that the death wish was reasonable. If the child would become feebleminded or paralyzed permanently as a result of the injury would they not be justified in feeling better about themselves and would it not be better for the child, herself, if she died without regaining consciousness? Instead of regarding such thoughts as reasonable they regarded them with horror and guilt as if they desired to kill the child. Such solicitude whether it arises from the parents' fear or from their feelings of guilt reinforces the child's pattern. Often adults who have suffered a serious prolonged illness in childhood continue to show this pattern. If they meet a disappointment they react by becoming ill, often with much the same symptoms they had when they were ill in childhood. Illnesses that involve the lower gastrointestinal tract have a marked effect on the pattern of the small child. They are often accompanied by loss of sphincter control which has to be re-established after he recovers. This second period of toilet training makes the future development of the child difficult because he prefers to remain untrained, even at the expense of being sick.

Can this reaction be ameliorated? It seems to us that an essential part of the treatment of a child for a serious illness should lie in the management of his convalescence. Kindly, consistently, and firmly he should be encouraged to derive pleasure from the things he can do for himself as he gets better, and the gratifications he obtains from being ill should be reduced to the absolute minimum. It seems better to err a little on the side of encouraging the child to do more than he is able.

A child who has suffered a painful illness in childhood may show a peculiar reaction later. He may act as if he were not subject to ordinary social customs and manners and may, without any feeling of guilt, do things which if done by the average person would overwhelm him with guilty feelings. This absence of guilt feeling comes about in the following way. The child has suffered great pain through no fault of his own. He has been punished without having committed any crime. Therefore he should have licence to commit crimes without any punishment. It is as if he lived in the times when some individuals believed that through the expenditure of a certain sum of money (in the child we are discussing, through the submission to a certain amount of suffering) they could buy absolution for all sins they might commit in the next year or two. It would seem to us to be desirable to have a child see a psychiatrist after he recovers from a very painful illness in order to prevent the development of such difficult reactions.

The child who suffers from an illness such as valvular disease of the heart or poliomyelitis, which leaves him with a permanent defect, is faced with a problem of reality in his adjustment. From that time on he no longer is like other children. He cannot do the things they do and therefore is really inferior to them. He is forced to compensate for this inferiority by developing other modes of obtaining success in life. Sometimes these compensations are not socially acceptable, as when a child compensates for a weak leg by making himself the leader of a delinquent gang or by giving up all physical and social activity and spending all his time reading and studying.

The degree of need to compensate, that is, the amount of the feeling of inferiority, seems to depend more on the extent to which the defect wounds the pride than it does on the actual extent to which the defect interferes with the child's life. For example, a child reacts more strongly to a cosmetic defect, and to the parents' attitude toward the defect, if the parents baby the child because of the defect. From the time the parents are informed that the child's illness will result in a permanent disability they should begin to help him lead a life as close to normal as possible. The physician should carefully evaluate the child's capabilities and should inform the parents in detail what the child should be encouraged and permitted to do. Here again it is better to err on the side of allowing him to be a little too active than inactive. The emphasis should be placed on what he *can* do rather than on what he cannot. Commiseration and maudlin sympathy are not only unhelpful but are injurious. The child has the defect; he has to learn how to live with it; and the physician, the nurse, and the parent should do everything possible to attain that end.

Some time ago one of us reported a study of the effect of operations on the child's development. Limitations of space prevent a full discussion of this subject here, but we feel it important to quote our conclusions:

Effect of Operations on the Child

Surgeons are well aware that operative procedures are associated with surgical shock, which is at times of serious import and which is more common after some operations than others . . . operative procedures are associated also with psychic shock in all children. This psychic shock stimulates the child's imagination, and the imaginative concepts increase the degree of the shock. To this shock the child reacts by attempting to rid himself of his fear, either by attacking its cause or by running away. Since neither reaction in childhood can furnish an adequate motor response to the sensory stimuli, the child is forced to deal with the shock by repression, which results in changes in his behavior and in his personality reactions.

Verbalization by the child of his ideas and feelings about the operation helps the motor response to be more adequate, but its inadequacy is increased if the child is not told that the operative procedure will be carried out, if he is not informed of its real nature or if he does not have the opportunity to discuss the products of his imagination about the operation and have them corrected by someone whom he trusts. If an outlet is denied, the operative shock affects his behavior and his reaction patterns in the future, although after a while it may be difficult to recognize the connection between the child's behavior and character and the operation.

Physical shock shows its effects immediately. Emotional shock may not express itself openly for some time. Therefore it is highly important that the physician and the parents of a child who is scheduled to undergo an operation inform him accurately concerning what is going to happen and what he will feel. After the operation the child should be helped to verbalize to the fullest extent his ideas about and his emotional reactions to the operation. *Such complete verbalization is the crucial procedure which prevents the development of excessive emotional reactions.* His ideas should be listened to carefully, and only after he has expressed them completely and in detail should any attempt be made to correct the errors of his imagination. His ideas should not be spurned, scorned or ridiculed.

Even before an emergency operation, some attempt is made to determine the physical ability of a child to survive the shock of the operative procedure. Such an evaluation is always made before an operation which is not done as an emergency, and in many cases if the child's ability to tolerate the procedure is not satisfactory the operation is postponed until his resistance has been raised. If the value of the operative procedure is dubious, it usually will not be attempted at all if the child's condition is unfavorable. Just as physical shock may result in death, so emotional shock may result in a lifetime of unhappiness; consequently, it seems valid to apply the same rules to determining the ability of the child to adjust to the emotional shock of the operation as are employed in evaluating his capacity to stand the physical shock.

If the operation is demanded by an emergency, to save the child's life, it must be performed, regardless of the emotional shock it may entail. However, such an emergency will seldom prevent one's telling the child that the operation is going to be performed and giving him an opportunity to verbalize his reactions after it takes place. If the history shows that the child has little capacity to tolerate anxiety, that is, that he has had unreasonable fears or other neurotic symptoms, then the operation should be followed by psychiatric treatment. If the operation is necessary but can be postponed for a little while without too great danger to the physical health and if a careful history reveals that the child already shows symptoms of neurosis or has suffered unusual traumatic experiences, such as deaths in the family, separation from his parents or exposure to adverse parental attitudes—treatment for the neurosis or study as to whether the child is reacting inadequately to the traumatic situations should be carried out before the operation. The introduction to the operation and the management during convalescence need more careful handling in the case of such a child than in that of a non-neurotic child.

If the history indicates that the child has undergone emotional trauma or that he at present is suffering from a neurosis, operations the value of which may be dubious should not be advised. There are many such operations—for example, circumcision because of masturbation, cytoscopic examination because of bed wetting at night without any other signs of disease of the urinary tract, tonsillectomy for enuresis, circumcision or tonsillectomy because of nervousness or fears, administration of drugs by injection (which could just as well be given orally) because of nervousness or fears in a child who shows some slight deviation from the normal in laboratory tests. For such a child treatment of the neurosis is the necessary procedure, and although the symptoms may cease as a result of such operation, their use may be followed eventually by a more serious neurotic condition which may be reflected in malformation and defects of [personality].

We conclude therefore that:

. . . operations on children produce emotional shocks and therefore should be performed only if absolutely necessary.

The degree of the shock to the non-neurotic child may be lessened by explaining in detail before the operation what will be done and how he will feel as a result, by giving him an opportunity to express his emotional reactions to the operation, and by allowing him to verbalize his ideas concerning the operation after it has taken place.

If the child already suffers from a neurosis or has been exposed to situations which would increase anxiety, he should not be operated on without treatment for his neurosis except as an emergency. Such a child should never be subjected to operative procedures for the relief of neurotic symptoms, for the value of such treatment is extremely dubious.

Every physician should be as aware of the necessity for dealing with the psychic life of the child during his illness as he is of the need for dealing with his physical condition. Every surgeon, particularly specialists in urology and in diseases of the nose and throat, also should be very aware of the intrapsychic effect of operative procedures either for diagnosis or cure and should consider them as important indicators or counterindicators of the state of the child's physical health. We have noted earlier that some cases of psychosis in children seem to have resulted from operations during the latter part of the first year of life. Operative procedures have particularly deleterious effects during the genital period, when all children have such marked castration fears. We have seen a number of boys of this age who knew that an operation of some kind—tonsillectomy, repair of a hernia, correction of a squint, etc.—was contemplated in the near future; regardless of what each knew of the anatomical location of the operation, each was convinced that his penis would be removed during the operation.

THE EFFECT ON THE CHILD OF THE BIRTH OF A SIBLING

Any change in a child's circumstances tends to have a traumatic effect on his development. It is interesting to observe that the child reacts adversely even to a change of residence. We once saw a child of less than a year whose digestion was greatly upset for nearly a week because the family had moved to a new house. A boy of seven immediately after the move to a new neighborhood had nocturnal enuresis for two nights. A girl of four was not certain, for sufficient reasons, that her parents loved her. When the family moved she tried to become a chair because she knew her parents would take the furniture with them while she was not sure they would take her. (It is interesting that unpleasant reactions with feelings of depression, etc., to a change of residence also become increasingly marked after the age of fifty.)

We believe that the traumatic effects of these moves are reduced greatly when the whole question of the move is discussed openly before the child, when he knows precisely what is going on and is allowed to participate in and express his opinion about the move. We believe also that the traumatic effects of all changes in the child's life—separation from parents, deaths, illnesses, the birth of new brothers and sisters—would be reduced if there were a similar full and free discussion of them before and with the child.

The birth of a new sibling in the family is one of the normal traumata to which many children are subjected. When a new baby is born in a family the older child in reality is deprived of a certain amount of the parents' time and attention. So much is being done for the new baby that the older child, contrasting the much smaller amount now being done for him, feels he is being deprived more than he really is. There is no question, however, that in many instances the parents are really more interested in the new baby and tend by their every action to demonstrate this preference to the older child. The older child reacts to his feeling of deprivation by a painful feeling of loneliness. This feeling is so acute that he has to do something to get rid of it. The child resists change; that is, he is disturbed by anything that will deprive him of his accustomed modes of gratification or by anything he thinks will deprive him of them. He reacts to this inner feeling of discomfort by feeling antagonistic and annoyed with the source of his deprivation. One way would be to mobilize his aggressive drives to change the situation. This method is expressed by strong feelings of jealousy.

If he is very young the child may show his jealousy toward the new baby by actually attacking him or trying to injure him. He may do the same if he is older, but is more likely to make derogatory remarks about him or to express wishes that he be sent away. If his parents object too much to his behavior or if he seems to feel guilty about his jealous feelings the child may still expresss them but in a disguised form: the baby is bad; or the baby cries a lot and therefore should be punished; or the baby had his toys and therefore the child had to hit him. (This is the psychological mechanism known technically as *defense through rationalization*.)

If the feeling of guilt is great the child may seem to have no jealousy at all. He may appear to have no feeling for the baby except one of love and adoration. He wants to participate in all phases of the baby's care, but if he is allowed to do so it is almost certain that some accident will happen to the baby through his clumsiness. He thus can exercise his desire to hurt the baby (of which he may be unconscious) by denying it and by feeling that he is too inept to do things properly. If his fear and guilt about his hostility are great he may deal gently, lovingly, and carefully with the baby, but become a bully toward smaller children at school or in the neighborhood. (He displaces his hostility onto a different object.)

In all of these instances the child is expressing his hostility to the baby. At the same time he may feel annoyed at his mother for daring to have another child. He may attack her physically or verbally, or he may refuse to give her any demonstration of affection; for example, he may refuse even to kiss her, as one girl who from the birth of her brother when she was three years old never kissed her mother until she was twenty-four. He may pointedly be affectionate to other adults in her presence, often those whom he knows his mother dislikes. In this behavior he says, "I won't love you, I will love people whom I know you dislike, because you don't love me any more." If he is too afraid or guilty about expressing this antagonism openly he may suddenly become naughty in his behavior toward his women teachers or other women who are in authority over him. (This again is a displacement.)

Another method by which the child soothes his feeling of loneliness is to act out a fantasy that he has remained *the* baby. Instead of openly expressing his jealousy he may become demanding of his mother's love and attention—the attention she seems to be giving the new baby. He may develop a feeding difficulty. He may suddenly become timid and fearful. He may resort to childish speech. He may start to wet or soil himself again. He may recommence finger sucking. He may have frequent attacks of minor illnesses about which he makes great complaints. There will usually be a combination of these reactions which will last for a varying period of time until he has learned to adjust himself to the new situation. There is often the possibility that he will make his adjustment simply by repressing his reactions without solving his problems, and that these repressed reactions will continue to interfere with his ability to adjust to the numerous jealousy situations he will meet later.

How early does the jealousy reaction appear? We feel from numerous observations that it begins as soon as the child learns that his mother is pregnant. This is often as early as the second or third month. Little pitchers have big ears, it is said; children do overhear conversations about the coming baby when the parents are unaware that they are listening.

It is reasonable, therefore, to expect that children will naturally feel jealous of a newcomer. The amount of the jealousy reaction can be increased or decreased by the parents' handling of the child during this period. In our experience the child who already is really certain of his parents' love does not have so much difficulty in making an adjustment. The parents who really love their child will recognize that jealousy is a normal reaction and will not punish him for expressing it. Instead they will protect the baby from harm by not leaving the two children alone together. As soon as the mother learns that she is pregnant she will begin to take the older child—even one of two or three years—into her confidence and explain to him what is about to happen. She will realize that the child is going to feel deprived and she will know that one way for a human being to overcome a feeling that he is not loved is to love someone else. She will see to it, therefore, that the child has a pet that will be his own, that he can play with and do things for, although he need not be required to look after it every day. She will encourage him in every way possible to try to be more grown up and to attempt more grownup pursuits—in short, to be more like the adult parent who can do and give, rather than like the baby who must receive and have things done for him. The child will undoubtedly ask many questions about sexual matters. These should be answered realistically for two reasons: (1) he needs the knowledge; (2) the discussion of sexual matters and the parents' answering of his questions make him feel more mature and more certain of his relationship with his parents.

After the new baby is born the parents will expect the older child to be jealous and will protect the baby from injury by him. They will explain to him the reason for the difference in the type of attention they pay to the baby and to him, stressing the fact that the older child is older and more like his parents. They will praise every new accomplishment by which he attempts more mature activity—and will abstain from criticizing the slips backward he makes. They will see that he has the prerogatives of an older child and will see also that there is a special time set apart for him in which he has his parents' whole attention. This will be gradually shortened as he gets older and becomes more accustomed to the new situation. If he is old enough to look after the baby they will not request him to do so, as is so often done to a degree that the care of the baby really interferes with the child's life.

If the parents follow these directions (which in most instances will occur to them from their own intuition) the traumatic effect of the birth of the new baby will be materially lessened, and the older child's adjustment will be made more satisfactory.

The birth of a new baby also serves as a marked stimulant to the sexual curiosity of the older child. This reaction is just as important as those of jealousy and regression. In the previous chapter we discussed the management of the child's sexual curiosity.

ADVERSE PARENTAL ATTITUDES

If the reader has been an observer of human beings he will recognize that parents are not all wise in the handling of their children and that some show a great deal more intuition about this than do others. In fact, as we have seen already, some parents seem woefully to lack any intuitive understanding at all. Also the reader will recognize that parents do not all feel the same way toward their children and that a parent does not feel the same way toward each of his children. Consequently he will be able to see that the concept that parents universally love their children wisely is a fiction—a theory really unsubstantiated by fact. The feelings of parents toward their children form a graduated continuous scale, starting from the parent who *really* loves his child and ending with the parent who *really only hates* his child. Since parental love is so necessary for the child and since the reasons why it is necessary have been discussed already, we intend here to consider only the effects of adverse parental attitudes. Though the scale of adverse parental attitudes is graduated and continuous, it seems necessary for purposes of presentation to classify them into four groups:

1. Parental (mostly maternal) indifference.
2. Rejection of the child.
3. Overprotection of the child.

4. Indulgence.

Similarly we classify parents who have adverse attitudes to their children into four types: (a) withdrawn and indifferent parents, (b) overstrict parents, (c) overstrict parents who feel guilty about their dislikes of the child, and (d) weak parents.

THE EFFECT OF PARENTAL (ESPECIALLY MATERNAL) INDIFFERENCE AND WITHDRAWNNESS

In Chapter I we discussed the effect on the young baby of maternal indifference and withdrawnness. Encountered during the first year or so of life, such negative maternal attitudes have relatively severe effects on the child at the time and on his ability later to develop adequately. Perhaps a certain percentage of cases of childhood psychoses result from these attitudes; there is proof that some cases of certain types of adolescent and adult antisocial behavior are their end products. So much has been written on the effect of maternal indifference that we need not do more than mention it here. However, the effect of paternal indifference and withdrawnness has not been described as frequently. The little boy whose father is indifferent and withdrawn has a not-very-adequate model of adult masculinity to identify with. The little girl with the same type of father may develop the concept that masculine love objects treat girls with indifference and withdrawnness.

THE EFFECT OF PARENTAL REJECTION

When we discussed the feelings of the boy toward his father and the feelings of the girl toward her mother during the genital period, we spoke only of the status of the child. It must be remembered that in the unconscious of all fathers and all mothers there are memories of their own oedipal conflicts and struggles. From time to time these memories and the drives behind them tend to break through into consciousness and the loving parent finds himself acting toward his child in a way which indicates an underlying feeling of hatred and competition or feeling consciously unreasonably antagonistic or jealous of the child. One mother of a four-year-old girl told her husband that unless he stopped being so affectionate toward his daughter she would leave him. So, there are more reasons for the child's fear of the parent of the same sex than the projection of the child's feelings toward that parent onto him. When we discuss adolescence we are going to see how often the unconscious oedipal feelings of the parent appear in their dealing with their child of the same sex. From time to time parents show irrational behavior and attitudes to their children based on their unconscious oedipal conflicts.

However, parents whose attitude to the child is one of rejection, and often parents who are overstrict, actually hate the child more than they love him. We wonder if the reader has ever considered the daily life of a child whose parents hate him. From the time he awakens in the morning until he goes to bed at night he is nagged, scolded, and frequently slapped. His attempts at conversation are received with curt, cold silence, or he is told to be quiet. If he attempts any demonstration of affection he is pushed away and told not to bother his parents. He receives no praise for anything he does, no matter how well he has done it. If he walks with his parents and lags a little his arm is seized and he is yanked forward. If he falls he is yanked to his feet. He is supposed to be seen and not heard. At mealtime he is either ignored or his table manners and inconsequential food fads are criticized severely. He is made to finish whatever is on his plate. (This is frequently done, and we think quite unnecessarily, by parents who really love their children; but they insist in a manner different from that of the parents who dislike their children. The latter insist not to help the child but actually to express their irritation with him.)

This same feeling underlies the application of all the routines of the child's life. It can be seen best in such a parent's handling of the small baby. Bathing, dressing, undressing, diapering, feeding—all are done in a rough, nontender manner. The child soon realizes that he can expect nothing but a hurt body or hurt feelings from his parents. He tries to avoid them as much as possible, and instead of wanting to see them and be with them—that is, instead of feeling love for them—he feels fear, loathing, and hatred. As a baby he cries when they go toward him; as an older child he often tries to run away but of course he is brought back and punished for running away.

At first he tries to stand his own ground, but as this attempt brings him discomfort he begins to try to avoid doing anything that brings punishment. Accordingly he has to abstain from the majority of activities, for there is practically nothing that he does that is not punished. His thoughts are rebellious and antagonistic; he fears that his parents may be able to read his mind and he knows if they do his punishment will be even more severe. He tries to stop himself thinking these hostile thoughts. When the repression is successful it is accompanied by a repression of all initiative and individuality. The sad part is that the child—every child—believes that all adults are like his parents. So to other adults and to society in general he behaves rebelliously and antagonistically or with complete acts of submission.

If the father dislikes the boy the mutual antagonism is greater during the oedipus situation, but the father is so much stronger and can enforce his hatred so much more painfully that the boy continually gives in. All his initiative and individuality disappear, and he learns that he can gain the most comfort by fawning on his father. He finds that this fawning attitude gets him some attention or at least avoids the pain of disagreement. He gets pleasure from it, and comes to desire the pleasure still more. He begins to find pleasure in being submissive, and even if the submission brings a certain amount of pain he puts up with it. The passive, submissive, fawning attitude from which he obtains pleasure gradually produces a feminine orientation to his father; that is, instead of leading the boy to identify with the father's masculine traits, and so grow into a man, it produces just the opposite effect. It enhances the desire of the boy to be loved by the father as if he were his wife. If the submission does not bring sufficient pleasure to make it profitable the boy may outwardly submit and store in his mind ideas of revenge. It is as if he said, "Now I am small and you are big and you can make me do things I don't want. Some day when I am grown up I'll be big and you'll be small and then I'll enjoy making you do things you don't want to do." Gradually as the years pass this fantasy of revenge becomes unconscious, but when the boy has a son of his own he may tend to treat him in just the same way his own father treated him when he was a boy.

The effect of rejection by the father falls on the boy's masculine activity, which it injures seriously. When the mother rejects her son it affects his relationship with the opposite sex. The boy wants his mother to love him and tries hard to please her. Still she rejects him. He then tries further to please her or becomes hostile and antagonistic and rejects her in turn. The latter reaction may cause him to turn his love to his father and assume a feminine attitude to him. It may cause him to reject all women and become homosexual, or it may cause him to be too concerned in pleasing the women with whom he falls in love.

If the mother rejects the daughter the effect on the latter is the same as when the father rejects the son. If the father rejects the daughter the effect is the same as when the mother rejects the son.

Rejective parents are usually harsh, domineering, and strict. If a parent does not reject the child but is a harsh, domineering person, the effect on the child will be similar to that of rejection. The parent who rejects his child may be conscious of his feeling of hatred toward the child and also conscious that his behavior toward him is the result of the feeling of hatred. He may be conscious of his dislike of the child and at the same time feel that this feeling is inadvisable and may consciously attempt to act toward the child as if he did not hate him. However, the attempt is usually unsuccessful because the force of the hatred will overcome the conscious attempt at action and because the child can sense the underlying hatred, for children are very intuitive—intuitive enough to sense the real attitude of adults. Then again the parent may be unconscious of his feeling of hatred and attempt to excuse his harshness with the alibi that children profit by a strict upbringing. If this excuse allows him to express his hatred fairly fully, the only sign of the hatred will be in the behavior of the child.

All parents feel differently toward children of the same sex and of the opposite sex. One mother said, "I can understand my daughter very well, but although I love my son, I don't understand him." We believe all parents feel this way to a greater or less degree and this attitude is understandable because the father having been a boy and having masculine reactions understands his son but doesn't understand his daughter as well. The mother having been a girl herself and having feminine reactions understands her daughter but her son not so well. In certain cases this attitude is intensified. The father or the mother may desire to have only daughters or only sons; if the newborn baby is of the sex the particular parent, for reasons stemming from his or her own developmental experiences, did not want, then the parent may try to eliminate the characteristics of that sex in the child and develop the characteristics of the opposite sex. As the reader readily can see, this results in at least a partial rejection of the child and produces great difficulties in the child's development.

Parental rejection may be complete; that is, the parent may dislike the child totally. It may occur during a certain age period; that is, a parent may dislike all his children during infancy but become quite fond of them when they arrive at school age. The parent may not dislike the child but may be antagonistic to certain phases of normal childish behavior. For example, he may be strict about finger sucking, or dirtiness, or untidiness, or masturbation, or independence. The child is not able to distinguish clearly between the parent's rejection of his traits and the parent's love for him as an individual, and so feels totally rejected.

THE EFFECT OF PARENTAL OVERPROTECTION

There is a type of parent who is completely unconscious of his hatred of the child. Some time early in the child's life he became conscious of his hate and dislike for the child and felt horror at having such—to him—unnatural feelings. This reaction of horror caused him to repress his feelings of hatred from consciousness. Soon thereafter he started to become troubled by fears that some terrible catastrophe might happen to the child. Now, he has a panic every time the child has the most minor ailment. He cannot permit the child to take part in any activity or sport in which there is the least element of danger. In fact he is content only if the child sits quietly and does nothing. He is incapable of applying the mildest discipline because he fears he will not be able to control himself and thus will injure the child. If the child is especially naughty he may punish him and then he does it so severely as to really hurt. In all of these fears and inhibitions the parent shows that he has the wish to get rid of the child but he keeps such wishes unconscious because he is so horrified by them. The child of such a parent is in a worse situation than if the parent openly and consciously rejected him, and the effect on him is more serious. We believe that some of the worst instances of maladjustments in children come from such an attitude.

THE EFFECT OF PARENTAL INDULGENCE

It is self-evident that the parent who indulges his child does not love that child with a real adult love. He knows that when he permits his child every liberty and every satisfaction he is not training him to be able to tolerate the many frustrations and deprivations that will be his lot in life, as indeed they are of all human beings.

Furthermore, although the parent grants all the child's requests that he is able to, we have seen in previous chapters that there are many wishes and desires that cannot be gratified. Such a parent, therefore, not only does not prepare the child to be happy in his future life but incurs the child's resentment because he will not gratify his unreasonable requests.

The son of a weak, indulgent father—and usually these terms are synonymous—develops exactly the same personality difficulties as does the son of a harsh, rejecting father. This result comes about in the following way. The weak father makes a poor model of masculine aggressiveness for the boy to copy. The boy does not have the opportunity to express his antagonisms to his father, not because (as with the cruel father) he will suffer retaliation of a painful nature but because he feels remorseful and ashamed to be hostile to such a kind, considerate person. The more kindly his father treats him the more guilty he feels about his aggressive antagonisms, and the tension continues until the conflict becomes so intolerably painful that he solves it by repressing not only his hostility to his father but all his masculine aggressiveness as well. A similar result follows with the girl whose mother is too weak and indulgent. If the mother is too indulgent to the boy he anticipates that he will be victorious in his struggle with the father and develops in the same way as the boy who has no father. A similar result will occur if the father is too indulgent to the girl. It might be stated in passing, however, that mild indulgence is infinitely less harmful to the child's development than a similar amount of strictness.

Parental attitudes toward children are a form of behavior and like all other behaviors have causes. These causes are varied; on the one hand, they may range all the way from simple lack of knowledge about children and their behavior to some disturbances in the parent-child relationship because of marked unconscious drives in the parent toward the child; on the other hand, they may result from definite parental illnesses—anxiety reactions, obsessive-compulsive reactions, manic depressive reactions, or schizophrenia. Adverse parental attitudes do not usually occur through ignorance but are symptomatic of the parents' maladjustment and must be treated as such.

Psychiatrists have noted that the types of neuroses most prevalent today differ markedly from those reported as most prevalent during the latter part of the nineteenth and the early part of the twentieth centuries. At that time marked cases of conversion and anxiety reactions and of obsessive-compulsive reactions were extremely common. At present these are rarely seen; what are seen are mostly personality disorders. Waelder believes that this change is the result of a real change that has taken place in parents' management of children. During the latter part of the nineteenth century and the early part of the twentieth century, parents were strict and trained their children to adjust to rigid routines. As a result a great deal of instinctual repression took place which manifested itself in neuroses with dramatic symptoms. About the time of World War I, parents were learning that such strict training produced unfavorable results and the pendulum swung far to the opposite extreme of indulgence and no real training at all. This opposite type of management produces an individual who is ill-equipped to bear the anxiety that results from the unavoidable frustrations and deprivations of life. He molds his personality in such a way as to avoid situations that will arouse his anxiety. The best type of management seems to be midway between these two extremes, with the parents' training inclining slightly to the side of indulgence; but at the same time good parents do not protect the child too much from the unavoidable and necessary frustrations and deprivations that occur through living in a real world inhabited by real people with real customs and mores.

THE EFFECT OF PREMATURE OR EXCESSIVE
SEXUAL STIMULATION

Over half a century ago Freud was surprised to find from the psychoanalytic investigations of his patients that there was as active a sexual life in early childhood as there was after puberty. He was impressed with the frequency with which sexual seductions by adults and older children occurred in the early childhood histories of his patients, and also with the fact that their neurotic symptoms seemed to start shortly after these episodes. In many instances he was able to corroborate from other sources that these episodes actually took place. Although he was later forced to reach the conclusion that many of the uncorroborated episodes might have been only fantasies of the little child, yet it is generally agreed, and from our experience amply proved, that actual sexual seductions have a definite effect on the child's development. The small child may be sexually seduced by an older child or by an adult of the same or opposite sex. If the child is a boy he may be masturbated, may be induced to attempt intercourse, or may be used as a passive object in one of the perversions. If the child is a girl she may be induced to submit to the same procedure, but more commonly, if the seducer is a male, she may be induced to permit vaginal intercourse.

It goes without saying that the child experiences a degree of pleasure during the seduction. A variety of other emotional reactions are often, however, combined with the pleasurable feelings. The child is afraid, partly because so much secrecy is insisted on by the seducer, partly because the child has probably been warned against exposing or showing an interest in the genitals, partly because the seducer may threaten him so as to force him to submit to the seduction, and partly because the experience is an unfamiliar one and he does not know what to expect. In many instances, particularly when a small girl submits to intercourse with an older boy, the experience will be somewhat painful. Combined with the pleasure there will be a great deal of excitement, and the child is left greatly excited and tense because the act itself is not likely to culminate in complete gratification and relaxation. However, the pleasure is so great, even if not complete, that the child does not mention the occurrence to the parents lest they interfere with a possible repetition of the experience.

It is interesting that the child often does not mention such an incident even though he has been somewhat severely hurt. This is strikingly different from the child's usual behavior, for almost invariably he will run to his parents for comfort if he has been hurt. Partly because of the incomplete gratification and partly because of the need to hide the experience from his parents the child begins to feel guilty, and often, in order to assuage this feeling of guilt, will begin to act in a naughty manner to induce the parents to punish him. The punishment relieves his feeling of guilt, as he expected it would, but the relief is only temporary and the feeling of guilt soon recurs.

We have seen a number of cases in which a child's whole personality seemed to change in the manner we have just described after a summer vacation. Careful study of these children has shown that some type of seduction had occurred either at camp or at some other place where the child was spending his vacation away from the parents. Therefore, we think that there should be more care in choosing camp counselors and more supervision in overnight camps.

As can be seen, the effect of seduction of this type is to bring the child into a state of intense excitement which is pleasurable but out of which he cannot obtain relaxation. He feels nervous and tense and attempts as soon as possible to repeat the experience in the hope of obtaining the complete gratification, which never comes, however, and so he is left constantly frustrated. This vicious circle attracts all his energy, leaving little or none for the other phases of his life and development; furthermore the knowledge becomes so painful that he is forced to escape by repressing all memory of the incident and all his sexual feelings. In order to maintain the repression he has to avoid all situations and actions that might remind him of the incident or arouse him sexually. He enters adult life, therefore, poorly prepared for sexuality because of this repression. Also, his first experience of sexual excitement has been associated with other emotional reactions—fear, guilt, pain, shame, feelings of disobedience, and the like—all of which are unpleasant and not validly connected with sexuality. When the repression occurs these emotional reactions are also repressed and if he later becomes sexually aroused the other uncomfortable emotional reactions are aroused also and make his later sexual experiences not as pleasurable as they should be.

Definite sexual seductions of younger by slightly older children are common, but because so much of the activity is really only sex play the traumatic effects are not very serious. Sexual seductions by much older children and by adults are less common but occur frequently enough to warrant the suspicion that such has occurred if the child suddenly becomes very frightened or quite naughty shortly after being alone with an older child or an adult for a period of several hours.

We have observed many instances where a child's neurotic behavior was produced through seductive experiences by the parents or other adults in the home. The father who allows and even encourages his little daughter or his little son to touch and fondle his penis, the mother who allows her little boy or girl to investigate and touch her genitals are exciting and stimulating the child too much, and the child cannot get adequate relief from this stimulation. Similarly, the mother who inspects her prepubertal son to see if he is developing body hair and the father who fondles his adolescent daughter's breasts is doing the same thing. It might be mentioned that some of these pubertal girls who have complained of this type of behavior on the part of their fathers actually have been welcoming this type of attention by appearing before him too often only partly clothed. These direct seductions by parents are more common than usually is recognized, and besides the excessive stimulation they increase the child's difficulty in solving his oedipal problems.

Indirect sexual seductions of children by their parents or nurses are very common. A mother bathes the genitals of her baby son most zealously in order to be sure they are clean. As he grows older she continues to do so. She may continue to bathe him, paying particular attention to his genitals, when he is four, five, six, seven, eight years old, and even older. (We have heard of instances where the practice continued even well past puberty.) This type of mother usually expresses great horror and disgust if the boy gets an erection through her ministrations. The child therefore is being pleasurably stimulated by his mother but at the same time has to repress any physical reaction lest she become displeased with him. However, through these indirect seductions the parent of either sex—for fathers show this form of behavior as often as do mothers—receives unconscious sexual gratification but of course would be horrified if the fact were realized consciously. There are parents who are obsessed with the ideas of cleanliness and will not tolerate any mucus secretion anywhere on the body of the child. The child's ears, nose, vagina (if a girl), and undersurface of the prepuce (if a boy) are rigorously cleaned daily. This cleaning, which of course is unnecessary, gives the child sensual pleasure, but if he attempts overtly to get his mother to repeat it she regards him as naughty.

Children are avid for sensual pleasure and once they have received it try to seduce the parent to give it to them again. A little boy of three, playing with a stick, fell on it and hurt his groin. His father, a physician, examined him carefully to determine whether he had injured his genitals. No injury was found, and in a few hours the boy was quite all right. Several days later when the father was sitting in his study the boy came in and said, "Father, I have a very bad pain here," pointing to his genitals, and dropped his pants down. The father, who was wise, recognized that the boy had no pain but was attempting to seduce him and be re-examined. He did not do so but told the boy he was all right and that he should button up his pants and go and play.

This type of attempt to seduce the parent is quite common with all small children. Less common are the instances, although they occur, where the child actually attempts to have intercourse with the parent. Such children later develop strong guilt feelings about these acts and try to repress their sexuality lest they repeat them. Similarly, older children who seduce younger ones eventually develop feelings of guilt and stop the seductive behavior. In many cases the feeling of guilt is associated with the fear of being found out. The fear and guilt may be so great that all sexual feeling has to be repressed in order that the child may feel comfortable. Such severe repressions have a detrimental effect on the future sexual life of the individual.

Another traumatic sexual experience that may have far-reaching effects on the child's future life is the observation of parental intercourse. When the child of three or four sleeps in the parents' bedroom he will be awakened by their movements and speech during the preliminary sex play. Children of this age sleep lightly. The room is usually half lighted, for the average bedroom is not really dark at night. The child observes what looks to him like a struggle between the two people for whom he feels the most devotion. He hears sounds that do not seem those of pleasure. He realizes that something is going on that he does not understand. He is interested and excited by the mystery. He feels frightened and bewildered. He is certain something terrible is happening, and because of these feelings he dare not express his emotional reactions lest the parents learn he is awake. If he is going through the oedipus period he wishes to participate with the most loved parent in whatever that parent is doing with the other parent. His jealousy of his rival is great. He feels resentment toward the loved parent because he is excluded in favor of someone else. He is thus filled with intense and conflicting emotional reactions which he tries not to express because he is interested in seeing exactly what goes on and because of his fear of his parents who seem so monstrous. Often the only form of emotional reaction he allows himself is to wet or soil the bed. The next day his memory of what happened during the night is so unpleasant because of the unexpressed emotional reactions that he has to repress the memory and the associated feelings. From this point on the repressed feelings begin to govern his daily activity and in adult life his behavior is very different from that of the person who did not undergo this experience. It seems to us most inadvisable for a small child to be subjected to this unnecessary trauma.

Although we, as well as other psychoanalysts, have been able to observe the effect of the sight of parental intercourse on the psycho-sexual development of older children and adults the question always is raised by the lay reader, "What about the children in families who, by force of circumstances, have to live in overcrowded slum quarters? Do they develop neurotic personalities and neuroses?" Greenacre has attempted one answer to this. She believes the situation often results in the development of delinquency. When we later discuss delinquency, we will refer to this again but here we can say that some cases of delinquency are the result of overcrowded slum conditions.

NUDITY VERSUS MODESTY

During the last forty years many educators and parents have believed that children would feel less shame about their own naked bodies and their bodily functions and be less concerned about them if all the members of the family, including the parents, went around nude or semi-nude without showing any embarrassment. They believed that through such an experience the child would grow up to accept nudity in himself and others as natural and reasonable. This belief arose partly as a reaction against the extreme emphasis placed by their parents on keeping the body covered at all times. These educators had forgotten that such emphasis in itself had been a reaction against earlier customs and manners during which semi-nudity had been the usual custom. The belief also stemmed partly from a misconception regarding certain discoveries made by psychoanalysts, particularly those concerning infantile sexuality and the sexual theories of children.

As a result of this misconception, many educators and parents began to believe that if the child was taught the facts about sex and could observe and know all about the naked body, he would not develop any neuroses. Of course this belief is fallacious, so we believe at this point it is desirable to present our point of view on the question of nudity and modesty in the home and the reasons for our opinions. The basis for our opinions is the data we have obtained from older children, adolescents, and adults during our therapeutic work with them, during which we have been able to review the unconscious effects of parental beliefs and behavior on their development.

Let us start with the oral period. We said during our discussion of it that the baby's naked body should frequently be held close to the mother's naked body during feeding times. This is for the purpose of *stimulating* the child's sensory apparatus of touch, warmth, and smell and to gratify his needs to be touched, to feel warmth, and to smell. This procedure helps him during the first part of the oral period to perceive his own feelings and sensations. The nudity is not so necessary toward the end of the period.

With the advent of the anal period the child's interest is intensely centered on his own and others' excretory activity. He wishes to come in to the bathroom when either of his parents is urinating or defecating and he desires and demands to see and hear what they are doing and what they have produced. The only beneficial effect of gratifying his demands may occur at the beginning of toilet training when through his desire to be like them he can use his observations as the way he should act himself. He already is dissatisfied with his size in comparison to that of his parents. His pride is hurt and he feels annoyed and resentful at them because he is not as big as they are. When he sees his father's larger stream of urine or the bigger size of the feces that his parents have passed and compares them with his own much smaller excretions, his pride is hurt further and unnecessarily and his jealousy and resentment is increased. It seems wiser therefore to exclude him from the bathroom when his parents are urinating or defecating. This may be difficult to do and it has to be done not as a prohibition but as a way of life. He has to learn automatically to accept many exclusions from the intimate life of his parents and this one will be only another that he has to accept even if he does not want to.

We have seen the great inner turmoil and conflict that take place in both the boy and the girl during the genital period and the shocks to his and her pride and the fears aroused by these shocks as the boy and girl learn about sexual differences. We have seen how sexually stimulating the mother is to the boy. One mother told us she had to stop dressing her four-year-old boy because he always had an erection during the dressing. We don't think anyone can doubt that the boy was aroused sexually by the closeness and the handling by his mother. The boy wants to see and explore his mother's body just as does any lover his sweetheart's. Physiologically at this age the boy differs from the adult lover in that he is not able to obtain real sexual satisfaction; therefore all that could happen if he were permitted to do so would be an intolerable increase in excitement to the point of painful discomfort with an increased amount of masturbation and the occurrence of violent attacks of rage—the way he obtained instinctual gratification during the anal period. Similarly the girl, if permitted to see too often or to explore her father's body, will develop the same painful tensions with no physiological capacity to obtain relief.

We have seen also that the increased excitement from the proximity of the parent of the opposite sex increases the hatred and fear of the parent of the same sex. The conflicts over the hatred and jealousy of the parent of the same sex are hard enough for the child to handle and too frequent and too close contacts with the parent of the opposite sex and too much opportunity to see the naked or part-naked body of that parent only increase tremendously the burden the child has to bear during this period and makes it more difficult for him or her to find an adequate and real solution to his oedipal conflicts.

We have seen that the fact that women and girls do not have a penis produces the fear of castration in the boy which will be increased the oftener he sees their naked bodies. We have seen the humiliation that the girl develops when she perceives that boys and men have a penis and she doesn't. This humiliation and all its attendant turmoil will be increased if she is exposed too often to the sight of the male genitals. We have seen that the comparison of her mother's breasts and pubic hair with her breastless, hairless body arouses her jealousy and hatred of her mother, which will be increased by too frequent opportunities to see her mother's naked body. The boy also is very jealous of the size of his father's penis compared to that of his own, and too frequent opportunities to see it only increase this jealousy and his sense of smallness. As a matter of fact, certain men, as a result of such experiences, find it difficult to urinate in a public toilet where other men are because they unconsciously are comparing the size of their penis with that of the other men and always to their own disadvantage. If the boy at the times when he is full of admiration and passionate love for his father is exposed to too frequent opportunities to see his father naked, he may become so engrossed in his admiration for his father's big penis that his horror at the penisless state of girls and women is increased—perhaps later to the point that he will regard all women with loathing and turn all his sexual desire and love to men—who have a penis. Of course there are other elements also that enter into an adult homosexual object choice. The same homosexual orientation may be produced in girls if they have too much opportunity to see and explore their mother's naked body during this period of development.

We have seen with the repression of the memories of the years before six, with the solution of the oedipus situation and the building of the superego that reaction formations of modesty, etc., develop in respect to the members of the child's family even though no education in modesty has been given. The parents should respect this developing modesty and not to try to break it down. If the boy or girl wishes to be alone when they bathe, go to the toilet, or dress and undress, they should be listened to and respected. Although repression keeps the memories of the oedipal situation unconscious, the oedipal struggle is not solved completely until the latter part of adolescence when the boy and the girl really fall in love and have their sexual desires directed to some person of the opposite sex and about their own age. Until this occurs the repression is still relatively weak so that from the genital period on until the latter part of adolescence, the boy and the girl should not be subjected to situations that tend to reinvigorate the unconscious oedipal desires. Parental nudity or semi-nudity in front of the boy or the girl tends to do this. The individual's modesty in the home needs to be not over-encouraged nor discouraged, but simply accepted. The mother who walks into the bathroom while her grammar-school or adolescent son is bathing, or into his bedroom when he is dressing or undressing, or who examines his genitals if he is prepubertal to see if he is growing pubic hair, and meets his protests with the statement that he is nothing new to her for she has seen all parts of his naked body for many years, is not helping him to grow up. Neither is the father who does the same with his daughter or examines her budding breasts if she is prepubertal.

It seems to us that it throws less strain on the psychosexual development of the child if both parents take care not to expose the child of either sex to too frequent sights of their naked bodies but utilize the natural modesty that all humans have to guide them. It seems wise also for the mother and father to have their son and daughter learn to take their baths by themselves and to dress themselves as early in life as possible, even though the bathing may not be exceptionally well done and the dressing may consume considerable time. Certainly both the boy and the girl toward the end of the genital period and thereafter are quite competent to do both. It is wiser to have each child during the genital period take a separate bath and undress and dress by himself than to have two boys, two girls, or a boy and a girl bathe together. In the present-day great vacational migrations that occur in America, we believe that families should be able to have separate hotel or motel rooms or other accommodations for the parents and the children, for the boys in the family and for the girls in order to avoid any sexual overstimulation of the children.

Parents must remember that the child is not a lump of clay to be molded by them but a living being with wishes, desires, drives, and feelings. They sometimes complain that their child does not respect them—and this often is true—but they themselves often do not realize how little they respect their child as another person. They would not treat their friends or even their servants with the same lack of personal respect they do their child. In many American homes there seems little respect for the rights of all members of the family. The father and mother both have their rights, which the child will learn to respect—and he usually does so without much injury. The child has rights which the parents should respect also. Only by seeing that each member of the family has his rights can a family live harmoniously.

THE EFFECTS OF A TRAUMATIC EXPERIENCE

What are the effects of a traumatic experience? If one takes a series of cases of children who show symptoms of a neurosis one finds that they fall into two groups: those whose neurosis started at a definite time and those whose neurosis seems to have been present almost throughout the child's whole life. In the first instance it is found always that the neurosis follows a traumatic experience, or several traumatic experiences, all occurring about the same time. In the second, one finds that mild traumatic experiences have been the child's lot throughout his life. The more severe the traumatic experiences the more severe will be the neurotic illness.

What course does the child's development take after a traumatic experience? Since such an experience is one that arouses intense feelings and strong emotional reactions with which the child is incapable of dealing, he will first feel anxious and helpless; that is, he will have an anxiety attack. This in itself is painful and in order to avoid the pain he will go through certain maneuvers. He will try to repress the memory of the traumatic experience, the feelings engendered by the experience, and the feelings, thoughts, and desires that seem to him to have produced the experience. In order to keep the painfulness of the traumatic experience repressed and to avoid doing anything that might cause a repetition of it, he may try to avoid all situations or actions that may remind him of what he has repressed. In technical language, he will impose inhibitions on himself.

The repression, when reinforced by the inhibitions, tends to break down and the repressed material begins to reappear in consciousness. Perhaps the repression of the impulses and ideas remains effective, but the feelings of fear break through. The child will then suffer from recurrent anxiety attacks and be unable to understand what it is that he fears. Perhaps instead of the feelings of fear his feelings of guilt may break through; then, feeling guilty without knowing why, he may be forced to behave in an overconscientious manner in order not to add to the guilty feeling; or he may tend to seek to assuage his guilty feelings by open naughty behavior which will cause him to be punished. If the repression of the underlying impulses breaks down, the impulses dare not seek their usual form of gratification lest the pain of the traumatic situation be re-experienced. Ordinarily in a situation where the child's inner impulses were frustrated of gratification he would attempt to find new methods of satisfaction; but any attempt to find new methods is banned by the fear that they might lead to a repetition of the traumatic situation. Under these circumstances the inner desires have only one course, namely to flow backward and seek earlier and now relinquished modes of expression.

Which one of these modes will the impulses find most ready for such expression? In the life of most human beings the course of development is not an even one. For example, if the child has had a short nursing period he will still be desirous of obtaining complete oral satisfaction; that is, the oral zone will still be energized to a greater degree than in other children. This zone will therefore continue to be a weak point, for the energy still attached there is held in check only by strong repression. When the inner desires at a later period are frustrated by the fear of repetition of a traumatic situation and so have to be repressed, they will be attracted by the energy still attached to the oral zone, and add their energy to that already there; the repression will break down and the child will attempt to find satisfaction from the use of the oral activities. This phenomenon is known technically as *regression,* by which is meant that the individual attempts to obtain gratification in a way that he found satisfactory when he was younger. For example, although he has long since given up finger sucking he may now revert to it. A regressive behavior of this sort is known as a *perversion.* A perversion may be defined simply as the use of an infantile form of obtaining sexual gratification at an age when sensual gratifications should be obtained in a more adult way.

If the child feels a strong antipathy to obtaining gratification through a perversion he may begin to show disturbances in the usual uses of his mouth. The attempt at gratification shows itself in a *disturbance* of oral function because by the time the child attains the age of which we are speaking he may have learned forcibly and definitely that it is not proper to use his oral zone as a means of obtaining this type of gratification. He cannot therefore extract pure pleasure from this gratification; but he has to feel pain in the attempt in order to bribe his disapproving conscience. It is as if he said to himself, "Look here, you are too grown up really to have pleasure from a babyish method of gratification so if you want that mode of gratification, instead of having only pleasure you will have to suffer pain for your desire to be babyish. Each time you wish to gratify your sensual impulses by taking something into your mouth you will vomit instead and at the same time you will feel nauseated just to show you that you shouldn't be a baby." This attempt to obtain gratification of an inner impulse in a childish way, and the punishment for attempting to be a baby again, form the basic structure of all symptoms.

As was noted above, energy will remain attached to an infantile sensual zone if there has been frustration of the optimum period of gratification. It will also remain attached if the pleasure of this type of gratification has been allowed to continue too long; for example, in connection with the oral zone if the child has been nursed over a very long period. This attachment of desire to a zone through which the infant normally experiences gratification, and which, because of too little or too much gratification, lasts long after the time when such modes of gratification have been relinquished, is known as a *fixation* on that zone. If in later life the individual experiences a severe frustration he will tend to show neurotic symptoms connected with that zone.

These are the main methods of reaction to a traumatic situation. However, as the child begins to use one or the other he has to develop modifications of them in order to get along better in life. Besides modifying these reactions he often combines several different methods of reacting, with the result that his neurosis develops a very complicated structure which often requires a long, painstaking piece of work to unravel. We have felt it necessary to introduce the concepts of traumatic situations at this point—and the reactions to the situations by anxiety, repression, inhibition, guilt, regression, perversion, and symptom formation—because not to do so would be to make the discussion of the true emotional illnesses during the genital and latent periods complicated and difficult indeed.

IRRATIONAL FEARS AND PHOBIAS

There are two disorders that are very frequent during the genital period—fears and phobias, and temper tantrums.

Childhood is a time of life when the human being is haunted by numerous fears. He is little, weak, and helpless, and the world in which he lives is filled with many objects and situations that can really do him harm. In fact, parents have to spend considerable time warning the child of objects and situations which, however attractive they are to him, are really full of deadly peril. The busy street, fire, sharp knives, sparkling broken glass, electric-light sockets, electric fans, and other appliances—all are fraught with real danger of bodily harm to the child, against which he must be protected until he learns how to protect himself. In addition to these real dangers (which interestingly enough the child often seems to disparage), the world of every child is haunted with unreasonable fears. He is overafraid of falling, of physical punishment, of accidents and injuries, of dying; he is afraid of rough games, bad people, magic, giants, corpses; of the dark; of being alone; of strange places and persons, deformities, lights and shadows; of strange noises, scary stories and movies; of ghosts, goblins, bogeymen; of birds, insects (harmless or otherwise); of multitudinous objects and situations which in reality either could cause him no injury or are not at all likely to do so.

Jersild in his exhaustive study of the subject found that only 19 of 400 children (comprising 25 boys and 25 girls at each age level between the ages of 5 and 12) admitted having no fears. The remainder of the 400 admitted one fear and often several. In a later paper he reported that three-year-olds admitted an average of 5.5 fears; four-year-olds, 6.3; five-year-olds, 4.3; and six-year-olds, 3.2 fears each. Children during the genital period were more commonly frightened by strange objects, persons, situations, and noises, by sudden unexpected visual disturbances, by animals and bad people. Boys of all ages were more commonly afraid of bodily injury, and girls were afraid of the dark, solitude, and strange sights and noises.

The unreality of these fears (for what sensible child could really be afraid of a butterfly, or of the motes floating in a sunbeam, either of which send certain sensible and intelligent children we have seen into a state of severe panic) indicates that they are not really fears but phobias. What is the mechanism of the phobia?

In the *phobia* the child is conscious of a certain feeling tone which we call fear, and he ascribes the feeling tone to the presence of the phobic object or to the dread lest the phobic object become present. No amount of sensible reassurance, even by an adult whom he loves and trusts, can reduce the feeling of panic or can change his assertion that the phobic object is the cause. In order to discuss the reasons for this compulsive type of reaction and the mechanism by which such phobias occur we will refer to the case we have presented in another book:

A four-year-old girl had a pronounced phobia of dogs. If one appeared three blocks away she became panic-stricken and rushed into the house or clung to her mother screaming. It made no difference whether the dog was large or small, friendly or hostile, good-natured or vicious; its appearance produced an anxiety attack. This fear of dogs did not follow any attack or injury by one, but began suddenly. When she was convalescing from an attack of pneumonia, she suffered a night terror. In the early hours of the morning she began to scream and did not seem to recognize any person in the room. When her father came toward her she shouted for him to go away. When her mother asked what the matter was, she said there was a dog under her mother's bed. When the father again approached her, she screamed, "Go away. You're a dog." After some little time her terror subsided and she fell asleep quietly. On waking the next morning she was perfectly calm, but from that day on her fear of dogs was present.

What happened to this little girl? She was sexually attracted to her father and as a result was jealous and antagonistic toward the mother whom she loved also. She had the wish to destroy the mother and rid herself of her by biting her to pieces. During her severe illness she had received a great deal of very pleasant care, affection, and attention from the mother, to which she responded with love. But she had also received increased care and kindness from the father and some actual physical handling which had increased her sexual attraction to him. The increased desire for the father in turn increased her hostility to the mother. She thinks, "If I were alone with father he would give me all the attention he now does plus all the attention mother gives. So why not plan to get rid of mother altogether?" But the little girl relishes the attention and kindness she gets from her mother. If she got rid of her these would cease. How can she get rid of the mother and keep her at the same time? The problem is too complicated for her immature ego to solve.

Why is this problem impossible to solve when it is a problem that every human being has to find a solution for, and for which the majority of children do find a satisfactory one? Most children are not exposed to the increase in feelings that were brought about in this little girl by her need for nursing care during her illness. Also, before she took sick she learned that her mother and father were not a united couple. They were superficially on good terms, but the mother was being induced by a former lover (whom she still loved) to leave her husband. On Sundays the mother refused to go with the father to visit his relatives. The father went and took the children; the child realized that this separation on Sundays and holidays was not a matter-of-fact occurrence but resulted from a difference of opinion. It is as if the mother were saying, "I can't get along with your father, let him go his way and I will go mine." At her grandparents' she heard much malicious gossip against the mother, with the constant theme that the father should not have married her and that the mother was not really interested in the father.

The mother stayed with the father for the children's sake and occasionally was troubled by conscious ideas of getting rid of the children. These ideas appeared more frequently in her dreams, indicating that she had a great but unconscious desire to get rid of them. There is no question that the child could sense this underlying feeling since, being largely conscious, it expressed itself in the mother's daily handling of the child. The child then felt somewhat as follows: "She is my mother but it is all right for me to want to get rid of her because she doesn't like me anyway and she really wants to leave father. He would be happier if she did leave. My grandmother and aunts all think so. Surely I would make a better wife for him than mother does and with me he would be much happier."

The child was thus all prepared for the possibility that her desire would come true; that is, she was certain that her wishes were magical and that in a short time they would act, the mother would disappear, and she would be completely happy. She took sick and she noticed that her mother was greatly concerned, that she did everything possible for her, and that she seemed worried about the illness. (It is to be assumed that the mother would be more anxious than usual because she would feel guilty about the possible fulfillment of her own unconscious wishes to get rid of the child.) This whole situation confused the little girl. She now thought, "I thought my mother hated me as I hated her, but now I find she loves me and tries to make me happy. I must have been mistaken. How could I ever have had such bad thoughts about my dear mother? Perhaps this illness itself and all the discomfort I am suffering are a punishment sent on me for my wickedness. But I still have these bad thoughts of wanting to get rid of mother every time father is nice to me. I have wanted to bite my kind mother at these times. I must be a dog. Perhaps mother is a dog too. Perhaps if she knew what I thought about her she would bite me. I wish I were a dog. Dogs can do all kinds of bad things, things that little girls are forbidden to do. If I were a dog and father were a dog we could do as we liked and then it wouldn't matter about mother. Mother likes dogs. Perhaps father is really a dog part of the day. (It is easy to see here how close such ideas approach to the superstition of the werewolf.) Perhaps mother is a dog part of the day. If they were both dogs I could stay away from them and then would not be so uncomfortable. My father really is a dog." And so, the dog phobia begins.

We do not mean that this little girl thought this all out consciously. We mean that if her feelings were translated into concepts the concepts would follow the line stated above. Anyone who knows children knows how frequently they play they are animals. If the adult joins in the game and pretends he is a dog or bear and if the game becomes too exciting one can observe the pleasure changing to a thrill and the thrill to a panic, as if the adult were rapidly transformed into the animal he is portraying. The pretense from the child's point of view ceases to be a pretense and the child suddenly loses all perspective of reality. The child enjoys pretending to be an animal because he admires the animal's courage, skill, power, and freedom from cultural restrictions.

In our opinion the closer the dread of the phobic object (in this case the dog) approaches a reality dread (in this instance, dogs really may bite or hurt a child) the less serious is the phobia. We have observed instances where the phobic object was something that did not exist in reality—such as a strange dinosaurlike animal—and in those instances the child was very sick emotionally. In all instances the choice of phobic object depends on an accidental concatenation of circumstances (in the case cited above, on the fact that the mother liked dogs) but the formation of the phobia is a result of the projection of the child's insoluble emotional conflict and has nothing to do with the phobic object itself.

This choice of phobic object is important, for both physicians and parents are often misled in regarding the phobic object as of great importance. We are thinking now of the number of instances where parents are certain that the cause of the child's anxiety is a movie he saw, a frightening story he read or heard, perhaps over the radio or on the television. We remember one little girl who developed an acute panic during the movie of *Jack and the Beanstalk*. The parents blamed the movie. Actually the movie would have had no effect on the child whatsoever if she had not been in the throes of an insoluble emotional conflict about her mingled love and hatred of her mother. Often in therapy with a child who has such an idea it is difficult to get him to realize that his difficulties lie in his feelings about his parents and are not the result of seeing a frightening picture.

At this point it might be well to mention that in our opinion there is a great deal of unnecessary commotion about the effect of horror movies, unexpurgated fairy stories, television Westerns, and crime plays on the mental life of children. A few psychiatrists have spoken out against these types of entertainment. Our experience through the intensive study of a number of children has led us to believe that a child who develops a phobia would have developed the phobia in any case whether he had been exposed to any of those forms of entertainment or not. He may pick a phobic object from such entertainment, if he is in the throes of developing a phobia, but he would pick something as a phobic object anyway. He could do so easily from a visit to the zoo, from seeing a butterfly, etc., etc. The choice of the phobic object has little or nothing to do with the phobic reaction itself. Children in the anal and genital periods and in early latency have many murderous fantasies and cruel ideas. This is why the original fairy stories were so enjoyed by them, so that scenes of violence will not put any *new* ideas into their heads. Of course, they should have such entertainment in limited doses. Similarly, children in the latency period are not incited to become delinquents by stories, movies, or television programs of crime. In fact, as they can read during the latency period, the daily paper furnishes real horror and criminal stories every day. The child knows that the movies and other stories and programs are make-believe—"play-pretend," which he understands very well. He knows also that the newspaper stories are real and could be imitated—but unless he already has a delinquent character, he will not attempt to do so. The newspaper stories may furnish such a delinquent character with methods. After a detailed and illustrated account of how the "Mad Bomber" of New York had made his bomb, several boys, obviously of delinquent character, in several places were injured though the explosions of similar bombs they were making in order to set them off in movie houses and other places. It might seem that the realistic—and known to be real—newspaper stories of crimes could be considered more unfit reading for children than could the play-pretend of the world of fiction and drama. All children at some time would like to run away. All children plan doing so in fantasy but we have never heard *Tom Sawyer* condemned because it instigated children to run away from home. Nor have we ever heard of or seen a child who ran away because he had read *Tom Sawyer*.

All little children have phobias. They disappear when the child has solved his particular emotional conflict. We remember one child· who solved his most dramatically. He got out of bed in the middle of the night, shot the bear that troubled him, and was no longer troubled by a phobia of bears. In reality he had apparently acquired enough courage to admit and play out his hatred of his father. These phobias are not prognostically serious but are what Freud calls "the normal neurosis of childhood." They become serious only if circumstances make the child's oedipus problem insoluble for him. In the case cited above, the insolubility of the problem lay in the fact that the parents had a real marital difficulty and so could not furnish the security of a stable home in which the child is compelled to work through his conflicting feelings to the satisfactory solution that was mentioned in the previous chapter. The oedipus situation was made insoluble by a traumatic experience. It is interesting— although Freud does not make any reference to its importance— that in the first case report in which a child's phobia was analyzed, the parents of the little boy later separated. Obviously if the separation took place, they had a marital problem at the time of the boy's phobia. Also, in Freud's case of the man who had the recurrent dream of the seven wolves and who suffered during his childhood from numerous phobias, being particularly panic-stricken by the picture of a wolf in a storybook, there had been definite traumatic experiences: the sight of parental intercourse (the most traumatic of all), the absence of the parents, the seduction by the older sister, and the quarreling between the servants.

The prognosis of the usual phobias of childhood is good. The child grows out of them. Reich points out that the development of a phobia is a sign that the ego is too weak to control the libidinal strivings. It really implies a splitting of the personality. Sometimes, perhaps always, this splitting is overcome by the accentuation of certain personality traits, which accentuation acts by unifying the personality, and this strengthens the ego. However, the unification may take place at the expense of further repression. This probably takes place with the resolution of all the phobias of childhood and if not too marked does not have a serious later effect; this combination results if the child has not had too many or too severe traumatic experiences. If there have been too many traumatic experiences or if they have been too severe, the phobia may disappear but the healing personality formation will show very serious scars of inhibitions, accentuated repressions, and regressions. Such a personality is predisposed to a breakdown later in life, as occurred in Freud's Wolf Man.

All the phobias of childhood merit consideration, if not necessarily treatment, since they indicate that the child is having difficulty in coming to terms with his inner strivings. It is not sufficient to pass them by with the light statement that he will grow out of them. He may need some help in order that his later adjustment may be as adequate as possible. Jersild and Holmes have made a study of the methods of treatment usually used by parents and teachers and group them into three classes:

1. Ineffective:
    (a) Ignoring the child's fears. This is effective only if the child is using his fear to gain the adult's attention.
    (b) Forcing the child into contact with the phobic object.
    (c) Removing the child from the phobic object or the feared situation, or offering him bribes to make him less aware of his fear.
2. Auxiliary measures, which are sometimes effective alone but work best if used in conjunction with other measures:
    (a) Verbal explanation and reassurance.
    (b) Practical demonstrations of the harmlessness of the phobic object.
    (c) Demonstrating examples of the lack of fear that other children have toward the phobic object.
    (d) Positive conditioning.
3. Most effective:
    (a) Helping the child to develop skills so that he will be able to cope with the phobic object or situation.
    (b) Gradually bringing him into active contact with the phobic object and into active participation in the feared situation.
    (c) Giving him the opportunity gradually to become aquainted with the feared object or situation under circumstances that permit him to inspect it and ignore it.

These methods deal only with the conscious situation. The child is afraid of dogs. Dogs are a usual part of civilized life, and are not often harmful. The child must learn therefore not to be afraid of dogs. We suppose in all phobias that these methods should be followed because it is essential that the child become acquainted thoroughly with all the realities of his environment, and learn how to deal with them. It is important to recognize that all the effective methods depend upon being used slowly and gradually—a very important point in all child training.

But these measures are only supplemental to the aid the child should receive about the real causes of his phobias. Since they center around his attempt to solve the oedipus situation there are ways of helping him do this. The parent of the opposite sex should gradually decrease the amount of physical attention he or she gives the child. This change comes about very naturally in teaching the child himself to look after his clothing and the care of his body. It is perhaps better to allow him to be a little less clean or to be occasionally constipated than to have the parent of the opposite sex help him out or pay too much attention to these matters. He should be encouraged to do things for himself and be given the opportunity to spend as much time as possible in association with children of his own age instead of with his parents or other adults. Sleeping with the parent of the opposite sex should be definitely discouraged even though the circumstances may be unusual, such as occur during traveling or visiting. The open expression of hostility to the parent of the same sex should not be suppressed if it is within reasonable bounds. Verbal hostility should be permitted without any retaliation either verbally or physically. Motor hostility against the parent of the same sex should also be permitted to some extent. At the same time the child should have the opportunity for a great deal of motor activity, and if during this activity he indulges in murderous games, such as war or cops and robbers, he should be allowed to do so without adult interference.

Sometimes—and this suggestion is advanced with great trepidation lest it be misused—an intelligent, understanding parent who is well aware of what is going on may talk with the child concerning the phobia, pointing out that his phobia is nonsense, that he is afraid of his feelings for the parent of the same sex, and endeavor to get the child to verbalize these feelings. This kind of discussion between parent and child will, over a period of time, result in the child's producing his sexual fantasies and his fears of castration. It will be a relief for him to talk about them. At times during the discussion the parent may assure the child that all children have similar feelings, fantasies and fears, and that all grown-up people had them also when they were children.

How can we determine when the phobia of an individual child may be considered pathological and merit professional treatment? There are several criteria. If the phobia is severe and is crippling the child's life, treatment is indicated definitely. For instance, the little girl who became panic-stricken after seeing the movie *Jack and the Beanstalk* spent the next month clinging constantly to her mother. She would not play with other children, and in fact would not stay anywhere unless her mother were with her. It would not do even if the mother were only in the next room. If it is known that the child has suffered a serious traumatic experience—acts of fate, adverse parental attitudes, or seductions—the case usually merits treatment even though the phobic manifestations are not very severe. Particularly where there are adverse parental attitudes treatment is imperative. As was mentioned earlier, if the phobic object is bizarre and the phobic reaction severe the case merits treatment.

What treatment should be applied? The really curative treatment will follow the lines so carefully described by Freud in his report on the case of Little Hans. Anyone attempting to treat a phobia in a child should read these *technical details* very carefully. In this connection also the report of Kubie is very helpful.

There are several successive steps in the treatment of phobia. The child must be convinced that his conception of the cause of the phobia, that is, his idea that he really is afraid of the phobic object, is nonsense. To convince him is usually quite difficult because such a concept makes the child admit he is ill, an admission that neither child nor adult wishes to accept. The conviction can be achieved either directly (for example, if the child has confidence in the therapist he may be willing to accept the idea from him), or indirectly as the child begins to understand and work out his conflict about his feelings toward his parents. The child must be helped to indicate to the therapist either verbally or in his play the precise nature of his conflict. This diagnosis is a rather fumbling process because the therapist is seldom able to read the child's unconscious as accurately as he may be able to read that of an adult, who co-operates to a much greater extent. The child is encouraged to be freer in expressing his sexual and aggressive feelings and the therapist attempts to relieve his sense of guilt about them. Treatment of childhood phobias proceeds along more clear-cut and more definite lines than does the treatment of many other childhood neuroses because the defense mechanism—projection—is a comparatively simple and uncomplicated one, and because little or no regression has taken place.

TEMPER TANTRUMS

Temper tantrums, along with fears and phobias, are disorders that are most frequent during the genital period.

If the phobia is the normal neurosis of childhood the temper tantrum may be considered the normal psychosis. Let us describe a simple instance of a tantrum which must have been observed by many of our readers who have any association with children. It is five-thirty and dinner will be served at six o'clock. The child desires a piece of candy. The parent refuses the request, telling the child that he will have dinner shortly and that he may have the candy after his dinner. The child again asks and is refused. The child demands that he get the candy now. The adult patiently refuses. The child begins to cry and scream. He stamps his feet, clenches his fists, begins to jump up and down, and hits or kicks at the wall or door. His frenzy increases. He throws himself on the floor, kicks and screams, pounds his head or his body with his fists or bangs his head on the floor. He pays no attention to what the adult says to him. Neither threats, cajolement, bribes, promises, nor scoldings make any difference. If he is severely spanked or placed in a tub of water he will stop. Otherwise he will continue for some time. His screaming gradually subsides into low sobbing, his hitting and kicking stop, he lies quietly for a few minutes, then gets up rather languidly. He sobs for a little longer. Perhaps he feels remorse for his behavior. He seems exhausted. After a little while he seems all right again. Of course the whole proceeding may be less severe but at times it is even more dramatic.

There are certain outstanding behaviors in this symptom complex. The first and most important is that the child is completely oblivious to reality and his surroundings. He neither hears nor pays any attention to anything that is said or done to him unless it causes sufficient shock to penetrate his consciousness. He acts as if he had given up all contact with reality, as he really has. It is this that makes his reactions comparable to those of the psychotic. In this state he uses a great deal of muscular energy directed either aimlessly or against his own body. (We once saw a child with a severe hematoma on her forehead which resulted from the pounding she gave herself with her fists.) Almost never does he attack the adult who has refused him. He cries and screams as if he were suffering the greatest torment. What has caused this reaction? He was to be frustrated for a period of about an hour from obtaining the piece of candy he wanted. Thus it can be easily seen that the reaction is out of all proportion to the apparent cause. Often his speech during the tantrum shows that he is reacting disproportionately. He wails, "You are an old meany. You *never* give me *anything* I want. You want the candy *all* for yourself. You don't want me to have *any* at all."

Before we discuss the significance of this behavior we feel it would be interesting to describe the usual reactions to frustration. These seem to make a series starting from the usual normal reactions and ending with pathological ones. When a person has been frustrated in obtaining something he wants, he first has a feeling of disappointment. This disappointment urges him to stop and consider whether he cannot get what he wants through some other method. If he believes he can, he then uses that method. If he can find no other method he considers whether it might not be possible for him to obtain the gratification he craves at another time, and if this seems feasible he waits until the new opportunity arises. If this is not possible he is often willing to take a substitute that will gratify his desire in another way; for example, if he can't get cake he may satisfy his hunger with bread. If he finds none of these possibilities open to him he begins to feel irritated, and this heightened annoyance may enable him to see possibilities of satisfaction which he had not observed before. If he does not, his irritation increases and he becomes angry, and because of this anger he tries to destroy the obstacles that interfere with his satisfaction. If these obstacles are human beings the feeling changes to hate and he tries to remove the human depriver or destroy him. If he cannot, and the need for gratification is very strong, he becomes enraged, tries to destroy everything about him, and eventually may try to destroy himself. Before this happens another reaction may set in. His rage may become so great that he may lose consciousness and have an epileptic convulsion.

It can be seen that the temper tantrum appears in this series as equivalent to the reaction that occurs just before the individual loses consciousness or has a convulsion. So again we are puzzled as to why there is such a severe reaction to a simple deprivation, and also why there is no attack on the ostensible frustrator, namely the adult who has denied the child the piece of candy. The child does make an attack but it is on himself. Therefore he and not the adult is the real frustrating person. In this, his behavior is realistic—just as all behavior is realistic. Furthermore, most of the force of the attack is directed against his head so that it must be his head that is depriving him. To all of us the head is the seat of self. Therefore it is the child himself who is the depriving person.

Why does the child react so disproportionately? He has been asked to postpone the satisfaction of his desire for a piece of candy for a period of an hour. Even if he is very hungry he knows he will get something to eat long before that time. Furthermore, he is not denied having candy. The denial is only for now. He acts and talks as if he had been denied any further candy for the remainder of his life, and as if the adult denied it to him in order that he have it all for himself. He thus accuses the adult of greediness. Now the child is really a very greedy person and has had to learn with much suffering that he has to control his greed. He does not want to do so but knows it would be better for him if he did. The best way to control greed would be to get rid of it altogether or to deny himself completely its gratification. It is as if the disappointment of the denial increased his desire for the candy. (This is the purpose of the feeling of disappointment.) Now he does not want one piece of candy; he wants the whole box. Furthermore, he does not want it later on; he wants it now. The disappointment therefore arouses his greed, over which he has not yet, being a child, very good control. The arousal of his greed overwhelms his sense of reality and, consumed by it, he withdraws his sensory contact with his real environment. The picture of his greed is not pleasurable to his idea of himself as a human being. He does not like himself as the base, greedy person he now appears. He tries to remain in control and project his greed onto the adult whom he accuses of wanting to have the candy all for himself.

This is not a satisfactory solution, so he would like to rid himself either of his greed (then he would never want any more candy throughout the remainder of his life, hence the feeling that he has been deprived forever) or of his controls (which were imposed by his parents and which he felt at that time were imposed not for his good but to satisfy their own greed). He has made his parents' training part of his own personality so that the only way to get rid of it is to beat it out of himself. This he attempts to do. Not only has he withdrawn from reality deliberately, but moreover, the intensity of the struggle within himself leaves little if any energy to maintain contact with the outside. Only as he becomes exhausted in the struggle or is able to reach a new adjustment of the problem does the temper tantrum subside. He becomes really remorseful for having allowed himself to get out of hand in this babyish fashion.

It would be expected from what we have just said that temper tantrums would be common in early childhood because at that time the child is only gradually learning to control his desires, and consequently is exposed to many and severe reality frustrations. So it is. Tantrums are less common during the latent period. There is a slight increase during the early part of adolescence because of the reactivation of the infantile situation. From that time on they gradually diminish, occurring in adult life only under the most unusual circumstances, as during a severe painful illness or under great deprivation. In reality many adults have temper tantrums, for though such persons are adult chronologically they are not so emotionally.

Since temper tantrums are universal in childhood their status as a pathological manifestation will be determined in the same way as is done for the phobias. If they are very severe and prolonged or if they occur too frequently, the child's development is not proceeding properly. There are always good reasons for pathological temper tantrums. If the child has been indulged too much and has been given little opportunity to learn to control his impulses, never having had the necessity to do so, his control system is weak and he reacts primitively to deprivation no matter how hard he wants to behave differently.

There is no question in our minds that a child needs some support from his parents' insistence (kindly imposed) that he learn to adapt himself to culture. It is usual to say that spoiling is the cause of temper tantrums, but in our experience severe tantrums occur in three types of conditions: (1) when the child has been forced to be too cultured; (2) when he has been forced to exert too much control too early; or (3) when he has been forced to become independent before he is really able to be so. The control system operates satisfactorily but the amount of unsatisfied hungers is great and deserves the title of starvation rather than greed. The child is too much on the side of his control system and regards natural and not excessive desires for satisfaction as an indication of his greed. If the parental demand for too early independence and too much control is the result of a rejective parental attitude to which the child tries to adjust by doing everything possible to behave in a way that will make life with his parents at least tolerable, his temper tantrums will be most severe.

Treatment in the first type will be directed toward helping the child gain more control of his infantile desires and making him want to get more mature forms of satisfaction which will compensate for the infantile forms he has to relinquish. He does not need psychotherapy by a psychiatrist so much as he needs mild training by a kindly, friendly, consistent teacher or nurse who can make him feel more pleasure in pleasing her than giving way to his inner impulses. For the second and third types treatment will be directed toward ameliorating the severity of the child's standards so that he will feel more comfortable in being his age. Children of this type require intensive psychotherapy by a psychiatrist. Under the influence of his benign presence the child is able to play freely and in doing so to learn that even adults do not regard the high standards he sets for himself as necessary. We would say that the main technique in this therapy would be to give the child freedom to be himself at his age level.

There is no treatment for the tantrum itself. Since the child is inaccessible to persuasion and reason it is perhaps best to put him in a room by himself and leave him until the tantrum has passed—not done as a punishment but simply because there is nothing else to do. There is no point in scolding or punishing him after the tantrum. The tantrum is not induced in order that he get his own way; hence it is wrong to grant his every request with the hope that he will not have a tantrum. Such appeasement is more commonly attempted than might be thought. Tantrums often occur in situations or under circumstances that are rather humiliating to the parents and many parents would rather give the child what he wants than risk the possibility of a tantrum. If the child becomes aware of this attitude on their part he will feign a temper tantrum when he wants something. The practice of ignoring the tantrum will cause the child to lose interest in feigning.

OTHER EMOTIONAL DISTURBANCES THAT OCCUR
DURING THE GENITAL PERIOD

Although phobias and temper tantrums are so universal during the genital period, children of this age may have other emotional illnesses. Toward the end of the genital period a child may develop a classical conversion hysteria or a classical obsessional neurosis. A child may develop tics or severe stuttering. He may begin to restrict his activities to a few interests with which he occupies most of his time. For example, we knew one child of four whose entire interests centered around the construction of model airplanes. He could build complicated models suitable usually for a much older child, and he did the work in the most exact and meticulous manner. He had little time or interest in playing with children of his own age and he was not interested in their usual games and pursuits. This constriction of the usual activities and interests of his age was his attempt to avoid the pain of his unsolved anal and oedipal conflicts.

It is not unusual for a boy during the anal period to wish from time to time that he were a girl and often to be pleased if he is allowed to dress as one. This is an attempt to imitate his mother, whose strength and abilities he admires. Usually this wish is short-lived. When the boy of four years of age or older desires to dress like a girl, to wear jewelry and make-up, he has met a problem in his oedipal conflicts which he can't solve in any masculine way. Instead, either to please his mother, who unconsciously wishes he were a girl, or to avoid his hatred and fear of his father he changes his psychosexual orientation from masculine activity to feminine passivity. He even may want his mother to remove his penis, as one four-year-old we knew did. Such a boy is severely ill and needs treatment.

It is during the genital period that the majority of cases of childhood psychoses begin. We will discuss all these conditions more fully later. When any of these conditions appear to be developing during the genital period, the child should be studied carefully to see whether the symptom complex really is a pathological one and so will continue, or whether it is a temporary disturbance of development that may correct itself. This study and the resultant diagnosis should be made by a competent child psychiatrist—in our opinion it would be done best by a child psychoanalyst. Also, if the condition really is pathological, the most effective treatment is psychoanalysis.

BIBLIOGRAPHY FOR CHAPTER VI

English, O. S., and G. H. J. Pearson, *Common Neuroses of Children and Adults,* Norton, 1937.

Freud, Sigmund, "The Analysis of a Phobia in a Five-Year-Old Boy," Standard Edition of the *Complete Psychological Works of Sigmund Freud,* Hogarth, 1955.

—— "From the History of an Infantile Neurosis," Standard Edition of the *Complete Psychological Works of Sigmund Freud,* Hogarth, 1955.

Jersild, Arthur T., and Frances B. Holmes, "Methods of Overcoming Children's Fears," *Journal of Psychology,* I, 1936, 75.

—— "Some Factors in the Development of Children's Fears," *Journal of Experimental Education,* 4, 1935, 133.

Jersild, Arthur T., Frances V. Markey, and Catherine L. Jersild, *Children's Fears, Dreams, Wishes, Daydreams, Likes, Dislikes, and Pleasant and Unpleasant Memories,* Teachers College, Columbia University, 1933.

Kubie, Lawrence S., "The Resolution of a Traffic Phobia in Conversations between Father and Son," *Psychoanalytic Quarterly,* 6, 1937, 223.

Pearson, Gerald H. J., "The Effect of Operative Procedures on the Emotional Life of the Child," *American Journal of Diseases of Children,* 62, 1941, 716.

—— *The Emotional Disorders of Children,* Norton, 1949.

Reich, William, "Character Formation and the Phobias of Childhood," *International Journal of Psychoanalysis,* 12, 1931, 219.

The Years Between–the Period of Sexual Latency

VII

Development of Personality during the Latent Period

W HEN one thinks of childhood or children, he usually thinks of a child between the years of five and twelve. When we are asked to think of our own childhood, we usually think of events that occurred at some time during this age period. Hence, generally (and to most of us), a child is a person of grammar-school age. If we have had the opportunity of observing a child year by year, we know that at the age of eight he is different from what he was at the age of three. At the age of three he was a little boy—now he is a big boy. As he is at the age of eight or ten, so in most ways he will be at fifteen, twenty-five, or thirty-five. He will be bigger physically, he will know more, but his patterns or reacting will be much the same—and very different from what they were at three or four years of age. So the child, as we usually think of him, is the child of the period known as that of sexual latency, or briefly, the latency period. How does it happen that the person is so much the same at eight, fifteen, and thirty-five—but so different from what he was at three or four?

When the human being is born he is simply a living creature. He is driven by two groups of instinctual drives. These are, on the one hand, the erotic instincts, whose aims are the preservation of the life of the individual and of the species and, on the other hand, the death instincts which arise from the need to return from the animate into the inanimate—essentially to reinstate the original inorganic state of being. The two basic instinct groups are seldom, if ever, presented in pure form. They usually appear in varying degrees of mixture. From birth these drives, in their rhythms, are demanding immediate gratification and the relief from tension which accompanies such gratification. These drives, so to speak, are encased in the body, whose neuromuscular systems react to external stimuli both of an unpleasant and a pleasant nature. The newborn living creature has a striving to gain pleasure and to avoid pain and also a compulsion to repeat former experiences, whether they are pleasurable or not, provided they insure the continuation of life. As he grows older he will retain these characteristics but he will usually not be conscious of them—they will remain in his *unconscious*. The part of the personality which repeatedly pushes for relief of tension and the gaining of pleasure is called the *id*.

As he has developed through the oral, the anal, and the genital phases, the child has gradually become not an "it" but a person who knows how he feels, directs his energy toward whatever goals he desires, and has his own likes and dislikes and his particular ways of reacting. He has been developing an ego or "I," which we know as the "self."

Against the demands of the instinct of pleasure-seeking are opposed the demands of the external world—whether these demands are made by the real physical world, by other human beings' needs for instinctual discharge, or by the demands imposed on the individual by the mores and customs of the social organization in which he lives and under which he grew up. It is as much the function of the ego to take cognizance of the mores and customs of the social organization in which it finds itself as it is to take cognizance of the real physical world. It is the function of the ego to arrange for adequate instinctual discharge in the light of its knowledge of the demands of society, which basically are opposed to the discharge and gratification of the instincts. If the ego is to do these things, the child has to develop an intrapsychic sense of morality which becomes automatic and unconscious. This unconscious intrapsychic group of concepts which serve as a personal measure of what is right and wrong is known as the *superego*.

The superego has its unconscious and conscious components. The latter are known familiarly as the *conscience*. Most people are aware of what is known as conscience because the conscience feelings are conscious and their presence and functions can be recognized introspectively. The conscience is a censor of behavior. Everyone has conscious ideals for himself and is aware that he tends to compare his behavior and feelings with these ideals and to feel pleased or displeased with himself, depending on how closely he approximates them. However, much of the superego is unconscious. This unconscious part also is a censor of moral behavior and is the core of what is often called integrity. It is during the latter part of the genital period that the main characteristics of the superego are formed. It arises from three sources. The most important is the solution of the oedipus conflict. The little boy hates his father for his greater size and competency and as a rival for the possession of the mother. He fears his father unnecessarily as the result of the projection onto his father of his own hatreds and jealousies. He also loves his father passionately. He resolves the pain of this conflict of strong and opposing feelings by introjecting—taking in and making part of his own psychic apparatus—the psychic image of his hated, feared, and loved father. This image is not the real father but the projection onto the real father of the little boy's own feelings toward him. This introjected image stands as a guardian to protect the boy against his instinctual impulses, specifically his hatred of his father, his jealousy of him, his desire to be the father's sexual rival, and his desire to possess the mother sexually. In short, it stands as a taboo against acting out his wishes to murder his father and his incestuous sexual desires toward his mother and sisters. Its severity depends on the character of the father, the intensity of the oedipus situation, and the rapidity with which the oedipus situation succumbs to repression.

A second part of the superego results from the incorporation of the parents', and later the teachers', real conscious and unconscious attitudes toward instinctual drives and toward reality. For the boy particularly, the father's attitudes are the most important; for the girl, the mother's. We call this identification with the parent of the same sex.

A third part of the superego arises from the culture in which the child is reared. In this part of the superego there operates the personal qualities of parents, everything that has had a determining effect on parents, the tastes and standards of their social class, and the characteristics and traditions of the race from which they spring. The parents' attitudes toward the child, toward his behavior and toward reality, in themselves are partly the product of their cultural milieu. Erikson points out that the different methods of training a child in different cultures are directed toward obtaining the ideal that the culture recognizes as desirable for all the adults. At each stage of psychosexual development the training is conducted in a way which eventually will accomplish the desired type of adult.

The superego is sometimes called the heir of the oedipus conflict.

Its crystallization as a part of the personality occurs as the oedipus conflict is solved. It is only after its crystallization that the child begins to govern his behavior through moral principles and begins to feel guilty if he violates the existing codes and inferior if he does not live up to them. However, even before the oedipus conflict is solved the child shows some evidences of morality. If he behaves, or wishes to behave in a way which he knows will not meet with approval from his environment, he suffers from unpleasant feelings—fear of the parent and of society, which are known respectively as objective anxiety and social anxiety. These controls, however, are not solidified into a part of the personality as the superego is. The child is quite capable of behaving in a moral way in front of the parents and in an exactly opposite fashion if he is sure that the parents will not find out. In the latter instance he will not suffer any feelings of remorse, guilt, fear, or shame *about his behavior* although he may be afraid lest the parents will find out about it. This objective anxiety is one of the precursors of the superego morality which will be imposed later.

Another precursor—one whose manifestations are closer to those of the superego—is illustrated by the morality learned by the child through toilet training. For a period the child acts as if he is under the influence of objective anxiety. He is clean as long as his mother is around; if she goes away, he lapses. Later, but long before the superego is crystallized, the child feels shame, embarrassment, and humiliation if he has bowel or bladder accidents even though his parents may be quite sympathetic with him. The toilet training values he has learned from his parents have become incorporated and his shame is the sign that he has offended, not his parents but the incorporated toilet training values. The incorporated toilet training has become part of his personality and stands in relation to his ego as the later superego does. Only at the end of the genital period does the personality have three well-formed, well-working basic parts—(1) the instinctual forces referred to as the id, (2) the ego or "I" which we know as the "self" and, (3) the ideals and dictates of society referred to as the superego—which it retains for the rest of the individual's life. It is this fact which makes the child at four different from the child at eight, and makes the child at eight much more like what he will be at fifteen, twenty-five, or thirty-five.

The period of latency follows the crystallization of these three parts of the personality. The word "latent" suggests that this period is a quiescent one in the development of the individual, and so it is, relatively. In comparison with the periods so far—the oral, the anal, and the genital—the latent period can be called relatively quiet. We have seen that the first three periods are unusually critical, that a great many events of emotional importance take place, and in rapid succession. The latent period is not without its conflicts, however.

The period of latency is roughly between five and one-half and twelve years of age. Careful observation enables us to divide it somewhat into two shorter periods. The first lasts from about five and one-half to eight years and during it the characteristics of the genital period are relatively strong. The second lasts from about eight to about twelve years of age. During the first period the child's oedipus conflicts are still close to the surface. He tends still to try to solve these conflicts by partially regressing to earlier stages of his development and through utilizing defenses against these earlier phases. He is trying to be on the side of his educators, that is, to be obedient. It is the desire to do this which makes the child of about six often behave as if he were a perfect soldier. Although he may deny it verbally, he wants and seeks the firm, controlling hand of an adult over him much of the time. Also he wants to be sure that this adult administers social justice—of a particular type. He is willing to relinquish any and all privileges provided that every other child has to relinquish the same privileges. Only in the latter part of the latent period can he allow other children to have as many privileges as himself.

This change evinces a reaction formation against his jealousy and envy and it is through such a reaction formation that the child begins to form an idea of social justice. In fact, all social justice—as we adults know it—is founded on such a reaction formation. Reaction formation, that is, *the ego wanting to do, and doing, the opposite* of what the instinctual drives would do, is one of the more important defenses against the instinctual drives which is used in the latency period. The use of this particular type of defense indicates that the ambivalence —for example, the almost equal force of love and hate in the child toward the same person—is very high at this time. Many of the child's defenses, particularly that of reaction formation which we can observe in his behavior, are his attempts to solve these problems. Also, he is trying very hard to bring to a satisfactory solution his conflict between his superego—which is being incorporated as a part of his personality—and his drives. Therefore, he shows alternation between implicit obedience and forceful rebellion. In the latter instance, however, the rebellion is followed by severe self-reproaches—a phenomenon which almost is a new trait in his personality although its beginnings have been evident to a slight degree earlier. In order to help himself to accept his superego, he falls back on earlier ways of thinking. His belief in the efficacy of magical rituals in thinking and acting becomes strengthened. He uses rituals in nearly every spontaneous activity in which he engages. All group games such as tag are governed by strict self-enforced rules which are like the proverbial laws of the Medes and Persians. Many of his routines have to be gone through in a ritualistic way so that he will suffer no injury from fate—that is, from his internalized superego. He allows himself from time to time to get pleasure from using the primary processes of the unconscious in the discharge of energy by indulging in sing-song nonsense rhymes and the like, which repeat the same "ideas" over and over. Around the age of six or seven, therefore, the child could receive pleasure in using repetition—the so-called rote memory that is used in mastering arithmetical tables and the like—to learn, whereas later such learning methods would be uncongenial to him.

At this time also the child's former fear of castration has been replaced by a conscious fear of punishment by death. For a while during this first part of the latent period he may not trust himself to keep his instinctual impulses under control. Particularly he fears that as he falls asleep and loses conscious control his impulses may become ascendant. At this time he may suffer from insomnia: he dares not fall asleep lest he do something which is forbidden. The way by which in the genital period he could solve some of his conflicts by projecting them into a phobia now becomes less effective and a new wave of separation anxiety, resembling that of the much younger child, may take its place. This may cause efforts to be close to the parents or sleep with them, which appears babyish.

After the age of eight, the child's conflict is less acute because the superego has become internalized and he is more used to its presence. He is able to direct more of his energy and attention to reality and to try harder to adjust himself to it. Of course, the more he attends to reality the sooner he observes that his parents are not the omniscient, omnipotent persons he once thought they were. He learns that they make mistakes, often are untruthful, are not as successful as some other people, and often are afraid—but he has tender feelings toward them and puts up with their frailties as well as with their merits. He no longer really confides in them but tends to discuss whatever problems are *important to him* with his friends. Occasionally he may consult some adult other than his parents, but only occasionally, because he observes they are as untrustworthy as his parents. Sometimes a parent shows concern and remarks that it worries her a little that her grade-school child keeps his thoughts so much to himself. He stays in his room a great deal, and even if he plays with others, she cannot find out very much what he is thinking or talking about. One hears this complaint more often from the parents of adolescents, since the adolescent is frequently sullen, close-mouthed, and difficult. He will not confide or share his life with his parents. This behavior is what should be expected. The solution of the oedipus conflict, which produces the incest taboo, causes the child to turn his feelings and desires from his parents to persons outside the home and to establish the presence of two different generations, for the child in turning away from his parents usually turns to companionship with other children. This is his first real step in establishing a social life and is important, for throughout his life his social life will be more with his peers than with much older persons. There is a great advantage in the parents' being interested in the child's interests and pursuits and being companionable with him, but the child as long as he is a child can never completely take his parent as a pal or as a close friend.

The advent of the latency period marks the beginning of the individual's friendships and loves outside of the home. During this period he begins to learn the complexities, pleasures, and difficulties of adjusting himself and his instinctual drives, both aggressive and erotic, to those of his peers; and by achieving this learning and adjustment he can begin to take his place as a member of their group; now begins his social life. In making this adjustment, children of the latent period tend to seek the company of their own sex, to have chums, and to form groups, gangs, and secret societies. Among themselves they advance their own theories of life, birth, death, adventure, particularly in relation to the question of sex, and they relate to these topics what they learn about the world in general. The gangs and groups, especially of boys, fight each other (either in a supervised way as in baseball or football games, or under the auspices of the school athletic plan, or else and more usually in warfare games—cowboys and Indians, cops and robbers), thus working off much hostility and aggression. Society usually provides more and better outlets for boys to work off their aggression than it does for girls. We doubt that girls have less aggression than boys but we suspect that they have less opportunity to work it off in acceptable social ways. Some people think this may be why their love for each other is more ambivalent than is the case with men.

CRUELTY AND AGGRESSION

We mentioned before that during the early part of the latency period, children tend to be little robots and welcome domination. As the counterpart of this attitude they also are bullies and tyrants. They want control, or feel that they can control, someone. A certain amount of this feeling is worked out in games, but even in spite of games the phenomenon of "being picked on" occurs during the grade-school period. Perhaps there is not much of it before latency because the play of young children is usually supervised, but there is always some of it. In the latent period, when girls and boys are less supervised by older people than during the previous periods, they can be extremely cruel to each other. They form cliques, punishing those they dislike by excluding them. They hate their rivals, verbally castigating each other because they want to feel important and because it is important to them that they affect other persons and affect them rather painfully. Boys and girls who do not have disagreements in play and who get along amicably all the time are probably the exception rather than the rule.

Actually children do not limit cruelty to each other. Often during this period boys will be cruel to grownups, especially if the latter are too weak or helpless to retaliate. Some accepted boyish pranks are directed toward older persons in the neighborhood, and these may merge into actual delinquency at times. This tendency results from a combination of several causes. The children, having grouped themselves together as children, have a common enemy, the adult. Also the children in one group or clique make common cause against those in another group or clique.

Any group, clique, or gang formation depends on the fact that the instinctual aggressions in each member of the group cannot be directed at any other member of the group, because they are his friends toward whom he feels love. His ambivalence, therefore, has to be split. The love goes to the other members of the group. The feelings of hatred have to be redirected and so each child in the group and the group as a whole must find suitable objects to serve as enemies. Group formation in itself is an important social phenomenon to help human beings deal with the ever-present problem of ambivalence. A group is formed around some kind of a leader, whether this leader be a person, a principle, or an ideal. Each member of the group loves this ideal or leader and expects to receive love in return. Because of this expectation he can love the other members of the group and feel much less hatred of them than he ordinarily would feel. The combined feelings of hatred of the individuals in the group are then at the service of the ideal or the leader, to be directed against other groups or other ideals. Extreme nationalistic attitudes are an excellent example of this sociopsychological mechanism, but its presence can be seen in all groups and best in well-organized groups which center around an ideal or a leader. The beginnings of group formation and its phenomena are seen first in the latency period.

One of the reasons for the rebellious attitude of children in the latency period is the fact that the old struggle of the oedipus situation is now displaced from the relations of the child to his parent of the same sex onto his relations to persons in authority—adults—outside the home. To this reason is added the need for the child to rebel in order to defend himself against his wishes to remain a subservient, submissive baby—an unpopular position even in grade-school society.

A third reason for the rebellious dominating attitudes lies in the facts that the child of this age has not developed enough skills to enable him to redirect his aggressive impulses into socially acceptable actions and that his erotic life has not matured enough to enable him to be considerate and thoughtful of other people.

In individual instances we can see that to the basic psychological reasons for the rebelliousness of children there has been added the fact that the parents themselves may not be good models of social behavior, or are not showing the interest and friendliness and giving the kindly supervision which the child requires. Often in our culture the latter failing is more common among fathers than among mothers.

We have mentioned that during the latency period children enter gangs and groups and we have discussed the reasons, but we have not yet considered the tendency during latency to get together in groups of the same sex. This tendency in the development of the human being for boys to seek the company of boys and girls to seek the company of girls is referred to as a "natural homosexual period." The sexes become segregated and each sex seems to have its own language. The children feel that their own sex is desirable and the opposite sex is more or less worthless and is to be looked down upon rather disdainfully. Boys say they do not like "those silly girls" who cannot play games. Girls say they do not like "rough boys" who do not have consideration. The fears of castration during the genital period cause the boy to be afraid of and therefore to dislike girls. The humiliation of the girl when she observes her penisless state during the same period causes her to dislike boys. When the genital period comes to an end these feelings continue during the latent period. Not until puberty, when the activity of the sexual glands gives a certain impetus to the erotic components of the personality, do boys and girls turn their interest to each other and emerge out of this homosexual period into heterosexual interests. Of course, society is not only permissive but encouraging of heterosexual interest at this age. However, we are sure the reader has seen boys and girls whose indifference to each other in the latent period changes very little at puberty, and these girls and boys are never able to show very much interest in the opposite sex at any time in their lives. Such persons usually have suffered severe psychic traumata during the genital period, which have made an adequate solution for the oedipus situation very difficult.

THE SCHOOL SITUATION AND THE ROLE
OF THE TEACHER

During these years most children are in grade school. They are years in which the family delegates a great deal of the child's training to the school system. In fact, a great many parents are often too relieved when the child enters school age. They rush him off to school with the expectation, or hope, that the school system will fill the child's time and direct his play, will solve his problems and answer his many difficult questions, and they are glad not to have to concern themselves so much with the child's development. The parents often consign to the teacher the major responsibilities for the child's development at this time. Some fathers and mothers actually say to the child when he asks a question, "Ask your teacher." Perhaps the reader has heard a parent say, "I'll be glad when my child gets off to school," as though the school were a kind of organization that will absorb much of the child's energy and relieve much of his insatiable curiosity.

During the latent period a great many situations and events occur that help the developing human being to form ideals for himself, to make himself a good citizen, to become a capable person, to mold himself into a considerate person. He develops a conscience about those ideals. Up to now the child has been concerned with weaning, toilet training, being neat and clean, and generally has been involved in a great many questions concerning sexual problems. During the latent period he begins to go to school, he acquires a larger vocabulary, he begins to read and to hear about the people who have lived before him and how they behaved. The parents are usually the most important people to the child during the first three periods of development and they still should figure as most important in the formation of the superego. However, when the child enters the latent period the parents' influence is supplemented by the educational procedure during the grade school. The school curriculum teaches the child about our national and international heroes and their achievements. He learns about soldiers, statesmen, writers, poets, inventors, and philosophers, and the important contributions they have made to society. He wants to be like these heroes because they have brought credit upon themselves, and he feels that if he follows the same kind of life and method of handling himself, if he does a similar piece of good work, he will bring credit to himself. And just as his history books relate the adventures of military heroes, so do his geography books tell about courageous navigators, his mathematics books reveal the intellectual ability of the mathematicians, his radio at home tells him about Superman and all the other "heroes" that manufacturers of contemporary products have enlisted in order to sell their wares. Motion pictures and television play their roles too. Possibly more regulation, for children, of both will be in order as time goes on, so that more suitable material may be available for them. The ultimate effect of these media upon the developing personality of the child is still not well understood.

The teacher and the personality of the teacher also exert a profound influence upon the mind of the child. Human beings of every age want to have heroes, and there is a great deal of hero worship in the world. It is said that there is more hero worship in America than in any other country. We worship our movie stars, our baseball players and our boxing champions. Just as adults need heroes to worship, so children need them even more, because the child's life is smaller and his interests less diverse. For this reason the teacher becomes an unusually important person. In fact, she can be the next most important person in the child's life—the most important being the parent—during each year or every year of school.

We need to pay attention to the personality of our teachers. Boards of education attempt to do so now, but in a too-limited way, and every once in a while the newspapers report controversies regarding the eligibility of certain teachers. We personally feel that only those persons who have mature personalities are desirable as teachers. Surely most would agree to that opinion, considering the important role teachers play in the formation of the child's personality. Nevertheless, it is a fact that some areas exclude women teachers after they marry, when through marriage and possibly having children of their own they may be in a better position to understand and inspire children than the unmarried teachers. We are all aware of the unfortunate fact that there have been and continue to be teachers who have no interest in children themselves but who consider teaching a fairly good vocation with short hours and long vacations in summer, and one having more prestige than office or factory work. And then there are teachers who, if they take interest in a child at all, do so to show favoritism for their "pets." Children sometimes suffer a great deal from this kind of teacher. On the other hand, the person who is really interested in teaching and inspiring children, in being a friend to all of them aside from imparting knowledge, can mean a great deal in the development of their personalities.

Uncles, aunts, neighbors, friends of the family may also play an important role in forming the child's personality. Perhaps the reader can look back and remember the interest of some person outside the family—perhaps a teacher at college, or a scout-master, or some friend of the family—which influenced him profoundly. The reason is that during the latent period a great deal of emphasis is still being put upon the process of imitation, or that process which is more intensive and more thoroughgoing than imitation—identification. Children will talk about being some prominent person. For instance, boys may talk about being a famous soldier or a noted flier. Girls may identify themselves with a nurse or a teacher or a movie star. In doing so they are playing the role of someone they have seen and admired, all of which contributes to personality building through the tendency of human beings to imitate and identify with older persons. This process goes on more intensely during the latent period than later. During puberty, for instance, children have come to the point of being rather skeptical about adults and feel that they have been through the age of illusions. Many have reached an age of regrettable self-sufficiency by the time they are fourteen. A great many adolescents feel it is silly and childish to be too interested in imitating other people and regard it as a sign of weakness. They too readily assume they can learn nothing more from adults; they feel they know practically everything already. Children of grade-school age, on the other hand, have not reached this stage. They are still willing to be interested in and inspired by other people.

We have discussed here the tendency of the child to form ideals. These become an unconscious part of his personality known as the *ego ideal*. A certain slight distinction is made in textbooks between superego and ego ideal. The superego pertains more directly to the concepts of right and wrong, the concepts that hinge around the do's and don'ts, the concepts that have a moral turn to them; whereas the ego ideal pertains more to the kind of person one wants to be, the kind of personality characteristics that one will have and that do not relate so specifically to conscience. Mannerisms, for instance, are picked up by children in imitation. The way other people walk, the way they dress, the words and pronunciations they use, are not characteristics directly related to right and wrong. These are matters of choice and undergo change from time to time and pertain rather to the ego ideal than to the superego.

We have sometimes questioned whether it is necessary to make this fine distinction between superego and ego ideal or whether the nature of the superego and its functions merely needed study to be understood; we feel that extra names do not substitute for study and understanding. Freud made the statement, for instance, that the superego was the heir to the oedipus complex. This statement referred to a boy's accepting the fact that he cannot possess his mother and must submit to the incest taboo which is a moral issue imposed by society. Having accepted this bit of social law within his mind as superego material, the boy then has to go through a further task of repressing his hostility to his father, using what good will is available to love him and imitate him and to regard his qualities as good. This latter task illustrates ego ideal, which has been called a precipitate of the superego.

PLAY AND WORK EXPERIENCE

Finally, another point to be taken into consideration during the latency period is the matter of play and work. Children need something to hold their attention during this period; they need to be occupied; they need something upon which to expend their energies. Some children seem to be naturally more resourceful about play than others. We maintain that the child who is resourceful at the age of eight or nine is the child whose mother was resourceful with him in his first few years of life. He has learned to play because his parents have helped him and given him some ideas about it in the beginning. We sometimes hear a parent say to the child, "Run off and play." The child does not know what to play with; perhaps he does not have any toy within reach, or has not known enough of the pleasure of playing with others to enjoy playing by himself.

Children of the latent period still need help with their play, and here is where the father and mother should participate. A boy of fifteen may be excluded from the baseball game simply because when he was seven or eight his father was too busy to play with him and get him used to throwing a ball in good form. Girls may not know how to enter into dancing classes, picnics, tennis games, or other activities because they were not helped by recreations with the mother when they were younger. Children become embarrassed about their lack of dexterity and poise in comparison with other children and become sensitive to remarks made about their abilities; if they are not left out of activities by others, because of sensitivity they may leave themselves out. Whenever we encounter a person who is suffering from a psychoneurosis or a psychophysiologic disorder, we ask if he enjoyed school. Practically never do we get an answer in the affirmative. The reason is not necessarily that the patient did not like the teacher or had difficulty in learning, but rather that he did not know how to get along with and be accepted by the group.

It is also important to help children enjoy work. It is difficult, we will admit, to have children do much work in the home. Primitive peoples teach the children to work along with them—the girls to cook and weave, the boys to hunt and fish. When our country was less industrial and more agricultural and with small trades flourishing, there were always things for children to do. They were expected to do them, and they got pleasure in helping the parents and working along with them. In the city today there is less work activity for children, but there is still an appalling disregard on the part of parents in helping children to work at what is available. Often mothers are in a hurry to get the dishes washed, or afraid a glass will be broken, or do not want the little girl around making a mess, so the child is never allowed to help about the house. At twenty-one some girls are most inept at cooking and homemaking.

Likewise, there are boys who are awkward not only at play but also in the use of their hands. They have missed the pleasure in working, not only in doing the thing itself but the pleasure of working with others. Some of the serious work difficulties we encounter in patients are among those who have never learned to work with pleasure on small things at home, even occasionally.

In the home of a friend we once saw a child whose father had brought him a present of a sandbox that had not yet been put together. The child wanted it put together, but the father did not want to do it at that time and kept putting the child off with such statements as, "We'll do it later." The child pleaded with the father, urging him to let them do it together. The father still insisted that he was too busy. Later while the child was out walking with his mother, the father hurriedly put the sandbox together: he wanted to be spared the trouble of having the child around, annoying him with his youthful awkwardness and eagerness to help! So the child had neither the opportunity to use his hands nor the enjoyment of the pleasure of work in the company of someone he loved. This was not a wise procedure for, as the reader can see, the father missed a real opportunity to have the child share the sandbox assembly with him.

Later in life this same father may be astonished that his son is not willing and eager to help him with some project of his business, and will think his son ungrateful for all he has done for him. The son's attitude will not result from the one instance of the sandbox but from the extension of the father's attitude described during the boy's childhood. When the boy had the energy and enthusiasm for work, it was not caught hold of by the parent and directed in a constructive way.

The progressive school has fostered the plan of the child working along with the adult—a close physical and emotional tie being interwoven with the activity. Whenever it is possible to work out such a plan in the home, it is important for the parents to sacrifice time and to create projects in which parent and child work together. The ritualistic sending of the boy or girl to do a piece of work for work's sake alone is of questionable value. One well-to-do woman we knew always had the idea that her son should have a paper route and deliver papers. She had been impressed with the stories of successful men who had started life as newsboys. She thought if her son could have some contact with newspapers when a boy his success as a man would be practically assured. So she sent him forth to deliver papers, work which he hated because none of his friends did it. He was alone and conspicuous and doing something obviously unnecessary, merely gratifying an impractical whim of his mother's that had no value in personality building. In fact, it was more harmful than beneficial because it was no fun—only an abstract discipline which caused him to lose respect for his mother's good sense. If she had herself gone to work in her own garden, for instance, and sought his help in something mutually creative, the result would have been better. He would have been helping her; he knew he was not helping her when he was delivering papers.

Before the child, psychologically already a rudimentary parent, can become a biological parent, he must begin to be a worker and potential provider. In the latency period the normally advanced child learns to win recognition by producing things. He has mastered the ability to use his hands and the techniques of locomotion. He develops industry, that is, he adjusts himself to the laws of the world of creative activity. He can become an eager and absorbed unit of a productive task. To bring a productive task to completion is an aim which gradually supersedes his childish whims and wishes. His ego boundaries include his tools and skills: the work principle teaches him the pleasure of work completion by steady attention and persevering diligence.

His chief danger at this stage, if there is one, may lie in a sense of inadequacy and inferiority. If he despairs of his tools and skills or of his status among his companions, his self-esteem suffers and he may abandon hope of the ability to identify early with others who apply themselves to the same general section of the tool world. To lose the hope of such "industrial" association leads back to the more isolated, less tool-conscious "anatomical" rivalry of the oedipal time. The child may despair of his equipment in the tool world as well as in his sexual power, and consider himself doomed to mediocrity or doomed to be cut off in relation to the others. It is at this point that the wider society of the school becomes significant in its ways of admitting the child to an understanding of meaningful roles in the world of men. Many a child's development is disrupted when family life may not have prepared him for school life, or when school life may fail to sustain the promises of earlier stages. If his aspirations are toward a career that involves mind training alone, he may have even more difficulty in acquiring confidence that he "knows how to do."

We have talked with college and medical students of both sexes who showed surprise when we said that the adolescent should be fairly well decided upon the kind of work he or she is going to do in his lifetime. Some students thought this was asking too much of the adolescent and argued that thoughts concerning a career occurred casually, perhaps during the senior year in college. We feel that not only should the adolescent be doing a great deal of thinking and planning about what he is going to do but also that the child in grade school should be given opportunities of learning perhaps by observing what people in various vocations—butchers, mechanics, engineers, doctors, and lawyers—do in order that he can at least make a start in thinking of where his place in the world is going to be. Nothing is decided all at once; at least nothing so important as one's life work should be decided without some thought and reflection. Therefore an interest should be shown by both the parents and the teachers in the child's play and work, to be certain that he is observing how the workaday world operates and considering where he can fit in.

These are some of the things we should think about in this so-called latent, quiescent period when nothing much is supposed to be happening and the children are "just attending school." As the reader can see, important situations and events occur which, if understood, can be made to be contributions to the child's personality, and which he can use to merge with what has gone before and with what is yet to come. If the events of this period are not understood or are neglected, they can leave a weakness in the personality which is corrected with great difficulty later in life.

SUMMARY

The latency period corresponds roughly to the years spent in primary school. Within it are confined the phenomena of physical and psychological growth which seem to stem from the tensions incident to a resolution of the oedipus situation. These include the continued identification of the child with the parent of the same sex as well as with other adults in positions of interest or authority such as uncles, aunts, teachers, heroes or heroines of books, movies, radio or T.V. personalities. During the latency period the child of either sex needs companionship, in order to feel that he matters. Games are necessary to utilize his energy in wholesome ways and to provide outlets for his aggressive forces. He needs guidance in order to incorporate a sense of fair play. His conscience—or superego—needs strengthening by an increasing awareness of his eventual social, moral, and altruistic obligations to individuals and society, be this through organized religion or through clearly stated family values.

We have seen how the parent, teacher, counselor, physician needs to bear in mind that certain forces within the youngster pull him backward at times while others propel him toward maturity. The former can largely be understood, accepted, and usually ignored while the forces pushing him toward greater maturity should be boosted in varieties of ways. This is a lonely, insecure, and difficult time for many children and there is a need for a good friend in both parents, if there is to be a steady, continuous maturation in the latency period. Personality patterns, good or otherwise, are being strengthened during these years and determine, to quite an extent, the reaction patterns of later life.

BIBLIOGRAPHY FOR CHAPTER VII

Bornstein, Berta, "On Latency," *Psychoanalytic Study of the Child*, 6, International Universities Press, 1951.
Cohn, D., *Love in America*, Simon and Schuster, 1943.
Erikson, Erik H., *Childhood and Society*, Norton, 1950.
Finch, Stuart M., *Fundamentals of Child Psychiatry*, Norton, 1960.

Flugel, J. D., *The Psychoanalytic Study of the Family,* International Psychoanalytic Press, 1921.

Gesell, Arnold, Frances Ilg, and L. Ames, *Youth, the Years from Ten to Sixteen,* Harper, 1956.

Pearson, Gerald, *Psychoanalysis and the Education of the Child,* Norton, 1954.

Redl, Fritz, *Children Who Hate,* Free Press, 1951.

VIII

Emotional Disturbances That Occur during the Latent Period

ALTHOUGH we have discussed the most common types of psychological illnesses that occur during each of the periods of infantile development, we have left the formal discussion of the neuroses, psychoses, and behavior problems of childhood until this point. Parents often are not as disturbed by many forms of deviant behavior in the preschool child as they become when this behavior is continued into the school age. Parents may even not be disturbed by the behavior of their child and sometimes may not be able to see that the child is ill, though the illness may be very evident to an objective observer like a teacher. The obsessional neuroses and many cases of conversion reaction do not appear in their classical forms until the internalization of the superego at the beginning of the latency period. Also many cases of phobias go unnoticed until the latency period. For these reasons we commonly see more children with neurotic manifestations during the latent and early adolescent periods than we see during the preschool period. However, recently, as parents are becoming more aware of early neurotic reactions in their children and of disturbances in development they are consulting child psychiatrists and child psychoanalysts more frequently for emotional illnesses during the prelatent period, when childhood psychoses usually begin.

GENERAL CONSIDERATIONS

Preliminary to a discussion of the neurotic symptom complexes in children, we shall discuss the methods of history taking in children's problems, the examination of the child, and some of the general principles that underlie treatment.

The medical approach to the study and treatment of emotional illnesses in children does not differ from the medical approach to an organic illness. It consists in the collection of data concerning the child and his illness (that is, the child's history and examination), the comparison between that data and the data that would be obtained from a well child (that is, the psychopathology), and the grouping of the data and its comparison with the data known to indicate the various forms of illness (that is, the diagnosis). Finally, it consists of a consideration of the measures that will help to restore the child to health and how to employ them (that is, treatment).

HISTORY TAKING AND DIAGNOSIS

It is advisable to have the parents or parent come without the child for the history interview. If the child is present at the interview, neither the parent nor the doctor will feel entirely free to discuss the child and his history. The child may become annoyed or frightened by some of the discussion. If he sits for an hour in the waiting room while the interview is taking place, he tends to become bored, to consider what terrible plans are being made for him, and to become frightened. All this unnecessary emotional turmoil is easily avoided by having the parents come alone.

Although there are certain questions to which the doctor requires an answer, it is better to start a history interview by asking the parent to tell all he knows and thinks about the child and his symptoms. With this general question and a little encouragement, the parent will usually launch into a description of both. This description will be infinitely more reliable and valuable than any history obtained by the question-and-answer method. As long as the parent continues to talk there is no need to interrupt except to ask for the dates of the various events he is describing. When the parent has related all he can, then the doctor can ask any questions that still remain unanswered. Not only will the history obtained through this method be more reliable than one obtained via questioning, but the doctor will also get more valid impressions as to the attitudes of the parents toward each other, toward the patient, and toward the other children in the family. The patient's history should be recorded chronologically.

The history should include a description and history of the presenting symptoms. In many cases there is one presenting symptom for which the parent brings the child, but it is improbable that it is the only evidence of pathology. It is necessary, therefore, to obtain a complete picture of all phases of the child's activity in order to ascertain the presence of other symptoms. This step is doubly necessary because the doctor may note certain phases of behavior which are undoubtedly pathological but which the parents may regard not only as nonpathological but even as admirable characteristics. Inquiry must be made concerning the child's adjustment in school, his educational achievement, his habitual emotional reactions, his fears, habits, and physiological status.

Having obtained this data, we next obtain the story of the life experiences to which the child has been subjected—acts of fate, parental attitudes, any excessive sexual stimulations, the importance of which we discussed in Chapter VI. At the same time we obtain the history of his psychosexual development.

It must not be expected that this history will be complete in any way. An accurate history of a psychogenic illness can be given only after the illness has been cured. This difficulty is inherent in the nature of the illness, which consists of an attempt on the part of the patient to avoid remembering and so knowing the painful experiences which have caused him to alter his psychological adjustments to his real life. Moreover, this history of the child is obtained mostly from the parent, who does not know all the details of his experiences, whereas the most significant data is obtainable only from the child himself. However, as much material as possible should be obtained from the parent, particularly regarding the child's psychosexual development and traumatic experiences and his objective reaction to the latter.

As much history as possible having been obtained from the parents, it is now necessary to examine the child. In most cases the examination must be threefold: physical, intellectual, and emotional.

First it is wise to have a psychological evaluation made by a competent psychologist.[1] A psychological evaluation is designed to furnish the psychiatrist with information not readily available either from the history or from initial clinical observations. Information obtained from psychological testing can include the following:

(1) *The nature of the child's intellectual functioning.* For the purpose of diagnosis and treatment it is more important to know *how* the child uses his intelligence than to know merely at which

[1] I am indebted to Dr. Sheldon R. Rappaport, of the Pathway School, Narberth, Pennsylvania, for most of these suggestions as to psychological evaluation.

level he is functioning. Therefore, a single IQ score is of little real value and may be misleading unless accompanied by a description of how the child utilizes the various intellectual skills on which the IQ score was based. An appraisal of the variability of the child's intellectual skills can supply diagnostic information concerning the sources of interference with the child's intellectual functioning. For example, it may give indications of excessive anxiety, ego constriction, faulty perceptual or conceptual skills due to cerebral insult, etc. An assessment of the variability of a child's intellectual skills also can furnish information concerning the difference between his present level of functioning and his premorbid or potential level of functioning.

(2) *Social development.* Information can be supplied as to the kinds of social skills the child has developed in everyday living. Such skills would include his ability to dress himself, care for himself at the toilet, feed himself, interact adaptively with other children, be independent of adult supervision, etc. The difference between a child's social and intellectual developments may furnish important leads concerning the nature of the child's difficulties or how much parental overprotection or deprivation exists.

(3) *Scholastic achievement.* In many cases it is helpful to know the grade level at which a child functions in the basic academic skills. By comparing the child's scholastic achievements with his intellectual and social developments, specific disabilities such as alexia may be uncovered. Such comparisons may also furnish clues concerning the extent or intensity of a child's emotional difficulties.

(4) *A cross section of emotional organization.* Psychologists now have a number of projective tests which have varying degrees of inherent structure. These range, for example, from unstructured inkblots, on which the child projects his inner feelings and thoughts, to ambiguous pictures, to which the choice of response is more delimited. By comparing the child's responses to these tests of various degrees of structure, the psychologist can give information concerning the characteristics of the child's psychic reactions and can give some indication of the severity of the illness from which the child suffers. Such information is often of value in helping the psychiatrist to decide the difficult question as to whether the presenting symptom, such as a phobia or temper tantrums in a young child, merits intensive psychotherapy.

None of the tests administered is meaningful or informative unless administered by a competent individual and unless the testing situation itself is conducive to reliable and valid testing. The best single criterion of competency today is that the psychologist be a diplomate in clinical psychology of the American Board of Examiners in Professional Psychology. The testing situation should be one in which press of time or other considerations will not vitiate the test findings.

The tests most commonly used today evaluate the four areas just enumerated: intellectual functioning, social development, scholastic achievement, and emotional organization.

Intellectual Functioning

(1) *The Wechsler Intelligence Scale for Children (WISC)*. This test is designed for use with children from 5 through 15 years of age. It measures 12 basic intellectual skills, of which 6 are verbal and 6 are nonverbal. From the child's scores on each of those skills three IQ's are derived: a Verbal IQ, a Performance (or nonverbal) IQ, and a Full Scale (or over-all) IQ. The variability of the child's intellectual skills, together with the discrepancy between his verbal and nonverbal IQ's, has proved in our experience to be of diagnostic importance. The diagnostic indications obtained, when integrated with the findings of the personality tests, have proved valuable in differential diagnosis of mental deficiency and psychosis, as well as of psychoses and neuroses.

(2) *The Wechsler Adult Intelligence Scale (WAIS)*. This has replaced the earlier Wechsler-Bellevue Intelligence Scale, and has been standardized on a population ranging in age from 16 to over 75 years of age. This test taps 6 verbal and 5 nonverbal skills, providing the same types of information as can be obtained on the WISC. Therefore the WAIS is used as an upward extension of the WISC.

(3) *The Revised Stanford-Binet Scale,* 3rd edition (1960). This is the test which has replaced the old Form L and Form M of the 1937 revision of the Stanford-Binet Intelligence Scale. The present revision of the Binet test covers the age range of from 2 years through adulthood and is comprised of selected items from Form L and Form M. It contrasts with the WISC and WAIS in that it is an age scale, whereas the others are point scales. Thus the Binet taps skills standardized only within a given age range for each child, whereas

the Wechsler taps the child's ability in each intellectual skill. The present Binet scores still are expressed as mental-age scores, but new tables provide deviation IQ's in place of the former ratio (MA/CA) IQ's. The new norms are based on the 1937 standardization adjusted for observations and changes made during the 1950's.

(4) *The Cattell Infant Intelligence Test.* This test, following the format of the Stanford-Binet, is divided into age levels, covering the age range of 2 to 30 months. Beyond 30 months, the test items are taken directly from Form L of the Stanford-Binet. Below 12 months of age the Infant Scale is regarded as being doubtfully valid, except for detecting extreme variations from normal intelligence.

(5) *The Minnesota Preschool Scale.* This test for preschool children consists of both a verbal and nonverbal section, and is appropriate for children 2 to 5 years of age. Like the Wechsler tests it is a point scale and yields an IQ. The nonverbal portion of the test is particularly helpful in examining preschool children who have speech or language difficulties.

(6) *The Arthur Point Scale, Form II.* This test can be administered completely in pantomime, and is helpful for children who have speech or language difficulties and are between 5 and 15 years of age.

In recent years there has been increased interest in evaluating children for possible brain damage. This in part is because the psychological tests offer a better prognostic indication of the paranatally brain-damaged child's learning potentials and what type of specialized educational techniques he needs than do neurological examinations alone. It has also been documented with many cases that frequently the psychological tests are more sensitive to an acute intracranial pathology, such as tumor or hemorrhage, than are at times even such neurological tests as the pneumoencephalogram. In reported cases, the psychological tests indicated acute intracranial pathology as much as six months to three years before they became evident on neurological tests.

There are no standardized tests exclusively for detecting brain damage. Most often, signs of brain damage are elicited from the relationship of subtests of the above-mentioned scales. In addition to those, there are several other tests which contribute to the psychological indications of brain damage. These are:

(1) *The Bender Visual-Motor Gestalt Test.* This consists of nine geometrical figures of varying degrees of complexity. The child

copies all nine figures on one sheet of paper; then the test cards and the paper on which he copied the figures are removed, and the child is asked to draw on a different sheet of paper all the figures he is able to remember. The copied drawings and the drawings from memory yield information concerning the child's emotional organization as well as the possibility of organic lesions being present. The one drawback of the Bender Visual-Motor Gestalt Test is that its validity with children under 8 years of age is open to question.

(2) The House-Tree-Person and the Rorschach tests, although they are projective tests used primarily to gain information concerning emotional status, often give additional signs of brain damage.

Social Development

The measure of social development most frequently used is the *Vineland Social Maturity Scale*. In this test the parent of the child is asked questions concerning the various aspects of the child's social skills and abilities to care for himself.

Scholastic Achievement

Perhaps the most widely used test of scholastic achievement has been the *Stanford Achievement Tests*. These tests measure the child's fundamental academic skills. However, children with reading disabilities often score spuriously high on group-administered, standardized tests such as these. This is because such tests provide short paragraphs of relatively simple difficulty and highly structured questions. As a result, the scores obtained in speed of reading and reading comprehension often place a child a year or more above his actual reading level. Because of this, individual tests designed to "diagnose" the nature of the specific subject disability are frequently also needed.

Emotional Organization

The projective tests most widely used today are: Rorschach, Thematic Apperception Test, Children's Apperception Test, Blacky Pictures, and House-Tree-Person. Used conjointly they offer information concerning the organization and strength of the child's ego functions, his psychosexual level of development, the relative intensity of his instinctual drives and defensive reactions, and certain highlights concerning the child's main inner conflicts. Although such information would be obtained through psychoanalysis (or psychotherapy) with the child, these tests provide the highlights of such information in a much shorter time.

It should be remembered that all psychological tests are no better than the individual administering and interpreting them, and that these tests provide only a cross-sectional study of the child which must be evaluated in the context of the child's history and clinical observations of the child. The psychological tests do not replace the considered clinical judgment of a well-trained and experienced child psychiatrist. The test findings should not be used as a laboratory manual for the treatment of a child. The treatment should particularly not be directed toward proving or disproving the psychological test findings, but should progress through the material given by the child, regardless of where it seems to lead.

The examination of the child's physical and emotional status is made by the physician. How should this be conducted? The purpose is not at this point to alter the child. If such is the doctor's purpose in the first interview with the child, he will not accomplish it except through a lucky guess, nor will he accomplish the important purpose of understanding why this child is ill and the nature of the illness. Unless he accomplishes the latter, he cannot embark upon a scientific treatment program. Of course all of us, as physicians, have the wish to cure our patients as completely and speedily as possible. If, however, this wish becomes more than a guiding urge and begins to compel us to act even before we know where, when, and how to act, then we ourselves are suffering from a neurotic compulsion to obtain relief for ourselves from some feeling of anxiety of which we may be conscious or, as is more often the case, unconscious. The successful therapist is one who has the wish and purpose to cure the patient as thoroughly and speedily as possible, but not the compulsion to attempt to do so without regard to common sense and scientific procedures. The young physician, just starting practice, has a greater and more understandable anxiety in this respect than the older, better-established one. Although this feeling of anxiety is understandable, the young physician should be aware of it and learn to cope with it, or his practice will suffer.

The real purpose of the examination is twofold: to ascertain with what kind of child the doctor will be dealing, and to help the child to feel friendly toward the doctor. These two purposes can very easily become mutually antagonistic and exclusive. In the child's unconscious, an inquiry into what he thinks and feels is regarded as an assault and the child reacts by an attitude of hostility to this unconscious feeling of being assaulted. If the physician is largely urged by the purpose of finding out about the child and pays little heed to the second purpose of the examination, the child becomes frightened and hostile and this purpose is not accomplished. If the physician is concerned mostly with having the child be friendly to him, he may avoid methods of finding out what the child is like and so the examination becomes stultified. Both purposes have to be maintained at the same time. Practically, it is desirable to pay more attention to the second than to the first purpose, for the result will not be as detrimental to the treatment of the child.

When the parent brings the child for examination, it is best to see the child alone. There is usually no difficulty in separating the child from the parent. Occasionally one meets a very upset, sick parent—usually suffering from a mild paranoid reaction—who will not permit the child to be alone with the physician. Occasionally the child is openly afraid to leave the parent. In most instances, however, if the separation is made gradually, the fear is readily overcome.

Which part of the examination—the physical or the emotional—should be made first? The physical examination should be made last; it should be done by telling the child that the physician has to know also about his physical health, with reassurances that he will not be hurt. Most physicians are accustomed to start with the physical. This approach is a mistake, since the physical examination produces so many frightening ideas in the child's unconscious mind. His unconscious regards the physical examination as even more of an attack than questioning is, and therefore it is no wonder that so many children act as if they dreaded the physical examination even when they know they are not going to be hurt. As every pediatrician knows, examination of the throat, ears, and genitals should be left till the last, and if the child becomes very frightened may be omitted unless there are definite indications that organic pathology in these organs may be present. Fear of the examination of these parts is due to the fantasies all people have in regard to them, fantasies that started at an early age, particularly in regard to the mouth and throat, as we mentioned earlier. We believe that when a physician is asked to examine a child for a definitely organic illness, it is well to spend a little time first getting acquainted with the child—a procedure that is often carried out by the pediatrician in his private office but seems to be invariably neglected in outpatient departments. Child psychiatrists and child psychoanalysts generally make it a rule not to do the physical examination of the child themselves but to have it done by a competent pediatrician. As we already have said, the physical examination stirs up a great number of conscious and unconscious fantasies in the child, and these fantasies will interfere with the progress of treatment.

In urban centers, laboratory specimens are usually taken by the laboratory worker, so the physician usually does not have to deal with this procedure. Laboratory tests should not be done routinely on a child but only when they are necessary. The decision in this respect has to be left to the judgment of the physician in the individual case. The electroencephalogram also is useful, although the results of the test are not as reliable as could be hoped for. Certainly when the electroencephalogram shows a disturbance in the brain waves, the pathology is more serious than when the e.e.g. is negative.

How does the physician proceed in making an examination of the child's emotional reactions? The technique of establishing a friendly relationship with the child consists in treating him as a reasonable human being. The small child often has difficulties expressing himself verbally, so it is well to have a small supply of toys on hand. Three dolls (father, mother, and baby), blocks (to build a house), one or more toy automobiles, airplanes, guns, some modeling clay, crayons, and paper are best. Usually it is sufficient to draw the child's attention to the toys and tell him he can play with them. Everything he does from that point on is of importance in understanding what he is like. In the record, one should list whether he plays with the toys or not, and if he does, what toys he selects and what play he performs with them. A preschool child's span of attention is short and may go from one kind of toy to another, but if he constantly wants to go back to his mother or if he seems bored with the toys, he is feeling anxious and this fact is important.

The child of school age (often this is true of the preschool child as well) senses something strange if a new adult tries to cajole him into being friendly. In our opinion, it is well to begin the interview with an older child by telling him who the doctor is and the kind of cases he treats, giving a short description of some of the problems that have been treated, explaining that the children all came to the doctor because they were upset and knew he could help them. We tell the child that we can only help him when we know as much about him as he knows about himself and therefore he will have to tell us everything about himself. We reassure the child about being hurt—unless we know he will have to be, when we make this fact clear. We assure him that the interview is confidential, that we are not going to tell his parents, teachers, or anyone anything he tells us. He can report this interview if he wants to, but we will not do so without his permission. We also assure him that he can tell us anything in any way he wishes and we will not criticize, scold, or punish him. We tell him that we do not expect him to believe this because he must have found already that adults frequently promise one thing and do another, but that we are going to try to be honest with him and he will be able to find out about our honesty only through experience. We then tell him that to help him we have to know everything about him and he can tell us starting with anything he likes. If he feels hesitant about talking, we have toys and perhaps in his play with them he will be able to show us himself.

Children's Play

In order to understand how the child's play shows his unconscious conflicts it seems to us advisable at this point to discuss the meaning of children's play. With the increasing number of psychoanalyses of children during which the intrapsychic reasons for the child's play have been carefully studied we know more about the mechanisms that are at work in the play of a child than Gross did when he propounded his theory that the play of the child was a recapitulation of human development or than Buhler did when she stated that play was important to discharge excess energy. Both of these theories still have validity but we are in a position to add other reasons. During the oral period the child seems to play with various objects. This play really is his attempt to investigate the world around him, to learn what that world is like and to get sensual pleasure from movement and touching. This play increases his knowledge of himself and his feelings and of objects in the world. Toward the latter part of the oral period he begins to imitate his mother and her actions. We say he is playing at clapping his hands. We have seen that this is not play but his beginning attempts at identification with his mother in order to be able to master his environment.

During the anal period when the child learns to master a situation such as climbing up a step he repeats the act over and over again with a manifest sense of pleasure. Part of his so-called play therefore is directed at mastering his environment. As we mentioned earlier, about this time as the child's muscular skills are better developed, he begins a new type of play. Freud observed that in this period when a child's mother left the house the child would play a game in which he threw a cherished toy away, brought it back, and threw it away again. The child felt unhappy and deserted by his mother. She went away and left him— threw him away. He had to be passive toward her going even though it was painful because he could not stop her. In order to overcome the painful feelings which he had to suffer passively, he became active toward his cherished toy, made it leave him as his mother had left him, brought it back and threw it away again. He found relief from his painful feeling of being deserted by his active desertion of the cherished toy. The earlier example we mentioned of the child at the dentist's has a similar reason. This form of play in which the child has to passively experience an unpleasant situation and then takes the active role in inflicting a similar unpleasant situation on another child or on a toy is a very common motive in children's play throughout childhood.

In the genital period and in latency we find a new motive entering into the child's play. He admires the ability and power of the adult to do as he wants. He would like to do the same himself but is told he cannot until he is grown up. He dislikes this waiting period and so from time to time he impersonates the grownup. He drives off to work in his toy car as his father does. He enjoys dressing up in his father's clothes (as the girl dresses in her mother's). In doing this the child is doing away with reality. No longer is he the little child but now in play-pretend he has become the adult. This flight from reality forms the basis for a great deal of children's play.

We have mentioned that after toilet training is completed the child begins to play with mud pies. In doing so he continues to pretend that he is playing with his feces which the precursors of his superego forbid him to do actually lest he suffer a feeling of shame. Through play-pretend he temporarily takes leave of absence from the precursors of his superego. After the establishment of his superego at the beginning of latency his play, particularly his dramatic play, usually is of this character. Both boys and girls, but more often boys, play killing games like cowboys and Indians, etc. They in play-pretend shoot and kill each other. If the boy who is shot falls to the ground and remains immobile too long, his colleagues become quite anxious and upset. He really may be dead. These types of games provide discharge for hostile and aggressive impulses whose aim is to kill and destroy, but this aim is carried out only through play-pretend which the participant can stop whenever he wants to. His superego forbids him to kill and destroy but through play-pretend he temporarily can take leave of absence from his superego and so does not have to suffer feelings of guilt.

The girl toward the end of the genital period and during latency can take care of her *baby* dolls, dress and undress them, feed them, often nursing them at her nipples. In this play she is taking her mother's place and getting rid of her mother but as it is only play-pretend which she can stop any time she wants, her superego cannot accuse her of wrong-doing.

These games reduce the pressure of the instincts by discharging them and so relieve the pressures from the superego temporarily. As a result the parts of the personality operate more smoothly.

As the boy grows older and comes to the beginning of adolescence, he changes his play from war play to athletic contests, which he continues throughout adolescence. In adult life these drives are expressed as competition and ambition. The girl's doll play in adolescence becomes an interest in real babies and housekeeping, which she continues into adult life. This progression shows the character of sublimations, many of which start in forms of play. If the child is deprived by circumstances, by parental disapproval, or by a too severe superego of these forms of play, his ability to sublimate suffers.

It must be remembered that real team play, the ability of an individual to relinquish his place in the sun in order to help someone else to make a play for the benefit of the team as a whole does not occur in the early part of the latency period and only very slightly does it begin toward the end of latency and the early part of adolescence. However, both boys and girls during the latter half of latency need help and instruction in the various skills necessary for team play and athletics. This should be given them by their parents. If this is not done, later on they become embarrassed about their lack of dexterity in comparison with other children, and if their lack of skill does not cause them to be excluded from participation in athletic pursuits by their colleagues, they themselves may refuse to take part.

Children of all ages learn many skills—muscular, social etc.—as a by-product of their play. During the genital period and latency a child changes from one type of play to another apparently without reason, because the intrapsychic motivation has changed or enough discharge of one emotional situation—passivity into activity, avoidance of reality, or leave of absence from the superego—has taken place. Both during the genital period and the period of latency most of the play should be unsupervised and not adult-directed. If too much supervision occurs, the child's need to play for emotional reasons is stifled.

Children in the latency period play a number of games—tag, hide-and-seek, etc.—for which rules are handed down from generation to generation. (The reader who is interested in this aspect will be interested in reading a recent book *The Lore and Language of School Children,* by Iona and Peter Opie, Clarendon Press, Oxford, 1959, which really is a "must" for anyone who works with school children.) Many of these rules go back generations, and the counting-out for "it" perhaps goes back to the choosing by lot of the yearly King God who took office in the spring and was killed and his successor chosen the next spring.

These rigid self-imposed and traditional rules fit the psychology of the child in the latency period very well. His life is full of self-imposed rituals—to save himself and other people from harm—just as is found in the severe case of an adult obsessional neurosis. Every telephone pole or every second one must be touched as the child passes; if he forgets one he has to go back and start all over again. This is a ritualistic defense against masturbation. Certain things must be touched and others not. A girl may not step on a crack lest she "break her mother's back"— a defense against her unconscious wishes to hurt her mother. An endless number of these normal activities of the latent child—which as we said we would find in the adult obsessional neurotic—could be catalogued by anyone who has observed school children. They serve—as they do in the adult obsessional neurotic—to reinforce the superego.

Play is a method of reducing intrapsychic tension, thus allowing the child's ego to understand and accept the demands of reality. For this reason children need the opportunity and space for play and the needful toys. These toys do not need to be too many or too expensive. The so-called educational toys are helpful during the late oral and anal periods and some building materials—erector sets, etc.—are useful during latency. Parents should remember that the toy given a child is *his* toy and he should be permitted to do with it as he likes, even to destroying it if he wants to. No adult is capable of knowing what is the particular instinctual need at any particular time. Neither can the child express verbally what this need is. He only feels he wants to do a certain thing. There are times when a child may not want to play or when he complains he does not know what to do. At these times usually his superego is in the ascendant and forbids any expression of the instincts. His complaint that he doesn't know what to do is a plea for his parents to take the responsibility in inaugurating some play so that his superego will not plague him as it might if he did it on his own. At other times the same plea may be for his parents to baby him a little. Children in the anal and the genital period really do not play much with other children. They accept their presence but go about their own concerns themselves. This is true also at the beginning of the latency period. There are times when the child in the latency period wants to play with other children. At other times he wants to be alone and play by himself. At others he simply wants to be alone. These changes of interest—most parents call them moods—should be respected. Just as the child knows when he is hungry—and as we mentioned earlier, actually knows the type of food he needs and knows when he needs to excrete—so he knows what form of activity he needs at a particular time.

Play helps the child in his adaptation to and acceptance of the demands of reality. It helps him to be a more responsible person, for its action in reducing intrapsychic tension frees the capacity of his ego for work.

After suggesting that the child talk or play we ask him if he wants to ask any questions about treatment or about ourselves. If he has no questions, we suggest that he go ahead. Everything he produces after this is important because what he says or does represents his reaction patterns. It may not be possible at this point to say what his type of play or conversation means in respect to the causative factors, but this information is not important at this time. More important than an estimation of the kind of child we have to deal with is an estimation of his reaction patterns.

Having examined the child and his environment, the next step is to come to a decision as to the direction of the major treatment emphasis.[2]

Is this child's illness the result of traumatic situations that are still operating or is it the result of situations that operated in the past—situations which the child has made part of his personality and to which he continues to react as though they were current? In many cases the traumatic situations—particularly those due to adverse parental attitudes—are still current and are day by day forcing the child to develop unhealthy reaction patterns in order to

---

[2] The reader should realize that the question as to who will treat the child or adolescent is an extremely important one. There are many well-qualified psychiatrists and psychoanalysts whose therapeutic work with adults is excellent but who have received little or no training in psychiatric work with children and adolescents and who temperamentally are not fitted to work with children. If possible, a child or adolescent should be placed in treatment with a psychiatrist or psychoanalyst who has been specially trained in child psychiatry or child psychoanalysis and has learned the specific techniques and methods used in working with children and with adolescents, as these methods differ considerably from those used in working with adults.

enable him to live with his own desires and the demands of his parents. In these cases treatment has to be directed toward the child's environmental situation, since he is little, dependent, and helpless and can neither change the attitudes in his environment nor leave of his own volition—if he runs away he will be brought back by the police. (The adult is in an entirely different position. If his environment is uncomfortable he can change it voluntarily, except, of course, in such circumstances as military service.) If the child's difficulties call for a drastically changed environment, the physician sometimes encounters difficulty in arranging that the child live in another home; often he will find this impossible.

If treatment is to be directed toward the environment—that is, toward the adverse parental attitudes—how can it be thus directed? As was mentioned earlier, the parents' attitude toward the child is a a form of behavior and therefore has to be treated as such. The more the physician understands the causes that have led to the adverse attitude toward the child the better he will be able to apply effective therapy. It is therefore decidedly helpful to devote some time to permitting the parents to talk about themselves and their life experiences. The several techniques of therapy by which changes in the adverse parental attitudes toward the child may be brought about are the same as those used in the treatment of neurotic persons. They are discussed in Chapter XVI.

Treatment for the parents does not necessarily always accompany treatment for the child. If the child is of preschool age, treatment for both parents and child must occur simultaneously because the child has to live with them. He is small and helpless and has to conform to their attitudes, and if he is cured of one neurosis and the parents have adverse attitudes he will have to develop another in order to get along with them. During the latent period it is usually best to follow the same plan. Simultaneous treatment is not so often necessary in adolescence; particularly in late adolescence, there is little real need for it as far as the child himself is concerned.

Although we are firmly convinced that adverse parental attitudes arise as a result of conflicts within their personalities we feel that some parents show what seem to be adverse attitudes toward the child simply because they are unaware of the propriety of certain phases of the child's behavior and emotional reactions. A parent may believe that it is improper for a child ever to become angry or fight and may with the best motives in the world curb every such display. If the parent knew a little more about human beings he would not condemn the child so severely, and thus what appeared to be an adverse attitude would disappear.

We wonder if such situations could not be prevented by courses in the grammar schools, high schools, and colleges in the emotional life of human beings. In grammar school and the early part of high school the courses might be confined to the emotional reactions of children and adults, and in the latter part of high school and in college they might be devoted to the emotional needs and reactions of children and to the relationships between parents and children. Such courses could very well be part of the social sciences. All this speculation presupposes that the teacher be conversant with the subject matter. The more contacts we have with teachers the more firmly we believe that they should be selected on the basis of the degree of intuitive understanding they have about human behavior, and that those who do not show a high degree should be asked either to undergo a personal psychoanalysis or to choose another profession. It seems curious that such courses have not always been included in curriculums. We wonder if this is not because adults—both parents and teachers—are unwilling to have children learn about the emotional reactions of human beings, because then they would realize that the adults also have emotional reactions and feelings as they do. The adults are afraid they might lose their authority if the children realized this.

There are some parents the adverseness of whose attitude toward the child cannot be ameliorated by treatment. There are other situations where the problem between the child and the parents, originally perhaps caused by the parents' adverse attitude, has reached such a degree of bitterness that no amelioration can be expected until parents and child are separated for some time. In these cases, if treatment is going to have any value for the child, he must be separated from his parents. We do not believe that in every case treatment for the child should enable him to adjust himself comfortably to any situation. We do realize that separation of the child from the parents produces another traumatic situation for the child, but we believe that this trauma can be dealt with during treatment. We do not believe that mere separation of the child from his parents is always a useful treatment measure, but we do believe that just as psychiatrists and social workers have erred in the past in considering it a treatment measure in itself, so they tend to err in the present in not utilizing it sufficiently as an adjuvant form of therapy.

Therapeutic separation of the child from his parents may be either partial or complete, and if complete may be either temporary or permanent. Partial separation is useful often in the cases of young children, those of preschool age. In large urban communities there are many families who live in small apartments on busy streets where the children have no play space. Often parents do not have sufficient money to hire a person to take the child to a place where he can play or to look after him so they can go out. In such situations the child, lacking opportunity for adequate play, feels shut in and becomes angry and resentful. He expresses this resentment through annoying behavior. The mother also feels shut in and resentful toward the child, and his bad behavior increases her resentment. A vicious circle rapidly develops which is popularly described as getting on each other's nerves. In such instances, if the child can spend part of the day in a day nursery or nursery school, where he has adequate play space, he feels less resentful and behaves better, and the mother, being less shut in, feels less annoyed at him. This breaks the vicious circle and their relationship improves. In some cases this partial separation is all that is necessary in the way of treatment. In others, treatment for the child and the mother can proceed more effectively as a result. It goes without saying that the teachers in the nursery school and day nursery must be well-trained professional people who understand and can deal adequately with the problems of child development.

This is one important use of nursery schools as a therapeutic aid. Nursery schools are becoming an integral part of American life and it seems important at this time to consider them as an educational and community function. We realize that nursery-school teachers may not agree completely with our opinion, but we believe we should present this opinion in order that the psychiatrist and the educator may be able to come to some agreement. In the first place we believe that under ideal conditions (to wit: the presence in a home of two parents; a feeling of love by the parents for the child; adequate knowledge on their part as to the needs of the child, as to what is and what is not important in child training; the ability to make practical use of that knowledge; sufficient space and opportunity for the child to exercise his energies; and the opportunity to play with other children of the same age and of both sexes) a nursery-school placement is unnecessary. If any of these factors are missing, the nursery school may be very useful in supplementing the deficiency. If it is necessary for the mother to work outside the home, the child of preschool age is better off if he is placed in a nursery school. Here he is supervised by trained adults who understand the needs of the child. If the mother has rejected the child or if both parents use unwise and unnecessary measures of child training, the child should have the benefit of a nursery-school experience. If there is a great deal of antagonism between the parents and the other children, the nursery school will make up these deficiencies.

It should be remembered that the placement of a small child in nursery school involves two traumatic experiences—the separation from the mother and acquaintance with new people. It is necessary for the child to weaken his attachment to the mother and to make an attachment to a new woman. During this period of adjustment he suffers anxiety and shows all or certain of the clinical symptoms; and his fears of being deserted, lonely, and not loved are increased. As a consequence the transition from home to nursery school should be made gradually so that he can become adjusted to the change without being hurt too much.

Any parent who contemplates placing his child in nursery school should give these facts about the traumatic possibilities in the placement serious consideration and determine whether the reasons why he intends to make this placement are sufficient to outweigh the disadvantages. Similarly, any physician who prescribes nursery-school placement for a small child should weigh all the pro's and cons.

In our opinion, as a treatment measure for certain problems and as a means of providing needful satisfaction for children who are underprivileged [3] in certain ways, nursery schools are an essential part of the educational system of urban communities. They are not essential in the suburbs or in nonurban districts. They should not exist simply as convenient places where parents can park their children while they are engaged in interests that exclude their family responsibilities.

[3] By *underprivileged* we do not mean living in a low financial status but we mean that the child, because of where he lives or with whom he lives, does not have the opportunities for adequate management, love, play space, and companionship.

In older children this type of therapy is accomplished through their compulsory school attendance so that as a therapeutic measure partial separation of this sort is valueless for them. In cases where there is a great deal of antagonism between the parents and the child, or where the management of the child or his problem by the parents interferes with the progress of therapy, a temporary separation between the two, at least until treatment for both can get under way, is desirable. Boarding schools, camps, and hospitals are all useful places for such a temporary separation. Which one will be selected depends largely on the child's symptoms, for this type of placement is not curative but is only an adjuvant to treatment. Children with marked chronic aggressive symptoms or delinquent behavior or those who have enuresis, or soiling, are not acceptable in most of these places, although hospitals are more tolerant of enuretics than schools or camps are. We believe temporary placement in a foster home—and by temporary placement we mean for a period of less than a year—to be inadvisable. The return home from a foster-home placement will be much more traumatic than will the return from a camp, school, or hospital. The foster home, being a home, has an aspect of permanence about it that is not the case with the other placements; hence the child, knowing that it is not customary to remain for years in a camp, school, or hospital, but, feeling that it might be possible in the foster home, tends to allow himself to form stronger attachments in the home than he does in the others.

Permanent placement of a child in a foster home is a serious procedure. The most important item is the personalities of the foster parents. It is for this reason that there are child-placement agencies, whose business it is to study foster homes very carefully before making a placement. If foster-home care is deemed necessary, one of these agencies should be consulted. It goes without saying that it should be the best one in the community. If the child shows marked chronic aggressive or delinquent symptoms, foster-home placement is usually valueless, for there are not many foster homes (or many communities in which such foster homes are located) that can tolerate the depredations of this type of child. The usual history is that after a short period of time the child has to be changed to another home and on top of his original troubles is superimposed the trauma of another broken relationship.

THE TREATMENT OF THE CHILD

The treatment of the child depends on the causes of his illness. If the child is languid, tires easily, is fretful, whiny, and undernourished, and if the examination reveals a definite vitamin deficiency or an anemia it will be obvious to any physician—but somehow, curiously enough, not so obvious to the parents—that the child's vitamin deficiency or his anemia must be treated. If the child is having difficulty in school and the examination discloses that his intelligence quotient is very much above or below the average, treatment will be directed toward a school placement that will be more adequate for his intelligence. If the examination discloses that the child's difficulty is an emotional conflict the treatment must be directed toward helping him to a better solution of the emotional problem.

How is this last treatment to be administered? From a study of the child's history and from the examination of the child it is possible to estimate the nature and extent of his emotional conflict. The child is not aware that he has such conflicts. He knows only that he has been brought for the treatment of a particular symptom. He has had the first interview, and regular treatment has been decided on. How is he to be approached? He is told that there is a cure for his symptoms and that it will lie in finding out the cause. The cause is due to some worries and fears he has—perhaps he knows about them, perhaps he doesn't. The only way to find out about them is for the physician to know him as well as he knows himself—much better than his parents know him—and usually better than he knows himself. Adults can talk and tell about themselves—so can children, but they usually find talking and telling more difficult than adults do. Therefore if he can't talk he can play with the toys in the playroom, as we saw earlier; in so doing he may dramatize his worries and fears and then the psychiatrist and he can talk about them. In this way the child can be introduced to treatment.

The aim of any method of treatment is to uncover the child's conflicts and help him understand and solve them. Since the therapist's activity is directed toward helping the child to express himself freely about his secret thoughts and feelings the child will need some time to develop a confidential relationship and the therapist often has to demonstrate three things—that he is *able* to help the child in his life difficulties, that he is friendly to him and *wants* to help him, and that the child is *ill* and needs help. As the child learns to develop a feeling of friendliness and confidence toward the therapist and as the latter begins to understand the worries and fears that are plaguing the child, he can begin to discuss them and their real importance with the child, correcting whatever misinformations he expresses. It usually will be found that the worries and fears concern facts of sexuality and feelings of anger and hatred, both of which the child regards as dangerous because they seem to threaten any comfortable relationship with the members of his family on whom he must depend for his existence.

It should be remembered that the vast majority of our knowledge of psychodynamics and psychopathology has come from psychoanalytic research and that most therapy is based on attempts to apply psychoanalytic concepts in forms of treatment which are not psychoanalysis. Psychoanalysis has a definite aim (making the unconscious conscious by bringing the patient's attention to the defenses he has established lest he know what his real thoughts and feelings are) and a definite technique—free association—which is the only one that will accomplish this aim. It is possible to bring certain parts of the unconscious to consciousness through nonpsychoanalytic methods and so doing often results in the relief of symptoms. This type of therapy is known as psychoanalytically oriented psychotherapy. In it the patient is influenced to a much greater extent by the therapist than he is in psychoanalysis. A great deal of therapy of children makes no attempt to bring the unconscious into consciousness but deals entirely with helping the patient to be more comfortable with his conscious thoughts and feelings of which he has become afraid. Here the influence of the therapist is used to a much greater extent. Each one of these three methods of therapy does help children with their emotional difficulties. We see no reason to cavil at the use of the influence of the therapist in helping the patient. This influence is exerted even if the therapist is very inactive in the treatment hours. It will be of great help to many children to be accepted by an adult as a person, an individual, and an equal. Children long for this relationship. A three-year-old whose grandparents had dropped in for a visit said to his grandfather, "Granddaddy, I want to talk to you." He then took his grandfather to his room and said, "I wish you'd speak to grandmother. She never invites me to her house for dinner."

In reality he had been at his grandparents' many times for meals but what he was saying was that he had not been specially invited to go there by himself. It always had been as a member of the group. When his grandmother said she would invite him he replied, "And I will bring my mother, my father, and my sister." He did not mind them coming but he wanted to feel he was an individual in his loved grandparents' eyes. He was able to verbalize what all children feel about the attitude of adults to them. When a child is singled out for individual therapy this need is satisfied and he develops a great deal simply from this satisfaction. The child in therapy thus develops a new object relationship and through this relationship can be influenced to be more tolerant of his own thoughts and feelings. This development is not a transference, as occurs in psychoanalysis. In the transference the patient brings into this new relationship all the difficulties and problems of his unconscious attitudes toward other people and these have to be made conscious to him.

Individual therapy demands a high degree of intuition, experience, and training on the part of the therapist. Also it is better if the therapist first has had a successful personal psychoanalysis. This combination of intuition, intensive training, and personal psychoanalysis are more important than whether the therapist is a school counselor, a social worker, a psychologist, or a physician. Psychoanalysis of children, however, is a highly skilled specialty and can be undertaken only by a person specially trained.

Group therapy also is useful for the treatment of children. Under the influence of the group an inhibited child becomes less inhibited, a delinquent child becomes less delinquent. Here it is the influence of the group situation which works the improvement. The therapist needs special training in this work.

Certain illnesses require specific types of treatment. We intend to discuss this under the appropriate illness.

At some point in this book the reader may say, "These descriptions of the emotional illnesses of childhood are very interesting and the discussion of their causes is very ingenious, but for each condition depicted there is advised a method of treatment that is often time-consuming and expensive. Is this really necessary? What would happen if the child were not treated? Would he go on being sick or would he get well? I have seen children who suffered from some of these symptom complexes and after a time, often when they became adolescent, all their symptoms disappeared and you would never have known them for the same children. Also I have known adults who seemed to be reliable and truthful who related that they had suffered some emotional illness in childhood or even had behaved in a chronic aggressive manner, and yet as adults they seemed to be adjusting fairly well. Do not psychiatrists as a rule regard these childhood maladjustments too seriously and prescribe treatment that is really unnecessary, for if nothing were done would not the majority of children grow out of their illness? Also are there not children who show no symptoms during childhood but who suddenly out of a clear sky become ill during adolescence, and are there not adults who in adult life suffer from a neurosis or psychosis who have been perfectly well adjusted during childhood and adolescence?"

In reply to the questions we agree that the reader's observations seem to be correct, but we would have to question him as to his understanding of the process of "growing out of." We have endeavored to point out that the child at birth is simply a bundle of instinctual desires which demand immediate and complete gratification. This gratification has to be supplied by some person other than the child because the latter is not well enough developed to obtain it himself. If the other person does not gratify him the child feels unhappy and uncomfortable—he feels anxiety. As the child develops more neuromuscular skills he does not need to suffer as much anxiety because he can gratify his own needs or can actively induce other people to gratify them. In this sense, therefore, as he develops he will grow out of many of his feelings of anxiety because he is less dependent on the whims of other people. A simple example: The baby is uncomfortable because he is hungry. He cannot obtain food for himself but has to depend on his mother to feed him. The child can feed himself but has to depend on his parents to provide the food. The adult has learned to work, knows how and where to obtain food, and gets it himself.

Much of this progress is due to the simple process of physical and intellectual development—the child grows out of his infantile and childish helplessness. This relief from helplessness is only one part of the process, however. Certain drives in all human beings are in conflict with each other, certain methods of gratifying certain drives are in conflict with the possibility of getting along with other people, and certain methods of gratification are in conflict with the social organization. In order that these conflicts shall be solved or at least in order that a working compromise shall be evolved, the inner drives have to be checked, redirected, and sublimated. These modifications are accomplished through the action of the ego and the superego. Each time that a drive has to be checked and then redirected or sublimated the individual feels anxious. With the appearance of the anxiety the ego has to develop new techniques by which the drives can obtain gratification through redirection and sublimation. As these new techniques become habitual they form part of the character of the individual.

This development of new habit patterns by the ego is also part of the process of growing up and of growing out of infantile behavior. Since each new technique as a method of avoiding anxiety becomes habitual we can say that all children grow out of anxiety situations. Is this growing out always equivalent to growing up, that is, to the development of new techniques that will allow the gratification of inner drives in a more mature and socially acceptable manner? We should like it to be so in every individual instance, but quite frequently it is not. The nature of the drive and of the environmental situation may be such that the ego has to seek methods of defense against the drive or against the dangers that would result from the environmental situation if the drive were expressed. These defense methods, such as reaction formation, also become habitual and form part of the personality. Thus the ego intimidated by the environment may first try to check any expression of the inner drive. This effort causes anxiety. The ego, in order to avoid the anxiety, tries to allow the drive expression—sufficiently disguised so as not to meet censure—or to allow its expression but at the same time to punish itself for the expression. We later will discuss the way this happens in the case of the child whose behavior constantly is antagonistic, destructive, defiant, and disobedient where the aggression is turned from the external world onto the self and a compulsion neurosis results, in which case the child has grown out of his direct expression of aggression and into a hampering and false conformity. In the first case he can use his aggressive drives, in the second, he cannot use them at all. The result is a growing out, *not* a growing up.

Another interesting example of growing out rather than growing up is found in the histories of childhood phobias. As we saw in an earlier chapter, the phobia is an attempt by projection to solve the conflict between the hostile and loving feelings for the parent of the same sex. The conflict between the feelings is painful and so both feelings are feared. The child's ego is too weak to deal with the situation; therefore he projects his feelings onto the phobic object, from which he can then stay away. Often as he approaches adolescence the phobia seems to disappear, but fairly soon after we notice that the boy, who while he had the phobia was doing well in school, now does poorly. He is no longer projecting his conflict. He is dealing with his aggressive ambitions by acting as if they did not exist. However, he no longer feels anxiety although he may be worried by his lack of success in school. He has not grown up and solved his phobia. He has simply changed his technique of dealing with it, and his basic problem remains unaltered.

As one follows the life history of a child with a severe neurosis one observes that spontaneous cure or cure produced by changes in the environment seldom occurs. True, the symptoms change and one group disappears—only, however, to be replaced by another group. Squeezed in the iron glove of his intrapsychic mechanisms, the individual ekes out a precarious existence, with at best a narrow margin of reserve for adjustment. If some common but rather marked change (such as change of occupation, marriage, loss of money or of a loved person, induction into the armed services) occurs in his life, his reserve adjustment fails, his defense mechanisms are no longer effective, and a neurosis develops whose symptoms are often the very ones that served in his original attempt to solve the problem. As the years passed he grew out of the neurosis into a complicated system of defenses, but has not grown up. These changes in symptoms correspond to the erection of the various types of defenses. After a period of years so many different types of defenses are superimposed on the original conflict that it may require a great deal of hard work for the psychoanalyst and the patient to discover the original conflict and the situations that brought it about.

The child who suffers from a neurosis thus may grow out of the symptom complex but he does not grow up, unless some kind of fate so alters the circumstances of his life that he has a chance to start over again. This does not occur often. It is interesting to observe that children often realize this themselves. They will tell you that everything would be all right if they could be born again, and some even seek religion because they feel religion offers them a chance of rebirth. Of course the child may be fortunate enough to obtain psychiatric treatment through which he receives a new solution to his conflict. We have never seen an adult suffering from a neurosis whose history did not reveal a similar neurosis when he was a child.

This capacity on the part of the ego to alter itself and take up new methods, use old techniques in new situations, and change its relationship to the environment, lethal as it becomes in the neurotic person, is both helpful and hopeful, for it indicates that with adequate help the individual's problems of adjustment can be solved. Indeed, were it not for this capacity and for the fact that the unconscious urges are always striving for expression, psychiatric treatment would be impossible and there would be little possibility of progress or improvement for anyone.

We have emphasized the importance of adequate therapy for the sick child, rather than letting the disease take its course, because we believe that sick children usually do not grow out of their sicknesses, that although they may grow out of one symptom complex into another, they may do so without actually growing up. We realize that our treatment methods at best are not as efficient as we could wish and that in many cases they seem to fall lamentably short of their goal, but they are the best we have at present. Only by use can they be made still more competent and efficient and perhaps less time-consuming.

We have mentioned in another connection one point that has to be observed carefully in the treatment of every child and adult. The capacity of the ego to change is an asset in treatment, but at the same time it is a liability. Its tendency is to try to use methods with which it is familiar; for example, the ego very often uses repression. Now in treatment the patient's ego may make use of this mechanism instead of finding a real solution for a difficulty. The therapist may be fooled by the repression into thinking that the patient is better whereas he is only less aware of his problem. Similarly the therapist may feel the naughty child has improved when he has stopped his naughtiness whereas he may only be developing a reaction formation against it.

The therapist also may depend too much on the patient's will as a mechanism for growing up. Often a child will suddenly state that he feels he does not need any more treatment and that he is going to stop. If the therapist is fooled by this behavior and regards it as a sign that the child feels capable of independence and is more grown up he may allow the child to set a termination for treatment. By looking carefuly, however, he may find that the child is about to bring a difficult part of his problem into treatment but that his ego shrinks from the task and suddenly determines to avoid thinking about or discussing it. The child would therefore leave treatment with his problems unsolved and perhaps more convinced than ever of the efficacy of his obstinate will power. By continuing treatment the therapist could gradually accustom the child to think and talk about his real problems and so learn to solve them. It is this preference of the ego to use well-tried techniques, rather than to learn new ones, that furnishes one of the greatest barriers to the success of treatment and that is responsible for its taking so much time. And the tendency becomes more marked the longer the problem exists, being most evident in persons past middle age who often can receive little real benefit from psychotherapy.

As a result of the experience both of many psychiatrists and of ourselves as well, we have come to believe that every neurosis in childhood is a serious condition and that the situation should be studied carefully by a competent child psychiatrist who can decide what type of therapy is most suitable for the individual case. If such a study were done in all cases and if the treatment were actually carried out, there would be a noticeable diminution in the number of breakdowns that occur in adult life.

ANXIETY STATES

During the height of the Christmas-shopping season it is common to see a small child standing in a department store among a group of adults, crying bitterly or perhaps screaming, with his face contorted by an expression of grief and terror, and inconsolable despite all the efforts of the adults to make him feel more comfortable. He is lost. If he is observed carefully it is found that his expression of terror mirrors the state of his feelings. He is really very frightened. He is restless and trembles. Both his pulse and his respiration are increased in frequency. He feels hot and cold alternately. He sweats profusely. If he is offered food he refuses it because he has no appetite. He may complain of feeling nauseated or actually may vomit. He may wet or soil himself or if he is old enough to control these activities he will suffer from diarrhea or frequency if the lost situation continues. If he should fall asleep through exhaustion his sleep will be restless, wakeful, and filled with frightening dreams.

A similar problem, though perhaps not quite so dramatic, is seen in the older child who has arrived for the first time at camp. He cries a little (usually with deep sobs that shake his body), stays by himself, has no appetite, may have diarrhea or urinary frequency, and sleeps restlessly the first night. When he is asked to describe how he feels he states that he feels afraid and wants to go home. Any adult who has been by himself in a strange city can verify introspectively the unpleasantness of this feeling.

Both of these children feel frightened in a strange, unfamiliar world. The feeling is one all children have when they are separated from the persons they love. It is very painful and upsets the child greatly. The fact has been particularly emphasized by the studies of the children who were evacuated from London before the blitz. It was plainly evident that the children were psychically more harmed by the separation from their parents than they could have been by the sights and sounds of the blitz.

A similar painful feeling that upsets the small child greatly is seen when the mother goes out to work. The child, even though placed in a good day-care center, becomes very frightened and many phases of his development and adjustment become upset. The following case is another good illustration of the same reaction. A father had decided to enlist in the armed services. He talked the matter over with his wife secretly lest his seven-year-old daughter be upset by the news that he was going away. Shortly after he had told his wife the date when he would leave, his daughter came home from school in the middle of the afternoon very frightened. She verbally attributed her panic to the fact that the teacher had scolded another child. Her sleep that night was fitful and broken by frightening dreams. The next day she refused to return to school and became nauseated and vomited when the parents tried to insist that she go. Although the parents thought they had discussed the matter secretly she had overheard and had become frightened by the knowledge that her adored father was going to leave her. Since she had learned a secret which she was not supposed to know she could not tell her parents why she was so frightened and therefore was not able to find relief by discussing the whole matter with them. (This case again emphasizes the concept we have tried to make clear in this whole book. It is better for children to know and to discuss their knowledge fully with their parents than for the parents to try to protect them from the knowledge of unpleasant facts.)

The feeling these children have is one of anxiety. The *feeling* is the same as the feeling of fear and is accompanied by the same bodily changes: trembling, restlessness, an increase in the rate of the pulse and respiration, alternating hot and cold sweating, loss of appetite, nausea, diarrhea, urinary frequency, and sleep which is fitful and broken by frightening dreams. (Sometimes these dreams become so frightening that the child begins to refuse to go to bed or if made to do so will dread falling asleep lest he have horrible dreams.) This reaction occurs when an individual believes himself to be in danger, either in a real danger or in danger of doing something or of wanting to do something for which he believes he will be punished either by physical pain or by the loss of love. In what real danger is the child lost in the department store, the child during the first day at camp, the child sent from London to the country, or the little girl whose father is going away? In all these cases the child is being separated from the person he loves and on whom he is dependent. He knows that he needs food, shelter, comfort, and love and he is accustomed to get them from his parents. In some cases, as in the case of the little girl, he desires the love of one parent much more than that of the other. These needs cannot be satisfied except by another person. He becomes afraid that if he is separated from this person his needs will remain unsatisfied and he will be uncomfortable, miserable, and perhaps die.

It is interesting that the child usually blames himself for the separation regardless of its real cause. He has done something or wanted to do something that is forbidden and now his feelings of loneliness because he is separated from his parents are his punishment. It is our constant experience that when a child is placed in a foster home because of the sudden death of his parents he denies that this is the cause. Instead he feels that he is being punished for some offense, perhaps as trifling as taking a piece of candy at a time when he was supposed not to. From this point on every desire for gratification will be regarded by him as something forbidden and dangerous and its presence will appear in his consciousness as a feeling of anxiety. It is the burnt child who fears the fire. These acute anxiety attacks.

then, are a signal that the inner desires and needs of the individual are in danger of not being gratified because their gratification is impossible owing to the environmental circumstances or because the person believes that if he tries to gratify them he will be punished. The purpose of the attack—that is, of the feeling of anxiety —is to warn the individual that he is in danger from his need to satisfy his inner desires.

Why is there such a danger? In the cases we have cited the danger lies in the fact that the child has been or is about to be separated from the person whom he loves and whose love he craves. He reacts to his feeling of anxiety by crying in order to bring the loved person back. If crying does not work he may attempt to cling to the loved person, as the child did who refused to return to school. If clinging is not effective he must find new love objects. He can do so if the separation that produces the anxiety is not permanent. If it is, then he must first undertake a period of mourning, whose purpose is to detach the bonds of love from the person from whom he has been separated. All these activities remove the painful feeling of anxiety.

Anxiety will arise, also, if the child wishes to do something or does something for which he believes the person whom he loves and from whom he desires love will punish him, either by inflicting physical pain or injury or by ceasing to love him. During childhood the child has many desires and impulses which he cannot be allowed to gratify in the way he wishes because such forms of gratification would be harmful to him and to his family, or would conflict too much with the culture in which he lives. Consequently children have frequent feelings of anxiety until they learn ways of gratifying their impulses which will be less dangerous and more cultural.

Naturally anxiety arises as a result of the oedipus situation. The little boy fears to love his mother lest he become torn by his feelings of jealousy and hatred for his father as against his love for the father and his need for the father's protection and favors. We have mentioned earlier with what frequency the child attempts to deal with this anxiety by developing a phobia. The anxiety engendered by this conflict is increased if there are real marital difficulties between the parents. For example, it would really be very painful if the little girl of divorced parents who is living with her mother should express her passionate devotion to her father. The mother, who may have been ill-treated by the father, would be very likely to become extremely angry at the child.

Even when the parents really love the child and are reasonable in the cultural demands that they place on him, the child will have frequent feelings of anxiety. If the parent is overstrict and demands that the child conform to too high a standard or if the parent rejects the child, the latter has a constant feeling of anxiety lest he do something that will snap the tenuous bond he feels with his love object. In these instances the anxiety results from the intrapsychic conflict—the natural need to gratify childish impulses and the fear that if he gratifies them he will lose the parents' love. This cause of anxiety is well illustrated in the case of a girl of twelve whose mother regarded any form of pleasure—dancing, movies, parties, association with boys, association with other girls, games, sports, or the like— as wicked and threatened to punish her or to expel her from her home if she engaged in them. Any time this child felt the desire to join with her companions in any of these activities she immediately became very anxious and frightened. In this case the anxiety was heightened by the fact that the mother actually did not love the daughter. She preferred the son, who was younger, and the girl had always to give in to him and go out of her way to see that he got the best of everything. If she did not do so her mother expressed extreme disapproval.

Anxiety feelings are increased if there is a long absence of one parent or the other or if the parents have been too restrictive or too indulgent. They arise, also, if the instruments for the expression of inner desires are incapacitated or if the child fears he will be punished if he uses them. If the small baby cannot suck his fingers because his hands are tied or because he is afraid they will be cut off if he does so, he cannot gratify the desire for nonnutritive sucking. The ungratified desire appears to him to be a very dangerous impulse and he reacts to its presence by anxiety. In fact his tendency is to try not to be aware of the impulse and to feel only anxiety if the impulse stirs. Since the impulse may be active all the time, he may be anxious constantly; we say he is jittery. The impulse may stir only at certain times and we say the child has acute anxiety attacks. Often these attacks occur at bedtime or when the child is asleep. If we observe a small child who of his own accord is in the process of relinquishing his finger sucking we find that he abstains all day but as he becomes fatigued puts his fingers in his mouth. Later he may abstain from sucking his fingers even though he is very tired, but may suck them as he falls asleep or in his sleep. The reason is that the control exerted voluntarily by his ego becomes weak as his ego becomes fatigued and to some extent is absent during sleep. Hence acute anxiety attacks are more likely to occur when the child is fatigued or asleep, although they may occur during the waking hours.

Acute attacks during sleep are known familiarly as nightmares or night terrors. We have used the example of finger sucking in the foregoing discussion. Anxiety attacks do occur because of finger sucking, as they may because of any other inner impulse whose expression is frustrated. (When the frustrated impulse is an aggressive one the feeling of anxiety takes a particular form which we describe as a feeling of guilt.) However, because the cultural restrictions in American society fall heaviest on expressions of childish sexuality, the most common source of this type of anxiety is some interference with masturbation. When a child has been severely punished for masturbating or has been frightened by the threat of what may happen to him if he masturbates, he will try to stop the masturbation. He may succeed in doing so during the day, but again when he becomes fatigued at bedtime or while he is asleep the impulse tends to get out of control. He is so frightened, however, that he cannot permit himself the gratification and struggles to remain awake or awakens himself from his sleep with a frightening dream, and thus endeavors to be sure he does not touch his penis. The content of the dream is almost invariably the repetition of the masturbation threat. He dreams that a ghost with a sharp knife is chasing him. The ghost is really his mother in her white nightgrown and the knife is the result of the threat that if he masturbates she will cut off his penis. The dream does not gratify the wish to masturbate but gratifies the punitive conscience and stops the masturbation.

Anxiety attacks occur often to adults when an active sex life has been interrupted for external reasons. Widowers and widows are prone to suffer from them, as are also married couples whom circumstances separate and whose morals forbid either extramarital relations or masturbation. Adolescents who stop masturbating either because of fears or because they are in love and feel masturbation is childish suffer similar attacks.

What is the result of an anxiety attack? This question would be more correct if put thus: What is the fate of the inner impulse that threatens to carry the child into behavior which he believes might cause injury or loss of love? or: What is the fate of the inner impulses of the child who really has been threatened with or exposed to loss of love? There has been a frustration and because of it the inner impulse cannot obtain gratification. The feeling of anxiety is painful, so the individual's aggressive activity is called into action. The aggression may be used to remove the frustration. The child may go ahead and obtain his gratification regardless of its cost or he may attempt to force the loved person to stay with him. If neither is possible or advisable the aggression may act by causing the child to change the method of gratification from the more primitive type (which would cause him to lose love) to a more mature type through which he can obtain gratification and retain the love of his love object at the same time. If a child is angry at his father he does not need to express his anger by killing or injuring him. These would be primitive methods of gratification and would result in the actual loss of the father and his love. Instead he can tell his father that he feels angry with him, and why. In this way he can express his anger and yet retain his father's love. The child gives up his finger sucking—a primitive method of obtaining gratification —because he wants to be grown up and to act like his father who does not suck his fingers. He begins to masturbate—a more mature method of obtaining gratification. He gives up his gratification from playing with his excretions (a primitive method) and gets gratification from playing with mud pies (a more mature method). The aggression may act by causing the child to find another love. (The child at camp becomes acquainted with the counselors, finds they are friendly, and his homesickness stops.)

If the aggression cannot direct the individual into activities that will remove the anxiety he tends to return to earlier forms of gratification. If his masturbation is too dangerous and he has to stop it he then begins again to suck his fingers or to wet the bed—both of which are more infantile ways of getting gratification than masturbation is. They are, of course, neurotic manifestations and consist in the return of the repressed. All neuroses start with some frustration which produces a state of anxiety. In short, all neuroses start with an anxiety attack.

So far we have stressed the fact that anxiety is a painful warning that the individual is in danger and that because of the pain he is forced to do something about the danger. A child has a very frightening dream and wakes in terror. He starts to cry and his mother comes and comforts him. Since he seems so frightened and clings so to her she decides to lie in his bed till he falls asleep. The next night the same thing happens. After this has been repeated several nights he again wakes in *terror* from a *frightening* dream. He *cries* for his mother and she gets into bed with him. Now the whole tenor of the experience has subtly changed. He knows that if he *wakes in terror* from a *frightening* dream his mother will sleep with him. This is very pleasant and comfortable and accomplishes his wish to possess her and to take her away from his father. He can well afford to suffer the *real* pain of the anxiety attacks in order to secure the secondary pleasure it brings him. The anxiety attack is no longer a warning signal; it is an end in itself. It has the dual purpose of gratifying an inner and partly forbidden wish (to possess his mother and separate her from his father) and imposing a punishment because the wish is forbidden (the pain of the anxiety). From a warning signal the anxiety attack has now become a neurotic symptom. This change can happen if the original dream which was so frightening was an incestuous one. The inner impulse (desire to possess mother) about which he was so frightened has become transformed into a gratifying experience about which he feels guilty. If such a situation continues the child soon learns to avoid paying attention to the attack as a danger signal. Every time he has a feeling of anxiety, he disregards the underlying reasons for the anxiety and instead uses the pain of the feeling to gratify another but prohibited desire—in this case his wish to sleep with his mother.

Treatment for anxiety attacks, whether acute or chronic, diurnal or nocturnal, lies in helping the child to become conscious of the nature of the inner impulses and in helping him to find acceptable ways of gratifying them. Sedation is useless as a cure. It is silly to force the child to overcome his fear reaction to a particular situation —for example, to make the child who says he is afraid to go upstairs alone do so—when the real problem is his fear lest he be separated permanently from his mother. It is equally silly to waste a lot of breath explaining to the child that there is nothing upstairs to be afraid of. The first step must be to ascertain from the child the nature of the danger which he feels threatens him. Since often he is only partly conscious of its nature he may be able to state it only in a vague way. He may say that he is afraid someone will go away. Often he may be entirely unaware of its nature, in which case the answer will have to be ascertained by studying his behavior. For example, if he becomes panicky only when he watches traffic it is reasonable to surmise that he is afraid of separation. Such a surmise must be substantiated by a close scrutiny of the family situation: is there a marital problem which the parents are contemplating solving by separation or for which separation would be a good solution? In such a case the child is entitled to be upset.

In our opinion all anxiety attacks in children deserve close consideration and severe anxiety attacks call for diagnosis and intensive psychotherapy. The main techniques consist in methods by which the therapist can learn from the child what are the inner impulses for which he fears he will be punished, and then to give him opportunity to discuss them and act them out; thus the impulses no longer feel strange, dangerous, and alien to his ego.

We all know from experience that we are sometimes puzzled, worried, and anxious when we do not understand something and that the anxiety disappears when we begin to understand, either through our own efforts and observation or through conversation with someone who does understand and who can explain it to us. The situation no longer seems strange but becomes familiar. We are particularly apt to be thus anxious regarding our feelings. In technical language, we are worried and anxious as long as a situation or feeling is isolated from our ego. It is interesting that although we experience this phenomenon daily it is our habit to place taboos upon the discussion of certain feelings and factual situations, and consequently expose our children to anxiety and leave their egos isolated from certain everyday facts of life. In America these taboos fall heaviest on the phenomena of birth, death, physiological processes, anatomical details, and emotional reactions and feelings (particularly the emotions and feelings of adults). Through withholding a free discussion of these matters we keep the ego of the child weakened, and thus leave him anxious and apprehensive whenever he comes face to face with them. Do we do this because we ourselves wish to maintain a position of supremacy and because we fear that if we enlighten him we will then lose our authority over him?

All children feel anxiety more often than adults. They meet so many strange and new feelings and situations with which it takes time to be familiar; they often have desires which they cannot gratify because they are physiologically immature. In our experience, however, they develop severe anxiety attacks only when they are exposed to unreasonable and unnecessary emotional strains, that is, to experiences which we have already discussed as being traumatic.

DISORDERS OF THE ORAL FUNCTIONS

The disorders of oral function include two broad categories, namely disturbances of the function of eating and disorders of speech. The disturbances of the function of eating may be classified as follows:

1. Inhibitions:
    (*a*) Anorexia (lack of appetite).
    (*b*) Dysphagia (inability to swallow).
2. Symptoms:
    (*a*) Rejection of ingested foods—vomiting.
3. Perversions:
    (*a*) Finger sucking.
    (*b*) Nailbiting.
    (*c*) Pica, the ingestion of nonnutritive substances.
    (*d*) Overeating.

DISTURBANCE OF THE FUNCTION OF EATING—
CASE HISTORY AND GENERAL DISCUSSION

There are children whose presenting symptoms involve the function of the mouth and the upper part of the gastrointestinal tract. Anxiety, the result of an intrapsychic conflict, may produce disturbances of the functions of these parts; or the anxiety may be removed by converting the intrapsychic conflict into a disturbance of these functions. We know that such a conversion takes place but we are not sure how it is brought about. The following case is a good illustration of what we mean.

A seven-year-old girl was referred to the Child Psychiatric Clinic because she was very tense, easily upset, suffered from feelings of nausea without adequate cause, was excessively clean, and had few friends. She vomited whenever she saw someone blow his nose, heard someone clear his throat, heard any conversation that mentioned blood, pus, or the like, saw food not carefully arranged on a plate, or saw cooked cereal. Both parents felt nauseated in similar situations. The father was easily sickened if the children were too "messy" or if some distasteful subject was broached at the table. The patient was excessively clean about her person. She refused to indulge in any play activity that would soil her hands. For example, her mother bought her some modeling clay and a sandbox but she refused to use either, saying she disliked the sticky, dirty feeling on her hands. She would not go to the toilet alone because she could not bear to touch her genitals, and when she took a bath her mother had to wash them.

She reacted with a great deal of anxiety to the idea of going away from her mother. When she was asked if she would like to go to camp she cried hysterically as though her heart would break. She said there were lions and tigers in the woods, that the counselors were mean people who wouldn't let her play or do anything she wanted to do, that they would stuff her full of cooked cereal and that if her mother really loved her, she would not want to send her away. It was clear to her that her mother was only trying to get rid of her. She did go to camp; there she was very well mannered and neat in appearance but inclined to be selfish, pious, and very avid for adult approval. She was apt to draw adult attention to the faults of others, holding herself up as a good girl. She showed decided likes and dislikes, excelling in things that held her interest but hurrying over those that didn't (washing clothes, making beds). Her craftwork was good, original, and neat.

At school she made good grades and was well liked by the teachers. However, she had to miss fifty-five days of a school term because of illness—usually due to nausea and vomiting.

She was the oldest child, having a sister of three years and a brother of ten months. In the interval between her birth and that of her sister, she had a rather close relationship with the mother. They were able to do things together, such as going through Woolworth's (which the patient dearly loved) or to the movies. In that interval, too, the family was in good circumstances financially. Her sister's birth came at a time when the family was suffering serious financial difficulties, and with the birth of the baby the mother no longer had the time to go places with her.

Both parents were intelligent, though not highly educated. The mother mentioned that when she was a child she felt the same as the patient did. For example, when she was only eight years old she was given the task of taking her father's lunch to him. He worked downtown and she had to take a long trolley ride. This made her feel a little carsick. She had to get off in front of a dentist's show window in which false teeth were displayed. This made her feel very ill, and she still continued to feel nausea at the sight of false teeth. When the mother mentioned something "dirty" that the younger children had done—as, when either displayed an interest in or desire to play with urine or feces—her tone of voice often expressed shock and revulsion. She disliked having the children play in water or with dirt and sand. She was obviously under severe emotional tension which seemed to be directly related to the fact that the family lived in a tiny three-room apartment. The father was supposed to go to bed at about four o'clock in the afternoon, which was impossible because the children kept waking him up. He would become furious and shout at both the mother and the children. The mother in turn would shout at him and the children, and then the children would shout at each other. Both parents said it was like a madhouse. The patient hated to come home from school and would dash out as quickly as she could. She was ashamed to bring other children home to play. The mother gave the patient little, if any, opportunity to participate in conversation. She seemed to expect the patient to keep still for unusually long periods while she engaged in rather long conversations on purely adult topics, and would become quite angry if the patient broke into the conversation.

The father's father was a strict, rigid person who did not allow his children to have any friends or to bring other youngsters home, even after they were in their teens. His mother was a submissive type, always attempting to shield her son from his father's harsh discipline. The only other child was a sister, who married and had children, but had periods of mental illness. The grandfather did not approve of the marriage of either of his children. The father had difficulty meeting strange people. He was a hard worker and very conscientious, but had no initiative or aggressiveness to help him get better-paid jobs. Before his marriage he did quite a lot of drinking. The mother had a tremendous amount of feeling about drinking because during her childhood there had been a great deal of friction because her father was a heavy drinker and abusive. So she stormed, nagged, or was coldly frigid when her husband drank, as though it were the most awful thing that could happen. There were many scenes and hysterical outbursts, which affected all three children, especially the patient.

The patient was a nine-month baby and was born after a labor of about an hour. She was bottle-fed till nine months, walked at fourteen months, talked at eleven months, was trained both for bladder and bowels at seven months, and got her first tooth at nine months. Because she had many sore throats she had her tonsils and adenoids removed at the age of five.

Her physical examination was negative, though for an entire year subsequent to it she had colds and a persistent cough.

Her psychological examination showed a C.A. of seven years, four months, an M.A. of eight years, ten months, and an I.Q. of 120.

This child was attempting to restrict, inhibit, and control her behavior in order to avoid feelings of anxiety and guilt. These restrictions and inhibitions made her behavior different from the usual behavior of children of her age and sex. Her behavior, however, did not bring any realization that she was different from other children or any feelings of pain and discomfort because of the difference. She regarded even her nausea as being correct behavior and not an illness. She therefore did not suffer from a neurotic illness but from a disturbance in her personality. This disturbance was partly of a hysterical and partly of an obsessional type. She was diagnosed as having a neurotic personality because of her necessity to avoid the suffering caused by feelings of guilt and anxiety. She made a virtue out of this necessity because through it she gained approval from her mother which she would otherwise forfeit. In brief, she altered her personality in order to avoid feelings of guilt and anxiety and then avoided any recognition of the resultant real suffering by finding satisfaction through her limiting personality reactions.

At this point, she saw herself as well and other people as sick. This mechanism made her feel that she had no need for treatment; this attitude made a difficult treatment problem which was increased by the fact that her parents did not regard her as neurotic but as virtuous and commendable. It is this type of case that for years goes untreated because adults often do not regard as ill the child who is shy, seclusive, good, overly conforming, and who needs constantly to please.

Such children are really very ill. A report from a teacher that John is a very good boy because his behavior and deportment are *excellent* may be regarded by both the teacher and parents as a sign that John is getting along well; but it is really a sign that John is a sick boy. The report and the praise he gets from the report satisfy him, however, and he gets pleasure where it would be better if he experienced pain. Perhaps only when such a person grows older and comes to realize that his character prevents his having a satisfactory adult life does he see that his deprivations and sufferings are the result of his own differences from other people.

What is the psychopathology of the girl? She shows certain definite groups of symptoms:

She is overfastidious in respect to cleanliness. So great is this overfastidiousness that it interferes with her recreational and social life, and has even reached the point where she is so disgusted as actually to feel nauseated with anything that verges on her idea of uncleanliness.

She is overconscientious to the degree of priggishness. Her main aim in life is to get adult approval at all times.

She shows marked anxiety at leaving her mother and is afraid consciously that strange adults will treat her cruelly.

She has learned that these pathological reactions have a value in her life. By her overcleanliness and nauseated disgust she can avoid doing things she does not want to do and still be certain of being thought an obedient and not a disobedient girl. Through these and through her priggishness she can demand that her mother and other adults allow her to have her own way. This use of her symptoms to gain control of situations is a secondary reaction and does not necessarily have much to do with the formation of her original behavior. We think it can be seen quite clearly that her symptoms are an attempt to avoid feelings of anxiety and guilt. If she stays with her mother she has no opportunity to feel anxious, while if she is away from her, she suffers from anxious feelings and frightening ideas. Her behavior about going to camp is an indication of her underlying problem. If she is good in school and to adults to the point of priggishness then they will keep her with them and not send her away. That is, her priggishness is an attempt to avoid the feeling that if she behaves like other children, all adults and particularly her parents won't like her. If she is overclean and overdisgusted with uncleanliness then adults and particularly her parents will approve of her and not send her away.

The girl's problem lies in a great feeling of anxiety lest she be disapproved of and sent away. We know from the history that her present behavior is one of which the mother approves and that the mother would disapprove of any other kind. We see no evidence that the mother's disapproval would cause her to expel the child from home, and even if she did, this intelligent little girl knows that she would be looked after and that civilized America is not filled with cruel humans and wild beasts. Why, then, does she have this fear? Taking first the fear-filled imaginings about camp, we see that they are concretized fears of bodily injury—being eaten and torn by wild beasts and mistreated by counselors. She fears, without reasonable basis, that bodily injuries will be done to her.

The mechanism is similar to that of a phobia. The child fears the phobic animal lest it do to him what he would like to do to the person whom the phobic animal represents. The girl is afraid that if she is away from her parents, she will act like a wild animal and tear and devour other people—probably children. Since the recipient of the aggression is probably a child, it is necessary to see what child. Since she knows none of the children at camp, it must be a child or children that she knows well, that is, a member of her own family. When we examine her behavior toward her younger sister and brother, we see that it is unnaturally good and kind and that there are no apparent signs of the anticipated sibling rivalry—which exists in all children, as Levy conclusively proved experimentally. Therefore we can conclude that she has felt at least the ordinary amount of jealousy and hostility toward them but has suppressed the expression of it and also repressed the knowledge of it from herself. Being repressed, the aggressive activity developed and grew, until to her mind it appeared frightening and dangerous and took on an importance that it really does not possess. Suppression of the expression and repression of the impulse does not get rid of the impulse; it only places it outside of the conscious control of the individual and so makes it a dangerous enemy instead of a useful servant.

But this child's hostile feelings are not all directed toward her siblings. Her overcleanliness indicates that she is trying to please the mother; it therefore covers a fear, the fear of a wish to disobey the mother and be dirty. The history shows that the mother toilet-trained the child early and overseverely. The child, resentful of the toilet training, acceded to the mother through fear of her displeasure and therefore repressed the resentment and hostility she felt toward her. This resentment, stored in the unconscious, attracts to itself all the other resentful feelings, which every little girl feels toward her mother—jealousy of the mother's relations with the father, of her ability to have a baby, of her more mature physical development, and the like. These other resentful feelings have had to be repressed because the first resentment was, but they serve to make the hostility greater and more to be feared by the child. In order to avoid any possibility of the resentment breaking through, the child agrees to alter her life and avoid all ventures which in her mind would be connected with hostile feelings.

The problem, therefore, in this case will be the treatment of the fear of her own hostile feelings so that she can use her aggression successfully in her life. As we stated above, there are two levels of this child's illness: the primary and deepest is her fear of her own aggressive impulses; the secondary is the value that she had found in the use of her endeavors to repress the aggression. This secondary problem has become so great that she now sees her sick behavior as a virtue and has no feelings of anxiety or discomfort about it. The first step in treatment, therefore, will be to convince her that her behavior is not virtuous but pathological. This may have to be done partly by the therapist, but is accomplished more successfully if the parents can be induced to co-operate and to look upon her over-cleanliness, her priggishness, her nausea, and her overconformity as pathological symptoms. They could help a great deal by refraining from praise of these acts or sympathy with them and by pointing out that they are symptoms of her illness and that she need not be so different from other people.

In this particular case the parental role was performed success-fully. The mother not only refrained from praising the child's symp-tomatic behavior but encouraged her to have fun being dirty, etc. (In some cases of the sort this seems to be enough, and after a year or so of experiencing the treatment the child loses his anxiety and is able to behave in a normal manner about his cleanliness and aggressiveness.)

The task of the therapist will be to encourage her to get pleasure from playing with dirty things—water, mud, clay, paints, and the like—and from acting out in play her aggressive feelings, that is her hostilities, resentments, etc. Meanwhile, she will be encouraged to express verbally her feelings toward her siblings, her mother, and her father, and the nature of the fears she has about such verbal expression will have to be ascertained and relieved. This is an over-simplified description of what might occur during therapy. In our opinion a child as sick as this child was should be psychoanalyzed. An analysis would necessitate her being seen three to five times a week by a psychoanalyst who specializes in the treatment of children.

This case illustrates one type of neurotic interference with the function of eating. There are a number of other types. Emotional disturbances of the function of any organ follow several patterns. If the use of the organ is regarded by the psyche as dangerous (it makes no difference whether the individual is aware of this dread or whether it is unconscious, but difficulties are more likely to follow if the latter is the case), then the individual will try not to use the organ (that is, he will use the mechanism of inhibition) or else will use the organ in a way opposite to its usual use, or else the use of the organ will be accompanied by pain and discomfort (this is the mechanism of symptom formation). If the function of one organ is inhibited because of the dread of using it, the desires that cause it to function may be displaced from that organ to another. There these desires are added to those that usually cause the second organ to function; thus the latter is used for purposes that ordinarily are accomplished better through the use of the proper organ (this is the mechanism of perversion).

ANOREXIA

We discussed many of the causes of anorexia in our discussion of feeding disturbances of the very young child. The same causes—improper preparation of food (food that is too hot or whose nature and consistency make it too difficult to eat), food that is unfamiliar to the child and that he is forced to eat suddenly, too much excitement at or just before meals, unpleasant experiences at mealtime, feelings of insecurity either because of separation from the parents (homesickness) or because of parental quarrels, hunger strikes which are reactions of rage against what the child regards as unjustifiable demands on the part of his parents—may result in loss of appetite during the genital and latent periods. To these, too, may be added reactions of disgust which take away the child's appetite. These reactions may be caused by ideas about the person who prepares the food or by ideas about the food itself. Years ago Ferenczi reported the case of a boy who suddenly developed a loss of appetite for his breakfast. Just before the symptoms began he had been told by his playmates that his parents performed sexual intercourse. The boy steadfastly denied this was so, but coming down to breakfast a day or so later he thought suddenly, "My mother prepared this food with her hands; with the same hands, she did 'dirty' things with my father last night." He felt disgusted and suddenly had no appetite.

Loss of appetite because of disgust with ideas connected with the food itself is universally experienced. This is the basis for many food fads—which are particularly common among children and which seem to develop without any reasonable basis—and for many cases of anorexia in small children. Pediatric experience testifies that no child reaches the age of seven years without having had some feeding problem and this universality of feeding problems is caused partly by disgust with ideas about food. If the reader has had the enlightening experience of dining with nursery-school children he will readily understand how these ideas arise. The children compare quite freely and without any feelings of disgust or shame the various articles of food to human beings and animals, parts of human and animal bodies, and human or animal excretions. However, as they get a little older and are being forced through cultural restrictions to adopt an antagonistic attitude instead of a predilection for cannibalistic and excretory interests, they have to develop feelings of disgust and shame toward these activities. These are displaced onto the article of food which had been associated in this way in their minds.

A simple example is seen in the varying attitudes of many adults and children toward drinking milk. Some cannot drink it at all. Others can drink it if it is cold but dislike it warm. Some can drink warm milk but not milk fresh from the cow. Others can drink it straight from the cow's teat. Some can drink human milk. The drinking of milk warm from the mother's breast is the greatest joy of the tiny infant, and it signifies a very special relationship with the mother and her breast. All of these attitudes except the last show varying degrees of repudiation of the joy of the infant and his relationship with the mother. The greater the disgust with the drinking of milk, the more the original joy in it and the relationship with the mother have been, the greater is the effort going on all the time to keep the memory of the period of infancy repressed. Anorexia of this type is not very important because it usually involves only certain foods and may not be permanent.

The treatment of all these types of anorexia is really comparatively simple. Find the cause, remove it, and give the child a little time to readjust himself to the changed situation. Every child has natural hunger which arises as a result of metabolic processes and which will reassert itself as soon as the inhibiting circumstances are removed. In the case of anorexia due to the child's disgust with certain ideas he has associated with certain articles of food, complete ignoring of the child's idiosyncrasy is the only necessary treatment. Even if the idiosyncrasy persists throughout life there are so many other articles of food that can be substituted that it seems unnecessary to pay attention to the food fad. Furthermore there is no single article of food the ingestion of which is essential to life and health. Very often if the idiosyncrasy is ignored the food fad disappears after a period of time.

Pediatricians will laugh at our statement that the treatment of anorexia is so simple. Theoretically it should be just as simple and easy as we have stated; but practically in many instances such treatment is impossible because there are two parents in the family, and their attitude toward the child's anorexia (or any other feeding problem he may have) after it has started complicates the therapy greatly. In fact, the attitude of the parents toward the child's feeding in itself may produce anorexia.

We have had a number of children ten or more pounds overweight referred to us for anorexia. The parent (often the mother, although fathers are not innocent in this respect) wants a child as large or as heavy as her friends'; she feels it is necessary for a child to learn to eat a big meal and to finish everything on his plate at mealtimes; or she has some inner need or anxiety that can only be ameliorated by a child who eats abundantly. Such a mother conducts the child's feeding in the following manner: A breakfast ample even for an adult is placed before the child. He is encouraged to eat it. As he becomes satisfied and portions are not finished he is given more encouragement to continue. At last, after great effort, he reaches the point of satiation and cannot take any more. The mother then feeds him the remainder, cajoling or threatening him until he takes it. At this point the overfull stomach cannot contain all the food and the child regurgitates part of it. The parent then prepares another equally large breakfast and tries to get the child to consume it. In order to please her he tries but regurgitates again. Another breakfast is prepared and the same process is repeated. Lunch and dinner are conducted in a similar fashion, and often because of the outrageous length of time each of these meals consumes there is really only an infinitesimal interval between the three meals. The next day, the child, being stuffed, has lost appetite for his meals, and not many days pass before he has no appetite at all. He would be able to regain an appetite only if he were starved for a day or so, when his real metabolic needs would assert themselves.

We realize that such exaggerated parental behavior is not very common but modifications of it are common enough. As a general rule, human beings do not have the same degree of appetite for each meal during the day. Some are hungrier for breakfast, some for lunch, some for dinner, depending on the energy they have expended and their metabolic needs. As a simple example, a person is thirstier and drinks more liquids on a hot day or during the hot portion of a day than at other times because the heat promotes loss of water from the body. Although parents may govern their intake of food according to their own needs, that is, their own hunger, they often forget that the child tends to do the same thing and they try to induce or force the child to devour three big meals every day instead of allowing him to eat as much as he wants at a given time. (Of course it goes without saying that the child should not be permitted to stuff himself between meals because he will then have no more hunger for his regular meals than a woman has for dinner who has spent the afternoon stuffing herself with nuts and candies while playing bridge.)

Often parents feel that certain specific articles, not varieties, of foods are necessary for the child and insist that he eat them. We believe that there are more superstitions about beneficial and harmful varieties of foods (that is, food fads) among civilized human beings than about anything else in life, with the possible exception of excretory habits. The child should eat spinach, he should eat rhubarb, he should avoid sugar, he needs green vegetables, fish will develop the brain, carrots are good for the hair, and so on ad infinitum. Any scientific basis for these ideas is at best tenuous. They take no account of the scientific fact that they are prevalent only in America and that other cultures have equally healthy people who have been raised by the application of entirely different sets of ideas.

We talk much about certain persons having a sweet tooth, others liking fruit, or meat, or cheese, but we seldom stop to think what these observations mean scientifically. A decrease in the chemical constituents (which are the fuel to produce energy) of the body is felt in consciousness as a sensation of hunger. If the decrease is in the amount of water we call the specific hunger "thirst." Similarly the general sensation of hunger is composed of more specific ones. If the amount of sugar necessary for the metabolism is decreased, a hunger for sugar develops; and so it goes with fats, proteins, salt, calcium (this is the basis for earth and chalk eating among certain children), vitamins, and the like. The individual may be aware of the need for the specific substance he requires; he may be able to say, "I feel hungry for a piece of meat." He may not be aware of the specific hunger. Instead he has a feeling of hunger and when he sits down to eat he selects certain types of food in preference to others. In fact, if the meal were composed solely of that type of food he would rise at the end of the meal feeling quite satisfied. The next meal he might not want any of that particular type of food at all. People differ from each other in their specific chemical needs. Some need (desire) sugar, some proteins, some fats. In the words of the well-known saying, "One man's meat is another man's poison." People differ also in their specific chemical needs from day to day. These needs, if they appear at all in consciousness, usually appear only as vaguely felt desires, and the feeling about them can be expressed verbally only with great difficulty.

If the body of an individual knows more about his real needs than does his conscious ego, how much more must the body of the child know about his real needs than does the conscious ego of his parent? The parent's attempt to dictate to the child what his bodily needs are distorts the ancient saying "Mother knows best" into a caricature far beyond the domain of reality. Several years ago Davis conducted a series of experiments with year-old babies. Each baby was given a tray with a large number of different varieties of food. The amount of each food was carefully weighed first. Then the baby was allowed to eat what he liked. After the meal the remaining portions of food were weighed again. For one day one child ate only bananas, another only meat, but when the results were estimated at the end of a year it was found each child had eaten a perfectly balanced diet. Gastrointestinal disturbances were fewer and gains in weight and height larger in the experimental group than in the control group.

From this discussion it is plain that parents do not need to be so concerned about the feeding of the child. It is the parents' duty to see that they provide three properly balanced, well-prepared, and attractively served meals a day, that the child does not have access to too much food between meals, and then to leave the child to do with the food what his hunger dictates. They can rely on the chemical needs of the child's body to govern the amount and variety of food ingested. Of course, if they themselves have many food idiosyncrasies which they mention constantly, they cannot expect the child to be even as free from food fads as the ordinary child, because an imitation of the parents in everything is an essential technique of the child's development. If besides offering the proper types of food they also see that mealtime is *not* the time or place for scolding or punishing the child for his behavior during the day, or for reprimands concerning his manners, or for the airing of parental quarrels, they can be sure that the child will not develop anorexia, except for the mild and specific anorexias about certain articles of food such as we mentioned above.

If they will adopt the same attitude when a feeding problem has developed or can learn from the physician to adopt this attitude as a means of treatment, the treatment of the anorexia will be quite easy. Some parents are afraid that if such a plan is carried out the child may go on a hunger strike and injure his health seriously or die of starvation. It may be that for the first few days in the treatment of anorexia, particularly if the parents have paid a great deal of attention to the child because of the feeding problem, the child will not eat at all, in the hope that he can coax back the attention that was so gratifying to him. However, if the parents will wait patiently the child's hunger for food will overcome his hopes of getting attention through not eating and he will begin to eat. He will never abstain from food long enough to hurt himself. (Such abstention only occurs in adolescent girls, who may commit suicide through starvation—a condition technically known as *anorexia nervosa*.)

The first step in the therapy of anorexia is the removal of the secondary gain, that is, the extra and gratifying attention the child has been receiving from his parents because of his lack of appetite. The institution of this step often reduces the degree of anorexia markedly and quickly (within two or three weeks). The second step is to ascertain the original cause of the anorexia and then to remove it. If it is due to parental unhappiness, steps must be taken to help the parents, either to a better adjustment with each other or to separation. If it is due to adverse parental attitudes these must be treated or the child removed from the home. If it is due to resentment by the child because the parents have demanded that he become more cultured, as we discussed in the chapter on illnesses arising in the anal period, his training may temporarily be allowed to lapse or at least be made less rigid. If it is due to such disgust with the person who prepares the meals as occurred in Ferenczi's case, the child must be helped to come to terms with the facts of sexuality. (This help is perhaps better given by a professional person than by the parents.) If it is the result of disgust with certain articles of food, then the physician has to decide whether he feels that the repudiation of these foods is a serious enough problem to warrant intensive psychiatric treatment for the child, since only in this way can this type of disgust be remedied.

A really serious situation may arise if the child for reasons of health—allergies, diabetes, or other sickness—has to be on a special diet that excludes certain articles of diet which he likes or which the body craves. The same problem faces the adult with a similar illness but the adult has greater ability to submit to deprivations than does the child, particularly the young child, who is governed more by the pleasure than by the reality principle. The child is bound to feel unhappy and resentful under these restrictions. He should not be scolded or punished for his resentment but should be helped to recognize that the parents understand how he feels about the situation. As much as possible he should be protected from seeing too many other people enjoying the foods he cannot have. This protection does not need to be carried to absurd lengths (for example, no member of the family eating any of the proscribed foods), but he should not be tantalized too much; and if it is at all practical the dietary restrictions should occasionally be relaxed. Finally, the physician should not prescribe too many restrictions at once. It is better that the child's health suffer a little than that his emotional development be traumatized too suddenly.

DYSPHAGIA

The refusal to take food into the body, the refusal to swallow food (for either conscious or unconscious reasons, that is, whether the child says he will not swallow it or cannot swallow it), is known technically as dysphagia. It may involve all foods or only certain articles of food. The inability may be complete or there may be only a difficulty in swallowing. Daily speech has translated this refusal to swallow food into psychological terms. We often say we cannot swallow some statement that we are unwilling to believe or that we repudiate. It is as easy under certain conditions to translate such a metaphor back into physiological terms and to be unable to swallow some food that reminds us of something we wish to repudiate psychologically.

Young children will frequently hold food in their mouths for a long time because they have an aversion to swallowing it and yet want to please their parents and eat it. This behavior usually results from the same situation we mentioned under anorexia, namely the child's disgust with the association he has made between the food and some other disgusting object. Another reason for the refusal to swallow certain articles of food or perhaps nearly all foods is jealousy of a new baby. The older child notices that the newcomer does not eat the same kinds of food he does but is given milk only. He wishes he were the new baby and then proceeds to try to act like him. He cannot eat any food but milk, and if other types of food are forcibly placed in his mouth he spits them out because he feels he can't swallow them.

Occasionally a child will refuse to swallow because of a more traumatic situation. We refer to the case we reported in *Common Neuroses of Children and Adults*. A child of six had a severe feeding disturbance. Although perhaps complaining bitterly of hunger she would sit and stare at her meal tray and then suddenly overturn it on the floor. If an attempt was made to feed her, she would knock the spoon away, spilling its contents. If her hands were held and she was fed, she would spit the food out. It made no difference whether or not the food was that usually liked by children—candy, ice cream, cake, or the like. The behavior was fairly constant although through pressure and forcible feeding she was given sufficient nourishment to keep her from starving, but she lost many pounds in weight. This behavior started rather suddenly at the age of four and apparently without cause.

Study of the child revealed first that she equated her ideas of food with the bodies of her parents, more particularly her father's. Next she equated food specifically with her father's penis. Then was uncovered the following episode in her life. A day or so before the food difficulty began, her father, who was a chronic alcoholic, coming home drunk, locked himself and the little girl in his bedroom, removed her clothes and his own and attempted to assault her sexually. He tried first unsuccessfully to introduce his penis into her vagina. The attempt caused the child some bleeding and pain. Then he committed fellatio—introducing his penis into her mouth where he had an ejaculation. The child was sexually stimulated but also frightened and hurt. She wished the experience repeated, but at the same time recollected the pain, fear, and disgust she had felt. Almost at once she displaced all her reaction of desire, fear, disgust and pain to her oral zone and began to feel toward any object such as food—which she desired to introduce into her mouth—the other painful and disturbing emotional reactions. She refused to eat when she was hungry lest in gratifying her desire she again be frightened, hurt, and disgusted. This story was obtained from the child, and following its full discussion and the abreaction of the experience, her behavior toward food became normal. The story was corroborated in most of its details by the mother.

Vomiting attacks without organic cause are common in both children and adults. Their purpose is to get rid of something the individual finds unpleasant. In the case quoted earlier in this chapter the vomiting expressed unconscious feelings of rage against the mother because of the strict way she toilet-trained the child; in other words, the mother had annoyed and upset the child, now the child would vomit in order to annoy and upset the mother, for the child knew that any stomach illness is upsetting to a parent (as we mentioned in connection with the illnesses associated with the anal period) and that vomiting made her mother feel nauseated. These feelings of rage were largely unconscious, but children may regurgitate deliberately, being quite aware that they are doing so, to get back at their parents. Sometimes the child may even express himself verbally by saying, "If you don't let me do what I want then I will vomit and you'll be sorry."

The reader must remember that when a child shows this degree of spitefulness and rage his parents have treated him in a way that would make any human being revengeful. The child does punish himself for these rage reactions by feelings of illness, and the more unconscious he is of their presence the more nauseated and sick he feels when he vomits. These unpleasant feelings are his attempts to punish himself for daring to feel angry and spiteful against his parents.

VOMITING

Similarly vomiting may be an expression of disgust either with some person or with some of his own ideas about articles of food. The child is simply acting out what the adult expresses in words: "It makes me sick to think about it."

Another cause of vomiting is seen in small children of both sexes and in older girls. The mother is pregnant and has morning sickness. The child is intensely interested in the coming baby, is envious of the mother, and would like to have a baby herself. She identifies herself with the mother and develops attacks of vomiting. She may or may not be aware that her attacks represent in her mind her wish to be pregnant. If she is aware of the wish the vomiting is simply a regurgitation and is unaccompanied by nausea. It is as if she were playing she were the mother, and because she is only playing she need not suffer any criticism or pangs of guilt. (One of the functions of children's play is to permit them to pretend to do things that are forbidden without feeling any criticism from their superego, since what they are doing is only "play-pretend.") If the child is unaware of the wish, the vomiting will be accompanied by nausea, and she will seem anxious and disturbed. And if she has a gastric upset from an organic cause, the anxiety she feels will be even greater. She has wanted to be the mother and have all her privileges, to do all the things she does. She has concluded that the best way to do this is to get rid of the mother. Since she felt guilty about these wishes she tried not to think consciously about them; that is, she repressed the wishes. Now her conscience has started to trouble her about her wishes even though she has repressed them. It is as if her conscience said to her, "You are a wicked child. At one time you wished to be your dear mother. Now your wish can come true. You can be your mother—in her pain and misery." The nausea and the feeling of anxiety therefore arise as a punishment by the superego for the hostile wishes.

A similar mechanism, that is, an identification with the suffering parent as a punishment for hostile wishes against that parent, is seen frequently in the headaches and other minor illnesses of children. The father suffers from migraine for which he receives care and sympathy from his wife. The son starts to develop headaches also. These are real and painful but are neurotic symptoms and not migraine. We often recognize this unconsciously in our attitude toward the boy. We say, "Poor child, he is just *like* his father."

Another type of identification with a parent in illness occurs. A little boy is passionately in love with his mother who suffers from migraine headaches, at which times he is solicitous of her and does all he can to please. However, because his passionate devotion produces too severe feelings of fear and guilt due to his intrapsychic conflict about his feelings toward his father, he endeavors to rid himself of his love for his mother. This endeavor results in another conflict between his love for her and his desire to be rid of his feelings of love for her. Instead of solving the conflict by detaching his feeling of love from her and placing it onto another object—say an aunt or a teacher—he changes the character of his love. The earliest type of love relationship in human life is identification. "I love you. I want to be like you." The later type is object love. "I love you. I want to do things for you and please you so you will love me." The boy we are discussing reached the beginnings of the second type of love, but under the influence of his fear and guilt he cannot maintain the position but instead regresses to the first type. Now, instead of looking after and doing things for the mother when she has one of her headaches he also has a headache. In this way he accomplishes several purposes: he can get attention from her without having to feel guilty at disturbing her when she is ill or without feeling frightened about his relationship with the father; he is able to express his positive feelings for her without having to feel guilty about them, since he is saying that he wants only to be like her, not to possess her; he can remain babyish without having to suffer loss of pride, since he is ill.

This identification with the sick mother, however, starts to produce further conflicts. If he identifies with the mother in her headaches he has to identify also with her passive feminine attitude toward the father. This makes him helpless in any competitive situation with the father and later with other men in authority. His attitude toward authority will be one not of respect or admiration or a desire to imitate but rather of a flirtatious attempt to get the authoritative person to like him. Such an identification can easily become a passive feminine attitude toward men and lead to overt homosexuality.

From what we have said the reader can see how important it is to pay serious attention to the child who tends to have the same type of illness as his parents. It is not that the child takes after the parent —as is so commonly the opinion—but that subtle psychological changes are occurring in his personality as a means of solving some of the difficulties in the oedipus situation. If the changes are of a helpful nature they can be left alone. If not—and certainly identification with the parents' sickness can never be an adequate method of solving a life problem—the child should be studied by a child psychiatrist and treatment instituted if necessary. We hope we have made it clear that the purpose of intensive psychotherapy is not to cure the child of the symptoms—for example, the headache—but to correct the subtle intrapsychic changes, which will thus help him to a better solution of his problem.

We have mentioned the fact that the child is ambivalent. He is able to love and hate the same person at the same time. This ambivalence is seen readily in all his behavior and is expressed in all stages of his development. During the oral stage he will kiss the mother one moment and bite her the next. If he bites her very hard he may feel remorse. (When an adult does something for which he feels remorse he may say, with a shudder and a faint feeling of nausea, "I feel sick about what I have done.") In the child—and sometimes in adults as well—the remorse, instead of appearing as a psychic feeling, may be expressed organically in attacks of vomiting. He feels antagonistic—perhaps because he is envious—toward someone he loves. He wishes to hurt the person by depriving him of some of his possessions—usually of some part of his body. The child then begin to feel remorse about these antagonistic feelings and in order to relieve his feelings of remorse he tries to make restitution to the person whom he feels he has injured. If the process takes place in oral terms his actions are as follows: He feels envious and antagonistic. He would like to devour (that is, take away and keep for himself) the object of whose possession he is envious. He feels remorseful and in order to quiet his remorse he would like to spit out or vomit up what he has taken away and devoured.

It is not unusual for children to think in oral terms. During one treatment session a boy of nine enacted the following play: He was a savage and captured the physician. After the capture he played that he tied him to the stake, lit a fire under him and burned him to death. When the physician was properly roasted he ate him and thought that now he would be able to perform the magic the physician performed. Here the play stopped, but if he had become remorseful he would have had to spit out or vomit up the physician's body in order to return to the latter his magical powers. If the child's reaction to the adult is unconscious or if he quickly represses it, the repressed energy may reanimate old oral patterns. These re-animated patterns appear as symptoms; in other words, a regression has taken place—a common cause of periodic attacks of vomiting in many children. Since the whole process—even, often, the feeling of envy and hostility and remorse for that feeling—takes place below the level of consciousness, the child has no idea why he has the attack of vomiting.

We believe that children have attacks of vomiting as an expression of remorse for antagonistic desires more frequently than is generally believed. Sudden acute gastrointestinal upsets are much more common in childhood than in adult life and may be caused partly by the child's tendency to eat anything that attracts him (this cause is usually assigned, without any real investigation) and partly as a manifestation of allergy; but we believe that the psychological cause we have presented may be at least as common. This is a subject that justifies and needs further research.

The treatment of dysphagia and periodic vomiting in children must follow the same lines laid down for the treatment of anorexia. If the dysphagia or the vomiting has been severe or long continued the child will be undernourished and will suffer from avitaminosis. In our opinion certain of the symptoms—weakness, tiredness, and emotional instability—shown by such children (or adults) are the result of the avitaminosis, and we believe it desirable to consider all cases where the feeding disorder has continued for any length of time as being complicated with a vitamin deficiency which must be treated. The symptoms of dysphagia or of vomiting must be treated as we advised for anorexia—by ignoring it. In certain severe cases this treatment cannot be given easily or safely while leaving the child with the parents, and it is better to have him hospitalized for a few weeks until psychotherapy can be instituted. In milder cases in young children the child may be entered in a good nursery school where the teacher is trained to observe him carefully and is accustomed to the proper management of children and their eating habits. It is often useful to have a trained social worker live in the home for several days in order to observe exactly what does go on there around and during mealtimes. Of course, in the presence of a stranger who is there to observe, no parent will behave in exactly the same way as she would if alone, hence the worker does not see what really goes on. However such a person is a great help to the busy practitioner or pediatrician. We say social worker rather than nurse because the majority of nurses have not had as intensive or extensive training in emotional conditions as the social worker has. Of course the ideal person to assist the physician along these lines would be a nurse who also has had training as a social worker.

During the child's separation from the parents a careful study of the whole situation must be made in order to find out the causative factors. If they are problems of the parents they must be treated. If a parent has shown persistent determination to overfeed the child the physician's advice may be helpful, but in certain cases it fails completely because the overfeeding is the result of a neurotic compulsion in the parent. Such a parent needs treatment for her own problems, of which the neurotic compulsion is only a symptom. If the main problem is the adverse attitude of the parents toward the child, the problem must be treated as such; at the same time in most cases the child needs psychotherapy as well in order to free him from the results of having to force his expression of his needs into unusual channels, necessitated by the need to get along with the parents.

One child whose case one of us has reported before had, among many other symptoms, attacks of vomiting. He had had to suppress any expression of his aggressive and sexual interests in order to get along with his mother, who had rejected him. During treatment he expressed a strong desire for the therapist to feed—that is, love— him. Later, when he was assured of the therapist's love, he was able to express his aggressive feelings and sexual interests both verbally and in play. As he lost his tenseness and became more like a normal boy, and as some treatment was carried on with the mother, she was able to feel more affectionately toward him and thus he was able to carry his increasing freedom to be himself into situations outside of the therapeutic hour.

If the problem is the result of the child's disgust with his own ideas, psychotherapy is called for. As mentioned earlier, it is questionable whether intensive psychotherapy is needed in mild and occasional food fads. Such cases are better left alone. If the problem is the result of an identification with a sick parent or of a regression to the oral phase (that is, if the vomiting or the dysphagia is a hysterical symptom), then psychoanalysis or at least intensive psychotherapy for both child and parent is necessary.

The question as to who should treat the child can be answered only on the basis of the severity of the child's symptoms. The results of the Rorschach test are most helpful, since they may reveal deepseated emotional disturbances that are not apparent on the surface, or they may reveal that the intrapsychic life is fairly satisfactory even though the gastrointestinal symptoms are severe. If the presenting symptoms are mild, not associated with too many other indications of personality maladjustment, and if the Rorschach test indicates a fairly stable emotional life, the case may be treated satisfactorily by the pediatrician or general practitioner who knows how to conduct the treatment. If the symptoms are severe or are associated with other symptoms, and if the Rorschach test indicates a serious personal disturbance, it would be wise to refer the child to a pediatric psychiatrist for consultation and treatment if necessary.

We have seen that the mouth has the two functions of ingesting food and of sucking and biting for pleasure. Both functions—and both are pleasurable—are continued throughout life and do not merit any social condemnation, nor can they be designated as perversions. The function of eating may become perverted if it is used largely to obtain satisfactions other than gratification of the need for food. Some time ago, one of us reported the case of a boy who ate enormously. His need for extra food was an attempt to satisfy his longing for the love of his mother and later his stepmother. Whenever he felt her lack of love he would gorge. In adult life one occasionally sees patients who complain of having excessive appetites. When the history is studied it is found that the excessive appetite began just after the sexual life was greatly curtailed. This phenomenon is well known to exist in eunuchs; it is observed often in women who have passed the menopause and in men of comparable age. In all of these instances the gorging is a regressive displacement of the need for love and sexual gratification from the genitals to the oral zone. The regression takes place either because the individual is afraid to get genital pleasure or because the circumstances of his life prevent him from satisfying his needs for sexual gratification or for love. In the case of the child, the treatment is not to prevent his eating, even though the overeating may be resulting in serious overweight, but to correct the cause, which is usually a lack of love, for which treatment must be directed toward the rejective parental attitude.

PICA

All children eat nonnutritive substances, a catalogue of which would include all substances that can be put into the mouth and swallowed. Their ingestion can be considered normal if it does not happen too often and if the child is not made ill. When the child eats nonnutritive substances to excess or almost exclusively the condition is known as pica. We have not seen many cases of true pica, but on the basis of those we have seen, we have come to the conclusion that pica usually occurs in children or adults whose diet does not satisfy certain bodily needs. Thus a child suffering from a serious feeding problem that results in a calcium deficiency may try to correct it by constantly eating the plaster off the wall. Similar dietary deficiencies seem to underlie the dirt eating that is endemic to some parts of the southern states. The treatment, therefore, will be directed toward the correction of the dietary defects. When these are corrected the pica will cease.

FINGER SUCKING

Finger sucking is a normal activity of early childhood and should not be interfered with. Here the physician may ask, "Does it not deform the mouth?" and "If a parent brings a child because he sucks his fingers must I not do something to stop the habit?" In reply to the first question it can be stated categorically that there is no proof that finger sucking deforms the mouth or jaw except under the most unusual circumstances, and that most of such deformities are either congenital or the result of adenoidal obstruction of breathing. In reply to the second question it can be stated as categorically that nothing—neither the use of punishment or scolding nor the application of nasty-tasting substances, bandages, or guards to the fingers nor the application of splints to the arms—should be permitted or suggested. The physician who conducts his practice in an honestly scientific manner will explain to the parent the facts concerning finger sucking and the inadvisability of preventing it. If the parent is dissatisfied and the doctor loses the case he can comfort himself with the assurance that he has been honest and correct in what he has done.

We can be sure that the parent who consults physician after physician for her child's finger sucking and who is not content with the honest advice she receives has an unconscious problem of her own about finger sucking. It may be that as a child she had a problem with her own parents over finger sucking and so does not let her child do what she wanted to do lest her parents punish her. It may be that she has an unconscious desire to suck her own fingers, a desire that is becoming strong because she is not obtaining genital gratification. In such cases any real treatment must concern itself with the parent's own problem, either her fear of her parents or her problems relating to genital gratification.

How long does the average child suck his fingers? It varies with the child. Some gradually relinquish the habit about the second or third year. Others continue till the age of five or six. Freud and Burlingham report that children who live in their own homes tend to relinquish the habit of finger sucking much earlier than do children who live in institutions, who tend to continue the sucking as a means of comforting themselves for several years longer. The process of relinquishing goes something like this: the child first gives up the habit while he is awake, but as he gets drowsy and starts to fall asleep it recurs. Later he abstains even when drowsy, but as he falls into sleep his fingers find their way to his mouth. Still later he ceases altogether. In some cases the child has a constitutional need to suck his fingers, which need is not as easily satisfied as in other children. In other cases the child continues his finger sucking because he is frustrated in some of his other needs. When a child continues his finger sucking past the age of four or five it is wise to study the home situation carefully to ascertain if there are adverse parental attitudes that are making the child too miserable and unhappy to permit him to give up his infantile forms of gratification. If such are found they should be corrected; if they are not found then the finger sucking should be left to the child to stop when he is ready.

Finger sucking, however, may be a symptom of regression to the oral stage. A child may relinquish all his finger sucking by the age of four years. Several years later, perhaps at the age of seven or eight, he may start again. This condition is entirely different from the finger sucking we just discussed. The child has progressed naturally along the path of his development and then suddenly starts to retrace his steps. The finger sucking therefore is an indication that the child has met an insoluble difficulty in his development and has attempted to solve the problem through regression. The real problem for the parent or therapist is the nature of the apparently insoluble difficulty that the child has met. In some cases, many of which were seen at the time when so many mothers were starting to work in war industries, the child feels unloved by the mother and his finger sucking is simply a motor cry, "See, mother, I am only a little baby, please stay with me and love me." In others, the child has become desperately frightened about his masturbation and has stopped it: if the genital stage of development is so dangerous he had better get his pleasure in a safer one, namely the oral. An interesting example is one we quoted in another book. A girl of fifteen had sucked her fingers since she was seven. She had not dared to stop sucking them because if she did, obsessional thoughts crowded into her mind that were of an unpleasant masturbatory character.

Here again, if the physician understands the pathology the treatment will be obvious. The child who returns to sucking his fingers because he feels insecure in his mother's love must be helped to feel secure. If the insecurity is caused by the birth of a new sibling in the family and if the parents are handling the situation of the older child adequately there is no need to take any steps but simply to wait until the child does feel more secure. If the insecurity is the result of separation from the mother then the mother must return to her family or a satisfactory mother substitute must be provided. If the finger sucking is the result of castration threats the child must be relieved from this fear. In the case just cited the nature of the unpleasant thoughts must be ascertained and the child's irrational conclusions corrected: she must be educated to a more reasonable view of her sexuality. In none of these cases is it ever necessary to do anything about the finger sucking itself. It will cease within a short time after the cause is removed.

NAILBITING

Nailbiting is very prevalent in America. It is surprising to note the high percentage of inductees at the induction center who give a history of nailbiting either in childhood or in adult life. It is this prevalence that inclines us, falsely, not to consider the habit as an indication of emotional instability. Dogs spend a great deal of time cleaning between their toes and around their nails with their teeth and possibly also biting at the nails themselves. They have no other way of attending to their paws. Children frequently break their nails playing and get rough edges. They feel a certain amount of discomfort when too much dirt collects under the nails. The skin beside the nail often gets slightly torn. The adult attends to these conditions by the use of nail file and scissors. The child is not anxious to use instruments that would take him from his occupations and interests when he has an instrument ready at hand, his teeth. Parents feel it necessary to stop the child from doing so and often err in trying to stop it too abruptly and too severely. When the practice is stopped gradually and the child encouraged to adopt more adult methods of manicuring and given time to learn them, he harbors little resentment; but when it is done in the way described he feels he is being picked on, becomes resentful, tends to continue the habit and even to increase it; thus a simple, childish procedure may easily become a severe case of nailbiting.

To repeat, despite the prevalence of the habit in the population we must regard it as a sign of poor emotional adjustment. Dr. Michael Lesse, who served during World War II as psychiatrist to the Submarine Training School of the Navy noted that the sailor who bit his nails was a poor risk for selection for services that required an ability to withstand long-continued and severe physical and emotional strains—especially in the submarine service.

Severe cases of nailbiting are motivated in part by the desire of the child to annoy and humiliate the parents—and the parents' reaction indicates clearly that the child does accomplish his desire. At the same time, the fact that the parents do get angry and that often the child bites his nails so deeply that the biting itself is painful, and the fingers afterward, indicates that there is another motive, namely the need to punish himself for his resentment. Severe nailbiting therefore has the structure of a neurotic symptom. Essentially it is an aggressive hostile act directed against one's own person because one is afraid to direct it against the real object. In most cases the real object is the parents, frequently the mother.

One little girl began to bite her nails as soon as she went to camp for the first time. She was a child whose mother had indulged and protected her; in fact, until she was five years old she was not permitted to play with other children. The mother also seemed helpless in the face of the child's demands, very often acceding to them when it would have been more sensible to refuse them. The child therefore had never learned how to get along with other people, and when she went to camp for the first time she felt a great deal of social anxiety, which caused her to want to regress to the satisfaction of finger sucking; but she felt this was too babyish. Nevertheless her hands crept toward her mouth. She felt angry at the mother for putting her in a position of being so anxious—that is, for sending her to camp—and angry because she had been babied so much. The child recognized that if the mother had not treated her so babyishly and had treated her more as an adult she would not now feel so helpless in a new situation. This feeling of helplessness made her envious of the mother's social poise (which in reality was not very great, although her daughter thought it was), and this envy increased her resentment against the mother. She was therefore in a conflict: if she expressed her resentment against the mother, then she would have no mother to fall back on to protect her against her feeling of discomfort when she was in a new situation and with strange people with whom she had never learned to get along; if she fell back entirely on the mother then she would miss all the pleasures and advantages of a social life and in the future of a life with the opposite sex.

The conflict was insoluble and so she tried to repress it; but she had to do something about the feelings connected with it. Tormented by her social anxiety, her hands crept toward her mouth as a symbol of her desire for the mother's babying and protection. At the same time she felt bitter resentment against the mother, so she began to bite the fingers that symbolized her. The greater the conflict between her two opposing feelings to the mother the more viciously she bit her nails, until they became sore and bleeding. Since the mother disliked the nailbiting, she could now add another motive when she came home: she could use it as a way of expressing openly her defiance and resentment.

In certain cases a conflict exactly similar to the one just described, also solved by the habit of nailbiting, arises if the parent has threatened or punished the child for masturbating. The child stops masturbating, bitterly resentful of the parent because he has to do so. His inner desires then take a regressive trend toward finger sucking. This regressive trend combines with the hostility and resentment, and nailbiting is the result. The child keeps it up because he knows it humiliates the parent whom he thus punishes for interfering with his pleasurable activities.

As was mentioned above, treatment for the common tendency of the child to use his teeth as a manicuring instrument is to teach him slowly and gradually, more by example than by precept, the use of other implements for manicuring. The gift of a manicure set and the gentle, regular manicuring of the fingers by the mother and occasionally, as the child grows older, by a professional manicurist are all helpful.

We are of the opinion that there are mothers who do not like to manicure their children's nails. They are not very gentle but go about it roughly in their desire to get the unpleasant job finished. This attitude makes the whole process unpleasant to the child. There are three parts of the routine of civilization of which most children complain—manicuring, washing or brushing the hair, and washing the face. Since the mother is not doing these things to herself, she is not guided by her own warning sensations, and the procedure accidentally becomes painful and the child gets slightly hurt. Furthermore, children are not as able to tolerate slight degrees of pain as are adults. Then, too, if the parent is annoyed at the child or if the child is being cared for by a nurse who has been forbidden to punish him and is annoyed because of something he did earlier, she may and often does vent her spleen on him during the toileting by pulling his hair, brushing it hard, cutting the nails roughly, and the like.

To these hurts that the child actually may receive during the manicuring is added his unreasoning inner dread that the scissors may really mutilate him. He becomes tense and fearful and tends to pull his hand away at inopportune times. Thus he may really be hurt; or the parent, fearing she may hurt him, scolds him for not keeping still. The combination of these two discomforts makes the child dislike the manicuring process and prefer to use his teeth instead. Such reactions can be overcome only by gentle, slow insistence until the child begins to take pleasure in his well-kept hands. We are a little skeptical, however, whether any child really cares much about his appearance until he reaches puberty and falls in love—when a revolution in his habits of personal cleanliness is usually produced.

Treatment for the severe types of nailbiting must aim toward a better solution of the child's conflict. He must learn to be less fearful of expressing his hostile feelings, if they are valid, and more able to dispense with his exaggerated need for dependency. When the emotional difficulties have been resolved the course of training that we mentioned for the first type may be instituted. Often, however, it is unnecessary, for the child is avid to be a grown-up person.

There is another point to be considered. Parents who bite their nails cannot expect their children not to follow in their footsteps. In fact it, would be a sign of inadequate development if the child did not do so. The parent may complain of the child's table manners, his neatness and tidiness, his food fads, his temper tantrums, his lying, his grammar, his use of slang or profanity, while all the time his behavior is a correct replica of that of the parent. It is not so strange that the parent should thus complain, for often he is actually unaware that he behaves in the way the child copies. Or he may feel it is correct for an adult so to conduct himself but incorrect for a child; or he may be displeased with the way he himself behaves and not wish the child to follow in his footsteps. (The last-mentioned reaction is seen often in parents recently immigrated to America.) In all of these cases the child is influenced much more by the parent's example than by his precepts and if the latter wishes the child to change he must change his own habits.

When the child attends school, whether it be nursery school, kindergarten, grade or high school, he tends to imitate the habits of the teacher of whom he is fond. These habits will be different from those of the parents, and the wise parent will welcome the tendency as a valuable contribution to the child's personality development, as helpful for his future life in a democracy where it will be necessary for him to be able to meet, understand, and get along with a wide variety of people. The unwise parent who is either bigoted and prejudiced or has the need to clutch the child too closely to himself will try to interfere; and the child will suffer a totally unnecessary conflict. Such conflicts are important during adolescence and will be discussed later on.

DISORDERS OF SPEECH

Speech is another function of the mouth and is a much more complicated one than either eating or pleasure sucking. As a result of a sensory stimulus arising outside the body, of physical changes within, or of instinct energy, an idea forms within the associational pathways of the cerebral cortex. If the idea is to be expressed in speech the stimulus innervates the speech centers in the cerebral cortex, which are in the left cortex in right-handed persons and in the right cortex in the left-handed. Impulses pass from here to the peripheral speech mechanism, which consists of two parts—the bellows or breathing apparatus which produces a blast of air, and the vocal cords, throat, tongue, lips and teeth which form apertures that can be varied in size and shape. The blast of air passing through these apertures produces the particular word sound desired. Disturbance of any part of this complex apparatus will injure the perfection of the speech.

The child learns to speak—that is, learns to modify voluntarily the size and shape of the apertures through which the blast of air passes—by imitating his parents. Through observation he learns that certain sounds made by the parent accompany certain actions and facial expressions, and produce certain results on other people. It is no wonder that the small child regards speech as magical—when he emits certain sounds he can cause other people to do what he wants! Through his observations he associates certain sounds with certain specific results, and when he hears these sounds he expects that the specific results will follow even if he has to bring them about himself. We say he has become aware of the meaning of words, that he has learned to obey commands, and the like. This learning occurs before he can speak himself. The child begins to think in verbal images and he understands words before he can use them. Then he begins to try to make similar sounds to express his verbal ideas and we say he is beginning to talk. He models the sounds he makes on the sounds he hears; therefore if the parents have a speech defect, if they have an accent, or if they talk very fast or very slowly, his speech will tend to copy them as accurately as possible. There are many children who when they enter school are sent to a speech-corrective class because their speech shows the well-ingrained habit of enunciating exactly like the parents. This speech fault is often found in children of foreign-born parents.

Some children tend to talk so-called baby talk and continue the habit for a long time, in most instances because the parents tend to talk baby talk to them and regard their use of the mutilated syllables as cute. Thus such children not only imitate the parents but continue to talk in this way in order to be admired. We feel it is better for children not to hear baby talk, since it may take much retraining before they can learn to talk correctly.

In order to imitate exactly it is necessary to hear accurately. Defective hearing is a frequent cause of speech defects, and in every case of speech disorder the child's hearing should be tested accurately. Auditory defects, like visual defects, even if fairly severe, frequently pass unnoticed in small children. Otitis media also seems to be increasing in frequency among small children in urban communities, although its severity and serious sequelae have been greatly modified by the use of antibiotics. The great number of draftees rejected because of auditory or visual defects indicates that it would be a wise precaution to have the vision and hearing of all children tested carefully as a routine before they enter school, and then to have instituted whatever corrective measures are necessary and possible. It is too bad to allow a child to go for years with an uncorrected but correctable sensory defect which distorts his whole knowledge of the world and makes it impossible for him to react as efficiently and accurately as can other children. A child with a speech disorder due to defective hearing should be given expert professional care. If the child is totally deaf, either because of some congenital condition or as a result of some serious illness during his first year of life involving either the middle ear or the auditory nerve, he will not talk at all. Most cases of muteness are not the result of any injury or defect in the speech apparatus, but of deafness. The deaf child needs expert training in learning to speak.

Cortical defects or injuries, if they affect the speech centers, produce speech defects. It is probable that many of the speech defects of mentally defective children are cortical in origin rather than peripheral. Speech defects that result from cerebral injuries are known as *aphasias* and have a specific symptomatology, which is not necessary to describe here because they are not commonly met with in children. We anticipate that in the future there will be more aphasias in children owing to the increased number of serious automobile accidents. Treatment for the aphasia is the problem of the neurologist and should not be attempted without at least a neurological consultation.

S. T. Orton has called attention to a specific and important type of speech disorder of cerebral origin. We know that the speech centers are in the left cerebral hemisphere in right-handed persons and in the right cerebral hemisphere in the left-handed. There is the anatomical structure for speech on both sides of the brain but the function of speech is located predominantly in the dominant hemisphere, whose presence is indicated by the handedness. If the child is congenitally left-handed the centers that control the function of speech will develop in the right cerebral hemisphere. Should the parent or teacher decide that the child should become right-handed and force him to learn to use his right hand in preference to his left, she will also be training the left hemisphere to become dominant. This process results in a conflict of dominance between the two hemispheres and is revealed in the child's suddenly starting to stutter. There are specific tests designed to determine whether this conflict of dominance is the cause of the stuttering, and treatment for the condition consists in retraining the child to use the originally dominant side of the brain and in retraining his speech defect. Unless both are done together no improvement occurs. We will discuss more fully the neurodynamics of this condition when we discuss (in Chapter IX) another discovery of Orton's called strephosymbolia.

The greatest number of cases of speech defect are the result of some disorder in the use of the peripheral parts of the speech mechanism, that is, the breathing apparatus or the apparatus that shapes the words. If the child has enlarged tonsils and adenoids he cannot be expected to speak well since the air passages are distorted. We seriously doubt that the so-called tongue-tie really interferes sufficiently to cause a speech defect. It may be so in occasional instances but certainly not as frequently as to justify the frequency with which frenotomy is performed.

If we suffer a painful injury to some part of our bodies, all of us will hesitate to use the injured part for a short period after the injury has healed and our first attempts will be made very gingerly. If this is the conduct of adults it is even more the conduct of children, who are not as tolerant of pain. Often with a child the dread of re-experiencing the pain remains for a long time and makes his action hesitant and consequently awkward and not well co-ordinated. It is a well-known fact that if a child starting to walk falls and really hurts himself he may abstain from any further attempts to walk for a long time, and his next efforts will show a great deal of timidity. When a young child painfully injures his mouth, cutting either his tongue or his lips, but particularly his tongue, he seems to develop a great deal of anxiety. (This is probably the result of the fact that he has injured an important part of his oral apparatus, which is almost as important to him at this age as his genitals will be later on. Often he even will refuse to let his mouth be opened in order that the extent of the damage be ascertained.) Thereafter he may cease to speak, and when he starts again his speech may be mutilated and in-co-ordinate and remain so for years. In technical language, he suffers from a traumatic neurosis. He has suffered a painful injury to his tongue or lips, organs whose use is part of the function of speech. He dreads any attempt to use the organ lest he re-experience the pain, so he inhibits the function of speech either totally or partially. (He also may repress the memory of the accident.) The treatment for such a traumatic neurosis consists in helping the child to uncover the amnesia about the accident. At the same time he is encouraged to use his mouth and tongue as much as possible.

Sometimes the traumatic neurosis is not the result of an accident but is inflicted on the child deliberately by the parent as a punishment for some misdemeanor. In one case the child began to use profanity, which he copied directly from his father who swore a great deal. The father, angered by the child's swearing, hit him brutally across the mouth. The child ceased talking and when he began again he used mutilated speech. Treatment for such a case must combine the two goals mentioned above with a lessening of the child's fear of the father.

The most common type of speech defect is stuttering. There is no need to describe the symptoms, for they are undoubtedly familiar to the reader. We sometimes find it most painful to listen to a stutterer. We feel annoyed and irritated and extremely desirous of helping him out and thus ending the pain of listening. Although some stutterers are extremely sensitive about their speech defect, even in some instances to the point of being unwilling to talk at all, the majority go straight ahead calmly and stubbornly to complete what they are trying to say.

The primary dysfunction in stuttering lies in the bellows which furnishes the blast of air for speech—that is, in the breathing apparatus. In order to speak clearly, smoothly, and rhythmically the breathing must be smooth and rhythmical. Anyone can demonstrate this on himself quite easily. If the breathing is increased in rate or if the rhythm is disturbed by muscular exertion it becomes difficult to speak, and if one forces oneself to do so the speech is mutilated and greatly resembles that of the stutterer. We have already discussed the fact that the respiratory apparatus in the very young infant is not well co-ordinated and that he learns to co-ordinate it only gradually as he gets older. We also pointed out that the startle reflex will suddenly throw whatever co-ordination he has achieved out of rhythm. (This happens also in adults when, due to being startled, they catch their breath.) In the child this sudden disorganization may last not only several minutes but even several hours or days.

In most children stuttering starts immediately following a sudden severe shock or fear. The child is startled and frightened at the same time; the startle reflex disorganizes the breathing rhythm; the disorganization persists and expresses itself in the stuttering. This causative sequence explains the well-known phenomenon of the stutterer who ceases to stutter when he sings or when in some other way he changes the pitch or tone of his voice. In fact, many cures for stuttering are based on imparting a different rhythm to the stutterer's breathing. If the child starts to stutter after a sudden fright and his fear reaction can be treated and overcome within a short time after it begins, his speech will become normal again, as David M. Levy has shown in his work with release therapy.

The sudden startle does more than cause a regressive disturbance of breathing. It causes an arrest of development and a regression to either the anal or oral stage. Some stutterers show marked sucking or biting movements as they speak which interfere greatly with the smooth enunciation of words. Others show marked anal characteristics and have the most difficulty in enunciating words that express sadistic drives. A case reported by Spring illustrates this type well. The stammerer, a boy of ten years, was engrossed with the shape of words. He said, "My throat is round and lots of easy words come through like sausages; some are liquid. When I get a word with a corner on it or a square word it sticks in my throat and I have to change the shape of my throat so it will slip through." Fenichel says, "The words have in addition the significance of an introjected object—the conflict which originally took place between the individual and the object is now expressed by means of a conflict between the ego and the speech apparatus or its speech products." Spring's case is an illustration. The boy stammered severely over the name of a teacher he disliked. He said the name had prickles on it—which clearly expressed the fear of being injured internally by the hated object, the name being the equivalent of the object. The name of the loved teacher on the contrary was liquid, therefore not dangerous, and was pronounced without stammering.

The regression causes the child to use speech no longer as a means of communication but as a vehicle by which his erotic and aggressive drives are carried, just as, during the oral stage, he used his mouth and during the anal stage he used his lower bowel and its media of feces and flatus to carry them. The regression tends to reactivate his old belief in his magical powers and his omnipotence. It tends to return him to the old conflict of ambivalence, the struggle between powerful erotic and hostile impulses toward the same person. He dreads the return of this struggle and tries to solve it by repressing his erotic drives and aggressive feelings. Lest his speech carry any of these charges he tries to inhibit its free, smooth flow. All this struggle goes on underneath the level of consciousness. It becomes what is called technically a case of pregenital conversion reaction. The child is conscious, however, of the inadequacy of his ability to speak, begins to feel consciously inferior, and thus more tense than he was before. This increased tension interferes again with his breathing rhythm and the stuttering becomes worse.

The stutterer has feelings of inadequacy as a result of his stuttering. He has great muscular and psychic tenseness which results from his fear lest he do or say something that will get him into trouble. He tries at one and the same time to speak the truth and to please the person to whom he is talking—often an impossible thing to do. He tries to pretend unconsciously that he has no hostile or aggressive feelings toward anyone. It is as if he said in his stuttering, "See, how can I be hostile or dangerous to anybody when I am such an ineffectual person that I cannot even speak plainly?" Increasingly he shows a tendency to emphasize the passive, submissive side of his personality. The suppressed aggression must find an outlet and it does so in the calm stubborn insistence by the stutterer that he finish what he is saying even though he knows that his speech causes his hearer great feelings of discomfort. Children often show their realization of this aggressive aspect when they imitate a stutterer for a few days in order to annoy their parents.

The following case illustrates the inhibition of speech—although the symptoms of stuttering did not occur. A boy had learned a slightly risqué song about eating beans. At a picnic where there were a number of girls he began to sing it. They were shocked and ostracized him. He became extremely embarrassed. Later, when he grew up it became necessary, in the course of his business, for him to speak in public; but each time he did so he felt embarrassed, being certain he would not say the correct thing. He had suffered a humiliating experience when he tried to express his anal sadism through speech. (The song had been a sadistic attempt to seduce his feminine audience.) Later he feared unconsciously lest he re-experience the pain of that episode when he spoke in public. (The speech was an attempt to seduce—that is, influence—his audience, just as the song was, and to him it had the same sadistic correlation.)

Stuttering of this type is the sign of a deep-seated emotional disturbance and if it has persisted a long time the mechanisms may become irreversible. No halfway measures of treatment are satisfactory. Speech retraining is woefully inadequate, for although most such methods depend on helping the patient to relax so that the breathing becomes better organized, he has great difficulty in relaxing because the cause of his tensions lies in his emotional conflicts. Psychotherapy may solve his emotional conflicts, but it is usually too superficial to be adequate to help him to a better solution of them. Psychoanalysis furnishes the best method of psychotherapy and must be combined with an intensive retraining of the speech, for the combination of the two methods can cure stuttering. However, if the case has been in existence for a long while the prognosis is poor. There may be improvement without permanent cure. Hence it is essential that the stutterer be brought for intensive treatment as soon as possible after his symptom appears. He should not be allowed to grow out of it, for it is extremely improbable that he will do so.

DISORDERS OF BOWEL FUNCTION

Constipation is the outstanding disturbance of the function of the bowel. What is constipation and what are its causes? In the human being at fairly regular intervals the peristaltic movements of the large bowel cause its contents to collect in the rectum. The individual then feels a sense of fullness and pressure. This is slightly uncomfortable, and as soon as possible—because the free exercise of this ability is curtailed markedly by culture—he goes to a toilet and relaxes the sphincter muscles of the anus, and the peristaltic action of the bowel ejects the contents from his body. What are these contents? They are not derived to any great extent from the ingested food, but mainly from the secretions of the gastrointestinal tract. Excluding vegetables and coarsely ground cereals, the contents have a fairly constant composition: water 65 per cent and solid material 35 per cent, the latter consisting mostly of desquamated epithelial cells and numerous dead bacteria. If the diet has contained a proportionately large amount of vegetable substances the stool will be rather soft and bulky because it is composed largely of cellulose—woody fibers that cannot be digested. As the cellulose content of the food is increased, the stool contains more water and solids, more of the ingested food is undigested, and more nitrogen is lost to the body. The increased bulk of this undigested residue stimulates intestinal peristalsis, the passage of food through the bowel is quickened, and the digestive ferments have insufficient time to exert their full action. Therefore too much vegetable food in man interferes with the processes of digestion.

If the call to defecation is neglected or impossible to answer, the rectal wall relaxes and the sensation of fullness—which we call the desire to move the bowels—passes off. At what intervals does the need to move the bowels arise? They vary with the individual's peristaltic rhythm. Some experience the desire to move the bowels once in twenty-four hours, others once in forty-eight, and still others once in seventy-two; individual variations are even greater. Alvarez does not consider that the condition should be called constipation until there has been no movement for over three days. Does constipation have any detrimental effect on the health? Alvarez has proved that it does not. The symptoms that do develop in cases of constipation—foul breath and tongue, impaired appetite, flatulence, nausea, loss of power of attention, depression, headache, insomnia, and irritability—are due to the distention and mechanical irritation of the rectum by the fecal mass. Masses of cotton wool packed into the rectum produce exactly the same symptoms—which as in the case of constipation disappear as soon as the mass is removed. The validity of these experimental findings was proved during World War II by Rickenbacker and his crew and by Dixon and his companions.

We have discussed the physiology of constipation thus fully because the thinking of many parents in regard to it is a mass of superstition. They call the child constipated when he is merely operating according to his normal rhythm, which may be a bowel movement every day, every two days, or every three days. More often they are certain that the child's health will be ruined if he does not have a movement—and a "good" movement (by which they mean a large one)—every day. Obsessed by this worry, they display a tremendous interest in the child's defecations, question him about them, and even inspect them every time they occur. If the appearance is not satisfactory they change the child's diet, adding the usual bulk foods —bran, fruits, or agar-agar. They forget that in doing so they are speeding up intestinal peristalsis and interfering with the process of digestion, with the result that the stool contains much valuable but unutilized food substance. Since the increased peristalsis is caused by mechanical irritation, such a diet tends to produce a pathological condition of the intestine. (We have seen at least one case of an adult whose intestinal tract functioned badly, with painful flatulence, lack of proper digestion of food, frequent diarrhea, and marked anal soreness, because she persisted quite unnecessarily in using such a diet for her so-called constipation.) The parents become determined that the child shall have a daily movement, and therefore require that he go to the toilet at a specific time to sit there till he has moved his bowels. They encourage him to exert voluntary effort through the contraction of the abdominal and chest muscles and the diaphragm to force the feces out of his body. (The only necessary voluntary effort usually required is the relaxation of the anal sphincter.) This straining is quite unnecessary and results in the forcing of large quantities of blood into the lower pelvic veins—particularly the hemorrhoidal ones. It produces congestion and certainly in adults is a frequent cause of piles. It is not unusual in such a home for the child to sit an hour or even more on the toilet trying to move his bowels. (We have known instances where the child was forced to sit there three or four hours.) He gets bored with sitting and sneaks a book in with him. Now he can sit and enjoy himself reading. When he grows up he spends a long time—perhaps even an hour or longer—sitting on the toilet reading.

In certain instances the parent comes to the conclusion that the child is not really trying—as he probably is not—and attempts to convince him of the dire effects that result from constipation. If the child believes her, he now takes over her attitude and spends his days in a turmoil of worry lest he be not able to move his bowels properly. In other instances the parent feels he is stubborn and punishes him for his stubbornness.

Of course such parents resort with great frequency to medicinal aids—saline preparations, which act by pouring liquid from the blood stream and tissues into the bowel; vegetable cathartics, which act by irritating the intestinal wall and increasing peristalsis; or inert, bulky preparations such as agar-agar, which act by increasing the bulk of the intestinal contents and through mechanical stimulation increase the peristalsis. Some of these have a nauseating taste; others produce irregular peristalsis which is felt by the unhappy child as painful cramps. (It is a pity that certain drug firms have disguised the taste of many cathartics with flavoring and have attempted combining them with other drugs to reduce the tendency to cramps. If the cathartic preparations were dispensed only in a more crude form there would be much less unnecessary and unreasonable self-medication.) However, this self-medication is not as disastrous in its psychological effects on the child as is the indiscriminate and unnecessary use of enemas and suppositories.

From what we have just said, one of the important measures in the treatment of constipation in children is first to determine whether the child is constipated or whether the constipation exists solely or largely in the parent's mind. In our own case as parents, we can honestly say that we never knew whether our children's bowels moved or not. Occasionally they would tell us that they were constipated and needed medicine, but apart from that no notice was taken of their bowel activities. We have not observed any ill effects resulting from this form of management and believe that if all parents would follow the same plan much of the so-called constipation in children would cease. Naturally the parent who follows this advice has the duty of seeing that the child's diet is adequate and that he has sufficient opportunity to exercise his body. These are only general measures of hygiene, however, and we are not sure if they have much to do with the regularity of bowel movements.

We realize that the reader who is unfamiliar with the studies of the last twenty years on digestion and excretion, or who is bound emotionally to a fecal fetish, will feel scornful of the views here expressed. We recommend that such readers read carefully the articles of Alvarez.

Although so many cases of constipation in children are really fictitious ones existing only in the parents' minds, true constipation does occur in children. For this there are two main psychological causes. One occurs in the child who has marked feelings of repugnance and disgust with any form of dirt, especially excreta, which are the result of a fear that if he moves his bowels even in the toilet his parents will punish him. This situation usually follows improper methods of toilet training. In this type of constipation the child has lost all sensory contact with his rectum and hence does not recognize when the organ is distended. Since his rhythm has been lost he should be advised to sit on the toilet once a day and try *for a few minutes only* to relax his anal sphincter. If he is unsuccessful he should stop and try again next day. He should be advised to be sure to go to the toilet as soon as he feels any perineal discomfort. A small amount of food containing cellulose or agar-agar should be added to his diet for a short time till his rhythm is re-established. He should be encouraged and even praised for playing with dirt, clay, sand, finger paints, or the like, and for getting himself dirty. If this encouragement can emanate from his parents, whose former actions have caused his accentuated feelings of disgust or repugnance, so much the better. If these simple measures fail after being tried honestly for a period of time, then the child needs a more intensive type of psychotherapy.

The second cause of constipation in children is well illustrated by the following case. A boy of seven would go for several days without defecating. Although he was placed on the toilet daily and appeared to try to move his bowels, there was no result except that he appeared to be in great pain. When his bowels did move the stool was not a constipated one, and his shrieking with what seemed to be pain was really from fear. This fear had several components. He had been rigorously toilet trained to the point where he had begun to think of any bowel movement as wrong and displeasing to the mother. He was insecure in her affections and had been made unhappy by the birth of a younger brother on whom the mother lavished attention. His jealousy of the brother was connected with his ideas about defecation, for he stated that if he moved his bowels he made men and boys in the toilet and then killed them by flushing them away. Therefore in his mind the flushing away of his bowel movements was the equivalent of murdering his brother, whom he hated because he was the center of the mother's attention, and killing his father, whom he hated for a similar reason, yet whom he feared greatly. The presence of the fear of the father was readily demonstrated by the fact that when the father returned home unexpectedly and caught the boy sneaking downstairs to talk to the maid (which proceeding had been forbidden) the boy almost lost consciousness on the stairs. The constipation also represented a strong desire for the undivided attention of the mother and grandmother, both of whom were overly concerned with the matter of proper toilet habits. Cases such as this one need intensive psychotherapy which must be directed toward first uncovering the child's fears of his own emotional reactions and feelings and then attempting to remove them.

Constipation in children does not usually wait until the latent period but begins at the time when the cause—be it the parents' attitude toward toilet training or fears the child associates with excretory functions—begins to operate.

Children—and adults—are extremely avid for any experience that brings sensual pleasure. We don't know the intimate lives of our children any more than we know the intimate pleasure lives of our friends. As we stated earlier, small children like to play with their excreta—feces or urine. They have a tremendous desire for sensual pleasure, which can be obtained readily by manipulation of the excretory organs. It is pleasurable to rub the anus and the surrounding skin and to introduce the top of the fingers or some other small object into the anus. Children constantly play at giving each other enemas. (This play is not so uncommon in adults, either. Every so often someone is seriously injured because a blast of compressed air has been forced up his anus as a practical joke.) Everyone knows that they postpone going to the toilet as long as possible (often so long that the internal pressure overcomes the contraction of the sphincter and the child soils or wets himself a little) and that they adopt many devices to retain the excretions. They hold the anus or the urethral opening, they hop and dance and stand first on one foot and then on the other. They even try to hold back the feces by standing on one foot and pressing the heel of the other against the anus.

This behavior is explained usually by saying that the child is so interested in his play that he does not want to take time to go to the toilet. The explanation is partly true, but partly only, since children often behave in the same way when the call for excretion arises when they are not particularly enthralled by what they are doing. The more important reason is that children derive sensual pleasure from the feeling of bladder or rectal fullness and from holding back as long as possible and then suddenly relaxing the sphincter. The number of excretory games of this nature played by children is legion. Of course one expects these games to be most common during the anal period, less common but still frequent during the genital stage, and still less common during the latent period and adolescence. Although less common, and when practiced certainly done in a secretive manner, they are often carried on even in adult life by persons who otherwise are eminently respectable. Their occurrence, therefore, during the latent period is natural and so is not a cause for alarm. Excessive indulgence in them occurs usually because the child has met some difficulty in progressing in his development and so strives to retain the pleasure activities of his infancy. Any treatment must be directed toward ascertaining the reason for the dread of continuing with his development. When this is corrected the excessive excretory play will decrease to a normal level.

DISORDERS OF BLADDER FUNCTION

Just as the historical monuments on a battlefield show where the struggle was most bitter and where the tide of battle ebbed and flowed, so the attitudes and behaviors of the average civilized human being toward the acts of urination (and defecation) are a series of monuments to the bitter struggle that has been fought out in the past between the child's wish to please his parents and his desire to perform his excretions where and when he desired. Few older children and adults, if any, are as un-self-conscious or unconcerned with the function of urination as are animals and little children. One child cannot urinate in front of others. He stands utterly unable to relax his urinary sphincter. Another, going somewhere with friends in a car, is too modest to ask that the car be stopped so that he can go to the toilet. He sits in silent misery and when the stop is made and he finally goes to the toilet, his bladder is so full that he has difficulty in starting to urinate and when he is about to finish the difference in intra-abdominal pressure is so great that he feels sick and faints. Another cannot urinate if he knows someone will hear him. One child refuses to use the toilet at school lest he get ill from germs and another will not use any public toilet for the same reason. Both endure misery till they can get home and relieve themselves. Another child may be perfectly willing to use a strange toilet but be too modest to ask anyone where the toilet is.

It can be seen readily that such attitudes are the most arrant nonsense socially and practically even though they are quite common. During World War I the greatest dread of many soldiers was that they be disgraced by being wounded while in the latrine. A more familiar example is the great difficulty and sometimes impossibility that many Americans find in urinating and defecating in bed, even though lying on a bedpan. When the child's wishes for excretory freedom succumb to the parent's wish that he be toilet trained they succumb completely, and thereafter when the whole procedure has become unconscious they continue to exert their influence regardless of present and practical considerations. These self-imposed inhibitions about the excretory functions are fairly marked in the latent period and perhaps are most imperative during adolescence; and it is always to be hoped that they will lessen as the individual enters adult life.

These attitudes are a sign of a certain degree of neurosis and are not the virtuous manifestations many parents think they are. Besides being bad for the child because of the great degree of unnecessary suffering they entail for him, they often serve as a too direct outlet for excretory pleasures which would be more valuable to him if they were more sublimated. There is no question that this excessive modesty and *nicety* interfere with the process of sublimation and therefore with the cultural development of the individual. If these attitudes are very marked it seems advisable to study the child carefully. He may have many other signs of unnecessary neurotic inhibitions and may need treatment.

The most frequent and distressing—to the parents and indirectly to the child—disorder of urinary function is enuresis. Enuresis is a condition in which the child who has been toilet trained, or has passed the age when toilet training should be completed, wets himself during the day or the bed at night.

Since toilet training is not expected to be complete before the age of three and a half, any wetting done prior to this time cannot be called enuresis. Neither can the term be applied to the occasional accident that all children have even after that time, nor to the incontinence which is only a minor symptom of some other illness, such as pyelitis. (The child who has pyelitis has tremendous frequency and urgency. The latter is so great that he may be unable to get to the toilet or to call for the bedpan quickly enough between the time he feels the urge to urinate and the time he is forced to let go.) The child who has enuresis is a healthy child, without any other signs of physical illness or symptoms related to a disturbance of urinary function. When his urine is examined it is found free from any pathological changes. This definition excludes, of course, all cases of bladder and kidney infection and those few cases where disease or abnormality of the spinal cord or vertebral column, such as spina bifida, may cause a disturbance of bladder function associated with disturbances in the motor and sensory functions of the legs and perineum. Nocturnal epilepsy may show itself only by the fact that the child has urinated in the bed during the night. Every case of enuresis should be studied carefully as to the possibility of its being due to epileptic convulsions occurring during the night.

Excluding these cases, which in actual practice are extremely rare, there remains the vast majority of children who suffer from enuresis and in whom no logically scientific physical cause can be found. There are a number of diverse causes for enuresis. In one type which is fairly common the enuresis is associated with other more important symptoms of personality maladjustment. If the patient is a girl she will have many fears, particularly of men; she will be extremely ambitious and if her ability does not exactly correspond with her ambitions she will become frightened and anxious. She must always be first in everything and particularly she must at least equal if not surpass any boy. Instead of showing the natural passivity of a girl she tends to be as active as a boy. On some occasions when she wets the bed, her urination will come at the climax of a dream in which she wants to urinate, but does so as a boy. In short, her whole life will be conducted on the principle that she is not a girl, that she will try in every way to be a boy. The basis of this idea is her fear of being a girl and having a feminine relationship to a man due to the fact that she is afraid of her father, particularly as a sexual person. As a small child she may actually have been overstimulated sexually by her father or have become frightened of him either because of the way he actually behaved toward her or because of her observations of the way he behaved toward other women. She fears to allow herself to have natural feminine feelings toward him and decides no longer to be a girl. She then tries to be a boy and as part of this attempt wants to urinate like a boy. She cannot do so, so she tries to express the wish in her sleep, and the enuresis results. She usually will stop wetting the bed at puberty with or without any treatment for the enuresis, but her fear of being a woman in relation to a man will continue and in her adult life she will tend to avoid men completely and be homosexual or to fall in love with a man whom she knows she can dominate. If she reaches the point of being psychologically able to have a child and has a boy she will tend to dominate him or even to reject him completely.

If the patient with this type of enuresis is a boy the clinical picture he presents is almost exactly the opposite. He, like the girl, suffers from many fears both in the daytime and at night. He is passive and retiring. He has no interest in any competitive activity, and if he does indulge he tends to deprecate himself when told he does well. He seems to have no pep, no backbone, and to be overwilling to let someone else take his responsibilities. In short, he prefers to "let George do it." This type of child invariably refers to his bedwetting with the expression "the bed got wet." He takes no responsibility for the situation. And there are parents and physicians who will agree with him. So much so that it is common to hear the statement that children wet the bed because they sleep so heavily, and in recent years attempts have been made, by the use of benzedrine, to help the child sleep more lightly: since he is more easily waked, he gets up and goes to the toilet and *therefore the bed does not get wet.*

Certainly such treatment does not answer the question as to why the child should have to urinate often during the night nor does it make any attempt to deal with the problem of the child's personality reactions. It can be seen that these are not masculine personality traits; in fact, when his dream life is examined it is found that his enuresis dream is one in which he urinates like a girl. In brief, in his behavior, personality reactions, and dreams he is trying to be a girl and not a boy, just as the girl was trying to be a boy and not a girl.

The reaction is caused by fear of the mother, who is usually a dominating and harsh person—so much so that he dreads to love her or any woman as a boy loves his mother; he feels he would be safer in loving her if he castrated himself and became a girl. One boy of six with enuresis stated that he had no wish to sleep in the mother's bed. It was too cold. On questioning, however, he explained that if he went into his mother's bed he would have an erection and she wouldn't like that at all. It was better for him to wet the bed because then she would never want him to sleep with her. Just as with the girl, the boy usually stops bedwetting at puberty. The reason seems to be due to the re-establishment of a more active sexual life at this time. However, although the bedwetting stops he carries his dread of women through adolescence into adult life.

The enuresis usually begins when the child has ceased masturbating through fear of punishment. The frightened cessation of masturbation causes a halt in the progress of the psychosexual development. Since the emotional development cannot progress it regresses to the stage immediately preceding the genital, namely, the stage of interest and pleasure in urination. The resurgence of the sexual energy at puberty overcomes this regression to some extent and the enuresis ceases. Of course all these reactions and feelings are unconscious or largely unconscious to the child. Certainly the connections between his fear of the parent of the opposite sex, his personality traits, and his enuresis are unconscious.

Treatment, therefore, will be directed toward the amelioration of his fear of his own sexual self in relation to persons of the opposite sex. It will not be directed toward the stopping of the enuresis, which after all is only an incidental part of the problem. Therefore the use of atropine, belladonna, alkalies, restriction of fluids at bedtime, waking and taking to the toilet, star charts, apparatuses that ring a bell when the child starts to wet the bed, apparatuses that occlude the urethra by pressure, operative procedures such as circumcision and tonsillectomy which are based on the theory that there is some mechanical irritation that causes the bedwetting—although they may stop the wetting, they are useless as attempts to cure this psychologically sick child. What is called for is intensive psychological treatment that will rid him of his fear of the opposite sex, and in our opinion this is best accomplished through a psychoanalysis, which will take a long time and will certainly have to be continued long after the bedwetting itself has ceased.

The symptom of bedwetting in these cases is often a peculiarly variable one. In some cases the bedwetting ceases after the child's first visit with the analyst, and never recurs. In others it ceases permanently after the parent makes the appointment with the analyst. It ceases frequently if the child is operated on. In other cases it does not stop until the analysis is almost completed. The cessation of bedwetting is not a reliable guide to the progress of the therapy. There are parents and physicians who regard the wetting as the main symptom and so desire to stop treatment as soon as it has disappeared; or they report marvelous cures through the use of methods that, to say the least, have no scientific validity. In these cases enuresis occurs only at night. There are included, also, cases in which the child has been toilet trained and then has relapsed, and cases where toilet training never seemed to have taken place. It is the commonest but not the only type. It is best designated *personality disorder with enuresis.*

We have not personally encountered any cases of the next type of enuresis but a number have been described in the literature on the subject. There is recorded the case of a boy who had enuresis mostly at night but also in the daytime for about two years. A year before the enuresis started his father died of tuberculosis of the bladder. Both the boy and the mother were very upset by the father's death, and to comfort each other they started to sleep in the same bed. Careful analysis showed that the enuresis was an unconscious attempt on the part of the boy to identify himself with the dead father. He had loved his father deeply and wished he would return. However his absence did bring certain advantages, such as sleeping with the mother, which he would lose if the father returned. The conflict in his mind could be solved if he were the father. He could retain him and at the same time get rid of him. Thus on the one hand he wanted to be the father because he loved him and on the other he wanted to be the father because he was jealous of him.

These two conflicting motives made him feel uncomfortable and guilty. It was as if his conscience said to him, "You have always wanted to get rid of your father and take his place. Now he is dead and your wish has come true. You will be your father. But your father was kind to you and loved you and you were a very wicked boy to desire to take his place. So now when your wish comes true you will be punished for your wish by being your father" (that is, by having bladder trouble as he did). This enuresis is a case of special symptom formation. The reaction mechanism is unconscious and responds best to intensive psychotherapy for the child. Usually psychoanalysis is the method of choice. Of course the boy should not be permitted to go on sleeping with his mother, and it would be well to ascertain if she is becoming too devoted to him and using him in her life to replace her dead husband.

Another type of neurotic enuresis may be illustrated by the following case. A little girl of five had been strictly and severely toilet trained much too early, after which she began to masturbate. The mother punished her for doing so. She then continued to masturbate but did not use her hands. Instead she sat on a rocking horse and during the rocking masturbated by sliding backward and forward on the saddle. One day she slid too far forward, the horse tipped and she was thrown violently against the pommel. The horn of the saddle bruised her urethra and for a day or two she suffered considerable burning on urination. Since she had acquired the injury during masturbation she dared not tell her parents of her discomfort. She worried a great deal lest she had injured herself permanently and inspected herself to see if she had mutilated her genitals. Since she could find no visible sign of injury she developed the idea that the injury was hidden inside, soon would burst forth, and then she could no longer hold her urine. She started to have some enuresis, which confirmed her fears.

Similar cases of enuresis—and these may include a few where the child wets herself both in the daytime and at night—may follow a painful sexual assault on a little girl by a much older boy or by a man. Since the child is hurt and yet excited she begins to feel guilty. Her guilt makes her believe that she has been injured in some way and that therefore she no longer has a physical organ to retain her urine. As a result of this belief she makes no effort to control her urination and whenever she feels the urge accedes to it on the spot. Since the child does not tell the parents of the sexual episode, the cause of the enuresis remains a mystery and can be uncovered only through intensive psychotherapy; the cure takes place when her erroneous beliefs are corrected. This type might be called *enuresis due to a fancied castration.*

Enuresis may be an expression of jealousy of a new baby, as in the following case. A boy of six and a half had the following history: He was toilet trained before he was two years old. When he was three the mother adopted another baby on whom she lavished much affection. The patient reacted by starting to soil and wet. The mother, much annoyed by this return of uncleanliness, scolded and punished him for it. When a friend told her she was not treating the boy fairly, she gave him more attention, and the soiling and day wetting stopped, although bedwetting continued until he was five. The boy was saying to his mother, "You give my new brother all your love and interest. He gets more attention than I do. See, I am only a little baby, too, and have to be cleaned and changed as he does." In cases such as this there exists, besides the organic plea for the mother's attention, a certain element of revenge. The child is well aware that his stained clothes add extra work of a distasteful kind for his mother and the maid. They may even complain a great deal about it, but he goes on doing it just the same. One sometimes even gets the impression that the child hears their complaints with a certain amount of glee. This type can be called *regressive neurosis*. The treatment should follow the course suggested by the friend of the mother. Of course the enuresis will not stop right away but will gradually cease after a moderately short period of time.

The revenge element is slight in the type of enuresis just described, but forms the most important motive in the next type, which includes most cases of both day wetting and soiling. (Soiling may also form a part of the symptom complex of the previous type.) In these cases the child's lot is an unhappy one. He is rejected by one or both parents. From the time he arises in the morning until he goes to bed at night he is nagged, fussed at, and criticized. Not uncommonly by the time he is ready to leave for school in the morning both he and his mother are in tears of irritation and rage —not over the bedwetting (although that comes into the picture) but over every detail of the daily routine. The father takes the mother's side or else remains aloof. The child has no one to support him against his nagging and unreasonable parents. He has few ways in which he can express his resentment of them. He knows that if he wets his clothes and the bed he will give his mother extra work and thus annoy her, giving himself the excuse that he cannot help his accident. Such a child often awakens at night and then wets the bed, instead of getting up and going to the toilet. He of course denies having been awake or having had anything to do with the wetting. It is only when he comes to have confidence in the therapist that he admits to having done much of it deliberately.

This is *revenge enuresis,* and its logical treatment is to change the parents' attitude toward the child, or if it cannot be changed to remove him from them. Often such a child has no enuresis during a stay in the hospital, in camp, or with friends (where the child is treated reasonably), but the symptom recurs as soon as he returns home. Such cases are difficult to treat because the rejecting parent has no incentive to change his attitude toward the child. In fact, he unconsciously welcomes the child's enuresis because it gives an added reason for nagging and abusing him. Similarly he seldom wishes to have the child placed because he will then lose an object on whom he can express his hostile feelings, and although he may bring the child to the physician for treatment every effort of the latter is thwarted.

In many papers published on the subject of enuresis attention is directed to the fact that a fairly large number of cases have low intelligence and come from poor economic and social levels. Any large hospital clinic for child psychiatry will have a number of cases of enuresis referred to it by other departments, but many of them do not keep their appointments, or if they keep one, never come back. Investigation often shows that the family is not at all concerned with enuresis. The child was brought to the pediatric clinic for some illness—a cold, bronchitis, or other—and only in the history taking is it disclosed that the child wets the bed. Further investigation shows that the parents never attempted to toilet-train the child, nor are they concerned in doing so. "All children wet their beds" is their attitude, and it is only as they approach adolescence that they gradually begin to toilet-train themselves. (1) In the majority of cases this attitude of the parents is due to their laziness and indifference to the restrictions of culture. (2) Sometimes the attitude is due to the fact that the parents also had enuresis in childhood and "outgrew" it. (3) In others, it is due to the fact that the mother gets sensual pleasure in attending to the physical wants of little children and is loath to have any of her children grow up.

There are three varieties of *enuresis from lack of training.* There is really no problem in the first group at all. The child eventually of his own initiative will establish bladder control. In the second group the outcome is usually the same. In either case the physician can do little or nothing about the situation because the parents want nothing done and feel his efforts are not necessary. Children in the third group are just as difficult to treat but the physician has more obligation to do so, since the attitude of such a parent is inclined to develop a babyish personality in the child which will make him unfit to be really successful in life. If treatment can be carried on at all it should be directed toward helping the parents find more pleasure in the child's development than in his remaining a baby.

Dr. Richard Silberstein of Staten Island differentiates between those cases of enuresis that return after a fairly long period of dryness and those that are present continuously from birth, the majority of cases. He would designate the latter as pervoid—like a perversion. In his opinion the child gets so much unconscious pleasure out of the wetting and the way it affects his relationship with his mother that he sees no reason to try to stop it. In these cases, as in the cases of lack of training, he treats the parents by counseling to the point where they become capable of using enough reasonable pressure and encouragement to get the child to stop wetting. If as a result the child develops anxiety or neurotic symptoms, he then treats the child.

There is one point about enuresis that has not been mentioned. Frequently when a child has enuresis the parents will tell you that other members of the family also had the condition in childhood. There is no certain explanation for this phenomenon at present. We can only make the assumption that such families show an inherited weakness in establishing voluntary control of the urinary sphincter. Whether this is due to the existence of a defect in the mechanism of voluntary control or to the fact that such persons possess a greater need to prolong the infantile pleasure of wetting cannot be stated definitely.

From the foregoing discussion it is clear that unreasonable punishment, shame, and scolding of the child because he wets his clothes or the bed are not only unnecessary but distinctly contraindicated. Such parental behavior serves only to focus the child's attention on his bedwetting, which can then give him a weapon for use against the parents, such as the weapon of anorexia that we spoke of earlier. It is better for the development of the child that the parents encourage him to be clean and dry as an attribute of being grown up and at the same time give him time and opportunity to do so.

BIBLIOGRAPHY FOR CHAPTER VIII

Alvarez, W. C., "Autointoxication," *Physiological Review*, 4, 1924, 352.

Davis, C. M., "Self-selection of Diet by Newly Weaned Infants," *China Medical Journal*, 43, 1929, 68.

Fenichel, Otto, "Pregenital Conversion Neuroses," *Psychoanalytic Quarterly*, 2, 1933, 94. Also Ch. VI in *Outline of Clinical Psychoanalysis*, Norton, 1934.

Ferenczi, Sandor, *Further Contributions to the Theory and Technic of Psychoanalysis*, Hogarth, 1926.

Freud, Anna, *The Psychoanalytic Treatment of Children*, Imago, 1946.

Freud, Anna, and Dorothy T. Burlingham, *War and Children*, Medical War Books, Ernst Willard, 1943.

Levy, David M., "Release Therapy," *American Journal of Orthopsychiatry*, 9, 1939, 713.

—— *Studies in Sibling Rivalry*, American Orthopsychiatric Association Monographs, No. 2.

Orton, S. T., *Reading, Writing and Speech Problems in Children*, Norton, 1937.

Pearson, Gerald H. J., *Emotional Disorders of Children*, Norton, 1949.

—— *Psychoanalytic Study of the Child, The*, Volumes 1 to 16, International Universities Press, New York.

Spring, William J., "Words and Masses: A Pictorial Contribution to the Psychology of Stammering," *Psychoanalytic Quarterly*, 4, 1935, 244.

IX

Emotional Disturbances that Occur during the Latent Period (*Continued*)

MASTURBATION

THERE is a type of masturbation that is a manifestation of a child's great unhappiness. It is known as *compulsive masturbation*. Such a child masturbates to the point of orgasm four or five times or oftener every day. He does not attempt to hide his act from observation. He unbuttons his clothes, takes out his penis and masturbates, possibly in public or before his parents or the teacher at school. He apparently feels little shame, guilt, or fear about his actions; or if he does, the feeling is not sufficient to cause him to stop. During the masturbatory act he has fantasies of which he may or may not be aware. Their content is not the simple erotic and aggressive fancies of the normal child but the sadistic and masochistic ones of the child during the anal period and includes ideas of obtaining pleasure through hurting others and through being hurt by them. Sometimes the ideas are associated with ideas of suicide, in which case the more he is warned that masturbation may hurt him the more he masturbates, since his desire is to injure himself. Sometimes when the masturbation is done publicly the child's underlying desire is to seduce the adult before whom he masturbates, in which case he has a serious intrapsychic problem and usually is living in a family situation that forces him to extreme efforts in order to adjust to it.

What is meant by this last statement? In the ordinary family where there is mutual love between the parents and between the parents and the child the emotional atmosphere is relaxed and happy. Quarrels and disagreements do occur but they are not constant; nor is the emotional atmosphere so tense that each member of the family fears to say or do anything lest he set off an explosion. The child does not have constantly to watch both his father and mother to determine if their mood is favorable, nor does he have to seek the refuge of his own room or of some corner where he can carry out his own pursuits in peace. The parents do things together and often they include the children in their recreations or plan interesting recreations for them. Together they go to the movies, to the zoo, or to a museum. Together, afterward, they talk about what they have seen. The child can talk with his parents about his interests if he wishes, though they make no attempt to pry into his affairs. At times the child prefers to play with other children and the parents feel no resentment, or he prefers to stay in his room and work at something in which he is particularly interested. He does not need to withdraw to his room in order to get out of the way. He knows when his parents wish to be alone or with other adults, and he respects their wishes even if unspoken because they respect his wishes under similar circumstances. The parents see that the child has ample play space and an adequate number of toys. Such a child has little need to feel lonely or unhappy, and therefore he is not so compelled to seek physical gratification from play with his own body.

The opposite is true of the child whose parents do not love each other, do not love him, or are too fussy and restrictive about what he does. We saw such a child recently. In the playroom, in spite of the many toys provided, he sits in a corner playing with his fingers or clothes. His behavior indicates that he is afraid he will be criticized if he plays with the toys so he prefers to play with his own body. He has developed the habit because of the unreasonable restrictiveness of his parents. In a home filled with adverse attitudes a child has to curtail everything he does lest he suffer from the wrath or disapproval of some adult. As a consequence he can find little pleasure in life except that which he is able to extract from his own body.

Treatment must be directed along two lines. First both in importance and in point of time there is required an intensive investigation of the child's intrapsychic life and of the interpersonal relationships in the family. (In the cases we have seen there has always been a serious marital problem between the parents.) If the problem of interpersonal relationships in the family seems insoluble or if it appears that efforts to solve them will take a long time, the child should be removed and placed in an institution. Second, the child needs intensive psychotherapy, usually of the degree of analysis. No other degree of treatment will be really beneficial. After treatment has been started the child should be cautioned against masturbating in public, and if he continues he should be excluded from the group until he ceases. Such treatment requires the services of an experienced child psychiatrist and should not be attempted by anyone else. Above all, operative procedures, prostate massage, bladder irrigations, and cruel and unusual punishments should never be used.

DISTURBANCES OF THE SPECIAL SENSES

We are dependent on our special senses for almost our entire orientation to reality and the external world, and a great deal of our sensual pleasure comes through their use. For civilized man, the most important special senses are vision, hearing, and touch. The other special senses such as smell and taste, though formerly more important than sight, have become relegated to the background through disuse.

Any of the special senses may undergo a type of disorder similar to those specifically discussed below, and their management will be the same.

DISORDERS OF VISION

Vision plays an increasingly large role in our life. Today's industrial and mechanical training, for example, is taught largely through the use of moving and still pictures. The sense of vision is a complicated one and can be disturbed in many different ways. Though the reader is probably familiar with the mechanics of the sense of sight we feel that the subject is so important as to warrant a brief review.

When the light rays pass from an object to the eye they enter by passing through the lens. This inverts the image of the object, hence when the image falls on the retina it is in an inverted position. The tracts that carry the sensations backward from the retina to the occipital cortex of the brain transmit the image in the same position so that as far as we can trace the progress of the impulses the image continues to be inverted. Furthermore, the image registered on one occipital cortex is the mirror reverse of that registered on the other. An F appears on one cortex as Ⱶ and on the other as ⅃. If the images of the two occipital cortices are superimposed (in order to make the single object we see consciously) the result is ⊥. As far as we can make out, the very small infant sees the world upside down.

We have no proof for this statement because we cannot learn from small infants how the world looks to them, but we do have some indication that it is correct from older children in their constant game of imagining a topsy-turvy world. In order that sight may be used as a means of orientation with the environment and with reality, such an impression must be corrected to correspond with external reality. This correction is a learned process. If a person puts on lenses that reinvert the image, he sees everything upside down for a short while and then quickly learns to see them in their correct orientation. This learning process comes about in two ways. The child looks at and touches an object at the same time. At first he sees the top of the object while his hand feels the bottom. After a few experiences of this kind he begins to try to see the object in the position that his sense of touch perceives. Gradually in this way he comes to recognize the true spatial position of objects and corrects the visual images of their position until he sees everything in its proper relation to space. Occasionally, following a cerebral injury or in those children whose learning is slow, it is possible to prove that the inversion of the visual image is corrected only psychologically.

The separation of the image on one occipital cortex from its reverse on the other takes place in a different way. Orton has shown that the image on the occipital cortex of the dominant side of the brain is retained while that on the undominant side is consciously elided and simply not seen consciously. The fact that such an elision can take place for purposes of convenience and clarity indicates that the conscious ego can readily alter or elide actual sense impressions—a fact that is well known. At best we only see what we want to see and actually do not see consciously what is repugnant to our minds, or what is associated with ideas that are repugnant to us or with feelings that cause us discomfort. Such an ability to repress and deny the evidence of our senses is not very possible before the beginning of the latent period, but it becomes increasingly possible thereafter. For this reason the mother's pregnancy state is revealed to the whole nursery school by the three-year-old child, while the ten-year-old child, much better able to reason, understand, and possessed of more knowledge than the three-year-old, is quite astounded when he is told that he has a new sibling. He never *noticed*—though he could not help but *see*—the change in the mother's figure. We have seen such an utter obliviousness to visual impressions of the mother's pregnancy even in an eighteen-year-old boy. This ability not to be conscious of visual impressions explains the vehement assertion of an eight-year-old boy that his father, whom he saw nude every day, had no body hair.

These disturbances in the conscious recognition of visual impression because of their association with repugnant ideas or unpleasant feelings are extremely common in the latent period and continue to be rather frequent in adolescent and adult life. The mechanism of repression is one of the reasons why teachers complain constantly of the lack of curiosity in children of school age. In some children the mechanism becomes so marked that actual disturbances of vision—blindness or partial blindness—result. In this case the usual condition is a concentric contraction of the visual fields—the child feels as if he were looking through a tube.

DISORDERS OF HEARING

Just as the obliviousness to visual sensory impressions is not due to so-called inattentiveness but is the result of a deliberate effort not to see, either voluntary and willed or automatic, so children's obliviousness to auditory sensory impressions also is not due to inattentiveness but to a deliberate refusal to hear. Children are notorious for their voluntary refusal to hear when they do not want to. A child is interested in his play. His mother calls him again and again. The child goes on playing. He has heard, and yet he has not heard; he does not respond because he does not want to. But when the tone of the parent's voice indicates that there will be a punishment in store if he does not come, he responds. He has an alibi for his behavior: because he has not heard he cannot be accused of being willfully disobedient. The more the child tries to make a picture of himself as a good, obedient child (that is, to inhibit his defiance of the parent), the more likely he is really not to hear when he is called. By repressing the consciousness of his sensory impressions he can be disobedient and relieve himself of any feeling of guilt about his disobedience.

This condition can result in the child's becoming actually deaf to all or certain specific sounds if they have been associated in his mind with former unpleasant experiences. For example, if the child has overheard parental intercourse and, because the feelings engendered in him by the sounds were unpleasant, has repressed the memory, then he may have to repress hearing any sounds that remind him of what he once heard. Children often react to this repression as if they were really deaf. (Since they cannot hear accurately they often compensate by developing a greater sensitivity of another sensory organ such as sight or touch. A similar compensatory reaction may follow the repression of the ability to see, or in fact the repression of the use of any channel of sensory intake.) The children who mask their deliberate defiance under the guise of deafness need some treatment for their exaggerated need to be good—a good course would consist in the parents' lowering, somewhat, their standards for the child.

DISTURBANCES OF MOTOR FUNCTIONS

Children are ordinarily more restless than adults. They cannot sit quietly for as long periods. They are more inclined to do things than they are to talk or to think. This restlessness is natural although there may be times when parents and educators find it annoying. However there are certain children whose restlessness is different from the average, in quantity or in quality.

We discuss at some length hyperactivity, fidgetiness, and tics or habit spasms.

HYPERACTIVITY

Some children are always getting into things, always on the go. Often they are so active that they remain thin, although well developed muscularly and having a good appetite. Their restlessness differs from the average child's in quantity. It usually is not associated with feelings of anxiety and may best be characterized as a state of hyperactivity.

In some instances this hyperactivity seems to be a constitutional trait. There are undoubtedly two classes of adults—indeed of children, of babies, and even of fetuses: those who are constantly active and seem to get most out of doing things, and those who are not so active but prefer quiet pursuits. The constitutionally active child tends to meet more restrictions from his environment than does the child who does not move so much and as a result he often develops antagonism toward the restricting person. This antagonism is met by further restrictions and soon a chronic aggressive reaction pattern develops.

The treatment for this type of hyperactivity is environmental. The child should have plenty of space and opportunity for muscular activity and he does best in a rural situation. When he reaches school age he should be placed in a good progressive school, particularly one where games and athletics form a prominent part of the school life. In order that chronic feelings of hostility should not be aroused it is important that there not be too many restrictions on his activity. It has been interesting to us to observe how frequently parents punish hyperactive children by making them sit still for long periods—several hours—or by tying them in one place. This not only increases the need for muscular activity but also causes the child to be uncomfortable and therefore hostile and antagonistic. It is probable that hyperactive children grow into hyperactive adults —the type who love tennis, golf, hiking, and the like, and who feel uncomfortable and distressed if they have to follow a sedentary occupation.

In other instances the hyperactivity is the result of an organic brain lesion. This type of restlessness became well known following the epidemic of encephalitis of 1919–1920. Its pathology is similar to that of the chronic aggressive reaction pattern due to brain lesion. Treatment consists of training new areas of the cortex to take over the task of control of the motor activity. This retraining is not accomplished easily and the prognosis at best is poor. It can seldom be done in the home but will be more effective if the child is in a controlled environment such as a hospital for cases of chronic encephalitis or a training school for the feeble-minded.

FIDGETINESS

The restlessness exhibited by the fidgety child differs from that of the average child in its quality. Such a child shows associated anxiety symptoms; his restlessness is not the carefree happy activity of the hyperactive (even if aggressive) child, in whom the hyperactivity is given free expression, but is an unhappy, partially controlled fidgetiness. He is like the child in the nursery rhyme: "Fidgety Phil, He couldn't sit still." He does not spend much time running and jumping but tends to sit still, with all his muscles in constant but inhibited action. He squirms, moves his fingers, hands, legs, or head, pulls at his sleeves or clothes, plays with pencils, table utensils, makes faces, and so on. In such children the restlessness is a neurotic symptom; that is, it is a sign of the presence of an intrapsychic conflict.

We again must draw the attention of the reader to the fact that it is a neurotic symptom only if the child is *really* restless. There are some parents who require a degree of inactivity which is impossible for any child or even an adult to attain. They believe in the old but outworn adage that children should be seen and not heard, and that the proper child is the child who sits still all the time. They regard a normal degree of activity as hyperactivity and accuse the child of restlessness when he really is not restless. The reader readily can see how quickly mutual hate can develop if this type of parent has a constitutionally hyperactive child. Treatment must be directed toward changing the point of view of the parents or toward rescuing the child from their restrictions.

However, there are children who are really fidgety and whose fidgetiness is the sign of an intrapsychic conflict. Long ago Darwin pointed out that animals become fidgety if they are excited, hungry, frightened or angry. Fidgetiness and restlessness form a large proportion of the symptoms of experimental neuroses in animals. The neuroses are produced by conditioning experiments in which the animal is required to discriminate between two closely similar stimuli, or to delay its response to a stimulus too long, or when, after being accustomed to being used as a test animal, the practice is stopped and its cellmate is used instead—in brief, when it is required to control its reactions too carefully or when it develops jealousy. Everyday observation will show that children, and adults also, become restless and fidgety when they are frustrated in satisfying some inner need or hunger and are unable for external or internal reasons to overcome the frustration.

Chronic fidgetiness in a child is a sign that he is being frustrated. Either his anger has been aroused and he is not permitted to express it or he has been refused satisfactions that he feels are necessary.

Frustration may occur when he has been placed in a situation where his jealousy has been aroused or when he is being asked to conform to impossible requirements. Such frustrating experiences make the child feel insecure and unhappy and as a reaction to these feelings he becomes chronically angry and has the urge to attack and annoy the persons in his environment. He does so overtly at times, while at other times he tries not to, although he is aware of what he wants to do. At such times he becomes restless because his desire to attack and annoy is greater than can be expressed through his actions, and the excess energy flows over to innervate the general musculature, producing unpurposeful motions. If he tries to remain unaware of his desire to attack and annoy and stops any attempt to put the desire into action the restlessness becomes involuntary fidgetiness. The more the desire to attack and annoy is prevented from being translated into action the more the restlessness becomes fidgetiness and spreads throughout the whole motor system.

What are some of the frustrating experiences that chronically fidgety children have undergone? In many instances the child has suffered one or more serious and prolonged illnesses in a short period of time, perhaps during one year. Such illnesses make the child more dependent on the parents and concentrate their love on him. The satisfaction in such a situation to the child's mind places a premium on being sick and dependent. When he becomes well organically he does not want to relinquish these gratifications. However, if he wishes to obtain gratification by being dependent he has to repress his desire to be active; activity's main vehicle for expression is the muscular system. In order to so repress, he has to place an inhibition on the purposeful use of his muscles. Instead of being active as he wants to be, he at the same time tries to abstain from activity, and the muscular innervation becomes more and more purposeless until a state of incoordination or perhaps tremor is reached. His desire to be active is increased by his illness, for as he lies in bed he does not have the muscular system well enough under control (because of weakness, medical prohibitions, and other causes) to use it to express his active impulses. Consequently the active impulses are stored up to be liberated later as he gets well.

After a severe illness children are often restricted unnecessarily from too active behavior by their parents, who fear a repetition of the anxiety and mental discomfort caused by the loved child's serious illness. Since muscular activity is a part of life, such restrictions tend to make the child restless, that is, to make him appear to have a purposeless excitement of the motor system. (This is clearly seen in the expression "tickles in his feet," used for a small child whose activity has been interfered with by a rainy day.) These restrictions also make the child angry. If he could express his anger verbally it would help, but his parents object. He tries to act angrily. The parents object. These emotional outlets being forbidden, the child tends to masturbate. If this outlet too is forbidden the desire to masturbate is changed to a desire to touch other parts of the body or to move in ways that will give genital satisfaction. This restlessness enhances the restlessness already present and causes a further conflict with the parents until a vicious circle is produced.

There are children who have suffered a number of traumatic experiences within a short period of time—a birth, a death, or a divorce in the immediate family, or marital difficulties in the parents' lives. Others have suffered from the continual expression of adverse attitudes by the parents. These adverse attitudes are similar to the situations that produce neuroses in animals that we mentioned above. A parent whose overprotection is based on rejection of the child frequently trains him in such a way that he has to make too fine a distinction between what is permitted and what is not. Or the parent may be overanxious to make the child conform too quickly, that is, to learn too soon to replace his use of the pleasure principle as a guide to life by the reality principle.

Treatment of these cases must consist of a search for the underlying conflict. It is not merely useless but harmful to try to coerce the child to stop fidgeting by threats, bribes, or punishments. It is equally useless and harmful to reduce the muscular activity by the use of sedatives such as phenobarbital. The fidgetiness should be ignored by the parents, the educator, and the physician. Instead, intensive psychotherapy for both parents and child should be instituted.

Years ago Freud drew attention to a type of person whose main defense is to act out impulsively a psychic conflict rather than consider it and deal with it rationally. If a series of persons living under essentially similar conditions—economic, social, and the like—is studied, it is found that accidents (such as fractures or wounds) occur only in a certain number of these persons. If the histories of this number are studied carefully it is found that they are frequently meeting with accidental injuries. When the accident itself is studied carefully it is found that it presents the picture of a deliberate attempt on the part of the individual to injure himself, though of course he is unaware that he has hurt himself deliberately. Further, it is found that persons who are prone to develop fractures are those who tend to act out or are unable to inhibit impulsive expressions of hostility. They usually have had to suppress their hostile feelings in deference to stern parents. Their muscular tension is great at all times. (It is interesting that this muscular tension disappears when they get relief from their feelings of guilt about their revengeful impulses—that is, if repression of the knowledge of the revengeful impulses has not taken place.) Ordinarily their muscular movements are stiff and jerky and they tend to act out their conflicts rather than consider them.

Similar accident proneness occurs among children. A child who is not accident prone can undertake a hazardous act safely, while an accident-prone child will get hurt in a situation that is not at all dangerous. When the psychic life of the latter is studied it is found that he is in the throes of an intrapsychic conflict which he attempts to solve through an impulsive act. Certain children have strong dependency desires. Such a child wishes to be babied and coddled, and to be free from the responsibility of doing anything for himself. This need for dependency is repressed into the unconscious because it is in conflict with the demands that he grow up and with his pride, particularly if the child is a boy. The repressed need is felt in his conscious mind as a fear that he will be a coward and unable to do the things that the other children of his age do. This feeling is painful and unacceptable to his conscious mind and he sets out to prove to himself that he is not that type of person. He can obtain such proof only through performing daring deeds. If there is a ditch he must jump the widest part. If he rides a bicycle he must ride on the most heavily traveled streets. As long as the need to prove himself brave is uppermost he can usually perform these acts safely, but if at any point the unconscious need for dependency becomes paramount he slips on the rim of the height, he falls in his jump, or he is careless in judging his distance from an approaching car. The accident occurs. Through the accident he obtains the attention and babying care he has longed for, but he can always excuse the result by feeling that he had no control over his failure. It was accidental, the result of fate.

In another type of conflict the child wishes to do something that has been forbidden by the parents or by his conscience. Instead of either acceding to the demands of his conscience and abstaining, or else getting rid of his conscience and going ahead without any feeling of guilt, he impulsively does the action and does it in such a way that he gets hurt. One boy was forbidden (unnecessarily) to play in a certain park. He went impulsively. While there he fell in the creek, lost his shoes and socks, tore his trousers, and injured his hand. When he returned home in this dilapidated state he had to confess where he had been and he received summary punishment. His sense of guilt over his disobedience and over his hostility toward his parents' orders haunted him so much that he could not have a good time without getting himself hurt. He compromised by acting in a disobedient way and getting himself punished for it. Accidents due to this type of psychopathology are frequent in accident-prone children. It is interesting that the child who, because of parental rejection, has never learned to love anyone and loves only himself does many dangerous acts safely. He is able to perform such deeds because his feelings of fear have been obliterated through a feeling of personal omnipotence which has been engendered through his self-love. Since he has no feeling of guilt he is able really to do quite dangerous things without getting hurt.

Accident proneness may also arise through an impulsive need to commit suicide. In children such an impulse is motivated often through a desire to take revenge on the parents by making them feel remorseful. This is well illustrated by the case of Tom Sawyer. Angered at Aunt Polly, he decided to go away and never come back; hence she would suffer permanent remorse for the way she had treated him. Had he drowned on his expedition—as it was thought he had—his revenge to his mind would have been complete. We say to his mind because in his fantasy he would not be extinct but would be able to observe what went on after his death. In fact the whole story of the episode (the flight, the report of the drowning, the secret return to watch the funeral ceremonies) resembles the usual suicide fantasy of the child—which he sometimes attempts to act out. Perhaps it represented a real boyhood fantasy of Mark Twain's. In many accidents the child escapes with injury only but sometimes the results are fatal.

We feel that children who show proneness to accidents need psychiatric study and probably treatment. The psychopathologies we have discussed are serious deviations from the normal and unless corrected can cause much harm and suffering to the individual and to his loved ones both in childhood and in adult life. They are not the types of psychopathology that can be expected to be changed by the simple process of growing up or by environmental change.

Children whose restlessness is an attempt to solve an intrapsychic conflict tend to become more restless in the late afternoon and evening. At this time their activity seems more aimless and in-co-ordinate; they are more liable to have temper tantrums and are more difficult to manage. As a general rule such a child is thin and pale. Parents often feel that the child is tired out by his excessive activity and think that if he rests during the afternoon he will be less tired, and therefore easier to control. The child is tired out, but his fatigue results only to a slight extent from his activity. The restlessness does tire his muscles, which are then less capable of serving as a vehicle for the expression of his aggression, but this simple physiological fact accounts for only a small part of the fatigue, for chronic fatigue is caused to a much less degree by physical exertion than by emotional conflicts. It is the interpersonal difficulties between the child and his parents or the child's intrapsychic conflicts that produce his restlessness and fatigue. If he were not restless at all he still would suffer from as great a feeling of fatigue. The treatment for the fatigue state in general is not physical rest but psychic peace. It must consist of measures that will make the individual more comfortable with his environment. Either the sources of discomfort in the environment (adverse parental behavior and attitudes) or those in the psychic life (unsolved intrapsychic conflicts) must be changed.

TICS OR HABIT SPASMS

When one observes a fidgety child one feels that he is fidgeting purposely, that he could control his restlessness if he tried harder. There is a group of conditions, however, wherein the impression received by the lay observer is different, wherein he feels that the muscular movements are not made purposefully by the child. These movements do not involve the whole of the child's body but only one or two groups of muscles. A child may blink his eyes, he may make grimaces with his mouth, he may turn his head spasmodically, or he may make jerky motions with his fingers or hands. It is always a group of muscles with a specific function that is affected and the movement caricatures an ordinary movement of expression.

A good example is the child who has attacks in which he blinks his eyes. He does not blink steadily but only in attacks that last for a few minutes and then subside. This is a caricature of the ordinary movement of blinking which we all make to protect the eye from injury, or to shut out the light because the eye is irritated. However, when this child is examined it is found that his eyes are not irritated by disease, foreign bodies, or visual defect. (Children who have defective vision may screw up their faces and blink their eyes in order to help them to see better. Neither parent nor child, however, may be aware that the vision is defective until some chance examination brings the defect in visual acuity to light.) It is true that we do blink in order to protect the eyes from injury, but it is also true that we blink in order to shut out repellent sights and to stop thinking unpleasant thoughts. We often say, about something that we do not want to think of, that we shut our eyes to it. Also we may shut our eyes and refuse to look if we feel that looking is wrong or that we will be punished for it. Such an attitude is illustrated in the well-known folk story of Peeping Tom and Lady Godiva. Thus we close or open our eyes in response to psychic activity and we may do so spasmodically as a result of an intrapsychic conflict.

An intensive study made of a number of children who suffer from spasm of the eyelids shows that the spasm is an attempt to solve an intrapsychic conflict. Often in these cases the spasm of the muscles stands as a monument to some former emotionally upsetting experience—such as some sexual curiosity for which the child had been punished or feared he would be punished but which he now has forgotten. Or the spasms of blinking began at a time when there was a slight irritation of the eye but continued after the irritation had disappeared because the motion became connected with a psychic conflict. Often these children show no signs of personality difficulties other than the spasms of the eyes, which may include spasms of the other muscles of the face. It is as if the entire psychic conflict has been crystallized into one group of symptoms and as long as it remains there the rest of the personality structure is unaffected.

After the symptom has been in existence for a little while its presence becomes noticeable to other people. The parents begin to insist that the child stop the movements and when he seems unwilling to do so—he really is not able to—they begin to nag, ridicule, and punish him. Other adults join in the nagging. The child's friends begin to tease him. This situation develops, usually, regardless of the cause of the child's disability. Even if he is suffering from chorea—which is an infectious disease of the brain—his parents may ridicule and punish him in their attempt to get him to stop the movements. The nagging and teasing are unpleasant to the child. He tries to stop and, finding he cannot, starts to become tense and restless. We say he is very nervous. A certain amount of the restlessness found in chorea is caused by this nervousness, which ceases as soon as the nagging and ridicule stop.

The child, being unable to stop the movements and finding the teasing and nagging unpleasant, begins to try to extract some pleasure from the situation. He begins to desire the attention he receives from his movements, and getting pleasure in this way he no longer minds the unpleasant part. It is remarkable how little shame or embarrassment such children feel consciously about the symptom, although they are ridiculed and teased constantly. In one case we observed, the child felt little shame about the symptoms because certain members of the family constantly remarked how cute his grimace was. Of course when the child comes to find that he enjoys the attention he receives from his blinking he is loath to give it up.

Blinking of the eyes is one of many types of movements that are designated as habit spasms or tics. They most commonly affect the head and neck, although they occasionally appear in the other extremities. Teeth grinding, whether during the waking hours or in sleep, is rather common in children. It represents a desire to injure by biting some person whom the child loves. (He feels guilty about the desire.) Rocking movements are common in babies. They express a desire for physical pleasure and of course are more pronounced in children who do not get sufficient satisfaction of this sort. Head knocking and banging occurs in older children, those at about one year of age. It is important in such cases to examine the ears carefully, for the child may have an otitis media but be too young to be able to tell that he is suffering, and so bang his head in an effort to get rid of the pain in his ears. Usually, however, he bangs his head because he feels resentful—and usually justifiably so—of some person but is too feeble to bang him. Since he cannot bang the person who has angered him he is reduced to banging the first person at hand, namely, himself.

Certain organic diseases of the central nervous system, such as chorea and the dystonias, produce localized spasmodic involuntary movements. These must be differentiated from cases of habit spasm and psychogenic tic because the treatment and prognosis are different. The diagnosis usually can be made through a careful observation of the movements and a thorough neurological examination by a competent neurologist. In some cases there may be a doubt as to whether the cause is organic or functional. It is better to treat these cases as if the cause were functional, for up to the present there is no curative treatment for the lesions in the central nervous system that produce spasmodic movements, whereas great improvement and often cure result from treatment of spasms due to psychic causes.

In the treatment of localized spasmodic movements it is necessary first to deal with the child's secondary gain from the symptoms, that is, the attention, painful or otherwise, which his family directs toward him because of his spasms. They should be advised to refrain as much as is humanly possible from any remark about his movements. The parental attitudes toward the child and the family situation in the present should be studied carefully; if possible, any adverse attitudes should be corrected or the child should be removed to another home. Both elimination of secondary gain and correction of parental attitudes should be undertaken in every case where a child shows spasmodic movements, whether the condition has an organic or a functional etiology.

Many children suffering from chorea are tense and jerky because the parents, unaware of the organic basis of the disease, nag and scold them constantly because of their "restlessness." Or the child may live in an unpleasant family situation and the chorea makes life a little more pleasant for him because it brings the kindly attention of the physician, often the comfort of several weeks in the more pleasant atmosphere of a hospital; or if he stays at home he is kept in bed and the parents make some effort to be nice to him because he is ill. When such children recover they find their life in the home more unpleasant by contrast, and they begin to wish they were ill again.

In our opinion certain cases of so-called recurrent chorea are really two successive illnesses—the first attack is a true chorea, and the subsequent ones are psychogenic copies of it. In all cases of habit spasm and psychogenic tic it is necessary to study the attitudes of the parents toward the child and to try to correct them if they are adverse. In addition, the child requires intensive psychotherapy, the purpose of which is to discover the impulses that underlie the movement and to remove the fear or distaste the child feels for the impulse. At the beginning of treatment he may be unaware either of the fear and its nature (punishment by physical injury or by loss of love) or of the impulse (curiosity, aggression, or the like). As he becomes aware of both sides of the symptom during treatment the fears can be removed and the proper and adequate use of the impulse can be pointed out to him.

The whole process consumes much time and energy for both the patient and the physician. Tics or habit spasms of long standing require therapy as intensive as psychoanalysis. However, like stuttering, the misuse of the muscles may continue even after the emotional problem is solved, in which case care must be taken that all the secondary gain has been removed from the child's symptoms. If they continue thereafter, it is advisable to suggest that the child go through a period of retraining in which he consciously tries to control the spasm. Although tics and habit spasms sometimes cease of their own accord, we do not believe that children grow out of them. Instead we think that they use a deformation of personality to solve their unsolved conflict and therefore, although no better intrapsychically, do not need the symptom of the spasm any more. This is a pity because deformation of the personality produces more real suffering in life than do single symptoms and is much more difficult to treat.

OBSESSIVE-COMPULSIVE REACTIONS

Little children are notorious for being unable to play together peaceably and happily for long periods. After a reasonably short while they tire of each other's company and turn to other pursuits or to quarreling. If the play is at all vigorous and exciting or if there is an adult present the quarreling starts sooner. The reason is that they are intensely individualistic and self-centered. They wish to be first in everything, to have the best and to be the most important, and they have little capacity to share or fill any role, no matter how necessary, in which the limelight does not shine only upon them. A great deal of childhood and adolescence is spent in learning how to limit and control this attitude in order to live happily with one's peers, all of whom have, basically, the same characteristics. It takes a long, hard process of learning before the child is able to know when it is desirable for him to consider the needs and desires of others, and when it is desirable for him to assert his demands for himself.

Usually it is only with the beginning of the latent period that the child begins to make contact with real social life with his fellows, and if the reader will watch a child of this age he will see the great variety of struggle through which he goes in his attempts to get along comfortably with his companions. He begins to take part in group games, and anyone who has observed these games formulated by children without adult aid will realize that they are governed by rules more rigid and unchangeable than the laws of the Medes and Persians. In the common and simple game of tag the child who is "it" is not chosen by any authority or by any system of democratic voting, but is selected by a method of counting out. This method—based entirely on chance—means that no one makes the selection, therefore there is no superior and each player has the same chance of avoiding being the unwished-for "it." Logically, therefore, there can be no recriminations, no hostility, and no jealousy, and if these occur they cannot logically be directed at any member of the group but only at malignant fate. Therefore the process of counting out, the leaving the selection to chance, is a magical method that avoids any personal participation in the result and removes any possibility of the arousal of jealousy or hostility within the group. In this way feelings of hostility within the group are checked and kept in control. Even counting is not always efficacious, for frequently the cry of cheating in the counting is raised by some child who has not yet learned sufficiently the rules of social behavior.

Another way which the child uses to socialize his urges is found in the previously mentioned game of walking without stepping on cracks in the pavement. The crack is symbolic to the child of an expression of some inner impulse which would meet with social disapproval. We are not sure whether the rhyme, "Don't step on a crack, Or you'll break your mother's back," is based on the same inner impulse—that is, hostility toward the mother—among all children who play it. To step on the crack is to injure the mother. The child uses the idea of stepping on a crack as a symbol of an inner wish and then avoids the expression of the wish by refusing to step on the crack. The impulse is displaced onto an action toward an indifferent object and then the child can avoid the action.

In addition to dealing with hostile impulses in this way, children often displace erotic drives from one object to another and then either perform or avoid performing an action upon that object, depending on whether the child *must* do it or *must refrain* from doing it. For example, touching is a pleasurable activity. In our culture quite severe restrictions are placed on children's touching. We find that the word *don't* is applied more often to children's touching than to any other single activity. The child is "don'ted" not only for touching his genitals but also for touching innumerable objects around the house, some of which are fragile and some dangerous —all of which curtails the amount of pleasure the child wants to have from the use of his hands. Children in the latent period have many touching games, such as the telephone-pole touching previously mentioned. If they are prevented from touching one or miss the proper one, they feel irritated and go back and touch it. They express their need to touch by saying they will have bad luck if they don't.

Children have a great tendency to bind themselves by vows. Sometimes the vows, voluntarily made, come to have such a hold on the personality that the individual finds himself unable to escape their influence. In many cases they are of a hostile, revengeful nature. A girl was rebuked by her father, when she tried to kiss him, because her breath was offensive. She became furiously angry at the rebuff and vowed never again to show him affection. Another girl vowed never again to tell her father anything about herself. As she grew up she found it impossible to be confidential with any man in authority, even though this attitude was detrimental to her. A boy vowed that when he grew up he would kill his father. When he did grow up he found it impossible to have a satisfactory relationship with his bosses.

He either attempted to do them some injury or else he behaved toward them as if no act of theirs could ever anger him. We feel that it is inadvisable for parents to induce a child to make a vow—to love mother always, to respect father always, to dislike a certain person always, to forgo certain forms of behavior always. The vow may attain control over the child's ego and the results may be disastrous to the individual.

It might be argued that all the rituals we have described are simply the expressions of excess energy on the part of the child. This opinion would fit in with one theory of play, that play has the purpose of using up excess energy. However, this theory does not explain the content of the play or the fact that the child feels irritated if the specific action is interfered with, as he feels irritated if he does not touch the proper telephone pole. Certainly part of the dynamics of play is the pressure of energy which needs utilization. The content of the play, however, indicates that the form of utilization also satisfies a specific need in the child's unconscious. In the touching games, he wishes to touch his or someone else's body. He represses this desire into the unconscious and then displaces it from touching the body to touching an inanimate object. He is unconscious of his displacement. If he touches the secondary object he feels pleasure. If his game is to avoid touching an object he is unconscious of the fact that he avoids because he is afraid of the punishment that he believes would result if he touched.

This process of learning to control the mode of expression of instinctual impulses—through games into whose composition rituals, ceremonials, and magical procedures enter—is a step on the child's road to the socialization of his desires and toward the sublimation of primitive impulses into cultural but pleasurable activities. It is after this stage that he becomes able to play real group games such as football and baseball, where team play is important and where rules are laid down that make the play for the good of the whole team more important than the play for the good of the individual player.

Thus during the latent period the child learns to control the mode of expression of his inner urges through the use of rituals, ceremonials, and magical procedures. His ego skills and abilities are not well enough developed yet to help him to control them in other more realistic ways. The personality of the child of this age level therefore has a strong resemblance to the personality of the adult who suffers from an obsessive compulsive reaction, and the reasons for the personality structures in both are the same, namely a weakness of the ego—in the child because of immaturity, in the compulsive adult because of extreme fear of his superego. In both cases the personality structure is brought about to avoid painful feelings of guilt.

The tendency on the part of children during the latent period to resort to rituals and the like in order to avoid feelings of guilt about the modes of expression of their inner impulses should be seriously considered by religious educators. Many children of this age turn to formal religion not because they understand or wish to lead better ethical and spiritual lives, but because the rituals and ceremonials of religion offer them temporarily an easier way of controlling the modes of expression of their inner impulses than having to learn how to deal with them from an ethical and sociological aspect. When such a child in the latent period is converted, then, having made his peace with his sense of guilt by having placed all responsibility for his actions on the *religious rituals* and *ceremonials*—not on religion—he can then behave as he likes without feeling any guilt about his behavior. He can continue to behave as he likes so long as he performs the necessary rituals and prayers.

He may not react to his conversion in this way. Instead he may rely on his religious beliefs to keep his erotic and aggressive impulses repressed. They therefore remain in a childish state of development and he never learns how to use them or deal with them in an adult fashion. It seems a great pity when a child in the latent period pledges his future life to the church in order to avoid the struggle he must make to socialize himself. If he is allowed to continue with this ambition he can be only an immature and inadequate minister of religion. It is fortunate that many religious educators are aware of the perils that lie in such a course, but unfortunately parents often are not, and give their sanction and even encouragement to such an ambition.

There are certain children who are unable to solve the oedipus conflict satisfactorily, particularly that portion of it that is concerned with aggression and hostility toward the parent of the same sex. Such children feel that the only way to deal with their guilt, aggression, and hostility is through the accentuation of the rituals, ceremonials, and magical procedures so common during this period.

The mechanisms, instead of serving them as a step toward maturity, become the dynamic forces by which life must be lived. The children develop all the symptoms of an obsessive compulsive reaction and behave in the same fashion and with the same difficulties as do adults who suffer from the same illness and whose symptomatology we will discuss later. The treatment for these cases will be intensive psychotherapy, preferably psychoanalysis.

NAUGHTINESS IN CHILDREN

All our readers are acquainted with naughtiness in children, but we wonder if they have defined what they mean by naughtiness. If they introspect carefully they will find that they have their own personal ideas as to what constitutes naughtiness. Each adult and each child has his own personal code, and any violation of that code by himself or others is regarded as naughtiness. For one, disobedience is the deadly sin, for another autoerotic sexuality, and for another untidiness. Overlying this personal code there is the code of the social organization, which is applicable to everyone living in that society regardless of whether the individual considers it appropriate or not. As a rule people do not violate their own personal codes, and regard those who do as being naughty, but they do not feel quite the same obligation to obey the social code and often violate it openly or underhandedly or countenance its violation by others. Even if they do not violate it they may feel that the code needs changing, and will work hard to bring the changes about; they seldom, if ever, feel that their own personal codes should be changed or feel any willingness to work toward changing them.

Ideally the code of parent and teacher should be exactly the same as that of the social organization that has been developed through long experience as the best way for individuals to live happily together in a group. Unfortunately the codes frequently do not agree. Parents are not content with the restrictions imposed by society, but have to impose others of their own. They may even be loath to accept the social code themselves, and so train the child to follow their code and to feel disrespect for society. A child may be considered naughty by the parents because he violates their own personal code, by the teacher because he violates her personal code, by the social organization because he violates the social code.

From the adult's point of view, naughtiness consists in the rebellion of the child against the code; in other words, the real sin lies in the rebellious unwillingness of the child to conform. The child is first and foremost an individualist and has little or no desire to conform to any code. We expect, therefore, that every child from time to time will show rebelliousness against being trained, and so will behave in a naughty fashion. Training in social living consists of two concomitant processes which proceed both consciously and unconsciously. The first is the amalgamation of the various partial and often divergent and conflicting erotic instinctual drives into a unified whole in order that their gratification will bring the individual person success and happiness, will ensure the perpetuation of the race, and will promote development of the ability to obtain gratification for these amalgamated desires without injuring or interfering too much with the other members of the group—parents, siblings, companions, superiors, peers, and subordinates—and their need to obtain their own gratifications. The second process is learning how to obtain the satisfactions mentioned above and at the same time live comfortably in the culture—that is, the manners, customs, and codes —of the society in which the individual lives. Unfortunately we tend often to lay too great emphasis on the latter and seem to forget the importance of the former; for example, we tend to lay great stress on training a child to select the proper fork instead of training him to eat adequately and in a way that will not be displeasing or disgusting to his fellows. American culture is somewhat restrictive but not too severely so in the matter of sexual gratification—its restrictions do not really interfere with an adequate sexual life. It does bear down more heavily on any attempt to freely exercise aggressive activities. Most of the legal enactments are directed against interpersonal aggressive acts, and even the legal prohibitions against sexuality are not against sexuality itself but against those components that are aggressive and hostile toward other persons.

As we said before, in the ideal situation the parents' and the educator's codes will be the same as the code of the social organization. The child, if he wishes to be a member of the group, must learn to conform to them. How does he learn? The natural answer to this question lies in considering the way in which the child learns to adjust to two situations: toilet training and the oedipus conflict. In both, the child gives up his independent individualism because he loves the parent—in the first because he loves his mother and wishes to please her and in the second because he loves his father and wishes to get along with him happily and peaceably. In neither instance does his giving up prevent him from obtaining satisfaction for his instinctual needs. In the first he can obtain anal gratification through sublimatory activities and in the second he can as an adult live a sexual life with another woman who is not his father's wife.

When the child loves his parents or, more accurately, when they love him, he tries to conform to their code and later to the code of the social organization. At times he finds conforming difficult and periods of rebellion and naughtiness occur, but they become less and less frequent as he grows older, until in adult life he conforms to the code of his culture automatically and without too much strain. Of course he must be given opportunities that will bring into relief the conflict between his individualism and the social code—for example, he will never become toilet trained unless he learns that toilet habits are an essential part of civilized life. Is anything more necessary than this general process of training by living together? Admonition and precept of course will occur, for it is natural for the parent to instruct the child verbally. Is it necessary to punish him when he fails to conform? Animals find it necessary to punish their cubs when the cubs decide to rebel against the parents' code, and it would seem that human beings need not be above learning from animals. However, children as a rule require less punishment than do beasts, because their capacity to love and to identify through love is greater than is found among the lower animals.

We have discussed these matters at considerable length because only by an adequate understanding of them is it possible to intelligently discuss persistent and chronic naughtiness in children and what can be done about it. Naughtiness is rebellion and rebellion is an expression of aggressive energy. Therefore we must look for the causes of chronic naughtiness when there are difficulties in dealing with the aggressive urges.

In an earlier chapter we described the various levels of reaction to a frustration. We noted that when a person's desire for gratification was frustrated he experienced a feeling of disappointment to which he reacted by mobilizing his aggressive energy in a rebellion against the frustration. If a child is in a state of constant naughtiness, that is, of chronic rebellion, we have to ascertain how the child is being frustrated. There are a number of situations where frustration may occur. Have the instinctual urges of the child been unnecessarily frustrated by the parents in the present or in the past? One mother obstinately determined that her child would not suck her fingers. She used every possible method to prevent it, because the child with great courage and tenacity refused to stop. However the mother's superior strength and ingenuity conquered. The child gave in, but from then on hated the mother with a deep, undying hatred and rebelled in every way possible. The mother succeeded in preventing the child's finger sucking, but at the same time, in ordinary parlance, ruined the child's disposition.

If the battle between this little girl and the mother had remained confined to this one situation the results might not have been so serious, but since the mother represented authority to the child she reacted in the same way to all authority outside her home because she anticipated that any authority would impose on her the unnecessary restrictions her mother did. It may seem strange to the reader that the child should regard finger sucking as so necessary that she could become bitterly antagonistic when the parent required her to stop it. It must be remembered that the parent who objects so obstinately to finger sucking usually objects as rigidly to other manifestations of infantile sensuality so that the child is really deprived of all avenues of obtaining sensual pleasure.

A more important question is why one child reacts by open and bitter hostility to his frustration when another accepts the frustration without too much hostility and another indulges in the prohibited activity either in secret or in fantasy, suffering an intolerable sense of guilt about the wicked behavior. The answer to this question seems to be in the type of ego that the child has developed. In the first child, the frustration increased the degree of hatred in her ambivalent feelings to her mother. In order to manage this ambivalence her ego regressed to the sadomasochistic stage of development to maintain some attempt at fusion of the aggressive and libidinal drives. This regression did not suffice. Even that type of fusion gave way and the aggressive drives expressed themselves in her rebellious behavior.

The best treatment for this type of naughtiness is to see that its cause does not occur. Children are entitled to an optimum period of satisfaction for their infantile pleasure needs. They cannot be expected to relinquish them too suddenly, but should be allowed to grow out of them. (By this we mean that they should have the opportunity to find more mature ways of obtaining the same pleasure, and that when they find them they will no longer be interested in the more infantile ways.) If the naughty behavior has been present only a short while it is relatively easy to deal with. The parent should apologize to the child for his unwarranted interference with the child's pleasure pursuits and should encourage him to indulge again if he feels so inclined. A case of stuttering might be cited as an example. The father and mother had interfered quite unnecessarily with the child's finger sucking. The child stopped it and immediately began to stutter. The father, recognizing where the fault had been, tried to encourage the child to suck her fingers again, and at the same time, because he realized that his daughter might be ridiculed by her friends if she did too much finger sucking, he laid in a plentiful supply of lollypops, the sucking of which was socially acceptable. Immediately the stuttering ceased.

The naughty behavior should be ignored. If the child is punished for it he will regard the punishment as unfair and will react against it with further rebellious behavior (naughtiness). Since such a reaction is usually in turn punished by the parent, the child feels more antagonistic and behaves in a worse manner. This secondary vicious circle is the cause of the great difficulty in treating this type of case when the naughty behavior has been present for a period of time. There has been so much battling between parent and child that the original cause is forgotten and both are aware only of the present mutual feeling of hostility. The parent is disgusted with the child and his behavior and the child hates the parent.

For such cases intensive psychotherapy for the child is required, often of the intensity of psychoanalysis. Even during an analysis, if the child lives at home, the constant daily mutual antagonism between child and parents adds fuel to the fire, which can counteract the effects of the treatment and so prolong it unduly or neutralize it entirely. Placement in a foster home is not practical because the child carries his hostile attitude toward the parents over to all persons in authority, which includes the foster parents. Foster parents who can accept into their home a badly behaved child—who may even be a neighborhood nuisance and continue so for some time—and not react with hostility against him are very rare. Practically it seems better to place such a child in an institution—such as the Southard School in Topeka, or Bruno Bettelheim's Orthogenic School in Chicago, or the Devereux School in Devon, Pennsylvania—where his naughty behavior can be ignored and where intensive psychotherapy can be carried on. The psychotherapeutic problem in these cases is to uncover the anxiety associated with the gratification of infantile sensual needs, to allow the child to gratify these needs as much as any child is allowed, and to help him from that point to proceed to other more mature forms of gratification of sensual pleasures. We do not believe that the treatment of these more severe cases should be attempted by anyone except a competent psychiatrist.

If the instinctual drives have not been unreasonably or unnecessarily frustrated it is necessary to look deeper into the parent-child relationship because here may lie one of the important causes of a child's bad behavior. Children not only resent the frustration of infantile sensual pleasures but resent more deeply a lack of love, or a decreased amount of love. It is common for older children to begin to be mischievous and behave badly about the time a new baby is born in the family. The older child feels that the attention necessarily given to the new baby is an indication that the parents love the latter more than they do him. His wish for love is frustrated and he begins to react antagonistically in order to express his displeasure. If the parents punish him for this reaction he feels more unloved and more antagonistic and behaves worse. Again the vicious circle mentioned before develops. If, however, the parents are wise they will ignore the naughtiness that sometimes heralds the arrival of a new baby and see to it that the older child is helped through his period of frustration in the manner we described in Chapter VI.

This illustration is simple but it indicates the difficulties that arise when a child feels himself unloved. What of those children who actually are unloved? Theirs is a very serious situation. Theoretically the earliest attitude of the human being toward his environment, human or otherwise, is one of hostility. The overstimulation of the sensory pathways during and after birth is felt by the baby as a painful frustration. Aggressive hostile drives are elicited by pain or by danger—the apprehension of danger being really a special type of pain. Since the infant's first connection with the environment causes him pain he must feel hostile and antagonistic to it. Then he learns to differentiate his mother from himself and begins to realize that she brings him pleasure; it is not till then that his feeling toward her changes from one of hostility to one of longing and desire to re-experience pleasure and comfort from her. This longing is the first budding of a feeling of love. It neutralizes the hostile feelings, causing the child to direct part of them away from the person of the mother and to combine part of them into a new relationship with her—a sadomasochistic one at this stage of development. Before this new relationship comes about, the child's feelings of love are directed entirely onto himself. A moderate degree of this state of affairs is plainly apparent in all young children. They are self-centered and love themselves and their own comforts and pleasures to a much greater extent than they do anyone else. It is even questionable whether anything approaching a real altruistic relationship with other persons is found before puberty. The binding of the feelings of love to the person of the child results in his feeling that he is all-important, omniscient and omnipotent, that he really is beyond all physical dangers, and that he must have everything he wants just when he wants it.

When the mother does not love the child she does not care to satisfy his needs for pleasure and comfort. She does what she has to do for him out of a sense of duty and often in a harsh and somewhat painful manner. Thus the child has no reason for changing his hostile attitude toward her or toward anyone else and no incentive for turning his love away from himself to others. He thus tends to remain very much in the same type of emotional rapport with himself and the environment that exists in the very small child, and his personality characteristics are similar to this small child's.

Children who are chronically rebellious because they are unloved show the type of personality reactions described above. Their attitude toward others is one of hostility. The environment is filled with many things to gratify their wants and needs and they tend to take them where and when they want them without regard to the feelings or needs of others or to the customs we impose on ourselves in order that we may live comfortably together. They behave, in actually dangerous situations, as if they were not afraid (as they are not, since they feel omnipotent). Since they have no feelings of love directed toward any object but themselves, they show no consideration for others and seem totally lacking in respect, sympathy, kindliness, gratitude, and the ordinary niceties of social intercourse. The presence of any of these traits or reactions, on the other hand, indicates that the child is able to love others, since the decencies in social custom and usage arise from our feelings of affection and love toward the other members of the group. Such capacity has never been developed in the unloved child. The child who is forced to develop in this manner is regarded by ordinary people, whether children or adults, as queer. They do not understand him, and because all their efforts to deal with him in the ways they have found successful in interpersonal relationships—that is, by kindness and sympathy—elicit only more hostility from him, they in turn become hostile to him. Their hostility calls forth more of his hostile feelings, until he and all members of his social group are in bitter conflict, which lasts as long as the *child* can maintain his hostile attitude and live in society.

In many instances the conflict with the environment ends in victory for the social organization, which either executes the hostile individual or incarcerates him for a longer or shorter period of time. The incarceration usually increases his hostility, with the result that when he is paroled, he emerges with only the determination to keep his part in his hostile acts hidden as much as possible from detection by the authorities. Such is the outcome in many cases. In others the painfulness of the counterhostility of society causes the individual rather suddenly to try to suppress the outward manifestations of his hostile feelings and if possible even his consciousness of them.

A similar attempt may be made by the child if he is moved from a hostile environment to one where there is some attempt to treat him understandingly, kindly, and decently. In the hostile situation nothing has been done to change the structure of the child's personality. It remains unchanged and he has only become *frightened* by the retaliation his hostile behavior produces. In the changed situation, he is beginning to make some attempt to change his personality structure, but his first steps consist only in attempts to inhibit the expression of his hostility. In both instances the change is sudden, and we know from our observations on other phases of child training—for example, toilet training—that if the child *suddenly* succumbs to the demands of the environment he does not learn to redirect and sublimate the instinctual impulses but suppresses them and keeps them suppressed by feeling and acting exactly in the opposite way; that is, whereas previously he was very dirty, now suddenly he becomes overscrupulously clean, and in this way nullifies any real cultural use of his instincts.

The chronically aggressive child who changes suddenly proceeds on exactly the same pattern: whereas previously he was defiantly rebellious he now becomes defiantly submissive; heretofore destructive, now he *never* destroys; previously antisocial and defiantly rebellious against the social organization, now he is asocial and defiantly regards the easy social customs of ordinary society as bad, coarse, vulgar, and indecent. He dare not react hostilely to a real injury. Instead he appears not to notice what has happened, or if he notices it he is unaware of any hostile feelings. He puts up with the situation meekly, but on some other occasion begins to feel angry where there is no cause. Thus he splits the emotional reaction from its cause. Since he is unconscious of his hostile feelings when they occur, even in circumstances where such a reaction would be valid, he begins to behave as if he had injured someone and tries to make a totally invalid atonement. If he is in a situation where the ordinary person would feel resentment he submits subserviently, but very soon does something that injures himself; thus his aggression which formerly raged against his environment in order to destroy it now rages as fiercely against himself with serious self-destructive tendencies.

In short, from being a chronically rebellious child he has become a compulsive personality. There was perhaps some benefit and happiness to himself, though not to society, in his former state. Now, at least, society does not suffer—though it receives no benefits from him—while he loses all benefit to himself and all chances of happiness. No cure has taken place. He has only developed a reaction formation as a defense against his inner feelings. These examples make it evident that any therapeutic measures directed solely toward the suppression of the aggressive reactions, if successful, tend only to destroy the child and his mental health and not to reform him to make him a useful member of society.

There is another group of chronically rebellious children whose condition is worse even than the group just described. In behavior they are the most violent, the most destructive, the most annoying, and the most unmanageable. Their life history is particularly consistent from case to case. The boy has a dominating mother or mother substitute, such as a grandmother. The father is a weak, ineffectual man or is absent from the home all or the greater part of the time. The mother dominates because she resents the fact she is a woman and not a man. This resentment is unconscious: were she aware of it, her lack of femininity would have prevented her ever marrying. Resentful of being a woman, she has no desire or use for the great compensation that a woman finds for her femininity—childbearing. She becomes pregnant accidentally. She loathes her state and often makes futile attempts at abortion. When the child is born she does not wish to see him but soon develops feelings of guilt about her rejection of him. She assuages these guilt feelings by developing an overprotective attitude toward her son. Through this protective attitude she crushes every attempt he makes at initiative, independence, and masculinity.

In order to avoid the pain of her displeasure the little boy suppresses all his masculine activity and accentuates all his passive attitudes. His attempts to imitate the father also increase his passive attitudes, for if the father is absent he has no man with whom to identify, and if the father is present his weakness and passivity make him a poor model for the boy. As soon as the boy's passive attitudes are well accentuated the mother begins to tease and taunt him for being such a sissy. This treatment hurts his feelings and he tries to prove to her that he is really masculine. In order to do so he has to accentuate his independence and his best method is to be defiant and rebellious. Thenceforth, every time he feels a passive impulse, which occurs commonly in men and which no one disdains, he suppresses it immediately and behaves in exactly the opposite way.

It is surprising, when one comes to know well such a young hellion who is the neighborhood menace, to find that he really is most interested in playing with dolls or doing housework, but that he keeps these interests to himself lest he be teased. Much of his annoying behavior is directed toward other boys or older men and has for its purpose attracting their attention to his person even though he may suffer pain as a result. Basically, of course, he has a great fear of women and feels more comfortable with men. He also has strong passive desires toward both men and women. When such a child reaches puberty he begins to be aware of his homosexual orientation, which he dreads because he dreads all love relationships. He represses it and gradually develops the classical symptoms of a paranoid state, usually of a schizophrenic type.

This last-mentioned type of chronically rebellious child indicates another source of the difficulty that such unloved children show in making an adjustment. We have mentioned already that one source lies in the fact that never having been loved, they have received no incentive to love others in return, and therefore their strivings to love remain attached to their own persons, while their hostile aggressive strivings are divorced from love and turned toward others. We mentioned also that in order to become socialized it is necessary for the child to fuse his hostility with love, and so to neutralize the destructive elements when the fused strivings are directed toward others. In short, one tremendous factor in the etiology of this condition is the child's inability to love. The child learns to redirect and control his aggressive impulses when he loves his parents, because loving them, he wants to be like them. The child who comes from a broken home does not have two parents to love and imitate. The child whose parents hate him has no incentive to love the parents and be like them. Since the identification with the parent is the basis for the formation of the superego and since the function of the superego is to control and redirect the mode of expression of instinctual urges in order that the individual may express them in harmony with the customs and manners of his social organization, these children tend to lack the inner light by which they can view their behavior, and so find pleasure in actions that would overwhelm the ordinary person with feelings of shame, guilt, and embarrassment.

There has been some controversy in psychiatric circles as to the status of the superego in these chronically rebellious children and adults. Are they people with little or no moral sense? Have they an overpoweringly severe superego along certain lines and consequently too little along others? Is their superego so severe that no matter how well they behave they are tormented by a sense of guilt and can assuage it only by being punished? We think the controversy is not very valid, for we feel that the naughty children include a number of types of personality structure, all of which tend to produce somewhat the same symptom complexes, just as a variety of different organisms if introduced into the body will all produce a specific type of fever; and we feel that etiological factors in a specific combination will produce a specific type of naughtiness, but our powers of observation are not delicate enough to distinguish easily one type of naughtiness from another.

In the first type we have mentioned (the child whose naughtiness is a rebellion against the unreasonable frustration of his infantile erotic needs) the child suppresses any attempt at gratification of his erotic desires because he must, and later in order to be comfortable he represses his awareness of the desire itself. His naughtiness at first is an overt rebellion against the parent's restrictions, and eventually a rebellion against his own self-restrictions of which he is aware only as he perceives them in projection, that is, as if emanating from the social organization instead of from himself. His personality structure therefore is one with an oversevere superego against erotic gratifications and an ego that rebels openly against those restrictions.

In the second type (that in which the child has been unloved and therefore never has learned to love) the personality structure may be formed in one of two ways. In one form the ego has learned through bitter experience that any attempt to love brings pain. Henceforth to avoid pain the ego shuns all love impulses except when directed toward itself. To love is not immoral; it is painful. Yet there may be actions and feelings which the individual feels it is immoral to do or feel and the awareness of whose presence fills him with shame and guilt—all of which indicates that a superego of a sort is present. It seemes to us that this condition arises in children who have not been totally rejected but have received some love. Perhaps the parental attitude toward the child has been one of overprotection rather than open rejection, or perhaps he has known at least a short period of time with some loving person. In the other form, one can find no real evidence of the presence of feelings of shame, guilt, or embarrassment about anything—no indication of the presence of a superego. In these cases the child has had no love and therefore has had no incentive to identify with the adult. Such children have no moral sense.

In the third type the ego fears the pain it will suffer if it gives in to passive desires. The superego is severely prohibitive of the homosexual orientation. Here an oversevere superego is definitely present and the ego is timid, weak, and ineffectual.

It is obvious that no treatment can be planned without considering the personality structure of the patient with whom the therapist is dealing. In the first type the treatment must be directed to an amelioration of the prohibitions of the superego against infantile erotic drives. For the two subtypes of the second group the aim of therapy and the methods employed will differ because of the different personality structure. In the first subtype the treatment will be aimed first at removing the dread of loving and second at ameliorating any misdirection or overseverity of the superego that may exist. In the second subtype the aim is to release the ability to love. The more an actual dread of loving is the motivating factor in the child's life the more probable it is that he will be helped best by intensive psychotherapy, especially analysis. The more the motivating factor is not a dread of loving but a lack of opportunity to love, the more the child needs not psychotherapy but an actual twenty-four-hour-a-day experience of being with people who love him.

It is difficult to introduce either subtype into the treatment situation, particularly if the case is severe or the problem of long standing. The attitude of the child usually is hostile and to this hostility is added the hostile reaction engendered by the fear of the strange adult, fear learned by long and bitter experience. As a result of his feelings of omnipotence the child repudiates any need for help. He has little apprehension about being rebellious and defiant—or if he has he uses it to cover his hostility with a superficial cloak of agreeableness. His defenses against treatment are almost perfect. It is necessary, therefore, to break down his defenses before one can begin real treatment of his difficulty. There are several ways of doing so. He can be treated in such a way that he has to change his chronic aggressive reaction to its opposite—a compulsive reaction—as has been described earlier. He can be allowed such absolute liberty that he breaks down in panic. He can be exposed to painful realities from which the therapist can rescue him. (An example of this treatment in a mild case is the child who steals but has no allowance. The therapist can arrange to have the parents give him an allowance of his very own, one that will be adequate for his needs and that he can spend as he likes without any parental interference.) The purpose of these methods is to get the child to realize that he is not omnipotent, that he is a sick child and really needs help and that the therapist really can help him. When this is accomplished the therapist and the child can work out the problem of the fear of loving. Since in most cases the condition usually has been in existence for a long time, treatment must be intensive and will be lengthy. For reasons we will discuss later the outcome of treatment is not always good even in the hands of the most experienced psychiatrists. Treatment for the third type will follow similar lines.

Therapy for the second subtype consists of placing the child in charge of some adult who can really love him. Such placement is made best in an institution because few foster homes or their neighborhoods can put up with the behavior of such a child. The presence of a person who loves him will call forth an answering love in the deprived child, and he will gradually pass through the same states in the control of his aggression as does the child in the ordinary home. It will not take as long after the initial contact is made, but it will take several years. As the process goes on one can watch with interest the development of the child's superego. His course must be watched carefully and if instead of a gradual growth of a superego he shows the development of a compulsive reaction he should be referred immediately for psychiatric treatment.

There is still a fourth type of naughtiness to be considered. The history is somewhat as follows. The child has been loved, both parents are alive and present, but the training has been rather strict. The child's infantile pleasure drives, such as sexual curiosity, destructiveness, and masturbation, have been prohibited. The child has conformed because he wants to please the parents. When the child is between four and seven the parents go on a trip, leaving the child with friends or relatives; or the child himself goes on a visit to friends or relatives for several weeks or months. The adults whom he visits are not as strict as the parents, and the child begins to partake of pleasures that previously had been forbidden. When he realizes that the time has come for him to return to the parents, he realizes also that he has to forgo these pleasures in the future lest he get into trouble. He avoids continuing them and tries to put the thought of them and the memory of the pleasures out of his mind. He does this best by beginning to think of his behavior as bad and punishing himself a little by a painful sense of guilt when he thinks about them. Pretty soon, instead of becoming aware of his desire when it is present, he feels only a sense of guilt. This is unpleasant and painful. He has learned from past experience that he always felt uncomfortable when bad and much better after his parents dealt out a sudden punishment such as a spanking. Having this experience at his disposal he proceeds to use it to assuage his painful feeling of guilt. After he arrives home, as soon as this feeling arises he looks around for some rule to break. The naughtiness is perpetrated openly in order that the parents may observe it, which they do, and then they punish him. It should be emphasized that his crime is never the same as that for which he is feeling guilty: during their absence he masturbated; now when he has a feeling of guilt he does not masturbate but may break a dish, spill water on the floor, or steal. As soon as he has been punished he feels better. His guilt feeling is assuaged. He is no longer naughty and seems happier. Obviously from the parents' point of view the punishment has worked. The child has learned not to be naughty.

After a day or two—perhaps more, perhaps less—the guilt feeling reasserts itself. He has now the added experience of the efficacy of a technique that will assuage the feeling of guilt. Again he is naughty, again he is punished, and again he feels better. From now on his life is a succession of this pattern—guilt, naughtiness, punishment, feeling better—and from the observer's point of view it is a succession of episodes of naughty behavior and of the child's never seeming to learn by experience that if he is naughty he will be punished.

It is a human reaction to try to extract pleasure from any situation or behavior. So the child, not satisfied with the negative pleasure of the assuagement of his guilt feeling, begins to get a thrill out of being naughty and to have a thrill superimposed on the pain of being punished. He begins therefore to add a masochistic pleasure to his need for punishment. Now he has two motives in his naughty behavior, and every time his parents punish him they only increase his desire for more punishment. If in desperation they desist from punishment his naughtiness increases until it is almost humanly impossible not to interfere. He begins to react in a similar way outside the home and by the time he has reached adolescence his main aim in life—of which he is unaware—is to receive punishment. Since ordinarily punishment comes less frequently to the adolescent and adult, his naughtiness increases until it becomes real crime and his adult life is a succession of alternating crime and punishment. He becomes a criminal because of a need for punishment.

There is no need to comment on how well the social organization functions in satisfying the need for punishment, because the entire social system is based on the principle that the pain of punishment will reform, whereas with this type of naughtiness the pain of punıshment is what the individual desires. It cannot be too strongly emphasized that in the vast majority of instances the individual is unaware of his need for punishment and consciously will ridicule the notion that his naughtiness is deliberately produced in order to get him punished. Occasionally a child will show awareness that he has a need to be punished, for one meets instances where the child will come to the parent and say, "Father, please whip me."

The treatment of the child whose naughtiness arises because he desires punishment will be aimed at discovery both of his sense of guilt and of the memory of the crime about which he feels so guilty. Then the guilt can be relieved. This requires intensive psychotherapy, analysis offering the best chance of cure. At the same time the parents will have to be cautioned along two lines: (1) The child's behavior may become worse from time to time during the period of treatment as he attempts to avoid analyzing his feeling of guilt by using his old method of assuaging it temporarily through punishment. This phenomenon always makes treatment difficult, since the child has so many opportunities for assuaging his guilt through naughty behavior. Too, the social organization may react violently against his behavior, and just at the point when the therapist is really making progress may step in and incarcerate the child, discontinuing the treatment. As a consequence, we feel that only the mildest cases of this type should be treated as outpatients, and that the moderate and severe cases should be institutionalized during the period of treatment. (2) The parents or parent substitutes will have to abstain from punishing the child as much as is humanly possible.

It can be seen that the naughty behavior in these cases has a definite beginning and occurs in episodes that suggest that from time to time the child is compelled to be naughty. As we have seen, there is a compulsion that underlies the symptoms.

A similar compulsiveness underlies the naughty behavior of the next type. There are certain children who seem to act aggressively without any reason and in fact do not seem to know they are behaving so until the action is almost over. Afterward such a child feels remorseful but also feels that nevertheless he could not help what he did: he did not want to do it, had made up his mind not to, yet here he is doing the very thing he had decided not to do. We saw a good example of this in a nineteen-year-old boy at a military induction center. The boy had a history of a number of arrests and short jail sentences for assault and battery. He did not drink. His difficulty lay in the fact that when he got in a crowd or was at a celebration he suddenly found himself getting into fights. He did not know how the fights started. He acted *impulsively* therefore, and so differed from the child who has a *compulsive* need for punishment. The child with a need for punishment has a superego severely prohibitive of a particular form of instinctual desire. If he violates the prohibitions of his superego and gratifies his desire he has to make amends by committing a different act for which he knows he will be punished. The impulsive child has a superego that prohibits a certain type of instinctual expression—often aggression. He gratifies the instinctual desire by circumventing his superego; that is, he allows himself to be overwhelmed suddenly by his desire, and can propitiate his conscience by denying his responsibility for the act.

The neurologically trained reader may say at this point, "I thought such cases were often closely akin to epilepsy, for which there is often an organic basis in some lesion of the cerebral cortex." This comment brings up a most interesting and complicated question regarding the naughty behavior of children. Does the behavior have a psychological basis or an organic basis, or is it the result of a combination of both? This is not just an academic problem but is important in considering the types of treatment necessary and the prognosis for any kind of treatment.

It is well known that children frequently become naughty after they have suffered from an encephalitis—whether the result of encephalitis lethargica or as a complication of measles, scarlet fever, or chickenpox. Naughty behavior also may follow injury to the brain as a result of fracture of the skull or of minute intracerebral hemorrhages produced by whooping cough, electric shock, or partial asphyxiation. In adults and older children it has been found that lesions of the brain often produce a change in the personality—a person with a mild, kindly disposition becoming irritable, quarrelsome, and hostile. In cats experimental decerebration just above the thalamus, as a result of which cortical control is removed, leaves the animal liable to violent attacks of rage and hostility for which there is no adequate cause. It appears, therefore, that reactions of rage and hostility are mediated through the upper part of the thalamus, but that these reactions are kept in check by the action of the cortex. Some of this cortical control seems to come from the frontal lobes, one function of which is to perceive what may happen in the future as the result of an act or impulse. If the controlling action of the cortex is partially or totally removed the rage reactions appear unmodified. Therefore children who have suffered from a cortical disease or injury, particularly if it involves the pathways from the frontal lobes, are less able to impose and in many cases are incapable of imposing any voluntary control over the expression of hostility, rage, and anger. A similar deficiency of cortical control exists in those individuals whose brain physiology is disordered, as in cases of epilepsy.

The problem is exactly the same as in the cases of chronic aggressive reactions due to lack of love, but in the first group the lack of control has a psychological basis, while in this it has an organic one. What can be done about these children? In many instances it is impossible to make any change in the organic dysfunction. Recently there have been reports of improvement by the use of benzedrine sulfate or dilantin in those cases where the electroencephalogram shows a disturbance in brain physiology. If further work bears out these studies we will be in a better position to deal with these cases. Although treatment for the organic lesion is seldom possible it must be remembered that the lesions usually do not affect the whole cortex, and that it is possible to train parts of the brain that are ordinarily seldom used to take over the function of the destroyed areas. Such retraining cannot be carried on at home or by educators not specially trained in the work. The best treatment is institutionalization in a proper hospital, of which a number are now available.

A second difficulty always arises with such children. Their behavior is annoying and adults tend to react to it with counterhostility, which only increases the hostile feelings and adds an impossible burden to any control mechanism they still possess. It has been found that the aggressive behavior of cases of chronic epidemic encephalitis improves when they are taken from their families and environment and hospitalized in a proper institution. Often they become quite docile and tractable while there, but as soon as they are returned to their families the old behavior reappears. The adults in the institution obviously were able to give such a child more objective, kindly, and understanding management than were the parents, and to this treatment the child tried to respond. However, as soon as this type of handling was removed the child felt no need to and perhaps really had no capacity to respond any longer.

The presence of abnormal electroencephalograms in a high percentage of naughty children makes one feel that in most cases there is a combination of organic and psychological causes. Those cases who do well with adequate psychotherapy perhaps have less organic damage, and those who do poorly, more. These observations also raise another interesting question. In some cases the history of the hostile resistive behavior goes back through the child's whole life. Mothers of certain of these naughty children state that even at two months of age the children were unmanageable. Are such cases due to a very early brain injury, to a state of rejection practically from birth, to an innate endowment with more aggressive urges than the ordinary child, or to some combination of two or more of these factors? We believe that each of these factors may be causative in certain cases. Cerebral injury either from intracortical hemorrhage or from anoxia during birth is not uncommon. (In fact, all children show blood in the cerebrospinal fluid after birth, indicating that a certain amount of hemorrhage has taken place.) In some the hemorrhage may be more severe than in others, and yet not so extensive or so located as to give definite signs of cerebral injury; that is, the child does not show a true birth palsy. It may be that some of the cases of chronic naughtiness in children are the result of this condition. There is no proof one way or the other for this speculation, but it is a theory that should be investigated thoroughly. Many observations have proven that a baby's reactions and disposition are easily influenced by the handling he receives even in the first days of his life, and since this attitude toward him is likely basically to be the same during the succeeding months and years, the rejected child is rejected every day of his life, and it is no wonder that his behavior seems to have existed from birth.

It is possible that some children are born with a greater endowment of aggressive energy. Certainly children differ in the degree of activity even in the uterus, and this difference is probably a constitutional peculiarity. Such an active child can easily become naughty, since often he is more restricted than the average child, and so more frustrated. Adults who desire quietness and peace find it difficult to tolerate his excessive activity and tend to scold and punish him more than is desirable. Social customs involve a great deal of orderly self-restraint, and involuntary violations of them on the part of the child provoke counterhostility, which makes the child feel that he is an Ishmael, and having the name might as well have the game too.

As we have already said, hyperactive children need more space for the expression of their physical activities and less rigid demands on them for inactivity, and should either attend a progressive school where constant physical activity is part of the program or else be allowed more freedom of motor action in the ordinary classroom. It is unfortunate to observe how seldom their need for activity is met, and how often parents or educators use their unconscious knowledge of this need to punish them. Often children give a history of being made to sit absolutely still on a chair for several hours as a punishment. Or if their hyperactivity has resulted in wandering away from home they have been tied in the back yard. Such punishment only increases their feeling of tension and makes them feel more resentful and frustrated. There is no way to control the hyperactivity itself, and all that can be done is to provide sufficient outlet for it.

When the resentful, naughty pattern of behavior has arisen as a result of unreasonable interference with the activity of the hyperactive child the treatment will fall into two phases. First, there must be treatment for the child's resentfulness. The aim of this will be to help the child to love instead of resent and to help him to regard his hyperactivity as a useful asset instead of a liability. Second, he must be given opportunity to use his hyperactivity successfully. The intensity of the psychotherapy directed toward the first aim will depend on the degree of the hostility present and on the extent to which it has deformed his ability to adjust socially.

There are many specific complications that arise in the management of a naughty child that do not occur in the management of a child who suffers from conversion symptoms and which must be taken into consideration in approaching its treatment. First, where should the child live during the period of treatment? Although we have discussed this already, we want to re-emphasize that in our experience if the degree of naughty behavior is at all serious from a social point of view, treatment does not stand much chance of success if the child remains at home. Foster-home placement in such cases is not desirable. It seems best to place the child in an institution before treatment is started, and usually this is easily done, at least temporarily, because the parents are so disgusted with the child's behavior. When the parent is rejective, however, and particularly if the rejection is unconscious and he suffers from a sense of guilt about his attitude, he often will refuse to allow the child to remain in the institution more than a few weeks. He removes the child—often just as the child is beginning to receive benefit from treatment—because the place is gloomy, because the child is with bad children who may corrupt him, or because the child is so unhappy. In these cases it would be well to have some form of legal commitment so that treatment would not be interrupted so inopportunely. It goes without saying that such institutions require a well-trained, carefully selected staff. Psychiatric treatment by well-trained psychiatrists must be available. The staff itself should consist of men and women who have been selected on the basis of an understanding of children and an ability to love. The hours of work should not be too arduous and there should be ample time and opportunity for recreation and social life.

In order to make an adequate prognosis the degree of organic causation must be considered and if possible, treatment given for it. The introductory steps to treatment are more important in these cases than in any other except delinquency. They should be carefully planned and sufficient time allocated for them. In all cases treatment of the parents should be carried on during the treatment of the child. If parent treatment is effective the child may return home after his treatment is completed. If not, or if only partially successful, it is better for the child to go to another home or boarding school; otherwise the child may develop another neurosis or personality disturbance in order to live comfortably with his family.

We realize that we are describing an ideal plan which is usually very difficult to carry out practically. Except in rare instances we lack the type of institution we described, and those that we have are not sufficiently numerous to deal with the number of such children that need them. We lack the trained and selected personnel required, and the salaries are woefully inadequate to attract such persons. These shortcomings apply both to state institutions and to those organized privately. We lack the power necessary to institutionalize and treat these children adequately because democracy has a tendency to lean more toward protecting the liberty of the individual than toward ensuring the safety and comfort of the group. Even our methods of treatment are in the experimental stage and although they prove adequate in individual cases we cannot lay down such hard and fast rules as we are able to do for the treatment of a case of appendicitis, for instance. In the discussion that follows, dealing with the complex problems of delinquency, we shall be describing a plan that should really be a function of the state.

DELINQUENCY

The chronic aggressive reaction pattern is really a subdivision of the much wider and more complex problem of delinquency. Etymologically delinquency means "falling away." A delinquent is a person who in his behavior "falls away" from the customs and mores of the social organization. In this definition the emphasis is laid on the falling away, while the customs and mores are regarded as static. It does not consider the reasons for the falling away, and since legally trained persons consider the problem from the standpoint of this definition they direct their efforts toward making the delinquent individual give up his tendency to fall away. In the past the sociologist has tended to consider the reasons for the individual's falling away, but because he has regarded the customs and mores as static and every delinquent individual as a sick person he has directed his efforts toward making the sick person well, whereafter he no longer will fall away.

The psychiatrist places emphasis on the reasons for the delinquent's not conforming, but in many cases may see that these reasons result from the static conditions of the customs and mores. He does not believe that all delinquents are sick people; in fact he feels that certain of them would be sick people if they behaved in an undelinquent manner and at that point would so treat them as to make them delinquent again. His efforts are directed toward curing the illness in those delinquents who are sick and in recommending that other disciplines, such as those of the sociologist, economist, educator, and psychologist, use their efforts to change the customs and mores which the culture has outgrown.

These various points of view seem to be contradictory, but the contradictions are more apparent than real. They spring from the fact that each discipline approaches the problem from a different and special angle and from the fact that the problem itself is so complex that it cannot be investigated by any one discipline alone. In fact, any attempt to investigate the facts underlying delinquency must combine the best skills of all the disciplines mentioned. No one discipline can claim the ability to understand delinquency or can offer a panacea for its amelioration. We hope we have made it clear that we realize we are in no position to hand down any dogmatic statements about delinquency, its cause and cure, and that what we have to say is more in the nature of tentative remarks, made largely in the hope of stimulating others to bend greater efforts toward trying to understand the problem.

What are some of the causes of delinquency? The first group of causes might be entitled "delinquency from force of circumstances." A child is hungry for carbohydrates, for instance. His parents have forbidden him to eat candy and give him only a small amount of sugar at meals. Since he cannot get the sugar he needs honestly, he has to steal it. In this stealing he has committed an act of delinquency because he has broken the prohibitions imposed by his family. Or an adolescent receives an allowance much smaller than that received by the other boys with whom he associates. The size of his allowance is the result not of his parents' being poor but of the fact that they believe the child should not have much spending money. The state law and the parents' opinion both prevent the child's working to supplement his allowance. He has only two courses open to him—to withdraw from his social life (which would be very unpleasant and also very unprofitable for him) or to steal to supplement his allowance. If he steals from his family he has broken their rules; if he steals from the neighborhood he has broken the law. In neither of these instances is the child sick. He dislikes his stealing. He suffers afterward from remorse. The three parts of his personality—id, ego, superego—are functioning together adequately, and one is not developed at the expense of the other. He is a normal, adequate person who is delinquent because circumstances (that is, his parents' incorrect opinions) are depriving him of necessities. Once he is allowed to have the necessities he no longer is delinquent.

This delinquency from force of circumstances is rather common in childhood, for many parents deal with their children according to their own superstitions which to them seem reasonable ideas. It is also not uncommon in adult life, in a culture that does not permit individuals equal opportunity to satisfy their needs. These needs are not excessive but the cultural or familial restrictions are. Treatment under these circumstances will aim toward liberalizing the attitude of the parents or of the socioeconomic structure, and is a task for the sociologist, economist, and educator.

Among any group of delinquents there is always a fairly large percentage who are feeble-minded. Their excursions into delinquency are the result of a combination of causes. The feeble-minded individual has a defective ego which makes him depend a great deal on other people. Hence he is easily led. His defective reasoning power—a function of the ego—makes him relatively incapable of distinguishing clearly in the matter of property ownership or the consequences of his acts. His ego defect makes it difficult for him to develop an adequate superego. The defect in the superego is increased by the fact that the mentally defective child as a rule does not receive as much real love and understanding from his family or companions as does the intelligent child, and he is more likely to develop some degree of a chronic aggressive reaction pattern. Furthermore, his mental defect makes it more difficult for him to learn to control his primitive reactions. If he falls into association with delinquents he rather readily follows in their footsteps, and is often used to pull their chestnuts out of the fire, so to speak. If anyone gets caught it will be he, and not the other, more intelligent members of the gang. Similarly, a mentally defective girl is more liable than an intelligent one to be free with sexual favors for a slight recompense. The delinquency of the mental defective is a problem for the educator. Above all, he needs training and supervision.

A certain number of delinquents are psychotic; their delinquency really would be correct behavior if their delusional world were the real one. The paranoid person who kills an imagined persecutor or the paretic who issues worthless checks for purchases he cannot afford under the delusion he is a millionaire would both be behaving in a nondelinquent fashion if the first was really being hounded to death and the second was very wealthy. Psychotic delinquency is not observed often in children.

We have already discussed neurotic delinquency—the individual who is delinquent in order to satisfy a need for punishment. His treatment is obviously a task for the psychiatrist.

A child reared in the culture of one of the tribes of New Guinea, for instance, will learn to observe the customs and taboos of his tribe even though they may include ritual murder. If he does not conform to them he is a delinquent. If he were transported suddenly to the United States, however, his obedience to the culture of New Guinea would be regarded as delinquency. Similarly, if a well-behaved American boy were suddenly transplanted to New Guinea his behavior would be regarded there as delinquency. In both cases the child has a normal superego—an adequate sense of guilt and of right and wrong—but the mores to which he has learned to react are different; in other words, his superego functions normally but its structure in New Guinea is different from its structure in America.

There are certain parents in America who bring their children up according to their own mores, which are different from those of organized society. Such cases flourish in certain areas in large cities —the so-called delinquency areas—and in isolated backward communities such as those where killing in feuds is regarded as a virtue instead of a crime. The child in such cases is a normal child. He has a normal superego, but through his identification with the parents the mores incorporated in his superego are different from those of the social organization. Therefore in the eyes of the social organization he is a delinquent.

It is more important to place emphasis on preventing the occurence of such a type of delinquency than on correcting it once it has arisen, and the sociologist and the educator are responsible for curing the social situation that is producing it. When a child has become delinquent through being raised in a delinquent environment his treatment cannot be successful as long as he lives in the delinquent environment and family. He must be removed to a situation where he can be induced to love a person who has a code closer to that of the culture. As a result of the new relationship the child will change the nature of his superego. The younger the child is, the more easily this change can be accomplished; the older he gets, the less likely.

Since we are so lacking in real knowledge as to the causes, types, treatment, and prognosis for delinquents, it seems to us that the following scheme for the management of delinquents might be adopted as a means of helping the individual delinquents, and at the same time furthering our knowledge. The scheme is ideal and has never been put into practice.

When the delinquent is arrested he receives a trial to determine his guilt or innocence of the criminal act. (In our Anglo-Saxon culture a trial is always given to adults, but not always to children. A child who is an onlooker may be picked up by the police even though he has no share in a crime. His protestations of innocence are not believed because all children tend to lie when accused, and he is treated as a delinquent.) If the individual is found guilty the task of the judge and jury is finished, regardless of the nature of the crime. He is sent to a clearing institution. Here are studied thoroughly his personal history, his physical, intellectual, and emotional status. His family and environment are investigated thoroughly by sociologists and economists. Finally all the results from these various studies are compiled and reviewed by a board that might consist of a criminologist, a lawyer, a physician, a psychiatrist, a psychologist, and a sociologist. This review is directed toward making a diagnosis as to the type of delinquency. If the data are insufficient to make such a working diagnosis the delinquent is remanded for further study.

This working diagnosis forms the basis for determining what shall be done with him. If his delinquent act is the result of force of circumstances only, he can be released immediately provided he can be returned to an environment where circumstances will not be so adverse. If he is feeble-minded he will be referred to a school for the feeble-minded, where if he is tractable and educable he can be trained. If he is untrainable he will be referred to an institution for the custodial care of the feeble-minded. If he has a psychosis he will be referred to a hospital for psychiatric treatment. If he recovers, he can be discharged; if not, he must remain under custodial care. If he is delinquent from a sense of guilt he is referred to a special hospital for the treatment of neurotic delinquency. Here he is offered the opportunity for treatment. If he accepts and it is successful he can be discharged. If he refuses or if it is not successful he will be transferred to a special custodial institution, the purpose of which will be discussed later. If his delinquency is the result of a delinquent superego he will be sent to an institution or a foster home where he can establish a relationship with substitute parents whose superegos are more in accord with the culture. If he does not improve he is transferred to the special custodial institution. Individuals whose delinquency is the result of lack of love are sent to a reformatory where they will meet a highly select staff who are able to love them and whom they in turn may learn to love. If an obsessive-compulsive reaction develops the patient is transferred to the institution for neurotic delinquents where he will receive psychiatric treatment. If the reformatory does not help, the individual will be transferred to the special custodial institution. The special custodial institution is for those cases that so far have not responded to treatment. On admission the whole case would be reviewed again.

This plan will offer a chance for experimental methods to be used and their efficacy proved, and for finer methods of classification to be developed. Those whom no methods of treatment seem to help would be detained for the remainder of their lives, regardless of the nature of the original crime. As can be seen, this plan requires the assistance of a highly selected and trained personnel and therefore would be expensive, but it seems to us that if some state would try it out for a period of five or ten years so much could be learned, and our ability to cope with and understand the problem of delinquency so increased, that it would be worth the expense. Further, the increase of our knowledge would lead to a more permanent and a less expensive plan for the future.

EDUCATIONAL DIFFICULTIES

His school life is the main activity of the child in the latent period. It is his vocation and will remain so during the greater part of adolescence. The presenting symptoms of adult difficulties of adjustment often appear largely or only in the vocational field. The same phenomenon occurs in school problems in children. We have received the impression that in the last few years an increasing number of children are having difficulties in learning their school work. This increase in problems of learning may be real or only apparent. It may be apparent because teachers are more aware that difficulties in learning may be problems and not the child's laziness or stubbornness. It may be due to changes in the methods of education that have occurred in the last few years. It may be due to the fact that parental pressure for education is stronger now than it used to be. It may be due to the changes in the laws concerning compulsory education. Some of these problems may be inherent in the difficulties in learning to read, write, and spell the English language; we have been informed that learning difficulties, particularly reading problems, are encountered only occasionally in Europe, with the exception of England. Whether this increase in the number of cases of learning difficulties is real or only apparent, there are children who have difficulties in their school work which range from unwillingness to begin or to remain in school, through examination anxiety, to failure in all or in some subjects.

UNWILLINGNESS TO BEGIN SCHOOL

At the time when the child is about to enter school for the first time, all children develop a conflict as to the advisability of this new step in their development. On the one hand, they are proud and pleased with themselves that they now have attained the age of maturity and are no longer little babies. (This attitude is seen also in the change from grammar school to junior high school, junior high school to high school, and high school to college or to getting a job. One little girl told us that she was glad junior-high-school classes ended at two-thirty so she could stand in the yard of her former grammar school and taunt the children for being grammar-school babies as they came out of school.) On the other hand, the children become aware of their reluctance to grow up. Also they are frightened as to how they will get along in the new situation and what it will be like. They often picture the new situation as very dangerous. (Here they are much like the intelligent ten-year-old girl who went into a panic at the idea of going to camp for the first time, because the woods were full of lions and tigers and the counselors delighted in being extremely cruel to all the children but on visiting days would pretend to be so nice in order to fool the parents. These ideas were partly rationalizations for the dislike of the change to a new situation which is characteristic of human beings throughout life. Everyone prefers the known to the unknown.) Although this attitude toward attending school for the first time is universal, certain children show it more markedly than others. These latter go into a panic on the first day of school, cry and scream, refuse to allow their mothers to leave them, and will not participate in any part of the classroom activities. This reaction may pass during the first day or may persist for days or weeks despite all the attempts of the teacher to make the child comfortable. In some of these cases the difficulty is not the fear of the new situation, although the child will state that it is, but is the fear of separation even for a few hours from the mother. The child is overwhelmed by an acute attack of homesickness—or better, mother-sickness. All nursery-school teachers have learned that a new child may show panic when his mother leaves, or that if he does not show panic and even if he appears to be happy in the new situation he will show a return to earlier forms of behavior, may begin to wet or soil himself again if he has been toilet trained, may revert to thumb sucking if he has given it up, or in general will lose some of his skills and abilities. So marked is this reaction that most good nursery schools at present allow the mother to stay in school a great deal of the time during the first few days and gradually encourage her to wean herself away from the child. The libidinal tie between the child and mother is very strong at the nursery-school age and the separation of the child from the mother is a very traumatic event. But by the age of five or six the child usually is able to tolerate the separation from the mother. If he cannot, as in the examples I have given, the cause lies in his feelings about his mother—he may have found his relationship with her so gratifying that he is unwilling to relinquish it, he may be afraid to leave her because he fears some danger other than the loss of his mother, in growing up, or he may be afraid of his hatred of her. An instructed teacher (or better still, a well-trained school counselor) usually can distinguish the results of the first cause from the results of the other two. In the first case the teacher or the counselor can help the mother to wean herself from the child and after the child has overcome his reluctance to leave his mother the counselor can continue to educate the mother in separating herself from the child. Cases which arise from the third cause usually need the study and help of a psychoanalyst who specializes in the treatment of children, but some of these cases can be helped by a well-trained social worker or counselor. Cases which arise from the second case usually require intensive psychoanalytic therapy.

In other cases which show the symptoms we are discussing, the difficulty arises in another way. In kindergartens and schools run on modern lines a new intermediate class of children has sprung up between the familiar groups of those who are intelligent, interested, and diligent, and those who are intellectually duller. These children are distinctly intelligent, quite well developed, and popular with their schoolfellows, but they cannot be induced to take their place in the regular games or lessons. They behave as if they were intimidated. The mere comparison of their achievements with those of the other children robs their work of all its value in their eyes. If they fail in a task or a constructive game, they develop a permanent disinclination to repeat the attempt and content themselves with looking on at the work of others. Secondarily, their idling has an antisocial effect, for, being bored, they begin to quarrel with the children who are absorbed in work or play. They behave in this way because they are afraid that their achievements will be compared with those of other children to their mortification. They thus impose an automatic check as soon as a particular activity results in a disagreeable impression. The fear that they will meet such painful comparisons interferes with their activity at school and with other children, and often forces them to avoid going to school or even entering school. These children restrict their activities and interests in order not to suffer the pain of failure. This reaction usually results from their earlier humiliation in discovering that their bodies and genitals are not as impressive as those of the parents of the same sex; in some girls it occurs when they realize that they do not have the penis that their male companions have. We intend to discuss more fully in another connection the type of child who frequently develops this defense mechanism. Often such children can be improved by educating them to develop skills in which they will be successful, and particularly by helping them to realize that such skills are obtained only through effort on their part and by encouraging them to put forth this effort. This help can be given by the teacher assisted by the school counselor. However there may be a few cases that also need analytically oriented psychotherapy.

There are other children who do not wish to go to school because the school represents the losing of freedom and of independence.

UNWILLINGNESS TO REMAIN IN SCHOOL

There are certain children who more or less suddenly develop an aversion to school to such a degree that they absent themselves. A girl of ten one morning refused to go to school. When her parents pressed her to go she became very anxious, almost to the point of panic. As they still continued to press her she became sick to her stomach and vomited. They allowed her to remain at home. The next morning she was nauseated when she awoke and could not go to school. After several days the parents again attempted to insist and the child became extremely panicky; when her father attempted to take her by force she ran to her room, got under the bed, and clung to the bed post.

Such cases are not infrequent and may occur both during the latency period and in early adolescence. Sometimes they are less severe than this one in that the child only feels ill—with nausea, abdominal pains, or headaches—every morning. If the parents allow him to stay home, he will do so; but if they insist, he will go to school from time to time. In our experience nausea and vomiting are the most common physical symptoms in these children. Often if they stay home from school the physical complaints disappear and the child goes about his usual activities unless the question of school attendance is broached; then the anxiety reappears. Frequently they do not mind other people knowing that they are not attending school and often will play outside unconcernedly.

In this last characteristic they differ from the next type of case. Here the child refuses to go to school because of anxiety and will put up considerable resistance if attempts are made to force him to go. A boy of ten could hardly bear to remain a full day in school. Usually he ran home after a short period of classes. During the time he was in school he could pay no attention to what was being taught. On some occasions his mother would escort him to the classroom but would find him at home when she returned from school. During the day he would not leave the house and even objected to running errands for his mother. When school was dismissed he would go out and play with his friends but never until the school day was over. He absented himself from school but remained at home. Technically his behavior could be labeled truancy, but the fact that he remained at home distinguished it from the usual variety of truancy in which the child absents himself from school without the parents' knowledge and in order to occupy his school day he goes downtown, pays his way or sneaks into a movie, rides the subway, window-shops, or plays with other truants in a different part of the city, returning home at the time that school is dismissed. Such children often make friends with delinquents who are truanting and may copy the delinquent behavior.

When cases of the first type occur in early adolescence they may indicate a deep-seated and malignant illness. Cases of the third type tend to indicate delinquency rather than illness. The seriousness of the condition depends on the causative factors.

A child may refuse to attend school because of learning difficulties or of an inability to learn; this cause more usually results in truancy than do the other two types. A child may truant because he believes he has no need to learn for when he becomes an adult he can use magic to divine things. There are certain children who feel that knowledge comes by magic and therefore they have no need to recall anything they have learned. The child may want to absent himself or may actually do so because his teacher really dislikes him and treats him badly or because he dislikes the teacher. He may be unable to get on with other children or there may be a gang or a bully who really are terrorizing and perhaps blackmailing him; such conditions are more frequent than most parents and many teachers realize.

In the case of the boy we cited earlier, his parents quarreled constantly and his mother, to whom he was much attached, threatened almost every day to pack up and leave the family. He really never knew when he left the house in the morning whether he would find her at home when he returned. When he sat in school he worried lest she had left already and so when the worry became unbearable he ran home to assure himself she was still there. Such conscious worries about the real family situation are frequent causes of this type of behavior.

The symptoms may result because of tensions within the child himself. There may be a fear of exploring, which is really a fear lest the child discover horrible facts; usually, forbidden family secrets. There may be a fear to learn about sex lest the child get into trouble from having such knowledge. (In both of these fears the teacher has to establish her trustworthiness and her willingness to protect the child from the parents' anger.) The symbolic function of reading often is affected by the fear of exploration. A reading inhibition may follow a threat against exploring his own or others' genitals. Learning itself may mean the giving up of primitive pleasures. The child may suffer from guilt lest competition mean the destruction of dangerous rivals. Bettelheim cites the case of a boy who refused to learn because he feared his hostility would bring him to the electric chair, but he might get off if he was so dumb he could not learn. The symbolic material may be personalized and regarded as a real enemy.

These tensions, although they may arise from many sources, may occur on the way to school and result in a need to run away or be worked out by violent activity before school starts. Every child suffering from fears about school goes through an intermediate period where he is trying to adjust to the classroom but is not yet adjusted to it. He needs special help in convincing himself that he need not run away or be afraid. The treatment for all such cases depends on the cause. We believe the teacher and school counselor need the help of the analyst in investigating the case and determining the cause. Many cases of the types due to anxiety or fear about the home or school situation and many cases of delinquent truancy can be treated by the teacher or the school counselor. Cases involving unwillingness to attend school plus physical symptoms usually are more serious and many of them need intensive psychotherapy by a child analyst.

EXAMINATION ANXIETY

All children have some degree of examination anxiety. The physical and mental manifestations of examination anxiety are closely related to those of fear, whose purpose is to alert the person for action. An individual anxious in this way will be conscious of some feeling of anticipatory dread, mental alertness, and tension. Physically he will produce some or all of the physical changes which in an external danger situation would equip him either to fight or to take flight. There are two types of examination anxiety. The first type is a stimulatory one and causes the student to strive toward success. If it brings success the anxiety is replaced by a definite feeling of pleasure. The second type of anxiety is not conscious and hence there is no incentive to drive for accomplishment and no subsequent pleasure in success. In fact, there is often a feeling that the success is unreal. The second type has an inhibitory action. In this type of anxiety, the fight-flight changes do not occur and the person has the helpless qualities of an infant: his mind becomes a blank, he is tremulous and distressed and unable to use his resources in a purposive way. Too much anxiety produces a paralysis of action and slowness in doing the examination.

One cause of examination anxiety is the fear of disgrace. The child dreads that his teachers and parents will find out that he has not applied himself diligently, will discover his shortcomings, and will humiliate him. If this fear is associatively connected in the unconscious with the memory of the humiliation the child suffered earlier when he discovered how much smaller his genitals were than those of his father, the examination anxiety will be enormously increased, even though he has applied himself diligently to his pre-examination studies.

Instead of the fear of disgrace, examination anxiety may be the fear of being found out and punished for lack of diligence. If the fear of punishment is associatively connected in the unconscious with strong fears of punishment by castration for masturbation, the examination anxiety will be increased because examinations are identified with proof of sexual capacity and failure is equated with impotence and castration.

There is another cause for greatly increased examination anxiety. To be successful in the examination is to progress onward in ambition. If this idea is connected associatively in the unconscious with the oedipus fantasies of killing the father and taking his place, and if these fantasies are not yet resolved but still dreaded lest the father retaliate in like kind, then there will develop fear of succeeding and perhaps also a desire to fail. Both of these appear in consciousness as greatly increased examination anxiety.

There are two sides to this question of examination anxiety to be considered. On the one hand there is the attitude, conscious and unconscious, of the examinee toward the examiner; on the other there is the attitude, conscious and unconscious, of the examiner toward the examinee. Examinations are a testing, a tormenting of the younger by the older. If assessment of knowledge were in fact the motive for examinations, then they would be given throughout life; but actually the attainment of the highest grades in professional life never depends on examinations. Examinations can be compared to initiation ceremonies which express the elder's envy and jealousy mixed with love and the younger's fear mixed with reverence and gratitude. In the initiation rites the hostility against the young men is based on the fear of retaliation which stems from the elder's guilt towards his own parents. "I rebelled against my parents and therefore anticipate that I will be paid back in kind by having my children rebel against me." While inflicting the cruelties, the elders also attempt to appease the youngsters and thus to forestall any retaliation. The appeasement is accomplished by impressing the initiates with the awesomeness and secrecy of the proceedings and by imposing upon them vows of silence concerning the rites, thus binding them in a bond of secrecy (from which women are usually excluded). It is therefore not surprising that the same tendencies should stand out in the relationship between the student and the teacher and examiner. An examiner, particularly a neurotic examiner, may make himself a severe, overstrict father, or a loving and over-lenient father; he may insist narcissistically that the student's views and methods of expression be like his own; or he may fear the candidate.

Every child suffers from examination anxiety. In children whose infantile intrapsychic conflicts are not well solved, it will be very severe, perhaps so severe that the child becomes paralyzed in the examination and either does very poorly, cannot complete the task, or refuses to take the examination. Children who show such severe types of examination anxiety need to be studied by a psychoanalyst. After the analyst has decided on the depth and seriousness of the problem the treatment in some cases may be carried on by the school counselor. In the more severe cases the child requires psychoanalytic treatment.

DIFFICULTIES IN LEARNING

A child may have difficulty in learning *because his intellectual endowment is lower than that of the average child*. Either as the result of lack of development or of disease or injury to the central nervous system, the cortical centers and the association pathways are not as capable of functioning as they are in the healthy child.

The causes of intellectual deficiency are so well known to psychiatrists, educators, and psychologists that they do not need to be reviewed here. It is not so well understood that an intellectually defective child labors under a difficulty in addition and in contrast to the organic one. He is slow in developing and is not able to identify himself with his parents as rapidly and as efficiently as the average child. Therefore his infantile anxieties are prolonged because he has less than the normal capacity to deal with them. The constant pressure of anxiety further weakens the development of his ego. His parents moreover cannot have as much real affection for him as they would for an average child because his defectiveness is a severe blow to their narcissism. In order to avoid the hurt to their narcissism, most parents refuse to recognize that the child is defective intellectually and they try, usually inadvertently, to distort the history of the child's development and may even go so far as to try to convince the psychiatrist that the child is psychotic instead of feeble-minded. This lack of parental affection further interferes with the development of the child's ego and with his acquisition of the skills for which he really may have capacity. He contacts the real world, therefore, with an ego weakened organically and weakened also by a defect in the ability to identify himself and a defect in the amount of love he receives.

We need not do more than mention that a frequent cause of school difficulty is the fact that *the child is not graded according to his intellectual capacity*. If his level of intelligence is different from that of the class—whether it be higher or lower is immaterial—he does not have the pleasure of success resulting from his efforts, or the pleasure of having to put effort into attaining success. As a result he works less and less hard; he becomes annoyed because as he sees it, other children receive preferential treatment—that is, they get higher grades—and this annoyance causes a feeling of hostility toward them and the teachers, which in some instances reaches the height of feeling that he is being persecuted. He expresses his hostile feeling in his behavior, which then gets him into trouble and often results in a real feeling of dislike on the part of other children and the teachers. Their attitude makes him more hostile and the vicious circle of hostility and counterhostility develops.

Instead of becoming openly hostile the child may try to get away from the irritating situation by truancy. If he goes by himself he gets into trouble with the school authorities and with his parents, to whom the school complains. If he goes with other children the same results occur, but in addition he may become associated with a gang of delinquents and himself become one. (This result obtains more frequently in children with a low intelligence level. We discussed this problem earlier; see page 323.) If he does not withdraw himself physically he may do so psychically, that is, sit in the classroom and daydream instead of attending to his work. From the psychiatric standpoint this last-mentioned reaction is more likely to result in serious maladjustment than the other two, in which the maladjustment is an open conflict between the individual and society.

The treatment for these cases is a proper regrading. But in the ordinary school setup this would mean that the child would be placed with much younger or much older children, where he would feel a difference in physical size and be treated differently by the other children than if he were with his peers. What he needs is to be placed in a special class or in a school where there are no actual grades—for example, a good progressive school.

Children whose total intellectual endowment is very superior may find difficulty in learning in the average educational setup, as Terman pointed out long ago. Their failure is the result of boredom. The other children in the class, whose intelligence quotients may be average or slightly above, may take about an hour to understand and master a particular problem which the child with very superior intelligence may be able to conquer in fifteen minutes. For the remaining three-quarters of an hour such a child has nothing to do and in order not to be restless and disturbing will spend his time in daydreaming. The daydreams soon become more interesting than was the problem solved in the first fifteen minutes, and instead of occupying only the unemployed time they begin to occupy the whole hour. Consequently such children learn little or nothing and at the end of several months their achievements are far less than those of the other members of the class. On the basis of their poor school work the teacher may believe they are intellectually retarded. They also have omitted learning certain basic fundamentals so that now when confronted by more complex problems, which the others in the class have the basic skills to solve, they fail utterly. This secondary failure drives them into more intensive daydreaming. The diagnosis and management of children whose difficulty in learning is the result of their intellectual endowment is the task of the teacher and the educational psychologist.

In our opinion entrance to school should be preceded not only by a thorough physical examination but also by an estimation of the intellectual capacity, and ideally of the emotional status, of the child. If his intellectual level is considerably less than the average he should be placed in a special class for backward children. The children in this class should have a careful estimation of all their intellectual capabilities and assets made, and their educational life should be planned on the results of this estimation. Children whose intellectual capacity is much above the average should be placed either in a special class for intellectually advanced children or in a good progressive school.

In either situation more attention should be given to helping the child in his social and emotional adjustments and in his physical and manual development than to the process of scholastic achievement. Ordinarily a child with a very high intelligence level tends to progress through school too fast. He may even graduate from high school at the age of fourteen or fifteen, which is too young to enter college, where he will be unwelcome in the social and recreational activities. With the school program adjusted to his total needs—physical, social, recreational, and emotional as well as intellectual—these unnecessary and painful difficulties of adjustment could be avoided. (It was to avoid the tendency to have bright children put all their efforts into intellectual accomplishments that Cecil Rhodes wisely laid down the requirements he did for selecting Rhodes scholars.)

If the child is gifted, and also exceptionally gifted along one particular line such as music, an added difficulty arises, for the parents and other interested adults often desire that the exceptional skill be highly developed and forget the other needs of the child. Here perhaps is the reason why so many great musicians and other artists are so often emotionally maladjusted individuals. It should be the care of those who are entrusted with the education of a genius to see that all his needs are met, and not just those of his talent. Sometimes we feel that not only should the life of such a child be planned carefully to ensure a well-rounded development of his ego and superego, but also that as part of his training he should have a period of psychoanalysis as a really preventive measure against personality unbalance.

Learning readiness is a determinant of learning ability. The abilities to learn to write and to do arithmetic develop as part of a maturational process. At certain ages all children are unable to learn any of these skills. As they grow older one or another ability becomes manifest.

Research educators have come to the conclusion that children are not able to learn to read until they have reached a certain stage of development, and that the age at which this stage is reached is specific for each child. It is therefore useless to try to teach a child to read before this stage is reached. It seems probable that it is reached when the intracortical connections between the various brain centers have reached a stage of maturity. The attainment of this stage is known to educators as *reading readiness,* and may take place anywhere between four and ten years of age. If the parent or teacher tries to teach a child to read before the stage of reading readiness the child does not understand what the whole procedure is about. He tries in order to please the adult, but without result. If the adult gets annoyed by his "stubbornness" or "laziness," the child tries harder, but again without success. Reading therefore becomes associated in his mind with a painful feeling of failure, and when his reading readiness appears, the past association with pain may make him try to avoid any contact with the subject. It may even be years before the pleasure he finds in reading becomes great enough to overcome the memory of the pain of the past. Or he may always be disinclined to read or always be a poor reader. The prevention of such a result will depend on not trying to teach the child to read before he is ready. If a reading disability has resulted from the failure to observe this rule the child should be given a rest from all reading for awhile and then be retaught to read under pleasant circumstances and in ways that will bring a quick sense of success, which will gradually outweigh the painful memories of past failures.

Similarly there must be a time when the child is incapable of learning to write or of learning to do arithmetic, and also there must be a time when through certain anatomical and physiological maturational processes he becomes capable. In some children this maturational process is completed later than in others without any pathology being present. The knowledge of this fact, however, is very necessary to educators who then will be able to spare the child the secondary emotional conflicts which would arise because he is forced to *try* to read or to master other skills before he is physiologically able to do so. Such conflicts may interfere with the child's ever learning a particular school skill.

Physical impairment (as fatigue, illness, or sensorimotor defect) hinders learning. It is well-known that children who constantly are fatigued because of lack of sleep, overstimulation, and overexertion do not learn as quickly and as effectively as unfatigued children do.

Chronic illnesses, particularly those in which toxic substances are circulating in the blood, or, as in anemia, the oxygen-carrying power of the blood is decreased, result in an impairment of the functions of the cortex and therefore the child with an average or better than average intelligence has an impaired ability to learn. Intellectual and neurological changes result from vitamin deficiency. In certain cases the child's difficulty in learning is the result of chronic avitaminosis.

Vision and hearing are the sensory organs most used in the learning of academic subjects; therefore, any defect in them—lens defects, partial or total deafness, for example—will interfere with the child's capacity to learn. Often in little children gross defects of this kind pass unnoticed for a number of years. Such oversight is less common today than it was several years ago because there has been a steady and desirable indoctrination of the public on this subject. However, the effect of slow eye movements on the capacity to learn to read is not yet so well known. Educators are aware that a good reader usually reads rapidly—that is, his eye movements are rapid—while poor readers often read very slowly as a result of slowness in their eye movements and they need exercise to speed up the rapidity of the eye movements.

The ability to learn to write, draw, model, and make things—that is, the ability to learn to use the hands in creative ways—may also be disturbed from physical causes. Some of these, like chronic illnesses, fatigue, and avitaminosis we have mentioned already. The effects of gross motor disturbances due to major cortical injuries are so obvious that they need only be mentioned. However, certain cortical or subcortical lesions (involving particularly the cerebellum and the cerebellar association pathways) may occur as the result of birth anoxia, birth hemorrhage, physical trauma, or some type of encephalitis. These may not be evident on clinical examination but may make it impossible for the child to do accurate work.

Orton has discussed an important and special type of reading disability—*strephosymbolia*. This condition shows itself in both the child's reading and writing. The child has great difficulty in learning to read because at one time he sees the letter E as E and the word SAW as SAW and at another sees E as Ǝ and SAW as WAƧ. At one time he will write NOT as *not*, at another as *ƚoᴎ*. Such children actually often read in a mirror better than when looking at the page itself. The reason is that the dominance of one cerebral hemisphere over the other has not been established. Therefore at one time the child tries to elide the sense impression from one half of his cortex and at another time tries to elide the sense impression from the other half. This uncertainty in dominance is sometimes associated with the fact that the child was innately left-handed and right-brained and was then trained to be right-handed and left-brained, which made it impossible for one cerebral hemisphere to attain definite dominance over the other. Such cases are readily ascertained when tested by the methods developed by Orton, who also has formulated precise methods of treatment for them. All cases of strephosymbolia should be placed in the hands of some person trained in the use of Orton's methods.

A small number of children with reading disabilities who show some of the characteristics of strephosymbolia nevertheless do not respond to the specific tests. The disability is the result of complicated emotional problems concerning the use of language—written, spoken, and read—as a weapon of offense and defense, and results from the child's reactions of guilt and fear about the uses of language. Such cases can be diagnosed and treated only by a psychiatrist, and the ideal treatment is psychoanalysis.

Improper or unpleasant conditioning experiences diminish the capacity to learn. The child may be encouraged to learn by using his desire for pleasure. He may be bribed with rewards he desires, the gratification of which gives him pleasure; or the subject to be learned may be presented in such an interesting fashion that its learning in itself is accomplished by a feeling of pleasure. He may be encouraged by using his desire to avoid pain. This method has been used for many centuries in the form of punishment, the infliction of pain, for not learning. If the child does not learn as quickly and as completely as the teacher feels he should, he suffers real pain so that he quickly comes to associate not learning with pain. This method often miscarries. The child may associate the teacher with the pain and come rapidly to hate him; then he will not learn. Or he may associate the pain with the subject matter to be learned and so may hate the subject and refuse to learn it.

Children whose ability to learn is disturbed by painful conditioning experiences need to be tutored in the subject by a skillful tutor under very pleasant circumstances. If this tutoring is not successful they should be studied by a psychoanalyst. Then tutoring should be supplemented by psychoanalytically oriented psychotherapy either by the school counselor—if he is trained to do this—or by a psychoanalyst, depending on the degree of repression of the conditioning experiences.

Object relations affect the capacity to learn. The need to learn, that is, to acquire ego skill and particularly the ego skills of an academic nature, arises from a number of sources. One important one is the need to identify with the adult. The child envies the power, self-sufficiency, and apparent freedom from fear of the adult and desires to be like him so as not to be tormented with his ever-present feelings of fear, inadequacy, and incapability. This psychic mechanism is one of the most important in the process of education.

The child of school age wishes to be able to do everything his peers do. If he observes that they are learning to read, their motives being as obscure to him as they are to them, he also wishes to learn to read. Competitive envy is a real intrapsychic motive in learning academic and other ego skills. A second more important motive lies in *the child's relationship with his teacher.* If the child loves the teacher he wants to please him. The best way he knows to please the teacher is to do what the teacher asks, that is, to be like him. Because he loves the teacher and wants the teacher to love him he identifies with the teacher just as he did as a younger child with his parents. In making this identification he learns the academic skills which he observes the teacher knows. As identification with the teacher takes place because the child loves the teacher any emotional reaction to the teacher of a different nature—such as hate, anger, or fear—will interfere with the identification and therefore with the learning process. A certain number of learning difficulties arise because the child hates or fears the teacher either because of the teacher's attitude toward him or because he displaces these feelings from another adult to the teacher.

If the child starts his reading when he has attained the stage of reading readiness he usually will be interested in learning. However, if he has interpersonal difficulties with his teacher—if the teacher dislikes him, is unnecessarily harsh and brutal, or is too impatient— then he falls into the same emotional reaction. His dislike for the painful experiences at his teacher's hands is carried over to the subject matter and he begins to dislike that and not want to learn it. He develops a reading disability. For reading disabilities due to this cause the ideal treatment is tutoring by a person who understands the importance of the interpersonal relationship for learning. Much of the tutoring consists in an introduction to the tutor—an introduction that has as its main purpose the development of a friendly relationship between tutor and child. When this has been accomplished the retraining in reading proceeds quite rapidly.

In certain cases of reading disability that we have seen, the beginning of the difficulty lay in an unpleasant *relationship between the child and the parent,* who, the child knew, had placed a high value on the ability to read. The child was angry and annoyed at the way he was treated and in revenge struck where he knew it would hurt most, that is, through the reading. Treatment for such cases must follow two routes: the unpleasant interpersonal relation with the parent must be corrected and later the child must be given special tutoring to bring him up to his grade level.

When a child has such an educational difficulty—usually a reading disability, whatever the cause is—we find that he is not as successful in his school progress as other children. As a result he begins to feel inferior. He tries to evade the inadequacy in various ways. He may, for instance, strain his memory prodigiously so that simply by sitting in class, listening to other children read, and paying careful attention to marks that will distinguish the page on which he is reading, he is able by memory to read the whole page with only a few mistakes. If he is confronted by exactly similar words arranged in a slightly different order on a page that has no distinguishing marks he is totally unable to read it. (We have seen children who had attained the eighth grade who were able actually to read only a very few words.) He may become totally disinterested in all schoolwork and proceed to develop compensations along other lines. He may develop feelings that the teacher is picking on him and that she is responsible for his deficiencies at school. All of these reactions are the result, not the cause, of the reading disability. They may have to be dealt with during any tutoring process, a point of which many parents and teachers seem unaware. The basic essentials of good tutoring are the ability to develop a good interpersonal relationship between the child and tutor and the capacity of the tutor to understand the child's behavior and reactions. It is the presence of this particular ability that makes one tutor successful in his work and another not, rather than whether the tutor knows his subject or uses the most advanced teaching methods.

Intrapsychic conflicts, whether perceived consciously as worries, as feelings of guilt, shame, and embarrassment, or as daydreams, or whether occurring in the unconscious portions of the ego, attract the attention to themselves and deflect it to a greater or less extent from all other external or intrapsychic constellations. Centering of the attention on the academic subjects to be learned and inhibition of the deflection of the attention to other internal or external situations is a necessary mechanism for a successful learning process. This centering may be interfered with by the attention being drawn to other external situations which the child finds important because they would serve as a means of gratification for some pressing instinctual desire or because certain instinctual desires forcibly are attracting the attention to themselves.

The intrapsychic conflicts may be classified into several groups.

We have mentioned already the boy who could not remain in school because he was worried lest his mother desert him. His case is an example of this type of learning difficulty. Excessive parental quarreling, broken homes, and the like all cause the child to worry; and this worry interferes with his ability to learn. Similarly, if the child's attention is engrossed with conscious feelings of guilt, shame, and embarrassment as the sign of fear of real detection and punishment or of superego disapproval because of some real or fancied "bad" act or failure, he is not able to attend to his school work and the result is a quite serious, although perhaps short-lived, decrease in academic achievement. It is unfortunate that these deflections of attention, from whatever cause, result in the child not learning the particular sections of the subjects being taught at the time the attention is deflected. The results of this lack of learning, however short-lived it may be, show consistently in difficulties in mastering later aspects of the same subjects; the individual may labor under inadequate skills in these subjects for the rest of his life unless he receives special tutoring in the parts he did not learn. It is the duty of the educator to see that this special tutoring is provided in all these cases after the conflict has been solved.

These conflicts or worries may be the result of conscious feelings of horror and fear. A girl of twelve began to fail in her school work. Shortly before the failure began she had been told by her friend about the phenomena of childbirth, the friend depicting vividly and with much exaggeration the painfulness and bloodiness of labor. The patient formerly had been quite satisfied with her feminine role and was looking forward with eager anticipation to the time when she could be married and have many children. Now these desires and anticipation became terrifying. She had to focus her whole attention on this conscious conflict so that she had no capacity to attend to her academic work and in consequence it became impossible for her to learn anything.

The child may be engrossed with a conscious conflict about his instinctual desires. A girl of fourteen rather suddenly began to fail in her school work. At this time she had become aware of a strong desire to masturbate, to which she succumbed at intervals. After each time, however, she experienced great remorse and fear—so great that she preferred to walk the floor all night lest by getting into bed and trying to go to sleep she might succumb again. Of course the fatigue on the next day interfered with her ability to learn. Her attention was focused night and day on the problem of whether she would masturbate or not and so was deflected from her task of learning. In this case the conflict was due to the strength of her instinctual desires and their demands for gratification. These desires were opposed by her fears of the results of the act and by her feelings that masturbation was morally wrong which were derived from superego prohibitions against the unconscious fantasies during masturbation.

The focusing of attention on daydreams may interfere with the ability to learn. During the first few days or few weeks at boarding school the learning ability of a child often decreases. If he is questioned it will be found that he is centering his attention on daydreams about his home and his family and has deflected it from the task of learning. He may not feel the unhappiness or anxiety which other children often feel in the same situation and which are usually the feelings that accompany homesickness in the first day or so at camp, because he is focusing his attention on pleasant memories; but his ability to learn suffers during this time. This type of focusing of attention on fantasy, and all other conditions in which escape from unpleasant intrapsychic conflicts to fantasy produces a similar focusing of the attention on the fantasy, produce learning difficulties in children.

Another type of focusing attention is a pathological process but results in an increased ability to learn instead of a failure in learning. A boy of nineteen explained that when he was younger he had found that if he felt deeply and expressed his feelings he was exposed to constant rebuffs by his parents, who favored his younger brother and who seemed to dislike him. About the age of nine the boy had decided that he would not allow himself to feel anything again but would allow himself to think only. In this he was caricaturing the old adage, "Look before you leap." Instead of responding to a situation with feeling, he thought the whole situation through very carefully before he acted. He focused all his attention on the process of thinking and of learning academic skills to increase his thinking ability. Since he devoted all his time to studying, his school grades were excellent. However, in his adolescence he began to notice that he had no friends, that his colleagues seemed to avoid him and ridiculed his scientific interest. It was this loneliness and unhappiness that brought him to treatment. In this case, in order to avoid many deepseated and painful intrapsychic conflicts and to avoid the feelings that are inherently a part of daydreaming, the boy focused his attention entirely on learning academic skills.

The child who is *too* interested in his school work and strains too hard at it is often a more pathological case than the one who fails because his attention is deflected away from learning. The diagnosis and treatment of the child who has difficulty in learning because he is worried or because he is daydreaming is the task of the trained teacher and the trained school counselor—in those cases, which are in the majority, where the worries and the reasons for the daydreaming are conscious. Carefully planned interviews, through which the child develops confidence to confide in the therapist annd then discusses his worries, frequently lead to a marked improvement in his ability to learn. The therapist, however, must be sufficiently skilled to distinguish these cases from those in which the learning difficulty is the outstanding symptom of a severe neurosis. As these disturbances appear more prominently in adolescence we intend to discuss them more fully in the chapter on that age period.

Too permissive upbringing contributes to another important type of learning and personality difficulty that is occurring with increasing frequency. In this type is included the new intermediate group of children discussed previously. Educators, and particularly progressive educators, in the last few years have become aware of a peculiar phenomenon in certain children. These children on entering school seem to lack any interest in learning. Instead of being interested in acquiring knowledge they seem interested only in the immediate gratification of their desires. Learning to read is boring because it requires effort and interferes with their immediate pleasure. No matter how hard the teacher tries to arouse their interest and hold them to this task by making it pleasurable, the results are slight or nil. In fact, these children will state openly that they do not intend to learn and that the teacher cannot make them. These statements do not sound defiant or stubborn but simply matter-of-fact.

More peculiar still is the fact that such children come from homes which appear to be the best. The parents are interested in the acquisition of knowledge but do not force their children to follow in their footsteps. They interfere as little as possible with the manifestations of the various stages of psychosexual development. Toilet training is done easily and slowly, there is no interference with finger sucking, masturbation, curiosity, or exhibitionism; in short, it seems as if they gave their children every opportunity for successful development. But when the upbringing of these children is studied carefully, two misconceptions are found. The child has been permitted to operate always on the pleasure principle. He has been protected as much as is humanly possible from any pain or any interference with the immediate gratification of his desires. The parents are not only extremely permissive toward his gratification but actually almost turn themselves inside out to see that he is gratified. They do not wish him to experience any pain or anxiety. These children therefore have not learned to tolerate any anxiety, particularly that which arises when the immediate gratification of an instinctual desire is prevented by reality.

This kind of upbringing is one of the typical and most frequent misapplications of Freud's findings. It reverses the whole parent-child relationship, for here the adult identifies with the aggressor, who in this case is the child, instead of vice versa. As a consequence the development of the defenses of repression, reaction formation, change of aim, and sublimation—in sum the development of the organization of the ego—is greatly retarded. Sexual curiosity is not changed into curiosity about the nonsexual aspect of the world but remains sexual curiosity, which is gratified constantly. Such children have no energy to learn at their disposal and their desire to learn cannot be stimulated even by making the subject to be learned as interesting as possible. They will begin to learn only when they are subjected to the slow educational process of being compelled both to postpone immediate gratification of instinctual drives and to tolerate the anxiety which necessarily must arise during this educational procedure. It is therefore the task of the skilled teacher to help them develop their personalities before they can learn.

THE EGO-DISTURBED CHILD

We mentioned earlier that the behavior of certain chronically rebellious children was caused by defects in the brain structure as the result of organic injuries or disease. Following the study of the behavior disorders which were found as the result of the epidemic of infectious encephalitis in 1919 and 1920, there were frequent arguments between psychiatrists as to whether the diagnosis of a particular case was that of the result of an organic lesion or not. In the early and middle 1930's, increased and improved psychological testing began to make clear that certain children diagnosed as intellectually retarded were not feeble-minded although they gave that appearance. Then in the 1940's child psychiatrists began to see what apparently was a new group of cases that did not fit any of the diagnostic pictures. We do not know whether this was because our diagnostic acumen was greater or whether this was a new disease syndrome. With our greater knowledge of disturbances in the ego and of the factors that influence ego development as a result of the pioneer investigations of Anna Freud, we are in a better position to classify and understand this group of cases than we were before. The development of and effectiveness of the ego functions may be affected in several ways:

Severe illnesses of the mother during the second half of her pregnancy, particularly if she suffers from chickenpox or severe metabolic illness, may cause cerebral injury to the fetus. Too rapid or too prolonged labor may have a similar effect due to multiple hemorrhages or destruction by anoxia in the baby's brain. Encephalitis—epidemic or as the result of severe chickenpox, measles, scarlet fever—in the first two or three years of life can produce cerebral lesions through the inflammatory process. Severe whooping cough during the same years can produce destructive multiple cerebral hemorrhages. Severe head injuries also may produce permanent cerebral injuries. After a year or so these brain injuries may show no signs on neurological examination except perhaps a disturbance in the electroencephalogram. As the ego does not have an intact nervous system to work with, its development and its functions are seriously hampered. The diagnosis in these cases needs the collaboration of a competent neurologist and a well-trained child psychiatrist, and their treatment requires the use of specific educational measures by well-trained educators with psychotherapy for the purpose of helping ego development. This means, of course, treatment by experienced child psychiatrists.

Some children develop the ability for specific groups of skills at a slower rate than others. In our experience this lag appears clinically most frequently in the language spheres. Certain children talk much later than usual. Others seem to be slow in attaining the ability to read, although their ability to learn arithmetic is the same as that of the ordinary child. From recent studies we have been making we have formed the opinion that many cases of reading difficulties fall in this group. The cause does not seem to be an organic lesion but rather that certain cortical areas do not develop at the usual rate. Such children quickly develop feelings of inferiority when they find they cannot do as well as their peers and so tend to give up trying to learn. Such cases need the services of skilled educators who have a real understanding of the emotional problems these children show.

In 1942 Bender described a series of children whom she judged were psychotic. They showed disturbances in every patterned functioning field of behavior and careful study showed that the ordinary physiological rhythms of daily living—sleeping, eating, elimination, growth, motor skills, reflexes, etc.—all had lost their normal rhythmical pattern. Reflexes such as are normal in the young baby remained unchanged as the child grew older. These children showed a great tendency for physical and bodily dependence on the adult. They had no clear body image and seemed to be unaware that their body had a periphery which separated it from the rest of the world. They either were mute or if they spoke, their speech was distorted by the dropping-out of connecting words and the use of neologisms. They were unable to make identifications with other people. At the same time they often were brilliantly artistic, intensely interested in music, and their memory might be phenomenal. Such children were anxiety-ridden personalities and developed many symptoms to alleviate the anxiety. Bender believed the cause of the anxiety was the severe disturbances just described and the effect of these on the perceptual and psychological functions.

The next year Kanner described a subgroup which he called early infantile autism. These children showed a preferred withdrawal from any contact with people, a compelling desire for the preservation of sameness, a skillful and even affectionate relation to inanimate objects and routines, a retention of intelligence, a phenomenal memory, a deep interest in music or art, and either mutism or the kind of language that did not seem intended for interpersonal communication. This language showed a reversal of pronouns—you for I, etc.—neologisms, metaphors, and apparently irrelevant utterances which sometimes simply are expressions of anxiety and sometimes can be traced to the patient's experiences. The condition usually becomes apparent about the age of two or three years. Both Kanner and Rank found that the mothers of these children who showed this kind of arrested and fragmented ego development fell into two groups:

(1) Those with diagnosed psychoses
    (a) patients with manic depressive psychosis who have had repeated hospitalizations and/or depressive episodes shortly after the birth of the child
    (b) patients with a schizophrenic psychosis with remissions
(2) Mothers who were extremely immature individuals, very narcissistic, and so incapable of mature emotional relationships.

In 1952, Mahler described another subgroup—the Symbiotic Infantile Psychoses. These children's psychosis becomes evident about four years of age. Their egos are poorly developed and are overwhelmed by separation anxiety—of a severe panic degree. These panic reactions are followed by an attempt to fuse themselves with their mother, with whom they have a delusion of oneness. The boundaries of the self and nonself are blurred, and their body image is not differentiated from that of the mother. Their reality testing remains fixated at the omnipotent delusional stage of development. For a full description of the behavior and personality of these children, the reader is referred to the original articles and to the Chapter on Childhood Psychoses in *Emotional Disorders of Children*.

We have presented this condensed description of the psychotic child because such cases are being diagnosed more frequently today and so we believe the reader is entitled to know such cases exist. We have kept the description brief because a complete presentation of the behavior of these children—and it would have to be complete for the reader to get an adequate picture—would take considerable space and is best read in the original articles.

From our own observations we think that in some of these cases the tendency to develop a psychosis is inherited. In others, it results from severe disturbances in the mother-child relationship in the child's early years. In a few others that we have seen, the psychosis followed operations in the second half of the child's first year.

The autistic child requires treatment which is a combination of methods of mothering, psychotherapy for the child, and psychotherapy for the parents, particularly for the mother, as Rank has described very fully. The disruption in the home caused by the presence of a psychotic child and what can be done about it has been well discussed by Moak in her book, *The Troubled Child*.

Between the cases of actual psychoses and the cases whose ego development is due to an organic slowness in development and maturation which we have discussed earlier there are a number of cases that show less marked forms of disturbance in the development of the ego which are caused by inadequate mothering in the early years but not to the degree that results in a psychosis. Weil has described such cases. All of these cases in which there are peculiarities in the behavior of the children need careful study by a well-trained child psychiatrist and special combinations of treatment.

BIBLIOGRAPHY FOR CHAPTER IX

GENERAL

Bender, Lauretta, "Childhood Schizophrenia," *Nervous Child,* 1, 1942, 138.
——— "Childhood Schizophrenia: A Clinical Study of 100 Schizophrenic Children," *American Journal of Orthopsychiatry,* 17, 1947, 40.
Bettelheim, Bruno, *Love is Not Enough,* Free Press, 1950.
Caille, Ruth Kennedy, *Resistant Behavior of Preschool Children,* Teachers College, Columbia University, 1939.
Cook, Stewart W., "A Survey of Methods Used to Produce Experimental Neurosis," *American Journal of Psychiatry,* 96, 1939, 1259.
Darwin, Charles, *The Expression of Emotions in Men and Animals,* Appleton, 1890.
Dunbar, Flanders H., Theodore P. Wolff, Edward S. Traber, and Louise

A. Brush, "The Psychic Component of the Disease Processes (including Convalescence) in Cardiac, Diabetic, and Fracture Patients," *American Journal of Psychiatry*, 95, 1939, 1319.

Freud, Anna, *The Ego and the Mechanisms of Defense*, Hogarth, 1937.

Friedlander, Kate, *The Psychoanalytic Approach to Juvenile Delinquency*, International Universities Press, 1947.

Kanner, Leo, "Autistic Disturbances of Affective Contact," *Nervous Child*, 2, 1943, 217.

—— "Problems of Nosology and Psychodynamics of Early Infantile Autism," *American Journal of Orthopsychiatry*, 19, 1949, 416.

Levin, Paul M., "Restlessness in Children," *Archives of Neurology and Psychiatry*, 39, 1938, 784.

Levy, David M., "Resistant Behavior of Children," *American Journal of Psychiatry*, 4, 1925, 503.

Mahler, M. S., "On Child Psychosis and Schizophrenia: Autistic and Symbiotic Infantile Psychoses," *Psychoanalytic Study of the Child*, 7, 1952, 286.

Moak, Helen R., *The Troubled Child*, Holt, New York, 1958.

Orton, Samuel T., *Reading, Writing and Speech Problems in Children*, Norton, 1937.

Pearson, Gerald H. J., "The Inverted Position in Children's Drawings," *Journal of Nervous and Mental Diseases*, 88, 1928, 449.

—— *Emotional Disorders of Children*, Norton, 1949.

Rank, Beata, "Adaptation of the Psychoanalytic Technic for the Treatment of Young Children with Atypical Development," *American Journal of Orthopsychiatry*, 19, 1949, 130.

Sayers, R. R., "Major Studies on Fatigue," *War Medicine*, 2, 1942, 786.

Schilder, Paul, "The Concept of Hysteria," *American Journal of Psychiatry*, 95, 1939, 1389.

—— "Psychic Disturbances after Head Injuries," *American Journal of Psychiatry*, 91, 1934, 155.

Weil, Annemarie P., "Certain Severe Disturbances of Ego Development in Childhood," *Psychoanalytic Study of the Child*, 8, 1953.

—— "Some Evidences of Deviational Development in Infancy and Childhood," *Psychoanalytic Study of the Child*, 11, 1956, 292.

ARTICLES ON LEARNING DIFFICULTIES IN CHILDREN

Bergler, Edmund, "Zur Problematik der Pseudodebilitat," *Int. Ztschr. f. Psa.*, 18, 1938, No. 4.

Bornstein, Berta, "Zur Psychogenese der Pseudodebilitat," *Int. Ztschr. f. Psa.*, 16, 1930, Nos. 3 and 4.

Fenichel, Otto, *The Psychoanalytic Theory of Neurosis,* Norton, 1945, pp. 180 and 181.

Freud, Anna, *The Ego and the Mechanisms of Defense,* International Universities Press, 1946.

Klein, Emanuel, "Psychoanalytic Aspects of School Problems," *Psychoanalytic Study of the Child,* Vols. III–IV, International Universities Press.

Landauer, Karl, "Zur Psychosexuellen Genese der Dummheit," *Ztschr. f. Sexualwissenschaft, U. Sexualpolitik,* 16, 1929.

Liss, Edward, "Emotional and Biological Factors Involved in a New Learning Process," *American Journal of Orthopsychiatry,* 7, 1937, 483.

——— "Learning Difficulties. Unresolved Anxiety and Resultant Learning Patterns," *American Journal of Orthopsychiatry,* 11, 1941, 520.

——— "Learning—Its Sadistic and Masochistic Manifestations," *American Journal of Orthopsychiatry,* 10, 1940, 123.

——— "Libidinal Fixations as Pedagogic Determinants," *American Journal of Orthopsychiatry,* 5, 1935, 126.

Maenchen, Anna, "Denkhemmeng und Aggression," *Ztschr. f. Psa. Padagogik,* 10, 1936, 276.

Mahler, Margaret, "Pseudoimbecility: A Magic Cap of Invisibility," *Psychoanalytic Quarterly,* 11, 1942, 149.

Oberndorf, C. P., "The Feeling of Stupidity," *International Journal of Psychoanalysis,* 20, 1939, 433.

Pearson, Gerald H. J., "A Survey of Learning Difficulties in Children," in *Psychoanalytic Study of the Child,* Vol. VII, International Universities Press.

——— *Psychoanalysis and the Education of the Child,* Norton, 1954.

Schmidelberg, Melitta, "Intellectual Inhibition and Disturbances in Eating," *International Journal of Psychoanalysis,* 10, 1938, 17.

The Approach to Adulthood–Adolescence

X

Development of Personality during Adolescence

WITH adolescence, there comes a resurgence of the instinctual drives which forces the personality—the ego and superego—to modify itself further until a new equilibrium is reached. The period of adolescence is one of increased conflict between the parts of the personality—the id, ego, and superego—and a certain period of time is necessary before the three parts of the personality are able to function again as a smoothly working whole. This time period extends for several years before and after the central organic phenomenon of adolescence, namely puberty.

EARLY ADOLESCENCE—PREPUBERTY

Adolescence begins gradually at the end of the latent period (about 10½ years of age) and terminates gradually with the beginning of adult life (from 18 to 21 years of age) in our culture. (Among many non-Western cultures it terminates shortly after puberty—fourteen to fifteen years of age.) In Western civilization and particularly in our culture the termination of adolescence is often prolonged through the mid-twenties by social and economic factors. There are individuals who reach physiological puberty before they reach psychological puberty, and others who enter upon psychological puberty before the corresponding physiological signs make their appearance. The physiological signs of puberty are more manifest and more definitely dated in girls—by menstruation—than they are in boys, hence it is easier to study clearly the psychological phenomena of prepuberty and puberty in girls than in boys. In fact, for some time we were not sure that the development of the boy during these periods approximated that of the girl at all. However, more recently the study of certain boys whose physiological puberty was delayed has seemed to confirm the fact that in certain ways the prepubertal and pubertal phases of the boy's development parallel those of the girl. It must be understood that the transition stages between the different phases are fluid, and attempts to delineate a period of development too precisely lead to the error of drawing too sharp lines. So in our discussion of any period we simply will try to highlight its important characteristics.

During the prelatent period the rate of physical growth was very high, as was also the rate of psychological and personality development. All of these rates of growth were retarded during the latency period, which in reality is not only a period of sexual latency but also a period of growth latency. With the beginning of the resurgence of the activity of the sexual glands there begins a resurgence of the growth process. This resurgence is accompanied by an intensification of activity in boys and girls. This intensified activity mobilizes the child's intellectual and artistic talents and his aspirations, his emotional ambitions, and his tendencies to search for objects outside his family whom he can love, whom he can hate, and with whom he can identify. He shows an increased sense of responsibility and independence and has a great need to be recognized as an adult. In short, the intensified drive to activity is placed at the service of the need to master the environment and is accompanied by an increase in neuromuscular and body development. Both sexes show this drive to activity at first. In the boy, it continues throughout the period of adolescence. In the girl, shortly after the prepubertal period the drive to activity is replaced by a trend to passivity which is usually noted as an increase in her femininity.

Now begins the battle for the recognition of his adulthood, which all through adolescence is so acute and painful because the child is still uncertain of his ability to fend for himself and is still, particularly in a civilized culture, in need of protection. He labors under an increase in the unconscious desire to remain a child—a desire all of us carry throughout life. Often it is possible to see these two conflicting drives—the need to be recognized as an adult and the desire to remain a child—in open operation. On one day a child behaves and speaks as if he needs no advice, suggestions, or help from anyone; there is nothing he is not capable of doing all by himself. On the next, the same child behaves and speaks as if he is hardly able to decide the simplest question for himself. Neither of these attitudes, although they both are directed at the parents, have anything to do with the attitude of the parents toward the child. They arise from the adolescent's inner needs. However, they both can become greatly accentuated if the parents either attempt too much domination or desire too much that the child remain a child. Thus an important conflict that the individual has to work out during adolescence is that between his desire to be regarded as an adult and his wish to remain a child. This conflict is one result of the newly accelerated growth process.

The accelerated growth process also produces other conflicts which are eventually corrected by the growth process itself but which are disturbing to the individual while they are present. The accelerated rate of physical growth eventually produces the body habitus of the adult individual. During the latent period the differences in body habitus among a number of children are not very great. Some are slightly taller, some slightly shorter, some slightly more slender and some slightly more obese. But by puberty or shortly afterward the classes of body habitus (endomorph, mesomorph, and ectomorph) are well differentiated. The rate of growth and the speed with which the final body habitus is attained differs from individual to individual. One will grow more rapidly than another. This variation makes for a new social difficulty. A group of boys who have been much the same size and strength during the latent period may become very dissimilar in size and strength during the early part of adolescence. They are no longer equally capable of competing physically with each other and in their social relations the relatively weaker and smaller ones find themselves at a disadvantage that they had not experienced before. The smaller and weaker tend to try to retain their equal status by too much admiration for their stronger and taller colleagues or by ridiculing their rapid growth—treatment which is resented bitterly by the ridiculed ones, who retaliate either physically on their ridiculers or else by withdrawing from social life. In girls the differences as to rate of development of the secondary sex characteristics cause a similar social problem and similar modes of reaction. In either sex, whatever the reaction pattern is, it is produced by the hurt to the pride— a very sensitive area at this time—caused by the realization that something has happened to make the individual apparently (though only temporarily, but the individual seldom takes comfort from this fact) less capable physically and physiologically than his peers. This social difficulty passes in time with the completion of growth, but is extremely painful to the individual while it lasts.

Not only are there markedly different rates of growth among various individuals, but there are also often marked differences as to rate of growth of various systems of organs in the individual himself. Often the skeletal system grows faster than its supporting muscles. Such disparity produces clumsiness and poor posture—neither of which the individual can correct without special exercising, usually in a group setting, such as camp or military school. His large muscle groups may grow faster than his finer muscle groups, so that he is badly coordinated; he is usually incapable of correcting this, either, by himself. His extremities may grow suddenly out of proportion to the rest of his body; his hands and feet may be relatively large. Usually this disparity is more harrowing to girls than to boys. The growth of his heart and lungs may be slower than that of the rest of his body so that his supply of oxygen is deficient and he feels constantly fatigued, even though perfectly well. We suspect the so-called chlorosis formerly so common in adolescent girls may be due partly to the complexity of the growth process emotionally and chemically. Individuals with these discrepancies in rate of growth of various systems of organs are clumsy, incoordinate, have bad posture, fatigue excessively, and lack all the grace of movement and of appearance that they had during the latent period. This awkwardness produces embarrassment socially and the individual, because he does not realize that it is due to incomplete growth and will be corrected *only* through further growth, begins to feel inferior and inadequate and humiliated because he cannot match his physical capacity with his ideal of himself and what he thinks other people would admire. His parents are often similarly unaware and share or promote his feelings. As a result, just like a person who actually has a permanent physical disability, the adolescent attempts to compensate for his "inferiority." He may overcompensate by ridiculing other people, by trying through exercises or diet to force his body to the impossible, by developing annoying behavior in order to attract attention even if unfavorable (he temporarily heightens his masochism), or by devouring knowledge so that his greater intellect will offset his physical condition. Or instead, he may withdraw from all social activity when there is any possibility of comparison between himself and others. He may alternate between overcompensation and withdrawal. Ridicule, scolding, attempts to make him do things which are impossible physically (such as constant nagging about his posture, which he could not change if he tried and which will improve as his growth continues), all increase the physical difficulties and heighten the feeling of inferiority. In these situations the conflict is between the real (for example, physical ability) and the ideal the individual has for himself.

While most of our readers, we believe, have some knowledge of the difficulties that the rate of growth produces in the motor sphere for the adolescent, they usually are not so aware that a similar increase in the rate of growth in the sensory sphere and the effect of the increased sexuality on sensations also produces temporary difficulties for the adolescent. During prepuberty and puberty there seems to be an increase in the ability to distinguish finer shades of color and of sound and an increased capacity to perceive stimuli from the external world. We do not know whether these increases result from an increased development of the sensory organs or the association pathways or from the erotization of the avenues of sensory intake due to pubertal changes. Perhaps it is a combination of both. Whatever the cause, the increase in perceptive sensitivity causes the individual to be flooded with new sensations and new feelings and new judgmental criteria of perceptions. This sudden flood of sensory phenomena and feelings requires time for digestion and assimilation, but no such time is granted—the flooding continues.

The change in sensory acuteness is one of the reasons for another phenomenon of puberty. One day the individual is bright and alert, interested and appreciative of the world, reacting to it, feeling it, singing its praises. The next day he may be apathetic, disinterested, irritable, unable to learn, often unable to apparently hear the simplest statement or see the most obvious detail. He appears heedless, unappreciative and negativistic. This condition may last for several days or weeks to be followed again by a period of alertness and interest. During the retarded period the individual has withdrawn from sensory stimuli by closing the avenues of sensory intake until he has digested and assimilated the previous flood of impressions. This process of assimilation and digestion has to occur because there is not sufficient understanding of what is happening or motor outlet to relieve the tensions of the incoming sensations. The adolescent does not understand why he "feels moody" or acts stupidly, nor, often, do his parents. The phenomenon may have little relation to any environmental changes. It is part of the process of growth and usually disappears as growth is attained. Analogously, somewhere around the seventh grade many children start to do poorly in school; this decline may last the better part of the school year. The next year they attain without trouble the degree of excellence that preceded the lapse. Obviously the family who can accept a certain degree of this without censure will help. But if it is too prolonged, then an emotional sickness pattern may be developing.

These effects of motor and sensory growth are matters of development and happen to everyone in a greater or lesser degree. They have some present consequences. They injure the individual's pride because he observes himself suddenly falling so short of his concept of himself. This observation leaves his vanity raw and smarting and is an important factor contributing to the fidgetiness, restlessness, mood changes, giggling, sensitivity, and easily-upsetness of the prepubertal person. The adult, parent or teacher, cannot help much with this conflict except by much understanding patience, some explanation that these difficulties will pass as the individual grows older (an explanation that is rarely fully believed), and as much avoidance of criticism and reprimand as possible. A positive statement of what the appropriate behavior could be and some friendly encouragement are helps that build self-confidence.

During the latent period the child has learned to strengthen his ego by developing for himself ideals—conscious and unconscious—toward which he strives. Such ideals were found originally in the parents, but toward the middle of the latent period adults outside the family begin to become more important as ideal figures. During adolescence this tendency is increased. Instead of wishing to be like the parent of the same sex the boy and girl attempt to be as different as possible. Although they may ridicule the parents at home they may still continue to speak about them away from home in a way that glorifies them. Heretofore, the parent, particularly the parent of the same sex, has been an ideal. Now in their minds the boy and girl shatter this ideal and turn their affection and interest from the parents to adults outside the family. The feeling of love toward the outside adult results in the numerous and short-lived "crushes" that are so frequent during early adolescence. The same intrapsychic process that originally went on in relation to the parents occurs here also. The boy or girl loves the adult, wants to please him in order to be loved, and identifies with him. From this point on, certain of the characteristics of this adult become a permanent part of the child. The effect of these short-lived deep attachments to adults outside the family is to give the individual ideals on which he can depend to strengthen his own ego by developing ego skills so that he can become a separate individual able to operate under his own steam.

This process of development is both inevitable and important. All of us, looking back, can see where a trait, a trick of speech, a mannerism, a way of dealing with a situation, certain interests or skills, were acquired from some loved and admired teacher, uncle or aunt, minister, physician, movie actor or actress.

This whole process is sometimes painful to parents. They would like the growing child to mature smoothly, evenly, quietly, gratefully and co-operatively at all times. But it must perforce be uneven, at times noisy, moody, resentful, and lacking in the appreciation of parental efforts that might be desired. To be given life may be a great favor, it is true. But to be asked to make all the necessary conformations to a society as complex and as demanding as ours is asking a great deal of the young. When they do conform and take inspiration and become persons of strength and competence, the parents can take credit for producing a work of art.

The differences that confront the adolescent raised in a Western culture and one raised in a different one are discussed in great detail by Hsu in his book *Americans and Chinese*. He says that the individual's search for security has a profound effect upon his attitude toward and relationship with other human beings, the supernatural, and material things. The Chinese finds satisfaction within primary groups, for example the family, and shows little interest in other attachments; the American in contrast finds little assurance of permanent security in human relationships and, therefore, seeks satisfaction elsewhere. These are the differing points of psychological orientation from which the two peoples have proceeded in fundamentally different social, political, religious, and economic directions. In consequence, the most serious problems of American life occur in the domain of human relationships while the most tenacious Chinese problems tend to center upon the natural environment: the lack of incentive to control it and the relative absence of internal impetus to alter anything that is established. Hsu points out that the world of Chinese children is not divorced from their parents' world. From the first, they are in contact with the Janus-face of mankind; they have impressed upon them the importance of obedience to social conventions; they learn the distinction between what their parents say and what the elders in fact do. By adolescence, they have learned most of the values of the culture, whereas the American adolescent is unprepared for the imperfections of the real world and so is disillusioned when he meets it. As a result his insecurity when face to face with reality is equally increased. The result is emotional turbulence, and because individuals differ widely it erupts in diverse ways. The milder reactions are sulky moods, quarrelsomeness, incorrigibility, hostility to parents, and many other forms of misconduct. The more extreme reactions are criminal, ranging from robbery and joyrides in stolen autos to sex orgies, narcotic addiction, and apparently unmotivated murder. The American adolescent's misconduct is likely to be the price of belonging to his own age group. Trouble with the law merely hurts his parents, whom he often intentionally disregards, but it earns him a firmer place among his own gang, and it is their rejection he fears. Under this compulsion, he is likely to do anything dictated by his gang. The misconduct of the Chinese adolescent is more of an individual matter: it is never dictated by the group, for the one group to which he is closely attached, and consequently the one group whose rules or commands have any real meaning, is the primary family group. If he gets into trouble, he not only incurs the displeasure of his parents and kinsmen, but moreover he receives little moral support from most persons his own age.

Besides these difficulties for the American adolescent, Hsu finds another one. American adolescents do not have a uniform basis of mores, taboos, and customs for reference. We have free speech, freedom of thought and prejudice and religion. One person can be a pacifist, another a militant; one can be an atheist and another a fundamentalist; one can believe in prohibition and another in moderation; any person can be a Republican, a Democrat, a Socialist, a New Dealer, and belong to any religious group he wishes or none. There is no single set of ideals on which the adolescent can depend.

It is well therefore for the adolescent to meet and know as many different kinds of people and ways of thought and belief as possible, and for him to take something from all of them regardless of the fixity or single-mindedness of the parents' ideals—for in this rapidly changing world no one can say what ideals will be most helpful ten years from now. However, if the parents are too set in their ways and are not flexible enough to understand that the ideals for which they live, whether these ideals be liberal or conservative, scientific or religious, may be all right for them but not for their children, the adolescent has an extra and unnecessary burden to carry. With an ego which feels weak and helpless and which he is endeavoring to strengthen through the acquisition of new ideals he now has to battle against unreasonable pressure from his parents. He may in response submit and allow himself to be overwhelmed by his unconscious wish to remain a child and so enter adult life unequipped to tolerate change.

The adolescent finds one source of solidarity in himself, through the development of ideals obtained from adults outside the family. He finds another source from his colleagues. During the prelatent period the child is an individual and cannot become a real member of a group. Group formation can happen only as the parts of the individual personality are crystallized. Even in the latent period real group formation is difficult—everyone, so to speak, wishes to carry the ball or be the pitcher, and there is little or no idea of real team play, of action not for the individual's benefit but genuinely for that of the team. With early adolescence, group formation becomes possible. The adolescent, particularly the adolescent boy, begins to develop a group life, which will be the basis for his future social life. These groups may be corner gangs, sand-lot teams, drugstore crowds, and after puberty, often fraternities and sororities. All too rarely do the Boy or Girl Scouts or the other adult-organized social groups play a real part in the group life of their members. That real group life takes place in self-organized gangs, and for a definite reason. The purpose of the gang or group is to repudiate adult influence and strengthen the individual's inner feelings of capability by his close association with his peers.

The course of social development, the development of new parts of the ego ideal, and the strengthening of the individual's ego do not pursue exactly the same course in the girl as in the boy. During the prepubertal period—10½ until puberty—the girl tends to dislike and attack the mother more openly than the boy does the father. The tendency of the boy is to stay away from home as much as possible or remain by himself when he is at home so that he does not allow himself the opportunity for quarreling. The girl is at home more frequently and so quarrels overtly more often with her mother. Along with this quarreling she tends more to select one special girl friend of her own age. The two are inseparable, they share secrets which cannot be told anyone else. The secrets they share among others include, of course, the sexual behavior of other people, contemporaries or adults, on which they tend to spy, and about sexual matters—sex differences, intercourse, menstruation, and pregnancy. The relationship is an unconscious monogamous homosexual one but this seldom reaches consciousness and rarely becomes overt. The purpose of this relationship is to help the girl to break away from her attachment to her mother, to turn this attachment toward a colleague as a friend, and to find support against her own feeling that her ego is too weak to allow her to function as an autonomous individual. It is thus an important step in her development. These friendships often last a considerable time. Occasionally triangles develop and arouse bitter jealousies and heartbreaks. The friendships tend to break up if one of the girls is sexually somewhat more precocious than the other and begins to be really interested in a boy.

We said earlier we were not sure that prepubertal boys go through a similar stage. However, one of us recently has studied several boys with physiologically delayed puberty and found such a tendency occurring, although not to the same degree. More often than in the girls the friendship situation may result in a few overt homosexual episodes, which are not of importance as indications of a strongly bisexual constitution. Perhaps there may be a cultural reason why boys do not show this stage of monogamous friendship as openly as girls. A prepubertal or pubertal girl may behave like a tomboy and there is little or no social condemnation. A boy of the same age who tends to show a great deal of affectionate interest in a boy friend is strongly condemned. The unconscious homosexual tendencies of the prepubertal and pubertal boy find their satisfaction in group horseplay, wrestling, teasing, and similar activities, which are more on the sadomasochistic level of development.

The pubertal girl tends to continue her friendships with other girls until she begins to fall in love, which she does more openly than does the pubertal boy. Because of her drive to passivity she has a greater tendency to give up everything for her loved one. On the other hand, some of her falling in love is simply to insure her "popularity," that is, to show to herself that she is capable of collecting hearts—like scalps to hang on her belt. The pubertal boy tends to develop more slowly along these lines. His rebellions usually are supported by the group, his friendships are less intimate, and his falling in love is often later than the female's.

Before discussing in more detail the development of object relations and the sexual life we wish to discuss the relation of the adult to the early adolescent's struggle to turn from his family and acquire new ego ideals and ego skills for himself. It is important that he develop wider ego ideals and the new skills he needs to live up to those ideals. In doing so, as we have said, he has to separate himself from his parents and so he selects the various activities of daily living—time of going out and coming in, clothes, and the like—as fields of combat. In the parents' mind and in the minds of other adults—teachers, for example, there is always the question as to the amount of responsibility he should be given and as to how much he should be subjected to adult control. We believe that there are many educational errors about this. People say they allow junior-high-school and high-school pupils student government. But on close examination it appears in the majority of cases the decisions are entirely teacher-controlled. Here adults say they offer the adolescent something which they really do not. On the other hand, perhaps adults tend to give him too much responsibility, such as school contracts, selecting his own courses, and other decisions which he may be incapable of handling wisely at the time. It is more certain that parents tend to worry too much about the adolescent; actually, if the development during the first seven years of the child's life has been satisfactory, the storms of puberty are not going to upset it. The best the parents can do is to avoid ridiculing and attacking, to help the adolescent not to overcompensate, and to allow him opportunities for developing his skills. Also it is better for them to tell the truth. For example, if the adolescent is staying out later than they want and they insist that he come home at the time they lay down, they should not claim that it is good for the adolescent (who knows?) but admit the reason that they do not wish their comfort to be disturbed.

As both sexes enter the prepubertal period there comes a gradual change in the individual's attitude toward the opposite sex. From the almost complete avoidance of the latency, there develops a secret interest, which the individual at first shares with no one and later only with his peers. This stage is followed by attempts to attract the attention of members of the other sex in a way by which the individual can disclaim any responsibility for the attempt. A boy, turning a corner and seeing several girls, immediately will go through a series of acrobatics—obviously to attract their attention. He can deny this motive to himself by saying he just felt like some exercise. The group of girls will start to giggle as he goes past—also obviously to attract his attention. About this time the individual usually is secretly in love with some adult of the opposite sex— teacher, minister, physician, aunt or uncle, older cousin, actor. As this phase passes he becomes more interested in individuals of the same age. The boy tends to begin his advances with teasing and horseplay—actually as if he were a sadistic two-year-old. The girls object vociferously to this, but want it—actually as if they were masochistic two-year-olds. About the time of puberty and after, love affairs of a romantic nature develop. These often are not responded to, or if they are mutual they are short-lived, but also there is often considerable heartbreak when they terminate. It is well for the adolescent to have several of these affairs because through them he learns the personalities of the opposite sex—a knowledge he has denied himself since he resolved his oedipus situation. If he allows himself sufficient opportunity to learn about the opposite sex in this way he is in a better position to fall in love later.

PUBERTY

The age of onset of puberty differs in different climates and in different races. In America it usually begins at the age of twelve and carries over to the age of fifteen, merging into postpuberty. It is generally accepted that the capacity for sexuality has begun by the time the child reaches puberty. Both the girl and the boy have within them a great many feelings of shame and uneasiness at this period. Menstruation is one of the most obvious signs of this change in the female.

At puberty there can be sharp differences between the boy and his mother and the girl and her father. Such quarreling is a strong defense against any recrudescence of the oedipal sexual wishes which are stimulated by the resurgence of physical sexuality. During early adolescence one may see some distorted recapitulation of the stages of the development of the libido during the prelatent period. At some time all early adolescents begin to show food fads, adopt diets and eating rituals, show alternation of lack of appetite and gorging, have occasional gastric upsets of unknown cause, and show interest in physical culture. There also can be similar distorted manifestations of the early anal sexuality—bowel difficulties, constipation, interest in cleanliness, overfastidiousness, fear of germs on the hands and other mild germ and dirt phobias, and the assumption that constipation is the cause of acne.

MENSTRUATION

In the female, puberty is marked by changes in body contour, widening of the hips, enlargement of the breasts, growth of pubic and axillary hair, and the onset of menstruation. At least several months, and sometimes years, are required for the regularity of menstruation to become stabilized. While this process is going on, psychological reverberations occur within the girl. A great many of these are caused by the unfortunate reactions to the growing-up process to which we have alluded in previous chapters and by the fact that children are not adequately prepared or educated for the various phenomena of life, particularly those concerning sexual functioning. In spite of a growing public awareness of the need for sex education and sex understanding we still have a poor acceptance of sexuality itself. It is superfluous to say that people in our culture do not have a wholesome attitude toward menstruation and that many taboos surround it. These taboos go back thousands of years into the beliefs of primitive man, some of which are difficult to trace; attempts to explain others are made through theories of anthropologists who have uncovered existing and ancient primitive beliefs, folklore, and superstitions.

Most primitive people seem to have felt a need to explain menstruation to themselves in one way or another. Some believed the phenomenon was brought about because the woman had been bit-ten by a snake or a wild animal. Some believed that she had had sexual relations with a god. No matter what the reason, all ancient tribes seem to have believed that the phenomenon made the woman dangerous to the men and that men should not come in contact with her during the time. Consequently many tribes had various cruel taboos for the newly menstruating woman. For days, and some-times for months, she was isolated in a hut without light and without company. Food was brought to her by older women, who them-selves had to remain secluded until some of the supposed evil in them disappeared. Even those tribes who do not carry out so stringent a rite nevertheless have rather strict taboos about the menstruating period each month. The man is not supposed to touch either the woman, her bed, or her clothing for a period of six to eight days after the menstruation has stopped, and then only after she has bathed in running water.

These stringent taboos of primitive people are still extant and little changed in various areas today, indicating that after thousands of years we are still under the influence of the beliefs of our primi-tive ancestors. Women are prohibited in some regions from canning while they are menstruating, the belief being that they will cause the canned goods to spoil. They are not supposed to plant seed, or tend or cut flowers, because it is assumed the flowers will wither and the seeds will not grow. They are not supposed to come in contact with pregnant animals on the farm because it is believed that the animals will abort.

This tendency in society to seclude and exclude the female while she is menstruating is still followed in the twentieth century by thousands of mothers who believe their daughters should go to bed and stay there for two or three days while menstruation is going on. If a mother does not insist that the girl go to bed, she feels she must prohibit her from going about socially, and even if she does not openly prohibit social life, she is still likely to discourage the girl from participating in it. If asked why she feels this way, the mother probably would not have any definite reason to offer. However, on pressing her for an answer we would very likely find that she feels menstruating women to be offensive in some way, and that men feel themselves repulsed or their esthetic sense revolted by menstruating women.

Another idea that mothers have is that the girl is in an unhealthy state during menstruation and so should not take part in ordinary social activities lest she do herself harm. Menstruation is a perfectly normal physiological phenomenon; it is not debilitating; and the loss of blood is trivial and soon made up. There is no reason at all why women should greatly disturb their existence because of menstruation. In spite of this, the fact remains that the effectuality and peace of mind of many women are spoiled by these old wives' tales, and by the implication that menstruation is a great misfortune, an illness, a shameful phenomenon, in some vague way disgusting and harmful to others.

Children invariably come to know that the mother is menstruating without having been informed about it. As with everything else connected with sex, children build up their own theories and may quite naturally develop the theory that since the mother bleeds she must be ill, that she has been injured, or that some peculiar sickness has taken hold of her. If this idea is coupled with the tendency on the part of the mother to be irritable or depressed or to take to her bed during the monthly period, then it makes the girl feel she also is bound to be incapacitated by menstruation during her lifetime. These impressions and ideas about menstruation which are laid down in the child's mind during childhood stay with her a long time and are difficult to shake off. Just as we have not shaken off some of our primitive beliefs of many hundreds of years ago, so the individual does not shake off the beliefs that he has acquired ten or twenty years previously.

If her castration problem was not solved during the genital period, the girl continues to be distressed because she does not have a male genital organ. She may maintain the belief until puberty that she is neither a woman exactly, nor a castrated individual. However, the true nature of her anatomy becomes more definite with the onset of menstruation. Women must, by then at least, accept the fact of their womanhood and give up the hope of being like the male, if that has been the tendency of their thinking in their earlier life. Girls who have not accepted the fact of womanhood may be extremely disturbed by menstruation. Often without any previous instruction, they are in no way prepared for the phenomenon when it occurs. Neither are they prepared for the fact, less abruptly encountered, that their breasts must enlarge, nor for the other changes in body contour. The female child particularly should have some explanation of her anatomy and physiology and the role she should play in life. If she has not had the instruction before puberty, certainly she should have it at this critical time. But all too frequently we may find this phase of life going by with neither the father nor the mother—certainly this role belongs much more to the mother—talking to the daughter, neither telling her anything about the meaning of menstruation nor explaining the role she is going to play as a woman. When the child is six or eight the mother usually believes that she will discuss the matter at puberty. When puberty arrives and the daughter starts menstruating, the mother thinks, "She is still a child. Why should I spoil her innocence?" So the girl is left to draw her own conclusions and struggle alone with the meaning of menstruating.

Menstruation is often distressing to women because of the nature of the discharge: they have a flow of blood from their bodies that lasts three or four days—more or less—and they cannot stop it. Women become psychologically disturbed because menstruation reminds them of the difficulty they had during the toilet-training period when they were made to feel shame and chagrin during the process of learning control of bowels and bladder. Much of the distress and uneasiness about menstruation that exists in the minds of women could be prevented if mothers would only come forward at this period and say, "You do not have to be worried about it. Menstruation is a normal phenomenon. It has the function of preparing the uterus for pregnancy and is part of the whole process of preparation for childbirth. It happens to all women. I am not distressed about it; I never have been; you should not be."

Even ten minutes of wise explanation would be extremely reassuring to daughters if mothers only had enough mental equilibrium to discuss the phenomenon. Medical students have said to us after hearing the explanations of body phenomena that they suddenly realized that they, themselves, had never had adequate sex instruction but had picked up bits of information here and there. Studies of college women show that many or most of them also have not had any instruction about sex or even any instruction about menstruation. The importance of imparting this information to women should be stressed because they do not stumble upon the correct facts by themselves.

Doctors are in a good position to instruct mothers in the importance of these things, because in the lay mind physicians are supposed to know everything about the human body and its physiological and psychological functions. Women will accept information from the family physician; in fact, there is no other authority to whom they can turn, no other person whose explanations they will accept as valid. They get more from him than from reading two or three books, for people are often more skeptical about what they read than about what they hear, though there are some who take the written word more seriously than the spoken word.

Some girls grow up looking forward to menstruation with anticipation, as if it were a badge of womanhood, and expect their mothers to look upon it in the same way. But when puberty comes they are disappointed: the mother ignores the phenomenon and implies, thereby, that they should keep the matter to themselves. So girls think about it alone and manage it to the best of their limited ability.

Many women suffer from extreme symptoms during menstruation and relate them directly to the menstrual period: fatigue, backache, headache, irritability, depression of spirits. We know of a woman who went to bed for two weeks each month. She had the theory that all the food she ate turned sour in her stomach because some poison invaded her body during the process of menstruation. This delusion was not peculiar to her but was only a slight exaggeration of current thought. She felt that menstruation was a toxic and poisonous process. When talking with her, one was impressed by the extravagance of her beliefs about the menstruating woman.

In the course of practice, doctors hear many strange ideas and beliefs surrounding sexuality and menstruation. They should reassure a woman who believes these tales by telling her they have heard them before. When she feels that the doctor is receptive to her feelings and ideas of menstruation, he will be in a position—after he has listened to her—to tell her it is her fear and false beliefs that is making her sick and keeping her in bed and not the glandular activity or the flow of blood.

NOCTURNAL EMISSIONS

The loss of seminal fluid during sleep, sometimes accompanied by an erotic dream, can be a source of great worry and concern to boys. Those boys who have had no adequate instruction or who have been allowed to be anxious about their body organs or about matters pertaining to sex have particular concern about it. They feel that the loss of seminal fluid is devitalizing to them, or that it represents a disease or illness, or that it is the outgrowth of too much preoccupation with the subject of sex. Though they worry about it they do not dare ask the father or mother or friend of the family about it lest the person question them too closely or lest they be accused of too much sexual preoccupation or masturbating. Often they continue on alone, worrying a great deal about these emissions of seminal fluid. Like menstruation in the girl, nocturnal seminal emission is a normal phenomenon in the boy and takes place from the age of puberty onward. It merely denotes the activity of the sexual glands and that sperm cells and spermatic fluid are being manufactured. Occasional release of fluid during sleep is of no pathological significance and should cause no concern.

All in all, boys probably worry less about seminal emissions than do girls about menstruation. Boys have the advantage of being able to talk more freely among themselves and of having more sources of information than girls. The majority of boys tend to accept the phenomenon rather philosophically. A few are concerned, and for these sexual instruction by the father or mother when they were younger would have prevented their worry and enabled them to accept the phenomenon. If imparting of these facts in relation to the body and its functions were better disseminated by the adult, the anxiety, uneasiness, and social awkwardness that children have at this age would be relieved considerably.

LATE ADOLESCENCE—POSTPUBERTY

Postpuberty is a period of life poorly understood and too little participated in by adults, though the reasons for this are not readily apparent. Everyone is aware of the fact that a great many misunderstandings arise between parents and their adolescent children. It is perhaps easy to understand why parents do not perceive the forces at work during the first years of life or even early childhood, but adult life follows postpuberty so closely that one would expect parents to remember better how they felt in their late teens and so be more understanding of the adolescent's problems. Many more parents want to help their adolescent children than know how to do so. They lack knowledge of what they should help with.

Between fifteen and twenty-one the adolescent must (1) decide upon a vocation and do some work in preparation for it, (2) effect an emancipation from his parents and family, (3) bring about a satisfactory relation with the opposite sex and begin to make some solution of his love-life problems, and (4) effect an integration in his personality for mature responsibility. If personality development has progressed fairly well thus far, these four aims should not be difficult to achieve, the adolescent should derive intense pleasure in their accomplishment, and his family should gain much satisfaction from helping him to gain these goals. But many instances of unhappiness, friction, and misunderstanding are precipitated between the adolescent and his parent while the adolescent is attempting to solve these problems, making the postpubertal years extremely stormy and even causing some adolescents to emerge from this period in a disorganized state of mind.

To some degree the adolescent is still a tractable, suggestible, modifiable personality, subject to change and amenable to help. Yet this possibility for change has its limits. Overly optimistic adults believe that the right environment and good advice can change any adolescent, no matter how maladjusted, and enable him to become an amiable and worthwhile citizen. But there are many adolescents who are stubborn, rigid, unimaginative, and hostile, with personalities already so limited that they are resistant to guidance, suggestion, or change. In any case, the adolescent is in his last period of dependence upon older people. The interest and wish to help on the part of adults diminishes rapidly as adolescence ends. Youngsters in their twenties are expected to be prepared to meet life and take over greater responsibilities. Those who go to college continue to have external developing forces in their lives but those who take jobs and marry at the end of adolescence must begin "giving to life" right away. Accordingly, the adolescent may be having his last chance to make use of the strengthening influence of parents and school to grow outward and expand. After adolescence, chances grow slimmer because he is supposed to be a mature individual able to take care of himself. From then on the environment is not so likely to be interested in him, or willing to offer the time and patience to help him.

CHOICE OF VOCATION

An outstanding educator once said, "An educated person is one who thinks more than is necessary for survival." This remark could be paraphrased to say that any *mature* human being is one who thinks more than is necessary for survival. Vocation tends to be thought of too narrowly as a means of survival, and too much energy is put into the preparation for a vocation from this specific point of view. Ideally, everyone should have at least two main vocations, perhaps three. These would be (a) the vocation of survival, (b) the vocation of parenthood, (c) the vocation of citizenship. Each one of these vocations has its own goal and purpose and needs its own preparation. Usually only the first is stressed and specifically trained for, while the other two are picked up along the way. It is true that some schools put considerable emphasis on citizenship training, at least to certain age levels. But many educational systems are still insisting that the lower grades stick to the three R's, and even at the college level emphasis is still placed on that which leads to technical efficiency. As for preparation and training for parenthood or home and family life—most of our educational systems pay no real attention to these subjects at all. The assumption seems to be that having grown up in a home and with a family, one learns all about their function by a process of osmosis. But this is a most faulty assumption. For in a healthy family situation there is much that the child does not see, hear or learn about. And in an unhealthy family situation, where much is lacking, it is even more important to study and know what healthy ingredients *should* be.

Fortunately most boys are rather adept at the work they choose and the matter of aptitude is usually less important than (a) deciding early enough in life what that work will be, (b) finding the means to pay for learning it and (c) developing an enthusiasm for it. Inadequacies in preparation often show up in the thirties and forties, when adults find they lack the personality qualities for leadership, when satisfaction in their vocation is lacking, or when they find that family and home life has more problems than they are equipped to deal with. Some young people would be better off at a vocational school rather than in college. If doubt exists, the advice of a vocational counselor is valuable.

With girls there is even more possibility for indecision and inadequate preparation for life. The increased interest in careers and the gratification that comes from them have put the woman of today into conflict with her biological role. Most women find it hard to encompass marriage, homemaking, motherhood, *and* career. Some can do it, but if it is done well it takes a combination of physical health, emotional health, training, and enthusiasm that few women possess. When they do so it represents a total personality efficiency that is certainly greater than that possessed by most men.

It can be seen, then, how important it is that parents should be articulate in the matter of their children's vocation. They should be more honest than most of them are in sharing with the children what some of their own conflicts and difficulties have been. They should point out that preparing for life is not simply a matter of learning to work to make a living and acquire luxuries, but rather that there are parallel vocations which have to do with being a part of the community and making family life and parenthood the constructive, deeply worthwhile satisfactions that they can be.

One of the most important ways of feeling worthwhile in this world is to be able to make a contribution to the social order through work. The deficiency of this feeling is illustrated by the case of the young man of nineteen who was failing in his college work. He was worried and gaining little satisfaction either in his social life or in his work. He was an only child who from early childhood had been shielded and protected from unpleasant realities. Whenever he asked questions, his parents said, "Wait until you are older." Whenever he wished to undertake a piece of work his parents asked, "Do you think you are strong enough?" When he began to discuss the matter of vocation, they said, "There is time enough. Just go to school." The only hobby he was allowed was golf, the one hobby in which his father indulged. When he went to college, he asked, "What am I going for?" His parents said, "We can decide later." Actually they had a career in mind for him but they were keeping it a secret because they wanted to make sure he was obedient, docile, and undemanding toward them before he was supposed to think of being somebody in his own right.

However, he got tired of all this. The day came—as it always does for children who are too thoroughly repressed—when he said, "I am getting discouraged. I do not know where I am going. I do not seem to have any part in decisions. When I ask questions, I get no answer, and if I come upon my parents when they are talking, they suddenly clam up. I have not been getting much fun out of life for the past two or three years. I am getting too worried about my health. I think things are going badly with me." This boy needed help to free himself from a neurotic pattern. One of the outstanding features of his case was the unrealistic attitude he had toward a vocation. His parents could not seem to function with the idea that he had to go out in the world to fill a complex role and that in order to do so he needed the opportunity to project himself into the future with freedom to think about being and working on his own. Hence, this preoccupation all through life with a vocational choice is a necessary matter of open discussion in the family. No age is too young to discuss it as a practical reality even though the final decision may take time.

EMANCIPATION

The problem of emancipation is a serious one in the personality growth of adolescents. Emancipation, positively carried out, is one of the great contributions to maturity. But certain factors that are inimical to maturation exist in the adolescent and in the parent. The adolescent has (a) the continuing emotional need to be cared for, (b) the reluctance to accept responsibilty, (c) the fear of criticism when responsibility is taken, and (d) the lack of desire to serve and co-operate with adults. In the parent, on the other hand, there exists—and it is usually unconscious—(a) the desire to retain dominance or control over the youngster, (b) the difficulty of sharing his love and loyalty with others, (c) the fear that he will come to harm in the outside world, and (d) an underestimation of the adolescent's strength to function independently.

These problems are usually greater in the mother, for very realistic reasons, although any one of these trends may appear in the father. If a mother's life is confined largely to the home it means that her normal, natural need to be important and to exert her influence is threatened as the child moves through the adolescent years and attempts to effect his emancipation. She may subscribe in theory to the dictum that adolescents must learn how to make their own decisions and function as independent human beings, but when the price for this begins to be felt in terms of her own lowered personal self-esteem and lessened importance in the home she may, all too easily, resort to restrictions and domination.

Emancipation normally proceeds slowly and takes many forms. It can be in the adolescent's choice of clothes, his choice of friends, his choice of books, his freedom to possess a key to the home and to come in and go out on his own, his choice of how and where to spend his vacations, his choice of school, driving a car, and so on. If parents—and fathers are parents, too—have made the home an enjoyable place to live in they need not worry that their youngster will seek other diversion to such an extent that he will stay out too late for his health or welfare. If they have taught sound values they need not worry that their child will make wrong decisions in picking his friends and his work. It is their good taste that will influence the taste of their youngster in choosing clothes or entertainment. And furthermore, if they do not set these standards by their own actions, it is unlikely that nagging or undue coercion will ever change behavior. Finally, it is quite important that the adolescent be permitted to make a few mistakes during his growth. If he insists, for instance, upon buying clothes that are more modish than practical he will probably learn more by having to wear them than he will by being restrained from indulging his impulse at the time of purchase. Wise parents will realize that youngsters must take on responsibilities for a time to prove to themselves and the community that they can take care of themselves and that they are not so weak as to overindulge, misbehave, or disgrace themselves, or fail to be responsible members of society.

Conversely, adolescents should also realize some of the strains their parents are going through. An individual nearing adulthood can surely understand that sullenness, disobedience, and secretiveness are hardly the intelligent way of gaining independence. Tact rather than rebellion goes a long way in improving family relationships. It is a wise adolescent who tries this method and who will probably find, to his own amazement, that harmony and understanding between himself and adults will improve.

A great many fathers and mothers imagine a young person, male or female, being carried away by sexual impulses. They feel the danger but can say nothing to their children about it. Instead, they issue prohibitions and make vague allusions about unspecified dangers. Had these parents been close to their children during the years preceding adolescence, and had they known what the children were thinking, they would not be so distrustful. An element of distrust has an unwholesome influence on the young. Adolescents need to be trusted more, with the adults expecting the best from them. Girls and boys should be helped in their battle for emancipation from their parents as an extremely important factor in gaining maturity.

A girl of eighteen who wanted to go to a seashore resort to work as a waitress presented an interesting problem involving emancipation. She was the oldest of a family of six. Her father was not earning enough money for her to have the same kind of clothes her friends wore, so she wanted to work to provide them for herself and prepared herself to do so. We had known her for six years and had found her reliable and trustworthy. Her father was most insistent that she not go to the shore. During our talk he became rather confidential about the real reason for his objection. "You know how it is, doctor," he said. "Men come in the restaurant, they like a girl's looks, they leave a large tip, then the next time they ask her to go out with them. That is the beginning of a girl's ruin. It ends in sexual promiscuity." We said, "Why do you think this?" and he answered, "I have good reason to know. I used to do this myself." He was judging the situation in the light of his own experience. We told him we would be willing to trust his daughter, even if he was not, and that if it would help him we would share the anxiety and responsibility connected with her going. He seemed relieved and let her go. She, of course, did well. From then on the girl was free to work every summer.

ADJUSTMENT TO THE OPPOSITE SEX

Courtship, marriage, marriage adjustment, parenthood, and responsibility in community life lie just ahead of the adolescent. Important in the preparation for these responsibilities is the necessity for both sexes to become accustomed to each other through association in work and play in order that they may learn to know each other and give each other the benefit of their emotional resources. A great deal of practice in living is needed to enable an individual to live a satisfactory and successful life, and should be encouraged during adolescence. Ordinarily adolescents get this practice through mutual participation in parties, dances, movies, concerts, theaters, picnics, and the like. This association tends to lead to physical expression in the form of hand-holding, kissing, embracing, and fondling, which are normal manifestations of human beings who are expressing themselves in a normal manner and who are preparing for future responsibilities. Adolescence is one of the last opportunities for having a good time with a minimum of responsibility, and this fun should be shared by both sexes. This fact is so obvious that the point seems hardly to need elaboration or defense. However, as everyone knows, in their efforts to adjust to each other and to develop a love life, adolescents are often thwarted by adults as well as by their own inhibitions.

Actually, the very term "adjustment to the opposite sex" indicates our awkwardness with this phenomenon of adolescence. We do not have a specific word for what it means and certainly the term "adjustment" does not imply anything very creative. "Courtship," "mating," and "lovemaking" are words that seem too premature and imply something too erotic or self-indulgent. Yet love should be "made," that is, "created," in the sense that young people should offer each other mutual admiration and share the pleasure of each other's company without being burdened with all the responsibilties of later life. Such companionship should develop, strengthen, and enable both sexes to know each other and enjoy each other and thereby prepare themselves, while still flexible and emotionally labile, for their adult life.

Various problems arise during postpuberty if parents object to any free, even though chaperoned, mingling of the sexes. They regard the girl or boy as having too much interest in the opposite sex and fear the young person will "lose his good name" or get a "bad reputation" by "running around too much." This terrible thing called "running around too much" is, of course, only an increased desire to be energetic, interested in life, and naturally they want to do it in association with the opposite sex. However, parents feel it can have bad consequences and they take this point of view without thinking through the factors involved. They are afraid, for example, that if young people come in too frequent contact with each other they may be prone to marry too young and thus be occupied sooner with their own financial support instead of being a source of support to the parents. They also fear that a young person may marry unwisely, or marry the wrong person, or marry someone "beneath him" —whatever that means. Moreover, they fear that there is a real danger of sexual indulgence before marriage and that this friendly proximity is going to be a temptation to sexual intercourse with the resultant danger of illegitimate pregnancy or disease and consequent disgrace.

Parents also have an unrecognized and unconscious jealousy that their offspring will have good times that they, the parents, missed. Consciously they are not that selfish, but unconscious jealousy is quite an important factor in each generation. In this country, members of each succeeding generation have had opportunity to mingle and enjoy themselves more freely together; thus each generation of parents, having had, as they feel, too little themselves, is jealous of its children and at the same time fears their promiscuous sexual behavior.

Much of the difficulty in understanding between parents and adolescents in this regard comes from the parents being frightened by newspaper reports or rumors about young people having illicit sexual relations. They fear the possibility that such activities will become universal, forgetting that if a child has been taught fair play, social responsibility, and a consideration for others, and that if they as parents have been sufficiently considerate of the child, when they ask him to give his consideration to their wishes in the matter of sexual behavior during adolescence he is likely to do so.

All too many parents do not give their children any sexual information, are not on a frank footing with them or close to them in sexual matters. Instead, a great mutual distrust exists. The parents focus fear and anxiety on the problem and become restrictive. They develop anxiety in the child's presence, do not have any frank discussion about the matter, and do not make any appeal for a sensible control of sexual impulses. Parent-child relations are in a sad state when a mother, hearing of a sexual indiscretion in some adolescent, is overcome by fear for her child, and at the same time has to admit to herself, "I never really told my child how I want her to conduct herself with boys. She has heard my opinion on a multitude of things and yet not on this important one."

If parents paid less attention to accounts of promiscuity they read or hear, and concentrated instead on their own relationships with their children, they would have little reason to worry about their children's sexual behavior. If they would encourage the sexes to mingle, to play and to work with each other with confidence, the young people would finally find themselves in marriage without disgrace and without harm to their character. We feel it is unnecessary to think that the race of human beings will have to stand always in fear of its sexual impulses. Surely our society can figure out a way of controlling sexuality rather than having it control its members and distort so much of its social life by sexual taboos and inhibitions which deprive people emotionally and which lead to so many unhappy marriages and divorces.

Doctors, teachers, and counselors are in a position to reassure parents about this matter of wholesome social life for adolescents and to see that young people have the opportunity to go about and to live out their desire to mix with each other without shame and anxiety.

Some parents, during adolescence, discourage friendships between boys and girls of the type called "going steady." They feel that a serious emotional investment of a young person in one of the opposite sex may lead to too severe disappointment should the friendship have to terminate. It may indeed, but it should be pointed out that when adolescents "go steady" they *are* in contact with one another and are having a necessary emotional experience, and this is what is most important. If and when separation comes, it may be an unpleasant disappointment but we again say that adolescence is a time for gaining experience in relations toward the opposite sex. If only short and superficial relationships are encouraged during adolescence, the deeper relationships later may be interfered with. Furthermore, though a disappointment in love during adolescence may be an unhappy matter, much may be learned from it—and the parents can be on hand to give their emotional support should it happen. It is important that young people come close enough together to learn how to evaluate each other in terms of compatibility, for in this way many of the disappointments of married life can be averted.

An important point to remember is that parents cannot expect the child of today to live by yesterday's rules and grow up a happy and satisfied person. Life changes too much for that. Young people always have to live more or less in harmony with current standards. Any parent who tries to bring up a child today on the standards of twenty-five years ago is likely to run into grief; he can take comfort from the thought that the same will probably be true twenty-five years hence.

Some parents who object to a free mingling of the sexes fear that it will precipitate an early marriage. We do not agree that closer association between the sexes necessarily influences young people to marry early. Society, as a matter of fact, might strive for early marriages. It is probably better for people to have their children while they are young, while they still can remember what it is like to be a child, and while they still have interests in common with their children. Also, children of young parents are less likely to lose their parents entirely through death or partially through chronic illness. Early marriage is not a bad idea from the emotional standpoint, yet it is looked upon by society in general as a luxury of questionable value rather than as the potential social asset it is. It has been said that late marriages may be wiser because people know better what they want. But they could be made wiser earlier without harm. A home that fosters ignorance about life, its values, and how to live it is no training ground for wisdom and happiness.

Perhaps parents' greatest concern for their adolescents is that they will have sexual intercourse, with the possibility of pregnancy and venereal disease. There is no doubt that here and there sexual activity is participated in by young people before marriage. However, we think it would decrease a great deal if young people had a careful sexual education in the first place, for many of them are drawn into sexual relations early from intense curiosity rather than from actual desire. If parents have not succeeded in educating the young person by the time he or she has reached eighteen or nineteen, they had better let him use his own judgment and avoid the arguments, hostility, and restrictions that can grow out of a battle over whether he is going to lead an active social life or not. When these battles occur, the young person builds up resentment, to say the least. Often he leaves home for good, and returns only at infrequent intervals for as long as the parents live.

Such a problem was caused by a mother who believed her only course lay in keeping the subject of sex from her daughter. She brought the girl up strictly and told her nothing about sex. The girl did not have a date until she was eighteen, and when she did she was chaperoned by her mother. When the girl went shopping by herself the mother warned her about men who cruised around in cars ready to abduct her into white slavery. In the mother's mind sex was everywhere and very dangerous and her own daughter, moreover, had dangerous sex impulses. She made the remark that if she could frighten the girl enough to get her through high school safely, she would be greatly relieved. She succeeded so well with her plan that when the girl reached the age of twenty-one she could not travel anywhere unless accompanied by someone. Moreover, she developed so many headaches and stomach-aches that a doctor had to be consulted who, in turn, suggested she see a psychiatrist. The fear, ideas, and emotions that the mother had instilled in the girl trying to keep her "safe" had finally resulted in making her so sick that she had adopted her own protection against the evil world.

INTEGRATION OF PERSONALITY

If an individual adjusts to work, chooses a mate, and becomes emancipated from his parents, he still may not be completely whole. He must be helped to see the necessity for participating in the life of the community and the nation and thus becoming a part of the world in which he lives. After all, society does not function entirely for the individual. The individual must function in relation to society as a whole, or society will eventually break down. Once this fact is put into words it becomes obvious, yet a great many families do not teach the child to perform any public service or to be any part of the larger world.

As an adolescent grows up he needs not only to be taught to think of himself and his own welfare but also to be accepting of people individually, to be tolerant of their foibles, to refrain from being too critical and too aloof, and to have a willingness to take part in community life. People everywhere need to acquire a feeling of greater willingness to help each other in order to achieve a better feeling of social unity, for only in unity will we have real social strength and health.

To integrate and develop the personalities of our adolescents, we need to modify considerably the philosophy of parents, which on the surface sounds very virtuous and magnanimous, to the effect that they give their children the best—the best education, the best of food and medical care, the best home, and the best clothes—in short, the *best* of everything to make them happy. Some stop here. Others go further and say they want their children to be useful, industrious, and successful for themselves. But all too few want them not only to be happy and successful, but altruistic—with a real concern for the person they will marry, the children they will rear, and the community and world they will live in, and with a real desire to make it a better place through their efforts.

These are some of the positive goals of postpuberty. Parents, educators, and religious leaders, we feel, should know how to foster these basic areas of personality development. We are telling our young people too little about life. They should be going out into the world with an urge to help, to give, to create, to care for and to care about. Only in this way will they find their existence emotionally rewarding and satisfying and play a role in a creative society.

SUMMARY

The period of adolescence reaches from prepuberty to about 21 years of age. It covers the period of time spent in secondary school and stretches into the college years. It is a time of finishing many of the patterns leading to maturity and must, of necessity, be an active, busy and even turbulent period of growth. During it, there are four large areas of action and decision: (1) gradual but increasing emancipation from family, (2) choosing and preparing for a vocation, (3) establishing some of the patterns of a heterosexual love life and, (4) integrating oneself for a life of service to others.

These four activities are "musts" to be worked on by adolescent and parents, if a reasonable degree of mental health is to be achieved. Their resolution puts emotional strains upon both. But, with thought, discussion, and a fair amount of good will on both sides, adolescence can still be a rich and strengthening experience, and one worth remembering with pleasure.

BIBLIOGRAPHY FOR CHAPTER X

Balser, Benjamin H., ed., *Psychotherapy of the Adolescent,* International Universities Press, 1957.

Blanchard, Phyllis, *Sex Hygiene for Girls,* Proceedings of the 27th Annual Meeting of the National Association of Principals of Schools for Girls, 1948, pp. 116–132.

Deutsch, Helene, *The Psychology of Women,* Grune and Stratton, 1944.

Farnham, Marynia F., *The Adolescent,* Harper, 1952.

Frank, L. K., et al., *Personality Development in Adolescent Girls,* Child Development Publication, 1953.

Howard, E. McC., *An Analysis of Adolescent Adjustment Problems,* "Mental Hygiene 25," July, 1941, pp. 363–391.

Hsu, Francis L. K., *American and Chinese, Two Ways of Life,* Henry Schuman, 1953.

Mead, Margaret, *Male and Female,* Morrow, 1949.

Mueller, Kate H., *Educating Women for a Changing World,* U. of Minnesota Press, 1954.

Pearson, Gerald H. J., *Adolescence and the Conflict of Generations,* Norton, 1958.

Sherman, Helen, and Marjorie Coe, *The Challenge of Being a Woman,* Harper, 1955.

Gesell, Arnold, Frances Ilg, and L. Ames, *Youth, the Years from Ten to Sixteen,* Harper, 1956.

XI

Emotional Disturbances That Occur during Adolescence

THE CHILD who has made a satisfactory adjustment in his infancy and childhood will nevertheless have some difficulties of adjustment in adolescence because the development of his ego is still far from complete and also because his superego may be still too much a simple reflection of the parents' attitude during childhood and not yet sufficiently modified by the influence of the social organization. The child who already has shown serious incapacities to adjust because his superego is too severe and his ego capacity proportionately too weak will be liable to suffer an increase of symptoms during adolescence. The child who has not made an adequate adjustment in the latent period cannot be expected to make a more adequate adjustment in adolescence. The child who seems to have made an adjustment in the latent period may find, as he experiences the new upsurging of the sexual life in adolescence, that his adjustment was a pretense and not a reality. On the other hand, some neurotic boys whose neurosis in the latency period has been symptomatized by great passivity and a strong tendency to latent homosexuality, that is, the unconscious desire to be a girl, may without treatment suddenly appear more masculine and almost completely recovered; the upsurging of the heterosexual impulses temporarily has overwhelmed the defenses against them which had appeared as symptoms. However, the original neurotic pattern may reassert itself toward the end of adolescence.

The emotional illnesses that develop in the prepubertal period of adolescence—between 10½ and 13 years of age—are the same as those that develop during the latent period. A description of the symptom complexes of the emotional illnesses of this period would be simply a recapitulation of what we have said before. During the pubertal period—13 to 16 years of age—the problems of the resurge of the sexual impulses and of the relative weakness of the ego defenses and of the pressures or lack of pressures from the superego produce a different class of symptom complexes. Besides the classical neuroses—hysteria, anxiety hysteria, and the obsessional neuroses—the clinical pictures during this period tend to fall into two groups—those which show impulsive actions and those which show ego constrictions—a limiting of the activities of the person in order to avoid conflicts. The emotional illnesses of the postpubertal period—16 to 21—are the same as those of the adult.

Adolescent neuroses, however, tend to have two peculiarities. The illness is either very stormy and the disorganization of the personality great—so that often there is difficulty in deciding whether the illness is a neurosis or a psychosis—or it tends to attack the personality so that the symptoms appear in the social and vocational spheres. The reasons lie in the resurgence of the sexual drives. If the resurging sexuality is very powerful or if the governing forces of the ego are too weak, the adolescent neurosis will run a stormy course which may cause the illness to resemble a psychosis, since there is a real danger that the inner drives will overwhelm the controlling mechanisms. If the forces of the superego are proportionately too strong, the ego will have to deform itself more and more as the resurging sexuality appears. Here the clinical picture will be a progressively severe personality disturbance.

The relative weakness of the ego makes psychotherapy of a neurosis in an adolescent extremely difficult, and often after a short period of therapy the adolescent patient stops treatment. Several years later, when he has entered into young adult life, he will get in touch with the therapist again with the statement, "Doctor, we started treatment years ago but we never finished it, and I think it is time we got it finished now." The usual story is that at the time of the first break the patient was about to confess some of his sexual experiences—usually his masturbation—but was too frightened to do so. This weakness of the ego in the adolescent neurotic produces still another type of difficulty. One day he gives in to his feelings of ego weakness and is clinging and dependent, wanting concrete help with situations that he is perfectly capable of dealing with, and the next he compensates for this feeling by protesting that he is more capable and knows more than any adult and therefore needs help from no one. Both attitudes, and particularly their rapid alternation, make it difficult for therapist and patient to establish a basis for mutual understanding.

On account of these weaknesses of the ego there is always considerable difficulty in determining the type of treatment most desirable for the neurotic adolescent. Shall we engage in intensive psychotherapy—the only treatment that in the majority of cases will really be of value—realizing that the patient's ego may be too weak to tolerate the unconscious ideas and feelings and that treatment may be inopportunely interrupted? Would it be better to adjust the environment as much as possible and wait until he has reached early adult life, when he will have more experience to help him in the diffiulties of intensive treatment? In many instances we feel that the latter is perhaps the best course, for the patient then will come to treatment with greater realization of his need for it and with more ability to undergo it. Since the attitudes of the neurotic adolescent are the product of traumatic experiences he suffered as a small child —frequently due to adverse parental attitudes—it is unlikely that they will have changed when he becomes adolescent. In fact they are likely to be more firmly fixed. In many cases it is perhaps better to deal with the problem by changing the residence of the patient— usually by placing him in boarding school. The school authorities will not have an easy time with him, but if he can be tolerated, he may be helped to grow up until it seems timely to undertake intensive psychotherapy.

NIGHTMARES

Excessive anxiety over sexual matters may take the form of nightmares. Sometimes the anxiety troubles the young person during the day as well, and may take the form of his believing himself to be the victim of a disease. At puberty children may go through a mild or even severe phobia, the content of which is that they have tuberculosis, cancer, heart disease, or possibly that they are going insane. If the anxiety manifests itself at night, it is prone to come automatically in a nightmare. The girl may dream of being pursued by a man, of being chased by an animal, of being run over by a horse or automobile. Both sexes often dream of being on top of a tall building or precipice from which they are about to fall. Nightmares grow out of a distortion of ideas relating to instinctual impulses and are usually concerned with the sexual or the aggressive impulses with which the young person is struggling at this period.

If at this time nightmares occur frequently, or if the young person has a fear of disease, he should be given particular attention by parents or doctor, because these manifestations are danger signals and not just phenomena of growing up, to be taken lightly or ignored. It is true that when the pubertal period comes to a close the anxiety in many cases does seem to disappear, but unless the problem has been talked over with the young person and solved it has not been absorbed but repressed, only to reappear in a more disturbing way later, possibly during the excitement of courtship or, for the female, at the time of the birth of her first child. It is a wise plan to deal with these evidences of anxiety at the time they arise. In a vulnerable child they arise early, and if not evident before can usually be seen during puberty when the activity of the sexual glands increases and menstruation begins.

DIFFICULTIES ASSOCIATED WITH EDUCATION

In an earlier chapter we discussed some of the causes of educational difficulties. It might be supposed that there we had discussed all the types and causes of learning disorders, particularly since we included the deflection of attention from the task of learning because of conscious and unconscious intrapsychic conflicts. However, it may be asked, "Does the concept of deflection of attention account for all types of learning difficulties based on intrapsychic conflicts?" Certainly deflection of attention interferes with learning but in itself it does not seem to account for certain cases of learning difficulties encountered particularly in adolescents; neither does it take into account the possibility that the learning process itself may be involved in specific types of conflicts between the ego and the superego and the instinctual life.

Freud pointed out long ago that the functions of the ego in the psychic sphere have their prototype in the functions of the ego in the physical sphere. The digestive activity of the body ego is the prototype of learning as a psychic-ego function. The digestive activity consists of four parts: (1) The taking of food into the body through a special organ, the mouth and the upper part of the gastrointestinal tract. (2) The digestion and assimilation of the food by a complex of special organs and their activities. (3) The putting out of the results of the digestive process, part being put out immediately as energy, part being stored for future production of energy, and part being excreted as unusable. (4) The energy formed through digestion is used by the ego in the functioning of the total individual.

Similarly, the learning functions consist of four parts: (1) The intake of information through the special senses and other parts of the sensory nervous system. (2) The correlation and association of these sensory impressions among themselves and with the memories of previous sensory impressions through the association pathways of the cortex and subcortex. (3) The putting out of the end products of these association processes through motor activities such as writing and speech. (4) The use of these end products by the ego in the successful functioning of the total individual.

Therefore, just as nutritive disorders may arise because of disturbances in the organs and their functions at any one of the four steps, and just as disorders of the organs and the functions of the gastrointestinal tract may result from organic changes or from the influence of emotional conflicts, so the learning process similarly may be disturbed. In gastrointestinal disorders, a disturbance in the function at one step is bound to result in greater or less disturbance at all the other steps. The same result also happens in disorders of learning. We would call the difficulties in learning we will discuss here *diminished capacity to learn because a neurotic conflict has involved the learning process itself.* These all are serious disorders. They are types to which not enough attention has been paid in the literature available to most physicians and teachers, partly because they furnish such baffling problems even to the experienced psychiatrist. They are not amenable to the usual methods of treatment but require very intensive psychoanalytically oriented psychotherapy or psychoanalysis itself.

SIBLING RIVALRY

The attempt by siblings to live together comfortably with their feelings of rivalry, envy, and jealousy produces a number of educational difficulties. If one child does good work at school for which he receives recognition from the parents, his sibling may feel quite hopeless of doing better work or of getting more recognition if his school achievement is equal to his rival's. He casts around to find a method of achievement which will win recognition in some field far removed from the educational field. As a result his studying will be done only in a mediocre fashion and he even may fail from time to time.

The opposite alternative may be chosen. If one sibling is not very interested in school but has his main interest in extracurricular activities—social life, athletics, or the like (for all of which he receives parental recognition), the other child may curtail his interest solely to school achievement. His success in study brings him parental recognition but along different lines than those of his sibling.

In both cases the child has chosen to exhibit differences in learning ability in order to avoid the painful competition with the rival and the painful feelings of hatred and jealousy.

ASSOCIATIONS WITH MASCULINITY OR FEMININITY

Learning of academic subjects and the use of such learning may have acquired for the child a specific masculine or feminine flavor as the result of the parental attitudes toward learning. There may be feelings of stupidity when there is an identification with the dull parent of the same sex. There may be intellectual precocity when there is an identification with an intelligent parent of the opposite sex. The person who has been rebuffed and emotionally traumatized by the stupid parent of the same sex may flee to an identification with the thinking parent of the opposite sex. Or he may resist such identification: if the mother is very interested in learning while the father is indifferent, the boy readily may come to regard the desire to learn academic subjects as a feminine attribute. In this way the desire to learn becomes connected with the passive receptive feminine desires which he dreads lest their gratification result in castration; such a desire has to be repudiated. If the child is a girl whose mother is not interested in learning and the father is, learning may become a masculine attribute and be used as a conscious substitute for the unconscious wish to have a penis.

FEELINGS OF GUILT

There is one type of adolescent maladjustment that we wish to discuss at length because it is a common one and extremely difficult to handle. It is a well-known fact that the beginning of adolescence has a definite though temporary effect on the learning capacity of most children. A child who has made good progress in school in the early grades often shows deterioration in the quality of his schoolwork when he reaches the seventh or eighth grade and for a year or so does not do so well; then his efficiency comes back to its old level. In some children this phenomenon is very marked; in others it occurs only to a slight degree. Its explanation seems to lie in two directions—in the acceleration in the growth of the central nervous system that occurs about this time (this growth is mainly in the associational tracts, and the learning difficulty results from the bewilderment that is produced by the number of these new associations) and in the increased sensitization of the sensory organs by the resurging sexual life (this makes the child keener in his perception but temporarily overwhelms him with new sensations).

There are adolescents, however, who do not recover from this setback. Their schoolwork becomes gradually worse. In the classroom such a child is inattentive: he daydreams or annoys his neighbors. Frequently he forgets to bring the right textbook, or has it open at the wrong place. When the teacher reprimands him he becomes sullen or attempts to justify his actions. Often his attempts at self-justification are couched in such a way as to provoke the mirth of the class. The reprimand does not improve the behavior, for after a few minutes he is acting in the same way again. His homework is neglected. He forgets to bring home the proper books. He has a dozen important pursuits—radio programs to be listened to, newspapers to be read, phone calls to be made, and so on—before he sits down to study. When he does sit down he turns the radio on. As bedtime approaches he becomes somewhat panicky because his exercises are not done, and he asks his parents to help. Since the hour is late they tend to do his work for him rather than just help him. If they refuse to co-operate he takes his unfinished work to school where he either neglects to hand it in or presents it with a great variety of excuses. In schools that use the Dalton plan this type of child gets far behind with his particular project. Laboratory notebooks are neglected and there is a mad scramble at the end of the time limit to get the work done. It seldom is completed.

The teacher, disturbed by the child's failure, calls in the parents for a consultation. The parents in turn are disturbed and begin to insist that the child devote specified hours to his homework. The child is usually engaged in some activity or other when homework time comes and gets started only after much parental nagging. By this time the parent is quite irritated and often sits with the child so he will not dawdle. The parent may try to help him with the work, but since by this time there is great mutual discord the session ends in violent quarreling. Of course the less work the child does, the farther behind he gets, until he reaches the point where to bring himself up to date, even with his required written work, would require two or three weeks' solid concentration. Even if he wanted to he could not get this extra work done, and the term ends as a dismal failure.

Only infrequently does the child fail on his examinations, since he does know much of the work. His failure is based on his day-to-day productions. When the parents talk to him about his work he blames his difficulties on the unreasonableness of the teachers, on the type of school he attends, on the annoying behavior of his class-mates, or he becomes sullen and angry. He expresses a desire to change schools, to leave school and go to work, or to leave home and go to boarding school. (The boarding-school proposal emanates more commonly from the parents than from the child. They usually feel that he needs discipline and believe he can get that in a good— that is, a strict—military school.) Often in these cases the teacher and the psychiatrist who see the case feel that the child must have a low level of intelligence and that the work is beyond him. A psychometric rating, however, usually shows him to be better than average. In fact, it is not uncommon to find that these children have intelligence quotients of 130 to 150.

The passage of time does not improve the difficulty—neither does the scolding and punishment by teacher or parents. In fact, the more the parents scold the child the less work he does. He is inclined to react to attempts at discipline in the school by absenting himself from classes—thus making matters worse. It is often painful for the adults who are interested in the child to see this bright and poten-tially able person making no use of his capabilities and heading with apparent recklessness toward a complete wreck of his future. This prospect is so painful that both teachers and parents resort to extreme degrees of nagging in order to force the child to avoid this fate. They feel that he is lacking in character, that he has no sense of responsibility and is incapable of self-discipline, and as a result they use every measure they can think of to get him to discipline himself and to take responsibility. (They often deal with the latter in a curious way. Because the child has no sense of responsibility they take on all his responsibility for him. If he dawdles in the morning they nag him in order to get him to school on time; if he dawdles over his homework they do the same. In both instances they forget that a sense of responsibility comes from taking one's own responsibility and that the best discipline comes from practical reality—for example, letting the child learn the unpleasantness of being late through being tardy rather than through admonition.) There is no question that both parents and teachers are correct in their evaluation of the situation. The child has no sense of responsibility and no self-discipline. But these are symptoms, just as his school behavior is a symptom, of an unconscious neurotic conflict, and until this conflict is understood and treated to a successful solution the symptoms will continue.

What is this conflict? The first point that strikes everyone about these children is that they act as if they had no ambition to learn and be successful in their present and future life, to be grown up and take responsibility for their daily lives, and to be self-confident. In fact they act not as if they had no ambition but as if their ambition was to do poorly rather than well. As one child said to us, "I see the better and do the worse." They seem to have placed an inhibition on their ability successfully to accomplish the ambitions of the ordinary American adolescent and to have directed their ambitional energy to accomplish successfully the opposite. Although they try as hard as they can *not* to be successful, their intellectual capacity often is so great that it nullifies part of their efforts. Through this procedure they are able to gratify two impulses of which they usually are unconscious: to express their spite at their mother's (and sometimes their father's) nagging, and to attract their mother's punitive attention to themselves.

In some instances these two desires are kept unconscious simply because the child has displaced the spite and the desire for attention from the mother onto the teacher. As one boy said, "If the teachers criticize me I will refuse to do any work for them." Here the spite element was conscious, but the teachers really were *not* critical of him; by his conscious behavior he was able to remain unconscious of the fact that his mother was the critical person. Another boy remarked that he would do no work for the teacher because she favored the other pupils. Therefore he was aware of his desire for her attention, but by thinking as he did he was able to be unaware that it was his mother's attention he craved. This desire for attention really is directed toward the mother, as is also the spiteful reaction. The latter is an expression of rage at her. (Usually the child is unaware of his rage at his mother, but the awareness is so close to consciousness that it does not take much time or skill to bring it to consciousness.) He may feel enraged at her because of her constant and irritating nagging or because he recognizes that she does not love him, and often he is correct in his judgment. We have found in our cases that the mother either has rejected the boy—or the father the girl—or has overprotected him because she has felt guilty about her dislike for him. In many of these cases the child had had a prolonged serious illness or a period during which he had in quick succession a number of less serious illnesses. During these illnesses his mother gave him a great deal of attention, often of a physical type, which he enjoyed very much. When he recovered she ceased her attentions because in reality they were no longer necessary. The child resented this behavior and became enraged at her. He may act as if he felt rage but this rage really is an expression of a sadistic form of love—the type of love that finds gratification *only* if the loved object is hurt.

In all of these instances the child does not love his mother with the mature tenderness of the adolescent. Instead his love is either extremely ambivalent, as in the first three instances cited in the two paragraphs above, or has regressed to the type of love natural to the anal period of development because he has become frightened or guilty about it, as in the last-mentioned instance. His active love relationship with his mother is either ambivalent or sadistic. If he is to be successful in carrying out the ambitions of the adult he must be an active person. If he is active he will hurt or destroy the mother whom he loves. If he does this he will feel very guilty. In order to avoid this sense of guilt it is better for him to inhibit all his activity. Therefore he has to inhibit his ambitions to be successful in school.

It is plain that he desires his mother's attention since he deliberately does the very things he knows will produce her anger and scolding; in other words, he tries to establish a passive receptive relationship with her. In this relationship he receives attention, coupled with her anger and the pain inflicted by her. Ordinarily we would expect that the pain and her anger would cause him to change his behavior, but they do not. Indeed, he often provokes a critical reaction from other adults, particularly his teachers, and although he complains similarly about their attitude he does nothing to change his own behavior which has produced it. He desires the attention so much that he is willing to put up with associated painful feelings. The pain still is painful, so in order to avoid the pain he endeavors to extract pleasure from it. He is able to do this by enhancing the masochistic attitude that brought him gratification during his anal phase of development. Although he is conscious of his wish to be placed in a military school where firm discipline would correct the faults he sees in his character, he revolts consciously against any awareness of his masochistic attitude because it hurts his pride. It appears in his behavior but his conscious mind repudiates the idea that his actions have this meaning. His ambition therefore becomes directed toward the gratification of his passive receptive desires, with the result that he can no longer be successful actively. His school progress ceases and he does not take responsibility for his daily life.

The history of these children is interesting. During the latent period they do creditable schoolwork but are tormented day and night by anxieties and phobias. They lie awake at night in terror of the skeleton that will come out of the closet, of the bear under the bed, of the ghost that will ascend the stairs. These symptoms, which they keep to themselves except when they become very disturbing, continue throughout the latent period until the beginning of adolescence. Then they stop, either suddenly, due to an effort of will, or gradually for no apparent reason. As the anxiety symptoms cease or lessen the schoolwork becomes poorer and poorer. The personality defects of which the parents and teachers complain therefore are symptoms that have developed to replace the anxieties.

The underlying conflict in these cases of school difficulty therefore is the same as that which underlies a phobia. We have noted that the preadolescent solution for the problem was a phobia. During the phobia the child's school progress was good. When the phobia came to an end the educational difficulty developed. In the cases we have seen the conflict resulted from an undue attachment to the parent of the opposite sex and an inability to solve adequately the resultant ambivalence to the parent of the same sex. In many of these cases the parent of the same sex is either overly proud and foolishly fond of the child or is indifferent and withdrawn, either as a result of the occupation followed or because of some emotional difficulty of his own. As a consequence the child has great difficulty in allowing himself to feel hostile toward this parent, who is either very kindly or very unimportant, and so has to repress his hostility, developing a strong sense of guilt in order to keep it repressed. As long as the child can project the problem—that is, as long as the phobic objects carry his conflicting feelings—he feels relatively safe from his problem. When the phobic mechanism fails because his ego dislikes the pain of the constant feelings of anxiety he has to adopt a new method of defense against the unsolved problem of the conflicting love and hate for the parent of the same sex.

To grow up, to develop skills that later will make for vocational success, to be ambitious and work toward vocational fulfillment, is to utilize aggressive desires about which the child feels guilty. Therefore it is better to inhibit them. The inhibition is effected by changing the ambitions and the skills needful to accomplish them into their opposite, that is, into an apparent absence of ambition and an incapacity for accomplishment. More basically, this inhibition requires that all activity be changed into its opposite—passivity. To please the parent of the opposite sex is equivalent to an expression of love. Love must not be expressed as such. The attitude, instead, must be one of *apparent* hostility—then there will be no feeling of guilt about the love. This apparent hostility, however, can be maintained only by partially repressing the love. The repressed love joins with the tendency to be passive rather than active and appears as a masochistic attitude which assuages the sense of guilt. The impression that the entire difficulty lies in the relationship with the parent of the opposite sex skillfully masks the true problem—the relationship with the parent of the same sex. So skillfully is this done that the child is really unconscious that such a problem exists.

We have tried to make clear that the renunciation of the phobic mechanism causes the ego to recoil from the problem which it feels too weak to solve. As a result of the recoil a regression takes place and a slow and insidious deformation of personality results (which could not occur if the phobic mechanism were retained). This deformation affects directly the main acts of the individual's life—in the adolescent appearing most markedly in the school life. (In the adult it appears in the vocation.) Once the ego has adopted the mechanisms of defense which deform the personality the process does not remain stationary but continues with more and more distortions.

The purpose of education is to train the ego in skills that will enable it to deal with the realities of life. The more complex the culture, the more skills and the more training for each skill are required. In our culture we tend to regard the struggle for personal existence as of utmost importance and spend years training the child in methods of earning a living. We have to do so because the degree of knowledge required for any particular occupation is great, and if the individual is to be successful he must acquire as much of this knowledge as possible. He must also know a great deal about society —its social organization, present structure, and historical background. On the other hand we seem to feel that the individual should be able without much help to acquire knowledge of his own inner life and impulses, to understand them, and to learn to use them automatically. In fact, we act as if we preferred that the individual think and learn about the former group of skills to the exclusion of the latter.

One of the authors recently had the opportunity to listen to a sermon given to college students. The preacher encouraged his audience to set up ideals for themselves and to try to attain them. These ideals were courses of action whose tendency would be toward self-control and self-denial. The speaker recognized that anyone following his advice would be very saintly and admitted that there was something unnatural about saintliness, but he extricated himself from the dilemma by endeavoring to prove that it was possible to be saintly and at the same time natural. In short, his thesis was that his audience must learn to restrict and to frustrate their inner impulses in daily life. He made no attempt to urge his hearers to learn about the nature of these impulses or how they might be gratified through socially acceptable methods of expression. Instead, he encouraged them not even to think about them but rather to pay attention to other things, saying there would be rewards and benefits to be received from following his advice.

Though the sermon was of a religious nature, the point of view is found in all education. Glover says education tells the child, "We want you to think about this group of concepts and concern your-self with performing this group of actions." We encourage him to follow our advice, but implied in the advice is the statement, though we do not add it explicitly, "We do *not* want you to think about this other group of concepts or to concern yourself with performing this other group of actions." We say to the adolescent, "You must think hard and work hard in learning your schoolwork." This statement really implies, "You must *not* think hard or work hard in learning how to get along with people of the opposite sex or how to lead an adequate sexual life." Osler made a definite statement to this very effect: that the medical student and the young doctor should put their emotions on ice, for a young man married is a young man marred.

Children understand that this implication exists in their parents' and teachers' emphasis upon education and often make use of it as a repressive measure against their inner impulses. One boy, after being punished for some childish sexual curiosity, decided that he never again could allow himself to have any physical feelings—such as had produced trouble for him. Instead, he would approach every situation through the use of his intelligence, that is, through the development of his intellectual skills. An adolescent girl who feared to compete with her sister (who had many boy friends and was not overly interested in educational matters) decided that she would solve the jealousy situation by giving up any interest in boys and devote herself entirely to her education—solve it, in short, by be-havior exactly the opposite of her sister's. These children fell back on the dichotomy which is found in education between learning and the gratification of inner needs and decided to accept it even more than does our culture, in order to protect themselves from the dangers they perceived in being human beings. Unfortunately their plan does not work; they do not escape the dangers that they perceive might occur if they try to satisfy their inner desires, for these dangers now become displaced onto the alternative (that is, the educational process) and the children do poorly in their school-work and in the use of their intellectual faculties.

Without treatment the prognosis in these cases is extremely poor, for each step in personality deformation serves as a temporary level of adjustment which produces a relief of tension for the time being, only to break down under its own strain—which breakdown is dealt with again by a further personality deformity. These temporary reliefs lull to sleep the individual's perception of his danger (that is, they reduce his anxiety) and perhaps it is only as he approaches middle age that he perceives that his life has not produced the same degree of happiness and success as has his peers'. In the face of this knowledge he becomes depressed and discouraged, and rightly so, because his rehabilitation at this time is extremely difficult and even if rehabilitated he has little real future to look forward to. This type of educational disability is a grave condition and should not be treated lightly nor subjected to half measures.

INHIBITION OF CURIOSITY

Only the very occasional person retains even the greater part of his early childhood curiosity. If for any reason curiosity produces pain instead of pleasure, the curiosity will be inhibited and the individual will have some difficulty in learning. If the child's early curiosity leads him to observe factual realities which (to him) are revolting, as the female genitals may seem to the boy or the male genitals to the girl, a more or less complete inhibition of curiosity may develop, depending on the degree of the child's reaction. An analogous inhibition of curiosity may take place if the observation arouses very strong erotic or hostile desires in the child (desires which he feels unable to deal with). The boy may react thus upon comparing the size of the father's body and genitals with his own; the girl may react in like manner upon observing that her mother has breasts or pubic hair, both of which the little girl lacks. It is such situations that cause all children to inhibit, to some extent, the pristine curiosity of early childhood by the time they reach the age at which they begin academic studies in school. If the early physically directed curiosity receives disapproval or punishment, the child, in order to avoid the feeling of displeasure, will inhibit his curiosity so that only a portion can be sublimated. The extent of the inhibition will depend on the severity of the disapproval or punishment.

The source of the inhibition may be oral. Psychoanalysis of certain children who have difficulty in learning has shown that there is a confusion in their unconscious minds between the desire to eat and the desire to take in knowledge. As small children they had suffered from some problem involving the upper part of the gastrointestinal tract. Either they had suffered ungratified excessive oral needs in infancy or they had become afraid of the results of oral gratification. Eventually the time came for them to displace the ability to take in from the physiological use of the mouth to the psychological use of the special senses, and then the dreads and fears that had been associated with the physiological mechanism of taking in were displaced also to the psychological ability to take in. Two types of oral difficulties which occur early in life result later in difficulties in oral processes involved in learning and difficulties in talking, reading, and singing. The first type exhibits idiosyncrasies toward food, either gluttony or more usually anorexia. In anoretic children all innovations in food are met with by active or passive antipathy. When food is ingested there is either rumination, regurgitation, or in extreme cases, vomiting. Often they need substitute oral gratifications such as thumbsucking. The second type is encountered when a very young child has frequent upper respiratory infections, has difficulties in dentition, or shows a delayed speech development. Later, children who have suffered from such early oral difficulty will have difficulty in learning because their ability to take in is inhibited by unconscious dreads and fears. Cases that may belong to these groups should be studied by an experienced psychoanalyst who has specialized in the psychoanalysis of children; those that do belong require psychoanalytic treatment.

INABILITY TO ASSIMILATE KNOWLEDGE

Disturbances in the assimilation and digestion of knowledge give rise to the most serious type of learning difficulty. These disturbances are not in the ability to take in knowledge, nor in the mechanism of oral incorporation, but they arise from disturbances in the ability to associate, correlate, and assimilate the incorporated knowledge, that is, in the ability to digest it. Children with this difficulty are characterized not only by a severe inability to learn, which makes them appear sometimes to be intellectually retarded, but also by a bizarreness and apparent incoherence in their thinking. Full discussion of these conditions lies beyond the scope of this book. A good illustration may be found in the book *Psychoanalysis and the Education of the Child* (Pearson) to which the reader is referred. Blanchard's studies seem to indicate that very serious reading disabilities that have a close resemblance to the reading disabilities due to strephosymbolia may often fall in this group. We believe also that this group includes cases which show alterations in the results of the psychometric examination like the following. A boy of the age of four had been examined by an extremely competent psychologist who was very experienced with children. He obtained an IQ of 50. At the age of twelve, after a long period of analysis, the boy showed an IQ of 110. His accomplishments later on showed that his real IQ must have been over 140.

Clearly there is a need for more adequate study of educational disabilities. We are of the opinion that when a child shows an educational difficulty the attitude of his teacher, his physical condition, his intellectual status, the attitudes and emotional conditions within his home, and his total personality should be investigated. It is only on the results of such an investigation that a valid diagnosis can be made and treatment instituted. We believe that all school systems, public and private, should have the opportunity to consult with physicians, psychologists, and psychoanalysts (or at least well-trained psychoanalytically oriented psychiatrists) about the problems shown by their pupils. In fact, we would go as far as to say that all school systems should have on their permanent staff as an essential part of the educational setup a team composed of one or more physicians, psychologists, and psychoanalysts. The school system *cannot* function efficiently if one or more of these disciplines is omitted. This team is needed in all schools, from the nursery school up to the university and professional school. The educator, after all, is a layman in these professional fields, and the considered judgment of this team should prevail in cases of difference.

IMPULSIVE BEHAVIOR

Impulsive behavior involves the adolescent—particularly in the pubertal period—in difficulties with the social organization, school discipline, and the family. A certain degree of impulsive behavior—either in the form of defiant rebellion or in mild forms of sexual experimentation occurs from time to time in many adolescents. However, if the impulsive behavior is marked or continuous the basic problem either is one of a delinquent character or is an attempt to solve an unconscious neurotic conflict. Behind the impulsive behavior may be a strong unconscious desire to remain a baby and not grow up. This unconscious desire is rejected by the adolescent trying to act as if he were an active, grown-up person who had no passive desires. In this attempt he impulsively may drink, smoke, or indulge in sexual relations to prove he is an adult. In other cases the impulsive behavior is an attempt at compensation for deepseated feelings of inferiority and inadequacy. Another reaction to these feelings may cause the adolescent of good family to associate always with other adolescents who are socially inferior or semidelinquent. In other cases the impulsive behavior is an attempt to defy an oversevere superego. The adolescent attempts to project his superego onto the authorities in his environment and then proceeds impulsively to defy them. In other cases the impulsive behavior through the thrill of living dangerously enables the individual to remain unconscious of his inner feelings of depression. In still others, the impulsive rebellious behavior is a plea for more love from the parents. A certain number of adolescent girls who become pregnant have this underlying motive. They feel their mothers do not love them enough and attempt by being pregnant to arouse their mother's interest. All such cases in which the impulsive behavior is an attempt at a solution of an unpleasant unconscious conflict require careful study and treatment by a child psychiatrist or psychoanalyst. This is particularly true in those cases whose impulsive behavior masks a depression. When this occurs the impulsive behavior often has a suicidal component and these patients may make a real suicidal attempt which unfortunately in some instances may be successful.

SOCIAL DIFFICULTIES THAT OCCUR DURING ADOLESCENCE

Every adolescent is confronted with a number of social attitudes with which he has to cope as well as with the problems of his own development. These center around his relationship with his parents and their relationship with him, and his own problems of homosexuality, masturbation, problems of premarital intercourse and intercourse substitutes, the attitude of society toward his needs, and his desire to establish an independent identity—to be a person in his own right—and the attitude of society which continues to regard him as a child.

RESENTMENT TOWARD PARENTS

A typical emotional problem of all these periods of adolescence lies in his feelings of resentment and impatience toward his parents. He may criticize his parents quite severely as to the way they dress, the friends they have, the manner in which they talk and entertain. His disapproval of his parents may reach such a degree that he refuses to speak to them for days, weeks, or months at a time. One seventeen-year-old we know refused to speak to his family for a year except in the form of an occasional grunt of recognition that he had been addressed. This resentment and feeling of being misunderstood may extend toward siblings and the greatest envy, rivalry, and sense of competition may prevail. When these emotions prevail too sharply in the home they often extend to teachers and to the school or college environment resulting in unpopularity, or failure, or both. This hostility is an accumulation of frustration garnered during the prepubertal period. It is the adolescent's way of coping with his pent-up resentment. It is, in other words, his hostility to parental failures and calls for patient understanding and wisdom in order to rectify adult errors. Calling a family council to discuss what's wrong is often an effective cure, for airing one's grievance is often the quickest way to get rid of it. Parents can do much to dissolve resentment if they will face the problem and explore, with the youngster, the best way to do something about it.

Instinctual strivings are strong during the adolescent period and tend to make it stormy and difficult. The boy or girl rarely has control and finesse during this period. Either the instinctual drives are forcing themselves to the surface in overt sexual or hostile activity by way of excessive masturbation, "girl craziness" or "boy craziness," promiscuity, excessive hunger for social affairs, truculence, pugnacity; or else there are reaction patterns to these instinctual drives in the form of asceticism, social withdrawal, excessive docility, overpreoccupation with religious activity, interest in health fads, joining up with "movements," moodiness, loneliness, self-pity, or an excessive identification with the "under dog." Any of these phenomena requires great patience and understanding on the part of the parents. In the usual situation these signs of continual conflicts will diminish after a period of time, as they are part of the phenomena of adolescence. If they continue or are very marked it is important to seek professional help rather than let the problem continue unsettled indefinitely.

However, it is well first for the parents to take stock of their own attitude to the adolescent. Are they inwardly resentful of the child becoming an adult? Do they want to make him live a life which will make up to them for their own feelings of dissatisfaction with their own limitations? Are they inwardly jealous of the fact that the adolescent has a life before him while they have nearly reached the peak of their own lives? These attitudes, conscious or unconscious, on the part of many parents add greatly to the adolescent's difficulties and constitute the conflict of generations which seems an inherent part of human life.

HOMOSEXUALITY

Another emotional problem of adolescence is the rediscovery of one's sexual nature, particularly the fact that all human beings have some degree of homosexual interests, usually much less than the heterosexual ones. Some adolescents are appalled at this discovery. Others think that they have a lukewarm interest in the opposite sex and are inclined to worry about whether they are showing some signs of homosexuality. The subject of homosexuality will be dealt with at greater length in another chapter. Parents should understand that the adolescent will have to work those problems out by himself. They should not inquire about them as this will make the problem more difficult. If the adolescent openly flaunts what looks like homosexual behavior in front of his parents or if he comes to them for advice he is acting impulsively in either case and he should be referred to a child psychiatrist, as he undoubtedly has a serious neurotic problem.

MASTURBATION

The very intensity and insistence of the sexual instinct makes it inevitable that there will be a good many sexual problems during adolescence. Some adolescents in the pubertal period discover to their consternation that the arousal of sexuality leads to a new impetus toward masturbation. They feel guilty and self-deprecatory about this. We have pointed out earlier that these feelings of guilt and fear of punishment develop because of the fantasies accompanying masturbation during the genital period, and although these fantasies are unconscious the resurgence of sexuality in adolescence revivifies them and they show their unconscious presence by the conscious feelings of fear and guilt about masturbation in adolescence. The adolescent has to struggle with this problem himself. Parents should not inquire as to the presence or absence of masturbation in the adolescent. They should recognize that masturbation is not in itself detrimental to a human being physically or emotionally unless he has been made to feel too guilty about it. Feeling guilty, he may dwell too much upon it and fail to have the psychic energies available for his social or academic life. If the adolescent flaunts his masturbation, making his parents aware that he masturbates or if he attempts to discuss masturbation with his parents, he is acting impulsively because of a neurosis and should receive expert help for the neurosis.

PREMARITAL SEX RELATIONS
AND INTERCOURSE SUBSTITUTES

For a number of generations adolescents in the Western World in the pubertal and postpubertal periods have struggled with the questions as to the permissibility or nonpermissibility of intimate physical sexual contact. These questions range all the way from ones about the propriety of hand-holding, embracing, caressing, and kissing through the matter of petting and necking up to and including mutual masturbation with orgasm and premarital intercourse. Sometimes the struggle temporarily has been solved by abstinence from any or all of these types of contact. Sometimes it is solved by a greater or less degree of experimentation. Each adolescent has solved it in his own way. If the degree of experimentation has increased over the past several decades to the point where, according to reliable studies, petting to the point of orgasm has become an acceptable solution to sexual tension in the lives of thousands of college students, the increase can be laid to several factors. If premarital sexual relations have become increasingly frequent with young people, one reason may be the factor of safety introduced by an increasing knowledge of contraception. Another more important reason lies in the fact that very late adolescents and early adults are still in a financially dependent position because of their educational life, whereas several generations ago, the man of 18 to 22 often had a gainful employment which permitted him to marry and have a family. Now these years often are consumed in his attaining an education so that the man or woman in college is asked to live in abstinence at the time that his or her sexual desires are most insistent. Another reason may be the relatively greater lack of supervision for the early postpubertal individual—16 to 18 years of age—partly due to the more available means of transportation than was possible several generations ago and partly the decrease in adult feelings about the necessity for supervision. A third reason may be the increasing degree of "going steady," which we think may be the result of the tendency of many urban parents to insist on boy-and-girl partners, dancing classes, etc., in the prepubertal period before the beginning adolescent psychologically is ready for them. It is a fact that for personality development to progress satisfactorily during adolescence young people of the opposite sex must begin to like to be together in various ways. This is a healthy and important concept. Dancing is, for instance, an almost universally accepted recreation in which considerable physical touch is inevitable. That it takes place to music and usually with some degree of chaperonage does not alter the fact that it is physical touch and is gratifying in a wholesome way, but actually only to the late pubertal and postpubertal individual, when the boy has solved his fear of girls and the girl has solved her attitude toward boys.

These social, economic, and educational factors add to the adolescent's struggles with his sexuality. As Bernfeld pointed out years ago, the attitude of society to the adolescent and particularly to his sexuality is one that seems directed to making a neurotic out of him. In the past, the majority of adolescents have reached their own specific solution for these problems of sexuality without becoming neurotic or delinquent. Even in the face of the added difficulties we believe that the normal adolescent will find a satisfactory solution for himself. Those who do not do so obviously are those whose behavior is the result of the impulsive conditions we mentioned before.

Parents, because of their close conscious and unconscious emotional relationship with the adolescent, are seldom in a position to give advice about the sexual problems of the pubertal and postpubertal periods. Some adult with a wide knowledge of adolescence and with good common sense may be able to. In *Life,* Vol. 51, No.

7, August 18, 1961, Anne Landers has presented what to us seems valuable advice for both adolescents and their parents—particularly the latter—advice which all school and college counselors, physicians, and others to whom the adolescent may come should read carefully. Of course her advice to the adolescent is on the side of the superego—for many adolescents benefit by outside support for their superego.

However the whole question of sexual behavior is only one part of a large question—that of ideals and values in our present society. As Kubie and Krutch have pointed out, it would be helpful to everyone if there were more real thinking and discussion of what the ideals and values in our society might be.

THE USE OF NARCOTICS AND ALCOHOL BY ADOLESCENTS

It has been reported that there is an increasing number of college students, of some high-school students and fewer junior high-school students who use alcohol, sometimes with the consent of their parents. This applies to the use of spiritous liquors and not to the graceful custom found among Europeans of the whole family drinking some wine or beer with their meals. In some cases the adolescent takes a drink that he feels he is forbidden to take as an expression of his rebellion against his parents and against the social order. In others, he does it to prove he is a man and no longer a child. The more our culture prolongs adolescent dependence, the more adolescents will drink from time to time from these causes. Some others do it to rid themselves of feelings of anxiety, depression, and tension. This group really may be increasing, concomitant with the present-day American tendency to try to avoid the danger signal of anxiety by the use of tranquilizers and other drugs. It is this last-mentioned group that may develop an addiction, particularly if they have the neurotic character structure which is found in cases of alcoholism.

Much public attention, especially in the newspapers, has been directed toward the use of narcotics by adolescents. This problem is in some respects similar to that presented by alcohol.

In this book, alcoholism and narcotic addiction are discussed in Chapter XV. Although these discussions do not contemplate specifically the problems of adolescents, the general principles apply to young people as well as to adults; and the emotional problems of adolescents that may manifest themselves via alcohol and narcotics are the same ones that manifest themselves via other symptoms and behaviors.

SUMMARY

The emotional disturbances that occur during the prepubertal period—10½ to 13 years of age—are largely similar to those we described during the latency period except that they may be more pronounced and more bizarre in their manifestations. (This bizarreness and severity is true also for the emotional disturbances during the pubertal period.) Besides the classical neuroses and the obsessional neuroses, the emotional illnesses which occur during the pubertal period—13 to 16 years of age—fall into two main groups: those characterized by impulsive behavior that gets the individual into trouble with his parents, the school, and the social organizations; and those which result from the limitations he imposes on himself in one or more spheres of endeavor. A large group of the latter cases have the symptom of failure or poor grades in school. The emotional disturbances of the postpubertal period—16 to 21 years of age—are a combination of those seen in the pubertal period and of those seen in adult life. All of these conditions require diagnosis and treatment through expert help.

The values and ideals of the social organization often increase the difficulties which all adolescents find in understanding and coming to terms with their reactivated sexual drives and their identity as a person in their own right. Unless the adolescent suffers from a neurosis, he usually works out these problems satisfactorily in his own way.

BIBLIOGRAPHY FOR CHAPTER XI

Bernfeld, S., "Types of Adolescence," *Psychoanalytic Quarterly,* 7:243, 1938.

Blau, Abram, "Prolonged Adolescence," *American Journal of Orthopsychiatry,* 24:733, 1954.

Coolidge, John C., Mary Lou Willer, Ellen Gessman, and Samuel Waldfogel, "School Phobia in Adolescence: a manifestation of severe character disturbance," *American Journal of Orthopsychiatry,* 30, 599, 1960.

Erikson, Erik, "Problems of Ego Identity," *Journal American Psychoanalytic Association*, 4, 56, 1956.

—— "Psychology of Adolescence," *Journal American Psychoanalytic Association*, 6, 111, 1958.

Fountain, Gerard, "Adolescent into Adult: An Inquiry," *Journal of the American Psychoanalytic Association*, 9, 1961, 417.

Freud, Anna, "Adolescence," *Psychoanalytic Study of the Child*, Vol. 13, International Universities Press, 1958.

Gardner, George E., "Present Day Society and the Adolescent," *American Journal of Orthopsychiatry*, 27:508, 1957.

Geleerd, E. R., "Some Aspects of Psychoanalytic Technic in Adolescents," *Psychoanalytic Study of the Child*, 12, International Universities Press, 1957.

—— "Some Aspects of Ego Vicissitudes in Adolescence," *Journal of the American Psychoanalytic Association*, 9, 1961, 394.

Glover, Edward, "The Unconscious Function of Education," *International Journal of Psychoanalysis*, 18, 1937, 190.

Krutch, Joseph Wood, "Life, Liberty and the Pursuit of Welfare," *Saturday Evening Post*, 234, No. 28, July 15, 1961, p. 18.

Kubie, L. S., "The Eagle and the Ostrich," *Archives of General Psychiatry*, 5, 1961, 109.

Pearson, Gerald H. J., *Psychoanalysis and the Education of the Child*, Norton, 1954.

—— *Adolescence and the Conflict of Generations*, Norton, 1958.

Rosenbaum, Milton, "The Role of Psychological Factors in Delayed Growth in Adolescence," *American Journal of Orthopsychiatry*, 29, 1959, 762.

Solnit, Albert J., reporter of the Panel on "The Vicissitudes of Ego Development in Adolescence," *Journal of the American Psychoanalytic Association*, 7, 1959, 523.

Spiegel, Leo A., "Review of Contributions to a Psychoanalytic Theory of Adolescence," *Psychoanalytic Study of the Child*, 6, 1951, 353, International Universities Press.

—— "Disorder and Consolidation in Adolescence," *Journal of the American Psychoanalytic Association*, 9, 1961, 408.

Emotional Problems of Living

XII
Work and Play

THERE are many conflicts confronting an individual about to start working and only a few persons are as fortunate as a young man we know who majored in physical education, liked sports, and was good at them. He had had experience in summer camps. He went to work directly from college as an athletic coach in a university and without any emotional jolt he made use of the aptitudes he had cultivated. He became successful and satisfied immediately.

Such a story is an exception. For many men and women the stress and strain of adjusting to work and its routines create many tensions, anxieties, fears and resentments. The reasons are varied and complex.

DIFFICULTIES OF ADJUSTMENT

Either emotional immaturities or lack of preparation may cause anxiety when a person starts his job. The resulting discomfort, mental or physical, is prone to make him feel he has not found the right work. Yet if his difficulty is due to inadequate preparation and he can recognize and repair this deficiency, he will soon become comfortable and enjoy his work and his associates. But, if he is emotionally too unstable, he is in for more difficulty. He may hate and fear to be given direction—especially if direction is given impersonally and without deference to his individuality. He may have a limited capacity for endurance. He may tire easily and feel overworked. If he has no understanding of his immature inability to perform along with the others doing comparable work, his tension may result in physiological disturbances such as indigestion, irritable bowels, headache or possibly heart palpitation. For this he may lose time at work with or without consulting a physician. For an instance, there comes to mind a young man who had been successful in the college atmosphere. He too liked sports and did well at them. He wore the clothes in vogue on the campus. He liked fraternity life and joined in every activity. But when he went to work he was miserable. He was given an excellent opportunity as one of ten young men to be trained as junior executives. But he did not like the regularity of hours; he did not like the cold, business-like attitude of his superiors; he did not like to be corrected when he made a mistake; and he even disliked wearing formal clothes to work. He felt he was being molded into a "type" of individual he did not want to be. He grew so resentful he had to give up the job. After some period of unemployment he obtained a second job and the same conditions prevailed. This time he learned to struggle and suffer through it, finally accepting the fact that he was undergoing "transition pains" in his change from college freedom to the atmosphere of work and responsibility.

A third man had an even more difficult problem. He came from a home where his parents were hard-working and conscientious but shy and inarticulate. He went through college with honors but never took part in social life nor took even the smallest responsibility for anything. He went into a large plant to work in the laboratory and after a few years he left the laboratory to assume charge of a group of twenty people as a supervisor. He found this task very difficult. He could not talk the language of the men and he felt strange and apart from them. He worried that he did not know enough about his work. He was afraid he might be shown up as lacking ability in front of the other men. He could not command the respect of the men and keep things running and he was sent back into the laboratory. He failed as a supervisor and was unhappy as a laboratory worker and blamed both his family and his education for not teaching him how to get along with people. He resented their failure in not helping him to adjust to adult life and blamed his anxiety on them.

A girl of eighteen, a high-school graduate without business training, could obtain a job only as a filing clerk. She found the work monotonous, her fellow workers uncongenial. The job held no prestige for her and was fatiguing. She gave it up, hoping to find something more "interesting." A series of jobs followed, each one more "tiresome" and "boring" than the next. She became discouraged and dissatisfied not only with her work but also with her environment and her life. She looked ahead to an empty future. During her psychotherapeutic interviews this girl discovered that she was fearful and shy and had little to offer her fellow workers or her employers. She had neither vocational skills nor social skills. She had been a lonely neglected child and had never learned to mix with others or be entertaining in any way. She needed not only self-understanding but also training in vocational and social skills.

These three cases of vocational difficulty illustrate how common it is for people to have anxiety, tensions, resentment, and dissatisfaction with their jobs. The source of these problems lies sometimes in the job but many times in the inadequacies of the individual who has not been taught the practical problems of how to adjust to work.

If we look first at what the individual wants from his work we might enumerate at least the following: (a) a consistent, dependable income, (b) respect, (c) care during illness and a plan for retirement, (d) a friendly climate in which he may state his views and obtain a hearing, (e) help with his problems from management, (f) a knowledge of how the organization runs from above, and (g) loyalty both to fellow workers (perhaps via union) and employer.

The worker who comes to the job anxious because he fears or resents authority inevitably blames the job itself when in actuality his conflicts stem from his early personality development in the home, or from a currently unsatisfactory home situation. His conflicts may arise from the following facts, one or several: (1) he never had friends while growing up and may wish to shrink away from human contacts on the job; (2) he fears exploitation, that is, fears doing too much; (3) he wants many people to recognize him; (4) he wants individual attention; (5) he wants his feelings considered in every situation; (6) he is incapable of putting himself in the other fellow's place; or (7) he fears anger, jealousy, and hostility in others and in himself; (8) he cannot endure the loneliness of anonymity on the job.

To meet the emotional needs of the worker and satisfy the needs of the employer for top production, much planning for the worker's adjustment and his efficiency is needed. Some methods currently being used include:

screening of new employees

indoctrination courses

job training

steady work

opportunity for advancement

pension plans

recreation programs

good communication between
  management and worker

good supervisor training

suitable placement of workers

paid vacations

modern plant with
  good equipment

hospitalization plans

parking facilities

safety

job rating

job analysis

Each one of the above considerations does its part in creating a better working environment for the employee and thereby enhancing working relations and mental health. But of all those listed undoubtedly good supervisor training stands as one of the most important. A good supervisor should know the kinds of feelings which trouble workers and be able to be a sounding board for them. He should be strong and capable enough to command respect and at the same time be fatherly enough to absorb complaints, soothe, placate, and establish a work climate in which the workers feel they will obtain a fair deal. He should know how to lead and at the same time how to appeal for the best the worker can give, both individually and in the group. He should be able to make decisions and avoid favoritism. He should realize that within everyone there remain certain dependent needs left over from childhood—needs for a man or woman who will function in leadership as the good parent is supposed to do—with patience, kindness, justice, and praise for conscientious efforts.

The worker in turn should be able to take direction, to accept being told "how" a thing needs to be done without resentment, and should realize that a reasonable degree of civility, a good attitude, and enthusiasm will probably be rewarded in the long run. It is by learning the value of constructive teamwork that mature workers develop.

Management should know and care more than it commonly does about people and their personality reactions.

Unions and their leaders have a great opportunity to exercise a constructive influence on the problems of both management and labor—provided they are not diverted too much by the gratifications of wielding power. If the worker can voice his needs and complaints, if management can listen, and if the union can speak articulately, there can be a great reduction in tension and improvement in teamwork, and working together can be more satisfying to everyone.

MEANING OF WORK AT DIFFERENT AGE LEVELS

Work offers the average American man several emotional gratifications. For example, it gives the young man an opportunity to get ahead—which means marriage, a home, children, a car, vacations, a savings account, prestige, and an opportunity to compete with his peers and show his abilities. However too few men take time out to enjoy their accomplishments. Too often they pursue these goals relentlessly at the time when children are young and most need companionship and attention. Kind and well-meaning young fathers often just do not realize the harm they are doing in leaving themselves out of their children's personality growth. The child in this modern world needs to know early in life that he is important to two people who love him and are interested in him. Further, the young father should be spending some time at play with his child so that a tie grows between them that will serve in some of the many instances when co-operation is necessary in family life. If the child is a boy he needs a father's interest and company in order that he may learn to think and act like a man through the process of identification. If the child is a girl, she too needs her father in order to eventually feel comfortable with and acceptable to other men. Case studies show that a girl's relation to her father when young does a great deal to establish her sense of comfort and acceptance of men and their acceptance of her as long as she lives.

Undoubtedly more of the understanding so necessary to successful marriage would be developed if the father played a more sympathetic role in the family rather than the very common one of the busy, overtired, harassed, self-centered success-pursuer. He could set a better emotional atmosphere for his sons and daughters if he balanced working and living when his wife and children are young. Many a child has said, "I wish father had been less prosperous and spent more time with me." And probably even more fathers say, "I wish I had spent more time with my children." For money made or success achieved by neglect of family is unlikely to bring the best happiness to anyone. Truly here is what has been called "ill-gotten gain." To change the situation demands wisdom and discipline on the part of the young man at work to do a better job of timing—the wisdom to spend time with his family and the discipline to be content to rise to economic success more slowly if necessary.

A plan which allows for a good balance of work, play, time spent with children, vacations, and the cultivation of arts and hobbies makes for a mature and happy man. It is a well-rounded family which knows the healthy and well-timed values of living. The mother, of course, needs to help plan in the division of the father's time and energy. Often she is less ambitious for material success than he but will readily—even gladly—join him in his ambition to make money and gain prestige. She, too, misses the values of togetherness in family life while this intense preoccupation goes on, but deludes herself that it can be made up later.

The older man tends to concentrate less on his work than the young man. As he grows older his interests turn more toward community affairs. He may join service clubs, take a greater interest in church activities, work for the community or in politics. In many ways he is prone to help the young while previously he had been concentrating on helping himself. He may take an interest in his middle years in younger employees and further their advancement by developing their potential abilities, particularly if he is not jealous or afraid of being pushed aside. He should interest himself in keeping up with newer advancements in order not to lose his usefulness. As he becomes older still, he may be used more and more in an advisory capacity and as a generally useful man to his organization. As he has more time he can become more useful in community affairs and should have the interest, inclination, and security to serve many valuable social institutions. (See Chapter XIV, Later Maturity.)

WOMEN AND WORK

The modern woman has great difficulty in her relations to work. Society does not offer her as clear a role as it does the man. First she faces the dilemma of whether she will choose a career or marriage. Then, can she actually choose marriage? Perhaps she will not be asked to marry and if she does marry, just what kind of work does marriage entail and how does she find out how it is done? If she leans toward a career she often has difficulty in putting all her energies into it because she is likely, and may hope, to be drawn into a marriage anyway and hence wonders if her career effort will have been in vain or nearly so. Because of these and other conflicts she has difficulty avoiding being a divided personality who is only halfheartedly preparing for anything. We have already indicated how important the prestige factor is in work. In the life of a woman a career has prestige; but once she is married, *being* a wife and homemaker has *little* prestige. It has its *advertised* joys, true, but it just does not have prestige. Since there are so many inexorable forces which bring most women into marriage the only course seems to be that a girl prepare for two careers, marriage being one of them. Certainly marriage, homemaking, and motherhood constitute a career and one that needs preparation—far more preparation than it is getting. And since there are other phases of life and various emergencies to be provided for it seems advisable for every girl to be able to do something whereby she can earn a living and enjoy it at the same time—be it nursing, secretarial work, teaching, social work, or any other work suitable to a woman.

Training for a woman should include learning how to cook, plan meals, buy food, sew, be a hostess, and make a home attractive. She should learn what children need for healthy personality growth. She should learn what men are like, what they are looking for in a wife, what their demands are likely to be, and what they are likely to put into marriage with the woman they choose.

Further, a woman needs to be taught how to be aware of and consider whether she has the personality qualities to match those of the man she is to marry; and whether, if she does not have them, to try to achieve them or to remain unmarried. (Few individuals ever seem to consider the fact that they might have an obligation to remain single and avoid parenthood because they are so ill-equipped for it.) Some brash people lie about their abilities and experience to get a certain job and are promptly fired when their inefficiencies show up. But there are many women entering the serious business of marriage and parenthood just as brazenly and dishonestly. It is as if they went to a factory to run a costly machine without having any training for it whatever. Even this analogy is inadequate, since an ignorant worker can wreck expensive machinery only once. But in our society an ignorant wife and mother can damage many lives year in and year out and no one has any method of stopping her. Somehow we seem to assume that along with the blessing that both state and religion give to marriage and parenthood come wisdom and kindness to those women who lack both love and a knowledge of their job. This ignorant and dishonest orientation to life must be corrected by our homes and by our educational and religious institutions.

However well she may be prepared for marriage, a career skill also is often necessary and important for the married woman. She may want and need to fill her time or augment the family income when first married. She may also need or want to work for the very pleasure and creativeness involved. She may want or need to work if her husband is in military service. She may need to help support the family if her husband should be ill. She may need a career skill if divorced or separated or widowed. And finally, she may want to return to work when children have grown and left the home. In an increasing number of families, particularly in the early years of marriage, women are working to help supplement their husbands' incomes. And interestingly enough, in many a household today the husband takes over a share of the housework while his wife takes over a share of earning money.

If a woman has not prepared for a career when young she seems rarely to have the initiative to do so later. In fact, she may not be able to afford the time or money or be able to make the necessary home arrangements to attend the educational institution which would fit her for a job she wants to do later. Early preparation is preferable and highly desirable. Even if never used, career preparation remains as one of those "security reserves" that has its place in getting one through life with less anxiety concerning security.

WORK SATISFACTION

The amount of satisfaction derived from work differs greatly in people. Some really hate their work and go to it with deep reluctance. To them work is always impinging on their happiness; it stands as a barrier between them and something else more enjoyable. Others derive great pleasure from work. They get a great satisfaction from working with their heads or hands, or both. A writer of an article may get intense satisfaction from bringing his ideas forth and arranging them in a logical and forceful way. To complete an article, to have it accepted and on its way, makes for a great satisfaction that compensates for all the tedium that goes with its creation. The pleasure of discovery for the research worker is one of the thrills of a lifetime. A student who has mastered his subject and his assignment has the double gratification of (a) knowing more and (b) pleasing his teacher. A cook derives great pleasure from the meals he creates, not only because they are a work of art but also because he anticipates the pleasure he will bring to the diners and the eventual praise and other rewards he will get for his work. The farmer thrills to get his planting finished, to see the crop grow and to harvest it. A cleaning woman may feel pleasure at leaving a home or office in spick-and-span order. A nurse finds pleasure because she knows she has made several people more comfortable as a result of her work. The telephone operator, the information clerk, the complaint taker—all take satisfaction from having given service, information, and emotional relief to tense and frustrated people.

Much of this ability to enjoy work (be it chosen or thrust upon one) depends largely upon home training and whether parents were skillful in getting their child to meet his obligations and carry them through cheerfully. It depends also upon whether a parent was generous in his praise, so that the child grew to enjoy giving of himself or giving service.

In some families the philosophy of child rearing is rather sterile and is a matter of "making the kids do what they are told or else!" In other families parents sense early that to create enthusiasm in work they must set a plan for their child embodying the following principles, and follow it through for years: (a) describe or demonstrate what is required, (b) be close by as much as possible when the work is done, especially when the child is young, (c) give praise generously for work done—the better done the warmer the praise. When this system is used the child incorporates within his mind the appreciative adult image and as long as he lives has a mental picture that work pleases, that work helps the world, that work is a satisfying, creative expression of body and mind, approved by everyone. Such a mental configuration enables people to neutralize to a large extent the drudgery, the monotony, the complaints, the boredom of any job. Be work ever so humdrum, the worker can glow with some pride over the facts that he has applied himself to it and that the world is a little more beautiful or that someone has suffered less and enjoyed more because of his effort.

The man who does not enjoy his work may believe he is in the wrong job—that fate was unkind not to place him elsewhere or make more education possible for him. He may feel he works with uncongenial people or for an unappreciative employer. Indeed he *may*. But nine times out of ten he could be happier with his lot and contribute more to it if he could discipline himself to: (a) give his best uncomplainingly, (b) work to satisfy his organization, (c) waste no time worrying over whether he is doing more than his share, (d) improve himself as he goes along by learning more and trying to do the job better.

Another phenomenon common in the current scene is the individual who is too busy, too tired, or both. He likes his work quite well—so well in fact that he puts in more time on it than he should out of an overeagerness for advancement and an inordinate need for praise and prestige. His excessive zeal to make money or accumulate possessions and his wish to gain power forces him to overwork. He has an inability to say no to appeals to "join" or "give." In the woman one often sees this type of personality setting too high goals of homemaking and perfection. She has strong compulsions that force her to be superior in both homemaking and career, or to have a large family and try to "do good" and "change the world" all at the same time.

Such people may be said to have conscious defects in judgment, and so they may; but they also have unconscious emotional needs which push them to such extreme endeavors. The result is that in spite of liking their type of work basically they turn on it in resentment because it saps too much of their strength or keeps them from the needed rest and relaxation that should pervade the life of everyone. Work, rest, and play should be so combined as to give life a balance.

SHARING WORK AND PLAY IN THE FAMILY

We have spoken about the conflict of the father who tends to throw his energies into hard work and make a career success when his children are young. We have spoken of the woman who has conflicts about career and marriage and who learns by trial and error how to be a wife and mother. There seems to be so much to learn and so much hard work to be done to meet even the ordinary standards of healthy family living that we often lose sight of the "good" life and what that means in terms of happiness and play. Some families seem to have found the secret of play and anyone who comes upon one of them should examine attentively what they have captured and should take and hold it for himself.

The formula, if it can be condensed at all, seems to consist of the degree and frequency to which parents are able to enjoy life at their child's level rather than insisting that the child always adapt himself to the parents' level. The following question list may make this clearer:

How often does the family enjoy a movie chosen by the children?

How often does the family do the things the children like to do on vacation?

How often does the family adjust a weekend or part of a weekend to the children and their friends?

How much are the children allowed to participate in choices such as the kind of car the family drives, what is to be planted in the garden, how a room should be redecorated?

How much effort is made to draw the children into and teach them how to help in family tasks, such as putting the house in order and washing the car?

It seems that enjoyable family life which insures pleasant, lasting memories and makes for harmonious cohesion is the family life where there is a sharing of play and work that takes into consideration the work and play needs of growing children. This tends to bring the father into the picture and make his time spent seem valuable and it gives the mother a feeling that homemaking is a worthwhile career. As for the children, here is their opportunity for some fun in conjunction with those two important older people who are so interested in them!

VACATIONS, PLAY, AND HOBBIES

Adults need play as well as children, although many do not like to think so. Some say, "My work is my recreation. I enjoy it so much I do not need anything else." But when we search for the meaning of play for adults we face a complex question. Just as people's attitudes differ about work, so they differ about play. For some, gardening is play—very relaxing play. For others golf is a continuous year-after-year thrill. They will play in the rain or in the hot sun and they look forward to the next game with the greatest avidity.

Vacations doubtless are the occasions when people play most effectively. Being relieved of work demands is very relaxing, and people often say it takes two weeks of one's vacation to become relaxed. They are relieved of such work-day routines as getting up at a specific time, watching the clock to get to work on time, dealing with big responsibilities, or making difficult decisions. Vacation relieves pressures. Coercion stops. Diversion or change is the important element of this play. The office worker may thrill to rowing a boat, diving, swimming, fishing, hiking in the mountains. And the man who lives in the mountains correspondingly enjoys the change of going to the city to ride the subways and see the museums and shows.

Some people get relaxation and diversion by being alone and reading or by doing odd jobs, while others who are too much alone at their work crave the company of people and good conversation. Play, then, is a kind of antithesis to work. It should provide a change from familiar things and introduce relaxation or, at least, new and different emotional climates. Bridge or mountain climbing can produce tension, true; yet the participant may say, "It relaxes me to play an evening of bridge," or, "I sleep wonderfully after a day in the mountains."

It seems then that the mind and body need a periodic change of pace. An adult needs to do and think about something enjoyable and noncompulsory occasionally. Play, or recreation, should really re-create something which the routine work day often inhibits— such as humor, a freer expression of aggression, love from others, a sense of being taken care of, taking better care of self, or a communion with Nature. Some play should occur for most people in the course of every day, every week, and every year. If play is thus sought and utilized, it should help to prevent that feeling of tiredness and frustration at work. Add play to the lives of individuals who are preparing for big responsibility and hard work schedules (it is not always possible to get hard-working people to add play to their lives late in life, if they have not become familiar with it earlier) and we will have a nation of healthier and happier people.

SUMMARY

It might be wondered why work and play are put in the same chapter. It was done because of an intuitive recognition that these two phenomena of life must be complementary. They must balance each other for health. Working and playing are learned in childhood through various activities, partly by imitation of parents and other elders and partly by the child sharing in what the parents do and enjoy. Traditionally, work has a more serious and worthy reputation. If one is to do a big job in life as a leader, he must *feel good about himself—be sure about himself*. What do these phrases mean? They mean that one must possess a combination of seasoned knowledge and goodness, that is, positive kindness with freedom from self-interest, cruelty, or vanity. With such attitudes a man will not feel guilty or anxious about criticism, when it appears.

In short, to be effective, one must know one's business as well as any of one's competitors and do it as well as one knows how. It is important to be comfortable and keep one's mind clear for all phases of work at all times.

Play has its place, also. Work will proceed better if there is a satisfying balance of work and play. Play is an event to look forward to while work goes on. Play permits a more relaxed, congenial, and gratifying relation with human beings. Work requires order and a discipline that is not only tension-producing but sometimes stirs up memories of an oversevere childhood home life that stirs up resentment. At any rate, play is a change, a diversion, a different pattern of activity and is performed in an atmosphere of greater friendliness that balances the severity of work tension. Hence, they complement each other admirably to make for a healthy balance. Work and play have a complementary action that should be better understood and utilized.

BIBLIOGRAPHY FOR CHAPTER XII

Childs, M. W., and O. Cater, *Ethics in a Business Society*, Harper, 1954.
Menninger, William C., *Psychiatry in a Troubled World*, Macmillan, 1948.
Viteles, M. S., *Motivation and Morale in Industry*, Norton, 1953.

XIII

Marriage and Sexual Adjustment

MARRIAGE should be one of life's very valuable maturing experiences. It offers an opportunity for personality growth to both men and women and serves to meet many important emotional needs. We have already stressed the importance of the role of parents and family in bringing an individual through childhood and adolescence and in giving him the support, security, emotional strengths, and ideas needed for later life. The individual, at adolescence, usually struggles to break free from the home and parental influence (and well he should), to function separately and on his own. He wants to be a free and independent agent, to make his own choices and assume his own responsibilities. But he soon tires of his independent existence and wants to re-enter family life, on a different basis. Instead of being the recipient of the care and kindness of parents he sets his sights on newer goals. Ideally, the young man wants to:

(a) *take care of* a mate

(b) assist in the emotional development of his mate

(c) give to his mate what is needed to promote her welfare and make her happy

(d) propagate himself and live his life over through his children

(e) maintain a home where he may come at the end of the day to rest

(f) obtain and give the happiness and inspiration inherent in the expression of love through physical contact with a woman

(g) create an atmosphere in which one or more people care about him and what he accomplishes and how he feels

(h) create an atmosphere that is conducive to self-development and maturation

Ideally, the young woman has the goals that fit and enhance these. These goals are an acceptance of adulthood and its responsibilities that emphasize what an individual puts in more than what he takes out of life. Since one out of four marriages ends in divorce in the United States, and since so many undissolved marriages are centers of friction and unhappiness, it leads us to believe there must be some great block to the process of "putting in." From the goals listed it appears that marriage and the home could be great, inspiring, and healthy institutions. They should be the great source-places of love. They should be productive in creating happiness. But since divorce rates are so high and so much marital discord exists, and since we see so many unhappy husbands and wives emerging sick and suffering from the home, we must conclude there is something lacking in the preparation for this important life adventure.

PREPARING FOR MARRIAGE

Unquestionably we are not giving sufficient time and thought in our educational curriculum for placing before the young of our nation the truth about the problems of living and the solutions for them. Probably no life event of equal importance is viewed with as little realism as marriage. We naively assume that learning to live with and getting along with our spouses in marriage is a natural by-product of our homes and our educational system. How naive this assumption is, is made abundantly clear when we realize that the following precepts are almost universally observed in our society:

If the family is in financial difficulty it is not considered proper to let the children know about it or participate in any attempted solution.

If in-laws are a problem one does not talk about it in front of the children.

If a disagreement arises between parents so that they have reached the point of not even speaking to each other, children are not supposed to know it! If, on the other hand, father thinks mother is a wonderful cook and homemaker, he may not extol her virtues before either her or the children, for fear of spoiling or praising her too much.

It is unduly sentimental or undesirably suggestive for parents to display any affection in the home before the children.

Sex activity, or any code of behavior about it, is a subject beyond the understanding of children, and one should rarely discuss the role it plays in normal living in the family setting.

Not only does the home proceed on these precepts, but parents do not even want the subjects discussed in primary or secondary schools. Relatively few parents support any courses in family life and sex education; and if they are presented in the school, the program rarely is given strong moral support.

Many colleges, with their students at the age group near to the realities of marriage and home life, consider their curricula too full of subjects of technical importance to give much time and prestige to courses on marriage and family life.

Many argue that "you cannot teach happiness in marriage in courses." It is true that one cannot teach all there is to know about marriage and home life in courses; but neither can all of law and engineering be taught in classes. Important principles can be taught, however, and the importance of this particular area of living can be emphasized so that the young people can begin to think of how they are going to be involved in marriage. We certainly must get away from the erroneous assumption that creating a happy home and rearing mature citizens is a job anyone can do without any thought or preparation whatever.

Some part of the curricula of every school year during a young person's formal education should be devoted to the study of "how to get along with people" and teachers should be equipped to integrate this information with home life wherever and whenever it is possible. The educational climate as well as the home climate should be one that permits the growing boy or girl to look into the future, at the home he will become a part of, as well as back upon the family he has come from. There is no need to be afraid of the future or ashamed of the past, and parents and educators should collaborate on this important aspect of living very seriously if they are to strengthen the home, strengthen the character of their children, prevent emotional illnesses, and raise the level of human conduct everywhere.

WHAT TO LOOK FOR IN A MATE

Few young people seem to know what to look for in choosing a mate. The one they want often does not turn out to be the one they need.

In a survey of college students, Clifford Adams, the well-known counselor on marriage, found the following things put first as most desirable in the persons they want to marry:

PUT FIRST BY SINGLE MEN		PUT FIRST BY SINGLE WOMEN	
Companionship	40%	Love	33%
Sexual		Security	27%
satisfaction	30%	Companionship	20%
Love	15%	Children	11%
Children	10%	Sexual	
Home	5%	satisfaction	9%

Note that the man does not mention security at all and that there is a great disparity in matters of love and sexual satisfaction. Such figures bear out the realities that married couples later discover— that men and women are looking for different things in different proportion and that they had better come to know each other early in life and learn to make some compromises with their desires. Otherwise many are in for disappointment.

Some disappointment may be avoided however, according to Dr. Adams, if the following ten points are used as a yardstick in measuring one's needs in relation to a prospective mate.

1. Will this mate bring you social approval?
2. Will this mate offer security?
3. Can this mate help you get ahead?
4. Will this mate embarrass you by nonconformity?
5. Will this mate be affectionate with you?
6. Will this mate be interested in your work?
7. Will this mate share your feeling about children?
8. Will this mate satisfy you sexually?
9. Will this mate work hard to make your marriage a success?
10. Will this mate talk things over with you?

If a would-be mate seems to be able to meet these needs, considerable assurance of happiness should be present. And a mate who could offer all these things would be a most mature, competent person. But with all of these attributes there could still be room for friction and disillusionment. Other points might be added such as:

Will this mate be understanding and kind if and when I fail to achieve all these points for a day or two?

When this mate talks things over with me, will we emerge with a better understanding or will he retain a stubborn persistence concerning his own point of view?

The temptation to improve one's mate or somehow to get him to give more of some personality quality into the marriage is almost irresistible. Theoretically, marriage is a living arrangement in which the participants grow, mature, become stronger and have more to give each other as they grow older. The challenge is for each partner to put in his love and his personality contributions and wait for the growth to take place, not trying to hurry the process unduly by nagging, complaining, quarreling, or broadly suggesting changes in the other. It· must be remembered that people will neither change much nor rapidly in marriage, but a little change for the better each year makes a big contribution to the happiness of a particular family and the development of the children in it.

COURTSHIP

It should be clear that courtship is a process of exploring a man and woman's personality rather than an attempt to win each other by each party concealing his less attractive traits. Courtship should be an honest search for the suitable mate.

It is repeating an old cliché to say that no one is perfect; but how many people are able to love and accept an imperfect person? That a mate should *approve of* and not try to *improve* the other is another timeworn phrase; but again, how many think of its wisdom and live accordingly?

Wise young people in courtship will test out some of their imperfections on each other rather than try to prevent their appearance. There is something human, yet essentially faulty and unwise, in "putting one's best foot forward" in the courtship days. It may help to win a desired mate, but it prevents using the courtship as a testing period for personality compatibility. It is human to hide one's disapproval of an irksome personality trait in one's fiancé, but it is folly to think that the marriage ceremony is going to cause its disappearance, or that marriage will make it any easier to live with. Irksome personality traits are usually even more difficult to live with after marriage since they are seen oftener and at closer range. So instead of trying to "make an impression" young couples might try "being themselves" instead. It is better to put courtship or engagement to this strain first rather than put marriage, with its greater finality, to the test.

MARRIAGE CEREMONY

The marriage ceremony is usually held in the presence of family and friends, but there are exceptions, as some couples find a simple ceremony by themselves more to their liking and more meaningful for each other than a large gathering. It is obvious that the marriage ceremony should be dignified. But in many instances, the ceremony has come to be a small part of the wedding and the wedding has come to be an affair that has many elements in it over and beyond the wishes, or emotional benefit of the young people. It has become a competitive affair between families, a phenomenon of social prestige, a gala emotional spree for the parents, a chance to make money for many people involved in the proceedings, a sentimental binge for family relatives on both sides or an occasion for a big party and paying off social obligations, with the poor bride and bridegroom helpless pawns in this traditional and grueling event.

HONEYMOON

A wedding often takes weeks of preparation entailing tremendous responsibilities and obligations for the bride and bridegroom so that by the time they start on their honeymoon they are emotionally exhausted, overtired, feeling obligated toward each other or to their families, and under a compulsion to have "the most wonderful time of their lives." The honeymoon, instead, is often an unhappy time and a sorry memory which some couples carry through their marriage for years.

It is difficult for bride and bridegroom not to feel some guilt over leaving parents. If the parents have overexerted themselves to afford a more lavish wedding than their income warranted, the knowledge of this adds to the guilt. One or both of the couple may be homesick. One or both may be made tense by the arrangements of travel and, last but by no means least, frightened by the problem of their sexual adjustment to each other. The bride may be fearful and emotionally and physically unresponsive. She may experience physical discomfort rather than pleasure. The man may be impotent or may experience premature ejaculation and suffer great shame and self-criticism. In either case, the sexual act falls short of any dreams of joy and delight. If both partners have difficulties but are mature, they may be willing and able to combine their goodwill with good thinking to effect a cure of the difficulty. But if only one of the couple fails and the other is impatient or critical, a barrier to later adjustment can be built up very rapidly—perhaps never to be removed without outside help.

PREMARITAL COUNSELING

If all the unhappiness and tragedies of the honeymoon could be made known it would be much more evident that more premarital counseling is necessary. Premarital counseling is a function that physicians, clergymen, and professional marriage counselors, as well as parents, have been performing for a long time, and it is a function in which more and more people should become proficient. Much counseling consists of an interview held sometime in the last few days or weeks before marriage. First, let us say that counseling, no matter how brief, is good—it is important and it is a pity that it occurs in the lives of so few when it is needed by so many. But in criticism of present-day methods it should be said that it is also a pity that it should occur as an interview just prior to marriage. It is difficult to integrate so much that is important in one interview. Premarital counseling ought to be a more natural part of living in our whole society—in the home, in school, in church, and in the doctor's office.

There are too many things said about marriage and sexual adjustment in marriage that detract from the happiness and pleasure that should prevail in it. For example, we hear that people "ought to marry," they "ought to propagate themselves," a man "*ought* to help a woman have a family," a woman "ought to take care of a man." We are told that people *ought* to legalize and sanctify their sexual needs and that they *ought* to provide a home for their children. Other commonplaces stress the inevitability of hardship and disillusion in marriage and sexual pleasure. "You will not be married long before you will be walking the baby at night." "You will be all tired out and harassed with children." To the girl it is said, "You will have to put up with your husband's sex desires whether you want to or not." What we need is marriage counseling that begins early in life and stresses the positive aspects of marriage and parenthood.

When parents show a joy in their children they are transmitting something which marriage counseling alone can never do. They are giving their children first-hand experience and the feeling that parenthood is a fine thing. They are transmitting the fact that family life can be a pleasant experience worth entering into and giving one's best to.

The churches, with their increasing emphasis upon family life, could include in their pattern of education the biological origins of family life. One woman in a church discussion forum said, "The reason we do not talk to our children about sex is because we do not know anything good about it." The church ought to be a safe and good place to talk about sex and the church members should have something good to say about it.

Any church program should have a forum for teenagers, as often as they need it, to help them with their problems of social and sexual adjustment. To a church interested in making its young people mature, might this not be a way of teaching them to deal with the realities of life? Some churches do this but their number should increase and their program be expanded to fit the needs of the times.

Parents should have a rapport with their children so that questions can be asked and answered freely at any age about marriage. For example, a son or daughter should feel comfortable in asking either parent such questions as: How much money should I be earning to get married? Must we count upon children coming right away and if not how do we regulate this? Can I hold down a job, run a home, and meet my obligations as a wife? How often do young married couples have sexual relations, and how do I know that I will be able to make this part of my marriage work out satisfactorily?

If the atmosphere of home, school, church, and doctors' offices were geared to the importance of marriage and its attending phenomena, there would be little need for last-minute counseling prior to marriage. But we find ourselves pushing premarital counseling as an effort to compensate for the fact that nearly everyone involved in the psychosexual growth process is shirking his job.

Every physician should be well informed and able to give premarital advice and instruction both in the physical and emotional sides of marriage. He is a counselor when he has acquainted himself with the problems of growth and maturity. He sees many young people in his practice and there are many opportunities to speak about the ultimate place of marriage and home in their lives. Such a discussion is not only helpful in itself but makes it much easier for the young people to consult the physician should they have any special questions just prior to marriage.

Premarital counseling by the physician may be a part of a premarital physical examination at which time he checks the presence of good physical health, takes blood tests, and ascertains if the sexual organs are normal. Sometimes he finds that the woman needs dilatation of the hymen—a membrane at the entrance to the vagina—to ensure that the male organ may enter. Or he may allay her fears as to whether intercourse will be a painful procedure. She may need reassurance as to the degree of spontaneous ardor and enthusiasm she can put into the act. The man, on the other hand, may wish to discuss the technique of intercourse, the length of precoital stimulation, the duration of intercourse, the best technique to use to give his wife pleasure.

In addition to discussion and counseling, there are many books that can be suggested for supplementing information on sexual adjustment in marriage. Included among them are *Marriage and Sexual Harmony,* by Oliver Butterfield, and *A Marriage Manual,* by Abraham and Hannah Stone. It has been truly said that books cannot teach what people cannot feel; but there are many good modern books on marriage that give structure to what married people feel so that, while they do not change people greatly, they help to facilitate discussion and understanding.

SEXUAL ADJUSTMENT

When sexual adjustment is unsatisfactory in a physically healthy person, the reason usually is either partial or complete impotence in the male, or frigidity in the female. Complete impotence in the male—that is, failure to obtain erection—is relatively rare. But partial impotence—in the form of premature ejaculation, infrequent interest, or partial and incomplete erection—is more common. Frigidity in the woman is more common than impotence in the male. The ability of women to have orgasm, according to the statistical studies of Kinsey, et al., in *Sexual Behavior in the Human Female* (Saunders), is roughly as follows: One-third rarely obtain orgasm in intercourse; one-third achieve orgasm about half the times that intercourse is entered into; and one-third have orgasm most of the time; a small two to three per cent have a spontaneous interest in sexuality and a capacity for orgasm equal to that of the average man. Orgasm, Dr. Kinsey points out, is not just a local genital response but a total spasmodic, muscular response involving all the body musculature and accompanied by altered physiological responses such as rapid and heavy breathing, rapid heart action, increased adrenal output, sperm ejaculation in the male, and intense physical and emotional pleasure in both (which may end in weeping for the woman), followed by pleasant lassitude, and a feeling of delightful closeness to the other.

The differences in capacity for this meaningful experience are thought to be partly innate (biological) and partly culturally determined. The female is not aroused sexually by as many stimuli as the male. She is rarely sexually aroused by sight of the male, by his clothes or his nude body, by pictures of him, or by erotic stories, literature, or conversation. All these things, or their analogues, are highly stimulating to the male. The woman, in turn, is stimulated by tenderness, caressing, a romantic story or movie in which tenderness and high devotion figure, and, finally, by direct touch, and by petting itself. But even here she may take more time than the male to be ready for intercourse, one sign of her readiness being erection of the nipples and a copious vaginal secretion. She needs to be made to feel a special female person in his eyes.

These wide differences in the excitabilities of the male and the female to intercourse and in their capacities for pleasure in the orgasm indicate how important it is that there be a wide dissemination of knowledge about each other and that they co-operate as fully as possible in order to make sexual happiness a reality in marriage. It has been said that when the sexual adjustment in a marriage is good it constitutes about ten per cent of the positive part of marriage, but when the sexual adjustment is bad it constitutes about ninety per cent of what is wrong in a marriage. Hence a husband needs to concentrate on the known factors that will make his wife receptive to physical love making—tenderness, compliments, appreciation, endearments, caressing, and plenty of time for her to become physically aroused before the actual act of intercourse begins. He should also know that the clitoris and the region just behind the clitoris are the most excitable areas of the vagina and that pressure with the penis against these areas is more important than repeated penetration of the vaginal cavity.

A wife should be free to participate actively in the sexual act, putting shame and modesty aside at this time for the greater value of mutual enjoyment. She should feel free to discuss with her husband (as well as he with her) what positions and what procedures bring most satisfaction. She should realize, unless she is among the two to three per cent who are as sexually interested as the average male, that if she wishes to have sexual harmony with her husband she will need, at times, to participate in the sexual act more often than she wishes and without complaint or reproach. And the husband must not expect the wife to do all the adjusting. He needs to be aware of the difference in his wife's sexual inclinations in comparison to his own. He should refrain from excessive demands and not reproach her for being "difficult." He should try to understand that her lack of interest is the result of nature and her training. He should not assume she does not love him if she is not as sexually interested as he. Neither should she assume he does not love her if he is too demanding with her too frequently. Both, under these circumstances, must try to meet each other half way.

Such biological or neurological differences as exist in the woman remain to be quantitated through further research. Much evidence points to the fact that social and esthetic taboos and the burden of chastity and the sanctity of the home are placed much more heavily upon the woman and reduce her spontaneity in sexual relations in marriage.

Recently, some wives of medical students remarked, "I think my husband is a great guy, but I wish he would see me a little more as a human being and not just a body or appendage for his gratification. I can understand when he comes home tired after being on duty in the hospital, or spends the whole night studying. But the next day when I would like to see some friends or go to a movie, he wants to spend the evening in bed making love. This is all right, but it does spoil a girl's hopes for her plans. Couldn't he ask how *I* feel? Do I have to fit into his way of life all the time? Aren't I a person too? I don't want to be treated like a chattel. One doesn't want to be a non-entity with any man. He would get so much more of what he wants, if he would just consider me a person rather than a convenient appendage to himself."

IMPOTENCE AND FRIGIDITY

The genital organs are the executive organs of much of the pleasurable exchanges in the marriage relationship. But often they cannot execute their function. They refuse to participate in the love act. We say the male is *impotent* when he cannot achieve an erection, or when he is unable to maintain erection long enough to effect entrance into the vagina and make at least a few coital movements before ejaculation occurs. We ordinarily speak of the woman as being *frigid* when she is uninterested in coitus or when, participating in coitus, she is unable to obtain any pleasure from it. A more specific description of the relative degrees of impotence and frigidity would be as follows:

MALE
1. Impotence complete with no interest in coitus.
2. Impotence complete but interest retained in coitus.
3. Premature ejaculation or excessively retarded ejaculation.
4. Inadequate or partial erection.
5. Interested in coitus but cannot always have erection when desired.
6. Potent but coitus had under protest.
7. Potent but coitus lacks pleasure.

FEMALE
1. Dyspareunia and vaginismus.
2. Vaginal anesthesia with aversion to coitus.
3. Vaginal anesthesia with no special aversion to coitus.
4. Mild pleasure in coitus but without orgasm.
5. Only occasional orgasm.
6. Occasional failure to obtain orgasm.
   (All usually accompanied by some lack of vaginal secretion.)

Thinking over these various degrees of emotional disturbance will enable the physician to estimate the severity of the case in question. Though not inevitable, it is certainly likely that the woman who has had a great deal of pain and distress with coitus would tend to have greater psychological difficulty with subsequent sexual experiences than the woman who has achieved some satisfaction in the relationship. The man who has no interest in sex relations whatever is, by and large, the most difficult case to treat: his impotence being a psychological disturbance, the physician will have just that much more work to do with him in order to bring about improvement in this feeling. The man who retains his interest in coitus but who is completely impotent may be more easily helped because of the fact that he has some feeling and some ideation centering around the subject of intercourse.

Premature ejaculation is not usually thought of as impotence but the results can be just as serious because the man has difficulty in having sexual pleasure and in giving sexual pleasure to his wife; if he ejaculates before intromission, he will be unable to bring about pregnancy in normal fashion. When ejaculation is unduly prolonged, the result may be very fatiguing to both parties and the pleasurable spontaneity of coitus is absent. The man with an inadequate erection is suffering from a very disturbing symptom that affects both partners, depriving each of pleasure and frequently causing him humiliation and feelings of inferiority.

The man who is interested in coitus but cannot always have an erection when desired has considerable capacity for the sexual relationship at all times but the capacity is of short duration. The man who has little difficulty in getting an erection but who feels and believes that sexual intercourse is debilitating and will do him harm and has intercourse under protest, worries about the result to his health and how it will weaken his vitality; such an attitude is naturally not conducive to conjugal happiness. Some men have little pleasure in coitus and give a history of having intercourse once or twice a month, sometimes as infrequently as once a year. If the wife is sexually normal, she is bound to find incompatibility in such a marriage.

Ordinarily we think of the frigid woman as having no feeling of pleasure; in addition to this lack there may be an actual feeling of pain in the vaginal muscles with attempt at entry, so that they are thrown into spasm. Such a woman is usually much sicker emotionally than the one who can at least go through the act of intercourse without these handicaps. As in impotence, there are varying degrees in frigidity also. The woman who has no feeling and does not want to be approached sexually usually also has the feeling that she is being exploited, and uses excuses like menstruation and the fear of pregnancy to avoid coitus. The woman who has very little feeling of pleasure in coitus but who, as she says, "does not mind it," usually feels she is quite normal and that she is very lucky not to have an actual aversion to the act. When such women are asked if they have sexual satisfaction, they often answer "yes" because they have never given much thought to the ecstatic pleasure of orgasm and, since intercourse is not distasteful to them, have taken it for granted that they have experienced all there is to enjoy.

Then there is the woman whose pleasure never reaches the point of orgasm, which is the end point of complete pleasure and is accompanied by varying degrees of involuntary muscular movements ending in relaxation and satisfaction. Some women accept the lack of orgasm as normal for their sex while others recognize that it is not normal and seek some improvement in their status. There are women who have orgasm once in every three or four acts of coitus, or who have great difficulty in achieving orgasm and achieve it only under special circumstances.

Finally, there is the woman who occasionally fails to have orgasm. She is not likely to come to a physician or seek his counsel; yet she may, since the decrease in prudishness about sex is causing young couples to seek a better sexual adjustment than the preceding generation demanded.

We would like to make clear the difference between impotence, frigidity, and sterility. These terms are often misused. Sterility in the woman means she is unable to become pregnant and sterility in the man means he is unable to bring about pregnancy in his wife. Yet there need be *no* disturbance in the capacity of a sterile mate to have sexual pleasure in the sexual relationship.

The sexual organs and the pelvic region should be energized and sensitized for the achievement of sexual pleasure. Yet many forces at work in society stand in the way of its achievement. Threats, admonitions, and ideas imparted from childhood onward tend to dam back the flow of psychic energy which would energize and sensitize the pelvic organs for sexual pleasure. In fairness to parents it must be said that they do not realize how much harm they are doing in frightening children and young people about sexual relations. Parents do not realize that they may cause the children to lead a fearful, unhappy, and perhaps childless existence as the result of these extreme attitudes. They should be told this fact, and in many instances it is the doctor who is in the best position to tell them.

CAUSES OF IMPOTENCE AND FRIGIDITY

1. Fear of disapproval or punishment:
    (*a*) Fear of criticism or ridicule.
    (*b*) Fear of bodily injury from some disapproving person other than the partner
    (*c*) Fear of pregnancy.
2. Hostility toward the partner:
    (*a*) A general resentment toward members of the opposite sex with a desire to do them harm.
    (*b*) The woman resents what she considers domination by the man.
    (*c*) The man is envious of the woman and her role in life and refuses to give her pleasure because of this envy.
    (*d*) A fear by one of the partners of injuring the genital organs.
3. Conflicting loves (usually unconscious):
    (*a*) The man loves some other woman and is unconscious of it (mother, sister); or the woman loves some other man (father, brother) and cannot accept husband sexually.
    (*b*) Latent homosexuality; i. e., persons of the same sex are loved rather than persons of the opposite sex.
    (*c*) Too much self-love. Love of another person is an overflow from self-love. In these cases there is no love left for the sexual partner.

Fear of disapproval is strong and deep in every human being. There are people who seem to be very much at home with the subject of sexuality and who tell jokes about it, yet somewhere in their makeup still retain a great deal of prudishness, prejudice, disgust, and fear of ridicule about anything having to do with sex. A great many people feel sure they are in love when they marry, which ought to mean the presence of a great deal of tolerance and acceptance. Yet when it comes to the matter of sex relations, the woman is very much afraid her husband will criticize something she might say or do in the course of sex play—and the same is true of the man. They may have this fear so strongly as to prevent sexual pleasure or sexual functioning. From childhood onward it is extremely common for grownups to tease children about their friendly overtures to each other. This leads to pain and embarrassment, feelings that are difficult to get rid of later in life.

The shortest definition of impotence and frigidity is the inability of a man or woman to have sexual pleasure. In order to understand the definition it is necessary to break it down into its various components and discuss them separately.

The fear of bodily injury applies to the person who, after entering marriage, still feels that he or she is going to be punished for doing that "bad thing." In other words, the marriage ceremony has not been able to break down the fears of being punished for sexual activity which such a person has carried with him all through life. He *still* fears punishment. A young couple consulted us when their sexual relations were going very badly. They were living in close quarters with the wife's parents. They were so conscious of this fact that when they got up in the morning they felt embarrassed about facing the parents when they went downstairs. They felt the parents knew of their relationship and as a consequence might punish or ridicule them. The thought made them unable to have sexual pleasure. They were considering a move to their own home and we advised them to hasten that move, after which their sexual adjustment improved.

Fear of pregnancy may be quite a serious factor in sexual pleasure. Many women still hold the erroneous belief that pregnancy will not occur when there is no sexual pleasure or orgasm. Thus women who fear pregnancy will inhibit sexual excitement, thinking to escape pregnancy in this way. Such old wives' tales have been in existence for centuries. In many cases both the man and the woman lack knowledge of contraceptives, or they are ashamed to seek it.

Hostility is another factor that frequently exists in marriage. It is assumed that only people who are in love marry and that the love they hold for each other is going to carry them along through life and solve all of their problems. Yet often people marry who are not in love as they think they are. Instead of acting from strong positive feelings toward the opposite sex they dutifully go through the social conventions. In a great many instances there exists a deep and unconscious fear of the opposite sex which in a subtle way prevents their obtaining sexual pleasure. There are also those, particularly women, who feel passionate for a few weeks or months and enjoy sexual relations. Then the enjoyment disappears and they wonder why. Actually their sexual desire was weak in the first place. It started out apparently normally but soon diminished in intensity when hostility in the form of "grim seriousness" or "coldness" caught up with them. Hostility is an important factor to be dealt with in helping people with their problem of impotence and frigidity.

Impotence in the male and frigidity in the female result from an identical personality disturbance. Despite the difference in anatomy, the cause is the lack of feeling in the sexual organs which prevents their functioning with pleasure.

With respect to hostility toward the partner, we will first consider resentment toward the opposite sex with desire to do harm. Resentment and hostility are fairly general attitudes; the physician cannot discover or measure these symptoms by asking about them directly. A better way to find out about a patient's internal hostility toward other people is to ask him how many friends he has or how many people he likes or how well he does in positively relating to people. This is a surer way to get at the truth, since few people want to admit they have active hostility. A great deal of hostility may actually exist in those married couples who boast that they never quarrel or say a cross word to each other. What they say may be true—because they never speak to each other! Many, many couples have hostility toward each other which is not recognized and cannot be admitted. The doctor may sense it but find it quite a task to make the patient consciously aware of its presence.

In one type of hostility the woman resents what she considers domination by the man, and the man is envious of the woman and her role in life and refuses to give her pleasure because of his envy. Men and women are envious and jealous of each other. It is quite well accepted that women are envious and jealous of men but it is not so well understood that the same holds true for men and that men are often envious and jealous of the role of women. One very simple reason explains why this can be so. As children grow up they are not told in a positive way what their role in life should be. For instance, to talk to a female about her role in life means to talk about motherhood and childbearing, and that is taboo in many homes. To talk to a boy about his role means to discuss family life and fatherhood in addition to career, and that, too, is taboo. In order to keep the whole subject of sex away from the minds of young people, parents do not prepare them for their respective roles in life, and as a consequence any pleasure and satisfaction that might be obtained from these roles are withheld at the same time. The children grow up without being positively related to the role they should play, without being enthusiastic about it, and instead are being envious and jealous of a member of the opposite sex. Attitudes of this kind are not close to consciousness, and in order to make them clear, the physician must use tact and understanding. Sometimes a woman overcomes frigidity after the birth of her first child. Through having a child she comes to see herself as being "as good as the man." She has finally obtained a substitute for the envied penis—the child.

Fear of injuring the genital organs is quite a common feeling. There is hardly a man alive who grows to the age of twenty-one without sometime having been told about harm that will come to the genital organs through intercourse with women. Also there are few women who have not heard stories about pain and distress in intercourse. Thus both men and women grow up with strong fears within them of the harm that results from the sexual act and specifically related to the genital organs. This again is usually an unconscious attitude. One of its most conscious forms is the fear of venereal disease. In many people this fear is so marked as to be crippling to wholesome sexual functioning.

Conflicting loves (usually unconscious), where the man loves some other woman or the woman loves some other man, are much more common than is supposed. Young people are brought up to love their parents and to feel positively toward them and often are warned not to have any emotional bonds with anyone else because to do so is to be sexually tinged and "wicked." In other families, where the sexual aspect is not so strong, it is regarded as disloyal and even sinful for a boy to become interested in a woman other than his mother or sisters. He feels a general disapproval when he makes dates or goes out with other women. The result is that when such a person, man or woman, marries (and some do not marry because this complex is so strong) a great deal of his emotional investment remains in his family instead of in his marital partner. He actually remains in love with or devoted to his mother or feels guilty that he has left home and married another woman whom he supports or with whom he sleeps. He feels this guilt every day. Some men are always attempting to relieve this feeling of guilt by visiting home frequently, giving money to a mother or sister that is not needed or necessary, or asking advice of one or the other—

all of which may be very annoying to the wife. Likewise there are women who never can seem to have a proper attitude toward their husbands. They not only cannot be tender or affectionate, having been taught that to be so is wrong, but they also cannot be loyal or have any respect for the husbands' opinions or desires. They refer all matters to the father or brothers to decide. These attitudes grow out of an improper and inadequate solution of the oedipus complex, which is the emotional tie that exists between the female child and her father or between the male child and his mother.

We emphasized earlier that these emotions are not only present but necessary and acceptable during a certain period. But for healthy development people must not remain fixed at that childish level of loving but finally get away from loving their own family and become able to love someone outside of it.

Fears of harm to the genital organs are remnants of a strong castration complex—a complex that exists in spite of the skepticism of some people. Some males unconsciously feel that the vagina is a fearsome cavity in which the penis will be lost, or squeezed, or bitten off. As boys they hear the untrue and fantastic story of the couple who became stuck together by reason of some unexplained contraction of the vagina, whereafter the penis had to be amputated in order to effect a separation. Women hear of the pain that can be suffered in intercourse. Both fear harm by way of venereal disease. As children they are warned not to touch each other's bodies—that to do so results in harm. Working with patients will in time convince those physicians who are skeptical that these constellations of ideas are important to understand and that parents should be made aware of them so that they can be handled adequately in childhood and not persist into adulthood and create the many problems that physicians see in daily practice.

Latent homosexuality is a condition of emotional immaturity. Remember, we do not love the opposite sex exclusively. There is some capacity for loving the same sex in everyone and there should be for any desirable social functioning. The emotions of some people, however, have been so completely steered away from the opposite sex and such a wall has been erected between them and their ability to love someone of the opposite sex that they are what we call latently homosexual. Perhaps the person does not actively participate in a homosexual relationship but he is emotionally attached to the same sex to a greater degree than to the opposite sex, and this feeling may result in impotence in the male or frigidity in the female.

Too much self-love is another condition of immaturity. There are people who grow up being so self-centered and demanding that they have nothing left over to give to anyone else, either in a sexual relation or in any other social relation. This lack does not necessarily come about through what we call "spoiling." When the word spoiling is used we think of a person who has been "loved to death" and given everything he ever wanted from birth onward. Actually that is not necessarily the case. When it is the case, the person comes out spoiled because no one ever trained him or requested him to think of others, to do things for others, or to consider their feelings. However, some of the most self-centered people are not necessarily those who have received a great deal. They are also the people who have had too little, who have lived in great emotional deprivation, whether in rich homes or poor, and the result of this emotional deprivation is to make them anxious and fearful. They are anxious and fearful because they feel that if they become too much interested in someone else, they will "lose out," they will "miss something," or they will suffer in some way. These people can never compromise or make plans that include the convenience of another. They can rarely say a kind word or rarely congratulate another person. Their conversation revolves about themselves, what they are doing and would like to do. A thought of making anyone else happy rarely enters their consciousness unless by chance it happened to make them feel good at the same time. Such people have been brought up to feel that they *give away* too much through participating in sexual relationships and as a result can easily be impotent or frigid.

TREATMENT OF IMPOTENCE AND FRIGIDITY

Since most cases of impotence and frigidity (aside from a few resulting from demonstrable organic disease) are caused by disturbances in emotions and ideation, then the cure must aim toward modifying the feelings such people have toward each other and modifying their ideas about sexual functioning. Other approaches have been tried, based on theories of causation. There is, of course, the very prevalent idea that impotence and frigidity are due to a lack of glandular substance and that supplying this lack would naturally have a good effect upon the condition. But persons suffering from impotence or frigidity rarely show any glandular deficiency and only very rarely does the giving of a glandular substance have a favorable influence. It used to be thought—and still is by some—that frigidity in the female is due to adhesions around the clitoris. This again is rarely if ever true. Operations that consist of grafting a glandular tissue substance to the male have been tried with limited success. When we come to evaluate the therapeutic effects of operation, we must not lose sight of the high degree of suggestibility associated with this form of treatment.

Therefore, if we are going to approach this subject from the psychological standpoint, we must take a very careful history of such persons, with particular emphasis upon the sexual side of their personality development, and try to bring out certain points. At the outset we want to know the attitude of the parents in the matter of sex. We have found that three general attitudes are taken in the home toward sex education. The best is to enlighten the children in a sensible way as they come to ask questions, telling them as much as they want to know and no more, being prepared to tell them the answer to what they ask—not limiting the imparting of the information to any one day or age period and then with a sigh of relief saying, "That is over!" It is fortunate when parents are sufficiently at home and comfortable with the subject of sexuality to see the child's interest in it when it appears and enlighten him as he wants to be enlightened. The result will be that by the time the young person has reached twenty years of age he will have gathered the facts slowly, integrated them well, and feel comfortable about the subject of sex.

The second parental attitude so commonly seen is a more negative one. An effort is made to condemn everything pertaining to sexuality and to stress the dangers of sexual indulgence of all kinds; sex is called dirty and disgusting. Bad though this sounds, however, it is not the worst attitude that can be taken.

The third attitude, in which the whole subject is completely ignored, is the worst of all. Families who refuse to mention or discuss sex, who treat it as a subject not of this world, one that no decent, self-respecting person would think of, do far more harm in the end than those who take the attitude of condemnation, bad as that is. For fathers and mothers who emphasize the dangers of sex at least recognize and accept some thinking on the subject, and ideas germinate that can be corrected outside and that can through fortuitous circumstances be overcome. But in families where no thinking is allowed at all, where sex is not even dignified by condemnation, the children have a very hard struggle in making a sexual adjustment. Since no one in authority even touches upon the subject, these children may have a great feeling of guilt or many mistaken notions about sex which they harbor within themselves. They are the children who do not exchange ideas with other children, and hence grow up ignorant, emotionally and ideationally empty, and with very little feeling about sexual functioning. They are the cases that are extremely difficult to treat because even when what the doctor says carries weight, he still has a difficult time combating twenty-one years or more of parental authority which has been saying that no right-minded person has any thoughts or feelings concerning sex. When the doctor starts to re-educate such a person he often finds nothing within the person that can respond to him and be utilized.

In questioning the patient, however, the doctor should ask specifically whether sexual matters in the home were regarded as disgusting, whether there was an effort made to separate the sexual function from the excretory function. He may ask whether there existed in the home a religious attitude strongly opposed to sexual thinking or functioning, whether love of the opposite sex and sexual expression were associated.

When a doctor begins to question people about sexual matters, they usually reply, "Everything was all right in my home," or "I had the average sexual education." Not until he questions them specifically is he able to help them to see in how many ways their thinking about sex was not average or normal. Even today there are many who believe that love is some pure ethereal feeling and that any physical expression of it is not a part of real love. The physician should ask whether fears were instilled over sexual expression, such as evil resulting from masturbation, the pain of venereal disease, or the shame and disgrace of illegitimate pregnancy. He should ask if sexual indulgence was pictured as hateful, frivolous, or dangerous. He should inquire as to whether the parents were in love with each other—a very important question—and also whether the patient ever saw demonstrations of affection between them.

The doctor should inquire into the parents' attitude toward other people outside the home who showed affection and ask whether there was any strong emotional tie to the parent of either sex. He may not get a very satisfactory answer to that question alone but by asking about the patient's behavior to the parent he will get a better idea of the emotional tie existing between parent and patient. He should learn whether the social and procreative roles of men and women were clearly outlined to the patient as he grew up, and whether the patient has a strong attachment to the same sex. Thus will the doctor be able to define for himself and for the patient the wrong attitudes and feelings existing in the latter that need to be changed. He must be able to describe to the patient the new attitudes and feelings that must be learned if the patient is to create the proper attitude for sexual functioning.

THE SEARCH FOR FEELING

Most everyone wants to feel more in this life. Even those who may talk in terms of acquiring more money or possessions do so because they assume it will make them feel better in some way. They behave as if feeling is everything. But feeling has to be secured in a certain way—brought about by certain life activities. For this, there are the early life experiences and their counterparts in later life experiences. The first and most important is the sensual acceptance of the infant at the breast by the happy, satisfied, devoted mother who feels her child is a most important creature. Later comes the child's achievements in school and the playground both in grade and high school, the friends made, and any special achievements. In another area of behavior, alcohol is one of the common later-life means tried for feeling. Sexual gratification is another. The feeling a man gets when he is accepted in the act of intercourse in the embrace of an attractive, warm, interesting woman is one of the most important feeling experiences in the world for him. It seems to be man's greatest achievement, but so far he has not consciously admitted it. He often spends much time and energy pursuing a greater self-awareness through sexual relations; he talks with his men friends about it. But, when he arranges things to achieve it, he is all too often severely limited in his ability to be "within it" in spirit because (1) he feels guilty about what he is doing, or (2) he finds flaws in the woman, or (3) flaws in himself, or (4) flaws in the beauty or goodness of the act. He isn't emotionally prepared to make the act meaningful, so he isn't able to make the woman feel she is important to him or doing anything important for him.

At the time of sexual relations there should be the highest level of emotional and spiritual communication. Most people do not talk much during the act—they feel. If they talk, they talk in terms of the pleasure they are giving each other or the charms of each other. They are lost in feeling, if they are capable of feeling. And the brevity of the act makes it very difficult for the people involved to make the most of it emotionally unless there has been proper preparation beforehand—a sincere exchange of ideas of what they each mean to each other as well as the meaning of the sexual act itself. So, the sex act all too often fails in its purpose. Man's second opportunity in being an inspiration to a woman fails—the first having been his infantile intimate relation to his mother at the breast. And if they fail each other in this close, intimate "love relation," they tend to fail everywhere to a corresponding degree. It is true that a man can become rich and make inventions, write books, and make speeches. But he may not know the joy of life—and somewhere within him he suspects this truth about himself. His evaluation of life makes it seem to have been a failure because it never had the intense meaning that a woman, and only a woman, can give to a heterosexual man. He always tends to doubt his power and worth unless he can get a woman to tell him of his importance to her and her body. If a man has the interest and the versatility to find the woman who will respond to him emotionally and intimately and at the same time will appreciate the importance of this experience to him, he will have a higher consciousness of his value everywhere.

A man should be taught to put this value high on his list of achievements. It is well to concentrate attention on this with men as well as with women. One can't expect women to enjoy the intimate pleasure of sexual relations, and the intimate pleasure of nursing their babies, without a man's interest and encouragement. If a man will show a woman what she can do for him with her body and spirit, she will probably know deep within herself the importance of giving her breast and her body to an infant son or daughter. Men look to women to be the creators of love and yet, with all the power men wield in society, they should take more of this responsibility upon themselves and look more closely at this creature from whom they expect so much and criticize so severely because she isn't able to give them a positive feeling of their worth as men.

A woman is much more handicapped than a man in being the leader here. Women who are able to give their love intimately to men are rarely rewarded for it. Instead they are often more or less despised, suspected of being capable of unfaithfulness or of becoming potential prostitutes, instead of being given respect and understanding they deserve for making the man's sexual pleasure the intense, meaningful thing he wants it to be.

What is the relation of all this to such important things as impotence and frigidity? If the needs that have been discussed regarding the search for feeling were more conscious and if such consciousness prevailed in everyday relations between men and women, more love, altruism, and family harmony would be sure to follow. A man will tend to successfully love physically the woman who meets his need for feeling. Having in her the source of this kind of feeling of intimate importance, he tends to feel calm, confident of his abilities, and willing to create good feeling in her for whatever condition or situation it is needed. She in turn responds to his feeling, and is able to be more the person he needs for his happiness and that of his children.

The treatment for impotence and frigidity is not easy, but some cases respond fairly well. A woman had been married for three years without sexual pleasure. She had come from a home where everything pertaining to sex was considered shameful and disgusting and where no one, particularly a woman, could take an active interest in sex or sex relationships and still be respected. The result was that though she was a woman of feeling and imagination, she took the attitude that in marriage the woman is to be used for the husband's pleasure and is never to make advances or take an active part in intercourse. After only two or three discussions with her, emphasizing the fact that women have as much right to sexual pleasure as men, as much right to discuss it and to make advances, she was able to participate to a much greater extent. In such discussions the doctor is sympathetically fulfilling the function of an authority—a function that should have been taken over earlier by the parent. All that was wanting was sanction for the sexual feeling and sexual activity.

There is another type in which some degree of impotence or frigidity is present and which does not need too much help. The husband or wife has become too preoccupied with his or her tasks, makes no time or opportunity for adequate sexual expression, feels that making a living or taking excellent care of the children and home comes first. The husband or wife is always tired, but regretful that sex relations are not what they were in the beginning, yet never gets around to taking any positive constructive attitude toward the problem. A discussion is usually needed for both husband and wife and suggestions made that they give some of the time and enthusiasm they are putting into everyday matters to plans for their lovemaking. In other words, they are expecting their love life to flourish without giving it any attention. It may not, and rarely does when so neglected. In this very hurried, hazardous world in which we are living today, satisfactory sexual adjustment in marriage is not easy to maintain. We do have to give some thought and allow some time for it. If couples do not take an interest in an occasional trip, a show, a movie, a night out in order to put themselves in the frame of mind for lovemaking, they may suffer a degree of frigidity or impotence.

In a problem of this kind, one or two discussions with the husband or wife are necessary first and then a discussion together. This is usually sufficient to improve their pleasure and ability for sexual functioning. When they learn that they cannot neglect giving some attention to their sexual relations, they usually take the doctor's suggestions and improve.

In sexual adjustment—as in many other problems—kindness and thoughtfulness on the part of each human being involved will solve many problems. Both the mystery and the suffering connected with sexual maladjustment could be lessened if each would have the generosity in his nature to be frank, listen to the other and try, *even though it hurts,* to be kind and meet the other's needs in the sexual as well as in the other relations.

ADJUSTMENT TO MARRIED LIFE

After the glamour and excitement of courtship, marriage, honeymoon, and beginning sexual adjustment have been passed through, a couple must settle down to the quieter tempo of marriage adjustment. Here some of the basic personality patterns of the young partners will assert themselves. It is a most fortunate thing for the marriage if these basic patterns have been positive in nature. We allude again to the psychological values of marriage. Marriage can be of tremendous psychological importance to both partners, and undoubtedly each one looks forward to it. The young woman hopes that her husband is going to be able to see her potentialities and help her to expand them by recognition, practice, approval, tenderness, encouragement, and acknowledgment. It is a sorry day for any marriage when the husband becomes so absorbed with his own work and problems that he begins to use the home as a boarding place and fails to see his wife as a growing, developing personality in need of his love and affection. It will be much easier for the young husband to fulfill these hopes if he has come from a family where he has seen such a relationship between his father and mother.

By the same token, a man looks to his wife to be interested in him and in his work, to praise his advancements and successes, and to appreciate his presence in her life. It is probably traditional that the woman is better equipped to appreciate the importance of her husband as an individual than he is to appreciate her as a person who needs to grow and develop. It has been taken for granted that the man needs to "rise in the world" and for this he needs recognition both at work and in the home. It has always been expected and acceptable for him to improve his lot but it has not been so clearly recognized that the woman in the family needs certain activities for her development also. Many tragic misunderstandings and divorces have come about because the husband actually did rise in the world and his wife did not rise with him. He studied and she did not. He traveled and she did not. His accomplishments were recognized both at work and at home and yet hers were not. She was somehow supposed to find happiness in taking care of the home and making her husband happy, in raising and caring for his children, entertaining and taking care of relatives.

There is a flaw in society's developmental philosophy concerning the young whereby the son is often given every advantage so that he may become a success but is rarely told that in addition to being a success he needs to encourage his wife and aid in her development also. A wife needs to feel that she is a partner in the marriage venture and she likes to feel that she too is permitted to grow and develop along with her husband. Consequently they should share as many things together as will contribute to their mutual development and give each the pleasure of shared interests.

Some couples read and study together. Others attend adult classes, attend lectures, or plan trips together. Whatever they do they should plan to keep communication alive. Some husbands are away from home all day and yet in the evening have nothing to report of interest. Other couples are too prone to discuss only the things which trouble or distress them rather than the things which they enjoy. Husbands and wives should check on their attitudes periodically in an attempt to discover whether they are either focusing attention upon the mate's shortcomings or else demanding more from the marriage than they are putting into it in terms of being an interesting personality, considerate, and co-operative.

It is highly desirable that a husband and wife know how to care for each other satisfactorily in these ways before they consider having a child. Actually when they become parents, they should not only be able to take care of each other well but they should have a reserve of love which will be available for the child. An infant, in the beginning, can do very little to make his parents happy if they are not already so. If they are happy as a married pair then they will be proud and satisfied to join others who have achieved the mature goal of parenthood. They will be glad to see themselves reproduced. They will be interested in watching their infant's daily development and his gradual capacity to recognize them. They will be glad to impart some of their personality qualities to him. At the same time the infant will make heavy demands upon both of them. He will demand a good deal of the mother's time which formerly was available for her husband. The husband must be willing to relinquish this time to his offspring. The infant will interfere with their sleep, since he must be fed at night and will awake early in the morning. He will interfere with their social life, since they cannot move about as freely without considering his needs for food and security. He will complicate their meal hours and their vacations, and all their plans will be confined, now that they have to consider the needs of a helpless young one. It takes maturity for a young couple to live with and appreciate this infant who makes such heavy demands on them. They will have to be well motivated in their role of parents and be able to look happily into the future in order to find the patience and devotion within themselves to meet the hour-by-hour needs of their infant.

Marriage, it would seem then, cannot flourish by itself. It cannot be neglected. Two people who enter matrimony cannot assume that because they have united forces they are going to be able to produce happiness for themselves or create a happy atmosphere in a home where their children can grow. Family life takes a great deal of thought and planning on the part of many people. Every child, from birth through adolescence, should be preparing for adult life. Boys and girls should grow up in homes which give them strength, comfort, and wisdom for later life. For at marriage they are merely stepping out of these homes to unite and continue the living process of their parents under a new and slightly different arrangement. What has been given to them they will pass on to their young. The process is never-ending and can be and should be quite meaningful and rewarding. Actually, all too many people fret, complain, and quarrel under the stress of it and find it frustrating and disappointing or at best unsatisfying.

A happy home is an asset to everyone in it. It creates mental health and maturity. In our modern society children are less of an asset to parents than they used to be in the days when families lived in more rural communities, perhaps owned farms or shops where the children furnished manpower. Today a much larger percentage of children must be loved, reared, and enjoyed for their own sakes. They need a long and expensive education, and it is probably safe to say that parents have to give their children more in many ways than was true a hundred years ago. However, the concept of dignity and worth of human beings has been constantly growing over the years, and the family is the place where it should continue to grow to even greater proportions. There is an inherent happiness in a marriage between a man and woman that is of much greater value than many people have realized, and if we add parenthood to this, people are given the means to a truly bountiful life.

SUMMARY

Since marriage is common for most people, they should try to make it as congenial and meaningful as possible. Few of those who enter it think of their parts in making it a positive relationship. They usually think of what they can obtain from it rather than what they can put into it. Consequently, with so much ignorance on the part of both sexes of what their partner wants and needs, it is small wonder they fail each other and fight more often than enjoy each other.

Marriage is a partnership in which work and play enter in a very practical way. Husband and wife have their work to do. When they have worked for a while, they should get together for play and the mutual enjoyment of each other's work. But few can share in this with any aura of romance and happiness. They tend to strip life down to its most unattractive essentials. If the wife talks about the children's school performance, the husband may feel left out and resentful. If he talks only about his office hardships, she may feel left out. They should strive to acknowledge each other and not merely bear griefs, sorrows, or conflicts together. There is an opportunity to enhance each other's development in a positive way.

There is a rhythm to marriage that few people are prepared for. It goes somewhat as follows:

1. the honeymoon—a time to have and enjoy each other to the fullest.
2. the first child—and with him the excitement and adventure of infancy and childhood.
   (a) the early developing years—P.T.A., boy and girl scouts, church and school activities to aid development.
   (b) young adulthood—as measured by socialization efforts in high school and college.
   (c) college years or other post-secondary school education—the independent-dependent phase.
   (d) the first job—and success that goes with it.
   (e) marriage—and success with this too.

Meanwhile:

3. the married couple's social life with friends.
4. the activity of mother as the children make their own lives. The community needs her, if she will respond, and both parents need each other to close ranks and entertain each other as the children move away.
5. the couple's management of the later years, with or without each other, which requires imagination and versatility if they are not

to fall back as a gloomy, heavy burden upon one or more of the children.

These are the rhythms of marriage with, of course, various unexpected breaks. The illnesses, the alienations, the divorces, deaths, infidelities, overinvolvement with family, alcoholism, and a myriad of other intrusions, disrupt a married life that was meant to be harmonious and constructive. An understanding physician can with vision and patience bring most of these marriages to be what they were supposed to be.

BIBLIOGRAPHY FOR CHAPTER XIII

Adams, Clifford R., *Preparing for Marriage,* Dutton, 1951.

Adams, Clifford R., and Vance O. Packard, *How to Pick a Mate,* Dutton, 1946.

Butterfield, Oliver, *Marriage and Sexual Harmony,* Emerson Books.

Dunbar, F., *Mind and Body,* Random House.

Fishbein, M., and E. W. Burgess, *Successful Marriage,* Doubleday, 1947.

Kinsey, A. C., *et al., Sexual Behavior in the Human Female,* Saunders, 1953.

Kinsey, A. C., *et al., Sexual Behavior in the Human Male,* Saunders, 1948.

Levy, John, and Ruth Monroe, *The Happy Family,* Knopf, 1938.

Mace, David R., "What Is a Marriage Counsellor?" *Bulletin of the Menninger Clinic* 18, No. 3, May 1954.

Menninger, Karl, *Love against Hate,* Harcourt, 1942.

Mudd, Emily H., and Aron Krich, *Man and Wife,* Norton, 1957.

Nall, T. O., and B. H. Davis, *Making Good as Young Couples,* Association Press, 1953.

Popenoe, Paul, *Preparing for Marriage,* Institute of Family Relations, Los Angeles, 1938.

Stone, A., and Hannah Stone, *A Marriage Manual,* Simon and Schuster, 1952 Rev.

XIV
Maturity and Its Problems

I N THE chapters dealing with marriage and work and play we have discussed various activities and problems of family life and living. Life is such a many-sided activity, however, that there are numerous other areas in which problems arise. If we could anticipate some of them and develop wisdom with which to meet them life might be more meaningful and less full of tension and conflict. Developing wisdom is difficult but does it not often come about in the following way? Information, plus experience, brings knowledge. Knowledge, plus experience and goodwill, brings about wisdom. In the course of acquiring this wisdom comes some degree of pain and suffering. The person who grows to be what is called "wise" and "mature" learns and is willing to endure the suffering that learning takes. Those who cannot grow also suffer. They have less mental health than those who live, learn, suffer when necessary, and find some joy and satisfaction in the process. The emotional problems of living are legion. We will discuss a few in this chapter.

THE MEANING OF MATURITY

Much has been said of maturity, yet it is still not easy to define. People are exhorted to be mature and yet the rules of maturity continue to be elusive. General agreement on the criteria of maturity is hard to come by, but the following concepts seem to be a part of the definition. The mature individual should:

1. Be able to work a reasonable amount each day at his job without undue fatigue or strain, and feel that his work is serving a useful purpose.

2. Be able to like and accept many lasting friendships; and be able to love and be tender and affectionate with a few close friends.

3. Have such confidence in himself that he is not harassed by guilt, doubt, or indecision. He should have enough confidence in

himself to be able to oppose impositions upon himself and his family.

4. Be as free of prejudice as possible and treat all men and women with appropriate respect.

5. Be able to give and receive love with joy in a conventional heterosexual way free of guilt or inhibition.

6. Extend his interest in an ever-widening circle from self to family, friends, community, state, and nation, and seek to take a part in contributing to the general welfare of mankind.

7. Be interested in advancing his own welfare without exploitation of his fellow man.

8. Be able to alternate work with play, recreation, reading, and the enjoyment of nature, poetry, art, and music.

9. Be free of undue body strains, stresses, and tensions when performing his everyday duties, as when confronted with adversity.

10. Be dependable, truthful, open-minded, and imbued with a philosophy that includes a willingness to suffer a little in order to grow, improve, and achieve wisdom.

11. Be interested in passing on his hard-won knowledge to the young.

These criteria of maturity should enable an individual to use his mind with enough efficiency to keep up his sense of well-being and thereby avoid anxiety and neurotic patterns of behavior. A mature mind creates and preserves mental health as it goes through life and has a reserve of mental health for every life period, including old age.

FRIENDSHIPS

Nearly everyone needs friends. Those who prefer solitude and the constant company of their own thoughts are exceptional. The average person is dependent upon friends for love, approval, comfort, inspiration, encouragement, entertainment, and at times, criticism. He lives, so to speak buoyed up, supported, and protected by his friends from noxious agents both within and without his personality. Who are his friends? Usually they lie outside the family circle. There is the old saying that fate gives us our families but fortunately we can choose our friends. A patient once gave this old saw a slightly different turn when she said, "If we were not relatives I'd say we hated each other."

It seems important to understand the relationship of friendship to emotional health and the investment we are making to a better way of life when we cultivate our friends. Further, it seems important to make a plea for more tolerance and understanding of friends.

As a goal we might say that by the time people reach middle life they need at least four persons with whom they consider themselves good friends. In the first years of marriage responsibilities are less and social circles are wide. But as the years pass, friendships have a way of narrowing down. And it is not too long before one finds that friendships have become few and far between. If one thinks of friends as supportive then one should have at least as many friends as a table has legs. One may argue that there are three-legged tables and stools, but these are usually a little unstable. One had better not fall below four for stability's sake!

We all have to watch out for a tendency to criticize our friends, to find them wanting, and either to ignore them or exclude them from our lives. In most instances it would be safer and better for our emotional well-being to be more magnanimous and socially altruistic; to cultivate patience, tolerance, and compassion with our friends. For friendship calls upon human beings to cherish each other. It calls upon them to invest a certain amount of psychic energy in others. This has been shown to be a requisite for mental health in most people. Too many friendships are allowed to dwindle without thought of their value because of lack of enthusiasm on one side, lack of patience or generosity, an unintentional slight, or lack of understanding of the importance of making the effort necessary to keep friendship alive. Friendship requires an output in time, energy, patience, even money—it will not stay alive indefinitely without some small effort—but it is worth it in the satisfaction, fun, health, and happiness derived from it. All the loneliness, boredom, and dissatisfaction of many people without friends makes it seem appropriate to point out these simple reminders.

One's best friends may be one's neighbors—certainly a desirable state of affairs. Some neighbors just do not have common interests and maintain only a most formal relationship with each other. When neighbors are friends, quarrels between their children, or borrowing of materials and equipment, may give more room for misunderstanding than with those friends who live at a distance. But when an individual speaks heartily and approvingly of his closeness with his neighbors and extolls their good qualities he is probably a person who has given considerable thought to that relationship and will profit from it correspondingly. A friendliness between neighbors creates an emotional healthy climate in which children may grow to advantage. These advantages are often not appreciated until contrasted with a neighborhood where families are feuding, and where name-calling, hostility, and deprecation poison the minds of growing children. Kindly neighbors on the other hand, who accept and approve of each other, seem to intensify greatly a child's trust in the world around him. Many simple small things add up to the total of a child's mental health, one of the most enriching being the freedom to "run in and out" of the homes of neighbors where he is welcome and where he obtains interest, kind words, and occasionally a gift of food. When neighbors reach a point where informality has ceased and where they are not close to each other's children, an undesirable sterility begins to affect the emotional growth of all concerned. Children need to be noticed and thought about and talked about in order to gain a comfortable healthy feeling of self-esteem. Grownups need the same thing. Friends give this to each other by talking about shared ideas, feelings, and experiences. Friends are more than a luxury—they are a necessity. They are important not for *what they can give us,* but because of what inevitably comes back when *we give ourselves to them.*

FRIENDSHIPS AND FAMILY

Some families are on very good terms with relatives after marriage. They see each other frequently and approve of each other—including brothers, sisters, fathers, mothers. Other families meet only out of a sense of duty, on the rarest of holidays, and when they do meet it is to discuss each other's success and accomplishments with envy, to regard each other's material acquisitions jealously, and to criticize the behavior of each other's children. Often, family gatherings are continued out of habit and tradition only, and all parties would be happier to have the time to themselves. Other families meet to gratify the emotional needs of a mother, a father, or "in-laws." Finally, there are other families who by common consent just never get together. One family of eight adult brothers and sisters lived within a fifty-mile radius for ten years and never visited each other. It is not hard to guess that this family did not have a happy childhood together. The best preventive of family alienation is to promote happy living when the children are young. A family of children who have enjoyed themselves while young will probably continue friendly relations later in life.

Some families find it very difficult to accept a son- or daughter-in-law. Parents take great pride in their child and are prone to feel that no outsider is quite good enough for him to marry.

In some families it would doubtless be more mentally healthy if they did not try to meet. Some courageous member of the family group needs to suggest that the gatherings be less frequent, and if this suggestion can be accepted each member could gradually feel free to go his own way and spend his time in ways that are more profitable and enjoyable to him.

Other families, however, have no real animosity toward each other and merely need some member of the family to make the effort of periodic reunion. Thus one family member may put forth more than his share of consistent effort toward unity and sociability, but it is a worthy project and an important one for him to shoulder.

There is no ideal solution for the "in-law" problem whether a family lives together or separated. A friendly relationship, if it can be maintained, demands the greatest understanding and patience on both sides. Young people have moaned, "I did not know that when I married I married my spouse's relatives also." A young person *always* marries his spouse's relatives along with the spouse, whether they live near or far away. They too have to take each other for better or for worse! Parents should do all they can to enjoy their children when they are young and in their teens so that when marriage comes they can relinquish them to their mates. Parents-in-law should as far as possible live their own lives and make themselves relatively unavailable to their married children unless needed. The tremendous number of misguided efforts at helpfulness which turn out to be a burden to young married people should make it plain to parents-in-law that they should redouble their efforts to stay out of the lives of their youngsters. But they mistake their own need for attention as being a need of their children. Only by keeping this important message before adults, however, and helping them to be more self-sufficient in later years will we create a wholesome freedom for young parents so that they can live their own lives independent of impositions from parents-in-law.

This may appear to be a callous recommendation that will spoil a beautiful family relationship by advocating too much independence—even aloofness—between family members. Actually it is a plea for better timing of the life cycle in order to enable parents to enjoy their own children when the children are young and help the children to enjoy their childhood; and it advocates that once childhood and parenthood are gone, adults should step back and relax and leave the young alone. If people can do that—and probably only when they can—will their children welcome them and find them useful in their lives. This timing desideratum poses a real problem in personality flexibility for the person growing older. But it is a problem that must be faced and dealt with, we believe.

THE COMMUNITY

Some families live much to themselves and seem never to stir around very much. There is little sign of life about the house even when children live in it. One rarely sees these people going out or coming in or even in their yards. They plant nothing. One wonders how they get food. If they live in apartments one rarely if ever sees them "on the way." They play no part in community affairs. They do not subscribe to community activities, nor attend community affairs. Some of them never even go to school affairs in which their children participate. Perhaps they do not even vote. They live as if the impingement of other personalities upon them was painful.

There are other families who are quite sociable in things which give them pleasure. They are seen more often but have little or no interest in the community. And there are those families who gravitate toward the things which put the community forward. They serve on committees, sponsor youth projects, are interested in schools, hospitals, new developments. They are called the "do-gooders" by the lazy and indifferent. But every community needs its interested citizens and there is a mental health and a satisfaction to be gained by this participation. Not only does every community need it but everyone in the community needs to do something, make some effort toward its progress. Such activity will keep him younger, more optimistic, more flexible, less lost within himself and less likely to be lonely and a problem to others as he grows older.

KEEPING LOVE ALIVE

Life can become disappointing to people at any age. Some become disappointed in childhood, others in adolescence, and a great many in the third and fourth decades of life. The frequent cause for this is that they cannot keep love alive or make love a reality. A child, for example, keeps hoping that a parent will approve of him and give a wholehearted acceptance to his activities. The child tries and tries. He works in school, practices his music and dancing, lives up to the moral code, and hopes that some day his parent will say, "Good work, child! You have worked long and hard to meet my expectations and I am satisfied with you. You have made me happy. I approve of you and all you have done to meet my demands of you." But too often this does not happen. This is one of the early disappointments in love.

Or the adolescent meets a girl who seems beautiful and desirable. Surely she will approve and accept him. But she is aloof, critical, distant, unaffectionate, inhibited, and complex in mood. So he sets his sights on marriage. Here, he is sure he will find love and acceptance—everyone says so! The church, the books, the movies, his parents tell him that in marriage his dream for love will at last come true. Here, in an atmosphere of intimacy and relaxation, mutual acceptance and approval will at last prevail! But does it? All too often not. Why? Because most human beings can only think of *wanting* love. They are not experienced in *giving* it. When a girl marries she wants her husband to give a large amount of his thought to her happiness. But he gets busy and forgets—or he assumes that since she is not actually complaining she must be satisfied. In any case he fails, periodically, to say something like this: "Are you satisfied, are you happy—are you living your life the way you want to? What can I do to make your life more desirable and meaningful?" She would appreciate this, and in turn might ask, "Am I making you happy? Is marriage to me what you wanted it to be? What can I do to make it better?" If this kind of inner searching could prevail, love might have a better chance of survival. Judging from the statistics on divorce and separation, love dies a slow (or rapid) death within the very institution that is supposed to foster love—marriage.

REACTION TO ILLNESS

Acute illnesses in the form of colds, measles, mumps, and other contagious diseases upset a home temporarily. They may cause temporary concern but they are usually soon over. However, chronic illnesses such as heart disease, poliomyelitis, or tuberculosis, that keep a family member in bed for weeks or months, put a greater emotional strain upon the family. They demand patience, extra care on the part of someone, rearrangement of budgetary plans, resourcefulness in entertaining and keeping up the morale of the sick one. Paradoxically while illness is a tragedy in its way, it may serve the family positively in that it makes members depart occasionally from their ordinary routines. They have an excuse to pause in their rush of obligations. Family members get better acquainted with the sick one. They show their mettle, and he shows his, and the need to sacrifice, to serve and support and encourage the sick one very often makes life more meaningful for everyone in the family.

Some illnesses are so prolonged and so serious as to sadden and burden everyone too much and too long. A family may have to look hard to find the inspiration therefrom and perhaps it cannot be found. Fate does not always seem just in dealing out misfortune; and a tragic, long illness takes its inevitable toll of human emotional resources. A wise physician, clergyman, or other counselor may help the family by pointing out how the illness is disrupting everyone and thus help the members to keep their mental equilibrium. Some physical illness and many mental illnesses may bring guilt. Family members—particularly parents—say to themselves, "What did I fail to do? What should I have done to prevent this?" Rather than face the implication that they had a part in producing the mental illness they complain against treatment efforts and demand the impossible from the physician. They might, instead of looking to the past or scolding the doctor, look to the present and ask "What can I do?" or "How can I co-operate?" and try to understand what is told them. The relatives of mentally ill people usually are implicated some way in the patient's illness. It is of little help either to deny the role or to accept and beat one's breast about it. The most helpful attitude is that of co-operation with the doctor in giving the history, co-operating with treatment, indicating a wish to be of help in any way one can, and then going about one's business as calmly as possible while the physician does what he can.

REACTION TO LOSS

Losses in life are many. We endow people and things with our interest and when they are taken away we suffer—often deeply. The more common losses are:

death of a mate	loss of home by fire or other damage
death of a child	loss of job
death of a parent	loss of savings
death of a sibling	loss of child to the armed services
death of a close friend	loss of youth
loss of child in marriage	loss of illusions
loss of child to a distant job	

It is difficult to say which is more traumatic—the death of a mate or the death of a child. Generally a husband or a wife is needed more for the actual essentials of family life. Either one's death is a great loss. Looking into the future alone is, in any case, painful. Husbands and wives become much more important to each other than they realize. Death points this up sharply and painfully. It enhances so much the appreciation of the one who is gone and can no longer feel the joy of being loved. So does the death of a child. We all withhold our love from the living and suffer so much when we are no longer able to give our love to the dead! When ties of interest are blocked and we are forced to withdraw our libido from the lost object we have cut off an important relationship—an interchange in mutual support and helpfulness—and we are the poorer and the more impoverished emotionally because of it. We need to re-establish ties but we do not want to. None seem to substitute satisfactorily for the one who is lost. But if we are emotionally healthy we accomplish it. Life forces us to do so in self-defense. We let the departed rest and take up life again with a little more love and appreciation for those who are left. When death comes, life seems all negative to those left behind. But slowly those who are left behind find that the departed one has left a gift—a greater sensitivity and appreciation of all others thereafter—a little greater appreciation of life and everything in it. The dead do not die in vain where love has prevailed.

Death of a brother, sister, or close friend has usually less poignancy than death of a beloved parent, a spouse, or a child. Adults should remember that the loss of a sibling has less meaning for a child than for the adult—especially if the survivor is a healthy, happy child—and that many of his morbid feelings about death are transmitted by the parents. The younger the child the less dependent he is upon a sibling and unless he, in some neurotic way, blames himself for the death he merely wishes the family would stop mourning and go about life as usual.

Loss of a child by marriage may cause feelings of depression in one or both parents—more often the parent of the opposite sex. We deplore the excitement of big weddings and wedding parties for the bride and bridegroom, but it has been pointed out that the celebration is really for the parents, who just cannot bear to be left without their child and use the wedding as a means to escape their mourning. They want their friends around them for at least a few hours to compliment and console them. Sometimes a parent will remain in a mildly depressed state for several weeks following the marriage of a child, but rarely is it a matter requiring medical treatment. The mourning ends in due time. The same reaction often occurs in a parent when a child leaves for military service or to take up a job at some distance. A period of social activity and a few letters generally cures the disorder.

Loss of home by fire, flood, or other catastrophe may precipitate a feeling of being deserted by the good powers and some depression of spirits may ensue, but the resulting activity necessitated by such a catastrophe is usually effective therapy.

Loss of a long-held job by business reverses or retirement may cause real anxiety and depression. It brings to the fore the feeling of not being wanted or needed any more and this results in a loss of self-esteem. Loss of savings can greatly threaten security and raise fantasies of physical hardship and social ostracism, with the same emotional result. A more imperceptible loss, but just as real, is the loss of youth, loss of attractiveness and physical agility, or loss of the dream that excitement or romance lie just around the corner. The latter is a disillusionment common to many in middle age, who feel empty and insecure as a result. Just as children keep hoping their parents will one day become magnanimous, so a wife keeps hoping her husband will stop drinking and become chivalrous—or he hopes his wife will stop nagging and be more attractive. Too often these hopes perish and the loss of them constitutes causes of depression not easy to perceive.

REACTIONS TO MIDDLE AGE

By middle life a man should have demonstrated his capacity for achieving some success in his business or professional career, and a woman should have demonstrated her ability as a mother and homemaker or have made good in her career. If success has not occurred, anxiety may result—taking such various forms as the excessive use of alcohol, psychophysiologic symptoms, pessimism, feelings of persecution and so on. (See Psychoneurotic Disorders, Chapter XV.) Many people become less active in middle life—"slowing down," they call it. Some slowing down may be natural, but it can be so extreme as to smother libidinal gratification. So it behooves those in middle age to remain active in the community, keep informed, discuss current issues with others, take a few adult-education courses, or renew themselves by taking a vacation in some place where they have never been before. New experiences keep the mind active and refreshed. The single man or woman may need to work harder to keep his or her life active and meaningful. Married family members have a way of impinging upon each other and keeping life busy, but it becomes easy for the single man or woman to be a recluse, and this has its dangers.

Family life will change at middle age as children grow up and leave for schools and colleges. Some parents can fill the gaps left by these departures by doing the things they have long wanted to do. Others are upset by the departures and feel lost and useless. Some mothers, for instance, in an effort to remain important, appeal to their youngsters to come home more often than is good for the latter's educational careers. Such parents should divert their interests into local affairs, no matter how hard a task this may be. Husbands should be interested and supportive but insistent that the mothers' lives cannot center too much on the children, and the clergyman and family doctor may have to add their counsel to this difficult situation.

MENOPAUSE

Just as the activity of the sexual glands comes on gradually at puberty, so it recedes gradually during menopause. The age at which this decrease in the activity of the sexual glands occurs varies between forty and fifty, forty-five being the average. The terms *menopause* and *climacteric* are both applied to this period. Critical events are always arising in people's lives. Puberty, adolescence, marriage, parenthood are all critical events occurring to both active and inactive people, and the menopause—and the changes associated with it—is just another event that has to be met.

In the past, thinking has not been very clear about the menopause syndrome. Many people have incorrectly ascribed to the cessation of glandular activity practically all the symptoms of the menopause. In discussing puberty we said that the onset of menstruation in the girl should be accepted with equanimity; that we should not expect this natural physiological function to interfere in any great degree with the woman's activities or with her emotional life; and that when people do not expect difficult menstruation, it generally will not occur. Such confident optimism is not quite so proper in regard to the menopause, for women who have lived unwisely between the ages of twelve and forty-two can build up a great many regrets over which to be irritable, depressed, remorseful, bitter, and pessimistic when the menopause appears. In addition to these mood disturbances, physiologic symptoms often occur in the menopause such as hot flushes, cold shivers, sensations of alternating heat and cold accompanied by perspiration, dizziness, cardiac palpitation, headaches, anxiety attacks, nausea, fatigue, insomnia, and loss of appetite. These symptoms may be either mild or severe, sometimes severe enough to necessitate going to a mental hospital.

Studies of the personalities of those suffering from severe menopause neurosis or psychosis reveal similarities in personality makeup. Such a woman tends to be sensitive and to live a rather isolated social existence. She has not been warm and gregarious, rather one of those women who proudly declare they never visit around much but stay at home and mind their own business. In other words, she has made a virtue of the fact that she was afraid to associate with people or that she did not like people sufficiently to be friendly. Usually she has been strict and pedantic in training her children, often excessively religious, meticulous about cleanliness, many times the excellent housekeeper in whose home no one can be comfortable. She has been sexually frigid, ungenerous, and prone to be critical. Such women take little from and give little to the world, so that by the time menopause is reached they not only have no more activity of the sexual glands, but they likewise have become emotionally and spiritually impoverished.

It is felt that the personality plays a larger role in the whole symptom picture of the menopause than the cessation of glandular activity in itself. The physician and the family used to think that any symptom that occured around this period of life was due to a deficiency in the ductless glands, and the remedy was a prescription for an ovarian glandular preparation, of which every drug house has at least one to three products. It is important to remember that a certain number of women go through the change of life without any distressing symptoms. Dr. J. P. Pratt of Chicago undertook to treat women suffering from menopausal symptoms by using two preparations, one oil with theelin and one oil without theelin. He asked his colleagues to send him patients suffering from the menopausal syndrome for him to treat with a glandular preparation while his colleagues made observations and reported the patients' progress. Dr. Pratt found that just as many women improved with the sterile solution—that is, the oil without theelin—as did with the solution that contained ovarian substance. Benedek and Rubenstein made studies of the menstrual period in an effort to determine whether a correlation exists between glandular activity and the accompanying psychology. Daily studies were made both of vaginal smears and basal body temperatures, together with psychoanalytic observations of the emotional life of the patients. When the findings were compared, it was found that certain types of thinking are associated at the various phases of the menstrual cycle. It is significant that in the first ten days after menstruation a woman's ideas about heterosexual activity and impregnation are much more active than they are in the last part of the menstrual period, when she is inclined to be much more passive and uninterested in sexual activity, more inclined to take care of herself than to want to undertake motherhood.

During the period of menopause some women become panicky with the thought that the energy which leads to sexual pleasure, romance, children, and motherhood is leaving them, and believe it can be replaced artificially by an injection. This feeling is true to the extent that the body has been producing a vital ovarian substance since the age of twelve and is now ceasing to produce it. But if a woman has not found love, romance, a happy marriage, enjoyment in her children, and interests to have made life worth while before she reaches forty-five, she is not likely to get these satisfactions from an injection of a glandular substance now. The same thing is true of men and their desires to find strength, joy, happiness, or youthful vigor through ductless glandular preparations. Nature does her best and provides people with the source of life (as sexual glandular substance is looked upon as being). However, one of the inconsistencies of human nature is that a man or woman erects many anxieties, fears, prohibitions, and prejudices, and deprives himself (or herself) of happiness until forty-five, and then, finding it disappearing, runs around madly trying to find a doctor with a syringe who will inject the means of happiness into him (or her). If a person has not found happiness and romance before forty-five, the chances are much more limited of finding them after.

In a problem of the menopausal syndrome the personality factor that has produced this menopausal symptom should be treated, and the doctor should not depend upon ductless glandular preparations too much, whether out of a bottle or a syringe. Women who are not enjoying bringing up their children, who are working too hard and taking life in deadly seriousness, should have it pointed out to them that if they continue this course, they are almost certain to be tired, disillusioned people at fifty. Doctors should give them a word of warning and thus help to prevent this serious emotional disturbance that comes with the cessation of menstruation.

A woman of forty-two began to suffer with irregularity of menstruation, headaches, indigestion, insomnia, nightmares, weakness, and fatigue. She was given replacement therapy for months without any change in her condition. The uterus was curetted to relieve the menorrhagia, but relief was only temporary. She grew more anxious, depressed and sleepless all the time, and finally became bedridden. When seen psychiatrically she said her most distressing symptoms were the terrible dreams (nightmares) and the palpitation, sweating, and terror that accompanied her awakening, which resulted in her remaining awake for hours afraid to go to sleep again. Her history revealed that she had a very rigid childhood training in both toilet and sex matters. Her life as a child was, as she put it, "a nightmare in regard to things like that." Her dreams were almost always related to these two functions: she would be in a public place and need to go to the toilet and be unable to find it and in panic would wet or soil herself or the environment; or she would be in a toilet and the bowl would overflow, soiling the floor, and she would be anxious about the possible punishment; or she would be in public partly clothed, and in a panic that she would be seen; or she would be chased by an ugly-looking man who she feared would assault her.

We explained to her the origin of these dreams and the ubiquitous nature of the conflicts, reassured her about losing her mind, got her to look upon sex and toilet training with less seriousness—with the result that her sleep became more restful, she ate better, her strength came back, and in two and a half months she was able to be up and about her work again after two years of suffering from what we regarded as an anxiety reaction rather than any glandular deficiency.

Since this is a book on psychiatry and since replacement therapy is a highly specialized treatment in itself, we refer the reader to any good current textbook on endocrinology for directions as to the careful study and management of cases that actually need endocrine treatment.

REACTION TO MIDDLE YEARS IN MEN

Whether men undergo a change of life similar to that of women is a question that has been raised in the past and that is still being argued pro and con by medical men.

We do not feel that there is anything in the man comparable to the menopausal syndrome in the woman. The cessation of glandular activity in the female is relatively rapid, usually taking place in two or three years. We have no evidence that sexual glandular activity in the male undergoes any similar sudden decline or cessation. The process in the male is much more gradual and goes hand in hand with all other evidences of aging. Consequently men do not have to undergo any of the discomforts of a too rapid readjustment of the ductless glands; nor do they have to face a particular crisis in their ability to reproduce such as women do with the cessation of menstruation.

It is true that at various ages men after forty can have *symptoms* akin to those of the woman at the so-called change of life. Like women, they can experience anxiety, irritability, depression of spirits, insomnia, digestive disturbances, headaches, tingling sensations in the extremities, but these disturbances are psychological in origin.

They conform to the neuroses of other age periods; to treat such a syndrome in a man with replacement therapy—which means giving ductless glandular substance by mouth or hypodermically—and ignore the personality and the life situation would be to practice medicine incompletely. When replacement therapy relieves a man of his symptoms, such relief is largely obtained on the basis of suggestion. For the large number of persons who would not respond to such therapy, the symptoms are liable to become worse because the diagnosis induces anxiety in such a person and produces unnecessary conflict. If he is not undergoing any crisis in the ductless glandular system, particularly in the activity of the sex glands, such a diagnosis may start him worrying. He may feel he is weak, become discouraged, and imagine his is a hopeless case. Men can be very sensitive to any implication that anything is wrong with their sexual power.

A man of fifty who was going through one such period of neurotic disturbance came to the doctor. He complained of insomnia, headache, inability to concentrate, depression of spirits, indigestion, worry over the future, and a great reluctance to mix with people, with a great desire to be by himself. His history revealed that he had a high-strung, irritable father and a more placid mother, and that he never liked school or mixed well. Later at work he never tried to make friends, always thinking he could get along without them. Instead of trying to cultivate friends, he kidded his colleagues and engaged in sharp arguments and criticisms with his friends when out socially. In this way he thought he would be "different, outstanding, and not one of the average mob." As a result he was not very popular. Now he felt people disliked him for this, yet he was afraid to be quiet and reserved in a group. He had to try to take hold of the conversation and "kid people," as he put it, in order that he be regarded as clever. In business he never asked a customer about his family or recreations but attended strictly to business and—strangely enough for a salesman—never told a joke. In other words, he never indulged in the kind of casual friendliness that goes with living and working. He considered it a waste of time and felt that he did not need to resemble other people in this regard because he would be outstanding in his own particular way. He planned to work hard and retire at fifty. Now he *was* fifty and he could not retire. A crash in the stock-market interfered with his plans and he never recovered financially. Even if he could have retired it would not have solved his problem. He would not have known what to do with himself because although he liked to work hard and keep to himself, at the same time he had the fear that he was going to lose his mind or that he was going to end in the poorhouse. This man had come to grief because he had lived a life that led to emotional impoverishment, and not because he was undergoing any so-called change of life.

To get well he had to be taught to take a different attitude toward people and seek his cure in better social and family relationships. His difficulty in concentrating, forgetting people's names, was merely an exaggeration of his tremendous lack of interest and his indifference to what was being said to him. It was not something new: he had been leading up to it for twenty-five years. He never cared about the thoughts and feelings of other people but only about furthering his own ends. Now his attitude had become a little more exaggerated and he found that it actually interfered with his work. His inner feelings, his misery, headaches, indigestion, were secondary conversion symptoms of his upset emotional state. These syndromes appearing in men, similar to the menopausal syndromes in women, are neuroses and not an outgrowth of any change in sexual glandular activity.

LATER MATURITY *

Few fields of human endeavor are more riddled with preconceptions, prejudice, and popular misinformation than the study of the process of psychological aging. The tendency of a vigorous, young, mobile, and productive culture such as ours to use its very recency of arrival on the world scene and its fresh memories of conquest, emancipation, and titanic accomplishment as the values and prototypes of human development has succeeded in overvaluing a somewhat ambiguous quality called youthfulness as the be-all and end-all of life. As a consequence, many men of fifty with a life expectancy half again as long as they have already lived view the next quarter-century as a barren time of unfulfilled hopefulness and regretful disappointment. Thereafter, metaphorically speaking, they

* By Maurice B. Linden, M.D., Director, Division of Mental Health, Department of Public Health, City of Philadelphia; Assistant Professor of Psychiatry, University of Pennsylvania School of Medicine; Chairman, Conjoint Mental Health Board, Southeastern Pennsylvania Region; Chairman, Committee on Aging, American Psychiatric Association.

may walk backward through life with their attention wistfully focused on their younger years, only to stumble eventually into later maturity with pathetic unpreparedness. The frenzied efforts to regain their balance and composure, the frantic scramble to find their bearings, may lead to a stunned perplexity and profound excited confusion from which they may have great difficulty emerging, if they recover at all.

This picture, with many minor variations, is seen so frequently in our culture that we have come to regard it as a logical expectation among older people. But we never quite know where to place our boundary lines for aging. While one man of fifty-eight is already rocking away his days into oblivion, another at seventy-eight is writing his history-making memoirs. Where one sixty-year-old has closed his last book and prepares to contemplate his dubious knowledge with smug self-deception, another at seventy-four is still wresting important secrets from Nature's locked stores. Many men at sixty-five have retired from life to indolent stagnation. An occasional man is found who has changed his life's work in the middle sixties and has thereafter followed a totally new skill into the nineties.

Now we must inquire of ourselves, "Who are the exceptions— the few, for whom every minute of life is a new experience; or the many, who, perhaps, have not fulfilled their potential?"

There is a widespread tendency among people to regard progress through life as an uphill development from infancy to some vague plateau of prime called middle life, followed by a general decline. This point of view fails to take into account the fact that different qualities and faculties of the human organism have different rates of achieving prime, and that—throughout most of life's course—for every faculty that has reached its zenith of achievement there is another that has yet to reach its highest developmental goal.

A generalized, indiscriminate decline is not a tenable notion, for the reason that an individual's intellectual, emotional, and behavioral growth consists of just such countless separate trends, each having its own particular rate of development and its role in human action.

This diversity can be illustrated with some special faculties that have already been studied carefully and treated statistically. Taking the sense of hearing as an example, we find that its peak acuity has been reached at age 20 more or less. In the field of vision, a variable peak development of quickness of visual perception, contrast sensitivity, and flicker-fusion sensitivity occurs around the age range 25–30. Reaction time in motor response shows peak achievement (shortest time) at about age 17. There is a decline in average scores on intelligence tests in the twenties with peak development around age 25. Certainly the greatest potential for childbearing occurs between ages 15 and 35, and concurrent with it is found the familiar constellation of behavior designed to enhance physical attractiveness. Due to social customs and the exigencies of reality the actual peak incidence of childbearing occurs in a slightly older age range.

Now, if we were to consider only the few abilities thus far enumerated as our base line for comparison, then obviously a person is "getting old" in each modality after age 30. But what do these elements of human capability taken together describe? We may justifiably conclude that they are part and parcel of man's sexual endowment, for are not sharpness of eye, acuteness of hearing, fleetness of muscular action, rapidity of calculation, and physical attractiveness all integrally related to the success of ventures into the social competition of courtship?

But obviously a man's total performance is not restricted to the small number of components just mentioned. Let us look further. Take, for example again, the field of motor response. It is found that *proficiency* of motor reaction achieves a plateau of peak development between the ages of 40 and 50. Considering once more the intelligence tests, we find that while there does appear to be a decline after 25 in performance and certain problem-solving sub-tests, subsequent losses are small, if at all, in *vocabulary, information,* and *similarities.* In fact it is found that vocabulary and the ability to define words in many people have not yet reached peak achievement in the age mode 60–69. Factor-correlation tests reveal that with increasing age there is apparently an increase in specificity of performance. And those who devise and give tests agree that the testing systems now available fail to allow for *increased knowledge* and *experience* of older people. In tests evaluating learning and memory it is found that the magnitude of loss depends on the nature of the test material—the least loss occurring in *practical* knowledge.

Already we begin to see that certain functions of mind and body that were just beginning in youth achieve increasing importance in the older individual, while the reverse of this is also true. Further considerations, however, are needed to give our panoramic view of human development a greater degree of completeness.

Studies of intellectual functioning disclose that significant contributions in chemistry, physics, biology, and medicine are made less frequently after age 60, but leaders in the fields of legislation, jurisprudence, diplomacy, military and naval strategy, religion, and education are significantly older. In a study of 2,607 scientists it was found that most made their major contributions between the ages of 30 and 70. It is not unimportant that more than 20 of these savants realized their major achievement after the age of 70.

Further interesting factors are found in the area of human attitudes and interests. Popular preconception now holds that there is an increase in conservatism and a restriction in interests in older people. However, a carefully controlled study of comparable groups of younger and older people failed to show any significant difference in conservatism on an attitudinal scale. And an even more important observation was made; that in a test situation to alter opinion, changes in the younger testees were probably due to uncritical acceptance of statements made by older authorities. Evaluation of a group of 2,000 nonpsychiatric office patients ranging in age from 10 to 90 failed to show any significant shifts in emotionality or instability in the older subjects. Investigators have been unable to prove an increased incidence in neuroticism or poor personal adjustment with increasing age at least up to about 60. Other studies also suggest that in later senescence such factors as economic security, late retirement, and congenial housing and living arrangements are important for good adjustment.

If we were to attempt to enunciate criteria of aging, we find, by employing the dissected segments of human behavior, that a person's vision is growing old after 25, but he is still young in proficiency of motor response. Or, he is aging in hearing acuity after age 20, but he is an infant in comprehension of government. His abilities to complete series, arrange pictures, and note opposites on circumscribed intelligence tests are declining after 25, but his vocabulary conceptualization is just developing. At 25 we might say a person is already too old to compete successfully in many gruelling contests of brawn, but he is young in the possession of practical information, specificity of performance, and the understanding of law, religion, and education.

Current attitudes toward the phenomenon of aging can be reduced to relative absurdities, because the values for comparison are ambiguous, too isolated, and biased. An effort to understand human behavior must take into account the total person and must relate him to the society in which he lives. It is in this realization that we find important clues for further consideration. In short, we may say that the younger a person is, the closer he is to his instincts; the older he grows, barring interferences, the more may his ego develop. Thus, while younger or less mature people are relatively self-centered, pleasure-seeking, and concerned with a somewhat narrow social outlook more related to self-gratification than to benefiting society, study suggests that normal older people have a broader social outlook, appear to be more altruistic, more protective of younger people, and more earnestly dedicated to preserving the indispensable systems of culture. Such attitudes, of course, are not lacking in younger people; they are present in a rudimentary state and are subject to further maturation.

This peculiarity of human beings may be related to man's unique acquisitions: a psychic organ for internal censorship and self-scrutiny, the capacity to idealize, complex verbal communication of abstractions, and societal organization with intricate cultures based upon postnatal transfer and recording of information. Whereas in other animal societies the adult has completed its usefulness following reproduction, the deposit of provender, and limited rearing of the progeny, human adulthood possesses a potential continuous post-reproductive usefulness. The probable natural tendency of the postreproductive mature individual is to turn to thought and activities that will preserve and improve a culture. In this sense the mature mind concerns itself with conserving social mores, transmitting and perpetuating judgment, fostering subordinate leadership, preserving archives of knowledge, sharpening and communicating skills, and maintaining and developing the indispensable tools of mankind.

Actually, the more a person matures the higher position on the social pyramid of responsibility does he occupy. If this be phrased in psychoanalytical concepts, then it is clearly seen that what we are considering here is degrees of object relationships, or degrees of capacity to love others than oneself. Let us trace this through life to later maturity. The infant is loved and someone is responsible for him. The child loves jealously, but is dependent. The adolescent loves experimentally and his sense of responsibility is similarly inconstant.

The young adult loves another person more definitely and develops a sense of protectiveness toward his mate. A little later in young adulthood his love and sense of responsibility embrace his family group. By middle adulthood his affection covers his family, and his responsibility is directed toward their social interests with the consequence that it includes proximal families. The later mature person then invests his love interest in his family of families, and his concomitant feeling of responsibility is projected onto an ever-enlarging body social.

In accordance with this sequence of events an increase in maturation should be paralleled by an increase in altruism and selflessness as well as of an intrinsic capacity to guide and to protect. The fact that what we have thus far discussed sounds like hypothesis and conjecture rather than demonstrable reality is mute testimony to the effect that there are very likely sociological and psychological events that frustrate full personality development in later maturity. Instead, we see a very large number of people with only a partial fulfillment of their ego potential and with frank emotional disturbances becoming manifest with aging.

For all men who may live to late and very late maturity there is a certain degree of inevitableness that physical and mental functions will decline. But the emotional disturbances of aging appear to be neurotically and culturally induced.

The physical nature of the aging process is a highly controversial area of study. The greatest difficulty lies in the problem of distinguishing biological-physiological aging from disease processes. Some extremists have concluded that all the changes in function that lead to death are pathological. They are thus drawn to the logical impasse that death is a preventable accident. It may well be that it is this type of thinking, conscious or unconscious, that has led many clinicians and investigators to employ a wide variety of treatment systems apparently directed toward fancied rejuvenation, "the fountain of youth" notion, and immortality. It seems far more prudent to heed the admonitions of able biologists and educators who have arrived at the intriguing philosophical paradox that death of the individual is a vital process.

The conviction forces itself upon us that man is a self-conscious animal whose love of pleasure and cultural immaturity have given him an exaggerated and expanded view of his own worth in the scheme of realities. If this point of reference is essentially correct, then we are further led to the realization that the illusions, over-valuations, and unilateral ambitions generated during the young periods of life are destined to succumb to disillusionment and dis-appointment.

The time of life at which an individual's self-deluding psychic devices may reveal themselves to him, when his egocentric ideals may become subject to vaporization, and when he comes face to face with inexorable reality depends upon the quantity of stress he can tolerate and the amount of mental energy available to him to poten-tiate his self-deceiving psychic armament. Any period of physio-logical change and upheaval thus becomes a time of great stress as well as a psychological event in which fraying defenses require special attention. The more a person's emotional energies have been bound to defensive measures, then the less are such energies available for personality repair. In a military metaphor, the soldiers who are repelling the enemy cannot simultaneously be the reserves.

The importance of the psychological implications of menopause in women has been discussed in a foregoing section. While we do not feel that there is anything in men quite comparable to the almost sudden cessation of certain glandular activities in women, it is likely that a more gradual series of involutional changes takes place in them. In both sexes there is witnessed a somewhat diminished sexual appetite with increasing years. Whether this indicates an actual reduction in primary instinctual energies, or a progressive increase in the psychological systems that conduct the instincts into secondary channels, cannot now be determined with certainty. The viewpoint presented earlier in this section suggests that the second sequence of events may be the normal one.

What constitutes normal aging from 65 to 70 on can be only vaguely sketched at best. Individual differences are great at this time of life. Some people are already senile in the early portion of this age period. In them the combination of factors to be described presently has already taken such a huge toll from their available resources that their losses are beyond replenishment. Others retain much, if not all, of their natural endowments into very late maturity, and they cease functioning as a a completely efficient unit only when death supervenes. An example of the latter type of person is found in the following very abbreviated case history which is remarkable because it differs so markedly from what our education and experience have led us to expect. Dr. David B. Schuster of Rochester, New York, reported a study of a 106-year-old man in a recent psychiatric journal. This man was born in 1844 in a hamlet that later became Atlanta, Georgia. His father was a successful lawyer who later became a judge and who was killed in a freak accident at the age of 70. His mother, of whom the patient spoke very highly, was the disciplinarian in the family. She died in 1932 at the age of 108. The patient described his parents as well mated; he had never known them to quarrel. At 25 he married a 17-year-old girl who bore him six children. His wife and youngest child, aged 15, died in the Iroquois Theatre fire in Chicago in December, 1903. He was so upset by the loss of his wife and child that for six months or so at the age of 59 he "couldn't settle down to anything" and traveled around the world. He was a brewery worker and brewmaster until in 1907, at age 63, he grew interested in changing his career and trained as a chef, later following this work in major hotels until he was well into his nineties, at which time a varicose ulcer condition of his legs forced him to quit work. Having lost almost his entire fortune in the 1929 market crash, he never did completely regain his losses. At age 101 he accepted public-welfare aid because it allowed him a certain amount of independence. "Never wild for women," he noted some decline in libido in his seventies and at age 106 he still had sexual interests accompanied by inconstant impotence. His physical condition was very good, showing only a mild degree of anemia and minimal impairment of heart function in addition to the periodically occurring leg ulcers. His mental-status examinations showed him to be of at least superior intelligence and functioning at an average level of efficiency. He gave the impression of being an alert, vital, and versatile individual with very strong resources whose main anxieties were concerned with a fear of regression and impotency. The patient accepted small amounts of money from his 78-year-old son, but refused to live with him because doing so would deprive him of his independence.

The outstanding features in this case study are the lack of dementia, the presence of emotional reserves enabling him to rebound from psychological hurts, and the very high degree of self-dependence. This man at the great age of 106 made up for his personal family losses by assuming and enjoying the role of patriarch in his community, which he was still able to do with deftness, finesse, and relaxed good humor.

We all know that only a small number of people have been known to fare as well and as long as the man in the example above. A much larger group of people in very late maturity show a progressively developing down-curve of functions both physiological and psychological. These individuals show a *psychological recession* that parallels *physiological recession* and which must be differentiated from the massive, almost sudden *regression* seen in the psychoses of the aged to be discussed presently.

The phenomenon of recession in very late aging yields a clinical picture that almost exactly resembles the stages of infantile psychosexual evolution in reverse. It could be described as a retracing of steps backward from adolescence to foetal infancy. These people as a rule are significantly older than those who develop severe emotional disturbances in late senescence, and they also usually are seen to go through the steps of recession somewhat more rapidly. Recession may be regarded to a certain extent as the final rapid decline before death, a decline that moves through area after area of psychological fixations. This recessive process is probably one of the reasons why the aged seem to resemble each other in behavior, but it also accounts for differences among them, when the fact is considered that all children have certain experiences in common as well as many that are highly specific within a given family. The process of psychological recession brings into prominence memories, values, and modes of behavior that were among the conscious experiences of childhood. These attitudes were apparently subsequently suppressed out of consciousness through the acquisition of acculturated ways of behaving, only to be uncovered again during the decline of physiological senility.

When the processes of regression in the severe sudden emotional catastrophes of late age and of recession in the somewhat gentler decline are not impeded, they eventuate in the following pattern of behavior that can be perceived clinically. There is first an upsurge of an adolescent type of rebellion that is closely followed by a return of increased sexual interests. The latter has as its companion a tendency for the aged person to fall in love with inappropriate people and to return to masturbation. The next step in decline is often a deceptive one, in which partial healing processes appear to have occurred.

People at this level function better socially. Their first panic has passed and some of their familiar ways of behaving have resumed effectiveness. However, they show a certain dependency and uncertainty and require frequent reassurance. This period can be called *senile latency*. As further recession takes place and the hastily repaired psychic defenses proceed to disintegrate, there is again an increase in sexual activity, this time accompanied by strong feelings of envy and jealousy that are very frequently disguised, distorted, and attributed to other people. The next stage witnesses a return to personal untidiness, incontinence of bowel and bladder, a tendency to hoard sundry, often useless, items, and a trend toward bellicosity as a defense against dependency needs and desires to be loved. Concurrently there is a progressive enfeeblement of the whole body and an advancing disturbance in the ability to maintain an erect posture. Language communication recedes to nonsense syllables; nutritive intake becomes limited to soft foods and fluids; rage reactions are enacted; continuous bed care becomes necessary, while the aged person at this infancy-like level wallows in his own wastes; cute, coy, and charming bits of behavior alternate with periods of abject detachment finally receding to complete withdrawal, obviously hallucinated thought life, and hyperirritability. The supervention of death then completes a life cycle.

Thus far we have seen many similarities between the recession of the aged and infantile progression. Akin to the stages of childhood development, those of senile decline do not necessarily follow precisely the simplified and schematic course as we have outlined it. There may be much overlapping, and so-called stages may run concurrently rather than sequentially. But there is one major difference between children and the aged. The latter have had what children are developing—a reasoning, responsible, experienced, and informed psychological organ that we call the ego. We shall see later on that it is this mental element that makes psychological treatment possible even among the very aged.

REACTION TO ADVANCING YEARS

If we are to understand the needs of people as they grow older we must take into account the multiplicity of factors that combine in their make-up. Many of the important elements contributing to the creation of a total personality have been discussed throughout this book. With respect to the matter of aging, certain considerations are essential here. They may be outlined as follows:

1. Attitudes toward aging
   a. Arising out of childhood
   b. Arising out of the social order
      and group (ethnic) variations
2. Neurotic problems
   a. Loss of defenses
   b. Intensification of defenses
   c. Psychological regression
   d. Psychological recession
3. Physiological involution and changes.

A leading motif in every individual's personality structure comprises the mental picture he has of himself, the psychological imagery he has constructed of his parents and parental substitutes, the ideals and attendant fantasies that are the substance of his ambitions, and an internalized indefinable composite of social trends that may be considered the cultural atmosphere in which he lives. Such items, with certain added psychological features, merge together in a person into what may be called his self-concept. In accord with this, many people have a feeling, sometimes conscious, sometimes secret, that they can never expect anything more out of life for themselves than was characteristic of their own origin. A successful business man of sixty, who was a first-generation American of foreign-born parents and whose father had been a common laborer, came to psychiatric care because of insomnia, irritability, feelings of impending doom, and a growing desire to avoid the company of other people. He was an intelligent man with great drive and much more native talent and ability than he acknowledged. During analytic psychotherapy, to which he devoted himself with the same intensity and eagerness that characterized his activities in the business world, he exclaimed one day with much emotion, "All my life I have felt that I have been living a sham existence—that my business isn't mine—my money isn't my own—everything would be taken away some day. Everyone would find out that I am just a fraud—that I am nothing but a European peasant who had no right to be anything but a worker in a steel mill like my father."

The manner in which people like this man are helped to get well will be reserved for the section dealing with the treatment of older persons. A study of his problems is pertinent here because it reveals a number of highly significant determinants of character that contribute to emotional problems during aging. This man discovered that every stage of his growth from early childhood forward had been characterized by twofold feelings of love and hate, acceptance and rejection, directed toward his parents and analogous representatives of culture. The love feelings permitted him to absorb their education of him as well as elements of their very personalities. The attitudes of resentment, repugnance, and rejection he felt toward them made him feel uneasy. He had later succeeded in removing out of consciousness the hostile impulses, but the guilt they engendered had given him lifelong anxiety.

His father, who spoke broken English and who had suffered some degree of cultural segregation in his community, was excessively proud of his own origin, but in sharp contrast he had always wanted his son to be an outstanding student, to speak English eloquently, and to rise to great social success in a business or profession. Exhausted, weakened, and with pathetic resignation, the father became a mere shell of himself physically and emotionally before he was 65.

The point became clear in treatment that the patient had been living in constant fear that he was in the shadow of his father's fate. His sleeplessness was his own effort to remain alert, alive, and active and to ward off the psychological death that sleep symbolized. The irritability was partly a re-enactment of his father's behavior in premature senility. The impending doom was in part his father's degradation coupled with a readiness to feel persecuted that had been instilled in him as part of his minority-group upbringing. The avoidance of people was a self-imposed isolation that resembled the loneliness of the late senescent state toward which he had felt relentlessly drawn.

The foregoing case history contains many elements, but for our discussion it is well to point out some of its most interesting factors, for there is a certain degree of universality of its principles. The rebellious, envious, and aggressive drives of the child toward his elders become repressed as he goes forward in life, but later in senescence, due to the frailty of threatened emotional defenses, these forgotten impulses make their appearance again. When such elder-rejecting attitudes occur in an elder, they clearly become self-rejection. Superimposed on this psychological component is another, the attitude that the external social milieu exercises toward its aged. American culture, which appears to place a very heavy emphasis on the values of youth, does not seem as yet to have integrated the quiet stability, dignity, and conservative philosophy of mature wisdom into its living pattern. Our elders are neither devotedly revered nor yet boldly discarded. Our general attitude toward the aged, with some exceptions, may be described as grudging acceptance. Such offhand tolerance of the elders amounts to scorn and disdain in youth. In senescence such learned attitudes are also perceived as elder-rejection.

A third factor of unmistakable significance is the changes in a person's circle of friends and loved ones that take place as he grows older. The children grow up and strike out for themselves, friends and relatives become numerically depleted through death, and the neighborhood community undergoes progressive alterations.

The American melting pot of ideologies and groupings is virtually a sociologic potpourri of cultures among which are various forms of family attitudes toward children and elders. As American children move beyond the circumscribed family confines into the greater external culture, their subsequent efforts to develop a new membership result in an intensification of feelings of rejection against their own origin. Confused identifications may result from this conflict and may develop into personality problems characterized by psychological inconsistencies, ambiguous ideals, and excessive defensiveness. Such internal problems often eventuate in long-smoldering ambivalent attitudes, which flourish into renewed intensity with advancing years.

The aggregate of rejections to which older people are exposed in our culture requires more personality strength than a large proportion of them possess. For to all the difficulty that elder-discarding causes there must yet be added the factor of the individualized neurotic traits and reactions that are the crop of emotional problems planted in childhood. Such neuroses are camouflaged during the childbearing period by superficial modes of behavior designed to enhance personal attractiveness and charm. However, when individuals enter the conservative stages of life, the covering behavioral systems become superfluous, are given up, and the real personality is revealed beneath. The real person, exposed to rejection, suffering a continuous internal readjustment to physiological subtleties, and without a *raison d'être,* may enter into a changed psychological state.

In spite of the actual physiological transformations that take place in senescence, the postclimacteric involution of various organs, the reduction in body substance, and the diminished metabolic needs, the commonly encountered *symptoms of aging* are to a very great extent profound attitudinal reactions. They are usually found to represent psychological distortions of counterculture rebellion, a failure to accept the inexorableness of aging, neurotic responses to frustration, tantrum equivalents growing out of loneliness, personal loss, and deprivation, and a frenetic blindness to reality and the future. Losing sight of his real attributes and resources, regarding whose value he always entertained neurotic skepticism, the senescent falls back upon his long-familiar ways of behaving. Partly due to his envy of youth, whose deportment he now attempts to emulate, and in part due to his having little choice in the matter because of his insufficient self-comprehension, he resorts to devices that he would be expected to have outgrown and which are therefore inappropriate, *passé,* and even ludicrous. Everyone is familiar with the middle-aged man who overexerts himself in games at the church picnic or who, in an inept burst of energy and resolve of a weekend, proceeds to renovate and re-landscape his and his neighbor's yard as well as the adjacent empty lot, only to discover after a week of lumbago and crankiness that "he ain't what he used to be." In the same category are the older women who overdress in the latest extreme fashions and generate a form of amused disappointment in those who view them up close, or the men and women of advanced years who fling caution to fate at a party and engorge themselves on rare liquids and rich snacks only to awaken the following day with ample reason for regret and self-reproach.

It is only a step from the unpleasant insights such experiences generate in the senescent to the condition of *partial surrender* in which neurotic disturbances appear. The very frequently encountered complaints such as insomnia, bowel difficulties, irritability, depression of mood, headaches, tingling sensations in the extremities, flushes, vague feelings of uneasiness, digestive disturbances, and a host of somatic preoccupations are to be viewed as being of psychological origin in a major proportion of older people. Many of the trials at treatment that employ palliative medications, endocrine substitution extracts, and manipulative measures do not alleviate causes; whatever benefit is obtained occurs largely through the power of suggestion.

When superficial treatment methods fail and suggestion is no longer effective the next step in *senescent decline* may follow. There develop feelings of hopelessness, isolation, friendlessness, uselessness, lowered self-esteem and reduced self-confidence. The panic and anxiety thus generated become terrifying and develop into a passively suicidal frame of mind. A great deal of emotional energy is then mustered for the purpose of re-establishing disintegrating emotional defenses. The mind thus occupied with repairing itself becomes further detached from external reality, which it is only too glad to avoid anyway. Simultaneously the frenzied efforts at reconstruction drive the individual to a state of emotional exhaustion. Clinically this is seen as lassitude, torpor, waning alertness, memory impairment, confusion, disorientation, and feeble restlessness. The interplay of psychological and physiological forces will ultimately produce the progressive breakdown we have termed recession.

The almost universally characteristic sequence of events that occurs among the senile and emotionally disturbed aged is as follows:

1. Cultural rejection
2. Self-rejection
3. Anxiety and panic
4. Psychophysiological exhaustion
5. Psychosexual regression and recession
6. Withdrawal of object interest (isolation)
7. Restitutive phenomena with enhancement of pathological defense mechanisms
8. Autistic and unrealistic preoccupations.

In many people much of the foregoing very likely can be prevented, or at least considerably postponed, when appropriate measures are employed in the manner soon to be discussed.

It is even probable that in many instances physiological aging can be halted to some degree as mental attitudes are favorably affected. In some instances, when it is clinically important to differentiate between a mild emotional disorder of late age and a psychosis, it is well to note that the point of transition occurs in the area of items 5 to 7.

RETIREMENT

An industrial leader, the president of a large and important business organization, recently said of his retirement, "One day I was the head of an empire. I was looked up to. Executives came to me for decisions. My judgment was law. It seemed that every major and minor problem filtered through my desk. I was key man. The next day I was nothing. I had to admit to myself that that vast organization could run without me, that I had no power, that nobody would care a tinker's dam for my advice, and that, were I to return to the business scene, I would merely be a sort of amusing and pathetic nuisance. For all my financial security, our fine home, the hunting lodge in the mountains, and the house at the shore, I began to feel lost, empty, dull, silly, and sorry for myself. Believe me, the readjustment has been troublesome."

A mother of four children remarked after the last child was married and left home, "I don't know what to do with myself. There just doesn't seem to be anything to do. The house always seems clean; very few dishes to wash; little shopping to do; and I hate to play canasta and go to luncheons all the time. The house is so quiet. Sometimes I could scream. I want to spend all my time with my grandchildren, but I know too much of that annoys my children."

Both of these people have retired from their career occupations and are faced with the challenge of a new way of life. Without foresight, without plan, without a pattern for continued usefulness, and without opportunities for keeping mental life keen and efficient, the likely outcome is an all too familiar picture in the American scene. There will be a sudden immersion in recreation of all kinds. They will travel, if they can afford it, until they tire of being the perennial tourist at whom every community ogles. They will play until play becomes a chore. They will relax until rest becomes work. They will be idle until life itself ceases to have meaning. Then there will be bickering between husband and wife. He will be underfoot and in the way most of the time from her point of view. Her shallow and gossiping chatter will grate upon his pleasant reminiscences. They will be two lonely people until he dies in a few years or becomes progressively senile. Then she will have all the prerequisites for her own psychological breakdown.

Retirement is a comparative newcomer on the scene of American living. It is the product of scientific and technologic advances that have lengthened life while shortening the work period. As an important phenomenon in man's span of life retirement has made its appearance mainly in the last half to three-quarters of a century.

While there are many possible reasons for withdrawal from principal occupations, such as illness, the transfer of an enterprise to mature progeny, and involuntary retirement due to incompetence, most people retire because of organizational policy and cultural tradition. There is some indication that the retirement-at-65 principle was an outgrowth of the financial depression of the 1930s when it became important to create job opportunities for younger people. However, the system has remained in force with a few exceptions; and with the constant extension of human longevity it is promising to become a considerable problem because of the many years of relative idleness thus created.

Clark Tibbitts of the United States Department of Health, Education, and Welfare has summarized the needs created by retirement as follows: ". . . the principal problems faced by the individual are maintenance of income to meet the requirements of active and healthful living; discovery of new occupations or social roles; finding opportunity for social contacts, companionship, and affection; maintenance of health; and procurement of suitable living arrangements." Many studies have shown that a majority of older persons manage to develop a satisfactory adjustment to retirement, but large numbers respond with bewilderment, anxiety, and feelings of frustration.

A major factor contributing to the tribulations of the latter group is the heavy valuation Americans place upon personal initiative and unaided individual effort. When success and making money are the prestige-producing activities, men tend to concentrate their efforts with great diligence upon the material goals, and they lose sight of the collateral niceties of life. Hobbies, recreations, reading, and the arts are underrated and avoided. As a result the leisure of retirement may later become quite esthetically sterile and devoid of an appreciation for the cultural wealth civilized men should treasure. Not only may this deficiency make retirement a nightmare for many people, but in addition it eventuates in a vicious, self-perpetuating system. The children, who naturally take example from the elders as well as from the dictates of a culture, thus have a dual stimulus to disregard the refinements of living. As a consequence the idle parent becomes an object of scorn, a feeling which is of psychological disadvantage to both parent and child.

In a subtle way the feeling exists that if a man takes any time from his career for hobbies, for recreations, or for otherwise deepening his personality, he is somehow being immoral or, at least, will come to economic ruin. For instance—unless medical students have changed since our day—the fellow who takes an evening off while the majority of the students are studying becomes the target for remarks that imply he will flunk out. Unconsciously the more conscientious students are jealous of his good times, and they try to make him feel guilty and uncomfortable. The same attitude is prevalent among business and professional men, and the result is that everyone tends to work hard, stay on the job, and keep up consistent effort in order to make as much money as possible.

In the same way a woman may take a marked pride in being a good housekeeper, in doing a good job with the children, and may criticize the woman who goes out too frequently. In many cases such women are making a virtue of a symptom, which is that they are actually afraid to go out. They feel anxiety when they go downtown in crowds or feel uneasy in a group of women. They may feel, for instance, that they should belong to the parent-teacher association, but disliking crowds and feeling conspicuous in them, they stay home and clean house and compliment themselves upon their diligence and ability to lead the busy home life. Diligence and work are important, but with nothing else to balance them people can come to grief later on because of a lack of more diverse emotional satisfaction.

The importance of prestige, status, and social recognition must not be overlooked in any age group and especially among the elderly. No man is complete unless he is part of a group. His social instincts and needs to be complemented direct him to seek give-and-take opportunities in group settings. Group living and group work grant each participant a membership. Contribution to social welfare and comfort yields gratification to the subscriber, because he thereby receives collective admiration and acceptance, the social equivalents of love. Retirement, which for many may mean departure from a sustaining group as in the case of our business executive, often is interpreted as threatened loss of love. Neurotic loneliness may be the outcome, particularly in those individuals whose lives have been characterized by a narrow social and intellectual horizon.

Retirement is often a greater threat to men than to women. This difference has many determinants, most important of which is the fact that a man's success in the business and professional world rests heavily upon his capacity to sublimate his instinctual drives. A woman succeeds in her normal role in family life through her greater nearness to her fundamental and natural endowments. Very often retirement for a man means fewer outlets for sublimation of emotional energies with a resulting potential for a greater measure of regression, anxiety, and symptom formation. For many women their usefulness continues largely unabated well into the later years.

A bright side to the problems of enforced leisure in later maturity is revealed by the fairly large number of people who discover in themselves hidden talents of which they were practically unaware in their earlier days. Arts, crafts, entrepreneur ventures, the guidance, care, and nursing of others, social-welfare and betterment activities, and many more become full-blown skills that bring to numbers of older persons hitherto undreamed-of social recognition.

Adult education not only helps older people to sharpen their skills, develop new hobbies, and remain abreast of world affairs, but it also has particular value in maintaining mental and emotional alertness. The significance of such programs is grasped more readily when it is realized that mental life is never stationary; if it isn't moving forward, it retreats. If a person is to progress at any age level, the continued psychological advance requires at all times a certain measure of ambition and aspiration based on socially appropriate wishes and fantasies. Intrinsic in education are many mental-health principles. For example, it tends to suppress primitive urges; it affords uses for free-floating mental energy; it diminishes natural fears by supplanting ignorance and superstition with facts and logic; it is usually a group endeavor that prepares its participants for group relationships; and it gratifies natively endowed curiosity. In addition, education offers information that broadens the vistas and horizons of the intellect and thus gives the striving set of psychological impulses material out of which to sculpt the dreams of intention. Educators who are currently planning to meet the needs of an aging population predict that in the future continuous education far into adulthood will be as much a part of our social order as schooling in childhood is now. The great advances in the sciences, technologies, and systems of commerce have increased the complexities of ordinary living, thus requiring much more knowledge and skill than present mandatory training and instruction afford. It is quite likely that the ordinary citizen in the future will have to do what members of the professions already must do, namely continue their studies throughout life.

Hobbies, which have assumed a position of prominence in the retirement period, have exemplified man's creative genius since prehistoric times, when men carved bone dolls and etched bison on the walls of their caves. The cultural wealth of mankind has doubtless grown out of human dedication to the perfection and elaboration of such humble experiments in the arts. There can be no question but that a hobby can encourage a sustained enthusiasm in the pursuit of experiences that add zest to life. There is small wonder that when regular occupations terminate, many people turn earnestly to one or many of the avocations that develop proficiency, adroitness, authority, and mastery. For all of its value and excellence the pursuit of a hobby may nevertheless unmask a problem, as exemplified in the following case history. John and Mary were regarded as a devoted couple by everyone in the neighborhood. He was a skilled machinist in a technical industry; she was a thorough housewife with many satellite interests. Both were warm parents to their two children although he left much of the discipline to his wife. Neighbors used the John-and-Mary household as the good example for the community; their home life was always so quiet, orderly, and predictable. After dinner each evening and on weekends John would repair to his hobby corner to do wood carving and a variety of handcrafts; Mary would hook rugs, tat, crochet, or knit nearby, while the children did their schoolwork. They sometimes spoke of the wished-for day when John would be retired and he and Mary would have lots of time to do things together. That day came and John attacked his hobbies with renewed vigor instead of engaging in the planned events with Mary. He persevered in putting her off. Insidiously, quarrels broke out between them and after a few years they were rarely on speaking terms with one another.

The John-and-Mary story reveals to us that for some people jobs and hobbies serve as neurotic compensations for emotional difficulties. Where a person escapes his poor marriage or a marital sexual problem by staying "on the job," his retirement may bring the difficulty closer to home and the deceptive neurotic mechanism may ultimately decompensate, following which the true state of affairs will be exposed.

THE TREATMENT OF OLDER PERSONS

As it is in all medical problems, prophylaxis is the best treatment for the special stress reactions that beset the aging person. All too frequently the physician as well as his patients have waited for a pathological process to start. Then intense treatment is begun, often to little avail. It is not superfluous to remind people in the earlier phases of life, much in the manner of the insurance salesman who advises financial readiness against illness or emergency, that they should be making emotional and ideational investments for later life. In most instances, unfortunately, this advice goes unheeded, for where it is accepted it is probably not needed. The problems of aging had their beginnings in early childhood relationships. The neurotic residues of the early years, that were covered over by activities of courtship, family rearing, and making a living, develop into full prominence when the chips are down in the great contests of later life. It is becoming increasingly clear that the gerontologist, the gerontologic psychiatrist, and the geriatrist can confirm with great precision the admonitions and recommendations of the child psychiatrist and analyst. Probably in the long run only the continued application of the best principles of mental hygiene and the ongoing emotional maturation of mankind will have any culture-wide effect on the enormous problems an aging population faces.

Still, inroads have been made at one end of the scale. The social betterment of childhood, the community awareness of needs for good family relations, the diminishing stigmatization of emotional disorders, the emergence of sexuality from ignorance to enlightenment, and community and governmental attack on social inequities, are all developments of comparative recency. The current world-wide campaign to obtain the facts and the problems of later maturity may yield new insights and solutions.

The need for cultural enlightenment regarding aging, the need for conscious preparation for the later years, the need for practical social and civic measures to reduce hardship and help promote comfort for the elder citizen, all spell out a long-range program.

The immediate need, that of treating the emotional indispositions of aging, is the here-and-now problem. This area is far more promising than many therapists hitherto have been led to expect. Those physicians who divest themselves of the fetters of cultural dogma find that gratifyingly large numbers of people in the sixth and seventh decades of life are quite susceptible to therapeutic measures that are essentially investigative and are directed toward the formation of insight. This type of treatment, however, should never be undertaken by a novice, for the development of appropriate rapport, the tactful uncovering of repressed material, and the management of the emotional relationship between the treater and the treated require the utmost skill and delicacy. People at this time of life, who need or seek help, are very often on the brink of depression or part way into it. Insights too rapidly produced and interpretations that are crudely and summarily made may mobilize intolerable guilt feelings that may lead to profound despair. A striking example of this is the case of an intelligent man in his middle sixties who sought help for insomnia, urinary frequency, irritability, and restlessness. His physician, a man of indisputable accomplishment and fame, talked to him for a few minutes and then casually gave him a current well-written and authoritative book on aging to read. Within a week the patient was in an agitated melancholia. He later told his new therapist, in the course of investigative therapy, that he had looked upon the behavior of his first physician as a severe social rebuff and that being given a book to read meant, "Go away. Don't bother me. You're an old man. Why not face it and try to grow old gracefully?" Incidentally, at the time this is being written, two years since the above event, this man has nearly overcome sexual impotency that had been present for 12 years, is enjoying his 35-year-old marriage with new gusto, and has made an even greater success of his business than he had ever expected. His analytic psychotherapy took nine months to achieve a practical goal.

Probably much larger numbers of people after age 50 can be treated intensively than is now realized. However, there are many more whose problems can be treated at more superficial levels. Reassurance, guidance, emotional support, and opportunities just to talk to a skilled listener (ventilation) are often effective when they are accompanied by genuine interest and understanding in the therapist. There is a far too prevalent feeling among physicians that the person of 50 and over has too little to hope for to be well motivated in treatment. This view is certainly an error, especially when it is recognized that at 50 life expectancy is about 25 years. It is very likely that the notion of hopelessness after 50 was born of interviews with depressed people. One psychoanalyst has made the intriguing observation that seventh-decade people respond more quickly to psychotherapy than those in the sixth.

The tendency on the part of physicians to drastically curtail life-long habits in the aging is probably not to be uncritically condoned. Such therapists seem to make a greater virtue of mere longevity than of living itself. While it is quite true that certain smoking, drinking, eating, and exercise habits may not be desirable in many somatic conditions, still the sudden removal or precipitous reduction of the outlets for tension may lead to an even more deadly fretful-ness. The aging should have every opportunity for normal living. In those instances where the future is really in doubt, empty, or without challenge, then such people should be encouraged and helped to live each day to the fullest extent possible.

The sex life of later maturity is still a poorly understood subject. Some younger counselors, with unresolved conflicts of their own from out of childhood, cannot tolerate the idea that older people may have sexual needs and wishes, with the result that unnecessary ab-stention and frustration may be imposed on their clients. It is edify-ing to discover that sex and love relationships are common topics of conversation in homes for the aged. A 70-year-old woman recently came to our attention for psychotherapy in association with the medi-cal management of her Parkinsonian paralysis. While unfolding her personal history she lamented the fact that the frequency of her conjugal relations with her husband had diminished. It should al-ways be kept in mind that the frustrated sexual wishes and the guilt they engender may intensify the depression in the surviving member of a marital pair separated by death. Social workers, volunteer aides, the family, and friends can do effective therapeutic work with older people by assisting them in finding appropriate companions of the opposite sex. Remarriages in later maturity are often stable and harmonious. The decrease in the psychological component of ag-gression that is concomitant with aging very frequently makes sex life after 65 both ardent and concordant.

For people who are moving into very late maturity, such facilities as day centers, recreational opportunities, Golden Age clubs, and sheltered workshops have both prophylactic and treatment value. Aged individuals whose mental faculties are unimpaired obtain much satisfaction from community service work of all kinds. Often the keen wisdom and lucid judgment they bring to the various conclaves they attend contribute materially to social welfare and betterment. Such arrangements obviously can be symbiotically fruitful.

The family problems that senility in an elder can create are not infrequently imponderable. A recent poll showed that 90 per cent of retired people preferred not to live with their children. Where the older person in a household has lost his self-critical faculties and his discriminative and reflective judgment is on the wane, there comes a point where his interferences may seriously hamper the lives and welfare of the younger members. While some families may be prone to virtually evict an elder prematurely by banishing him to an institution, many keep the emotionally disturbed oldster overly long, because of feelings of affection, obligation, or guilt. Both situations are unfortunate; the first heralds regression; the second delays the application of definitive care.

Modern mental institutions, certain outstanding homes for the aged, and some hospitals are able to restore fair numbers of senile psychotics and psychotics with cerebral arteriosclerosis to community usefulness. When necessity requires lesser goals, then the aim of treatment is humanitarian—to produce insofar as possible in the very aged some return of self-sufficiency and independence, increased tranquillity, and a potential for happiness.

Even in the presence of organic brain damage of very late maturity much of the behavior seen is consequent upon psychological reactions to the process of aging. Psychological alterations promise a degree of reversibility, but this does not follow automatically. Whether such functions are reversible depends upon (1) knowledge of their origin; (2) insight in patient and therapist into their nature; (3) an incentive in treater and treated to do something about them; (4) the amount of irreversible physiological damage also present; and (5) a well-developed setting with a therapeutic atmosphere affording supplies for emotional needs.

The main psychological pain from which the emotionally disturbed aged suffer is due to a rejecting environment, intrapsychic and external; isolation; regression; and pathological mechanisms for psychological defense.

It is evident that a treatment program for the aged must contain the following direct counteractants:

1. Removal from a covertly or overtly rejecting environment to an accepting one. The greater the emotional disturbance, then the more is there a need for institutional care. A well-conceived plan of therapy implemented by a trained and indoctrinated personnel team is essential.

2. Resocialization. Group living, even if at first resisted, is a valuable counterisolation agent and helps bring about a return of cultural values.

3. Activity. When productive, recreational, and entertaining this factor is the safeguard against stagnation, and it combats regression.

4. Psychotherapy. Many forms of human relationship possess psychotherapeutic elements. While individual treatment of the aged is often desirable, group psychotherapy lends itself especially well, since it contains all the elements of a therapeutic program. The development of deep insight is much less exigent than the need to diminish the urgency of sick defenses. The latter permits more wholesome functioning to resume supremacy.

The following is a good example of the efficacy of treatment of the aged. A 75-year-old widow had been hospitalized for 12 years in a bitter, hostile, suicidal and depressed mood that caused her to be irritable and seclusive. Passionately vituperative and sharply sarcastic, she had been permitted to recede into an utterly meaningless institutional life, merely waiting and hoping for death. Severely limited by joint pains and weight loss, she was able to hobble only short distances for her bodily needs. She had not been seen to smile in 12 years. Placed on a routine medication (oral metrazol [R] and vitamins) that is known to stimulate the release of emotional energy, she became sufficiently alert and hungry for social experiences to enable her to be coaxed into attending group psychotherapy sessions. In a few months she became a fairly pleasant, affable, and charming group member. At a doughnut-and-cider party she ate heartily and asked to kiss the therapist. Progressively she gained weight, was much more physically agile, and became a leading raconteur in social gatherings. She obviously enjoyed life during the following months and developed a peacefulness and good humor that she had not known for a sixth of her life.

At the time this is being written there are more than 17,000,000 people over 65 in the United States. Nearly a third of our total population is over 45. Those are unprecedented figures. Whereas the errors in our psychological past can be undone in each of us only with great difficulty, we all possess a certain degree of autonomy of purpose in shaping our future. This is our personal investment in the problems of later maturity and one of the major reasons why we must prepare ahead for that day, a mere generation from now, when the "over-65's" will number 25,000,000 and about *half* of all Americans will be well along in senescence.

SUMMARY

Maturity includes a solution to a multitude of problems, depending upon how much responsibility an individual undertakes. It involves many things. Maturation means:

(1) making oneself a congenial and helpful marital partner,

(2) being a warm, wise, and helpful parent,

(3) being a friend to at least four people,

(4) being a useful and congenial worker with one's superiors and colleagues,

(5) supporting one's family and friends helpfully through illness and adversity, if needed,

(6) doing one's work uncomplainingly,

(7) being generous and uncritical of others, unless criticism is really beneficial (doctor, lawyer, minister, teacher, employer, coach, supervisor, or authorized counselor can advise professionally. Unsolicited or unauthorized criticism usually does more harm than good),

(8) being able to see and advocate a harmonious solution to problems in the family and outside as well,

(9) entering later years able to take care of oneself emotionally, that is, being able to entertain oneself, to entertain someone else, and to entertain a new idea. This maturity makes physical incapacitation bearable; and who among us does not suffer this at some time or other.

BIBLIOGRAPHY FOR CHAPTER XIV

Benedek, Therese, and Boris B. Rubenstein, "The Correlation between Ovarian Activities and Psychodynamic Processes," *Psychosomatic Medicine* I, 1939, 245–270.

Cowdry, E. V. (ed.), *Problems of Aging,* Williams and Wilkins, 2nd edition 1942 and 3rd edition 1952.

Freud, Sigmund, *Civilization and Its Discontents,* Hogarth Press and the Institute of Psychoanalysis, 1949.

—— *Mourning and Melancholia,* in *Collected Papers II,* Hogarth, 1934.

Gumpert, Martin, *You Are Younger Than You Think,* Duell, 1944.

Lawton, George, *Aging Successfully,* Columbia University Press, 1951.

Lawton, George (ed.), *New Goals for Old Age,* Columbia University Press, 1944.

Liebman, Joshua L., *Peace of Mind,* Simon and Schuster, 1946.

May, Rollo, *Man's Search for Himself,* Norton, 1953.

Menninger, K. A., *Man against Himself,* Harcourt, 1938.

—— *Love against Hate,* Harcourt, 1942.

Menninger, W. C., *You and Psychiatry,* Scribner, 1948.

Otto, Max, *Science and the Moral Life,* New American Library, 1949.

Overstreet, Harry A., *The Mature Mind,* Norton, 1949.

Pratt, J. P., discussion of an article entitled "A Syndrome of Estrogenic Deficiency," by Philip J. Schneider, *American Journal of Obstetrics and Gynecology* 3, 1936, 782.

Saul, Leon J., "Emotional Maturity," Lippincott, Second Edition, 1960.

Schuster, David B., "A Psychological Study of a 106-Year-Old-Man; a contribution to Dynamic Concepts of Aging and Dementia," *American Journal of Psychiatry* 109, No. 2, August, 1952, 112–119.

Tibbitts, Clark, "Retirement Problems in American Society," *American Journal of Sociology* 51, No. 4, January, 1954, 301–308.

XV
Mental Illness

THUS far we have traced the progression of a human being from infancy on through the various stages of personality growth and development. One attains psychological maturity —which is another way of describing mental health—by successfully passing through these various stages.

This process of growing up and adapting to life is never entirely easy and comfortable, even under the best of circumstances. The most normal of us will go through occasional phases of seemingly distorted or bizarre behavior, such as temporary periods of anger with our best friends or feelings of being misunderstood and persecuted. Yet, if our early training and environment have been proper and healthy, we will soon overcome these difficulties and our personalities will continue on their paths to maturity.

Unfortunately, however, many people fail to make satisfactory adjustments between the needs and demands of their own personalities and those of the environment in which they live. These persons are tense and in conflict as a result of unresolved childhood problems and when their faulty pattern disturbances become crystallized and exaggerated, they become mentally ill. It is the purpose of this chapter to discuss the various categories of nonorganic mental and emotional disorders.

There are four broad classes of such disorders, and each of them, in turn, is subdivided into several categories. The broad classes are:

1. Psychotic disorders
2. Psychoneurotic disorders
3. Personality disorders
4. Psychophysiologic disorders

It must always be borne in mind that the dividing lines between these groupings, and particularly between their various subdivisions, are not sharp and clear. Many people who are mentally ill exhibit symptoms of more than one type of disorder. In fact, the classic case which can be completely pinpointed almost never appears. Nevertheless, the groupings and their subgroupings are valuable aids in both diagnosis and treatment.

PSYCHONEUROTIC DISORDERS

Neurotic symptoms are universal. No human being is without them. Everyone is aware of experiencing tension and being beset by conflicts. The normal individual lives fairly comfortably with his conflicts; the neurotic cannot. He cannot cope in a healthy, comfortable manner with his inner, unconscious conflicts and he develops a state of anxiety felt as tension. The cause, indeed the very nature of this anxiety, is largely beyond his conscious understanding. In many neuroses the tension of conflict (anxiety) acts through the autonomic nervous system and then in addition to the common emotional states of fear, frustration, and repressed hostility an individual may suffer symptoms such as palpitations of the heart, sweating, faintness or weakness, vomiting or diarrhea. Anxiety, further, often creates *chronic* physical dysfunction of certain organs of the body as well.

In contrast to one who is psychotic, the psychoneurotic (or neurotic; the terms are synonymous) does not lose his grasp on reality, or his ability to relate to those about him. He usually retains a measure of social adjustment, his judgment is not affected fundamentally, and he has a full awareness that he is ill, albeit he often erroneously ascribes his sickness to some organic ailment.

In short, a psychoneurotic disorder is an attempt on the part of an individual's ego to find some solution to its unconscious problems. The struggle is set off by emotionally charged situations with which the individual is unable to cope and for which he cannot find a solution.

Psychoneurotic disorders are subdivided into six categories. Again, it must be remembered that the boundaries between them are not sharply defined and overlap. The six categories are:

1. Anxiety reactions
2. Dissociative reactions
3. Conversion reactions
4. Phobic reactions

5. Obsessive-compulsive reactions
6. Depressive reactions

ANXIETY REACTIONS

The primary symptom of anxiety reaction is, of course, anxiety itself. Anxiety may best be described as an extremely foreboding sensation of dread. It is such a common symptom in our society that almost everyone has suffered it at times, at least to a mild degree.

Anxiety is a basic and fundamental symptom of every type of psychoneurosis. The psychological and physical components of anxiety are similar to those of fear. But anxiety differs from fear in that there is no actual danger threatening. In other words, the stimulus of fear comes from without; that of anxiety from within. In an "anxiety attack," so called, there occurs a nameless feeling of impending disaster while the pulse becomes rapid, muscular tension increases, and all the familiar symptoms of actual fear occur, such as palpitating, sweating, and weakness.

The essential purpose of fear is to act as a warning signal to the individual that he faces an external danger which must be overcome. Anxiety is a similar sensation or warning that some threat or danger is present *within* the individual. But since this inner "danger" is unconscious, it cannot be dealt with as can outer realistic danger. The individual recognizes that he is in an uncomfortable state of dread, but he does not recognize what he can do to achieve relaxation with attendant psychic and physical comfort. The person with anxiety can be thrown into as great a state of panic—with undesirable physical manifestations—as if, for instance, he were frightened by a truck bearing down on him, or as if he were being held up by a gunman. It has been repeatedly said that those who suffer from a severe anxiety would cheerfully trade it for any type of organic pain.

The roots of anxiety lie in childhood. We know that lack of a healthy emotional atmosphere in early life hampers and retards healthy personality development. We know too, that the more emotional security an individual has during the formative years of childhood the less anxiety he will be likely to have in later life. For instance, one suffering from an anxiety reaction invariably reveals that his parents were unable to give him constant, mature affection and protect him from stress, so that he suffered repeated exposure to unpleasant tensions. As a result, he lived in an unstable and uncomfortable emotional atmosphere from which he could never learn to face some of the dangers and responsibilities of ordinary living. Such an unhealthy atmosphere not only impedes healthy ego growth but perpetuates immaturity and insecurity.

Anxiety will often manifest itself early in life. A child, for instance, who is afraid of the dark or is frightened of being alone is already suffering from anxiety. His relationship with his mother has not been secure enough to enable him to keep the feeling of her kindness, goodness, and protection with him when he is alone. When a child shows anxiety by not wanting to go to school, it usually means that he cannot take with him the memory of his parents' acceptance and he therefore cannot imagine that his teacher or the other children will make him feel secure and accepted at school.

A nineteen-year-old girl working as a secretary came for treatment, stating her problem in the following way. "I'm so ashamed of coming for help. The truth is I'm scared of everybody and everything. I wake up in the morning dreading the day. I'm so tense worrying about the office I scarcely can eat anything for breakfast and keep it down. When I get on the bus to go to work I am uneasy. I do not want people to look at me! I'm afraid the bus may have an accident. When I get to the office building it is an effort to go up in the elevator. When the telephone rings I wonder if I can handle the person at the other end of the line adequately. When the boss buzzes, I'm in a panic lest I have done something wrong. My heart beats like a scared rabbit. I sleep restlessly and dream of being with people who do not like me or who reject me. Sometimes I awake in a panic. All this leaves me exhausted and unhappy. What shall I do?"

This is a typical history of an anxiety reaction at age nineteen. If the patient were ten years older before being seen the anxiety would probably have attached itself to an overconcern about the safety of her children, or her husband, or her ability to help them, or protect them properly from danger. But the common denominators are usually to be seen in the formulation "I am not good enough. I am not capable of coping with the world. The world is unfriendly and unsafe."

So what do we do for these people? Details of treatment will be discussed in the chapter on treatment, but since we have just finished depicting the *origin* of anxiety and then depicted the *persistence* of anxiety in this particular case a few very fundamental concepts of treatment can be pointed out at this time:

1. Tell the story of the origin of anxiety in childhood to the sick and troubled person.

2. Indicate thereby that he has a continuance of an old condition and not a disease as such.

3. Get him to see that his cure lies in a new orientation to the present, a better use of the acceptance of people in his present environment who do not want to hurt, frighten, or be punitive.

4. Help the anxious one to accept himself and to accept others as offering more than his nonreasoning and nonpunitive early environment.

It is one of the paradoxical things about mind activity that the anxious person who is weakened by anxiety and literally "hungering" for acceptance has such difficulty in taking it and making good use of it. Once a person has been made to feel guilty or even excessively modest or skeptical of the good intentions of others, an unfortunate pattern has been established which all too many times requires professional help from very skilled psychiatrists.

DISSOCIATIVE REACTIONS

Amnesia, fugue states, somnambulism, and multiple personalities are the symptoms found in dissociative reactions. They are the means by which an individual deals with his anxiety. He is, in other words, walling off certain areas of his mind from consciousness in order to deal with his conflicts. Dissociative reaction is one of the most sensational and dramatic neuroses known and the one most sure to make newspaper headlines.

The person with a dissociative reaction has a conflict, as do all psychoneurotics. This internal, unconscious conflict is "triggered" by an environmental situation which is intolerable to him. He tries to escape this uncomfortable, anxiety-producing situation, and thus he develops his symptoms. He closes off a portion of what was previously conscious memory and feeling, and may even become totally unaware of a certain period of his life. He may even upset his conscious awareness of what is going on about him and enter a dreamlike state where he is out of touch with reality. In other words, he represses or forgets large or small segments of his experiences. It is a sort of "selective forgetting" which operates beneath his conscious awareness and without conscious intent.

Amnesia is a fairly common phenomenon. Hardly a day goes by in any large city when at least one amnesic victim does not come to the police station saying he does not know who he is, where he comes from, or what he has been doing. The victim has dissociated the events of a certain period of time from the rest of his mind. He has lost his memory about an incident or period of time because it threatens to expose to consciousness unwelcome material. He has segregated certain ideas and emotions from the rest of his mind and for the time being the remainder of his mind cannot control the split-off ideas or feelings.

A truck driver came to the hospital suffering from amnesia. It subsequently developed that he came from a town two hundred miles away where he had been involved in an accident. A suit had been brought against him, he had lost it, and money was to be taken from his pay each week to pay the damages. This loss occurred at the same time as his wife became quarrelsome because she felt he was not giving her enough money. He knew he would be in trouble with his wife when she heard the court decision. He remembered walking out of the courthouse and down the steps and from then on —nothing. He lost his memory completely for two days and found himself in the hospital unable to recall what had occurred in those two days.

This man's experience is called a "circumscribed" amnesia. A period of time is repressed and all that comes before it and all that follows it is remembered. It is as if the particular traumatic situation did not occur, for the patient has no memory of it. However, when the amnesia extends backward and the individual is unable to remember anything of his previous life up to a certain traumatic event it is called "retrograde." When the amnesia extends from the traumatic situation forward, it is called "antegrade." An amnesic may live for years in his dissociative state until, finally, some highly charged emotional situation restores his memory, or until adequate psychotherapeutic measures release the repression.

Simple examples of dissociative reaction fall within the personal experience of everyone. Forgetting a person's name when one knows the person well; forgetting places and dates, only to recall the correct name or time later are all examples of what Freud called "the psychopathology of everyday life." Such incidents are temporary repressions of unconscious, conflictual material. Perhaps the person's name is linked in some way with an individual whom one does not like but where there is guilt about the dislike, or possibly, the place has an unconscious similarity to a place whose recall would be unwelcome in consciousness.

Somnambulism or sleepwalking is another symptom of dissociative reaction. It is most common in childhood but can appear at any time in life. In the typical somnambulistic state the person gets up during his sleep but contrary to popular notion, has his eyes opened and is apparently aware of what is happening. However, he seems not to understand as well as he would if he were awake. He may or may not respond to questions and may or may not return voluntarily to bed where he resumes his normal sleep. Such a person may be involved in danger because he cannot evaluate what is going on about him. For instance, he may climb out of high places without realization of the danger involved. If he were to be awakened he might lose his balance and get hurt. It is not any more difficult to waken an individual when he is sleepwalking than when he is in a normal sleep. Usually the proper solution is to lead him back to his bed where he can resume his normal slumber. The next morning he may or may not remember vaguely what happened or he may remember it as a dream.

Multiple personalities are a relatively rare type of dissociative reaction. As a matter of fact they are so rare that they seldom occur except in literature. Dr. Jekyll and Mr. Hyde provide the well-known fictional example. There are two changes in personality, each of which in turn controls behavior. Essentially in an individual with a dissociative reaction there is the alternate appearance of different facets of personality. On one occasion an individual may seem shy and inhibited and on another occasion quite aggressive and forward. This alternation may appear from day to day or for periods of weeks.

The *fugue state* closely resembles amnesia. An individual in fugue may disappear, live elsewhere for months or years as a completely different person, marry, raise a family, and become an accepted member of the community, but suddenly one day "remember" his original personality. Such fugue states are rare and occur only infrequently.

When an individual is *in a stupor* he withdraws from his environment and does not respond to what is going on about him. This is often a temporary though inadequate solution to a psychologically traumatic event which has occurred immediately preceding the onset of the stupor. It is as if remembering and communicating are too painful and to avoid pain the individual plunges himself into this temporary withdrawal.

Therapy. Most people believe that the most important step to be taken with an amnesic person is to restore his memory. It is as if this restoration of memory will promptly solve all of the individual's problems. Unfortunately, it will no more do so in the dissociative reaction than in any other emotional problem. It is the individual's basic personality patterns and conflict that need changing. He must be shown how to relate to his present environment and recognize his symptoms as a childish attempt to escape the realities of living. He needs to find a more mature level of adjustment and learn how to cope with his life situation. Relief of symptoms may temporarily appear to help such an individual, and it may restore him to contact with his environment. But without psychotherapy that gives him insight and adds to his ego strength, he will inevitably return to all of his painful memories and when this occurs he is always vulnerable to a return of symptoms.

CONVERSION REACTION

Conversion reaction is a type of psychoneurosis characterized by the individual's tendency to represent his inner psychological conflict by means of symbolic somatic disturbances. To understand this reaction one must understand the ability of the individual to express in some portion of his body the *unconscious* conflict from which he is suffering. Examples are the sudden and dramatic occurrence of paralysis, loss of sensation in an extremity, or even such symptoms as blindness or deafness. Here the conflicts causing anxiety are being "converted" into physical symptoms. And these symptoms serve to lessen conscious anxiety and meet the immediate need of the individual to find a solution, though it be distorted and pathological, of his unconscious conflict. It is typical to find a sudden onset of symptoms in conversion reaction and these often occur in a setting of unusual emotional crises.

In past years the ocurrence of conversion reaction was quite common. The sudden loss of sensation of an extremity, or paralysis, blindness, or deafness was frequent. However, such histrionic symptoms are not as common today and there is more likelihood at the present time of finding individuals developing a more subtle and insidious involvement, such as a psychophysiologic phenomenon. In conversion there is a fairly sudden leap of the psychic conflict over into a part of the body under the control of the voluntary nervous system. In psychophysiologic conditions the somatic dysfunction is more likely to be produced by prolonged psychic stimuli operating by way of the involuntary nervous system. In Victorian society these conversions were apt to occur in naive individuals whose upbringing had been extremely strict, particularly from a sexual standpoint. The present-day trend in our more sophisticated society is toward less dramatic and less obvious acting out by the body. It has become increasingly frequent to find such symptoms developing in situations involving workmen's-compensation or medicolegal situations. There has been so much written and portrayed in cartoons about the emotional factors involved in the more dramatic symptoms that these become less "available" to most potential psychiatric patients today.

The symptoms of conversion reaction are exceedingly variable. They can mimic almost any disease conditions, although usually in a crude way. As we have mentioned, the onset of these symptoms is often dramatic, occurring during a period of emotional stress. Therefore it is not uncommon to find a widespread outbreak of conversion symptoms occurring in many people during earthquakes, fires, and wars. Not infrequently, however, in the neurotically disposed individual the conversion symptoms gradually become evident as an outgrowth and superimposition upon a physical injury or disease which has, in the meantime, been cured. Conversion symptoms are an example of "somatic compliance" where the body, through injury or illness, "complies" with the needs of the neurosis by providing an expression of the conflict. Generally speaking, the types of conversion symptoms are divisible into several categories. They are motor symptoms, sensory symptoms, and autonomic nervous system symptoms.

Motor symptoms involve the various voluntary muscles of the body. Most characteristically they involve an entire extremity, as, for example, a paralysis of one or both legs or arms. An illustration is seen in the soldier at the front who on being ordered to attack finds himself unable to move his legs. On the one hand he is deeply fearful of injury if he goes with the attacking forces and yet his conscience unrealistically forbids him conscious realization of his fear. His particular solution to the conflict is the paralysis which comes on as an unconscious "answer." It is literally impossible for him to move, even if his life is threatened.

Sensory symptoms involve various areas of the surface of the body or one of the special senses. The sudden onset of blindness or deafness may signal the development of conversion reaction. It is interesting to note that the symptom is produced through the unconscious of the individual and that therefore he is not aware of its true meaning.

Patients often have an event around which they date the onset of symptoms. Usually something can be adduced as an introduction to the symptom picture. A girl of eighteen felt a fishbone stick in her throat while eating a meal. The bone was removed by her in the usual manner but she continued to feel a "sticking sensation" and concluded a piece of it must have remained. She went to her family physician, who saw nothing, but she was not content until she had seen a nose-and-throat specialist. He too informed her there was no evidence of any bone fragment. She then began to demand that an X-ray study be made, but by this time the family physician called in the psychiatrist. The latter assured her that since all had been found healthy in the physical sphere that the next logical step was to inquire into her personality and try to ascertain why her interest was continuing to focus on the sticking sensation. It developed that she was in a contentious home situation and that a boy friend was importuning her for a sexual experience. She was being made tense by increasing pressures from both areas and her discomfort disappeared after four sessions of expressing her fears, conflicts, and resentments over these situations and learning a few techniques for coping with them.

A conversion reaction represents, as we have mentioned, an expression of a forbidden impulse and the prohibition of this impulse at the same time. This conflict can be dramatically and meaningfully symbolized, as a rule, through motor or sensory symptoms. These symptoms are usually more evident as such to the outer world than to a person's own personality. For instance, blindness may be obviously suspect in the person who "will not see" a given unpleasant situation. The almost theatrical and totally incapacitating symptoms, such as general paralysis, are widely recognized by both the medical profession and the layman today as frequent manifestations of emotional problems. The general practitioner who visits a home in which the eager, developing adolescent has a sudden paralysis in a healthy body almost automatically begins to wonder what frustration phenomena are going on. The *autonomic nervous system symptoms* are less obvious in their manifestations and less dramatic. An inability to control a home or work problem satisfactorily very often results in an inability to control some part of the gastrointestinal tract, particularly the lower bowel. Helping the patient to cope with problems will result in a returning control of bowel function.

Another factor of no small importance in conversion reactions is the existence of an injury or a minor organic ailment which allows focusing of the symptom in this particular area. An example is the individual who receives a blow on the head which, although of minor severity, occurs in a situation of great emotional stress. If such a person has a conversion type of personality, it is not unusual for him to develop a chronic headache of functional nature as a result of the initial blow. Such conversions are very common. A young housewife of twenty-three had failed to hit the chair when she went to sit down one day and hurt what she alluded to as "the end of my spine." It was impossible to determine just where the injury had been sustained but she began to complain of "pain in the back." The pain was in the lower lumbar spine. She was thin and slight of stature and had been told she did not "look strong." She was found from many examinations to be free of any evidence of organic disease. Her emotional problems and conflicts were many. She did not like housework. She did not want children "very much." She was frigid and merely endured sexual relations. She was sorry she had given up a good job to marry, as being at home was not very interesting.

All these conflicts had to express themselves in some way and in some spot. As she came to understand how unhappy she was emotionally and began to ventilate some of this unhappiness and resign herself to marriage and the acceptance of the wife-and-potential-mother role her pain in the back disappeared.

Sometimes these cases become even more complicated psychologically if litigation is involved. The hope for financial recompense for injuries (real or imagined) sustained, or the easier life afforded by insurance payments may prolong symptoms or even help to prevent recovery. As one physician put it, "Some cases are very hard to cure if compensation sets in." In order to avoid this complication, which is called *secondary gain,* prompt and skillful handling and the utmost honesty and co-operation on the part of physicians, lawyers, and insurance companies are mandatory.

PHOBIC REACTION

Phobic reaction is a type of psychoneurosis characterized by the presence in an individual of one or more unexplained, severe, and unrealistic phenomena of avoidance of places or situations. Phobic individuals suffer an extreme degree of anxiety, to the point of panic accompanied by somatic responses to anxiety, whenever they are confronted with the phobic situation. Phobias are much more common in the general population than is ordinarily suspected. Exaggerated fears of high places, animals, closed spaces, dirt, germs, public speaking, and other such phenomena are some of the most common examples. Many of them never come to the attention of a physician because the individual literally learns "to live with his fear." He avoids the phobic situation and thus remains comparatively free from anxiety. Medical attention is usually sought by an individual only when he develops a phobia which seriously affects his ability to carry on with his ordinary daily activities. It is quite remarkable, however, the number of people who will arrange their lives for years on end so that they need never venture out on the street alone or ride in a public conveyance or attend a crowded function. These self-imposed limitations in order to avoid phobic situations become an integral part of a person's life. He accepts them, plans his life around them and, in a great number of instances, never seriously considers seeking medical help.

Phobias have been called the "normal neuroses of childhood" because of their being almost ubiquitous during this period of life. Most youngsters suffer at least a transitory phobia or two, most often during the fourth, fifth, and sixth years. It is at this time that the child is involved in his oedipal struggles and the phobia is an attempt to handle the anxiety which is generated. The youngster is disturbed by unconscious stirrings of rivalry feelings toward the parent of the same sex. There is, on the other hand, within the youngster a preponderance of love and affection toward this same parent. The little boy who is envious and jealous of his father's relationship with his mother nevertheless loves, admires, and is affectionate toward his father. In the effort to "solve" this uncomfortable situation of mixed feelings, the anxiety engendered by the feelings toward the father becomes detached from the father and displaced onto some external object, situation, or thing. This latter can then be avoided and the father can be more comfortably accepted by the youngster. The little boy may suddenly develop an exaggerated fear of dogs and refuse to go anywhere near one, even though it is a friendly and harmless pup. Phobias, particularly in children, may also be of things which exist only in fantasy. For instance, it is not uncommon to find a little girl, struggling with her negative oedipal feelings toward her mother, developing a fear that witches will visit her during the night.

The widespread occurrence of transient phobias during childhood is a phenomenon which owes its occurrence to the immaturity of the growing personality. The ego of the child, as yet incapable of mastering all instinctual impulses, is hard pressed to control oedipal strivings. It therefore follows that even the comparatively normal child, during the process of development, may resort to the pathological mechanism of phobia formation, without such a symptom necessarily indicating the degree of pathology which it would in an adult when the ego is expected to have attained greater maturity. There are other youngsters, however, who develop more incapacitating, chronic phobias which may disappear after two or three years or may even last into adult life. Such children and adults are lacking in security. It is true that they have displaced some of their original fears of childhood onto objects and situations, but it is also true that their earliest years have lacked sufficient security to enable them to thoroughly and efficiently overcome and work through their early fears.

A typical example of phobia is presented by the young woman who fears riding in elevators. She is unable to give any clear explanation of what she fears. She is only aware that whenever she enters an elevator and the doors are closed she becomes panicky. She ordinarily avoids every situation which might require riding in an elevator. She would rather climb many stairs than enter an elevator. Should circumstances necessitate her riding in one, she becomes extremely apprehensive and fearful. She feels closed in, unable to catch her breath, certain that the elevator will plunge to the bottom of the building, or certain that it will become stuck between floors and she will be trapped.

There are innumerable possible phobias and only some of the more common may be mentioned here. *Claustrophobia,* a fear of enclosed spaces, is one of the most common. A patient suffering from this symptom is unable to remain in a closed room or confining space unless, perhaps, he is sitting or standing near an open door and realizes that he may make his exit at any time. However, if he finds himself in a situation where all the exits are closed or where he would create a noticeable disturbance should he attempt to leave, he then begins to suffer marked anxiety. Many of these people, for instance, can attend a moving-picture theater as long as they sit near the back and in a seat next to the aisle. In such a position it is possible for them to leave at any time. The mere recognition that they may leave often is sufficient to forestall the development of the anxiety. The essential underlying difficulty is an inner awareness on the part of the individual that he literally must control his own impulses while he is insufficiently secure about his ability to do so. The combination causes him considerable anxiety. If he is near an exit, there is an inner awareness that, should his impulses become uncontrollable, he may then leave. If one were to ask such a person what impulses he fears, he would not be able to give a clear answer, but would only state that he knows he feels safe if he is certain that there is an opportunity to leave whenever he wishes. A fear of crying out unexpectedly or of falling down in a helpless state are two of the most common fantasies.

Agoraphobia, a fear of open spaces, is also extremely common. An agoraphobe is unable to venture out on the street alone. He also is unable to give any clear reasons for his fear. He feels comfortable and his childish insecurity is allayed only if he has someone accompanying him. He often fears that he will faint or that some unpleasant thing will occur to him which he would not be able to manage unless accompanied by someone else. He may, for instance, fear the possibility of heart attack and feel that he will probably die on the street unless accompanied by a friend. Such people, like the claustrophobes, fear their own inner, childish impulses. The agoraphobe fears his exhibitionistic and other sexual impulses, as well as the expected hostility of the people in the world. It is as if he feels that he could not control himself if alone, nor could he save himself from the expected indifference or even ill will of people. He feels inwardly as if the added presence of a more mature ego than his own will save him from giving way to his inner impulses and therefore also from punishment from the hostile world.

It is possible for an individual to be phobic of almost anything and the basic underlying mechanism is very similar in all of these phobias. They represent the patient's inner insecurity and conflict. His anxiety is bound to the phobic situation and if that situation can be avoided, he may make a superficially satisfactory adjustment. There is often a similarity in characteristics between the phobic individual and the person with a conversion reaction. Both often appear outwardly to be friendly, warm, and attractive people. However, continued association with them usually brings to light their childishness, immaturity, self-centeredness, and general insecurity. This superficial attractiveness and geniality is a sort of an outer layer which these individuals do not ordinarily maintain with close relatives and friends. At home they are prone to be moody, inarticulate, aloof, and they know little of the simpler joys of living and little of the potential security that lies in close friendships and trust in others.

As the phobic defense reaction spreads and becomes more severe, it begins to include more situations and things. The individual loses himself in preoccupation with himself and his own problems and his own state of mind. Eventually many such people literally limit themselves to their own homes, avoiding people, avoiding the outside world, and avoiding work. They become increasingly dependent upon those about them and yet more difficult to please. All of this makes a vicious circle because, although the person is seeking security, his own tendency to be wrapped up within himself prevents others from providing even a minimum of his sought-for security.

A word should be mentioned here about the hostile element of a phobic reaction. The individual, by virtue of his incapacitation, often immobilizes those closest to him and warps their lives as well as his own. A housewife who is unable to shop, unable to answer the door, fearful of the telephone, or phobic of entertaining guests may constantly harass her husband with innumerable and unreasonable requests. She may require that he come home from the office to quiet her anxiety. She may find herself developing a panic if she attempts to go out, and "solve" this by requiring her husband to be her chauffeur constantly. Such persons are ordinarily completely unaware of the underlying hostile and dominating element in their phobic living pattern. The treatment of phobias is usually somewhat prolonged and complex and will be taken up in the chapter on treatment.

OBSESSIVE-COMPULSIVE REACTION

The obsessive-compulsive reaction is a type of psychoneurosis in which an individual suffers from unwelcome repetitive ideas or impulses to perform ritualistic acts. Such persons, for instance, may be tormented by recurrent blasphemous or obscene thoughts or the need to perform apparently useless acts such as touching certain objects in a ritualistic way, dressing in a particular order, counting doors, steps, or some other such similar gesture. The repetitious thoughts are called obsessions, while the actions are called compulsions. While such a person may realize these thoughts or actions are irrational, he must continue them in order to relieve emotional tension.

The frequency of mild obsessive or compulsive rituals in the general population is much higher than is ordinarily expected. Superstition falls within this general category. Such things as knocking on wood, throwing salt over one's shoulder, or avoiding walking under a ladder are examples of minor and usually nonincapacitating obsessive-compulsive reactions. Particularly during childhood, in the age group of seven to perhaps eleven, are these things seen with a remarkable frequency. As long as such simple acts or thoughts do not seriously disturb the individual's efficiency, productivity, or love life, they are relatively innocuous. However, if they are magnified and involve much of the individual's daily experience, they can become tremendously incapacitating and interfere seriously with everything the individual tries to do.

The obsessive-compulsive reaction stems primarily from difficulties encountered in childhood, particularly during the anal phase. It can be best understood by reviewing the various characteristics which contribute to the anal phase and how the child behaves during this period. The youngster from perhaps one to four years of age is first and foremost ambivalent. By that is meant that he literally loves when he hates and hates when he loves. He has not yet reached the level of psychosexual development where he can truly be said to love someone directly and consistently. To clarify this, one need only watch a three-year-old with his mother for a short period of time. He accepts, enjoys, and at times even seems to return some of the warmth which she shows him; but in only a few moments he is furious with her because she has frustrated a desire of his or made a demand upon him. One senses very clearly that in his relationship with his mother he is the important person and he places his gratification far above hers. The three-year-old girl who is very maternal with her little brother will, a few moments later, show great hostility to him because of something he has done to one of her toys. Such unstable relationships as these, which alternate from obviously positive feelings to severely negative ones, are characteristic of this age level and normal at this time of life. Only gradually during the next few years do they begin to reach a more stable and mature level.

A married woman of thirty-five came complaining of living a life of slavery to the following compulsive acts. She would have to go down to the cellar several times a day to ascertain whether the gas heater was working properly. She feared that escaping gas due to a faulty mechanism might blow the house up. She also had to wash all the dishes extra meticulously, and if guests came in the home she would after their departure have to wipe all the furniture they had used with a mild antiseptic solution. She said, "I know it's silly, but I can't be contented inside unless I do it." In addition to these things, she was most scrupulous about locking the doors at night and would occasionally have to get up in the middle of the night and check on them. She was most reluctant to leave the house at all, lest she forget something "that would burn the house down or do some damage."

We see here this woman's continuous efforts to show herself and others that she was not a "careless, dirty, thoughtless, heedless, harmful woman." On the contrary was she not demonstrating how clean, careful, and considerate she was? Mothers frequently are obsessed with fear for the safety of husband or children even as a result of their own violence.

There are three main tasks to accomplish therapeutically. The first is to help the patient understand the behavior as similar to and a derivative from the conflicts of the anal period. This is not easy for the patient to come by; it is incredible theorizing to him at first. The second thing he must do is abreact some of the emotion bound up in these conflicts. He must set himself a goal of normal (average) behavior in similar circumstances and make himself live it until he has become convinced that: (a) he is not as bad as his childlike superego believes, and (b) that he is accepted by others as good when he forgoes his rituals, learning all the while that no catastrophe occurs.

Therefore, in summary, we see that the obsessive patient is inwardly urged toward messiness, rebelliousness, stinginess, violence, destruction, and all of the other anal characteristics. Yet his rigid, puritanical superego forbids expression of even the slightest tendency in these directions. His ego, therefore, is hard put to maintain intrapsychic peace and resorts to various mechanisms of defense. The result is a cold individual leading a rigid, constricted, unemotional type of life often filled with numerous ritualistic thoughts and actions. He draws his feeling of virtue from strictness with himself and others, asceticism, and worry, rather than from a feeling of genial, warm love of others.

DEPRESSIVE REACTION

The most prominent symptom of the depressive reaction is a chronic state of dejection or despondency accompanied by a tendency toward self-depreciation. It typically follows some environmental condition which might ordinarily be expected to produce a temporary unhappiness, but not unhappiness to as severe a degree nor for as prolonged a period as is found in the individuals affected. The death of a close relative, an economic failure, or some other unfortunate crisis in a person's life often immediately predates the depressive reaction, but the reaction is both more marked and more prolonged than would be expected in the reaction of a normal individual under similar circumstances.

The person with a neurotic depression is essentially a chronically unhappy, usually complaining person. He withdraws from many of his previous activities yet is still amenable to relationships with others and, consequently, to psychotherapy, in contrast to the more disturbed people who suffer from psychotic depressions. The person with depressive reaction may still be able to carry on the most important of his daily activities. For instance, he may still be able to work and to relate on a limited scale to his family, but the joys ordinarily derived from these activities are greatly diminished. He no longer shows any zest or interest in the things he does, but rather goes through them mechanically and almost automatically.

An example of depressive reaction was shown in a married woman of forty-one who stated to her physician, "I am unhappy and miserable. I get up in the morning and the day holds nothing for me. I do not like to take care of my house and I do not want to undertake anything else. It is my husband's fault. He is a selfish man. He has never considered me. We have always lived where he wanted to live and done what he wanted to do. He never spent any money on me or tried to make me happy. My daughter is married and has moved away and I have nobody. I should do something useful, I know, but I am no good at anything and I am too lazy to learn. I have one good friend. I hang on to her and bore her to death, I guess. But I just get lonely by myself. I think I have been this way since my daughter got married and left home. While she was there I felt I had an ally, I guess. But my husband does not care. He travels a lot. But even if he were home he could not cheer me up. I guess I never made much of my life but how could I with a man like that? Life is so dreary and meaningless I'd do away with myself if I had any courage but I'm too weak even for that. It doesn't seem as if I ever was very happy."

We see in this patient an ambivalence in relation both to herself and to her husband. She capriciously pities herself and then blames herself and expresses a fairly continuous resentment toward her husband. She obviously misses her daughter yet later admits she was jealous of her daughter's opportunity to make a better marriage. This was her first depressed phase. She slept well, ate well, and had no intense suicidal preoccupations, had no motor retardation, and had little surface guilt feeling. Such features distinguish her from a patient with a psychotic depressive reaction. She presents the frustration and decline in sense of well-being that beset so many people in middle life. She is a woman limited in outlook and lacking the imagination and goodwill to make the necessary adjustments to her daughter's marriage and her husband's preoccupation with business.

Her emptiness and many reproaches were alienating him but she could not deny herself the relief she found in complaining and projecting (some at least) of her own inadequacies upon fate and upon others. Such a case in a woman at this age is often called a menopausal neurosis, but this woman had no menstrual disturbances. (As we have already pointed out, the emotional symptoms of the menopause are largely psychogenically determined, anyway.) Physical examination, of course, revealed no somatic pathology. With psychotherapy and encouragement to take on some voluntary community work she improved without shock treatment. Sometimes the latter is necessary, but most cases of psychoneurotic depressive reaction should respond to a psychotherapeutic approach which combines the following features:

1. Give the patient an opportunity to ventilate resentment.

2. Help her to see the futility of reproach against either persons or fate.

3. Help her to see the defects of her childhood psychosexual growth which have made her so unresourceful with her later life.

4. Help her to see the potentialities within herself of rising above her regressed and petulant state of mind.

PSYCHOTIC DISORDERS

A psychosis is a severe form of mental illness characterized by an extensive disorganization of the personality. In a typical psychosis the individual loses his contact with reality and reveals severe disturbances in many areas of his contact with life. A psychotic reaction is a much more complex and serious abnormal type of personality reaction than is a psychoneurotic reaction. The psychotic, as his personality disorganization progresses, becomes incapable of making a social adjustment. He loses his grasp on reality and often must be hospitalized. As the ego of a psychotic breaks down, unconscious material is allowed expression in its rawest form, and its expression is bizarre, disorganized, and difficult to understand. The loss of reality means an impairment of the ego's ability to perceive, integrate, and realistically act upon events taking place in the world. Things are misinterpreted because of the presence of strong conflict within the psyche which has altered the integrity of the individual's ego functions.

We discuss specifically the psychotic disorders of the schizophrenic and the manic depressive type.

SCHIZOPHRENIC REACTIONS

Schizophrenic reactions are characterized by a marked difficulty in interpersonal relationships and usually involve a strong tendency to withdraw from reality and a fundamental disturbance of personality organization. The patient has slowly begun to weaken, and finally break, his ties with reality and with those around him. He retreats into a world of his own making since to him the real world is no longer tenable. He suffers a disorganization of his thought processes so that to the normal person he seems odd and bizarre.

The idea and the emotion are not synchronized in him as they are in the normal person, but rather the two seem disjointed. He is apt to laugh when there is nothing humorous or become irritated when there is seemingly no reason. If he is paranoid he seems to find hidden meanings in every action or expression of others. Attempts to build up a relationship with him often meet with failure since he seems to retreat before every approach. His efforts to work lack vitality and direction and his avowed goals (if any) fail to materialize. He may be merely cold and withdrawn or he may be obviously suspicious and irritable. Essentially there is the element of oddness, bizarreness, and strangeness that is apt to mystify his associates and make them feel vaguely uncomfortable.

Although the onset of schizophrenia may have seemed to be very acute, gradual changes in the individual have probably been taking place for months or even years prior to the appearance of the most obvious symptoms. It is not unusual to find that such a person has never socialized well, has been rather shy and retiring, cold and moody and at times irritable, and has led a limited social existence. Gradually these characteristics have increased in intensity until he has become more asocial, withdrawn, irritable, and given to temper outbursts if frustrated. He has become careless in appearance, sloppy in his work habits, lacking in his sense of responsibility, careless and obscene in his language at times, and increasingly suspicious of everyone. When the final break with reality becomes complete, delusions and hallucinations usually make their appearance and emotions and thoughts tend to become more unrelated and speech more irrelevant and illogical.

Etiology. The cause of schizophrenia has already been indicated, in that it is a relationship defect inherent in the pattern of living and in the quality and quantity of interpersonal values in a family. The schizophrenic never felt fully accepted from earliest infancy onward and everything he has tried to learn and everything he has tried to do has lacked meaning and satisfaction thereafter. His social ineptitude, his bizarre behavior, and his delusions and hallucinations are the logical results of a personality that has never been given the necessary personality equipment for living life. This has been the main trend of thinking by psychiatrists regarding the etiology of schizophrenic reactions for the last twenty-five years or more. In the nineteenth century schizophrenia was regarded as a defect in brain structure and there is now a return of interest to the theory of basic neurological defect. Bender feels that the importance of a basic neurological defect is crucial at least in some cases, and while she does not ignore nor even minimize the importance of the family constellation psychologically, she feels that even in the most normal family atmospheres there are some children with a basic neurological defect which cannot be overcome and will overwhelmingly condition the child toward schizophrenia.

Treatment. Regardless of etiology, which is as yet unsettled, there is a great deal of evidence to support the theory of psychological (emotional) defect due to a family atmosphere which is pathological in itself. The family, particularly the mother, in the period of infancy gives too little love and affection. There is a paucity of joy and happiness. Too much is expected of the child, too little reward given. There may be too much morbid thinking in the family atmosphere—too little reassurance around various phenomena such as sex, birth, death, war, disease, injury, and so on.

Treatment must take the form of replacement of defective emotional lacks, repair of broken attachments, correction of distorted thinking, and encouragement to face immaturity and struggle through to a healthier maturation process. Various drugs have been and are being used by some to make the patient accessible. But, once relationship with the environment has been established, a prolonged psychotherapeutic relationship with a skilled therapist is necessary for months and often years in order to strengthen the personality to the point of functioning efficiently. In fact, a person who has once been ill with a schizophrenic reaction may again need some helpful support at crucial, tension-producing periods in his life, and he, as well as his family, should accept this fact.

The best arrangement we know of at the present time is a small, homelike environment prepared to: (1) take an interest in the patient, (2) like what is likable about him, (3) share in his present and past suffering, (4) understand his emotional and personal needs and, (5) fill the role of family members who have defected in his growth experience. An environment providing daily psychiatric therapy, with assistants who can understand and carry on what is needed for the patient, will do the most to rehabilitate the schizophrenic back to health.

The most successfully treated schizophrenics (who remain well and function effectively) seem to achieve two things. They find a corrective atmosphere, which supplies what was defective during the original family growth effort. And they acquire the ability to abreact, i.e., talk out with feeling the original defective family relationships. Schizophrenics who can do this (differing little from neurotics) go on to health and success. Those who can not be helped to see and appreciate these basic fundamentals of a cure remain locked up in their defenses and, hence, remain ill.

MANIC DEPRESSIVE REACTION

Manic depressive reactions are more benign psychoses than schizophrenic reactions, inasmuch as the pathological state of mind is usually circumscribed and self-limited. The patient suffers from an exaggerated mood of depression or elation which lasts on the average from three months to two years if untreated. The condition is called "manic depressive" because the patient is vulnerable not only to depressions but also to manic episodes. One phase, however, can occur without the other. Some patients, for instance, have several depressive periods throughout their lives while others have several manic attacks and some alternate between both. The patient who suffers from depression complains of fatigue, loss of appetite, loss of zest for living. Everything he undertakes is a great effort. Ambition and energy are lacking. Sometimes there is insomnia and restlessness and there are practically always feelings of unworthiness and guilt and sometimes suicidal thoughts and drives. The condition, while similar in nature, is more severe in degree than the psychoneurotic depressive reaction.

The manic patient is overactive, excessively alert, sleeps little, is overtalkative, full of plans, often writing long letters and making excessively numerous phone calls. Often there is poor judgment in the spending of money and there may be unconventional romantic and erotic interests. The manic individual is often amusing for a short period of time and then his excessive pressure of speech becomes tiresome.

Physically the manic depressive patient is free of actual disease. In the depressed patient the body physiology is slowed down and in the manic patient it is accelerated. These two phases as described are the extremes of mood change and together have been called the *affective reactions*.

Although the incidence of patients admitted to mental hospitals with manic depressive reaction is less than schizophrenia, the figures remain large. The Bureau of Census found that a formidable per cent of all patients admitted to mental institutions were suffering from this particular type of disturbance. As in schizophrenic reactions, there are many patients in the incipient stages of this psychosis who never reach mental hospitals but who remain burdens and problems to their families for many years. Milder evidence of manic behavior or depressive behavior ordinarily does not lead to hospitalization, but is certainly capable of disrupting family life for months and even years.

Differential Diagnosis. Manic depressive reactions may not always be recognized for what they are. In the depressed phase of the illness, the sufferer may focus so much attention upon symptoms such as fatigue or faulty function of the gastrointestinal tract that organic disease is persistently looked for and the emotional state overlooked. In the manic phase of the illness, overactivity of the thyroid gland may be suspected as the cause of physical and mental overactivity. Actually both the manic and depressed phases may be seen when syphilis invades the brain tissues and causes structural change. These points are just a few which illustrate how important it is to seek the best advice when mood swings affect a family member.

Complications. One of the foremost complications of the depressed phase of this illness is suicide. There are about 17,000 suicides annually in this country and many of them occur while in the grip of depression. Part of the examination of a depressed person is to ascertain whether he has suicidal intentions. While he may occasionally have them and conceal them, generally he is quite frank about them and welcomes both an opportunity to talk about them and seek protection from them. It is not harmful to speak about suicide, for discussion does not condone the idea nor does it shock or hurt the pride of the sick person. If the question is asked calmly and matter-of-factly along with others it has no special significance beyond a rational seeking of information. If the impulse to self-destruction is strong, then obviously the patient needs protection. This usually means entering a hospital for mental illness, where people in such a state of mind are understood and treated.

Those patients who enter into the manic phase of this illness—the milder state often being called hypomania—are in certain danger from which they too need protection. Being exuberant, overactive, and expansive, they plan and carry out adventures which may bring financial loss as the result of defective judgment, or romantic activities which bring criticism, embarrassment to relatives, and regret to themselves later. Commitment to a mental hospital may seem hard for relatives to carry through, but if they understand these inherent dangers they will realize it is for the patient's best interests.

Fortunately, the manic depressive reactions are relatively rare—more rare than psychoneurotic or psychophysiologic reactions. They are not discussed in detail in this book. Enough has been said, however to indicate that they are emotional problems of living—serious ones at that—and to sensitize the reader to their presence.

Etiology. Manic depressive reactions were once regarded as hereditary. With the more intensive study that has taken place during the last fifty years of the various factors that go into making up the human personality, the consensus seems to be that a manic depressive reaction is due to a failure in adjustment to life and the symptoms are the unfortunate results of efforts at repair. The depressed patient's self-criticism is both the criticism he received as a child and the criticism he feels others should be giving him now for a life he has lived inadequately. The manic patient's boastfulness, pseudosociability, and overactivity are pathetic efforts to try to catch up with a life he has not lived in the way he unconsciously wished.

Treatment. Both phases of the manic depressive psychosis respond quite well to electroshock therapy. Eighty per cent of the cases of depression and a smaller number of manic cases return to a satisfactory contact with reality after six to twelve shock treatments given every other day. A psychotherapeutic treatment, if available, would be preferable. However, few areas have the psychotherapists necessary for a long treatment process.

PSYCHOPHYSIOLOGIC DISORDERS

The term psychophysiologic refers to those conditions caused by the physiological expression of chronic and exaggerated emotion, much of which is unconscious. It seems wiser to use the term *psychophysiologic* rather than the term *psychosomatic,* because the latter has come to indicate so many different ideas that it lacks the specificity required in a scientific classification. On the one hand, the term psychosomatic indicates an approach to the patient which is as old as medicine itself and infers the consideration of man as a unit rather than as separate psyche and soma. On the other hand, psychosomatic is a term which has more recently been used to indicate a certain group of physiological disorders whose etiology often stems from psychological problems. Many terms such as organ neuroses, cardiac neurosis, and gastric neurosis have been used for these and related conditions.

It seems advisable here to recall the broader implication of the old term psychosomatic. It indicates that each man possesses a psyche and soma, and what occurs in one system influences the other. Man reacts, in other words, as a unit, and it is basically impossible to consider one of these systems without considering the other. When a man is angry this event is not purely psychological. There are equally important somatic components which are easily measurable and demonstrable. Similarly, one cannot consider a cirrhotic liver without taking into account the fact that it belongs to a man with a wife, three children, and a mortgage, and that the man's emotional state depends upon his physical well-being and ability to meet the demands which his environment places upon him. In other words, we do not find a specific disease, but rather a human being who is suffering from some pathology.

While it is true that astute practitioners of the art and science of medicine have always approached their patients from a psychosomatic viewpoint, it nevertheless remains true that many of the most important advances in understanding relationships between mind and body have come during relatively recent times. In the past many physicians excelled in their ability to produce improvement, particularly in certain patients, because of their intuitive understanding of the great importance of the emotional elements in such patients' illnesses. Particularly within the last two decades, however, our increased understanding of these matters and improved techniques of research have added a firm scientific foundation to what originally was part of the art of medicine.

The psychophysiological conditions, then, as we here use the term, refer to those conditions in which the physiological (or eventually even the pathological) dysfunction is brought about by a chronic emotional state present in the individual. We know that there is a close interrelationship among the autonomic system, the endocrines, and the psyche. This is an extremely complicated relationship, but it is recognized that a disturbance in one of these systems is capable of producing changes in the other two. What we are concerned with particularly are chronic disturbances of the psyche which subsequently produce changes through the autonomic or endocrine systems and thus eventually lead to physiological and possibly pathological bodily disturbances. When a normal individual becomes angry, certain autonomic and endocrine changes occur. His sympathetic system becomes more active, his adrenals increase their output of adrenalin, and the body makes preparation for either fight or flight. In such a situation the physiological functions remain in a constant state of preparation for fight or flight. Blood pressure is elevated, sympathetics are hyperactive, and other such mechanisms are constantly alerted. If this situation continues over a period of days, weeks, months, and years, certain physiological changes eventually become pathological and the tissue damage becomes apparent. Eventually the entire process reaches a stage of irreversibility because of the actual organic damage that has ensued. At this point, although we have a truly organic condition, it is nevertheless psychophysiological in its origin.

The classification of psychophysiologic disorders is as follows:

> Psychophysiologic skin reaction
> Psychophysiologic musculoskeletal reaction
> Psychophysiologic respiratory reaction
> Psychophysiologic cardiovascular reaction
> Psychophysiologic hemic and lymphatic reaction
> Psychophysiologic gastrointestinal reaction
> Psychophysiologic genitourinary reaction

Psychophysiologic endocrine reaction
Psychophysiologic nervous system reaction
Psychophysiologic reaction of organs of
    special sense

Typical Case Presentation—Psychophysiologic Gastrointestinal Reaction

Social and Psychological History:

Infancy (Age 1–2): Mother pampered him. Father ignored him.

Childhood (Age 2–6): Timid, shy. No special interests.

Grade School (Age 6–13): Fearful and tried to hide this by limited participation in play.

High School (Age 13–18): A poor mixer. Participated in a few sports. Little interest in studies.

Adulthood (Age 21): Married a gentle, competent woman in early twenties. Went to work in a small industrial plant where father had worked. Felt like "the kid," unaccepted; did not know how to make friends. Could not share in camaraderie of the men.

Parenthood (Age 25): Son born. While he was deriving so little emotional satisfaction from work, he was also ignoring the potential pleasures in enjoyment of his wife and child. His psyche was becoming impoverished and empty and life was more burdensome, formidable, and anxiety-producing.

Etiology:

The unfulfillment of emotional needs necessary for security resulted in anxiety, became more and more disturbing to body physiology.

Careful physical examinations, X-ray, and laboratory studies were negative. But the distress he suffered made him feel that something toxic or "sick-producing" was being overlooked. After eighteen months of suffering, he stopped work and this event caused the treatment to be changed from antiacids and sedation to psychotherapy.

Psychotherapeutic Process:

1. Kept in foreground the examinations, which revealed no tissue pathology.

Symptomatology:

Began to have anorexia in the morning; nausea after trying to eat. This was followed by distress after lunch and dinner; alternating constipation and diarrhea. A few weeks later he developed griping pain in abdomen. After two months of symptomatic treatment he developed fatigue so that work became an additional burden. One month later he began to sleep poorly. Six weeks later he began to feel that the griping pains meant ulcer or cancer. He worked under great anxiety, saw many doctors, and tried various self-medications, to no avail.

2. Used charts to show autonomic nerve distribution to glands, blood vessels, muscle tissues, and organs.

3. Called attention to emotions which disturb organ functions.

4. Pointed out his need for friendship and interest but also how he was missing it by fear of people and not knowing how to be friendly.

5. Gave him specific formulations of dynamics as learned from history as follows: "To get strength for healthy body-functioning again, you need security through better human relations. The men at work are willing to accept you if you accept them. Your wife and child need a cheerful man who will notice and appreciate them rather than one who worries about his digestion. Let your physician have the responsibility of deciding whether your body is sick or well. You relinquish that responsibility into trained hands while you do what you can learn to do: namely to offer yourself to people in such a way that they can help cure you."

6. "Your body's distresses are secondary to your mind's need for love and goodwill and the sense of physical well-being which comes from good social relations. Take your wife and child out, go to the movies, invite your friends in. Begin that golf playing you have wanted to do. You do not need to suffer if you will begin new habits of thinking and acting."

7. "You need to live in friendly relations with people so that you make up to yourself for some of the lack of love and interest denied you by your father during your childhood. You should accept the fact that for health you need a wider range of interests and personal contacts for healthy living than either your mother or father required."

Effects on Symptomatology:

Some reduction of anxiety began when he received tangible explanation for symptoms. Doubts would creep in and he would ask, "Are you explaining the cause of all my trouble, as I feel 'wrecked' in my bowels?"

He would be reassured and then able to run his mind a little more in the direction of personality self-improvement. He slept better. He began golf with a little less fatigue. He protested, however, at the idea of increased social activity. His wife liked dancing while he did not. So he needed encouragement to learn. He had never played cards so he learned—reluctantly—but he learned. He needed to be shown and convinced that a more altruistic and well-rounded personality would be productive of better health.

Improvement in symptoms is always convincing and one of the physician's best allies in psychotherapy.

His upper and lower bowel quieted down: the griping pain stopped, appetite returned, and digestion became comfortable. Three weeks after treatment began he was back at work, albeit with some residual symptoms, but in three months he was symptom-free.

PERSONALITY DISORDERS

Personality disorders form a large and heterogeneous group of emotional problems which are characterized primarily by abnormalities in an individual's mode of behavior or action. Personality, as an all-inclusive term, encompasses the sum total of an individual's behavior which is peculiar to him. Each person creates certain impressions on others about how he will react to various situations. For instance, one individual becomes recognized by his associates as being aggressive and dominating, while another is labeled as shy and retiring. It is with the deviations from the normal behavior pattern that personality disorders are concerned.

When an individual, in the process of growing up, perpetuates within himself inner immaturities and conflicts, thus leaving a certain deficiency within the over-all structure of his personality, he may reveal his emotional problems in any one of four general directions. (1) He becomes psychoneurotic (thus developing defenses against his immaturities and neurotic symptoms); (2) he becomes a personality problem (thus displacing his conflicts toward the outer world by acting them out in his pattern of behavior); (3) he develops psychophysiologic disorders (thus draining his chronic emotional tension off into autonomic channels and producing eventual organic pathology); (4) he becomes psychotic (thus suffering ego disintegration with loss of ability to face reality).

The patient with a personality disorder is one whose behavior deviates from normal because his immaturities are finding expression in his behavior rather than being dealt with in any one of the other three methods.

We discuss those personality disorders called paranoid personality, antisocial reaction and dyssocial reaction, and those leading to the misuse of alcohol and drugs and to unusual sexual behavior.

PARANOID PERSONALITY

The paranoid personality is the person who is extremely sensitive in all his relationships, with a tendency to be suspicious of the motivation of everyone. He relates much of what is said or what goes on about him to himself and attributes to other people a dislike of himself, and would like to reproach or punish them for this imagined neglect or hostility. Whenever anything happens his first concern is whether or not there was anything in the occurrence directed against him by someone else. These individuals are oversensitive, envious, jealous, stubborn, possessive, and quick to feel a lack of attention on the part of others. They seem to start on the basic assumption that no one likes them and everyone is out to do them harm, and subsequently they find in their environment innumerable "realistic" reasons to believe this. They complain loudly and bitterly against all the imagined slights and rejections which they feel are thrust upon them. Their primary difficulty is an extensive use of the mechanism of projection. Basically they are bitter and hostile against the world but they project this bitterness and feel that the world is bitter and hostile to them. Unfortunately, the world usually does become bitter against them eventually because of their tendency to be so suspicious and resentful. This, of course, makes it easier for them to find reasons to "prove" that they are disliked and maligned.

These patients have suffered great deprivation of affection during their early years. However, rather than succumb to an attitude of discouragement and defeat, they "come out fighting" at every pos-sible occasion and feel that they have not been treated fairly. Their favorite attitude seems to be, "Nobody is going to push me around." They are often an extremely disturbing and antagonistic element of society. On many occasions they go further than fighting for themselves and take up arms against various social injustices so that they become "crusaders." They may take legal steps to protect their personal rights and to correct what they consider to be unfair circumstances directed against them. They have often been, as a result, referred to as "litigious personalities." They are quick to resort to lawsuits and other legal procedures, so as not to be denied their "basic constitutional rights." The result of this tendency is often a long series of lawsuits over relatively minor points. These people are usually of sufficient intelligence to have made themselves adequately aware of legal procedures so that their cases cannot be dismissed without expensive trials, suits, and so forth.

Such individuals sometimes reach the degree of unreality where they are truly mentally ill and require hospital care. However, most of them are merely regarded by others as obnoxious, queer, and difficult to deal with. They are referred to frequently as being mentally ill, but such a label, although perhaps seriously meant, cannot be adequately substantiated as far as legal procedures are concerned.

Establishing this point is complicated by the fact that, should anyone make known to such an individual that he is considered mentally incompetent, it will only lead to further resentment which the patient seems to enjoy expressing. Essentially such people are extremely individualistic in their approach and therefore are better dealt with tactfully. They cannot be changed. They can only be temporarily placated. They have a great need for attention and consideration stemming from their early deprivation. In a way, their behavior seems directed toward forcing everyone to give them their due consideration, attention, affection, and recognition which they missed earlier in life.

Treatment. As was stated, persons with a paranoid personality cannot be changed by their families or employers. They are with difficulty changed by anyone and then only in special circumstances. Let us suppose that such a contentious personality held a good position which he needed. He might, if told he had to seek professional help or lose his position, be willing to work with a psychiatrist and look within himself and try to change his personality pattern. With such pressure upon him he might possibly open his mind a little to the statement, "People are not out to hurt you. You are just demanding more in terms of consideration than the situation offers to anyone." It is very difficult to enable such a person to understand his deep hunger for love. While such a need may be obvious to everyone else it has only sinister meaning to him. Any explanation of the love he needs seems to him to represent the intolerable accusation that he is childish or sexually perverse and he usually has to reject interpretation. Magnanimity in his environment by everyone concerned helps to keep him going and keeps him placated but it is quite a strain upon those supplying it, since rarely if ever is there any gratitude forthcoming for the utmost kindness and understanding displayed.

This particular emotional condition seems to illustrate very well indeed that intelligent, capable, superior people may suffer serious personality distortions from childhood vicissitudes. No organic brain defect has ever been found in these people and no drug or other treatment has ever been of the slightest value in changing their oversensitive, truculent attitude.

ANTISOCIAL REACTION

There is a certain group of individuals within our society who are extremely self-centered, hedonistic, and living primarily upon the pleasure principle. They are callous people who have little regard for the rights and privileges of others. They want what they want when they want it and give no thought to the other person from whom they are taking. They lie, steal, fight or use any other means which seem to them most advantageous to gain their own ends. They profit little from experience or punishment and form extremely weak relationships with others. They have no loyalty to anyone except themselves and primarily love only themselves. They reveal a remarkable lack of a sense of responsibility. They are inconsistent except in their seeking for their own pleasures. Such individuals as this have been classified in the past as "constitutional psychopathic inferiors" or "psychopathic personalities." Most of them give a history dating back to very early childhood of an attitude which obviously did not take into account the feelings of others. They have never attained a real devotion or sincere relationship with anyone. They often have drifted, again seeking their own gratification.

Such persons, when confronted in the psychiatric interview, rationalize the greater part of their behavior. They admit only what they feel the interviewing physician already knows. They minimize or, if possible, deny other things which they feel may not be known. They attribute to themselves relatively high motives in many cases. If they are frustrated, as can happen during an interview, they become irritable and resentful. The emotional instability of these patients is notorious and they are easily stirred to anger. If they have sufficient courage, they will attack; otherwise they will quickly find other means out of the plight. Many of them are capable of making excellent initial impressions, only to be found later to have meant nothing of what they originally said. Such people as this have often achieved, by one means or another, relatively respectable standings, perhaps even in the professions. They then go about their business of hedonistic pleasure in such a way as to quickly run afoul of society's rules and mores. They may attempt to show guilt when punished but really do not feel it. Essentially the majority of them lack a stable social conscience and do not benefit from the repeated difficulties consequent on the same antisocial act. Their problem presumably stems from an extremely early and relatively severe lack of parental warmth, often combined with excessive parental punishment. They have been unable, early in their lives, to form a stable relationship with their parents. Their ego growth has been deficient and has been distorted to the point that they are extremely narcissistic and egocentric. If such a person marries, he often marries someone who has some need for him as an auxiliary ego—as someone to live luxuriously, carelessly, and hedonistically for him when he cannot. Or, the person he marries is too dependent or too afraid of social condemnation to break with him. Antisocial personalities involve other people who later would like to be rid of them but fear some unscrupulous retaliation from them.

Treatment. Society's method of "treatment" of the antisocial personality is incarceration. However, this tends only to confirm the antisocial person's conviction that it is not worth while loving anyone. He is treated, in many instances, with cruelty and deprivation which enhances his feeling that loyalty ties are useless. Such an individual really suffers a severe basic personality inadequacy. It is extremely difficult to establish a therapeutic relationship with him and this, of course, is necessary prior to any real maturation. These persons are infantile in their emotional lives and relate on this basis to others about them. They are willing to listen, to agree, and to try to seek their own ends from the therapeutic relationship. However, the minute anything is asked of them or they are put under any pressure in the treatment situation, they are apt to pout, to become irritable and even rebellious. If they are seen on an outpatient basis where they are responsible for their own lives, they frequently miss appointments, particularly if the material discussed has not been to their liking. Any small slight or irritation produced by the psychiatrist results in their refusing to return. They have such a lack of superego (sense of social responsibility) that they suffer little guilt from their repeated transgressions toward other people. There is little that motivates them to continue therapy and they prefer to seek their own satisfactions by the infantile acting out which they have always used. The therapeutic prognosis for such people is extremely guarded. Sometimes limited gains can be made if they are treated on an inpatient basis where their daily activities can be controlled so they cannot get into trouble. However, innumerable patients of this type have begun therapy on an outpatient basis, only to quit because of the anxiety produced or to commit some antisocial act for which they were subsequently incarcerated so that therapy could not proceed.

DYSSOCIAL REACTION

This category is represented by the individual who disregards the social rules and regulations and frequently runs into conflict with the law because he comes from an environment in which such practices are considered the normal and usual thing to do. There are certain isolated segments of our population in which various behavior standards are a great deal different from those accepted by society in general. At times this variance is within a family and at times within a small group of society. The patient with this dyssocial reaction may have little conflict within himself and be a relatively mature individual from the standpoint of his own family or small segment of society. However, his values have been so distorted and disturbed by them that he is unable to live in peace with the rest of society. It is interesting to note that psychological testing of such an individual may reveal a relatively mature pattern because the relationship between id, ego, and superego seems to be free from conflict and there is little demonstrable immaturity present. However, this same "mature" person may, at the same time, be chronically involved in conflicts with the law.

Treatment. The slum areas and other underprivileged portions of our population are fertile breeding grounds for dyssocial reactions. There, youngsters, particularly during their adolescence, often come into conflict with the law. The majority of their contemporaries are doing the same thing and for them to try to abide by the usual rules and regulations of our society would be extremely difficult. Their parents often talk freely about stealing or lying or cheating and these youngsters absorb the same values. The therapeutic milieu which is to be of benefit is one wherein they can learn some of the more stable, useful, and accepted social mores. It is for this reason that such places as Father Flanagan's Boy's Town are extremely useful to this type of delinquent adolescent. Such youngsters are not emotionally sick in the true sense of the word, but merely have never been exposed to an environment which teaches them the proper modes of behavior. They are able to introject and take into themselves such improved methods of behavior if they are surrounded by the proper environment. They are usually capable of loyalty and good relationships and, if placed under the care of mature individuals, they are capable of changing their behavior in such a way as to be able to get along with everyday society when they return to it. These individuals have a much better prognosis in general, especially if they can be removed from their pathological environment, than do the antisocial reaction types.

ALCOHOLISM

It has been estimated that there are over one and a half million people in the United States who are social problems by reason of the excessive use of alcohol. This is a large number of people, and they constitute a tremendous social problem. Everyone is familiar with the proverbial alcoholic who spends all his money on liquor, leaving his family without food or clothing and often physically abusing them as well. The picture is truer to life than we like to realize.

Every person with an alcoholic problem has a personality difficulty. Every alcoholic is an immature, insecure, oversensitive and anxious person who is suffering from marked feelings of inferiority, unable to meet and enjoy people socially or unable to get on with his work without the support of alcohol in fairly large quantities. This indictment against the alcoholic sounds serious but with rare exceptions it is true. The reason some do not as yet generally accept it as true is because they often see the alcoholic at his best rather than at his worst. They see him before he has drunk too much, when he is genial, friendly, often full of compliments, telling jokes and amusing people with his wit. But after he has a little more to drink his wit becomes monotonous and his stories cease to hold the center of attention, whereupon his sensitivity comes to the fore, he drinks some more in order to cover up his feelings of chagrin, and finally he becomes so objectionable that he has to be removed from the scene.

The use of alcohol in large quantities is an indictment against society and shows a lack of maturity in that society. Unquestionably too many people need alcohol to produce friendliness and a state of mind suitable for social intercourse or for carrying on their work, which means they are not fundamentally mature enough or friendly enough to carry on these functions without alcohol.

Drinking together, no matter what the beverage may be, is a symbol of friendship and goodwill and has a place in our civilization. Just as drinking and eating mean so much to us when we are very young, so they continue to have their place throughout life. As hosts we serve tea or coffee or wine or beer or liquor or a soft drink as an evidence of friendship. The drink produces a pleasant sensation within and we feel emotionally warmer toward each other. This custom has a definite place in our society. However, as time goes on, either because life grows more complicated or because it makes more demands, people seem to need more alcohol in order to be friendly in the company of others or in order to get work done.

Why do people have to drink excessively in order to help their personalities accomplish what they are supposed to accomplish without any such help? A regression to an oral activity takes place in the alcoholic. The habit of drinking—having something go into the mouth and down the throat—has a great deal of meaning for these people. In infancy we were warmed and made comfortable by drinking milk and being nursed by the mother. And in the same way that these attentions quieted the anxiety of the infant, so does drinking liquor fulfill the alcoholic's present need. Alcohol acts as a narcotic and raises the sense of well-being; it affects the brain and deadens for the moment the painful impressions of unhappiness that have been built up with the years. For instance: A man enters a roomful of people. He feels strange, awkward, out of place, unwanted and uncomfortable. He is reluctant to get into conversation with anyone for fear of being regarded as silly or dull or stupid. Then he has a drink or two which dulls his anxiety and lo! a miracle occurs: he begins to feel interesting and important and worth while and to achieve a greater sense of comfort and well-being. He says to himself: "If two drinks work so marvelously, six will make me practically a genius." And so he continues, always hoping to reach the point of genuine ecstasy and well-being—of inner security. But he never achieves this happy state. He just gets drunk instead.

As we have already pointed out, the alcoholic personality has had early life experiences of great deprivation so that he or she grows up feeling insecure and unable to cope with responsibilities. He reaches a point where he says, "Nothing ordinarily seems worth while. It is only when I am drinking that life seems bearable." If our experiences are pleasant and satisfying enough, we do not need to lean too heavily upon alcohol to make us feel buoyant and able to function from day to day.

Let us look at the matter of the personality of the alcoholic from the standpoint of sexual development. We have already said that the alcoholic is immature and that he seems to have strong oral trends. These grow naturally from the tendency to keep children dependent. Many parents fear that if the child is allowed to be aggressive and curious and has his curiosity satisfied he will grow up to be a problem in management or will leave parental authority too soon, and so he is kept anxious and dependent. Because of this mistaken attitude, young people are kept from knowing the facts of sexuality and from developing into loving self-reliant individuals. All of which makes child-rearing easier (in the early years at least), but with disastrous results to the child's personality, to his social development, and to his genital level of functioning—which is the goal of life in successful home and family formation.

Grown people cannot remain dependent in attitude if they are to be successful with life's problems. It is this attitude of dependency that is present in the relation of the alcoholic who marries a maternal type of woman. He senses she is going to excuse him and take care of him. He works at his job for a year or two, drinks more and more and enjoys her less and less. His interest is only in the bottle, and he neglects his obligations. After each drinking bout his wife is prone to excuse him and thinks, "Poor fellow, it is too bad." If anyone objects to his behavior and tries to make him a responsible person, his wife sympathizes, smuggles liquor in for him, condones his behavior, and gives no co-operation.

Such a wife may complain about her husband's drinking and seem to want him cured, but actually she needs to continue to indulge him. She does not want to make him stand up and be a man for two main reasons common to most human beings. One is the tendency to indulge others in those things that are important to them because we like to be indulged ourselves. The other is the fear of arousing the other's hostility and reproaches when something is taken away from him. However, if the wives and families of alcoholic men want to help them, they should not mind reproaches.

When men come to indulge themselves more and more in the oral gratification of drinking, in the association of others who are likewise heavy drinkers, and in the mistreatment of their wives, they show themselves to be immature sexually, acting like irresponsible children rather than like men who have an adult genital attitude toward the world. We were once asked by the court to examine a man who had been drinking. He was married and "doing very well at it," as he put it. We pressed him with questions about his attitude toward his wife and his marriage and when he finally saw what we meant he said, "If I had to choose between a woman and a bottle, I would take the bottle every time."

To summarize: First, the alcoholic is made to feel warm, comfortable, and glowing inside with the alcohol, partly through the physical activity of drinking and partly through the physiological reaction within him. Second, the alcohol reacts upon the mind so that it becomes possible to fantasy more pleasantly. Third, it deadens some of the pain of anxiety and depression and makes the task of socializing temporarily easier.

The more the alcoholic uses alcohol, the more he is going in the direction of all drug addicts, becoming more and more dependent upon it—be it a narcotic, a sedative, or anything that gives him a "lift." He neglects to concern himself with the satisfactions to be gained through contacts with human beings and from work. The final result is that alcohol is the only thing that satisfies him and the getting of it his chief concern—like the infant whose chief concern is obtaining milk and being nursed.

The question arises with friends, family, and doctor—what shall be done about this condition? A specific case in this regard is a man of thirty-three who was the youngest of five children. His mother was a sensitive, empty, narrow-minded person who had little to give the children and who as she grew older became extremely bitter about life; by the time this youngest son came along she had only bitterness and criticism for him. Her chief pleasure seemed to be in making sarcastic remarks and in driving the children to a point of confusion—whereupon she would give them a severe verbal berating. She rarely left the house but stayed at home and complained about the neighbors and her husband, quarreled with the children and had almost no motherly feeling toward them, and particularly toward this boy. The father was a fairly capable businessman whose wife was too severe for him. He sacrificed the children, and particularly this boy, to her mental state, and instead of standing up for the children and defending them against her, he always took the attitude, "Let's keep the peace. You know how mother is."

In spite of this atmosphere the boy got through high school and wanted to go to college. His mother disapproved, and again, instead of backing up the boy, the father said, "You know how your mother is. Let's keep the peace because mother will make it too hard for us if we don't." This, on top of all the other disappointments he had had, made the boy so bitter, resentful, and dissatisfied that he took to drinking in increasing quantity. While under the influence of alcohol he would become irritable and pugnacious because his irritability and hostility toward his mother came forth. He had been brought up in such a hostile family environment that he could not feel friendliness anywhere. He held a job for a short time but gradually worked for shorter and shorter periods, eventually getting into a state that would require a long period of rehabilitation; that is, if it should be possible to cure him at all, because alcohol may be the last support a potential psychotic holds onto before going insane. Some people are mildly alcoholic all their lives and are fairly successful. Others go downhill rather rapidly when the underlying neurosis or psychosis is severe, and they may go all the way from apparent success to complete failure in three or four years.

Treatment. Various attempts to cure alcoholism were made at one time with the use of drugs, whose purpose was, on the whole, to make the taste of alcohol obnoxious. Another attempt that is still sometimes used is to put a drug into the alcohol which will make the drinker sick and in this way build up an association between alcoholic indulgence and feeling sick and miserable which will induce the person to leave it alone.

The latest and best of these drugs is one called Antabuse (tetraethylthiuramdisulfide). Any discussion on the treatment of alcoholism would be incomplete without mention of this drug. If patients are given appropriate doses of this drug, they react violently to the effects of alcohol. The autonomic nervous system is thrown out of balance; the patient suffers from remarkable nausea and vomiting as well as palpitations and other symptoms. The theory behind the use of this drug is that its effect produces such a remarkably distasteful reaction if alcohol is imbibed that patients are thereby discouraged from drinking. The ordinary patient can be maintained on a dose of perhaps a half gram a day after having been given a half gram three times a day for a couple of days and then gradually tapered off to the maintenance dose. Patients are ordinarily given a carefully controlled "test" with this drug after they have been put on a maintenance dose. They are allowed to see, under a controlled situation, the violence of their reaction to alcohol, and this also contributes to their abstinence in the future.

There are several disadvantages to the use of this drug. In the first place it is not a real "cure" for alcoholism. At best it must be utilized in conjunction with psychotherapeutic interviews. Its use also requires the permission of the patient and his willingness to participate. (It is relatively easy for the noncooperative patient to surreptitiously reject his Antabuse or even regurgitate so that he will be free to imbibe alcohol.) It is also essential that both the patient and his family realize the extreme toxic effects which can result from an excessive intake of alcohol while taking this drug; even death may result. It is essential that the patient have frequent examinations by a physician which should include laboratory studies and especially those involving the status of the blood and blood-producing areas. It should be remembered that the chronic alcoholic patient is a psychologically disturbed individual whose emotional problems make him a questionable candidate for the use of such a dangerous drug. Only under the most optimal conditions where both the patient and his family are cooperative in the treatment procedure may Antabuse be utilized as a temporary crutch while psychotherapeutic endeavors are being made.

To help an alcoholic, he must first be made to understand himself and his reasons for drinking. He has to be shown why he is failing with life itself, and then helped to be more of a success. This education may be done by the doctor working with the patient alone or in a small group with the same problem, in private practice or in a sanitarium, or by contact with an organization called Alcoholics Anonymous. Those sanitaria that have been most successful with alcoholic cases are the ones where individual attention is given to the patient not only in regard to a physical program but also to his personality problems. His anxieties, fears, emotional needs, and anything in the immediate environment that makes him feel distressed and which he cannot face are discussed with him. Then an effort is made to trace these anxieties back to the original situation that created them, and patient and doctor set to work to correct them as far as is possible.

Some years ago we heard an alcoholic who had been in a great deal of trouble say, "I have not a friend in the world. I do not trust anybody and I can tell you in a fairly short time why I have come to feel this way." He went on to relate experiences where he felt his friends had let him down. The point was that in all these experiences he was unduly sensitive to what was done and said. Furthermore he did not have enough goodwill in his own makeup to forgive these things and to realize that he was not being turned down so completely after all. People who come to sanitaria for the treatment of alcoholism feel they have been badly treated. If one word is said against them they respond by feeling justified for having used alcohol to try to find a little happiness in a world that has been neglecting and mistreating them for so long. They have to be shown that it is not the world that is so bad but their sensitivity and fear of the world.

Another favorable factor in sanitaria lies in the fact that others are there who are also alcoholics. When patients find others with similar problems, they are more willing to work and struggle with their own. It is easier for them to find that they can get along without alcohol. Thus self-respect and loyalty to family and friends increase, and they leave the sanitarium with new ideas and a new perspective on themselves. Their success is often due to the fact that attention has been focused sharply on their personality problems. The best of these sanitaria have the atmosphere of a fraternity, where fraternal feelings are carefully cultivated. A strong personal entreaty is made to "stay on the wagon," and staying on the wagon is made to look as attractive as possible. Also, the appeal to stay on the wagon is made for the sake of the sanitarium itself. And so patients leave with the feeling that they cannot fall into old ways because of loyalty to the sanitarium and to the doctor in charge.

Many have been helped by the organization called Alcoholics Anonymous, branches of which exist in many cities. It might be of some value to doctors to see how the organization is run and how it aims to help the man who is drinking. At their meetings the general problems of alcoholism are discussed. In addition, the drinkers themselves may get up and discuss their personal problems. This group feeling is vitally important. They feel that they belong to something and someone, and that feeling acts as a sustaining force through the week between meetings.

Each utilizes his concept of God and religious action in his own way. They are asked to take an interest in and help each other, and thus reduce the great degree of egocentricity that is so characteristic of alcoholics. Together they learn to function effectively without alcohol. Nearly everyone who has difficulty with alcohol has to stop drinking entirely. He cannot drink even a little. He cannot drink beer or ale with its small alcoholic content, for before long he will reach the whisky stage again. The only thing to be done is to leave it alone entirely.

Alcoholics sometimes attempt psychoanalysis, which involves intensive work on the personality and seeing the patient as frequently as every day. The doctor, on the other hand, who treats the alcoholic in his usual office practice by psychotherapy should not be surprised if he is not successful, for the patient may not have adequate motivation for a treatment requiring so much self-study and emotional deprivation combined. It is not of much help to send alcoholics to a large mental hospital to stay for a while, for very little is accomplished, and often the only benefit derived is that they are without alcohol for a time and that their families are temporarily relieved. Mental hospitals are filled with psychotics and others suffering from severe personality disorders, and alcoholism is so subtle and so difficult to treat in a mental hospital that these hospitals do not relish taking alcoholics as patients. It can be seen that the treatment of the alcoholic requires full co-operation from all concerned, for the personality illness underlying alcoholism is serious and requires great patience and resourcefulness.

USE OF SEDATIVES, STIMULANTS, AND NARCOTICS

A cause of some concern to the medical profession and others interested in mental health and social welfare is the increased tendency of many individuals in our population to use both sedative and stimulant drugs to aid themselves in maintaining a desired sense of well-being.

Human beings may become addicted to a variety of drugs. Such drugs have in common the fact that they induce a false sense of well-being and, at least temporarily, minimize the stresses and strains of the world and also lower the level of inner anxiety. The addict has become extremely dependent upon the repeated and chronic use of drugs. At times, with certain of the drugs, there are physiological changes which will produce severe symptoms should the drug be withdrawn. Other drugs have no such painful physical withdrawal symptoms, but nevertheless are difficult for the addict to leave alone. Almost everyone who becomes an addict does so because of underlying personality difficulties. Addicts are unable to tolerate the tensions and frustrations of ordinary living and resort to the use of a drug in order to escape. Since removal of the drug only places them again in the difficult anxiety-ridden state present before the addiction, such patients are extremely difficult to cure.

The barbiturates are among the *sedative drugs* most commonly used to promote sleep at night as well as to relieve tension or "the jitters" during the day. Much of this drug taking is self-directed and while it does not produce an addiction syndrome as do opium and other narcotics, yet a dependency on one's "sleeping pill" or upon a drug for relief of tension can become serious and difficult to give up.

The insomnia sufferer often has a superstition that needs clarification. He believes that eight hours' sleep are necessary to maintain health and that any marked departure from this routine is inimical to health. This belief just is not true. *Rest* is important to the maintenance of health but whether one is unconscious during the rest period is important only from a comfort standpoint, not from a basic health standpoint. Granted, it *is* difficult for a person to lie quietly awake in bed during the night while the rest of the world seems to be sleeping. But if he *would* lie quietly the necessary repair to his fatigued body would take place. The insomniac is not suffering from wakefulness per se. Rather, he suffers from his worries, body tensions, and fears. A person with insomnia has fear of an unsuccessful contest against sleep much as a student has fear before an examination. Just as a worried businessman will doubt his ability to carry a given deal to success, so the insomniac doubts his ability to sleep. Fear of ill health, fear of meeting some unpleasant memory or fantasy in the unconscious as revealed by a dream, a lack of security at work or in the social world, fear of harming someone or being harmed by vague forces within himself, all are causes of insomnia. Barbiturates anesthetize the insomniac against these fears. The insomniac should be treated psychotherapeutically instead. Barring actual pain, sedatives should be used sparingly, say at such times as the night preceding or following an operation.

Psychiatric treatment is indicated for insomnia as opposed to the continued use of sedative drugs, which will not effect a cure. The widespread use of sedatives is, like the excessive use of tobacco and alcohol, a phenomenon of "the times." To some degree the individual of today is a victim of greater tensions than have previously been known, but at the same time he has some choice over the degree to which he should indulge himself in relieving these tensions.

The *stimulant drugs* are directly opposed to the sedative drugs. They aim to quicken rather than deaden the senses. They aim to excite rather than to quiet, to animate and exhilarate rather than to produce lethargy and calm. Stimulants are used by some people to induce pleasant fantasies and an artificial sense of well-being and competence. They may produce hallucinations. Some rational use of stimulants is attempted—although not without danger—by workers who try to work overtime or who are threatened with sleep by the monotony of their work or who go to work insufficiently rested. Accidents sometimes result from the impaired judgment produced. Others use stimulant drugs to induce a "jag," to "pep" them up, to overcome a morning hangover or a dull, apathetic, slightly depressed feeling. Some individuals use sedatives (barbiturates) and stimulants (amphetamine) alternately, the latter to give a feeling of exhilaration and relieve fatigue and the former to calm down and induce relaxation. Such self-directed medication and tampering with the sense of well-being shows questionable wisdom. The sense of well-being should be natural, self-induced and self-perpetuating in the person who has undergone healthy personality development.

A drug often experimented with and all too often used regularly for its exhilarating effect is *marihuana*. Under its influence there is created a sense of well-being, even euphoria. Other effects are visual hallucinations and an altered sense of space and time. While using marihuana, judgment and moral sense are impaired and it is often associated with delinquent and criminal behavior. Laws prohibiting the growth and sale of this drug exist and many people work at their enforcement. In spite of this, however, there seems to be a demand for the drug by those who cannot find life interesting enough through the ordinary channels of work and play. Treatment for the habit is enforced withdrawal and psychotherapeutic treatment of the personality.

Morphine and Opium. Morphine enjoys the reputation of being an extremely valuable drug in the practice of medicine. It is exceedingly unfortunate, however, that it must also be branded as a dangerous drug because of the malignancy of the addiction which it is capable of producing under certain circumstances in certain individuals. The latter statement is also true of several other related drugs, such as opium, heroin, and some of the newer synthetic preparations such as demerol and dilaudid. These drugs are capable of producing a euphoric state, not only allaying pain but removing all the worries and cares of reality. So attractive is this state of being to certain people that they repeatedly resort to the use of drugs in order to attain it. In some cases the initial administration of the drug is given by a reputable physician and is directed toward the amelioration of some type of physical pain. The individual because of his inner psychological difficulties remains chronically in need of further doses of the drug, even though the root of the pain has been removed. Other patients begin the use of the drug through association with addicts. Often the drug habit begins insidiously with the individual taking small doses occasionally in order to produce the longed-for feeling of well-being. There is an increase of the dose ultimately and the patient tends to become more tolerant of it so that larger doses become necessary in order to produce the desired effect. Many addicts reach a daily dose that would be fatal to a non-addict. The person who becomes addicted to morphine or one of the related drugs has many similarities to the alcoholic from a psychological standpoint. There is a deep craving for an elevated sense of well-being which the patient attempts to satisfy by using the drug. The ordinary frustrations, disappointments and difficulties of routine living are too difficult for such people and they resort to the creation of an artificial world of their own in which they are not beset by all of these problems. Unfortunately, in the morphine addicts as the required dosage increases, the patient has more and more difficulty obtaining his supply. This often results in the patient becoming completely untrustworthy and getting himself involved in various nefarious schemes in order to obtain the drug.

These patients often try in every way to conceal their addiction from all but their fellow addicts. Many become experts at feigning physical illness of a type that would ordinarily require morphine. They put on such a convincing show that the physician prescribes morphine for them without recognizing the true nature of the difficulty. It is exceedingly rare that a true psychotic picture results from the use of morphine or any of its related substances. It is true, however, that sufficient doses of these drugs are capable of producing hallucinations, at least temporarily. The most obvious personality disturbance which is seen is the gradual disintegration of a sense of responsibility, duty, and obligation. These patients reach a stage where their primary aim in life is to insure their daily needs of the drug and they are willing to go to almost any lengths to meet this need. Contrary to popular belief, the use of morphine and the allied drugs does not lead to an increase in criminal activity other than as a secondary result of the patient's attempts to insure his daily drug supply.

The stopping of a drug in an addict, particularly if he has been taking moderate or heavy dosages, results in severe withdrawal symptoms. These symptoms come on during the first day and terminate, as a rule, after about a week or ten days. The patient becomes increasingly agitated and there is apparent a remarkably heightened sensitivity to temperature, both hot and cold. There are gastrointestinal disturbances, especially nausea and vomiting, as well as diarrhea. All of these symptoms are accompanied by severe abdominal cramps. There is an increased irritability, and fits of crying and temper reactions are not uncommon. Patients in the throes of withdrawal symptoms suffer a great deal and often plead for a dose of their drug or try to utilize any means at hand to obtain a fresh supply. In weakened, emaciated patients with malnutrition or other physical difficulties, it is not impossible for death to occur from exhaustion during this period. The symptoms are thought to be an aftermath of morphine's inhibitory action on the sympathetic nervous system, there being a compensatory heightened activity of that system coincidental with the withdrawal. This heightened activity following the removal of morphine is thought to be the basis of withdrawal symptoms.

The treatment of morphine addiction is an extremely difficult problem and even under the best circumstances is not successful in many cases. The most extensive experience is that of the group who are working at the United States Public Health Service Hospital in Lexington, Kentucky. Many types of therapy have been proposed but the biggest difficulty still remains that of insuring the patient's freedom from relapse in the future. The drug may be withdrawn abruptly, rapidly, or gradually. Generally speaking, abrupt withdrawal may be utilized only in those individuals in good physical health who have been taking relatively small doses. Rapid withdrawal is the most popular method and is accomplished ordinarily in a period of one to two weeks. The patient is given initially a daily divided dose of three to four grains of morphine; this is gradually cut so that at the end of one to two weeks he is taking no drugs at all. He is not told the amount of the drug that he is getting during the withdrawal period. Gradual withdrawal involves five to six weeks during which the dosage is more slowly diminished. Some workers feel that the administration of daily small doses of insulin is of benefit in reducing the severity of the withdrawal symptoms, but this is somewhat questionable. Physical means such as tub baths and packs have some value, especially in that they result in the patient's receiving more attention, which is beneficial. Any other measures of a similar type are obviously useful in most cases.

It goes without saying that the successful treatment of morphine addiction must take place within the confines of an institution. Addicts are extremely adept at obtaining supplies of the drug and may do so even in a well-guarded and -maintained institution. Psychiatric workup and psychotherapy form a cornerstone in the successful treatment of morphine addiction. Addicts need an extensive follow-up. They require help in rearranging their living and also prolonged therapeutic efforts directed toward furthering their insight into their own personalities.

Cocaine. Cocaine is not resorted to by drug addicts nearly as often as morphine and its related drugs. Many of the features of addiction are similar, with one exception: the prolonged use of cocaine has more deleterious effects and may more often produce a psychotic picture. At times certain addicts alternate between the use of cocaine and morphine. Initially, cocaine produces a feeling of euphoria, an increased psychomotor activity, and a sense of well-being. As its effects pass, the patient is left with a "hangover" which involves weakness, irritability, and restlessness. Commonly found in the prolonged use of cocaine are paresthesias which give the patient the sensation of bugs crawling under his skin. There is a progressive deterioration seen in cocainism where the patient at times becomes hallucinated, agitated, and terrified. There is a loss of social and moral responsibility and the patient becomes oriented primarily around attempts to obtain additional supplies of his drug.

The withdrawal of cocaine does not lead to the violent symptoms seen in morphine withdrawal. Treatment, however, must obviously be undertaken in an institution where it can be assured that the patient cannot obtain any further supplies of his drug. Successful treatment must also be accompanied by psychotherapeutic interviews similar to those required in morphinism.

SEXUAL DEVIATION

In the teaching of medicine the subject of sexual perversion is often left relatively untouched. The reason for this omission may be that the general practitioner does not often meet an individual who is behaving in a sexually perverted way. When he does, however, it is important that he know something about the patient's way of acting and that he be able to take an understanding attitude toward him.

Doctors are sometimes heard to express themselves most violently on this subject, saying they would have nothing whatsoever to do with a sexually perverted individual. We believe greater tolerance than this is necessary. There is no reason to reject a person because he has a problem of behavior in the sphere of sex. The best way to handle such a person is, first, to listen to his story and, second, to be able to help him understand something about the ideas and motivations that lie behind his behavior. The doctor may not readily cure the patient of his perversion but he can give him some reassurance, comfort, and advice. And it is important for physicians and others to make themselves acquainted with the causes of sexually perverted behavior.

There are no fixed concepts about the normality of sexual behavior; they vary greatly from individual to individual and even in heterosexually mature persons. There are people whose behavior is such as to approach perversion, and sometimes is actually regarded as such by them. Among the various forms of perversion are the following: *fetishism*, which consists of deriving erotic satisfaction from loving objects instead of people, such as a piece of a person's clothing, a lock of hair, a shoe; *homosexuality*, obtaining gratification by practicing intimacies with a member of the same sex; *sadism*, obtaining gratification by inflicting pain and cruelty upon another person; *masochism*, obtaining sexual satisfaction by the opposite procedure—having pain inflicted upon the self; *voyeurism*, obtaining gratification by looking at other people; *exhibitionism*, obtaining sexual satisfaction by exposing the self to the gaze of others; *bestiality*, obtaining sexual satisfaction by contact with animals; *pedophilia*, obtaining satisfaction by the seduction of children.

These behaviors are some of the more frequent of the unusual ways of achieving sexual gratification which come under the heading of sexual perversion. There is another phenomenon which lies in the realm of the normal love life of men and women: the tendency for one partner to bring the mouth in contact with the genitals of the other partner—called *fellatio* when it is the penis and *cunnilingus* when it is the vagina. This act may give pleasure not only to the one who actively carries it out but also to the more passive participant.

There are many definitions of a sexual perversion. A sexual perversion is not easy to define. It has been defined as a gratifying sexual activity which consistently defeats the aim of procreation. While this would apply to the perversions described, the same definition would include both masturbation and heterosexual activity in which contraception is practiced. Furthermore, accurate and dispassionate study of sexual behavior shows that some of the irregular or unusual ways of sexual gratification are quite common among society's most successful and well-adjusted persons. So in describing and discussing these more unusual ways of sexual gratification let us try to remove the term perversion, as far as is possible, from the category of opprobrious epithets.

Why does society become so upset about any type of sexually perverted behavior? The first important reason is that people feel it is unesthetic and conflicts with our culture's idealistic values. The second important reason is that if all sexuality were carried out in perverse behavior, the aims of procreation would be defeated and we would soon die off as a race. The latter is only a theoretical possibility but it still alarms people.

Actually, society condemns sexually perverse behavior without knowing exactly why. People lead their sexual lives in private, and how they conduct their sexual relations need be none of any others' business. Nevertheless, society has a tendency to be upset about it, as if this type of behavior contaminated everyone in some way, and people act as though condemnation could bring about its reduction. We would like to make clear that society can never bring about the reduction of perverse sexual behavior through condemnation or through punishment of the sexually perverse individual, whether by excluding him from everyday life or from society or by bringing him into court and putting him in jail. These attempts do nothing to change him; he will go on with his perverse behavior just the same; society will never understand what caused it and hence will never cure it.

In a way, society has no more reason to condemn the sexually perverse individual than it has to condemn an individual soldier for killing in wartime. For he is driven on by strong instinctual forces of which he is not aware—forces of which doctors and scientists have to be aware if they hope to alleviate the problem. The sexually perverse person is often hated, lonely, and in serious conflict about *his problem*.

HOMOSEXUALITY

Homosexuality is one of the end results of the psychosexual growth of an individual as it shapes itself in the family setting. Sometimes (but not necessarily) this is contributed to by persons outside the family, in order for the individual to become homosexual in orientation. The degree of homosexual orientation and activity in any given individual may vary. For instance, a person may be predominantly heterosexual and yet have only one or two homosexual experiences in his life. But because of these activities he may worry about being homosexual and he may be labeled homosexual by others. Yet the proportion of homosexuality in his personality may be very slight.

Dr. Kinsey, in writing up his studies of sexual behavior, presented the graduations in homosexual orientation by means of a heterosexual-homosexual rating. Definitions of the ratings were as follows:

0 = entirely heterosexual.
1 = largely heterosexual, but with incidental homosexual history.
2 = largely heterosexual, but with a distinct homosexual history.
3 = equally heterosexual and homosexual.
4 = largely homosexual, but with distinct heterosexual history.
5 = largely homosexual, but with incidental heterosexual history.
6 = entirely homosexual.

The Social Problem. Homosexuality presents several social problems. First, deeply rooted prejudices bring out fear, hostility, and condemnation of the homosexual of either sex by the majority of people. This is because the activities by which the homosexual achieves sexual gratification are seen as different and therefore alien, perverse, and unesthetic. There may be some deep resentment on the part of society that homosexuality carried far enough will destroy the race, but we have never seen an individual who showed much emotion concerning this theoretical possibility. Some adults, especially parents, sometimes justifiably fear that a homosexual person will seduce the young into homosexual behavior. This happens but it certainly is not a characteristic of all homosexuals.

There are other problems, however, which still trouble society at large. The emotional make-up of the homosexual puts him, often enough, at variance with heterosexually orientated people of either sex. There is a lack of sympathy, empathy, or sometimes even mutual interests, so that there is a "clash of temperaments" that is disturbing in either social gatherings or in work activity. Furthermore, the tendency to try to get their emotional needs met by heterosexual people to whom they may be attracted provokes anxiety and sometimes revulsion. Moreover, their emotional involvements with others are sometimes so important to them that they attempt undesired importunities or even blackmail to retain control of a relationship. This has caused enough known disasters to give the homosexuals as a group an unsavory reputation with many people. Finally, there is a tendency in the homosexual, greater than in other neuroses certainly but possibly no greater than in other sociopathic personality disturbances, to be self-indulgent to an extreme degree. This causes them to demand special treatment from family, friends, or paramour. It can reach the proportion of a degree of social parasitism which more disciplined and responsible members of society resent. One can see why the homosexual is not a very welcome member of heterosexual society as a whole. Recently there has been a movement in the direction of being more understanding, less afraid of and less punitive toward the homosexual.

Personal Problems of the Homosexual. The percentage of personal problems is not as great as one might suppose. In the first place, the majority of homosexuals are eminently satisfied with their orientation. They were a long time developing their form of relation to other humans. And insofar as nearly everyone goes through some conflict in rationalizing and accepting himself as a sexual being, the homosexual in most instances, when he discovers the trend of his sexual impulses, finds them as acceptable as do his neighbors find their heterosexual impulses acceptable. There are exceptions to this, of course, but all people tend to justify what attracts them, pleases them, and gives them gratification. The fact that homosexuality is not popular is soon turned into the compensatory camaraderie of belonging to the rejected minority group. To this may be added a conviction that the homosexual orientation is the better one. So, the homosexual rarely mourns his lot or wants very seriously to make any change in himself. He may find himself unhappy, depressed, and frustrated at times but he rarely blames this upon his homosexuality. He blames it on the lack of understanding or the lack of generosity of someone else.

Etiology and Psychopathology. As far as we can ascertain, homosexuality, as well as the other sexual deviations, is the result of emotional growth deviations. We are excluding rare cases of physical sexual anomalies such as hermaphrodism. The main factors are the interactions of the emotional life which give the child his identification with the parent of the same sex and the circumstances which give him the freedom to love and enjoy the parent of the opposite sex, and to identify with an emotionally mature parent of the same sex. Some of the conditions which predispose, but will not necessarily cause, a child to grow toward homosexuality are:

1. A boy who is ignored and/or rejected by his father, so that he is emotionally unable to identify with a man.

2. A boy who is overindulged by his mother to an extreme degree—who is made her companion too long and too exclusively, so that he comes to feel only women's interests and has been excluded from a man's world.

3. A boy who has had a cold mother and a rejecting father also,

and is so deprived of affection that he takes on the role of woman (mother) himself and acts out his psychological problems through his homosexual activity.

4. A girl who has had a cold and rejecting mother, or a mother who radiated a lack of pleasure in being a woman, wife or mother. The mother offers nothing attractive to identify with.

5. A girl who has had a doting father who, wanting a son, has encouraged and praised all masculine interests and pursuits on her part and discouraged her feminine qualities.

6. A girl who has had a father so cruel, cold, or abusive toward her and her mother that she fears, hates, and renounces men.

These are broad patterns of family constellations that have been shown to contribute to homosexuality. Identification is both a subtle and a powerful force, as is the hunger for affection and understanding. Moreover, the human mind is very selective in its grasp of that which will gratify.

Treatment. A physician can treat only that which causes the patient discomfort and, hence, which he wishes to have treated. Hence, treatment can be carried out successfully in the person who wants treatment very badly. No one else can send a homosexual for treatment, nor is it likely that anyone could demand that a homosexual obtain treatment. It is not an easy task for a homosexual to achieve success even when very dissatisfied with his way of life. The only treatment suited to the condition is a treatment that will change personality values and trends—and that is psychotherapy in the form of psychoanalysis or other well-applied psychotherapy in the hands of a skilled and experienced psychotherapist. There can be no quick cure in the average case. Time and enough sessions to bring about a complete awareness of the early life forces in the family which set the deviation into motion are necessary, followed by a phase of treatment in which the patient accepts the goal of mature sexuality and analyzes away his resistances against reaching it.

Prognosis depends mainly upon (1) the seriousness of the patient in getting well, i.e., the strength of his motivation, (2) the skill of the therapist, (3) the basic self-disciplinary capacity of the patient as shown in other facets of his life. A good work history or a history of loyalty to others would indicate strength to change. A history of repeated self-indulgence without social accomplishment would speak against success in therapy.

Families have a universal tendency to temporize on the treatment plans suggested. They are afraid of making the mental patient unhappier, or more worried about himself, or angry at them if they insist on treatment. This thinking is detrimental to the patient, and the physician should discourage it. It is known today that mental illness does not cure itself and that postponement makes the task of treatment more difficult. If the physician has in his practice a patient with a mental problem that he cannot treat, he should recommend prompt treatment by a specialist. If the family does not co-operate, the physician should not condone waiting for cure to occur spontaneously, or letting himself be exploited into halfway measures to keep the family comfortable. To do so is not too unlike giving morphine to allay the pain of an infected appendix. Everyone may be more comfortable for a while, only to face more serious complications later.

SUMMARY

Mental illness, acute or chronic, divides itself mainly into three classes:

1. The psychotic, who becomes fragmented and disorganized and is unable to think clearly and logically, to act competently, trustfully, and efficiently. He may be out of touch with reality and express illogical, unrealistic ideas or have communication with personages other than those in the immediate reality.

2. The neurotic, who is concerned with an inability to control fears or dispel recurring morbid thoughts. He is able to be in touch with reality but his morbid concentration with his fears and phobias rarely allows him to enjoy healthy, happy patterns of living.

3. The psychophysiologic, who cannot divest himself of some personal theory or belief about the sick state of his heart, head, gastrointestinal tract, or his body's energy system. He thinks, "I am a sick man and you doctors don't know either how to find it or how to cure it."

Treatment of mental illness, whether major (psychotic) or minor (neurotic), or related to body distress (psychophysiologic), or of a purely personality or sociopathic nature (behavior disorder), requires a carefully planned treatment scheme with or without the hospital milieu. It is a part of the physician's job to arrange this plan, state it clearly, and seek co-operation for it.

BIBLIOGRAPHY FOR CHAPTER XV

Aichhorn, August, *Wayward Youth*, Viking, 1935.

Alexander, Franz, *The Neurotic Character*, International Journal of Psychoanalysis, July, 1930.

———— *Psychosomatic Medicine*, Norton, 1950.

Bender, Lauretta, "Childhood Schizophrenia: A Clinical Study of 100 Schizophrenic Children," *American Journal of Orthopsychiatry*, 17, 1947.

Dunbar, Flanders, *Psychosomatic Diagnosis*, Hoeber, 1948.

Fenichel, Otto, *The Psychoanalytic Theory of Neurosis*, Norton, 1945.

Freud, Sigmund, *Mourning and Melancholia*, in *Collected Papers*, Vol. IV, Hogarth Press and the Institute of Psychoanalysis, 1949.

Hall, Radclyffe, *The Well of Loneliness*, Garden City, 1928.

Hinsie, L. E., "Schizophrenias," in *Psychoanalysis Today*, edited by Sandor Lorand, International Universities Press, 1944.

Hoskins, Roy G., *The Biology of Schizophrenia*, Norton, 1946.

Kinsey, Alfred C., et al., *Sexual Behavior in the Human Female*, Saunders, 1953.

Saul, Leon J., *Bases of Human Behavior*, Lippincott, 1951.

Scheflen, Albert C., *Psychotherapy of Schizophrenia: Direct Analysis*, Thomas, 1961.

Weiss, Edward, and O. S. English, *Psychosomatic Medicine*, Saunders, 3rd ed., 1957.

XVI

Treatment

THE TREATMENTS of psychiatry can be divided into several types. One of these is *institutional treatment,* which is used when mental illness is so severe that the patient can no longer live comfortably with himself and others in the community. Various treatments used in the hospital are hydrotherapy, electroshock, insulin shock, surgical therapy, and occupational therapy. Additionally, art therapy, recreational therapy, music therapy, and industrial therapy as well as psychotherapy are used. These treatments are usually given in cases of psychotic disorders.

For psychoneurotic disorders, certain psychoses, personality disorders, and various psychophysiologic diseases the treatment of choice is psychotherapy and is usually carried on as office or clinic treatment.

Psychotherapy includes anything that is said or done by a physician which is aimed at favorably influencing the thinking, feeling, and acting of the patient and helping him toward happiness, efficiency, and health. Almost every physician uses some psychotherapy.

The individual in need of psychotherapy is one who has failed adequately to meet his life situation. The goal of psychotherapy is to help the patient make a more realistic and therefore a more mature adjustment. The methods used in psychotherapy are varied but at the present time most psychotherapy is psychoanalytically oriented, at least to some degree.

More specifically, the foundation used in all conscious psychotherapy is the life history of the patient, which reveals that he is functioning in certain ways at an immature level.

Certain people do not want psychotherapy and may even resent the fact that it is needed or recommended, the reason being that before very much psychotherapy can be given the individual has to accept the fact that he has, to a more than average degree, a personality liability such as fear, anxiety, jealousy, or selfishness. Psychotherapy requires the co-operation of the patient, and the physician generally gets it because the patient is suffering and he wants to feel better in his body or mind or he wants to be a more successful or a more effectual person. Wanting these things, he is generally willing for the physician to make him aware of his immaturities and to make some effort to overcome them.

Psychotherapy is not a popular treatment. There are a few people who do not mind being reflective about themselves and having their difficulties pointed out. Such people want to learn and they are sincere about it, but they are in the minority. Most people, however, have what they call pride—a sense of importance and of their own completeness—and when the physician makes any implication that they are childish, that they are reacting to life in an immature way, that they are emotionally weak, that they ought to do better in some way, the medicine is not easy to take. In applying it the physician has to use a great deal of tact, understanding, and kindness. Helping people too quickly to see too much about that part of them that is immature and socially unacceptable may have the unfortunate result of making the treatment so painful that they refuse it. To get good results this state of mind should not be aroused. Good psychotherapy tries to avoid rejection on the part of the patient. The physician accordingly takes care never to give too much of the truth at one time or more than the patient can emotionally digest. The patient can take truth and use it best when it is mixed with a good deal of kindness and understanding.

An important part of treating the psychoneuroses and the adjustment problems of human beings is to understand human personality, how it forms, and the possible deviations from the average it may take. To get this understanding requires a study of the life history of the human being, a study of social pressures and demands, and a knowledge of the varieties of traditional and conventional conflict which we have discussed in the preceding chapters. A psychotherapist must have some ideas of the average in human conduct, a kindly but objective point of view as to what is fair in the relationship of parent to child, husband to wife, employer to employee, and so on.

There is no question about the fact that people can be changed—some more rapidly than others, it is true, but they *can* be changed. Moreover, the person in trouble, the person who has suffered pain and distress in mind and body, is going to want to change if it means a restoration of his happiness or health or both. More and more people are becoming willing to consult the psychiatrist when necessary and to utilize what psychiatric understanding and therapeutic ability is possessed by the family physician.

HISTORY-TAKING PROCEDURE

Just as the chapters of this book have given an ontogenetic study of man's emotional development generally, we must in treatment or in counseling use history-taking as a rapid means of studying and knowing the particular individual, his needs, how he has met them, and his resulting conflicts.

To aid in history-taking, the following outlines can be used and modified, as the case demands and time permits.

Family Background

1. Age, birthplace, and occupation of parents.
2. How would you describe the temperamental traits of your parents, individually, with the following as a guide: depressive, cheerful, irritable, conscientious, indifferent, prudish, tolerant, optimistic, pessimistic, unfeeling, affectionate, understanding?
3. Would you say they had a broad or a narrow outlook on life?
4. Did they encourage you in your plans? Did they praise and reward your accomplishments?
5. Would you consider that you had come from a well-adjusted family?
6. Did their attitude foster any feeling of inferiority?
7. Did their attitude foster certain of your ideals?
8. Is there any history of epilepsy, migraine, alcoholism, psychosis, neurosis, or invalidism in your immediate family?
9. If so how do you look upon them—with tolerance, shame, indifference, or with what emotion?
10. Do you feel that their presence has produced any effect upon your career from a psychological standpoint or otherwise?

Personal Early Development

1. What has been told you of your progress in nursing, weaning, walking, talking, dentition, feeding, bowel and bladder training?
2. What has been told you of early developmental incidents, such as thumb sucking, breath-holding spells, tantrums, bedwetting, spasms, night terrors, idiosyncrasies as to diet, fears?

3. Did you have any illnesses during childhood that have left a residual physical or psychic change or both?

Attitude Toward Family

1. Did you have any special attachment to father or mother?
2. Did you have any timidity before or antagonism toward either parent? If so, when and why did this come about?
3. Have you been on a frank or formal footing with your parents?
4. Are you an only child? If not, what is your position among the siblings? Age, occupation, success or failure of siblings in chronological order.
5. Are you aware that this factor has made a difference in your career?
6. Are you on friendly terms with siblings? If not, on what grounds is there difficulty? On the other hand has an older sibling been especially friendly and a source of inspiration?
7. How did you take births and losses (by death or separation) in the family?
8. Do you feel you are emancipated from home and parents?
9. Along what lines do you still turn to the home for advice and decision?
10. What person, inside or outside the family, has been the greatest influence in your life this far?
11. Have your grandparents, uncles, aunts, cousins, or any friend of the family played an important role in your childhood or later life? How did this come about and by reason of what characteristics in the person mentioned?

School Adjustment

1. Did you have any difficulty in school attendance because of illness, unwillingness to attend, actual truancy, or other reason?
2. Was there any one year, or period of years, that you failed or made consistently low grades, in marked contrast to your usual ability? If so, can you assign any reason for this?
3. Did you have any special educational disabilities, such as inability to memorize, inability to use figures or to calculate, etc?
4. Was there any one teacher during your school career to whom you were unusually devoted? Was there one whom you particularly disliked? If so, of which sex was this teacher? How do you account for the intensity of feeling?
5. Would you say any teacher had exerted a marked or permanent influence upon your personality? How?
6. During school age were you often involved in neighborhood mischief

or actual delinquency, such as stealing, setting fires, etc.? If so, was this your own trend or due to gang influence?

7. What was your ability to mix? Were you an active member of the group? A leader or follower, or did you entirely dislike and avoid group activity?

8. How were you regarded by the other children? Were you teased and belittled, or admired and looked up to?

9. Was your school life a satisfactory balance of social, athletic, and scholastic attainment? If not, do you now see any ways in which it might have been made so?

Sexual Development

1. Trace the evolution of your sex life as far as possible in terms of concrete situations and reactions, with the aid of the following questions.

2. At what *ages* and on what *occasions,* and from what *sources* have you acquired sex information?

3. Has your environment given opportunity for sex orientation?

4. How much active interest and curiosity have you shown?

5. Have much misinformation and misinterpretation been involved?

6. Are you conscious of much shame and secrecy about sex?

7. How was it acquired and how has some of it been lost?

8. At what age did you become aware of your sex organs and their functions?

9. How did puberty make itself felt in your case?

10. What sex preoccupations or sex adventures did you have *before, at* or *after* puberty? How were they initiated and what do you estimate to have been their effect upon you?

11. Has masturbation been a special problem for you?

12. Have nocturnal emissions ever been a source of worry to you?

13. Did any special *person, event,* or *group* influence your sex trends?

14. Through what change of theories and views regarding sex have you passed?

15. How frequently are you preoccupied with sex fantasies? Of what type?

16. Have you many dreams concerning sex matters?

17. Have you had any sex experiences with your own sex, or any sex experiences of any sort whatever which you would consider abnormal, or any inclination toward such?

18. What situations give rise to sex tension and what method or methods have you attempted for relief and regulation of tension?

19. Has any part of your sex activity given you a sense of guilt?

20. What is your present sex code or goal? Do you think it differs from

that of the rest of your family? Is it satisfactory to you?

21. Does sex tension interfere with your work?
22. To what extent has the concept or urge of family formation entered into your sexual preoccupations, if at all, and at what age did it appear?
23. To what extent do *affection* and *broader human interest* enter into your sex preoccupation?
24. What in your opinion are the outstanding social sex problems?
25. What is your attitude toward them?
26. What is your conception of an ideal adult sex life?
27. What is your attitude toward monogamy?
28. Do you feel that you have any sex problem at present?
29. What is your attitude toward these questions of your sex life?
30. What should be the ideal attitude toward the sex topic, especially indiscretions or sexual perversions in patients?
31. Do you believe children should receive sex instruction, and at what age?

Mood Reactions

(It is realized that an evaluation of these reactions can, in many instances, be only approximate. Try, however, to make your answer as specific as possible.)

1. Are you naturally cheerful or inclined to depression or worry, or is this variable with you?
2. Are you usually aware of what produces the changes or do they seem to come from a clear sky?
3. Are you optimistic or pessimistic?
4. Have you a good sense of humor? Are you stubborn?
5. Are you serious-minded or inclined to be frivolous?
6. Do you get sullen or sulk, or hold resentment? Can you be cheerful or gay at will?
7. How do you react to disappointment, to trouble, to competition?
8. Are you irritable, impatient, fault-finding? If so, what conditions any of these traits? Can you relate them to particular topics?
9. To what extent are you influenced by the emotions and moods of others? Give example.
10. Do you think we can expect to modify moods, and if so, how?
11. What does the word "sentiment" suggest to you? What are your most important sentiments?
12. Are you fearful of the outcome of your projects, and do you indulge in forebodings, or are you usually confident?
13. Are you easily frightened? Are you quick-tempered?

14. Are your feelings easily hurt?
15. How do you react to success in others? Is it easy to congratulate them?
16. Can you work steadily for hours at a time, or do you feel concentration difficult?
17. Under what circumstances do you work best—i.e., by schedule, impulse, under pressure, or how?
18. Have you always the energy you wish for, or does this fluctuate?
19. Are you benefited greatly by rest periods or vacations?
20. How do you spend occasional holidays?
21. Is your attention easily distracted?
22. Can you make judgments easily or are you vacillating?
23. Does your performance during a day keep pace with what you have planned, or do you find performance lagging behind plans?

Social Adaptability

1. Are you timid, shy or tongue-tied in the presence of the opposite sex?
2. Are you at ease in the presence of older people?
3. What is your reaction to authority? Do impolite or unkind remarks of people in minor official positions upset you?
4. Are you independent in thinking and making your own decisions, or do you like to have help from others?
5. Are your decisions *impulsive,* due to *circumstances,* or *well thought out?*
6. What is your type of friendship—many or few, lasting or changing, warm or cool, reserved or confiding, protecting or dependent?
7. Are you married? Are you engaged? If not, when and under what circumstances would you contemplate marriage?
8. Are you interested in being a parent of children?
9. To what extent are you conscious of egoism or altruism in yourself? Has this ever been brought to a real test?
10. How do you take advice or criticism?
11. Are you inclined to seek sympathy or to pity yourself?
12. Are you overmodest or overconfident?
13. Do you often feel at a disadvantage compared to others?
14. Are you satisfied with the way the world has treated you thus far?
15. Do you dislike adapting yourself to new surroundings?
16. Are you able to co-operate well with others?
17. Are you tactful? Are you ingratiating?
18. Do you have a conviction that you are always right?
19. Are you a good loser? Do you like to talk of your accomplishments?
20. Do you seek or shirk responsibility?

Sense of Reality

1. Are your plans for the future clearly or vaguely outlined?
2. What factors caused you to choose your career?
3. To what extent do you think success depends upon effort, and to what extent upon chance and circumstances?
4. Do you rate yourself as imaginative, idealistic, visionary, practical?
5. Do you like or dislike responsibility?
6. Are you superstitious?
7. Are you frank and honest with yourself; that is, can you acknowledge a mistake and attempt to correct it?
8. Have your plans up to now worked nearly as you would have liked or have you felt yourself thwarted or disappointed?
9. Do you plan well? Can you direct others? Is your advice frequently sought?
10. What is your attitude toward money? Are you saving? Do you spend wisely? Are you generous? To what extent is making money your aim? How do you react to economic uncertainty?

Health

1. Illnesses, operations, accidents, and circumstances leading up to them.
2. Length of convalescence.
3. Age at which each appeared.
4. When was physical health last checked up?
5. Do you worry about health?

Neurotic Tendencies

1. What circumstances bring out uneasiness or blushing?
2. Does physical comfort mean a great deal to you?
3. Is food an important item to you?
4. Have you any special sensitivity to certain foods, either esthetic or symptomatic?
5. Have you a special fondness for alcohol? Is this related to a mood disturbance?
6. Do you take medicine or drugs regularly or in large amounts?
7. Do you suffer from constipation?
8. Are you much affected by unusual sights, odors, or sounds of either a pleasant or disgusting or unpleasant nature?
9. Have you any unusual demand for system and order? Does disorder in your surroundings or interference in your plans or routine annoy you?

10. Have you any special fears, anxieties, or compulsive ideas or actions?
11. Are you overconscientious? Are you superstitious? Are you overfond of gambling?
12. Do you have any specific acts, habits, or thoughts which are a source of worry, doubt, or remorse to you?
13. How do you react to being ill or to inquiries about your health?
14. What games and sports interest you? Have you indulged intensively in any particular ones?
15. What type of reading do you like? Do you consider yourself well read?
16. Are you interested in politics, sociology, art, music? What is your favorite diversion?
17. Have you any special religious interests? How does this compare with your early training in religious matters?
18. Have you any special interest in any cult, philosophy, occultisms, etc.?
19. Have you any special interest in the factors at work in the development of mankind, such as history of race with regard to civilization, literature, language, and thought?
20. What are your concrete interests in sociological problems?

Synthesis

1. Do you feel that your personality is well harmonized, with a suitable distribution of energy into work, play, relaxation, fantasy, art, literature, religion, philosophy, science, and concrete life?
2. What have been your greatest difficulties and handicaps? To what extent have you been able to trace their origin to early experiences?
3. Do you have any sources of comfort during disappointment or discouragement? How do they act?
4. What means of personality change have you tried, either upon yourself or others? With what success?
5. State one or two concrete difficulties you would like to modify in the next year as an example and test of what is possible, and under what conditions it may be possible.

When the history has been taken the physician must be able to pick out the factors of significance, weigh them carefully in connection with the physical and laboratory findings, and arrive at a diagnosis. If a personality problem is present, with or without structural pathology revealed by laboratory study, then psychotherapy in some form is usually the indicated treatment. To use drugs, physical therapy, or surgery on a neurotic illness is contraindicated. It sometimes gives temporary relief but symptoms return and each time are harder to cure even if psychotherapy is later instituted.

PSYCHOLOGICAL TESTING

Before deciding upon the type of psychotherapy to be used, or even after the patient has begun therapy, it is often necessary to call upon the skills of the psychologist for the intelligence and personality measurements at his command. Sometimes patients give the impression of greater intelligence than they possess and vice versa. Their intelligence tests may show signs of a slipping downward from earlier levels as well as defects in special areas such as reading, vocabulary, and computing. Test findings give clues as to the cause of special problems encountered or fortify clues already found.

Projective personality tests such as the Rorschach, T.A.T., or draw-a-person test show special areas of emotional and ideational preoccupation. They also show degrees of ego strength or weakness which will help the decision as to what type of psychotherapy shall be used, if any. Some conditions worsen under treatment, or at least have a very slow recovery rate. Therefore it is always most judicious to assay the situation carefully for the benefit of patient, family, and physician (for fuller discussion see pages 192–197).

HYPNOSIS

A special form of suggestion is hypnosis. In this form of treatment it is suggested to the patient that he go to sleep. A certain number of patients can do this at the suggestion of the physician and hypnotist. While they are in the sleeping state, suggestion can be given to remember forgotten events, to dispense with certain symptoms, or to get rid of a troublesome condition. Hypnosis has always been and still is a difficult therapy to control, and though one of the oldest of the psychotherapies it still awaits development. Freud began his psychotherapeutic work with hypnosis but abandoned it in favor of free association in the waking state. The results of occasional cases treated with hypnosis are dramatic, but it has limitations—imposed by a *resistance* present in all human beings against allowing any large amount of affect-bearing material to emerge at one time from the unconscious. Once unhappy situations are over and done with the patient does not wish to live them over unless absolutely necessary and he must be given time or some other alleviating force to help him.

Hypnosis has always been an interesting phenomenon, containing potentialities for good, and has never fallen entirely into discard. The technique is not easy to master and good results are obtainable only by a few. Theoretically it has psychotherapeutic possibilities but it has to be further developed in order to be more generally applicable and give better results.

NARCOSYNTHESIS

Narcosynthesis was used extensively in the combat theaters of World War II as a combination of drug therapy and psychotherapy of various psychoneurotic states following combat. The patient was given a barbiturate drug, sodium pentothal or sodium amytal, intravenously at a slow rate until a seminarcosed state was induced, during which most patients were able to relive the traumatic battle experiences with release of powerful and intense emotions. With the aid of the psychiatrist the patient was able to synthesize the emotions and memories that produced symptoms. With each treatment an additional quantity of emotion was released, and through utilization of the psychiatrist as friend and substitute for his childhood family and his service buddies the patient was able to establish a working relation with reality again. This treatment is reported to be strikingly effective in reducing the permanent crippling effects of neuroses and in enabling many men who would otherwise be completely incapacitated to take up some activity again. It is indicative of the advances of psychiatry between the World Wars to see so much emphasis put upon the crippling effects of fear and of psychologically traumatic experiences, and to see the wide-spread importance that is being put upon psychotherapeutic treatment, which is replacing punitive, mechanical, and electrical treatments.

Just how effective narcosynthesis is in facilitating the treatment of civilian psychoneuroses remains to be seen, but we know that the experiences with war neuroses have added greatly to our knowledge of neurotic and psychophysiologic conditions.

PSYCHOANALYSIS

Of the various psychotherapies employed, psychoanalysis is the most intensive, highly structured, and prolonged. It should be remembered that most psychotherapy of other types is patterned in some way after psychoanalysis; nearly all have borrowed from it. Although not everyone in the field of psychiatry would agree that psychoanalysis is the most effective treatment, we think they would agree that it is the most intensive and specialized form of psychotherapy.

Psychoanalysis was originated in Vienna in the 1890's by Freud. It grew out of work on conversion hysteria (conversion reaction in modern terminology) by Freud and a colleague named Breuer. These two men began by using hypnosis. Under hypnosis the patient was able to recall events of his early life which he could not remember in his waking state, and to some degree he was able to integrate the part he could remember under hypnosis into his existing personality.

Treatment under hypnosis was difficult to control, so Freud eventually abandoned it and adopted the technique of free association. In free association the early experiences of the individual, his deeper attitudes and ideas, are gradually revealed to himself and to the doctor through a process of the patient's saying whatever comes to his mind. Sessions are usually one hour a day, four to five times a week. Thus psychoanalysis was carried out in Freud's time and today is still unchanged as to procedure. Once the diagnosis has been made and the doctor and patient have agreed that psychoanalysis is the therapy of choice, a treatment program is made. The patient lies on a couch, with the doctor sitting behind him at the head of the couch, and the patient proceeds with the technique of free association. The patient allows his mind free play and expresses whatever thoughts, feelings, and ideas come to him. No limit is put upon the patient regarding what topic he may discuss or concerning who or what he may talk about. What comes forth may seem rather meaningless for a few days. Soon, however, the patient's main problems begin to take shape. Under this technique and with the doctor's aid, the patient comes to learn more and more about himself.

Psychoanalysis has been used during the past fifty years by an increasing number of physicians who have studied the technique. It has been followed in England, Germany, Hungary, Switzerland, the Scandinavian countries, India, South America, and Japan. Although this form of treatment has spread very widely throughout the world it has been met with considerable resistance. Yet in spite of all condemnation, it has come to gain more and more respect from the medical profession. Doctors do not always like its ideas but they have come grudgingly to respect its use as a therapeutic tool.

To practice psychoanalysis a doctor must have a medical degree plus two or three years' experience in psychiatry in an accredited hospital; he must have a knowledge of all types of mental illness; and he must undergo a personal psychoanalysis himself. In addition he must attend seminars and lectures on the theory and practice of psychoanalysis for a period of two years, part of which can be done while he is having his own personal analysis. Finally, he must analyze two or three cases under the supervision of an experienced psychoanalyst. The preparation needed to train a psychoanalyst takes a long time. Therefore joking references to the effect that a psychoanalyst is able to find out all about a person in two minutes are ridiculous. The shortest time needed for any investigation and readjustment of emotional trends which could justifiably be called psychoanalysis would be six months to a year. Usually it takes from one to two years and may even go on longer. This may seem on first thought to be a fantastically long time but when one considers how resistant human personality is to change he must realize that any effective re-educational therapy would have to take that length of time.

In psychoanalysis one has to take into consideration certain phenomena: (1) the importance of childhood experiences in determining later personality reactions; (2) the unconscious mind (by that we mean experiences that take place early in life and remain as impressions in the mind even though no longer consciously remembered, and exert a force in determining the reaction pattern). The ability of a patient to be well must come through *his* awareness of the unconscious forces within his personality so that he may bring them into orderly arrangement and direct them properly for his own happiness and efficiency. The person who can be psychoanalyzed is thus necessarily one who has a certain amount of healthy personality; certain deeply psychotic people cannot be analyzed because they do not have enough healthy personality left to understand what is going on and with which to effect a cure.

The phenomenon of *transference* must be regarded as one of the most useful in psychoanalysis. Transference is the tendency in every human being to relate the emotions and attitudes that have developed during his growth to those people in his immediate environment. A simple example of transference would be that of a man who came from a home where his father was a fussy, arrogant, domineering person. As a man the patient has never been able to get along with his boss or any other figure of authority. In the analytic situation he transfers to the analyst hostile feelings of the type he originally felt toward his father, and accuses the analyst of the same arrogant treatment he suffered at the hands of his father.

Everyone, whether he has a neurosis or not, is in need of friendship and help in working out a happy and successful existence. If the parents have tried to help and be friendly, even though imperfectly or unsuccessfully but with the child's interest at heart, he will transfer a desire for help, friendship, guidance, emotional support, and interest. Such transferences are called *positive*. If during his early development the parents have not had his interest at heart but have been cold and indifferent, have disappointed or frustrated him, then he has probably developed a corresponding unfriendliness and suspicion and distrust. As one might expect, the more positive the transference the more quickly and easily can help be given, whether it be in the form of enhancing the patient's sense of well-being or correcting false ideas. When the transference is negative, then part of the work of the psychotherapist is to help the patient understand the origin of his negative feelings and work toward making them more positive. Improvement in a neurosis of a permanent nature is dependent upon an increase in the capacity for satisfying personal social relationships.

A patient will often try to cover his childish patterns of behavior by an air of humility when he comes to his therapist. However, when people are given a chance to lie down and speak their minds, the tendency is for them to expose their real selves. This tendency is important to the patient and likewise to the psychoanalyst, who is sitting there listening. Once people start free association and begin talking about themselves, they find out that they are more petty, childish, selfish, afraid, inconsiderate, and resentful than they ever imagined they were. As this material (thoughts, feelings, ideas) begins to emerge from deep in the mind there are forces which tend to slow up and prevent its appearance. This is called *resistance,* and the analyst needs to be skillful in understanding the ways in which patients reveal resistance as well as the ways to help them overcome it.

As childhood feelings are re-enacted in the analytical sessions, a high degree of emotional tension emerges. This discharge of emotion associated with the recall of a repressed memory is called *abreaction*. This differs importantly from the everyday *acting-out* of emotions in the lives of people not in treatment, in that in the latter there is usually only *discharge* of emotion without understanding of its infantile origin and hence no insight accrues and no personality change follows.

As the treatment continues and the patient becomes increasingly aware of immature trends in himself he naturally wants to correct them. We can safely assume that all human beings want to be better people if they are properly shown how. At this point the healthy part of the personality plays its part and enables the patient to make the resolve to be more courageous and generous, to exert more goodwill, to renounce jealousy, to be more constructive and less self-centered. As psychoanalysis progresses the patient becomes more aware of himself and at the same time resolves to behave in a better way. If he is a fairly strong individual who is not too sick, these resolves come of their own accord and little help is needed from the outside.

If the patient comes to the psychoanalyst with fear or headache as a symptom, he soon finds he does not talk much of his fear or his headache but he concentrates on his relation to the world at large and to the people in his environment in particular and analyzes his emotional trends. Thus psychoanalysis is a treatment involving a gradual looking into the personality, a sort of catalysis and yet a synthesis going on at the same time. As the analysis proceeds, with the doctor's help the patient learns the structure of his makeup. His relations to his parents and others become clearer, and his struggle to achieve a more altruistic pattern toward life begins.

Most neurotic people feel very sorry for themselves and in their analytic hours may take the attitude that "nobody cares for me. I am miserable and no one tries to help me." Psychoanalysis has been described as the holding of a mirror to one's face. So when these childish attitudes predominate the patient has to learn what the nature of that childishness is and that such an attitude does not work well with people but causes them to turn away from him instead of helping him. He has to adopt a better and more mature reaction pattern, go out to people and do something for them instead of waiting in a passive way for something to be done for him. During this time he has the analyst's help in interpreting his personality and the structure of his neurosis, and by his very presence the analyst helps him in his new resolution and with whatever he wants to achieve through the analysis.

Briefly that is what psychoanalysis accomplishes. To learn it thoroughly a doctor has to make a special study of it. It is a postgraduate course, and one that cannot be learned in medical school. A student may learn something of what it *does*, but to know how to apply it and to master all the things that go to make up its technique takes special study.

DREAMS

The interpretation of dreams forms an important part of psychoanalysis and psychotherapy and is a part of the study of the human mind. Freud showed that dreams are an attempt on the part of the mind to live out its wishes and to solve its conflicts. It might also be said that dreams are a way of revealing to the dreamer, and to the doctor to whom he reports them, what is going on in the unconscious. Mental activity goes on all the time we are asleep. When we can recall a piece of this activity we call it a dream; so a dream, strictly speaking, is one or more thought processes we remember after waking. We dream every night and may remember nothing of it, but mental activity goes on all the same. Sometimes the fragments of a dream seem fairly real or closely related to the events of the day before, or the week before, or even years before.

Dreams vary greatly in character. Understanding the dream can be a means of help in understanding the unconscious. For instance, a patient may insist on telling the doctor that he is a very friendly fellow, that he never quarrels with anybody, that he cannot think he has any aggression in his makeup. But on watching his dreams the patient may find that in them he is always quarreling with someone, that he may actually be hurting someone, even making an attack upon the person with a gun or a knife. Through dreams, patient and physician see the other side (the unconscious side) of the personality at work. As another example, the physician may ask a patient if he is interested in sex and be told that he never thinks about it. However, in watching his dreams the doctor sees that they have a definite sexual coloring.

The dream can be used by patient and analyst to better understand past experience, often portrayed in symbolic form, and current wishes, as well as current conflicts and future hopes. The mechanisms of condensation, displacement, and symbolization are operative in the dream and the progress of some patients is greatly enhanced through their use, while others do not find use of the dream as valuable as transference analysis.

The dynamics of Freudian psychoanalysis and the dream form the basic understanding of most of modern psychotherapy.

We cannot enlarge too much upon dreams here, but a knowledge of dreams and their mechanisms is necessary for a psychotherapist. With the dream as one of the means of understanding the unconscious mind, patient and doctor work toward an ever greater ability for the patient to see himself, his personality assets and liabilities, and the problems of life he has to meet.

PSYCHOTHERAPY

As we have already stated, psychotherapy is patterned after psychoanalysis and uses psychodynamic principles in understanding the patient and his problems and in trying to make him better able to know himself: his emotional needs, his weaknesses, his personality defects, his areas of conflict, his causes of frustration, the traumata of both childhood and later life that have impaired his happiness and efficiency. When these are known, he has to be helped to see and appreciate his strengths also, which he can apply to overcome his weaknesses.

Case History—Psychotherapy

A case that illustrates some of the concepts of psychotherapy is that of a girl of nineteen who woke up one February morning with an anxiety attack. She woke up fighting for her breath, with her heart palpitating, with sweating, with a sense of constriction in the throat, and with nausea. She felt as if she were going to die. A doctor was called who after administering treatment said, "It is a good thing you called me because a certain number of people with this ailment die before they wake up." Since she had eaten pork the night before it was assumed she had been poisoned by the pork, which was of course a possibility.

However, emotional storms that set up an anxiety attack, hard breathing, and disturbances in the gastrointestinal tract can cause violent symptoms without the presence of poisoned food at all. At any rate, these attacks continued. From February to August she had one almost every day. She saw about ten different doctors, each of whom said she had no organic disease and that she was "nervous." She got no better. In fact, she grew worse and began to build up in her thoughts theories of what was wrong. She could picture that the nerves in her body were curling around her heart and that in one of these attacks the nerves would be so affected that they would constrict her heart and she would die. Another theory she had was that the poison from the pork had not gone entirely out of her system and that what remained was causing the attacks. She did not believe she was nervous at all but thought she had a disease that the doctors could not discover.

She finally came to the accident dispensary. The medical resident was called and he spent some time with her. He recognized the fact that she had an anxiety attack and he told her what it meant. He said, "Your illness arose in the following manner. You know when anyone is afraid the heart beats faster and the person may have some difficulty in getting his breath. This fear can also make people sick to the stomach and cause other even more bizarre sensations. *That* is what you have and that is *all* you have, *nothing else.*" Of course she had a physical examination and laboratory work was done, but the nature of the attack made the resident feel that the real pathology was an anxiety attack and that the girl needed reassurance and explanation of the cause of the symptoms. In other words, she needed some education about the nature of an anxiety attack which no one theretofore had given her. All that the doctors had said was, "You are nervous. Go home and do not worry about yourself." The result of this twenty minutes' talk with the resident was that she went home and had a full night's sleep, the first in several weeks. Although the reassurance had not worked completely and had not cured the condition, talking to her in this way gave her enough reassurance for the time being to persuade her that she did not have the conditions she had been imagining and hence that she did not have an organic disease.

However, the resident realized that a person suffering from an anxiety attack has quite a lot of personality difficulty and so he referred her to us in the psychiatric department. We learned that she was the second child in a family of three: herself, a sister three years older, and a brother five years younger. The father was a fairly cheerful man who had been a policeman at one time and who told the children all the dangerous things he met in his work. He used to tell his daughter about the dangers of a girl going about a big city and how a girl must watch out against boys who would only deceive and betray her. "Never trust a boy until you are married to him," he said. The mother was also a fairly cheerful, optimistic type of person with considerable friendliness and gaiety in the home and especially with the patient, who was an attractive child. Very little was expected of the girl and everything was made easy for her. She was dressed well and was the showpiece of the family. Her sister was a little envious and jealous of her and said, "I do not see why everyone likes her better than me. I guess it is because she laughs so much and is never irritable."

Stories used to be told in the family about such things as the world coming to an end. When our patient heard them she would hide under the stairs and think of the house falling in and people dying and being imprisoned. When she got to school she talked among the girls and they told her how disgraceful it was that many girls had illicit sex relations, even getting pregnant and sometimes dying in childbirth. Acting on instructions from her teachers, her older sister would go through considerable handwashing and tooth brushing as a prevention of disease. Our patient saw this and did likewise.

When she became seventeen years old she met a young man three years older than herself and they began going together. Finally they decided to be married without telling either family about it. They went to a magistrate, went through a ceremony, and supposed they were married. Marriage was a very difficult thing for this girl because she had been brought up in a home where there had been much discussion about the fear of pregnancy. It would have been difficult enough if she had had an open, accepted marriage with the approval of both families; but the secrecy of the marriage did a great deal to make her feel anxious. In addition she had married a man who had an attachment to his mother. He could not bear to tell his mother that he was married. If he even hinted at it his mother became quite excited and talked down the idea so that he did not dare tell the truth. After a year they found out that something was wrong with the marriage papers and that they were not married at all. Thirty days later the girl had her first anxiety attack, after which a great change took place in her disposition. From being a cheerful, buoyant, happy girl she became moody, had temper outbursts, and even scratched and bit people. From her first attack until she came to the hospital six months later she went through a most difficult time. It was then that the resident saw her and reassured her and thus effected a reduction in anxiety and an improvement in symptoms.

However, reassurance alone is rarely enough to cure neurotic symptoms of this type. It has to be followed up by re-educational therapy which helps to re-educate the patient in more mature ideas and feelings for living. We have said that two things tend to make people anxious—fear of harm and fear of the loss of love and affection. Our patient had been a "good girl." She had repressed many sexual and aggressive impulses. Yet she had been taught very little about the facts of life; her home life had been made very easy; and now, at nineteen, she was faced with a great deal of responsibility. She was brought to the point where she had to use her personality assets, assets that had not been very well developed. First, she had to face the prospect of an adjustment to a man sexually. Second, she had to face the possibility of an immediate pregnancy, and everything she had ever heard about these matters had been unpleasant and fearful. Third, she had actually to wrest her husband away from his mother. If she revealed the marriage both families might make a row. Wanting approval herself, she yet had to put herself in the position of having to petition her mother-in-law and to face the fact that she might get a "beating" from her for stealing her son. Fourth, she had to face the responsibility of planning a home. All during the so-called marriage she had managed to stay well. But when she learned that the marriage was not valid, that she had been "living in sin," and that if she had any feeling for her husband at all she would have to go to the mother-in-law to try to take her son away from her and bring about a satisfactory ceremony, she was faced with a situation that she was completely incapable of handling. It was in this setting that she had her first anxiety attack and the ones that followed.

Our patient's anxiety attacks were not accidental. An anxiety attack is *never* accidental. It means that there has been a long period of faulty living and that re-education is required. Re-education in this case meant, first, to make her feel comfortable with the sexual problem and, second, to give her help with her normal aggression so that she would be able to step forward and deal with her mother-in-law and utilize her aggression in a mature way. The question of marriage would have to be discussed with both families, a ceremony satisfactorily performed, and help given in setting up a home. She had to be able to say to her mother-in-law, "I want your son for myself." Up to this time, her husband had been only half hers, the other half catering to his mother's whims. She had a great deal to work out for herself and little courage to do it with. No acceptable utilization of aggression had been cultivated in her. She had been babied and petted, and at no age trained to face responsibility or to anticipate the responsibilities of the twenties, thirties, or forties. She had to be educated to meet them.

When such a patient comes to a doctor he must have her continue to visit him for psychotherapy. Even though the symptoms of anxiety attacks are sometimes brought in abeyance a case of anxiety reaction is not made *well* quickly and the patient should come to the doctor at intervals, at least once a week. When he or she comes for treatment the doctor should not examine the heart or take the reflexes or the blood pressure just to make an impression. Instead he should concentrate upon how the patient is living and how managing his or her personal problems. In the case of our patient, for instance, he must ask how often she has seen her husband during the past week, what his attitude about the marriage has become, how far they have progressed in discussing the problem with both families, if she has seen her mother-in-law, and what she is doing about the latter's disapproval. He should discuss with her some of the childish incidents that made her a timid, anxious girl, as well as more current material, and point out to her how her present fears of her husband's mother are the fears she had as a child toward her parents and teachers. If the husband and his mother are so emotionally bound together that he cannot take the interest in her that a mature man should, then she had better face this fact and accept the necessity of living alone for the present and making other plans for the future.

Many people need help over a critical situation like this. They often remain in a bad social situation which gives them no pleasure and satisfaction, only grief and frustration, but they cannot, without help, make the decision to move out of it. A physician doing psychotherapy must be able to help a patient test out the positive and negative aspects of his real life situation and if the positive ones indicate that they can furnish sufficient ego gratification, then they must be utilized to their fullest extent. If there are not enough positive factors to keep the personality alive and thriving, then a change in direction must be taken. Too many people live on from day to day and week to week, never being able to mobilize their aggression to the point of asking for what is needed to keep them happy and healthy.

In the case of our patient it was most important for her peace of mind and health that the husband have the capacity to emancipate himself from his family and take the patient as his wife with full resolve. For this reason, an interview with him was necessary in order to find out his intentions toward the patient, his sincerity, his maturity of outlook. If he were the type that could make her a home and appreciate her as a woman she would have a strengthening force available, and the doctor could utilize this force in his discussions with her, pointing out that anxiety, being born of insecurity, can be neutralized when security appears in one's life. By discussing with her the difficulty in managing her life and offering at the same time the interest and guidance of a friend, the doctor would strengthen her emotionally and prevent any further recurrence.

Anxiety symptoms can be most incapacitating. In the six months before seeing us our patient not only had these attacks and other symptoms (such as dryness of the throat and irregular menstrual periods) but also had ideas of having been permanently "poisoned" by the pork, of having "nerves constrict her heart to death." Such ideas are actual delusions in the making—and delusions which once fixed make the personality more difficult to approach and help. Ideally such a person should have psychoanalysis, for when a breakdown occurs so early in life, a great deal of interest and re-education in ideas are needed to stabilize her and make her strong and a good mother. She needs a great deal of thinking about herself, a great deal of help to do the various things that are necessary if she is to become capable and stay well. However, psychoanalysis is a long, expensive treatment and sometimes the best we can do is to utilize what psychoanalysis teaches us in the direction of what we call *re-education*.

As it turned out in our case, the husband was interviewed and he was able to express his love for his wife and ignore his mother's demands upon him. They had another ceremony, took an apartment, and our patient, with the benefit of new information and the security offered by her husband, became free of symptoms.

Over the years, efforts have been made to improve the techniques of psychotherapy. The psychoanalytic model remains the popular one. But modifications are made for some patients who either do not adapt to efforts to uncover infantile experience or those whose resistances are not responsive to ordinary efforts at interpretation. Some patients must learn what they have to learn from the interpretation of day-to-day experience and in the immediate transference relationship. This means a therapeutic relationship that is intense with immediate affect, and the psychotherapist of today is, in larger numbers, equipping himself to do this. An example is given to show this:

A patient had been seeing a psychotherapist three times weekly for a year, giving an immense amount of data about her family, her early life, and her worries about her competence as a wife, mother and neighbor. But all of this had no effect in improving her condition because she was unable to make any positive emotional acknowledgement of the therapist as being helpful. The relationship remained cold, sterile, impersonal, joyless, negative, unproductive. Her second therapist noted this and wished to work on this important point and discover why it was so and alter it. The patient protested and said, "Don't you want to hear about my worries? What good will it do to talk about your value to me as a person?" But she was not allowed to escape from the subject of her negative feelings toward the therapist, and she discovered thereby the causes for her worries about being seen, heard from, and regarded as "queer," and "not a person."

Many people are afraid of relatedness, friendliness, closeness, personal warmth, lest they be rejected or exploited. Modern man suffers greatly from loneliness and isolation and yet he fears to leave his self-centered self-preoccupation and acknowledge the value of another. Psychotherapy can speak directly to and about this condition in the patient. Men and women would like to make some more immediate human relationship that would have meaning for them and the psychotherapist can offer them this opportunity. Often when such a relationship is attempted, the patient and therapist will soon see which events in the patient's history made the matter of relating in a warm and constructive way so difficult. On the other hand, a historical recounting of events may avoid the matter of any *immediate relationship* that has feelings of respect, dependency, criticism, or approval in it, and it is out of dealing with these feelings that sincerity and authenticity are brought about in the patient.

For the psychiatrist to expect the patient to give significant data or feelings merely by being invited to do so does not always result in any material that contributes to self-revelation on the part of the patient. It takes a capacity for inter-emotional dialogue with both parties participating and being quite honest with each other.

Example: An attractive brunette, 30-year-old housewife and mother of three children had been suffering for five years with depression and anxiety attacks and fear of harming her children. She came of a large family with much contention and both financial and emotional insecurity. Her need for discovering the importance of relatedness was deemed great. She had been hospitalized for two weeks and was on a fortnightly clinic schedule. A cancellation came one day and she was called and given the appointment a week sooner than expected.

Patient on arrival: You had me thinking on the way here this morning.
Dr. About what?
Pt. Why you gave me this appointment a week early.
Dr. What did you think it might mean?
Pt. That I was very unstable and in danger of cracking up.
Dr. That's a worrisome meaning to put to it all right. But you were wrong.
Pt. Really?
Dr. Yes. There was a cancellation and I told the clinic secretary to see if you wanted it.
Pt. It relieves me to know that.
Dr. Didn't any positive meaning in connection with it cross your mind at all?
Pt. No, I never can put any good meaning to things.
Dr. Well now, you have seen you don't always have to think the worst. Actually, I was thinking of you. I know you worry a lot. But I wanted to help you improve as fast as you can. But it never crosses my mind you could get worse.
Pt. It's hard for me to let anybody give me anything good.
Dr. Why?

Pt. It makes me feel so dependent and weak like a child.

Dr. What's so bad about that? We are all ages inside.

Pt. Yes, but I'm trying to be 30.

Dr. I don't despise the child in people. Actually, I think it usually makes them more interesting, if they don't overdo it.

Pt. Maybe—maybe I want to overdo it.

Dr. Possibly your lonely childhood gives you reason to. But you won't always want to overdo it. Meantime, try to accept what you are. I do, both in you and myself.

We see here a rapid interpersonal dialogue tuned to the present reality, but that arrived at being a corrective emotional experience without explicitly saying so. There had already been discussion preceding this interview about the lacks in her early upbringing and family life. She found it hard to express any hostility toward and criticism of her parents. The therapist was trying to intensify the present phenomenology with corrective emotional and ideational interchange. How much or how rapidly this can take place, and whether it can take place without the more prolonged experience of psychoanalysis needs scientific comparison and documentation. But it seems to be effective in many cases. Certainly, people grow by current dialogue, even without uncovering past history. The uncovering of past history may be more important in those patients who are always asking "why"—those who seem to be demanding a reason for remaining in psychotherapy. For those who merely seek a growth experience without being too concerned about why they have a problem the more existential, current, phenomenological psychotherapeutic interchange may be adequate if used actively and comfortably by the therapist.

The successful psychotherapist must get into the lives of emotionally ill patients—not by taking them to a ball game or by paying the rent but by asking them enough questions about themselves and getting them to talk about themselves to find out what they need for emotional security and then showing them how they can get it. Sometimes he needs to help them by seeing other members of their families who may hold the key to their happiness and security.

INSTITUTIONAL TREATMENT

Institutions, while generally thought of as being places for the seriously mentally ill, nevertheless have a place in the treatment of psychoneurotic reactions in adults, in cases of alcoholism, in certain psychophysiologic conditions, and in certain personality disturbances. In some cases of children's neuroses it is better that—if treatment is to be most effective—they be taken out of the home and placed in an understanding environment. In certain adult cases an institutional environment is necessary while the psychotherapeutic treatment is going on because the patients will accept routine and restraint upon their self-indulgence from strangers which they will not accept from their families or which they cannot manage while living by themselves. Moreover, the emotional security offered by friendly, accepting, nonpunitive physicians and ancillary personnel is of invaluable help in re-establishing ego strength when it has been lost.

PSYCHIATRIC SECTIONS IN GENERAL HOSPITALS

There is an increasing trend to set aside a section of the general hospital for the treatment of emotionally ill people. There are many types of emotional illnesses which can be helped in this way. Patients suffering from some neuroses, psychoses, or psychophysiologic illnesses are too disturbed to make progress in ambulatory treatment and yet they are unsuited for the conventional mental hospital. They have less reluctance to come to a general hospital, where the section for emotional disturbances is relatively unstigmatized. There they are grouped together where everyone, patient and personnel included, works toward the goal of improvement undistracted by medical and surgical procedures going on around them. If they are unduly anxious and insecure they have the protective influence of the hospital atmosphere, nurses and doctors. If they are too completely under the influence of morbid thoughts and feelings these can be worked on daily by the staff of psychiatrists, psychiatric nurses, and other personnel. If they need a rest and recuperation from too much social or work pressure they can stay in their rooms behind closed doors. But if they need to socialize, mix, practice contacts with other people, that too can be arranged. A great advantage over ambulatory therapy is that patients have more forces carrying them along to health and less time to become lost, as one patient put it, in "a negative impression of myself." They are exposed continuously to a psychotherapeutic environment and in addition have psychotherapeutic help individually with their own unique personality structure.

GROUP PSYCHOTHERAPY

Partly because of the paucity of psychotherapists and partly because under it some people make better psychotherapeutic progress, the practice of doing psychotherapy in groups of ten or twelve persons has grown. It has been used in dealing with frank neuroses as well as in personality disorders of varying severity, and has been used somewhat with psychotic patients. It began as a therapy in 1905. It utilizes many of the dynamic principles which have already been mentioned in regard to individual therapy. It makes use of the transference of one patient to another patient as well as to the therapist and it also makes use of the interaction of the patient with the group as a whole as well as with each individual member. The group functions as a surrogate family, with the same ego frustrations and with the same opportunity for mental catharsis. Resistance plays its part also and needs to be dealt with as in individual therapy.

It has been stressed that group therapy is not alone a time- and money-saving technique. In fact, these advantages are only by-products of the procedure. It has its own positive values and may be advantageously combined with individual psychotherapy. Group psychotherapy teaches the individual to share and to participate. He learns that he gets back from the group in proportion to what he puts into it. He has to give love in order to get it. He has to put forth effort to get ego satisfaction. He can learn to become more objective as he abreacts emotion and is not penalized for it. Some therapists feel that some patients can work out problems in group psychotherapy which they could not work out in individual psychotherapy.

In summary then: (a) Group therapy has an important place in present-day psychotherapeutic treatment. (b) Cases for it should be chosen carefully by a group therapist possessing understanding, experience, and empathy for emotionally ill people. (c) While individual psychotherapy is often the first choice, group therapy will meet the psychotherapeutic needs of many patients. (d) A few patients are actually aided over and above individual psychotherapy by the group experience. (e) A combination of the principle of individual psychotherapy plus the psychodynamics of family life will prevail in the treatment session and demand skillful handling by the group leader.

EMOTIONAL DISTURBANCES THAT ACCOMPANY
ORGANIC ILLNESSES

We can hardly leave the subject of treatment without touching upon the problem of emotional disturbances in illnesses that are not psychogenic. In an earlier chapter we discussed the importance of the effects of organic illness and operations on the emotional life of the child and we assume it is understood that the discussion applies to adults as well. When an adult becomes seriously or painfully ill he is confronted suddenly with the fact that his body is not under his control, that he can be made uncomfortable by influences he cannot avoid, and that his life, of which he has felt so certain, may come to an end. Like most human beings he has spent his time avoiding facing the fact that *he* as a *person* can suffer pain and death, and now when he is forced to face these facts as applied to himself his self-confidence is rudely shaken and he becomes greatly frightened.

These fears—particularly the fear of death—overwhelm the sick person with a feeling of helplessness and make him look forward eagerly and pathetically to the visit of his physician as if the latter held the keys of life in his hands. The fact that the patient feels that an interpersonal relationship is an important help in overcoming the fear of death indicates that this fear is based to some extent on a dread of loneliness. Much in the writings of poets and novelists —who, as Freud says, are often closer to recognizing the unconscious than other people are—expresses the loneliness of death. The fear of death is often responsible for the constant and unreasonable complaints of patients, or for the dissatisfaction that causes them to shift from one doctor to another, or for the exaggerated respect they frequently show for their medical attendants, or for the shift made by many persons with minor chronic illnesses for treatment by the medical profession to various forms of faith healing like Christian Science, whose appeal lies in the supernatural denial of the reality of death and pain. It motivates also in large measure the painstaking search carried on by the medical profession for remedies that will cure, as well as the too optimistic reports of panaceas in some medical literature.

In this connection the nurse is often the physician's alter ego. So much of the nursing care essential to the adequate and rapid recovery of the adult patient is a practical method of banishing the patient's apprehension. It is as if the patient said, "Now I know mother and father are interested in me. I am sure they will protect me from death."

The handling of the patient's fear of death, which often shows its existence only by a feeling of panic and discomfort, is part of the art of medicine. Only in part can it be taught didactically; it consists of an intuitive understanding of the patient's needs as well. From a practical standpoint, however, we believe the following suggestions are helpful in dealing with the situation.

First, the patient should be made as comfortable and free from pain as possible.

Second, the patient should be made as comfortable in his mind as possible. The physician's best way to do this is to allow the patient sufficient time so that he can discuss his worries, fears, and complaints. Too often the physician is too interested in ascertaining what is occurring inside the bodies of his patients, whereas he might be more helpful if he was more interested in learning what was in their minds. This outpouring itself is helpful, and if the doctor finds that some of the worries are based on misconceptions it is his duty to correct them, for doing so will often relieve some of the patient's anxiety. Physicians frequently are loath to take the time to do these things, perhaps because of other patients' needs, but they should employ a nurse for this purpose even when nursing care to the physical body is not strictly necessary. The patient can then express himself throughout each day to the nurse and she can correct his misconceptions.

Third, the patient should be taken into the doctor's confidence regarding his illness, the means that must be taken to make a diagnosis and to effect a cure, the time that these means will consume, and the fact that recovery is not delayed but aided by the measures being undertaken.

Fourth, the reasons for specific directions, such as staying in bed, should be discussed with him. It may be argued that discussing physiology and pathology with the patient tends to center his mind on himself whereas he would be better off to think of other things.

This view is correct so far as his relations with other laymen are concerned, but it is not correct in the special relationship between himself and the doctor.

PREVENTION

Achieving Mental Health. To effectively reduce some of the many serious emotional problems of living we need to have more people informed and actively concerned and working in an effective way to create mentally healthy environments in which people can live and work and rear their children. Hence the creation of mental health should be a community concern and not merely the concern of a few. In April 1949, The Group for the Advancement of Psychiatry published its Report No. 8 entitled, *An Outline for Evaluation of a Community Program in Mental Hygiene.* From this report we quoted the following, which will show the extent of the need and the possibilities of citizen activity.

EVALUATION OF COMMUNITY PROGRAMS
FOR MENTAL HYGIENE

I. Introduction

In recent years the public has become increasingly aware of the problems of mental health and illness. The dissemination of statistics regarding the prevalence of mental illness, the dramatization of neglect of the mentally ill, and the realization of the effectiveness of the newer methods of therapy, have all served to emphasize the magnitude of the problem of mental ill health. It is now becoming generally realized that although the cost of care of the mentally ill is great, not nearly enough funds have been spent in this field to bring the problem under control.

Mental health can be defined as a state of well-being, of efficiency at work, and of harmony in human relationships. Mental hygiene is any activity which contributes toward raising the general level of mental health. Although from this point of view almost any human activity has its mental hygiene aspects, nevertheless certain measures are more deliberately aimed at the mental health target. Such measures include both general community activities bearing upon the opportunity of the individual to achieve satisfactory social and personal adjustments, and specific community facilities for the treatment of the mentally ill.

II. Evaluation of Mental Hygiene Activities at the Local Level

A. GENERAL ACTIVITIES INFLUENCING MENTAL HEALTH

1. Prenatal and Well-Baby Clinics, Day Care Centers and Nursery Schools. (a) Are they available to all? (b) Are they adequate in number? (c) Are the staffs adequate in numbers and preparation of personnel? (d) Are the staffs—doctors, nurses, teachers, social workers—oriented to the mental health implications of the program at each center? (e) Do they serve as sources of referral to specialized clinical facilities, including psychiatric facilities?

2. Schools. (a) Do the school buildings meet the physical requirements to carry out the educational program? (b) Are they adequately staffed by qualified teaching personnel who are economically and professionally secure? (c) Have the teachers had instruction in preventive psychiatry to aid their orientation to the emotional needs of each child? (d) Do educators provide good classroom instruction in mental health principles? (e) Are there facilities and personnel to meet the special needs of retarded, educationally gifted, and physically handicapped children? (f) Is there an adult education school stressing special educational and social courses including normal personality development? (g) Is there a good Parent-Teacher program, and does it include psychological as well as educational planning for parents, teachers, and children? (h) Are state and local educational consultants utilized? (i) Are budgetary provisions sufficient to meet the needs of the school system? (j) Are there available diagnostic, counselling, and guidance services for adults and children, and are the personnel adequately trained and oriented to mental health principles?

3. Recreational Program. (a) Are the community recreational programs adequate in scope, and sufficiently diversified to include all age groups? All social strata? All minority groups? (b) Are the staff and their consultants aware of the mental health implications of a broad recreational program? (c) Are school and community recreational programs integrated? (d) How are the activities of the Boy Scouts, Girl Scouts, Y.M.C.A., Y.W.C.A., and similar organizations integrated into the community recreational programs? (e) Is use made of the consultation resources of the National Recreational Association?

4. Industrial Health. (a) To what extent have industries in the community developed industrial health programs? (b) Are management and labor mutually interested in and informed of the effect of personnel selection and personnel practices on mental health? (c) Is there mutual recognition by management and labor of the effect on mental health and working morale of human relations within and outside of the industrial

plant? (d) Are industrial physicians and personnel management sharing their responsibilities for mental health?

5. Welfare Agencies. (a) Are the budgetary provisions for the public and private social welfare agencies sufficient to provide services for all who need them? (b) Are the agencies staffed by professionally accredited, trained workers, and is there provision for in-service training? Does training include an understanding of interpersonal relations and personality difficulties? (c) Is there coordination of social welfare agencies with each other and with health, educational, and recreational programs? (d) Do the social welfare agencies utilize and cooperate with psychiatric facilities in the community? (e) Are ministers, physicians, and educators in the community oriented to the kind of service social work agencies are prepared to give?

6. Courts. (a) Do the criminal courts take into account the influence of environmental and emotional conflicts in the offender? (b) Is probation administered under a staff trained in case work techniques? (c) Do the courts comply with the standards of the National Probation Association? (d) Are informal hearings held for juvenile first offenders? (e) Is there an official psychiatric courts clinic to advise the court regarding the issue of insanity and to counsel the court regarding sentences? (f) Are the Domestic Relations and Civil Courts aware of the environmental and emotional factors influencing mental health?

7. Public Health. (a) Is there a full-time, trained public health officer, and is he aware that mental health is part of the total public health program? (b) Does the public health educational program include mental health? (c) Is the public health nurse oriented to emotional factors and mental health aspects of her work? (d) Does the community have a Health Council, including health, welfare and educational organizations? (e) Is adequate attention paid to emotional and social factors in the special clinics such as for the crippled and spastic, rheumatic fever, tuberculosis, venereal disease, and cancer? (f) Is hospitalization, when indicated, readily and conveniently available? (g) Are educational and vocational counseling available to those suffering from chronic or limiting illness? (h) Is convalescent after-care properly supervised?

8. Lawyers. (a) Are there lectures in psychiatry in the local law schools? (b) Does the local Bar Association recognize the significance of and stimulate interest in the mental health and psychiatric aspects of legal problems? (c) Is there effective liaison between the local Bar Association and the local Mental Hygiene Society? (d) Is the legal profession oriented to the use of social welfare agencies, psychiatric consultation, and marriage counseling facilities in the community?

9. Clergy. (a) Are courses in preventive psychiatry and mental health

included in the preparation of divinity students for the ministry? (b) Is the local Council of Churches aware of current thinking on the relation between psychiatry and religion? (c) Does the Council of Churches encourage the Clergy to acquire this understanding?

10. Communications. (a) Are the people connected with the press, radio, and movies in the community well enough oriented in psychiatric understanding to give proper evaluation to material that passes through their hands? (b) Are reliable sources of information such as a local Mental Hygiene Society, or qualified psychiatrists available to these professions? (c) Are the public libraries well stocked with the best books on the problems of mental health? (d) Do librarians feature this material and make it easily available to the public?

11. Socio-economic Factors. (a) Are adequate housing facilities readily available for all who need them in the community? (b) Are employment opportunities accessible in accordance with the composition and density of the population of the community? (c) Are racial and minority group tensions and the concomitant economic and social discriminations held to a minimum in the community?

12. Problems of the Aged. (a) Is the institutional care of the aged based upon current ideas of group living as embodied in the cottage or colony plan and stressing the importance of the individual to the group? (b) Is there a foster home for the aged? (c) Is vocational guidance and retraining available to the aged? (d) Are the personnel of institutions for the care of the aged oriented to mental health principles, and is psychiatric consultation available for residents of the institutions?

B. SPECIAL ACTIVITIES INFLUENCING MENTAL HEALTH

1. Lay Groups Concerned with Mental Health. (a) Is there a Mental Hygiene Society in the community consisting of an organized group of lay individuals interested in the education of the public in mental health problems? (b) Does the Mental Hygiene Society or its equivalent have at its disposal adequate professional psychiatric advice and guidance? (c) Does it serve as a stimulant and as an integrating body for all other groups in the community who become interested in mental health problems? (d) Does it keep executive and legislative bodies in the community and the state informed of local mental health needs? (e) Does it keep the public informed of legislation pending at the community or state level regarding mental health problems?

2. Professional Groups Concerned with Mental Health. (a) Is the County or District Medical Society aware of the importance of emotional factors in physical illness, and does it foster a program of psychiatric orientation for the general practitioner? (b) Do local psychiatrists or the

local Psychiatric Association maintain effective liaison with general practitioners and other specialists in the community? Do they foster programs designed to keep each other abreast of latest developments in their special fields? (c) Does the local Psychiatric Society in liaison with the Mental Hygiene Society provide lecturers for the education of the community in special or general mental health problems? (d) Does the County Medical Society have a committee which cooperates with state mental hospital?

C. TREATMENT FACILITIES

1. Outpatient Services. (a) Are there available in the community psychiatric clinics for adults and children staffed by qualified personnel? (b) Do the public and private (voluntary) hospitals which operate outpatient clinics also provide properly staffed psychiatric clinics? (c) Are the emotional implications of organic disease recognized in the general medical and surgical clinics? (d) Are budgetary provisions sufficient to meet the needs of an adequate psychiatric treatment program in the community? (e) Are there qualified psychiatrists in private practice and do they meet the needs of the community?

2. Inpatient Services. (a) Are there adequate facilities for the care of psychotic (insane) patients in public and private mental hospitals? (b) Are there adequate facilities for the care of nonpsychotic (neurotic) patients in public and private mental hospitals? (c) Are there adequate facilities for the care of psychotic patients in public and private general hospitals? (d) Are there adequate facilities for the care of nonpsychotic patients in public and private general hospitals? (e) Do these services meet the standards of the American Psychiatric Association? (f) Are budgetary provisions sufficient to provide services for all who need them?

III. Evaluation of Mental Hygiene Activities at the State Level

A. GENERAL ACTIVITIES INFLUENCING MENTAL HEALTH

1. State Agencies Parallel to Local Community Services. (a) Does the state level counterpart (Bureau of Education, Welfare, etc.) stimulate the growth of local services? (b) Does the state level supervise and regulate local activity? (c) Is there coordination between state and local agencies? (d) Are budgetary provisions at the state level sufficient to provide adequate services? (e) Is there a training program for various mental health personnel?

B. LEGISLATION AND ADMINISTRATION

1. Commitment Procedures. (a) Are mental patients ever held in jail pending commitment to a mental hospital? (b) Is commitment made on

a medical rather than a trial-by-jury basis? (c) Do laws differentiate between the mentally ill and the criminal? (d) Are there established qualifications for physicians who commit patients to mental hospitals? (e) How closely do the state commitment laws approximate to the model commitment laws drawn up by the Group for the Advancement of Psychiatry?

2. Organization of State Mental Health Office. (a) Is there centralization of authority over State Mental Hospitals? (b) Is provision made for inspection and licensing of private mental hospitals? (c) What is the relation between the state mental health authority and the state health officer? (d) Are budgetary provisions sufficient to maintain a central mental health authority and to carry out the functions of that office? (e) Does the mental health office maintain a division on research? (f) Does it maintain outpatient services for adults and children in areas which cannot be serviced through locally developed facilities? (g) Does it maintain an educational program? (h) Is the state taking advantage of the financial aid available to states and communities under the National Mental Health Act administered by the Public Health Service of the Federal Security Agency? (i) Is the state mental health program in research, education, and outpatient services adequately coordinated with the national program established by the National Mental Health Act?

3. State Legislature. (a) Is the state legislature adequately informed of the needs of all mental health activities? (b) Does the state legislature accept responsibility in principle for a broad state program in mental hygiene? (c) Does it give adequate financial support to the program?

C. SPECIFIC SERVICES

1. State Mental Hospitals. (a) Do the hospitals conform to the standards established by the American Psychiatric Association and the American Hospital Association? (b) Are the budgetary provisions sufficient to meet the needs of all patients needing services? (c) Are there facilities for follow-up care of discharged convalescent and recovered patients? (d) Are there adequate provisions for the specialized care and resident therapy of pre-psychotic and psychotic children? (e) Do the hospitals have Boards of Visitors from the community who come regularly?

2. Institutions for Feebleminded and Epileptic Children. (a) Is there provision for the care and training of retarded children? (b) Is there provision for the care and training of epileptic children? (c) What provisions exist for their after care? (d) Do the provisions meet the standards of the American Psychiatric Association and the American Hospital Association? (e) Are budgetary provisions sufficient to carry out the program?

3. Penal Institutions. (a) Is the general attitude of the prison punitive or correctional? (b) Is a classification service available? (c) Is there a functioning parole system?

4. Reformatories. (a) Is the general attitude punitive or correctional? (b) Is a classification service available? (c) Are there provisions for supervision of parole? (d) Is the budget adequate for its needs? (e) Is provision made for continual evaluation of results?

5. Training Schools. (a) Are psychiatric services available for the study of the juvenile offender? (b) Is there an actual and effective program of rehabilitation? (c) Are provisions made for a normal scholastic education? (d) Is there provision for supervision of parole?

6. Youth Authority. (a) Is a modern concept of a youth authority in effect? (b) Does the youth authority have absolute authority to do that which is for the best interest of the offender? (c) Is provision made for continual testing of results?

IV. Methods for Gaining Information

A. MAKE PERSONAL VISITS TO THE LOCAL AND STATE AGENCIES AND INSTITUTIONS IN QUESTION.

B. LOOK CAREFULLY AND ASK QUESTIONS.

C. CONTACT THE EXPERTS ON THOSE ACTIVITIES IN THE COMMUNITY:

1. General practitioners and the district medical society.
2. Local or nearby psychiatrists, and the psychiatric department of the state university medical school, or nearby medical school.
3. Local educators—superintendents of schools and teachers.
4. The local public health officer.
5. The director of the Council of Social Agencies as well as directors and personnel of other social welfare agencies.
6. Local business men and industrialists.
7. Local labor leaders.
8. School nurses and visiting nurses.
9. Local judges and lawyers or local Bar Association.
10. Friends who have had occasion to use psychiatric services in the community, either for themselves or their families.
11. The local Council of Churches.

D. CONSULT THE LIBRARIAN AND ASK FOR READING LISTS.

E. CONSULT THE ADMINISTRATIVE OFFICER RESPONSIBLE FOR THE MENTAL HEALTH PROGRAM IN THE STATE.

F. CONSULT THE LOCAL REPRESENTATIVES ON THE STATE LEGISLATURE AND THE MEMBERS OF THE LEGISLATIVE COMMITTEES ON MENTAL HEALTH, HOSPITALS AND BUDGETS.

G. WRITE TO THE NATIONAL COMMITTEE FOR MENTAL HEALTH, 10 COLUMBUS CIRCLE, NEW YORK 19, N.Y.; AND TO THE STATE MENTAL HYGIENE SOCIETY FOR PERTINENT LITERATURE AND ADVICE.

H. WRITE TO THE AMERICAN PSYCHIATRIC ASSOCIATION, 1700 18TH ST., WASHINGTON 9, D.C., ATTENTION CHAIRMAN OF THE COMMITTEE ON COOPERATION WITH LAY GROUPS, FOR ASSISTANCE IN THE PROJECT.

This outline is designed to aid any group in learning about the mental hygiene activities of its own community, and in planning for their improvement. In any concerted attempt to raise the level of mental health in the community, the first step must be a familiarity with the existing mental hygiene activities for the sake of evaluating their effectiveness or their deficiencies. The next step is a long-range plan for the improvement of the current situation. Finally, it is necessary to initiate concerted action by all interested groups in the community to bring the long-range plan to fruition.

Counseling. As the relatively small number of psychiatrists available work largely with those who are seriously mentally ill in hospitals, clinics, and offices they have, in the main, been aided in their work by counseling efforts made by various groups and individuals in fields other than psychiatry. In fact, many psychiatrists have helped to train these groups. Psychiatrists are interested in the creation of mental health, fostering it and maintaining it, and preventing mental illness. Many people have a hand in promoting individual development toward mature personality.

The Teacher as Counselor. One of the most fruitful times to create mental health is in the early school years. There has been an increasing trend in education away from the sterile teaching of facts and figures toward the teaching of concepts that would aid in the personal and social growth of the child. School architecture, for example, has been modified to meet this need—and teachers and other personnel are fast learning to make the best use of it. Among the many advantages of this altered approach has been the observation that better intellectual performance follows an emotional climate that fosters security and enjoyment of the total learning experience. Of course, such a climate should prevail in the home, but the school too should be equipped to carry on the maturation process as well as to impart knowledge. Should the home be an emotionally unhealthy one, the school will be in a position to help remedy the situation a little at any rate.

One of the least complicated and most popular mental-health school plans was started by H. Edmund Bullis in Delaware. He developed lesson plans for use in the sixth and seventh grades. These lesson plans were organized and published in two books called, *Human Relations in the Classroom* (I and II) (Hambleton Co., Wilmington, Delaware, 1948). The classes are led by the teacher, who chooses a topic from the book such as, "How Emotions Are Aroused," "Our Unpleasant Emotions," "Submitting to Authority," "Why Daydream?" The children enter the discussion and learn from each other various ways in which emotional problems can be handled.

More extensive methods are being used in various other areas. Some involve rewriting textbooks in order that the personalities and emotions of those who made history can be studied along with the facts of what happened. Other plans call for discussion groups with teachers, discussion groups with parents, training courses for teachers. Since the authority to make changes emanates downward from the superintendent through the principal to the teacher, it is evident that any modifications in curriculum that are meant to help the emotional maturation of the pupils would have to be accepted by and permeate the whole system, including the school board, personnel, and parents. References are given to others than the Bullis Project. These projects will and must become more widespread since the old adage that "an ounce of prevention is worth a pound of cure" is nowhere more true than in the mental-health field. The teacher who is alert to the many emotional needs and problems of young growing children can be an effective counselor and use the class group in a manner that will help the individuals in it and prevent mental illness. Those interested should read Report No. 18 of the Committee on Preventive Psychiatry of The Group for the Advancement of Psychiatry entitled, *Promotion of Mental Health in the Primary and Secondary Schools: an Evaluation of Four Projects,* January, 1951. (Available for 10¢ from the Group for the Advancement of Psychiatry, Publications Office, 104 E. 25th St., New York 10, N.Y.) One of the projects described in this pamphlet is the so-called "Force Project" designed for the better preparation of high-school students for work and family life.

College Counseling. At the college level there is possibly more counseling activity proportionately than at the primary and secondary school level. It is part of the effort to aid in the maturation of the college student and to prepare him to adapt more fully to the life that he must plunge into directly after leaving the protection and relative simplicity of the college campus. The college student is still an unfinished product and college personnel can do much to help him grow emotionally if they are concerned about this phase of their responsibility and know how to counsel individually as well as to utilize subject matter to foster individual development. A teacher may feel: "I am employed to give thirty-six lectures on history. That is what I am paid for—that is what I do." But what of the twenty-five students who may be taking this particular history course? Possibly they have families pressuring them for high performance. Possibly they wonder how they will make use of the course in the future. Possibly they wish it could become more alive and interesting. Or they may wish the instructor would reveal more of his personal philosophy about life in addition to teaching events and public figures. College youngsters have a great desire to come closer to older people who have been solving some of the problems that the students themselves will face very shortly. The students, some of them at least, want to come a little closer to their professors after class or in class discussion, and if they can, the experience helps the student and should add to the professors' pleasure of teaching. Some professors feel burdened with work and say, "I haven't the time for talking to students. I have my own life to lead. Besides I don't have the answers." Students are looking for an opportunity to exchange ideas with an older person or perhaps they are looking for a listener, someone who will care enough about them to listen to them for a few minutes. They feel the need for a friend.

The college counselor has many roles to play. For example, families of college students may need some guidance. Some families take thought only as to the frequency with which they can see their son or daughter. They do not care about his friends, his recreational life, his self-growth. They want him around when he is not actually in class and feel they deserve to have him. The student in turn is caught up in some residual sense of obligation to keep his family happy and so he must forgo friendships and activities in the college in order to placate a family that poorly understands the valuable experience of emancipation. One mother insisted that her son leave college because the administration would not let him have a car to come home weekends. This kind of parental dominance is, of course, inimical to healthy personality development.

Colleges differ in the degree to which their administration, organization, and personnel can meet the emotional needs of individual students and their families. More and more colleges are employing psychiatrists, psychologists, and social workers to promote student health and correlate the home and the college influence. Deans, professors, and heads of departments are trying to gain more knowledge and insight both of the student and of themselves so that they can act as catalytic forces in the lives of these thousands of youngsters in need of inspiration and guidance. Dr. Lawrence Kubie, in an article in the *Harvard Alumni Bulletin,* "The Forgotten Man of Education," has made an eloquent plea for what he calls "understanding in depth" to be instituted at the college level. He feels that instead of a college program emphasizing more chemistry, more history, or more technological research, we should emphasize *more knowledge of people about themselves* and more awareness of the important values in living. Instead of an aimless, listless, passive acceptance of class routine a college student should be developing an independent, self-motivating personality increasingly capable of utilizing the freedom which a free society offers. To develop it he may need to rebel judiciously against overprotective parents and other authorities and learn to make decisions and choices of his own, accepting and discharging responsibilities in miniature which the world will demand of him in full measure later. To bring forth this kind of student requires a mature, wise, able, altruistic faculty member who, understanding himself and liking students, functions to some degree in a parental role and counselor role as well as in his teacher's role. Such a role should not be unduly stressful, for it can add to the zest of the job. Thus, when a student says, "I'm finding this course hard to grasp. Should I change?" or, "I'm not making friends the way I would like," or, "I wonder if I shouldn't go to a college farther away from home?" then the instructor can hear him out and counsel him on some of the pros and cons of the question so that he will be in a better position to come to a decision as to what to do.

The Religious Leader as Counselor. Religious leaders of all faiths are attempting to improve their capacity to counsel people on personal problems. The religious leader of today is becoming increasingly aware that the healthy personality makes the best use of religious teachings. He is also aware that religion needs to be introduced to the human being when he is young. He knows, further, that the family is the source-place of love and that if a family cannot learn to love, its children run a greater risk of delinquent behavior, divorce, separations, and other asocial ills than do children in other more happy families. So, in addition to preparation for the more traditional duties of the religious leader, instruction in counseling is being given in an increasing number of theological schools, usually in conjunction with some psychiatric center. Some religionists still feel that Sunday School attendance, or church attendance with Bible reading and prayer, is sufficient of itself to make mature personalities; but case studies show that study alone—even study of the Bible—and exhortation, nay, even confession, are not enough. Man needs some opportunity to express his true self in a setting that will help him see his conflicts and understand their origin before he can reorganize his life in a constructive manner and make better use of his religion.

Pastoral counseling is not an easy skill to acquire or to practice. It is difficult, for instance, for a minister to take a definite stand on moral issues from the pulpit and then take on a sufficiently nonjudgmental role in his study to meet the needs of a given case. Furthermore, he must have the skill to know when an emotionally disturbed individual is in a prolonged grief state or is suffering from a pathological depression of spirits. In marriage difficulties he can be caught between the narrow line of a simple moral defection and a pathological personality reaction. A high degree of both skill and humility is required in this very important collaborative effort between the professions of psychiatry and religion.

The Supervisor as Counselor. Among the many people who are developing an increasing interest in mental health—although they probably rarely think of it under that heading—are probation officers, police officers, building and apartment-house managers, and office and plant supervisors. These people want to understand people to avoid tensions on the job, increase efficiency under their regime, make people happier, and make the job more pleasant for all concerned. Regardless of motive, there is no question that the psychologically adept and mature person in any walk of life can help immeasurably those with whom he is associated.

A supervisor or anyone in a position of authority surrounds himself with most if not all of the attributes that originally surrounded the parent. To some people a police officer is a friend, protector, helper, a man (or woman) interested in the best interests of the community as a whole. To others a police officer is an enemy, a tyrant, a punitive and unreasonable man, trying to make life as difficult and as frustrating for people as possible. The supervisor of an office, store, restaurant, or factory also attracts to himself this varied collection of attributes which are replicas of the worker's experience as a child and growing adolescent. The supervisor may be a "good guy," a "right guy," a man or woman who will understand, protect, and intercede as mother or father did. On the other hand he may be regarded as self-centered, interested only in his own advancement, or only in pleasing those above him because they pay him or will advance him. The supervisor has a difficult task. Psychologically, he is parent to a group of workers who want approval for what they do. They look to him for fair play in judging their disputes and differences. They expect him to represent them, if necessary, before higher superiors. They want him to be interested in what they do on a holiday, to be impressed if a new child is born, to applaud if someone in the family receives honors, to be concerned if they are sick, to protect them on their lack of work output if they are not feeling well, to warn them on any approaching changes in routine, and to ask them kindly to co-operate in case changes do occur. They do not expect ridicule from him for their personal idiosyncracies and they expect him to understand and interpret their personal reactions to higher authority. In other words, every leader of people in this nation—even in the smallest office, department store, and production unit—is being silently asked to be a generous, magnanimous, wholly understanding person. How many are prepared to be so? The number who are could well be increased. Courses for supervisors are given in larger communities under various auspices. Everyone who leads and directs people should know about personality and personality needs and meet these needs as far as he can. It is easy to make fun of, scold, ridicule, and fire people. But to work with a man and understand his personality and make it a better one, contributing constructively to the group effort, is a real challenge to a supervisor. To be a supervisor is a reward perhaps—but it is also a great responsibility and a great challenge. Business organizations today are arranging training for their supervisory personnel through various means. Some of this is done by on-the-job training courses, or by institutes or courses to which their personnel are sent in relays, through enrollment in intensive, specially arranged training periods set up by a university or some organization in human relations. No attempt is made to make the supervisor any kind of expert, but rather a more sensitive, alert, psychologically understanding, capable group leader.

THE CLINICAL PSYCHOLOGIST

Among the many associated scientists working in the area of human relations we need to give a prominent place to the clinical psychologist. Under this category come many people who are identified with vocational guidance, vocational counseling, remedial reading, personnel selection, psychological counseling, and so on. Specialists in this field are most capable and gifted. There has been some problem between the physician and the psychologist in working out the area of operation for the clinical psychologist. In colleges without a medical-psychiatric department and in industries who turned first to psychology for the handling of their adjustment problems it has developed that the clinical psychologist often finds himself involved in the handling of people whose functioning or behavior is disturbed, temporarily or chronically, and in whom mental, emotional, and physical factors are at work that require the diagnostic and treatment skill of a medically trained physician. Granted that it is difficult at times to be precise in defining who is a psychiatric patient, there does exist a problem in making sure that the sick person gets the best available care.

Psychology has been defined as "the systematic study, by any and all applicable and fruitful methods, of organisms in relation to their behavior, environmental relations, and experience. Its purpose is to discover facts, principles, and generalizations which shall increase man's knowledge, understanding, predictive insight, directive wisdom and control of the natural phenomena of behavior and experience, and of himself and the social groups in which, and through which, he functions. Psychologists seek to provide a basic science of human thinking, character, skill, learning, conduct, etc., which will serve all the sciences of man (e.g., anthropology, sociology, economics, government, education, medicine, etc.) in much the same way and to the same extent that biology now serves the agricultural and medical sciences."

There are now a great number of practicing clinical psychologists who are members of the American Psychological Association. They work in the fields of both retarded and inferior children, speech and reading difficulties, experimental and diagnostic work in mental hospitals, child and adult psychiatric clinics, personnel and counseling activities and vocational guidance. Because of the acceptance of psychoanalytic concepts psychiatry has become more psychological and therapy is heavily psychotherapeutic. This trend has brought some added drive within both psychiatry and psychology to develop diagnostic techniques and criteria, and much has been accomplished by the clinical psychologist in this area. The following have been adjudged fruitful areas for collaboration as well as for independent action by the psychologist and psychiatrist:[1] (a) the development and refinement of diagnostic devices for the detection of various types of maladjustment and abnormality; (b) the nature of personality structure and psychodynamics; (c) the classification, clarification, and delineation of syndromes of maladjustment; (d) the relationship of attitudes, feelings, conflicts, emotions, etc., to physiological malfunctioning such as found in psychophysiologic illnesses; (e) experimental psychodynamics—the reproduction of psychopathology in controlled settings; (f) the nature of the psychotherapeutic process; (g) the development of new therapeutic techniques.

In July, 1949, the Committee on Clinical Psychology of The Group for the Advancement of Psychiatry (functioning with consultants from the field of psychology) published a report in which they concluded the following:

This committee does not feel that the association of clinical psychologists as psychotherapists with general practitioners or medical specialists other than psychiatrists is ordinarily a wise arrangement. This separates the clinical psychologist from his logical professional associate, the psychiatrist. It provides medical but not psychiatric safeguards. Many medical specialists and general practitioners have not had sufficient training in psychiatry to make an accurate psychiatric diagnosis, nor do they understand the management and treatment of psychiatric conditions.

[1] Group for the Advancement of Psychiatry, Report No. 10.

The report goes on to outline the prescribed course of study which the field of psychology is trying to develop for clinical psychologists —a graduate program of four years leading to a doctoral degree.

After obtaining his degree (Ph.D.), the student is in a position to undertake clinical work in an approved psychiatric hospital, clinic or institution, where further supervision in advanced and specialized aspects of the clinical field is available. Any intensive training in psychotherapy is obtained after securing the Ph.D. degree.

After five years of experience, the candidate becomes eligible for examination by the American Board of Examiners in Professional Psychology. At least three of the five years should have been spent in centers where supervised training is provided. On the candidate's passing the examinations, both oral and written, and meeting the requirements as to ethical standing and experience, the Board will issue to him a diploma qualifying him as a specialist in Clinical Psychology.

In conclusion, then, this committee believes that the clinical psychologist will be able to make his most effective contribution to the total area dealing with mental health and emotional adjustment if he works in direct association with psychiatrists. In such a relationship his maximal effectiveness to persons in need of help will be assured.

This publication is Report No. 10, entitled *The Relation of Clinical Psychology to Psychiatry,* and is obtainable from The Group for the Advancement of Psychiatry, Publications Office, 104 E. 25th St., New York 10, N.Y.

It should be emphasized that this report does not restrict the psychologist in his counseling activities any more than the clergyman, the college instructor, or the teacher is restricted where the fostering of healthy personality growth is concerned. It does try to delineate some safeguards in the area of psychotherapy where the welfare of ill people is concerned.

THE PSYCHIATRIC SOCIAL WORKER

In the total treatment of mental illness the part played by the psychiatric social worker is considerable. For more than twenty years the clinic teams both of adult psychiatric clinics and of psychiatric clinics for children have included the social worker. In modern psychiatric practice we no longer think of the patient in terms of his psychopathology alone but we think of him as a human being functioning in a social environment involved at all times in a complicated system of interpersonal relationships. His inner tensions and conflicts are always being influenced for better or worse by his social matrix. The psychiatric social worker in a majority of instances uses the concepts of the psychological and social sources of emotional illness. She is also prepared to assist the other members of the clinic team in becoming aware of other therapeutic resources which may be inherent in the community and utilizable for the welfare of the patient.

Treatment plans may include certain members of the patient's family as well as use of resources in the community. The social worker often arranges for these services and may participate in them herself in co-operation with the psychiatrist. Often the psychiatric social worker, through case-work interviews with the patient before, after, or at stated times during the psychiatric treatment of the patient, may be of direct assistance in arranging such practical matters as finances, jobs, places to live, school or camp placement, or medical examination. At other times, case-work treatment may be undertaken independently of any psychiatric treatment of the patient. Sometimes psychiatric case work with one or more members of the family may be indicated in connection with planned consultation with the psychiatrist.

Social case-work procedures make fewer psychological demands upon the patient than psychotherapy, but the range of application is much wider than the latter. Such co-operative work between the psychiatric social worker and the psychiatrist can be intricate but also rewarding. The psychiatric social worker may bring to this working relationship a consciousness of shifts in the feeling of persons on whom the patient must depend and of their responses to changes in the patient. The social worker's awareness of environmental factors can be of great help in planning what is needed for the patient's progress and welfare. Good co-operation between psychiatrist, social worker, and psychologist both in the psychiatric hospital and in the outpatient clinic combines for the best treatment program for a large number of the patients.

THE DOCTOR

The doctor who is a general practitioner or specialist in some other field than psychiatry may need some encouragement to act as counselor. Many such doctors do not fulfill this role because they feel they do not have the time, or they do not believe in psychiatry, or they have no flair for working with people, or they are not sufficiently concerned about people's emotional problems to develop any kind of counseling technique for helping them. In such cases the doctor claims ignorance of being able to help with personal problems, or he gives direct advice in a few words. Often, however, this advice is worse than admitting ignorance, for quick off-the-cuff unconsidered recommendations can do considerable harm.

Actually a very few principles can start the physician on the way to counseling and he can gradually add to his skill by reading and listening to the procedures of others. To begin with he might observe the following few principles: (1) Listen to the patient's story and get the facts. (2) Try to distinguish, from the patient's expressed wishes and from the language of his symptoms, what are his emotional needs. (3) Discuss with him how these needs came to be unfulfilled and also how they might be met now and in the future. (4) Continue in additional sessions to discuss his unfulfilled needs and encourage him to work to find a solution. (5) Study a book that covers the subject in greater detail, such as *Psychotherapy in Medical Practice,* by Maurice Levine (Macmillan), and the necessary knowledge and skill will come with a sharing of experience with experts and further study.

Families need so much counseling these days, in every part of their activity from rearing the infant to coping with an aged member of the family, that it is difficult to be a practitioner of medicine and not be a counselor. An estimated thirty-five to fifty per cent of medical problems have a large emotional factor in them, and it seems like a necessary part of the physician's equipment to have an understanding of basic counseling techniques.

CONSULTING A PSYCHIATRIST

In our modern world the psychiatrist is playing an ever increasing role. More medical-school graduates are entering the specialty of psychiatry than ever before, and large psychiatric training centers are preparing more and more specialists to cope with the great demand. Psychiatrists are being utilized by colleges and universities and consequently more families are being introduced to the idea that their child is "seeing a psychiatrist." Many parents have long since become used to this idea and have actually sought out the psychiatrist and welcomed his help. On the other hand, there are some families who feel that it is a matter of shame and insult to be told that their child "needs to see a psychiatrist." To them this advice carries the implication that the child is weak-minded and that in some way they have failed to give stability to their youngster. They suffer a great sense of inadequacy. However, it should be emphasized that rearing children is a very difficult and complicated process and anyone from any walk of life can fail in his responsibility as a parent.

A child may be unduly shy or may have been overprotected in spite of his parents' best intentions. Or he may be immature as a result of misguided attempts to be helpful. If parents are too busy, a child may fall into poor study habits. Parents may have to move about from place to place because of their work, and the changes may affect a child's security. Changes from one school to another may interfere, for instance, with his social development. Because of reasons such as these, even loving, devoted, and thoughtful parents may fail to enable their child to adjust himself to the complex demands of living.

The specialty of psychiatry is relatively new. Modern dynamic psychiatry is little more than fifty years old. It has had its own difficulties in gaining necessary wisdom and knowledge, yet it has trained and placed within the medical profession men and women who understand and treat the many complex phenomena that arise from problems of human behavior in its most subtle manifestations.

It should not be considered a disgrace to see a psychiatrist. Seeing a psychiatrist rarely means mental illness of the kind that requires either brief or prolonged removal from society. The psychiatrists of today treat a wide variety of human problems, such as the child who has difficulty in reading or the child who is lonely and eats too much and becomes obese. Psychiatrists interest themselves in the college student who is homesick or who cannot study, as well as in the businessman who is overtired and suffers from headaches. Psychiatry believes in trying to sensitize everyone to problems in human adjustment before they become too serious. Consequently, we make a plea for co-operation with the psychiatrist when problems no longer seem soluble by ordinary means.

SELF-DEVELOPMENT

Gloom, pessimism, apathy, inactivity, feelings of inferiority, self-pity, self-criticism, and hopelessness about life not only limit an individual's effectiveness but also make him an unattractive and even burdensome member of society whether he be at work, at home, or at play. We are inclined to believe there is a great deal of truth in the words of Abraham Lincoln to the effect that a man is about as happy as he makes up his mind to be. A person needs to think well of himself and be in a fairly continuous rewarding relationship with life and people in order to avoid the distress of lowered self-esteem. An individual cannot afford, if he is to keep his emotional health, to withdraw interest and permit his self-esteem to fall for long periods at a time. We realize that we are speaking as if an individual could regulate this emotional attitude solely through his own will power. True, he cannot exercise complete control through will power; but he can learn facts about himself and others that will make improvement easier. We believe people should be happy and are entitled to pursue happiness; but being happy is less the purpose of our existence than conducting ourselves in such a way as to deserve happiness. If people could achieve this conduct ideal, there could be a constructive integration of the world's religious philosophies and at the same time some of our most pressing social problems could be solved.

In "normal" living the imaginative, optimistic man or woman is often regarded with suspicion. A new idea is labeled "bizarre," a wealth of ideas is regarded as "erratic," and optimism is thought of as "unsound" or "unrealistic." People avoid moods of depression because they are painful, and so too they seem to want to avoid excursions into happiness, elation, and its accompanying wealth of ideas because these seem impractical and disturb complacency or the commonsense practicality. But optimism, positive thinking, and mutual approval are necessary to everyone and man must dare to cultivate them in spite of criticism.

Any discussion of self-development returns us to a discussion of the growth of personality within the home and in the educational framework. A child's confidence, imagination, and sense of well-being develops slowly and gradually every day that he lives. If he is approved of he gains confidence. If he is loved and appreciated he is happy (meaning that he is able to love himself and maintain a sense of well-being). As he expresses his ideas about what he would like to do or be and what he would like to create, one of two results may occur. He may be encouraged, so that his ideas grow and flourish. Or, on the other hand, he may be condemned or ridiculed, whereupon he may well withdraw his dreams and hopes back inside himself. If he does the latter he may dream of enhancing his potential abilities but lack the confidence or fail to develop techniques for putting them into execution. Here is clearly seen how important the roles of parent and teacher are in the development of healthy personality through support and encouragement. Who knows what a child may become! Of course, *all* cannot be laid at the door of parent and teacher. For whatever their failings, an individual emerges, at the end of his teens, to be a person in his own right with a personality and a capacity to improve.

Too often, however, this capacity for self-improvement has not received sufficient attention in our philosophy of living as propounded by home, school, or church. There comes a time in each individual's life when he must take a hand in his own self-development and build upon what society has given him.

The *first* need for self-development is to realize that he has an obligation to tolerate anxiety, in other words to accept the distress that self-criticism is bound to bring and try to discover how it may be useful in planning future activities.

Second, when he has seen by way of criticism (his own or that of others) that he is lacking in some personality attribute, he should *practice* acquiring it.

Third, if he does not know how to improve he should consult those who are in a position to give him understanding of what he needs. They may be, variously, psychiatrists, religious counselors, social agencies, marriage counselors, or those who give such courses in self-improvement as were pioneered by Dale Carnegie but are now offered in many adult-educational programs. *Above all,* the real point is to avoid *self-satisfaction* ("I guess I'm all right as I am"), *despair* ("I'm a mess and I'll never be any better"), and *rationalization* ("It is so hard to improve. I do not see how I can begin this year").

Everyone should try to envision the concept that personality growth takes: (1) effort and activity, (2) imagination, (3) courage, (4) capacity to tolerate and utilize the suggestions of others, (5) the willingness to "take" what happens and integrate it into a more positive, constructive approach to life.

In this way the average "normal" person may use his ordinary life experiences as stepping-stones to personality growth and as means toward self-development rather than as the "closing of doors" called regression. Anne Morrow Lindbergh, in her book *The Steep Ascent,* said:

People "died" all the time in their lives. Parts of them died when they made the wrong kind of decisions—decisions against life. Sometimes they died bit by bit until finally they were just living corpses walking around. If you were perceptive you could see it in their eyes; the fire had gone out. Yes, there were a lot of people walking around who were "dead" and a lot of people killed who were "living." She couldn't explain it any more than that. But you always knew when you made a decision against life. When you denied life you were warned. The cock crowed, always, somewhere inside of you. The door clicked and you were safe inside—safe and dead.

And usually it was fear that made you pull the door shut: emotional fear of becoming involved with people, of loving too much.

Let us take a case in point: Joan W., who had a happy and adjusted infancy with a normally devoted and supporting mother and father. Her first contact with the world outside her home came when she started kindergarten. There she met her first criticism from her teacher for talking out of turn. This nettled her and she was inclined to renounce school, but her mother prevailed upon her to try to meet the teacher's expectation with good co-operation. In early grade school Joan was reproached for lack of diligence in studying arithmetic and spelling, but by this time she was inclined to study harder on her own accord. She continued to make her way through elementary and high school—sometimes accepting the invitations offered to meet the demands of teachers, school, and parents, sometimes ignoring them. At last she and her growth met the greatest of all tests when she married a man whom she greatly loved and admired but who had great expectations of her. He wanted her to go to a distant city with him. This prospect required her to face the loneliness of being by herself most of the day and of meeting and making new friends. The thought caused her to shrink and even consider going back home, but she met the new challenge and conquered her anxiety by facing the new situation squarely. Soon there were children. Each brought new experiences and new compensations. She was almost daily brought face-to-face with her fears or her inadequacies, but each one that she met and mastered gave her an added awareness of her strength and the satisfaction of accomplishment. Her husband approved of her efforts, while the school and her friends approved of her children. She gave of herself but she was *given to* by others, and she knew that this giving is most of what there is to living and keeping up a level of psychic comfort that we call "normality."

Some people may derive their satisfactions in more glamorous and interesting ways but to have a healthy sense of well-being one must (1) start life with a sense of security, if possible; (2) accept new responsibilities all the time; (3) be able to endure some sense of inadequacy daily; (4) keep that sense of inadequacy neutralized by warm, enriching friendships and constructive activity (work); (5) keep in step with the changing demands and gratifications of each decade of life; (6) visualize future goals; and (7) build up a reservoir of pleasant memories and be resourceful and useful to others so as to neutralize the disillusionments of the aging process.

Middle age brings imperceptible changes, disappointments, and losses which require a flexible compensatory psychic mechanism. Parents lose children to college, to jobs, and to marriage. They lose friends by death and by moves of various sorts. They lose physical attractiveness and they lose pleasures through physical debility. These are just a few of the many threats to the disturbance of the desirable level of psychic equilibrium we call "normal." They must be compensated for by new knowledge, new skills, new wisdom, new scenes, new usefulness, new outlooks, new undertakings—in other words, by self-development.

There is a positive value in memories of past joys that is being lost in today's rushing, busy civilization, and so we conclude this book with a quotation from C. S. Lewis that we recommend for those times when a few restful moments can be found for contemplation.

A pleasure is full grown only when it is remembered. . . . When you and I met, the meeting was over very shortly, it was nothing. Now it is growing into something as we remember it. But still we know very little about it. What it will be when I remember it as I lie down to die, what it makes in me all my days till then—that is the real meeting. The other is only the beginning of it. You say you have poets in your world. Do they not teach you this?

SUMMARY

The treatment of emotional illness can be divided into three categories:

Physical: Electro Convulsive Shock Treatment, Hydrotherapy, Massage.
Chemical: Insulin Shock (subshock treatment by insulin). Psychotropic
  drugs, Psychotomimetic drugs (sedatives, tranquilizers).
Psychotherapeutic: Educational treatment, psychoanalysis, psychotherapy.

Electro convulsive therapy has declined greatly from its once widespread application. It is now known to be of some value in 4 out of 5 cases of depression, at any age, that are resistant to psychotherapy. Hydrotherapy and massage are of definitely limited value and, unless combined with psychotherapy, are of little value in mental illness.

Insulin shock therapy has gone out as a specific treatment of schizophrenia, acute or chronic, and is rarely recommended any more. Drugs which simulate psychotic symptoms, such as L.S.D. 25, Psilocybin and Mescaline, while interesting, have not demonstrated their usefulness in treatment in spite of some publicity to the contrary. To produce psychotic-like symptoms is not effective as a curative agent to anyone. The psychotropic drugs which produce alteration in mood and sense of well-being have temporary value while in the system. But they have not been shown to have curative potentialities unless combined judicially with psychotherapy. This awaits more experimentation. Merely to dull the senses does little to reduce *the cause* of anxiety or tension. Hence, the value of the tranquilizers to cure has been overrated, we feel. Some patients seem to get no positive effect from tranquilizers and some get a negative effect. When a positive effect occurs, it has been our experience that a similar effect could be achieved with greater benefit to the personality in the long run by a few hours of psychotherapy.

The aim of self-development efforts is to get an individual to carry his own weight in life's forward progress. If we must be a pill-taking humanity to get the world's work done and achieve greatness, then we are in trouble. The human being has unused potentialities for maturation toward the "good," the "saner," the "more mature" life. This could be the life of serenity, competency, versatility, altruism, generosity, and concern for others. In short, man can work, play, and love without electric shocks, stimulants, sedatives, or tranquilizers. The family can be its own "medicine" for the young. When it fails, then the medical profession and its ancillary personnel should supplement what the family failed to give in healthy potential.

BIBLIOGRAPHY FOR CHAPTER XVI

Arbuckle, Dugald S., *Teacher Counselling,* Addison-Wesley, 1950

Horney, Karen, *Self-Analysis,* Norton, 1942.

Kubie, L. S., *Practical and Theoretical Aspects of Psychoanalysis,* International Universities Press, 1950.

——— "The Forgotten Man of Education," *Harvard Alumni Bulletin,* February 6, 1954.

Levine, Maurice, *Psychotherapy in General Practice,* Macmillan, 1942.

Lewis, C. S., *Out of the Silent Planet,* Macmillan, 1943.

Lindbergh, Anne Morrow, *The Steep Ascent,* Harcourt, 1944.

Otto, Max, *Science and the Moral Life,* New American Library, 1949.

An Outline for Evaluation of a Community Program in Mental Hygiene, Group for the Advancement of Psychiatry. Report No. 8, April, 1949. Publications Office, 104 E. 25th St., New York 10, N.Y.

The Relation of Clinical Psychology to Psychiatry, Group for the Advancement of Psychiatry, Report No. 10, July, 1949. Publications Office, 104 E. 25th St., New York 10, N.Y.

Stolz, Karl R., *The Church and Psychotherapy,* Abingdon-Cokesbury, 1943.

Index

Horney, Karen. *Our Inner Conflicts.*

Horney, Karen. *Self-Analysis*

Inhelder, Bärbel, and Jean Piaget. *The Early Growth of Logic in the Child.*

James, William. *Talks to Teachers.*

Kagan, Jerome, and Robert Coles (Eds.). *Twelve to Sixteen: Early Adolescence.*

Kasanin, J. S. *Language and Thought in Schizophrenia.*

Kelly, George A. *A Theory of Personality.*

Klein, Melanie, and Joan Riviere. *Love, Hate and Reparation.*

Komarovsky, Mirra. *Dilemmas of Masculinity: A Study of College Youth.*

Lasswell, Harold D. *Power and Personality.*

Levy, David M. *Maternal Overprotection.*

Lifton, Robert Jay *Revolutionary Immortality: Mao Tse-tung and the Chinese Cultural Revolution.*

Lifton, Robert Jay *Thought Reform and the Psychology of Totalism.*

Meehl, Paul E. *Psychodiagnosis: Selected Papers.*

Piaget, Jean. *The Child's Conception of Number.*

Piaget, Jean *Genetic Epistemology.*

Piaget, Jean. *Play, Dreams and Imitation in Childhood.*

Piaget, Jean. *Understanding Causality.*

Piaget, Jean, and Bärbel Inhelder. *The Child's Conception of Space.*

Piaget, Jean, and Bärbel Inhelder. *The Origin of the Idea of Chance in Children.*

Piers, Gerhart, and Milton B. Singer. *Shame and Guilt.*

Piers, Maria W. (Ed.). *Play and Development.*

Raymond, Margaret, Andrew Slaby, and Julian Lieb. *The Healing Alliance.*

Ruesch, Jurgen. *Disturbed Communication.*

Ruesch, Jurgen. *Therapeutic Communication.*

Ruesch, Jurgen, and Gregory Bateson. *Communication: The Social Matrix of Psychiatry.*

Sullivan, Harry Stack. *Clinical Studies in Psychiatry.*

Sullivan, Harry Stack. *Conceptions of Modern Psychiatry.*

Sullivan, Harry Stack. *The Fusion of Psychiatry and Social Science.*

Sullivan, Harry Stack. *The Interpersonal Theory of Psychiatry.*

Sullivan, Harry Stack. *The Psychiatric Interview.*

Sullivan, Harry Stack. *Schizophrenia as a Human Process.*

Walter, W. Grey. *The Living Brain.*

Watson, John B. *Behaviorism.*

Wheelis, Allen. *The Quest for Identity.*

Williams, Juanita H. *Psychology of Women: Behavior in a Biosocial Context.*

Zilboorg, Gregory. *A History of Medical Psychology.*

Liveright Paperbacks
PSYCHIATRY AND PSYCHOLOGY